The Evolution of the Costumed Avenger

The Evolution of the Costumed Avenger

The 4,000-Year History of the Superhero

Jess Nevins

 PRAEGER™

An Imprint of ABC-CLIO, LLC
Santa Barbara, California • Denver, Colorado

Library of Congress Cataloging-in-Publication Data

Names: Nevins, Jess, author.
Title: The evolution of the costumed avenger : the 4,000-year history of the
    superhero / Jess Nevins.
Description: Santa Barbara, California : Praeger, 2017. | Includes
    bibliographical references and index.
Identifiers: LCCN 2016041967 | ISBN 9781440854835 (hardcopy : acid-free paper) |
    ISBN 9781440854842 (ebook)
Subjects: LCSH: Superheroes in literature. | Heroes in literature. |
    Literature—History and criticism. | Pulp literature—History and
    criticism. | Comic books, strips, etc.—History and criticism.
Classification: LCC PN56.5.H45 N48 2017 | DDC 809/.93352—dc23
LC record available at https://lccn.loc.gov/2016041967

ISBN: 978-1-4408-5483-5
EISBN: 978-1-4408-5484-2

21 20 19 18 17   2 3 4 5

This book is also available as an eBook.

Praeger
An Imprint of ABC-CLIO, LLC

ABC-CLIO, LLC
130 Cremona Drive, P.O. Box 1911
Santa Barbara, California 93116-1911
www.abc-clio.com

This book is printed on acid-free paper (∞)
Manufactured in the United States of America

Contents

Acknowledgments

My thanks to the many scholars and academics whose work I've plundered while writing this. As the cliché goes, all the good stuff is theirs; any of the errors and omissions of this book are mine alone.

I have to acknowledge two authors in particular for their influence on this book. Both Pete Coogan and Chris Gavaler preceded me in writing about the roots of the modern superhero, and even though I disagree with both of them—in some cases substantially—I hope both will understand that I'm doing so with respect, and in a very real sense standing on their shoulders rather than trying to kick them in the head.

Many thanks to my comics-minded scholarly friends (and scholarly minded comics friends) for serving as sounding boards: Abe Binder, Kevin Maroney, Greg Morrow, Jason Tondro, and Chad Underkoffler. Thanks to the other beta readers for criticisms and suggestions: Brian Baer, Richard Becker, Benito Cereno, Kai Friese, Denny Lien, and Ariana Osborne. Thanks to Chris Sims, the Internet's Foremost Batmanologist, for answering Batman questions for me, and to Robin Walz and Kristin Thompson for helping me answer my *Judex* question.

My sincerest thanks to Michelle Martinez for article assistance, and to Barbara Mitchell of the Tomball Public Library for Interlibrary Loan assistance. And no thanks to the Interlibrary Loan Department at Lone Star College, who pale in comparison to other libraries' ILL departments I've dealt with, much less Barbara Mitchell's: *a chúl an lámh a thabhairt duit, agus is féidir leat a chur faoi thalamh I ifreann seacht domhain.*

And, of course, many thanks to the editors at Praeger and the copyeditor who corrected my many mistakes.

This book is dedicated to my wife Alicia and my son Henry.

Introduction

It's somewhat of a tradition in studies of this sort for the author to describe their personal history with the genre or medium or artist—"I started reading *Legion of Super-Heroes* in 1973," "The first novel I read to my son was *The Hobbit*," "I was first in line for the first Can show in Cologne in '68"— that sort of thing. It's intended, I suppose, to show how close the author is to the subject, or how they have always truly been *involved* with it, that they are one of the *insiders*, and so what they have to say is said with special authority because of that long involvement and insider status.

Is such a declaration necessary here? Perhaps, perhaps not. I've been reading superhero comics all my reading life—I did start reading *Legion* in 1973—but I came to many of the heroes I describe in *The Evolution of the Costumed Avenger* much later and acquired scholarly knowledge of them in some cases only as a middle-aged adult, or even while writing this book. I hope this does not make you, Dear Reader, look askance at the following or view it in some ways as less authoritative.

Suffice it to say that while I may not have the insider status of an official comics scholar, nor the long involvement with large portions of my subject here that the academics I cite do, *The Evolution of the Costumed Avenger* is nonetheless the product of a lot of thought on my part, in some cases going back decades, and of many years of research. I trust you'll find the arguments I make worth reading despite my arriviste status, and the evidence I assemble persuasive.

Why I'm Writing This

I've always had an interest in the lesser-known characters of popular culture, the second rankers, the ones who stand behind the leads, living heroic lives on their own but being swallowed up by posterity faster than the leads are. It's why I spent so much time on Sexton Blake and Nick

Carter and Nelson Lee in *The Encyclopedia of Fantastic Victoriana*—everyone knows about Sherlock Holmes, but who remembers his competitors in the 1890s, 1900s, and 1910s? It's why my *Encyclopedia of Pulp Heroes* exists—to bring attention to the thousands (literally; over 6,000 of them) of characters, forgotten about now, who nonetheless had their heyday alongside the Shadow and Doc Savage. It's why I assembled *The Encyclopedia of Golden Age Superheroes*, about a motley crew of do-gooders who never got the publicity of a Superman, Batman, Captain America, or Captain Marvel, yet nonetheless nobly fought evil for a short while.

So I'm naturally interested in the idea of a history of the superheroic characters who came before the superheroes. That many of them—Beowulf, King Arthur, Robin Hood—are hardly unknown is beside the point: What would I discover about them if I actually looked closely at them? What forgotten characters lurk within their heroic universes?

Unfortunately, an initial search of the literature didn't turn up a book on the subject—not exactly. A great deal of time and effort has been spent on writing books about the history of superheroes, beginning with Superman and going up through the time of the book's writing—there's a small but distinct market for such books, and new additions to the collection of superhero histories seem to regularly appear—but far less time and effort has been spent on the cultural and literary history of what I'm calling the "protosuperheroes," those heroic characters with elements of the superhero about them who existed before Superman's debut in 1938.

I had high hopes for two recent books in that regard. Peter Coogan's *Superhero: The Secret Origin of a Genre* and Chris Gavaler's *On the Origin of Superheroes* each seemed promising when I opened them, and although each has individually excellent elements and chapters, neither gave me what I hoped for. While both touch on the protosuperheroes who appeared before Superman and *Action Comics* #1, neither do so in a programmatic or diachronic way, nor in any sort of depth. Clearly, if I wanted such a book, I was going to have to write it myself. And so here I am, and here you are, reading it.

What I'm Not Writing

This book is primarily the history of a character type, the protosuperhero. It's not—well, I can do no better than steal Peter Coogan's words from the Author's Foreword to *Superhero*:

> It is not . . . a semiological analysis of the superhero . . . nor a social history of comic books and superhero comics . . . nor a look at superheroes as myth . . . nor a cultural analysis of one superhero . . . nor an art historical

analysis of the graphic design of superhero comics . . . nor a multi-disciplinary critical approach to a superhero . . . nor an ethnography of comic book readers . . . nor a discussion of what superheroes tell us about ourselves . . . nor the application of literary theory to superhero comics . . . nor is it a "superheroes and" book of the sort that seems popular at the moment on superheroes and physics, science, philosophy, religion, spirituality, and so forth.

It is not, then, an attempt to address the way the superhero genre narratively and ritualistically resolves basic cultural conflicts and contradictions . . . it is not an examination or explanation of the *meaning* of the superhero.[1]

Nor is my book Coogan's book, which he describes as "an examination of the superhero genre as a genre."[2] (I address this notion in Chapter 1.) No, what I'm doing is tracing the history of what I'm calling the "protosuperhero," and how the varieties of that character influenced (from a greater or lesser remove, and to a greater or lesser degree) the superhero. Those looking for an analysis of themes and meaning will need to look elsewhere, I'm afraid.

Where I'm Going

In Chapter 1, I discuss the operational premises of the book: the difficulties with defining the term "superhero" and how best to resolve those difficulties, the difference between an ordinary adventure hero and a superhero, what characters can be considered influential or liminal without actually being a superhero, and the historical schema—the Costumed Avenger and the Übermensch—that I'm applying to protosuperheroes.

In Chapter 2, I discuss the protosuperheroes who appeared from the beginning of popular culture—*The Epic of Gilgamesh*—in 2100 BCE to 1500 CE. Costumed Avengers, supermen, and other protosuperheroes from Western folklore and myth are covered, as are Robin Hood, the masked highwayman of reality and ballads, and the protosuperheroes of Arthuriana and "traditional" epics.

In Chapter 3, I cover the protosuperheroes who appeared between 1500 and 1829, the year when the modern British police force was established. The rise of the sorcerer hero is addressed, as is the "modern" masked highwayman, the secret society hero, and the Gothic Hero-Villain.

In Chapter 4, I split my coverage into its two tracks. In this chapter, I discuss the history of the Costumed Avenger in the 19th century. I discuss the importance of detective fiction and the casebook, Western dime novels, and post–Civil War masked vigilantes.

In Chapter 5, I cover the history of the Übermensch in the 19th century, from magic characters like the Rosicrucian heroes to those supermen influenced by the monster characters of 19th century fiction. Mesmerists, aliens, and *doppelgängers* are discussed.

In Chapter 6, I move into the 20th century, and cover the explosion of Costumed Avengers in popular fiction from 1900 to 1938. The effect (such as it was) of the Scarlet Pimpernel is discussed, as are the pulps.

In Chapter 7, covering the supermen of 1900–1938, I discuss the effect of the pulps and science fiction novels, both British and American, the existence of posthuman bodybuilders and "Physical Culture" movement, and Philip Wylie's Hugo Danner, the father of Superman.

In Chapter 8, I discuss the early years of superhero comics, from Superman's debut in 1938 to the United States' entrance into World War II in December 1941, and how the medium of comics and the genre of superhero comics developed during those three and a half years.

In Chapter 9, I discuss the various "ages" of superhero comics that have passed since Superman's debut, from Golden to Metamodern, and how the superhero has developed during those ages.

In Chapter 10, I discuss how the superhero has been portrayed in film and television from the 1940s through the shows and films of 2016.

In the Epilogue I discuss the discouraging current state of superhero comics.

Last, in the Appendix, as a way to demonstrate the international reach of the protosuperhero, I list all the pre-Superman international (non-American, non-British) Costumed Avengers and supermen who were influenced by—rather than being an influence on—the protosuperheroes covered in Chapters 4 through 7.

On Statistics

In Chapters 4 through 8, I make use of a range of statistics to support various statements and arguments or simply as references. I will whenever possible cite where I got these statistics from, whether from the Internet Movie Database (http://www.imdb.com) or other sources. However, many of the statistics were compiled by me, either for *The Pulps* or for this work, and were based on information and notes gathered while writing this or other books. Any uncited, unsourced statistics are original to *The Evolution of the Costumed Avenger*.

Sidenote, on Ideology and Usage

Like it or not—and there are plenty of academics and writers who don't, never mind the substantial number of readers who reject this notion—the language we use expresses our ideologies. Writing in "politically correct"

English (whatever that means) expresses a certain ideology—but then, so does writing in "standard" English. Default positions—the status quo—have their own ideological and political assumptions, more covert if no less pronounced than openly political stances. So too with spoken and written languages and vocabularies. Once this is understood, the only recourse is to choose which languages and vocabularies best express your own political positions.

So I use "he" and "she" alternately rather than "he," on the grounds that I choose not to use a default expression that excludes the entire female sex. Too, I use "BCE" (Before Common Era) and "CE" (Common Era) rather than "BC" and "AD," because I wish to avoid the specifically Christian orientation of "Before Christ" and the theological claim of "Anno Domini" (to paraphrase Patti Smith, it may be the year of somebody's lord, but not mine).

Finally, whenever possible I am listing the creators of individual heroes when I first mention the hero. Admittedly this disrupts the flow of the text—it is much clumsier to write "Jerry Siegel and Joe Shuster's Superman" than to simply write "Superman"—but the history of the comic book industry has been one of individuals and corporations denying creators due credit for their creations, and I refuse to be a part of that, even if it makes my own text less smooth than it could be.

CHAPTER ONE

Operating Premises

Before we begin exploring the history of the protosuperhero and the superhero, from the beginning of recorded human history to the modern day, we must ask, and answer, the obvious questions: What is a superhero? Who counts as one? Who doesn't? Who is a part of the superheroic tradition and lineage predating Superman—and who, for the purposes of this book, doesn't count?

These are questions that seem to have obvious answers, but even a moment's reflection gives pause, for the obvious answers are riddled with exceptions. So I'm going to have to delve deep—deeper, perhaps, and at more tedious length than previous writers on the subject.

The Problem of, and with, Definitions

Inevitably, in a project like this, the author is called upon to define (and defend) his or her premises and to explain what will be included and, perhaps more importantly, what will be excluded. This is particularly important in a book that attempts to trace the history of an idea. Edges need to be laid down, and those things that are external to the project need to be put on the outside, where the author will not deal with them.

The problem with doing this, in the case of *The Evolution of the Costumed Avenger*, is that the idea itself grows fuzzy and nebulous the closer one gets to it, until, at the core, one is grappling with fog. What, after all, is a superhero? What particular elements make up the superhero? As might be expected with a cultural archetype whose modern commercial roots stretch back at least to the 1930s—and, as we'll see, whose cultural roots stretch considerably farther back than that—there have been thousands of stories about superheroes published in comic books and books and broadcast on radio, television, and film, both in the United States and around the world. The writer who wants to grapple with the definition of the superhero has no paucity of primary texts to deal with. But unlike other cultural archetypes, the superhero cannot simply be defined by setting (like the cowboy) or profession (like the private detective). A basic working definition of the superhero does not, in fact, exist, and for a very simple reason: any definition of the superhero, no matter how intelligently and cleverly phrased, inevitably excludes superheroes who already exist, and thereby proves itself to be useless. Any list of required elements, any definitional schema, will exclude those characters who have appeared as superheroes in superhero texts but do not have the required elements and do not fit into the schema.

Raglan, Rank, and Campbell

The issues of and problems with definitions are hardly unique to superheroes, of course, and none of us who have written about superheroes and attempted to define them to our and our readers' satisfactions are groundbreakers. Academics, when writing about traditional legendary heroes, the subjects of epics and myths and folktales, have already done substantial work in creating and applying definitional schema.

The landmark work in categorizing classical mythological heroes, and delineating the common patterns in them, was Otto Rank's *The Myth of the Birth of the Hero* (1914). Rank writes:

> The hero is the child of most distinguished parents; usually the son of a king. His origin is preceded by difficulties, such as continence, or prolonged barrenness, or secret intercourse of the parents, due to external prohibition or obstacles. During the pregnancy, or antedating the same, there is a prophecy, in form of a dream or oracle, cautioning against his birth, and usually threatening danger to the father, or his representative. As a rule, he is surrendered to the water, in a box. He is then saved by animals, or by lowly people (shepherds) and is suckled by a female animal, or by a humble woman. After he has grown up, he finds his distinguished parents, in a highly versatile fashion; takes his revenge on his father, on the one hand, is acknowledged on the other, and finally achieves rank and honors.[1]

Rank was focusing on the heroes of classic myth, although the list of heroes he examines shows he was not limiting himself to simple Greco-Roman myths: Sargon, Moses, Karna, Oedipus, Paris, Telephos, Perseus, Gilgamesh, Kyros, Tristan, Romulus, Hercules, Jesus, Siegfried, and

Lohengrin. But Rank's schema was written with the intention of applying it to the range of mythical heroes, rather than modern cultural heroes.

One of several responses to Rank's work was Baron Raglan's *The Hero: A Study in Tradition, Myth, and Drama* (1956). Where Rank was influenced by Freudian theory, Raglan's central influence was James Frazer's *The Golden Bough* (1922). Raglan (applying his schema to Robin Hood, the heroes of the Norse sagas, King Arthur, Hengist and Horsa, Cuchulainn, and the heroes of the *Iliad*) writes:

> The hero's mother is a royal virgin; his father is a king, and often a near relative of his mother, but the circumstances of his conception are unusual, and he is also reputed to be the son of a god. At birth, an attempt is made, usually by his father or his maternal grandfather, to kill him, but he is spirited away, and reared by foster-parents in a far country. We are told nothing of his childhood, but on reaching manhood he returns or goes to his future kingdom. After a victory over the king and/or a giant, dragon, or wild beast, he marries a princess, often the daughter of his predecessor, and becomes king. For a time he reigns uneventfully, and prescribes laws, but later he loses favour with the gods and/or his subjects, and is driven from the throne and city, after which he meets with a mysterious death, often at the top of a hill. His children, if any, do not succeed him. His body is not buried, but nevertheless he has one or more holy sepulchers.[2]

The most influential of the responses to Rank's work was that of Joseph Campbell, who counted not just Freud, Rank, and Frazer among his influences, but also Carl Jung and his model of the heroic archetype. Campbell, in *The Hero with a Thousand Faces* (1949), writes:

> The standard path of the mythological adventure of the hero is a magnification of the formula represented in the rites of passage: separation–initiation–return: which might be named the nuclear unit of the monomyth.
>
> A hero ventures forth from the world of the common day into a region of supernatural wonder: fabulous forces are there encountered and a decisive victory is won: the hero comes back from this mysterious adventure with the power to bestow boons on his fellow man.[3]

Later in *The Hero with a Thousand Faces*, Campbell sums up the hero's life and journeys:

> The mythological hero, setting forth from his common day hut or castle is lured . . . to the threshold of adventure . . . then the hero journeys through a world of unfamiliar yet strangely intimate forces, some of which severely threaten him (tests), some of which give magical aid (helpers). When he

arrives at the nadir of his mythological round, he undergoes a supreme ordeal and gains his reward. The triumph may be represented as the hero's sexual union with the goddess-mother of the world (sacred marriage), his recognition by the father-creator (father atonement), or his own divination (apotheosis) . . . The final work is that of the return . . . At the return threshold the transcendental powers must remain behind; the hero re-emerges from the kingdom of dread . . . The boon he brings restores the world.[4]

None of these models is without its critics, but as rough guides to the heroes of myth they are quite useful, even if only as starting places. However, their utility when applied to superheroes (the closest modern equivalent to mythical heroes) is limited. The central problem in applying Rank, Raglan, and Campbell to the superhero is that all three were evaluating traditional myths and legends of mortal heroes, and these myths and legends inevitably ended with the hero's death. The hero's cycle, in these myths and legends, has a beginning, middle, and ending. The same cannot be said of the modern superhero, the vast majority of whom eternally operate—thanks to the exigencies of the market and the demands of the consumer[5]—in the middle phase of their career. Rare it is to find a superhero with a definite, limited three-part story arc to their lives; even dedicated superhero fans can probably count such characters only on the fingers of one hand.

Because of this, and because of the emphasis that Rank, Raglan, and Campbell place on endings—either death or completion of the hero's journey/story arc—their models ultimately can't be applied to modern superheroes.

21st-Century Attempts at Definition

Critical works examining superheroes in the 20th century rarely attempted to define superheroes, being concerned instead of tracing the then-forgotten and obscured history of the genre. For writers of this era, the definition of a superhero was obvious and could be taken from any dictionary. It's not until the Internet era that definitional arguments begin to arise, and it's not until the 21st century that cultural critics began seriously examining the matters of definition, inclusion and exclusion.

The first writer to tackle the definition question at length was Peter Coogan, in *Superhero: The Secret Origin of a Genre*. Citing Judge Learned Hand's words,[6] Coogan provides four core elements for the superhero: mission ("prosocial and selfless, which means that his fight against evil must fit in with the existing, professed mores of society and must not be intended to benefit or further his own agenda"),[7] powers, identity ("the identity element comprises the codename and the costume, with the secret identity being a customary counterpart to the codename"),[8] and costume ("the iconic representations of the superhero identity").[9] Coogan's exploration of his actual definition of superheroes is comparatively brief; the majority of his time is spent in applying his definition to various characters and explaining why they are or are not superheroes.

In Rosenberg and Coogan's *What Is a Superhero*, a number of writers, many of them professional superhero comic book writers, provide varying definitions. Alex Boney writes, "But at his core, the superhero is—and always has been—a response to the rapid, dizzying forces of early 20th century modernism."[10] Kurt Busiek (creator of *Kurt Busiek's Astro City*) writes, "The primary hallmarks of the superhero are *superpowers, costume, code name, secret identity, heroic ongoing mission*, and *superhero milieu*. If the character has three of those six, he or she is probably a superhero."[11] Stanford Carpenter writes, "Superheroes need superior villains to raise the stakes of the heroic struggle by putting culturally defined value systems in high relief."[12] Danny Fingeroth writes:

> Someone has or obtains enhanced power—physical, mental, magical, mechanical—and then, either through good character or a difficult, transformative rite of passage, realizes that power confers on them an obligation to some section of humanity, if not all of it . . . it follows that a superhero is a figure who embodies the best aspects of humankind, differing from a heroic real person or even a fictional non-super hero due to . . . a nobility of purpose, which is what makes him or her not a super*villain*.[13]

Most recently, Chris Gavaler, in *On the Origin of Superheroes*, declines to engage with the difficulties of definition altogether:

> Superheroes are the ultimate amalgams, all-swallowing über-characters that consume other genres like black holes. They defy conventional definitions because they contain too many conventions. If that nondefinition sounds cowardly, philosopher Ludwig Wittgenstein plays the same game with "game" (what traits do marathons, chess, and solitaire share?) . . . definitions work like erasers. I prefer the pointy end of the pencil.[14]

Gavaler's approach results in an essentially all-inclusive definition, one almost tautological in its inclusiveness—a superhero is a superhero because she is a superhero and because Gavaler includes them in his book.

We can do better than that, while still avoiding the difficulties and contradictions and limitations that Coogan et al. create with their definitions.

A More Useful Approach

Ultimately, none of these approaches satisfies or works because there are *too damn many exceptions to the rules.*

A superhero cannot be defined solely by superhuman powers, because Batman, to name just one, has no superhuman powers. A superhero cannot be defined solely by costume, for a number of superheroes, like the 1990s iteration of DC's Starman (as created by James Robinson and Tony Harris and appearing in one of the most aesthetically successful extended superhero runs) often appeared wearing no costume. A superhero cannot be defined solely by a mission statement ("fighting crime," "supporting the oppressed"); like a number of characters of the 1940s, Joe Simon and Jack Kirby's Captain America is primarily a soldier, fighting in a war, rather than a crime fighter. A superhero cannot be defined by having an alternate or dual secret identity; heroes like Stan Lee and Jack Kirby's Fantastic Four are public heroes, while Arnold Drake, Bob Haney, and Bruno Premiani's Robotman has no secret identity. A superhero cannot be defined as being generically distinct from characters of other genres; too many examples of superheroes to name appear in other cultural genres (but see below). A superhero cannot be defined by the end result of her actions; comic superheroes like E. Nelson Bridwell and Joe Orlando's Inferior Five are incompetent, but are nonetheless superheroes despite their inability to catch the bad guy. A superhero cannot be defined as someone who appears in superhero comics or films; the superhero, perhaps surprisingly, is common in many different modes and commercial genres and media. A superhero cannot be defined as someone appearing in anything branded and sold as a superhero text; superheroes have become pervasive enough to appear in works branded and sold as "mainstream" or "literary." And so on.

The fact is that considering the superhero through a binary lens of "is/is not" is not the most useful approach to defining what a superhero is—not useful aesthetically, not useful critically, and not useful on the most basic level of accuracy. (After all, a definition of superheroes that actually excludes superheroes simply doesn't work.)

A more useful approach to addressing the vexed question of the definition of superhero—and "vexed" is indeed the appropriate adjective, given that every critic of superheroes seems to have their own definition, few of which are mutually inclusive with other critics' definitions—is to consider superheroes on a continuum and to apply fuzzy logic to the matter.[15] Fuzzy logic is a mathematical, engineering, and philosophical approach that arose in the 1960s. In philosophy, fuzzy logic is applied to statements like "Many writers are poor," which use imprecise vocabulary to create a statement for which the law of the excluded middle ("either 'x is true' or 'x is not true,' there is no in-between") does not apply. Because "many" and "poor" are ambiguous and subjective, "many writers are poor" can be partially or mostly true rather than simply true or not true.

Applying this approach to the definition of the superhero frees us from the requirement to craft a definition that will inevitably fail. Instead, what needs to be done is to identify the individual elements that make up the continuum of superheroes. The more of these elements a character has, the more of a superhero she is (and the reverse is true as well), but *there is no ideal, Platonic form of the superhero to be reached*—there is no "pure" superhero to whom all others are compared. Not even Superman, the iconic superhero, is the ideal form of the character type.

Heroenkonzepte

The notion of a cluster of these elements being used to define a hero is not a new one. However, it is found in the study of more traditional heroes rather than in the study of superheroes. Rüdiger Bartelmus, in *Heroentum in Israel und seiner Umwelt* (1979) coined the neologism "heroenkonzept" to mean "the combination of motifs such as the divine paternity and superhuman capabilities of a hero, which was used in Mesopotamia and throughout the eastern Mediterranean in antiquity to legitimize dynastic rule."[16] Bartelmus's *heroenkonzept*—which has no direct English equivalent, and which I trust readers will forgive me for using here—will be recognizable to superhero consumers: each superhero has his or her own *heroenkonzept*, however scanty or deep. We simply need to define the most important elements of heroes' *heroenkonzepte*.

A comprehensive list of such elements would be extensive. The most important elements, briefly described, are as follows, albeit in no particular order:

- an **unusual origin story**. This needn't be the exceptional birth of traditional mythical heroes, and often is not; but most heroes have a unique moment in their lives when they realize that they must become a superhero or superheroine.
- a **superpower**—that is, abilities that are in the realm of science fiction and fantasy rather than reality (superstrength, invulnerability, flight, and so on)—abilities that real people simply can't possess because of the limitations of real-world biology and chemistry and physics.
- **extraordinary skills and abilities**, from fighting to computer hacking to juggling, and everything in between. The superhero with extraordinary

skills and abilities is not just good at what she does, she is *extraordinary* at it, up to the peak of human ability.

- **extraordinary technology**—which is to say, technology that does not exist yet but may someday exist (and is therefore science fictional) or that will never exist because it violates the basic laws of science (and is therefore science fantasy).

- a **distinctive weapon**: offensive (a bow and arrow) or defensive (a shield), real (a gun) or science fictional (technologically advanced suit of armor) or magical (a cursed sword).

- a **distinctive appearance,** whether a full-fledged "pervert suit" costume (in the scabrous phrase of writer Warren Ellis), a distinctive piece of clothing, like a mask, a unique body type or part, or simply an instantly recognizable body state (like being nude except for a loincloth).

- a **code name**, often (though not exclusively) thematic of the superhero's origin and/or powers and/or costume.

- a **dual identity**, whether secret (few know that Batman is actually Bruce Wayne) or public (everyone knows that Reed Richards is Mr. Fantastic).

- a **heroic mission**. In this case, the mission must be selfless (not performed for personal gain) and aimed at aiding the oppressed, whether victims of crime or of the aggressions of "evil" men and women, monsters, governments, and/or states/nations. The character's motivations must be heroic in the modern sense of the word: selfless and done in service of and for the benefit of others. *This is perhaps the single most important of all the components listed here*; the number of selfish superheroes is minuscule, and even they are, on balance, more self-sacrificing than not. The heroic, selfless mission is of signal importance, and figures who lack the heroic mission are automatically on the lower, "lesser" end of the superheroic scale, if they can even be called heroes at all.

- **extraordinary opponents**. These opponents need not have superpowers, extraordinary abilities, extraordinary technology, or any of the other elements of the superhero listed here, but the opponent must be distinctive in some way from ordinary, realistic criminals, even if only by the number that the superhero faces at any one time.

- **lives in a world where there is law enforcement and a government,** however corrupt or incompetent.

- **operates in a world in which crime/oppression/evil is clear cut and obvious**. There are no moral gray areas in such a world and no crimes, like the poor man stealing bread for his starving family, which are legally wrong but morally/ethically right.

- **operates in a world in which law enforcement/the government is not capable of controlling or defeating crime/oppression/evil**.

- operates under the assumption that law enforcement/the government is capable of holding and confining a criminal once they are apprehended.

- operates under the assumption that vigilantism is welcome or at least tolerated by general society as well as law enforcement and the government.

- is finite and can be killed. Without the risk of death as a possible result of her actions, a superhero is merely a superbeing.

- does not kill. The superhero refrains from undue violence, and never murders his opponent(s), no matter how justified the killing would be. Execution is the prerogative of the state, not the individual.

This list can be expanded, of course; there are as many underlying assumptions and elements to the superhero as there are superheroes. But as a starting place it works, I think, to show ways in which various characters can be seen as superheroic, whether to a greater or to a lesser degree. No superhero has none of these elements; no superhero has all of them. Brought together, they form the basis of each hero's *heroenkonzept*. There is no prescribed formula for being a superhero, just an endless variety of *heroenkonzepte*.

Gods and Epic Heroes, and What They Are Not

The use of the superhero element continuum does bring with it a new set of problems. Not least among these difficulties is the reality that not using a binary definition means that virtually any heroic character can be considered "superheroic" or just "protosuperheroic" if he or she has one or more elements listed on the continuum—even if that character is not what anyone would normally define as a superhero. Using the continuum rather than the binary threatens to make the term "superhero" so fuzzily vague as to be useless in critical and historical discourse. Clearly, more qualifying is required if we are to attempt to track the history of the idea of the superhero.

Writers and critics have usually taken it as assumed that the line of descent of the superhero ultimately begins with the stories of the gods, and goes from there through the epic, culture, and adventure heroes until manifesting itself in the protosuperhero. As we'll see in Chapter 2, however, the first protosuperhero is distinct from the gods—created by them but not one of them—and the tradition of the protosuperhero evolves separately from the oral and written traditions of godly stories, legends, and myths. (This is in addition to the gods' inability to meet some of the most important criteria of the superhero listed above, of course.) The tradition of the protosuperhero, growing out of multiple separate traditions and being assembled from many different components, is ultimately that of mortal men and women, not immortal beings—who may have a heroic, selfless mission (rare among immortals) but are immortal and cannot die—and therefore don't risk anything by their actions, which leaves them far less heroic than those mortal men and women who risk everything on a daily basis to fight crime and evil.

So we will set aside the gods and their divine minions, angels. (Gavaler argues that Milton's *Paradise Lost* provides the "archetypal superhero plot."[17] But angels, the action heroes of *Paradise Lost*, cannot die, are backed by the power of the divine, and lack agency. They are hardly heroic in the modern sense.)[18] Epic heroes, culture heroes, historical heroes, and adventure heroes are somewhat more problematic. They aren't superheroes, of course—the first superheroes appear centuries after these heroes—but protosuperheroes.

That's what Chapter 2 is for. I'll be looking at the most important—and more vitally the most influential—of these heroes on a case-by-case basis and determining whether or not they count as protosuperheroes. But, as a general rule, just as the more elements a character has, the more superheroic she is, so it is true that the fewer of the superheroic elements a character has, the less superheroic he is, and the farther down the superheroic spectrum he is. I choose not to determine a minimum number of elements a character must have to make them a protosuperhero rather than merely an adventure hero, but surely there is a minimum limit, whether one or three or however many, and surely the selfless mission *must* be present for the character to be considered at all. Epic heroes et al. may fit the definitions of Rank, Raglan, and Campbell for their particular genres, or may match the famous description of Northrop Frye in *Anatomy of Criticism* for particular modes,[19] but superheroes are a different case.

The "Superhero Genre"

That said, what case, exactly, are they? I mentioned above that superheroes cannot be described as being generically distinct from characters of other genres, on the grounds that too many examples of superheroes to name appear in other cultural genres. This declaration undoubtedly raised the hackles of some of my scholarly readers, who may have written their own books on the themes and meaning of the superhero genre. Peter Coogan, in *Superhero*, spends practically the entire book teasing out the meaning of the superhero genre as a distinct genre.

Sadly, I'm forced to disagree with all these writers, on what are, I think, very simple grounds. The argument that literary genres have hard, discernible, defensible borders seems to me to be an insupportable one. It's a holdover from Renaissance literary theory, which posited that genres were fixed and essential and separate literary forms, a theory that the Romantics only partially rejected. Worse, this notion of genres as having firm borders leads to unfortunate ideas of generic purity and essence and limitations; as Jacques Derrida says, "As soon as genre announces itself, one must respect a norm, one must not cross a line of demarcation, one must not risk impurity, anomaly, or monstrosity."[20]

Instead, literary genres are best regarded as having extremely fuzzy edges and should be imagined as part of a massive, three-dimensional (or perhaps four-dimensional) Venn diagram/globe of overlapping and interacting genre spheres. One can't spend the time arguing that a detective novel set in the future isn't science fiction, or isn't a detective novel. It's both. A Regency romance with steampunk elements is still a Regency romance, it merely is *also* steampunk (or science fiction, if you prefer). An insistence that texts that inhabit multiple genres simultaneously can only be described as belonging to one genre is neither helpful nor accurate. As Derrida and Ronell write, "Every text participates in one or several genres, there is no genreless text; there is always a genre and genres, yet such participation never amounts to belonging."[21]

When it comes to superheroes, this insistence—understandable, as those doing the insisting are trying to establish superhero stories as a separate and distinct literary genre, which means that it would be academically acceptable to study it—quickly leads to some problematic places. Peter Coogan argues for strong borders between the superhero genre and other genres, as a way to disallow characters like Buffy the Vampire Slayer, Adam Strange, and John Constantine from the superhero genre:

> Their strong ties with other genres, it can be argued, should exclude them from this cross-genre or borderline-genre status. As I have argued, this identity convention often works to signify whether a story with some superhero elements falls within the superhero genre or within another genre, and these heroes lack the identity convention. Strong identity markers are the clearest way to place a story within the superhero genre, although such markers need to be backed up by the presence of other equally clear conventions.[22]

Coogan's eagerness to defend genre boundaries by disallowing superheroic characters leads to some critical difficulties: cross-genre superheroic characters like cowboy superheroes, including Roy Thomas, Gary Friedrich, and Dick Ayers's Ghost Rider and Bill Parker and Pete Costanza's Golden

Arrow, or Steve Englehart and Jim Starlin's Shang-Chi the Master of Kung Fu (a martial arts superhero), or Len Wein and Bernie Wrightson's Swamp Thing (a horror/monster superhero), or Jerry Siegel and Bernard Baily's Spectre (a horror superhero), all of whom are superheroes by any common-sense definition, are defined by Coogan as not superheroes because they don't meet the criteria he sets forth based on their other-genre markers.

It is preferable to regard superheroes on a continuum or spectrum rather than as a binary "is/is not," for the reasons given above. This approach is equally preferable when it comes to a consideration of the superhero genre. A genre that is forced to include occult horror (in the form of sorcerers like Stan Lee and Steve Ditko's Dr. Strange and Gardner Fox and Howard Sherman's Dr. Fate), gritty street level detection (via Bill Finger and Bob Kane's Batman, or Stan Lee and Bill Everett's Daredevil, or Brian Bendis and Michael Gaydos's Jessica Jones), science fiction (Stan Lee, Larry Lieber, Don Heck, and Jack Kirby's Iron Man), and science fantasy (Jerry Siegel and Joe Shuster's Superman) because of its constituent characters is not a genre whose borders are secure or whose genre markers are consistent. Critic James Nicoll wrote, of the English language, that

> the problem with defending the purity of the English language is that English is about as pure as a cribhouse whore. We don't just borrow words; on occasion, English has pursued other languages down alleyways to beat them unconscious and rifle their pockets for new vocabulary.[23]

The superhero genre should be looked at in a similar light, as a voracious thief of a genre that takes from other genres to expand and glorify itself. The superhero genre is at its most superheroic—is the most *itself*— when it has elements of the superhero and elements of other genres cheek by jowl. It becomes a mosaic rather than a solid—it becomes a genre that is vast and contains multitudes.

The Two Categories of Protosuperheroes

Ultimately, of course, the superhero *does* develop into something unique and distinct, something that, to paraphrase Supreme Court Justice Potter Stewart, we know what it is when we see it. The modern superhero takes some combination of the elements listed above, combines them into a *heroenkonzept*, and appears in colorful (literally and figuratively) stories, and has done so without ceasing since the debut of Superman in *Action Comics* #1. There were comic book superheroes before Superman, but he was the culmination of the many trends that led up to his debut, and the reification of the concept of the superhero. There have been thousands of superheroes published, in a staggering variety of forms, and any attempt at coming up with a categorizing schema that includes them all is doomed to failure.

However, the same cannot be said of Superman's predecessors, the protosuperheroes. Dozens of them there were, as I hope to demonstrate, but by the 19th century they can (both accurately and usefully) be said to fall into two categories, and it is these categories that take up Chapters 4 through 7. There are a few notable exceptions to these categories, as I address in Chapter 4, but the vast majority of the protosuperheroes of the 1829–1938 era—the decades that did so much to shape the protosuperhero and indeed the superhero itself—fall into these two categories.

First is the Costumed Avenger. The Costumed Avenger is any character who wears a recognizable and consistent costume while fighting crime or evil. As mentioned in the *Heroenkonzept* section above, this "costume" does not have to be a superhero-style bodysuit, but can be simply the same mask or the same set of similarly colored clothing. Characters who regularly use disguises fall into this category as well, with their disguised selves being their "costume."

Second is the Übermensch. The Übermensch is any character who has abilities that are impossible in our world, from various psychic abilities to greater-than-human physical abilities to magic powers. I'm borrowing the term from Nietzsche without also taking the meaning he applies to it. It would be preferable to use the word "superman," but DC Comics already owns the trademark and copyright to that one. I've no wish to confuse matters or readers, but "superman" isn't available to me, so I trust my readers will indulge me in the use of a German term rather than in the trademark/copyright-violating "superman." I will, though, use "supermen" instead of "Übermenschen" and "superwoman" instead of "Überfrau." DC Legal hasn't gotten its hooks into either of those. Yet.

Who Gets Left Out

In this book I've chosen the dawn of recorded literary history—Mesopotamia, four millennia ago, and *The Epic of Gilgamesh*—as my starting place and moved forward from there. I've done my best to be as inclusive as possible, as I hope a brief perusal of the following chapters demonstrates. But, even with the best will in the world to be as encyclopedic as possible, I still left some characters and indeed some cultures out. Here's why.

The Evolution of the Costumed Avenger: The 4,000-Year History of the Superhero is, as the title indicates, the history of the idea of the superhero, traced across time. In the beginning this history is intermittent, even spotty, but eventually it becomes a definite lineage—a river with many tributaries, if you like, but still a distinct river—with a definite narrative through line. It starts in Mesopotamia, expands to the Middle East and the Mediterranean, and then makes its way through Europe to England and then America.

It does not, regrettably, have any branches farther east or south. African and Asian protosuperheroes are left out of this book, as are the protosuperheroes of the American First Peoples. The truth is that, for all the commerce and traffic between European cultures and those of Africa and Asia and the Americas, when it comes to the protosuperhero, that traffic is one way. Specialists in the fields of the literature of those regions will undoubtedly object and point out the various ways in which African or Chinese or Japanese literature influenced Western literature, but those influences did not extend to the protosuperhero. In this book I talk about influence and transmission, and neither can accurately be said to apply to the protosuperheroes of the non-Western world. Much as I'd love to include the heroes of Firdawsi's *Shahnameh*, Väinämöinen and Lemminkäinen, the heroes of Chinese *wŭxiá* fiction—or for that matter their Song Dynasty predecessors, Judge Bao and the monk Jigong, and Ozidi of the Ijo—they simply aren't relevant to the history of the superhero. They developed in parallel to the superheroic tradition, and usually in isolation from it, and a good book could be written about the protosuperhero outside of the West. But this book is not that book. (However, see this book's Appendix for a list of mostly non-Western 20th-century protosuperheroes.)

CHAPTER TWO

From 2100 BCE to 1500 CE

The canard that superheroes, like all expressions of popular culture, don't deserve studying or academic and critical attention has been disposed of for long enough that I hardly need to address it here.[1] Only the most conservative and backward of cultural commentators would bother to make such a claim, and scholars of superheroes give that assertion scant attention these days. But the assertion that the antecedents of the superheroes were gods, demigods, and epic or folkloric heroes receives equally scant attention, even by the most perceptive writers. It's simply taken as a given and treated as received wisdom.

This chapter is intended to serve as a corrective to that. That there's a connection between the mythical and literary heroes of yore and the superheroes of today, I do not deny; but what that connection is, and who is a part of it—which characters form the lineage of the protosuperhero—deserves closer examination than simple unthinking acceptance.

2100 BCE is a logical starting place: it's the date of the oldest written version of a Gilgamesh poem and therefore the starting place for heroic literature and protosuperheroes. 1500 CE is somewhat more arbitrary, but it is arguably the starting date for the Renaissance in England—Frederick Artz, in his still-useful *The Mind of the Middle Ages*, picks 1500 as his closing date—and the figures of the Renaissance, the Enlightenment, and the early 19th century are numerous enough to deserve their own chapter.

The protosuperheroes that appear between these two dates lay the groundwork for both the Costumed Avenger and the Übermensch, and by the end of this time period the stuff from which actual superheroes would be made has been produced. But that's jumping ahead.

Hazy Beginnings

We'll never know the beginning of popular culture. Writing was invented somewhere between 3100 BCE and 2900 BCE, with humanity's first literature, Mesopotamian, appearing somewhere between 2900 BCE and 2334 BCE, but oral traditions precede Mesopotamian literature, likely to a considerable degree, and there's the small matter of uncountable centuries, possibly or probably millennia, of popular culture in Stone Age and then Bronze Age civilizations of which we will likely never know anything. Oral traditions disappear all too often with their cultures, and even the clay tablets that the Mesopotamians inscribed their cuneiform on are not eternal or unbreakable. So while it's probable that civilizations before the Mesopotamians had mythic heroes and monster-slayers and godlike men (and perhaps women) as part of their popular culture, we will probably never know about them.

So we perforce begin in Mesopotamia, that area of the Middle East stretching from the Mediterranean to the Persian Gulf, across parts of modern Lebanon, Syria, Turkey, Iraq, Iran, and Kuwait. "Mesopotamia" is actually the broader use name for the region, which hosted various empires—Sumerian, Akkadian, Babylonian, and later the Neo-Assyrian and Neo-Babylonian—across its heyday, from the beginning of written history to the fall of Babylon in 539 BCE. We have a surprising amount of literature from these empires; generations of scholars and translators have made it available to us, so that we know, for example, a fair amount about the mythologies of these empires.

The outstanding document of these mythologies, and the first epic of world literature, is *The Epic of Gilgamesh*. As with many premodern epics, *The Epic of Gilgamesh* was not the creation of one person, not the product of one civilization, and not the product of a specific time period. *The Epic of Gilgamesh* developed over a long period of time and incorporated material from several different cultures and languages, evolving from stories told by the Gilgamesh cult, which worshiped the historical Gilgamesh, king of Uruk (ca. 2750 BCE).

What readers know of as the *Epic of Gilgamesh*—the fullest version of the epic—is actually the version in the Akkadian language from first millennium Babylonia and Assyria, with gaps filled in by older material. So dating *The Epic of Gilgamesh* is not as easy as dating *Iliad* or *Odyssey*; the nearest approximation we can come to is in centuries rather than decades. Scholars choose 2100 BCE because that's the date of the oldest copy of a Sumerian Gilgamesh poem.

And that's where the superhero begins: over 4,000 years ago, in the Middle East, in competing versions of an epic poem.

The Epic of Gilgamesh

The Epic of Gilgamesh is the story of Gilgamesh, the king of Uruk. Created by the Lady of the Gods, "two-thirds of him god and one third human,"[2] Gilgamesh helped create the walls of Uruk and is the city's protector as well as ruler, but he tyrannizes the people of Uruk, forcing new brides to sleep with him on their wedding night (*droit du seigneur*) and harrying the men "without warrant."[3] The people of Uruk complain to the gods, and the goddess Aruru responds by creating "Enkidu, the hero,"[4] a hairy primitive man who lives in the wilds with the animals.

Enkidu is seduced by the temple prostitute Shamhat, losing the friendship of the animals but gaining in its place "reason, and wide understanding."[5] Shamhat begins the process of civilizing Enkidu, bringing him to a shepherds' camp and instructing him in the ways of men, and Enkidu becomes the shepherds' watchman. When Enkidu learns of Gilgamesh's tyranny, he challenges Gilgamesh to a fight. But Enkidu is not the equal of Gilgamesh, and after battling him he is forced to acknowledge that Gilgamesh is his superior. The two then become best friends. Gilgamesh proposes to go to the Forest of Cedar to kill the ferocious, monstrous Humbaba.

With the assistance of the sun god Shamash, Gilgamesh and Enkidu succeed in killing Humbaba. When they return to Uruk, the goddess Ishtar, attracted by Gilgamesh's beauty, asks Gilgamesh to be her husband, but he declines on the grounds that her former lovers suffered unfortunate fates. Enraged, Ishtar persuades her father, the god Anu, to send the Bull of Heaven to Uruk to kill Gilgamesh. Gilgamesh and Enkidu instead kill the Bull and mock Ishtar. The gods then decree that Enkidu must die, and Enkidu, after suffering nightmarish visions of the fate of the dead, becomes ill and dies.

Gilgamesh, traumatized by the loss of his best friend, holds a great funeral for him, and then wanders the Earth in search of the immortal Uta-napishti, who can teach Gilgamesh the secret of eternal life. Gilgamesh travels to the end of the world and at length finds Uta-napishti, who lectures Gilgamesh on the duties of a king but eventually tells him that the secret of eternal life is a plant at the bottom of the sea. Unfortunately, a snake steals the plant, and now despairing—for he will never be able to find the spot where he got the plant—Gilgamesh returns to Uruk, where he sees the walls of Uruk and believes that they will be his lasting monument.

The First Protosuperhero—Not Who You Think

It is of course extremely anachronistic to apply the standards of modern superheroes to characters from long-past cultures. (A weakness in my entire approach to this book, admittedly.) When judging characters, we must take into account their historically contemporary standards.

In that respect, Gilgamesh is ultimately the hero of *The Epic of Gilgamesh*. He is certainly intended to be. Gilgamesh was, after all, the subject of the historical cult of Gilgamesh, and *Gilgamesh* stresses that Gilgamesh is "He Who Saw the Deep,"[6] "Surpassing All Other Kings,"[7] and "heroic."[8] He is certainly the epic's protagonist, and the story of the *The Epic of Gilgamesh* is of Gilgamesh's maturation from a callow youth to a contemplative middle-aged man. The Mesopotamians used the *Gilgamesh* to teach its readers, both students and royalty, the values of their culture through the words of the gods, the words of Uta-napishti, and the deeds and misdeeds of Gilgamesh himself—but the message taught is "do the will of the gods, fulfil your function as they intended."[9]

Gilgamesh certainly falls into the category of epic hero because of his deeds, and unlike many other epic heroes he changes over the course of the epic, becoming mature and good where he begins the epic as a tyrant and abuser of men and women.

But none of the preceding make him protosuperheroic. As discussed in the first chapter, of epic heroes, mythic heroes, legendary heroes, and culture heroes, none are automatically protosuperheroes, largely because they lack a significant—a necessary—number of the basic superheroic elements. Most vitally, Gilgamesh lacks the heroic mission and the selflessness that are arguably the essential elements of any superhero—he lacks the heroic intent. Gilgamesh tyrannizes the men and women of Uruk from sheer self-indulgence. Gilgamesh's motivation for killing Humbaba is gaining fame and glory. Gilgamesh rejects Ishtar's advances out of self-interest, and kills the Bull of Heaven in self-defense. Gilgamesh goes in search of Uta-napishti because of a fear of death, not because he wants to share the secret of immortality with everyone. Gilgamesh's actions are superheroic; but his intentions and personality are not.

Enkidu, on the other hand, has the superheroic elements as well as the superheroic intent and selfless mission. He is created by Aruru in response to the complaints of the tyrannized men and women of Uruk—his origin has a selfless mission encoded into it. Once civilized by Shamhat, he volunteers to become the watchman of the shepherds' flocks—not for himself, but for the shepherds. When he hears of Gilgamesh's brutality toward the men and women of Uruk, Enkidu volunteers to go to Uruk and stop him—not out of a desire for fame and glory, but because it is the right thing to do. Enkidu acts selflessly, for others—not for himself, as Gilgamesh did. It is Enkidu, not Gilgamesh, who is the great-grandfather of all superheroes, the archetypal protosuperhero.[10] That he becomes, in essence, the sidekick of Gilgamesh—the first sidekick in literature—does not render Enkidu any less heroic in the modern sense of the word, nor does his accompanying Gilgamesh on their (epically heroic, but ethically neutral) adventures lessen his protosuperheroism.

Of course, Enkidu is primarily an epic hero, like Gilgamesh, and can only be described as a "protosuperhero"—the term I'm making use of for those pre-Superman characters who have individual elements of the superhero's *heroenkonzept*—rather than as a superhero. Still, Enkidu has the unusual origin story, the superpower, the extraordinary skill, the distinctive appearance (his hairiness), extraordinary opponents, the finite/mortal status, and most of all the heroic mission. He has the superheroic elements, a distinct *heroenkonzept*, and the selfless mission. He is both epic hero and protosuperhero—the first such, and the only one for a long time.

Egyptian Mythology and Poems

But, of course, succeeding cultures did not look to Enkidu for a heroic role model. They looked to Gilgamesh, which is why the protosuperhero did not reappear for so long.

The Pharaonic Egyptians developed in parallel to Mesopotamia and for long centuries afterward—from the Old Kingdom (starting ca. 2690 BCE) through to the end of the Roman era (641 CE)—were influenced by the Mesopotamians, in areas ranging from architecture to ceramics. But a prominent exception to this, an area in which the Pharaonic Egyptians developed on their own, is in their mythology and cosmogony. One notable difference between Mesopotamian mythology and Pharaonic mythology is the role of men. As seen in the *Epic of Gilgamesh*, the role of men, as personified by Gilgamesh and Enkidu, is to do the will of the gods, but also to restrain the gods and their creations; the gods are great, but Gilgamesh and Enkidu are in their way significant as well. But in Pharaonic mythology the role of men is minor. The myths focus exclusively on the doings of the gods, the creation of the world, the Osiris myth, the quarrel between Horus and Set, and the journey of Ra across the sky. Pharaonic mythology and culture produced no epics about mortals, no *Epic of Gilgamesh*, no *Iliad*, no *Odyssey*, and the more-than-human figures in the myths and legends were gods, not men. And gods, again, don't count as superheroes.

Mortals do—heroic mortals—and heroic mortals are notably lacking from Pharaonic Egyptian mythology. However, ancient Egyptian literature, both predynastic (from ca. 6000 BCE) and dynastic (from ca. 3100 BCE), does have the occasional mortal hero, in poetic and fabular form. I'm differentiating between ancient Egyptian and Pharaonic Egyptian literature because the literature of ancient Egypt, in its various genres, predates the "classical" mythology of Pharaonic Egypt by millennia and existed and was consumed during and after the Pharaonic periods. The popular conception of ancient Egyptian mythology is the product of the Pharaonic era; ancient Egyptian literature, with its mortal characters, is much older.

Looking at ancient Egyptian literature from the perspective of a critic in search of legendary mortal heroes, the modern reader is most likely to be struck by their relative absence. The genres that the ancient Egyptians wrote in—moral teachings, prophecies, funerary texts, epistles, hymns—did not produce tales of heroic mortals. Their biographical works about historical figures often made those individuals into heroic figures with heroic accomplishments, but these works were intended to be told as fact rather than fiction. The "Prayer of King Ramesses II" (ca. 1285 BCE) has an epic gloss, presenting Ramesses II as a legendary warrior ("Did I not fill your temples with my spoils of war?"),[11] but the prayer is presented as a work of autobiographical, historical fact rather than as a work of fiction. In general, while the ancient Egyptians did have primitive forms of genre literature, these genres were culturally relevant to the Egyptians—travel stories, *königsnovelle,* and mythological stories—and the hero tale was not.[12]

The ancient Egyptians did, however, have a few works that we might think of as heroic fiction. Foremost among them, what at least one critic calls "the finest piece of literature to survive from ancient Egypt,"[13] is the anonymously written "The Tale of Sinuhe," whose coherent, traditional form dates from the 12th Dynasty in the 20th century BCE. "The Tale of Sinuhe" tells the story of Sinuhe, a courtier who runs away from an attempted coup to live in exile in Upper Retenu (northern Palestine and Southern Syria). While there, he serves King Amunenshi and fights for him against the Easterners who are plaguing Upper Retenu, in particular slaying in single combat a rebellious Retenu chieftain, "a champion without contenders/Since he had overmanned them, every one."[14]

For all its heroic content and influence, however–and there are obvious echoes of and parallels to "Sinuhe" throughout the Old Testament[15]— "Sinuhe" is merely a protoepic featuring a culture hero, albeit one nearly as old as *The Epic of Gilgamesh.* Sinuhe himself lacks the elements of the superhero listed in Chapter 1, more so even than Gilgamesh, not to mention Enkidu. This does not detract from Sinuhe's heroism, of course; it just excludes him from the lineage of the superhero, which is the focus of this book.

Samson and the Wild Men

The biblical Book of Judges dates to circa the eighth century BCE, but the core of Judges, the hero stories, go back a century or more before.[16] So Judges, and more specifically the story of Samson, can be traced back to ninth century BCE sources—well after the "The Tale of Sinuhe," but some centuries before the Greek myths. Although the influence of Egyptian culture and mythology on the Bible is well-known and needs no elucidating here, it should be noted that there was no Egyptian source for Samson or even influence on him. Samson, instead, is the more or less direct descendant of Enkidu, who is the archetypal "wild man" of ancient Near Eastern folkloric tradition.[17]

The wild men have certain elements in common: hairiness, unusual size, remoteness from human civilization, identity as a foreigner/nonnative, primitiveness in his weaponry, unrestrained aggressiveness and lust, relationship with (and secret knowledge of) wild animals, insanity, outsider status (when compared to civilized warriors), and vulnerability to being made civilized through the lure of a woman.

Obviously these elements can be seen in *The Epic of Gilgamesh* in Enkidu.[18] Equally obviously, these elements can be seen in Samson. By no means the only wild man of the Old Testament—individuals from Adam to Nimrod to Nebuchadnezzar match the description of the wild man[19]— Samson is nonetheless the most significant example of the Old Testament wild men and arguably the closest the Bible has to a protosuperhero. Saul killed his thousands, and David his ten thousands, and Goliath to boot. Elijah could outrun a chariot and call down fire from Heaven. Moses controlled nature, the wind and the water. Josheb-basshebeth, Eleazar, and Shammah were David's *gibborim* ("mighty men"), and Shamgar's slaying of 600 Philistines with an ox-goad[20] implies superstrength and the use of a distinctive weapon. But they are all ordinary adventure heroes and culture heroes, albeit with the addition of one or two protosuperheroic elements. It is Samson who has the *heroenkonzept* and most of the elements of the protosuperhero.

The story of Samson, though from the Old Testament rather than the New Testament, will be familiar to most readers: a barren couple are visited by an Angel of the Lord, who promises them a special child as long as the couple follows certain rules and makes their son a Nazarite, one who takes special vows of abstinence, including refraining from wine and liquor, not cutting the hair on one's head, and not becoming ritually impure. Samson is raised as a Nazarite and is empowered by the Spirit of the Lord on various occasions: in killing a young lion and numerous

Philistines, bursting the cords that the Philistines bound him with, slaying more Philistines with the jawbone of a donkey, and then judging Israel for 20 years. It is only when Samson is seduced by Delilah and tells her the secret of his strength, and his head is shorn, that the Spirit of the Lord leaves him and he loses his superhuman strength. He is then blinded by the Philistines and imprisoned. But his hair grows back, and when he prays to the Lord his strength is restored to him, and using all his might he topples the house that he and the Philistines are in, killing himself and 3,000 of the Philistines.

Samson would seem to meet the protosuperheroic criteria listed in Chapter 1, just as Enkidu does. He has a *heroenkonzept*: an unusual origin, a superpower (and "in post-biblical Jewish tradition Samson does acquire gigantic dimensions"),[21] extraordinary skills (fighting), a distinctive weapon (the jawbone of the donkey), the equivalent of a costume in his long uncut hair, an extraordinary opponent (the lion), and he is finite and can be killed.

What Samson's *heroenkonzept* lacks is the selfless mission: he does what he does for the Israelite nation rather than for the objective good of everyone, and indeed his entire life is the fulfillment of the divine mission decreed for him before his birth—"He is to begin to deliver the Israelites from the hands of the Philistines."[22] From the point of view of the Israelites, Samson is a kind of superhero, but from the point of view of the Philistines, he is a supervillain—and how many superheroes fail this kind of viewpoint test? Not many; war heroes like Captain America and most of the Golden Age superheroes do, of course, but they have other elements of the superhero scale to make up for it. Samson does not, and ends up in the middle of the superheroic scale.

Moreover, structurally and thematically Samson remains "permanently liminal"[23] until his death, an insider of the Israelites but also, by virtue of his wild man status, a permanent outsider as well.

> Just as, however, wilderness is never a terminus for Israel but, as Talmon put it, a liminal place of transformation, the wild man Samson too represents a means to an end. Wild men typically have an instrumental role in narrative. They solve problems for society (usually unintentionally and solely in reaction to egocentric appetites or personal slights), winning battles and slaying dragons, but, often, find no place in society for themselves . . . by single-handedly killing several thousand Philistines, Samson completes his destructive mission. The destruction is the prelude to the creation of a nation in its own right, but the task of building up and maintaining culture belongs to others. For the permanently liminal hero Samson, there is no place after he has torn down the temple of Dagon at Gaza.[24]

Thematically, one of the stories of superheroes—perhaps *the* story of superheroes—is the story of outsiders, by virtue of birth, personality, or superhuman abilities and powers, negotiating their liminal status and eventually being accepted by and incorporated into society; though, because of the perpetual second act in which the great majority of super-heroes live, this acceptance and incorporation never fully takes place. The story arc of Samson is of a liminal character who remains liminal until his death, a state of affairs applicable to the classic Western cowboy hero[25] but not to superheroes.

The "Heroes" of Greek Mythology

Greek mythology did not develop in isolation. There was substantial traffic between Greece and other civilizations, both materially and cultur-ally. The Greeks took much from Egypt, not least from Egypt's myths, and while the Greek sources don't explicitly acknowledge the Egyptian myths until the fifth century BCE, "it is probably right to think of Egyptian mythology as part of the general myth-ritual *koine* (shared language) of the eastern Mediterranean and western Asia."[26] *The Epic of Gilgamesh*, whose fingerprints can be seen all over Greek poetry and myth, has as extensive an influence, just as the Mesopotamians more generally influ-enced Greek arts and crafts.[27] But what the Greeks took from *The Epic of Gilgamesh* were themes, episodes (the Sumerian epic "Gilgamesh and Agga" has direct parallels in the *Iliad*),[28] verses, and arguably the cycle of Heracles stories—just not the superheroic *ethos* of Enkidu. Numerous ingredients ultimately became the stew of the Greek myths, but one searches through them, too, in vain for Enkidu's morality.[29]

However, Greek culture and mythology did give us a wide array of myths about mortal heroes as well as the *Iliad* and the *Odyssey*, and it is natural to turn to them in search of more protosuperheroes.

But after examining the Greek myths, starting with Hesiod's *Theogony* (ca. 700 BCE), one is forced to conclude that there, too, one searches in vain for the influence of Enkidu. What motivates the Greek mortal heroes is self-interest, the lure of sex or gold, the prospect of renown, the pursuit of excellence (*aretē*). Selfless, ethical, and benign motivations are rare. Consider:

- Achilles is a warrior who lusts after fame and has a large ego. (His love of Patroclus and his occasional thoughtful introspection are his only redeem-ing qualities.)
- Amphitryon acts to avenge the deaths of his beloved Alcmene.

- Atalanta acts out of a desire to avoid marriage and then out of love for Meleager.
- Bellerophon captures the Pegasus and kills the Chimera as part of his duty of expiation for the crime of murder.
- Cadmus follows the orders of the oracle of Delphi.
- Daedalus constructs the labyrinth for his king and makes his wings so that he and his son Icarus can escape imprisonment.
- Hippomenes acts out of love for Atalanta.
- Jason goes in search of the Golden Fleece so that he can take the throne of Pelias.
- Meleager kills the Calydonian Boar because his father tells him to.
- Narcissus acts out of pride and self-love.
- Odysseus's primary characteristic is his *mētis*, or "cunning intelligence." He is motivated throughout the *Odyssey* by his desire to return home.
- Oedipus kills the Sphinx to claim the throne of Thebes. His actions to end the plague of infertility are taken because it is his kingly responsibility to do so.
- Orpheus presents gifts to humanity but descends into the underworld to retrieve his dead wife out of a selfish love.
- Pelops acts out of love for Hippodamia.
- Perseus originally acts out of a desire to protect his mother Danaë from her suitor Polydectes, but then kills the sea serpent Cetus to claim Andromeda as his wife.
- Pirithous acts out of friendship to Theseus and a desire to claim Persephone as his wife.

The list goes on. Inarguably, some of these characters have protosuperheroic elements—Achilles with his magical invulnerability, Perseus with his magic weapon (the Medusa's head)—but they emphatically do not have the heroic, selfless mission. Selflessness is in fact not a consideration for them at all. Their primary goal is *aretē*, the quality of excellence in performing a function. For warriors, that meant "strength, bravery, physical courage, prowess. Conversely, there was no weakness, no unheroic trait, but one, and that was cowardice and the consequent failure to pursue heroic goals."[30] Secondary to *aretē* is order, control, stability; "the maintenance of order whether on the field of battle or in the household, was tantamount to the continuance of society; its absence spelled the end of civilization itself."[31] Selflessness is not present in this *ethos* at all. As is the case with Gilgamesh, some of the actions of the Greek heroes are superheroic, but their morals and intentions are not.

Missing from the preceding list are four figures who deserve separate examination. The most obvious exception, and the one who seems to be closest to an archetypal protosuperhero in the Greek myths, is Heracles. After all, he has several of the superheroic elements listed in Chapter 1: he has superpowers, his divine strength and later magic invulnerability; he has an extraordinary ability at fighting; he has a trademark weapon, his club; he has a trademark costume, the skin of the lion of Nemea; he has extraordinary opponents, including the monsters of his 12 Labors; he has an unusual origin story—he is the son of Zeus and is the enemy of Hera from before he is born; he is finite and can be killed—the Heracles cycle of stories ends with his death and divine apotheosis.

His *heroenkonzept* is full of superheroic elements. He seems to meet most of the prerogatives for a protosuperhero, in fact. Except—and this is an absence we will repeatedly see throughout the centuries and the next few chapters—Heracles is missing what I argue is the most important element of all: the heroic (in the modern sense of the word) mission and selfless motivation. The mixture of heroic (in the classical sense) capabilities and psychological flaws—the fact that his life history is a litany of misdeeds as well as triumphant acts—is what makes Heracles so fascinating a character study in the myths, but it is those flaws and misdeeds that render him inadequate (to say the least) as a protosuperhero.

Consider: as a child he kills the serpents in self-defense; he murders his tutor in response to criticism; he kills the lion of Mt. Cithaeron so that he can have sex with King Thespius's 50 daughters; he fights for Thebes out of loyalty to his wife's father; he murders the usurper to his father-in-law's throne; driven mad by Hera, he murders his children, two of Iphicles's children, and, according to some sources, his wife; he enters service to King Eurystehus—and performs the 12 Labors of Heracles—in order to purify himself and to achieve immortality; he frees Prometheus with the permission of Zeus, who wishes Heracles to gain renown; Heracles gives his wife away and murders Iphitus when Iphitus suspects him of stealing cattle; he enters service to Omphale, the Queen of Lydia, to expiate his crime, and has adventures in her name; he kills Trojans, Spartans, and others to avenge previous insults; he fights the giants at the bidding of the gods; he wrestles the river god so he can marry Deianeira; and he dies as a result of infidelity.

Hardly the career of what we would call a superhero, is it? Heracles was of course a hero to the Greeks, and the subject of a cult after his death, but for his martial capabilities and achievements rather than his personality, psychology, or motivations. No, Heracles is an epic hero, and what the Greek poet Pindar called the *heros theos* (hero-god),[32] the half-divine mortal destined for ascension to godly status, but he is no protosuperhero—he is on the far lesser end of the superheroic continuum.

Another possible candidate for protosuperheroic status in the Greek myths is Theseus. Like Heracles, he has a superpower, divine strength, being the son of Poseidon; Theseus (like most Greek mythical heroes) has an extraordinary ability at fighting; he has an iconic weapon, the staff that he took from the outlaw Periphetes; he has extraordinary opponents, including the wild sow of Crommyum and the Minotaur; he has an unusual origin story, being raised in secret with the purpose of returning to Athens and claim his kingship; he is finite and can be killed—the Theseus myths end with his death and later existence as a ghost.

In his first adventures, Theseus kills bandits, bad men, and the wild sow of Crommyum out of self-defense; he captures the Cretan Bull by order of King Aegeus; Theseus kills the Minotaur voluntarily, to put an end to the tribute of youths sent to Crete; Theseus abandons Ariadne after she helps him kill the Minotaur; he becomes king of Athens and establishes democracy; he abducts the Amazonian queen and fathers a son with her; he defeats the Amazons when they try to take revenge for their queen's abduction; he takes part in the hunt for the Calydonian Boar and was a member of Jason's Argonauts, though neither event was done for noble goals; he fights the centaurs on behalf of his friend Peirithous; he tries to carry off the goddess Persephone and is trapped in the underworld until he is freed by Heracles; Theseus kills 50 sons of a usurper to the throne of Athens; he curses his son based on a false accusation; and he is exiled from Athens and dies from falling off (or being pushed off) a cliff. As a ghost, he aids the Athenians at the Battle of Marathon.

As with Heracles, Theseus's career, told thus in summary, reads like the history of a flawed individual (by modern moral standards) rather than the deeds of a protosuperhero. What Theseus has over Heracles is his one instance of notably selfless behavior: volunteering to kill the Minotaur so that the every-seven-years sacrifice of Athenian boys and girls will be put to an end. Presumably, Theseus *also* sought glory and renown—what Greek hero did not seek fame, or preferred to hide his accomplishments?—but the myths are clear: his motivation, in this one case, is what we would now call heroic. But on balance Theseus, like Heracles, is an epic hero rather than a protosuperhero—on the continuum he is less superheroic rather than more, even if he is more superheroic than Heracles.

A third candidate is Prometheus. Originally, in Hesiod's *Theogony*, Prometheus's motivation for reserving the best part of a sacrifice for humans and for giving fire to humanity is rebellion against Zeus; there is nothing particularly benign or selfless about it.[33] On the other hand, the unknown author (traditionally thought to be Aeschylus) of the three Promethean plays, *Prometheus the Fire-Bearer, Prometheus Bound,* and *Prometheus Released* (ca. 450 BCE), following the views of the cult of Prometheus, portrayed Prometheus, though still the enemy of Zeus, as being full of selfless love for humanity, which is why he saves humanity when Zeus wants to destroy it, why Prometheus steals fire from Hephaestus and brings it to humans, and why he teaches them the various arts. Prometheus is notable for his selfless benignity toward humanity, a feature none of the other divine beings possess, and which is certainly a protosuperheroic motivation.

But otherwise Prometheus is a poor fit as a protosuperhero. He is not mortal, instead being the son of a Titan and incapable of dying. (His punishment for stealing fire is delivered to him while living, as opposed to those mortals who are punished in the afterlife; and this punishment—to have his liver ripped out and eaten by an eagle—which would kill an ordinary human, heals after the eagle leaves.) Prometheus has distinctive iconography—the flame—but no trademark outfit or weapon. His opponents (the gods themselves) are unusual, but he acts as a thief (and benefactor to humanity, true) rather than as a vigilante. Prometheus lives in a largely lawless society where individuals rather than a state or government enforce the law. Prometheus is certainly morally good, but equally certainly not a protosuperhero.

The fourth exception, and arguably the one closest to the superheroic ideal (if lacking the protosuperheroic elements), is Hector. In Homer, of course, Hector is thoughtful and even courtly, though still a warrior on behalf of Troy. But starting with the *Ilias Latina,* the first century CE abridged version of the *Iliad,* poets and commentators, including early Christian writers, transformed Hector into something else, a paragon of knightly virtues, until in the 14th century he was designated as one of the Nine Worthies, the most chivalrous of all historical warriors. The Nine Worthies' membership was three pagans (Hector, Caesar, Alexander), three Jews (Joshua, David, Judas Maccabeus) and three Christians (Arthur, Charlemagne, Godfrey of Bouillon), but even among such august company Hector was viewed as special. "As the oldest he seems also to be *primus inter pares.* In representations of the Nine Worthies he is sometimes shown gesturing as though he is their spokesmen."[34] Medieval romances even made Hector into Achilles's superior, with Achilles only able to kill Hector with a cowardly blow from behind. From the 14th century to the 16th century, Hector and the Nine Worthies are the archetypal chivalrous knights, although by 1596, in Shakespeare's *Love's Labour's Lost,* they are the objects of comic scorn rather than respect.

Does this make Hector a protosuperhero, though? As one of the Nine Worthies he had recognizable iconography (the symbol of one or two lions on his shield), but he lacks the other elements, even the distinctive weapon. He is courtly and wise, chivalrous and noble—but not selfless. If, as I argue, the heroic, selfless mission is the minimum requirement for inclusion in the list of superheroes, then Hector, though one of the Nine Worthies, doesn't qualify.

Nectanebo II

Nekht-hor-heb, a.k.a. Nectanebo II, was the last pharaoh of Egypt's 30th Dynasty, ruling from 360–342 BCE. The facts of his life, as related by the Greek historian Diodorus of Sicily, are these: nephew of the pharaoh Teos, Nectanebo II rebelled against his uncle's rule and defeated both Teos and another pretender to the throne, then spent years defending Egypt against the Persian Achaemenid Empire. Nectanebo II was ultimately defeated by the armies of Artaxerxes III, accompanied by Greek mercenaries, in 342. Artaxerxes marched into Memphis, and Nectanebo fled to Upper Egypt, then to Nubia, and then disappeared, his final fate unknown.

So much for the historical Nectanebo II. Egyptian folk legends told different stories about him, stories of the reason for his disappearance and for his eventual return. These legends came together to form what Martin Braun calls the "Nectanebus Romance."[35] In the *Nectanebus Romance*, which Braun dates to the third century BCE, Nectanebo summons his armies and his magical powers to destroy the invading Persian army, only to have "an epiphany of the gods from which he gathered that the gods themselves were leading the hostile forces against him," that they personally "guided the ships of the hostile barbarians."[36] This epiphany was too much for Nectanebo, who knew he could not fight against the gods and chose not to, which is why he fled. A later version of this legend, influenced by the *Nectanebus Romance*, would appear in Manetho's *Aegyptiaca* (third century BCE), about Pharaoh "Amenophis" fleeing from the rebellious priest Osarseph.

This *Nectanebus Romance* would be just another lost work of historical fiction, and Nectanebo II just another dead king, except for its immediate influence on three BCE texts and Nectanebo II's second- (or perhaps third-) hand influence on the development of the protosuperhero.

The first text was the *Demotic Chronicle*, a series of oracular prophecies dating from the third century BCE. The *Chronicle* claims to have predicted Nectanebo II and that he will return:

When, after the flight of Nectanebus, the hated Persians once more took over Egypt, the heart of the people was crushed, and only hope and fond memory could sustain their spirits. They thought of Nectanebus with sorrow and affection as the last of their native Pharaohs, and in him all their hopes for the future came to be focused. He had gone, no one knew where. Perhaps he was only sleeping for the present, like Frederic Barbarossa in the great Kyffhäuserberg; but, like Frederic and other famous champions of old, he was destined—yea, the prophets and the oracles had declared it—to return again in the person of a younger and more vigorous king, who would drive out the enemies of Egypt and liberate the people.[37]

The second text was *The Dream of Nectanebus*, written in Greek in the early second century BCE. In the (fragmentary) *Dream of Nectanebus,* Nectanebo II dreams that the gods are abandoning him, due in part because he has not finished building the temple of Onuris (Anhur).

And the third text was the *Alexander Romance* (see below), which incorporates some of the *Nectanebus Romance*—we can never know how much, although as Braun points out, "Would not the origin of the Alexander Romance become much more intelligible, if one could assume that it was preceded by a Nectanebus Romance with which the former competed and which it strove to displace?"[38] In the *Alexander Romance* Nectanebo II uses his magic to disguise himself and seduce Olympias, Alexander's mother. Nectanebo II thus becomes the true father of Alexander and is his tutor for a dozen years, until Alexander—for reasons that the *Romance* does not make clear—kills him. Nectanebo II's personality in the *Alexander Romance* is ambiguous, both good and evil, some distance from that of the protagonist of the *Nectanebus Romance*.

The influence of Nectanebo II on the development of the superhero—besides being the earliest example (albeit an isolated one without influence) of the Sleeping King/King Under The Hill character, most prominently seen in comics in Captain America's return from the ice in *The Avengers* #4 (cover date March 1964)—is in Nectanebo II's role in the *Alexander Romance* as a sorcerer, not an evil sorcerer, but as a character of both good and evil, and even (despite his actions with Olympias) more good than evil. This quality of ambiguity, leaning toward a positive portrayal, is practically unique in the ancient world with regard to sorcerers—in Exodus Moses defeats the pharaoh's sorcerers with the help of God, not through magic of his own—and, via the *Alexander Romance*, sets up the prototype of the sorcerer hero that would later appear in medieval chivalric romances, from Maugis to Merlin of the Arthur stories to Melissa in *Orlando Furioso*. At a farther remove, this character type would appear during the 19th century, as we'll see, and becomes common in superhero comics (see Dr. Strange, Dr. Fate, and so on).

Aeneas

Following the Battle of Actium (31 BCE), in which the ships of Octavian defeated the combined fleets of Mark Antony and Cleopatra, Octavian became the undisputed de facto ruler of Rome. To commemorate his victory, Octavian commissioned a poem from the poet Virgil (70–19 BCE). Virgil worked until his death to finish this poem, which was nearly complete at the time of his death. The poem, *The Aeneid*, was published two years later, to acclaim, and posterity deems it the greatest of the Roman epics.

The Aeneid tells the story of Aeneas, son of the Trojan prince Anchises and the goddess Venus. Aeneas was not Virgil's creation: Aeneas appears in *The Iliad* as a favorite of the gods (even Poseidon, who hates the Trojans), he is specifically stated to have survived the Fall of Troy,[39] and in the centuries after *The Iliad*'s creation and propagation stories circulated about Aeneas's travels and exploits, including the founding of Rome. *The Aeneid* fleshes out Aeneas's story, telling of the escape from Troy, the attempts to find a new home for himself and his fellow survivors, the landing at Carthage and Aeneas's year-long affair with Dido, the queen of Carthage. *The Aeneid* further tells of Aeneas's flight from Dido at the instigation of Jupiter and Venus (leading to Dido's cursing of Aeneas and the eternal enmity between Carthage and Rome), the return to Sicily, the funeral games organized for Aeneas's father, Aeneas's descent into the underworld, and the Trojans' eventual arrival in Latium, where Aeneas becomes betrothed to Lavinia, the daughter of the king of Latium, defeats the forces of Turnus, king of the rival Rutuli, and kills Turnus himself, who Lavinia had originally been promised to.

There can be no question of the influence of the *Aeneid* on Western culture, high or popular. Not just a cornerstone of the canon, the *Aeneid* was for centuries required reading (and memorizing) for anyone wishing to learn Latin or to be well educated. The number of works it influenced is high, including (possibly) *Beowulf*, *Sir Gawain and the Green Knight*, and *The Faerie Queene*. Aeneas was one of the archetypal characters of later heroic literature, just as the *Aeneid* was the source of themes and incidents.

But it cannot be said with any accuracy that Aeneas is either a protosuperhero—he lacks nearly all of the superheroic elements of Chapter 1, even and especially the heroic mission element—or specifically influential on the development of the superhero. Male heroes in general, yes, but superheroes specifically, no. His primary attribute, *"pius"* (piousness), did not communicate itself to later protosuperheroes—the secondary aspect of *pius* is dutifulness, but that has never been in short supply among heroes, and Aeneas's sense of duty is to his family and country rather than to a heroic, selfless mission. His other attributes— patient endurance, charity, and faith—are likewise commendable but not particularly superheroic. Aeneas does not even have a legendary weapon. Moreover, in the medieval tradition Aeneas was not only responsible for abandoning Dido but was a traitor to Troy, having engaged in secret dis- cussions with the Greeks and even being responsible for opening the city gate to them in exchange for a promise to be spared.[40] To the Romans, Aeneas was a culture hero, but later critics saw him as crucially flawed— his abandonment of Dido was not justified by his piousness—and no one today would see him as a protosuperhero, not least because he lacks nearly all of the elements of the superhero listed in Chapter 1.

Aeneas falls into the same category as several of the characters in this chapter: an influential epic hero who lacks a superheroic *heroenkonzept* and whose halo of influence never quite reached the superheroes.

The Noble and Just *Latrones*

The influence of Aeneas and the *Aeneid* was as mentioned heavy. But there was another cultural archetype in the Roman Empire that is of par- ticular relevance to the history of superheroes: the *latrones*. Literally trans- lated as "bandits," the *latrones* were no mere thugs or thieves, but instead were active threats to the social and moral order of the Roman state.[41] The *latrones* were widespread—indeed, one writer speaks of the "ubiquity of banditry"[42] in the Roman Empire—and long-lasting writers from Juvenal to Pliny the Elder wrote about them.[43]

While the *latrones* were on the whole no better or worse than bandits across the ages, one aspect of them deserves our particular attention: the contemporary perception (whether or not it was a reality is a subject on which modern writers differ) that they were what E. J. Hobsbawm, the author of *Bandits* (1969), the landmark work on the subject, calls "social bandits": "The point about social bandits is that they are peasant outlaws whom the lord and the state regard as criminals, but who remain within peasant society, and are considered by their people as heroes, as champi- ons, avengers, fighters for justice . . . and in any case as men to be admired, helped and supported."[44]

The idea of the noble peasant outlaw can be traced back at least to Phar- aonic Egypt, with the peasant thieves known to the Greeks as *boukoloi* and to the Egyptians as "Asiatics" or "herdsmen." Though "desperate" (read: violent and rebellious) and perhaps practicing human sacrifice and canni-balism,[45] the *boukoloi* also provided role models for noble outlaws in Egyp-tian fiction (from the fourth century BCE) and then in Greek romances.[46]

Two of the *latrones* in particular stand out as having some of the fea-tures of the protosuperhero. Julius Maternus, active (according to the his-torian Herodian) in the mid- to late second century CE, deserted from the Roman army to become a bandit. He accumulated both followers and loot, and was successful to the point that the Romans viewed him not just as a criminal but as an enemy of the state. Maternus's response was to step up his activity and—this must be emphasized—to begin freeing prisoners from prison, regardless of whether they were guilty or not.[47] Maternus's ultimate goal, according to Herodian, was to depose Emperor Commodus—a goal at which Maternus failed due to betrayal—but his methods on the way toward that goal were, at least at times, motivated by rebellion against an oppressive government entity, the Roman state.

Even more Robin Hood–like was the character of Bulla Felix ("Lucky Amulet"—a code name rather than his actual name). The historian Cas-sius Dio describes Bulla Felix as an actual person; later historians view him as a myth.[48] According to Dio, Bulla—active around 205–207 CE—led a band of more than 600 men and "was never seen when seen, never found when found, never caught when caught."[49] Bulla robbed from the wealthy and gave some loot to artisans after making use of their skills, disguised himself in order to free some condemned men from death in the arena, and sent a message to Emperor Severus, telling him to feed his slaves so that they would not be forced to turn to a life of banditry.[50]

Maternus and Bulla Felix, and the Hobsbawmian social bandits of antiquity as a whole, are in many ways a far cry from noble Enkidu. As Shaw and Grünewald write, their perceived motivations were mixed, being active agents against the state, loot-interested criminals, and heroic Robin Hood–style social levelers. But as this book hopes to show, the lineage of the protosuperhero is a confused and hectic one, with multiple vectors leading up to Superman. Enkidu, the moral Übermensch, is one; so, too, the social bandits like Maternus, Bulla Felix, and Robin Hood, who are—let's call them great-uncles of Batman. Not directly related, but a part of the family tree. And while any *direct* influence of the *latrones* on the stories of Robin Hood would be purely speculative (and likely without merit), the *latrones* are the earliest and most prominent example of the Hobsbawmian social bandit, a cultural archetype found worldwide, and a heavy influence on the Robin Hood stories and thus on modern superheroes.

Alexander the Legend

Alexander III of Macedon (356–323 BCE) was the conqueror of the known world and established an empire that stretched from Greece and Egypt to India. His recorded life is colorful enough and full of individual anecdotes that read like something out of an epic poem or adventure novel.[51] Naturally, that wasn't enough for readers, who demanded more about him, stories and narratives that would place Alexander in the lineage of epic heroes of yore. These stories began during his lifetime but became vibrant and flourishing some centuries after his death and were gathered together in the *Alexander Romance*, an anonymously written work credited to "Pseudo-Callisthenes" in some sources. The exact date of composition for the *Romance* is unknown: "component elements of the *Romance* were already in existence in the third century B.C.,"[52] but scholars continue to place its coherence into a discrete whole in a date range of 323 BCE to the third century CE.

Its individual elements include Egyptian tales, Jewish tradition, and the work of Greek and Roman historians and travelers/fabulists. These individual elements came together to form the *Alexander Romance*, which began as a Greek text, was translated into Latin and expanded, and then, following another Latin version written by Leo the Archpriest of Naples in the 10th century CE, became the medieval version of a best seller, appearing in all the languages of Western Europe as well as Armenian, Middle Persian, Russian, Arabic, Malay, and Mongolian. With the exception of the Bible, no other work was more frequently translated in the Middle Ages[53]; its influence on later writers was considerable. As late as 1683, the Alexander of the *Romance* was making appearances in European literature, although by that time translations of the historical accounts of Alexander were supplanting the *Romance*.

Pseudo-Callisthenes's *Alexander Romance* begins ordinarily enough by telling the reader how Alexander's real father was not Philip but was instead Nectanebo II, the last of the Pharaohs, disguised as a god. Various ordinary exploits follow—the (unhistorical) conquest of the Romans, the founding of Alexandria, and the attack on the Persians. But from there the author of the *Romance* enters mythic territory, telling the reader of how Alexander defeated giants (the Phytoi, 24 cubits tall, with "hands and fingers like saws"),[54] hairy wild men (the Oxoli, "as wide as a spear"),[55] talking trees, and many-eyed beasts, and how Alexander eventually traveled to the Land of Darkness. Later versions of the *Alexander Romance* go still farther, with a battle with a god in the form of a dragon, a trip to the land of troglodytes, Alexander's construction of a gate of brass and iron that will keep out the Unclean Nations, Gog and Magog, and even his flight up to heaven in a griffin-drawn chariot.[56]

Much of the Alexander of the *Alexander Romance* is standard epic hero material, but he does have two elements of the protosuperhero about him. He has a distinctive appearance, both his lion's mane of hair (perhaps a deliberate reference to the "wild man" tradition mentioned in the Samson section) and his mismatched eyes. And he has superhuman strength. But he lacks the selfless mission, the most important superheroic element, and in general his *heroenkonzept* is missing most of the superheroic elements. If Alexander is a protosuperhero, he is certainly on the "less superheroic" rather than "more superheroic" end of the spectrum.

How the consumers of the *Alexander Romance* regarded Alexander varied over time and as various cultures attended to the Alexander myth and altered the traditions for their own purposes. So the medieval Alexander becomes a romantic knight, chivalrous toward ladies as well as heroic and courtly, where centuries before he was closer in actions to the historical Alexander. Similarly, readers' attitudes toward the mythical Alexander varied: he is generous, but as a result of *hubris*; he rides into the sky as a result of pride and curiosity (both bad for medieval habitants), but also as a result of his soul striving toward heaven. For the Syrians he was a Christian, for the Jews a Jew, in Arabic a Muslim, in the Christian Middle Ages an admirable heathen who is an instrument of God. By the 14th century Alexander was regarded as one of the Nine Worthies who represent the righteous knightly virtues,[57] and this portrayal of Alexander would influence how historians viewed him up through the late 20th century.

Once again, however, we're on a branch of the superhero tree that doesn't bear fruit. Alexander—the legendary Alexander, the protosuperhero—was a part of Western culture for centuries, well into the Renaissance. He was the archetypal example of the magical adventuring hero for centuries. But his influence is questionable when it comes to superheroes. As a larger-than-life adventure hero, he provided an example for all later fictional heroes, and in that respect the fictional Alexander was quite influential, even at some many centuries' remove, on superheroes. But as a protosuperhero (albeit one on the far end of the heroic continuum) to be modeled upon, his influence was much less.[58]

Beowulf, the Thor-Wolf

This much we know about Beowulf, and the poem named after him: it exists, and he's in it. Everything else seems debatable: the etymology and meaning of his name (Bee-Wolf? Thor-Wolf? War-Wolf?), the date of the poem's composition (which scholars have placed at anywhere between 340 and 1025 CE, with circa 650–800 or late ninth to early 10th century currently being the two scholarly choices), the poem's author (layperson or cleric?), the poem's provenance (Denmark? Germany? Anglia? Wessex? Northumbria? Mercia?), even the poem's audience (secular or monastic?).[59] The sources of the poem and the influences on it have been fiercely and repetitively argued by scholars for over a century. Even the meaning of the poem depends on the listener or reader, rather than being something generally agreed-upon.

For the purposes of this book, though, all of that seems of secondary concern. What matters are *Beowulf*'s content and its influence.

The poem's major focus is on three events. Beowulf of the Geats arrives at the hall of Hrothgar, king of the Danes. Hrothgar's hall in Heorot is being attacked by the monster Grendel. Beowulf kills Grendel, then, when Grendel's vengeful mother attacks the hall, Beowulf slays her as well. Fifty years later, in Geatland, Beowulf kills a dragon but is mortally wounded in the battle. When he dies Beowulf's followers cry that "of worldly kings he was the most benevolent of men and the kindest, most generous to his people and most honour-bound."[60]

Certainly Beowulf has protosuperheroic elements. He has a superpower, greater-than-human strength; he has distinctive weapons, his sword Hrunting and then the giant's sword with which he kills Grendel's mother; he has extraordinary opponents; he is certainly finite and can be (and is) killed. But his *heroenkonzept* is at bottom not appreciably different from that of other epic heroes. Externally *Beowulf* certainly seems like a protosuperheroic tale; rather than a quest narrative like *Epic of Gilgamesh*, the tale of a divinely directed life like Samson's, or a travel narrative like *The Alexander Romance*, *Beowulf* is a story of three fights of increasing difficulty against increasingly powerful foes—a plot basic enough to function as a three-issue story arc for any superhero's title.

But *Beowulf* has elements that elevate it beyond a mere heroic slugfest with monsters, into literature, and at the same time disqualify it from consideration as protosuperheroic, and leave Beowulf on the "less superheroic" end of the superhero spectrum. Most notably, *Beowulf* is heavily elegiac, beginning with the funeral of Scyld Scefing and ending with Beowulf's admission that all his kin are gone, and then his death, "finally lamenting how even the noblest spirit must succumb ultimately to the mutability of earthly things."[61] *Beowulf* is an epic poem, and Beowulf an epic hero, and the structure of epic poems and the fate of epic heroes tends toward a third act death. *Beowulf* is a particularly grim and foreboding example of these: "the destruction of the king's hall and the death of the king imply the end of the Geat nation."[62] In this *Beowulf* is most un-superhero-like. *Beowulf* builds toward its third act, without which the first two would be mere boasting. Superhero texts by their very nature and by the exigencies of the marketplace and the consumers' demands deny this third act, reject elegies, reject grim and foreboding and a final ending, in favor of hope and rebirth and continuation. *Beowulf* is everything that superhero comics are not.[63]

Too, the dominant *ethos* of *Beowulf* is a far cry from modern superhero ethics, and not essentially dissimilar from those of the Greek heroes: "the fundamental ethical code of the poem is unmistakably secular; it is the warrior code of the aristocracy, celebrating bravery, loyalty, and generosity, with the hero finding his only immortality in the long-lasting fame of great exploits carried out in this world."[64] The heroic mission of the superheroes is entirely absent; glory is all, in *Beowulf*. Historically critics have tried to call *Beowulf* a Christian poem, and certainly there are Christian elements to it, but it is not a Christian poem: "apart from the references to God there is little to it that is really Christian; it deals in fact with the values of pagan Germanic society: loyalty unto death to the chosen leaders, the sacredness of the ties of blood-kinship and the duty to avenge a dead leader."[65] Beowulf is a paradigmatic hero for his culture, but his culture's values are a far cry from those of ours and of superheroes.

Nor can *Beowulf* be counted as influential on the development of the superhero. The poem lay unexamined for centuries, the Tudors having little use for the products of the Saxons. It wasn't until 1807 that an English scholar called attention to the poem, and not until 1815 that the first printed edition of the work, the *editio princeps*, was published. (After that, *Beowulf* studies took off, and got another boost from an obscure academic named J. R. R. Tolkien in 1936). Beowulf, though preceding Roland, King Arthur, and the other heroes who followed him, was not an influence on them and was unknown to their authors; following the Norman Conquest, *Beowulf* and its heroic lead were simply forgotten about.[66]

So Beowulf cannot properly be called an influential character in the history of the protosuperhero. He is on the lesser end of the protosuperhero continuum, and on the family tree of the superhero, Beowulf is a sprig rather than a major load-bearing branch.

Roland the Martyr

As with *Beowulf*, there are insoluble mysteries about *Chanson de Roland*, the *Song of Roland*. To quote one scholar, "none of the poem's 'vital statistics'—its date, its author, its sources—have been established conclusively, and although scholars have labored long and hard over these problems, their solution remains as remote today as it was half a century ago."[67] What we do know for certain is that there was a historical Battle of Roncesvals on the afternoon of August 15, 778; that among the men killed was "Roland, prefect of the Breton Marches"; that Roland's name appears on the back of two eighth or ninth century *deniers* (gold coins), on whose front is Charlemagne's name, which would indicate that Roland was a man of importance in his lifetime beyond that of a mere valued warrior; and that a *chanson de geste* ("song of heroic deeds," a type of French epic narrative poem) about Roland was copied down sometime between 1129 and 1165.

Everything else is assumption, though often on relatively solid scholarly grounds and based on facts. Some of those facts point more or less convincingly to the *Song of Roland* having been composed sometime at the beginning of the 12th century.[68] A man named "Turoldus" put his name at the end of the *Song*, in the line "Ci fait la geste que Turoldus declinet," an ambiguous line that means that Turoldus either composed *Roland* or copied it down. (Scholars are divided on this matter, as with so much else about *Roland*.) If Turoldus only copied *Roland* down, then the theories of a proto–*Song of Roland* may be true, placing the dating of the legend of Roland's death earlier than the 12th century. Likewise, while we can never know the full list of influences on *Roland*'s composers, there are "faint echoes"[69] of the *Aeneid*.

At least there is a physical *Song of Roland* that we can turn to, for certainties that otherwise escape us. *Roland* tells the story of the Battle of Roncesvals. Charlemagne's armies, after having conquered all of Spain in seven years but for the city of Saragossa, have been lured back home by an offer of peace from the Muslim king Marsilla. Roland, Charlemagne's nephew, volunteers to lead the rear guard protecting Charlemagne's armies on their way out of Spain. The Franks are betrayed by Roland's stepfather Ganelon, and, after a fierce battle, Roland, his best friend Oliver, Archbishop Turpin, and the rest of the Frankish rear guard are wiped out. Charlemagne avenges this defeat by vanquishing a second Muslim army and killing Balignant, the emir of Babylon. Ganelon is put on trial, and after a trial by combat to determine his fate, he is found guilty and torn apart by horses.

In terms of influence, *The Song of Roland* was one of the central heroic texts for Western Europe. It was well-known throughout the Middle Ages and the Renaissance and was a direct influence on Ariosto's *Orlando Furioso* and through it on Spenser's *Faerie Queene* and later writers of epics and heroic works. As far as influential fictional models of heroic masculinity go, Roland has to be ranked with King Arthur and Robin

Hood, not least because of the unbroken continuity of influence of *Roland*, something not the case, as we've seen, with Beowulf. One can argue that the self-righteous, empowered-by-rage-and-unshakable-confidence male superheroes—into which category fall characters from Captain America to Gerry Conway, Ross Andru, and John Romita Sr.'s Punisher to Stan Lee, Larry Liebert and Jack Kirby's Thor—are direct descendants of Roland, much more so than Beowulf or Enkidu.

So is Roland a protosuperhero? He's an epic hero, intriguingly different from the epic heroes described by Rank and Raglan and Campbell, but he lacks many of the superheroic elements described in Chapter 1. He doesn't have an origin story, a superpower, a distinctive appearance, a code name, or extraordinary opponents. He does have a distinctive weapon, the sword Durendal, and he does have a heroic mission—of a sort—but otherwise he lacks the attributes of the superhero.

Interestingly, however, he has a sidekick, his best friend Oliver, who is "wise" where Roland is "bold." And to a modern observer, looking for protosuperheroes, Oliver seems to be a better choice than Roland—however anachronistic such a judgment is.

However, one of the major traditional debates about *The Song of Roland* is whether or not it is a tragedy. Roland, Oliver, and all the Franks in the rear guard die, after all, and the poem emphasizes the fact that Roland is told by Oliver (who sees how overwhelming the enemy numbers are) to blow his olifant (horn) and summon help—something Roland refuses to do, preferring to die (and to have all his 20,000 men be killed) at the hands of the Saracens rather than disgrace himself by asking for help. Critics traditionally have seen this choice as hubris and decided that since Roland et al. die, that *The Song of Roland* must be a tragedy, and that therefore Roland's actions are the result of his fatal flaw, vanity. Oliver, the "wise" one, seems to have more respect for the lives of his men, and therefore to be more heroic, in the modern sense.

But the current critical consensus[70] is that *The Song of Roland* is not a tragedy and Roland is not a flawed figure; he is a martyr, deliberately sacrificing himself, his friends, and his men so that Charlemagne, who the poem stresses is wearied of war with the Saracens, will rededicate himself to the Christian Crusade. This, current critics stress, is the preferred inscribed narrative of the poem—what the poet's intentions were—and how the contemporary audience would have received it.

Taking this into account, then, the dominant characteristic of Roland becomes not his boastfulness, but his Christian faith, and his willingness—even eagerness—to die for the cause as a martyr, a characteristic that, while extreme to modern eyes, is nonetheless selfless, and a medieval version of the superhero's heroic mission.

So, perhaps surprisingly, Roland ends up on the "greater" end of the superhero continuum.

Medieval Heroes

The popular culture of medieval Europe was full of heroes, appearing in epic poems, romances, *chansons de geste*, ballads, and a variety of other forms of heroic narrative. That many of them are unknown today and continue to exist only between the covers of poorly circulated books and in rarely viewed Wikipedia entries does not mean that these heroes did not have their heyday and their period of influence or were in some way unworthy—it merely means that these heroes' life spans were, for various reasons, not as lengthy as that of Beowulf and The Cid and the rest.

Most of these heroes, who have names like "Aiol," "Girart de Roussillon," and the "Swan Knight," were the products of the Continent, and while substantially influential on German and French culture, even into the 19th century in some cases, they did not have a similarly strong halo of influence on English heroic culture, and therefore cannot be said to have contributed to the lineage of the protosuperhero. Too, most of these heroes are merely epic heroes, rather than protosuperheroes. But there are a number of exceptions to both points, characters who contributed something to the lineage either through sheer influence or through some exceptional protosuperheroic quality or element.

There was a great French metacycle of texts about Charlemagne, from the 12th century on, most tying into both the historical life of Charlemagne as well as the *Chanson de Roland*. Two such were the anonymously written *chansons de geste Fierabras* (ca. 1170) and *La Destruction de Rome* (ca. 1190), the latter of which is a prologue to the former. They tell of Fierabras, a massive Saracen warrior and son of Balan, Emir of Spain. Together the two conquer Rome, kill the Pope, carry off holy relics, and battle with Charlemagne and his 12 paladins. Oliver, though sorely wounded, eventually bests Fierabras, leading him to swear to become a Christian, after which Balan dies and Fierabras is given half of Spain. (This is specifically said to happen three years before the "treachery of Roncevaux."[71]) There was no historical source for either Fierabras or *Fierabras*, but the *chanson de geste*'s influence was such that there was an English version in rhyme, *Sir Ferumbras* (late 14th century) as well as other retellings of Fierabras's story across Europe through the 18th century.

Fierabras's significance lies in his protosuperheroic superhuman strength and his status as an (eventually) heroic Saracen, a forerunner to the later knights of color in the Arthurian mythos (and therefore to the nonwhite superheroes of the comics).[72]

Another pair of *chansons de geste* tying into the Charlemagne metacycle are *Renault de Montauban* (end of the 12th century) and *Maugis d'Aigremont* (ca. 1225?). *Renault de Montauban* is about the quarrel between Charlemagne and one of his vassals, Beuve d'Aigremont. Dragged into the conflict are Aymon, Beuve's brother, and Aymon's sons, one of whom is Renault. Beuve is treacherously murdered, and a war between Charlemagne and Aymon's sons follows, with peace arising between the two sides only at length. One of the main characters in the poem is Maugis, a sorcerer knight and an ally of Renault et al.; he becomes central enough to the poem that peace between Charlemagne and Aymon's sons can only be achieved if Maugis is disempowered. An unnamed poet seized on the popular reception of *Renault de Montauban* and especially Maugis and wrote *Maugis d'Aigremont*, a prequel explaining Maugis's origin (though Beuve's son, he was raised by the fairy Oriande of Rocheflor and taught necromancy by Oriande's brother Baudris), how Maugis won the intelligent horse Bayart, how Maugis fought with and was reconciled with his brother Vivien, and how Maugis inflicted a magical defeat on Charlemagne. Although *Maugis d'Aigremont* had a life span of centuries in France and the Low Countries, it was unknown in England; not so *Renault de Montauban*, which was translated into English in the 14th century and flourished for four centuries. (Renault would become "Rinaldo" in Ariosto's *Orlando Furioso*.) Maugis's influence rests in his role as a magician hero, the successor to Nectanebo II and the predecessor to Merlin, but more noble and proactive than either. The line of magician heroes runs through Maugis to the sorcerers of *Orlando Furioso* on its way to Dr. Strange, Dr. Fate, and others.

Yet another tale tying in to Charlemagne, which eventually became influential in England, is the *Roman de Robert le Diable*. The original version of it comes from the first half of the 13th century, with the *Roman* being set down in the second half of the 13th century, and English editions appearing in the 15th century. The story is about Robert the Devil, the father of Rijckaert (Richard), one of Charlemagne's best knights. As a young man, Robert was a hellion. His parents could not conceive until his mother promised any child of hers to the Devil, after which the mother immediately gets pregnant. The child quickly grows and displays superhuman strength and limited invulnerability, but his behavior is reprehensible, and as a teenager and young adult he engages in rape and murder for years. It is only when he discovers the secret of his parentage that he confesses his sins to the Pope and does penance. When the Saracens attack Rome, Robert puts on a suit of white armor and defeats the Saracens, eventually marrying the daughter of the emperor. The *Roman de Robert le Diable* was popular in England in the 15th and 16th centuries under its own name and as the romance *Sir Gowther,* in which form Shakespeare made use of it for *King Lear.*[73] Robert the Devil, with his superstrength and limited invulnerability, is an Übermensch *avant la lettre,* although he lacks the selfless mission of an Enkidu.

The Cid

Unlike Roland, we do have some of the facts of the life about Rodrigo Diaz de Vivar (ca. 1043–1099), the Castilian knight and military leader known to the Moors as "El Cid" (the Lord) and to Christians as "El Campeador" (the Champion). De Vivar fought the Moors nobly and well, served his Castilian kings faithfully, served Muslim rulers when his Castilian king exiled him, established an independent state in eastern Spain, and ruled over that for the final five years of his life. When he died, he was so respected that even a longtime foe of his, a Muslim, called him "one of the Miracles of God."[74]

Legends spread about de Vivar in the decades after his death and songs were sung about him. In 1207, one "Per Abbat" (Abbot Peter) "escrivió" the poem *El Cantar de mio Cid,* or *The Song of the Cid.* As with Turoldus and *The Song of Roland,* there is considerable scholarly debate about whether Abbot Peter composed/created *The Song of the Cid* or merely copied down a preexisting poem or song, one (it's argued) that may go back as far as ca. 1175.

The Song of the Cid tells the story of Cid's exile—he is accused of keeping some of the Moorish tribute owed to the king—the Cid's raids on Moorish territories, his defeat of King Yusuf ibn Tashfin and the capture of Valencia, and the restoration of the Cid's honor. The princes, the nephews of the king, marry the Cid's daughters, but the princes are cowards who insult and abandon their wives, leading the Cid's men to fight them in a duel. Later, the princes beat the Cid's daughters and leave them for dead, leading the Cid to seek justice. The princes are defeated in another duel, this time mortally, and the Cid's daughters are married to the kings of Navarre and Aragon, thus beginning the union of Spain.

The Cid's *heroenkonzept* is marginally protosuperheroic: the unique weapon (his sword Tizona), the extraordinary fighting ability, and the code name. In this respect, he is perhaps the least protosuperheroic of the figures described in this chapter. He had no superhuman abilities, nor a selfless mission, nor even a distinctive appearance.

But no description of the lineage of superheroes would be complete without including him, because of his cultural influence. Certainly he became the national hero of Spain, appearing in ballads and epic poems over the course of centuries, and even in a play by the French playwright Corneille, which was well received in Paris in 1636. The legend of the Cid never disappeared. But his influence on the lineage of the superhero came from the interest in him aroused in the 19th century after Robert Southey's translation of *The Song of the Cid* into English in 1808. The Cid became one of the standards against which medieval knights and other heroes were compared. The Cid became an icon of heroism, similar to (if more literally foreign than) King Arthur—a *prieux chevalier*, a patriot, full of self-control and magnanimity and dignity, an uncompromising Christian (similar to Roland), a mature man of wise judgment and courtly manners, a loyalist to his king despite the king's suspicions of him, "embodying virtues at once martial and civic, a law-abiding citizen as well as a good family man and a brave soldier."[75] The Cid became an archetypal and definitional hero in the 19th century, and the important fictional heroes of that century—who were in turn heavily influential on the early superheroes—were influenced by him.

The Cid is the least protosuperheroic figure in this chapter, but had a longer and stronger influence than many others.

The Matter of Arthur

One can argue a great many things about King Arthur and the knights of the Round Table: their historical origin, their members, their continuity, their meaning, and so on. Scholars do, and the bibliography of Arthuriana grows every year. But what cannot reasonably be argued is the influence of Arthur et al. on modern superheroes. After all, the very idea of a team of superheroes is Arthurian (plus, of course, Greek, derived from Jason and the Argonauts),[76] and what's more superheroic than a superhero team? Who is more noble than Arthur and his knights, a nobility that was directly inspirational on superheroes?

But describing the historical background of the Arthur myths is something that can be, and has been, argued and debated, endlessly. So the following is the briefest possible version of what is usually described at far greater length: from the mid–first century CE to the end of the fifth century there were a number of historical warriors and rulers in what would later be Great Britain and Scotland whose names were either "Arthur" or something that can be closely translated as "Arthur." Legends about them grew, and written sources began incorporating them, starting with the Welsh elegy *Gododdin* (ca. 600). Major works that summarized and further developed the legends of King Arthur and his knights followed: Nennius's *Historia Brittonum* (ca. 829–830), Geoffrey of Monmouth's *Historia Regum Britanniae* (1130s), and Sir Thomas Malory's *Le Morte d'Arthur* (1485). (This is in addition to the Continental romances of the 12th and 13th centuries about Arthur et al., such as those by Chrétien de Troyes [late 12th century], which were drawn upon by Malory.[77]) Following Malory, and especially following Alfred, Lord Tennyson's *Idylls of the King* (1859–1885), the single most influential modern retelling of the Arthurian tales, the Arthurian mythos became an integral part of British culture, with a vitality that lasted well into the 20th century, when comic book superheroes were created.

The story of King Arthur, at least in its later iterations (Malory and afterward), is well known. At some point in the distant past, King Arthur ruled over Britain from his castle, Camelot. He led the knights of the Round Table, his band of dozens (and in some cases hundreds) of heroic men, against the forces of evil. His men sought for the Holy Grail, and one of them actually found it. Eventually Arthur dies fighting his son, Mordred, in the final battle at Camlann.

The character list of the Arthurian legends is substantial, and entire books have been written listing and describing just the cast. Rather than attempt to list all the Arthurian knights who qualify as protosuperheroes, then, I'm going to list the protosuperheroic elements and briefly describe which Arthurian knights had those elements. (Characters from *The Faerie Queene* will be dealt with in Chapter 3.)

The **unusual origin story**: the numerous knights who did not know their identity until they joined the Round Table, or were born from unusual families and had extraordinary adventures before joining the Round Table, or being defeated by a knight of the Round Table and made to serve Arthur and/or convert to Christianity; Addanz, Perceval's great-grandfather, descended from fairies; Alain the White, whose father, Bors, is seduced (with the help of a magic ring) by the daughter of King Brandegorre of Estrangorre, and fathers Alain the White, who when grown joins the Round Table and goes on the Grail Quest; Arthur himself; Brangemuer, son of a fairy; the Giant Without A Name, son of a dwarf, suckled by a unicorn, baptized and knighted by Arthur; Lot, the product of a secret affair, who learns his lineage via a secret ring and piece of parchment, and uses both to gain entry into the Round Table; Merlin, the son of a devil or incubus, who loses his father's evil spirit upon baptism; Mordred.

The **superpower**: In the Welsh lore of Arthur, "Arthur and his warriors are giants among men, they can run lightly across the tops of reeds and can hit a fly with an arrow from the other side of the realm. They create fire with their bodies and carry knives as big as bridges and crush mountains under their feet."[78] There are a number of knights in Arthuriana with superpowers: Achilles, the descendant of the Greek hero, who shared his predecessor's general invulnerability and foot weakness; Agar, who magically healed Tristan; the Amorous Knight, who magically healed Arthur; Brandin of the Isle's spells; Eiddilig the Dwarf, who could shape-shift; Elïavrés, the sorcerer knight; Erec, who thanks to his mother's spells is immune to magic; Gawain, whose strength grows in the morning and shrinks in the afternoon; Godilna's ability to heal any wound; the Green Knight's immortality; the spells of Mabon the sorcerer knight; Menw, the enchanter knight; Merlin's magics; the nameless magician at King Pelles's court; and Tristan, who can shape-shift and make superhuman leaps.

Extraordinary skills and abilities: obviously, most of the knights of the Round Table were unusually good fighters. Kancor is an extraordinary scientist and artisan.

Extraordinary technology: not relevant in the medieval world of Arthur et al.

The **distinctive weapon**: Every knight with a named weapon, beginning with Arthur's sword Excalibur, falls into this category. The number of magic swords in the Arthurian mythos is substantial. In addition to them, Alardin's magic shield, which restores lost flesh; Arthur's magic ring; Excalibur's scabbard renders Arthur immune to losing blood while wearing it; the Avenging Lance or Bleeding Lance; Eiryn the Splendid's invisibility-granting mantle; Sir Fergus's shield, which protected its bearer from death; Fimbeus's magic belt and victory stone; Gawain's ring, which quintupled his strength; Melion's magic ring, which allowed him to become a werewolf; Perceval's magic shield; the stone that grants Peredur invisibility; and Wigalois's magic armor.

The **distinctive appearance**: One could argue that every knight falls into this category, because of their heraldic emblems. But even and above those, certain Arthurian knights are unique in their appearance or even named based on their appearance: Agravain, who has a misshapen body; Antelan, the dwarf knight; Bilis, the lord of the dwarfs; Druidain, the hunchbacked dwarf; Evadeam, the Dwarf Knight; Gareth, known as "Beaumains" because of his pretty hands; Glewlwyd, of the enormous size; Groadain, the dwarf; Groing Poire Mele, of the tiny nose; Morfran, the remarkably ugly; Sanddef, the astonishingly beautiful; and Tristan, the dwarf.

The **code name**: As with the distinctive appearance, a number of Arthurian knights are known by epithets rather than their real names: the Amorous Knight of the Savage Castle; the Black Knight, a.k.a. the Fairy Knight; the Black Knight who killed Cahus; the Blue Knight; the Bold Knight; the Brown Earl; the Coward Knight; the Gay Gallant; Great Fool; the Handsome Coward; Ironside; the Knight of Baladingan; Knight of the Green Shield; the Little Knight; the King of the Lake; the King of the Red City; Knight of the Castle of Three Roses; Knight of the Field; Knight of the Golden Quilt; Knight of the Green Shield; Knight of the High Mountain; Knight of the Horn; the Old Knight; the One with the Golden Bow; the Pensive Knight; the Poor Knight; the Red Knight; the Ugly Hero, a.k.a. the Black Knight, a.k.a. Acanor, a knight with black skin; Unarmed Knight; and the White Knight (several knights bore this name).

The **dual identity**: the Black Knight, Lancelot's alias for a short while; Black Knight of the Black Lands (Perard); the Blue Knight, Sir Persaunt's alias; the Chevalier Malfait (Ill-Made Knight), Lancelot's alias for a time; the Fair Unknown, Guinglain's name for a time; the Good Knight Without Fear (Brunor the Black); the Green Knight, a.k.a. Bercilak of the High Desert; the Green Knight (Oriles); the Handsome Prisoner (Brian of the Isles); Knight of Ladies (Meriadeuc); Knight of Maidens (Gawain); Knight of the Cart (Raguidel); Knight of the Circlet of Gold (Perceval); Knight of the Dragon (Sir Segurant the Brown); Knight of the Golden Arms (Gawain); the Knight of the Ill-Fitting Coat (the other Brunor the Black); Knight of the Litter (Lancelot); Knight of the Mill (Peredur); the Knight of the Parrot (Arthur); Knight of the Questing Beast (Palamedes); Knight of the Sleeve (Miraudjis); Knight of the Spring (Sir Atamas); Knight of the Surcoat (Gawain); Knight of the Tower (Sir Atamas); Knight of the White Shield (Perceval); Knight of Triple Arms (Jorans li Febles); the Knight of Two Shields, Beaudous's alternate identity; Knight with the Black Shield (Tristan); Knight with the Eagle (Wigamur); the Knight with the Fair Shield (Fergus); the Knight with the Lion (Sir Yvain); the Knight with the Surcoat (Gawain); Knight with Two Swords (Balin the Savage); the Mute Knight, Peredur's alternate identity for a time; the Offensive Knight (Gawain); One Without a Name (Gawain); Red Knight (Perceval), Red Knight (Perymones), Red Knight (Pelleas), Red Knight of the Red Lands (Ironside), Tantrist (Tristan), the Ugly Burned One (Guares the Black); Unbridled Heart (Lionel); the Unknown Knight, the son of Arthur; the Wicked Knight, Lancelot's alternate identity for a time; and the White Knight (Lancelot).

The **heroic mission**: As I argue in Chapter 1, the heroic mission is the most important element of each hero's *heroenkonzept*, the minimum requirement for a hero to be considered as a protosuperhero. Every knight of the Round Table has a heroic mission, because the rules of the Round Table, as first mentioned in Giovanni Boccacio's *De Casibus Vivorum Illustrium* (1355–1362) and later described in Malory, are clear. Boccacio has the rules as follows:

1. To never lay down arms;
2. To seek after wonders;
3. When called upon, to defend the rights of the weak with all one's strength;
4. To injure no one;
5. Not to attack one another;
6. To fight for the safety of one's friends;
7. To give one's life for one's country;
8. To seek nothing before honor;
9. Never to break faith for any reason;
10. To practice religion most diligently;
11. To grant hospitality to anyone, each according to his ability; and
12. Whether in honor or disgrace, to make a report with the greatest fidelity to truth to those who keep the annals.[79]

Malory has as his rules of the Round Table:

To never do outrage nor murder;

Always to flee treason;

To by no means be cruel but to give mercy unto him who asks for mercy;

To always do ladies, gentlewomen, and widows succor;

To never force ladies, gentlewomen, and widows; and

Not to take up battles in wrongful quarrels for love or worldly goods.[80]

These rules, this *ethos* of medieval knightly heroism, are followed by all the knights, although individual knights sometimes break the rules and have to atone for it.

Extraordinary opponents: Boars, hounds, and lions; numberless giants, named and unnamed, male and female; numerous sorceresses and wizards, named and unnamed; numerous dragons; Afanc, the lake monster; the Beautiful Giantess; the beast who tormented the King of Suffering and his children; the Black Hag; the Black Hand; the Black Hermit; the Black Serpent of the Barrow; the abominable Boncu; the demon of Bright Fountain; the seven-headed Burlow-Beanie; Caradoc the Huge; the fearsome Cath Palug, a.k.a. the Chapalu; Dagon the sorcerous demon; the demon of the Bright Fountain; the devil-cat that Arthur slew; the devil-woman who tempted Bors; Escanor, the large, son of a giant and a witch, who shared Gawaine's waxing and waning strength; Felon of Albarua, a monstrous knight with an enormous head; the fiends of the Castle of the Most Ill Adventure; the Fish-Knight; the Formidable Knight; Garlon the Red, who could turn invisible; the ghost knight who wounded Gaus; the griffins in the Castle of the Griffins; Guengasoain, the invincible; the hag of Dunostre; the Hags of Gloucester; the incubus who fathered the Questing Beast on the sister of Galahad (not the Grail Knight Galahad, the other one); the dwarf Juran; Karrioz the marrowless pagan beast knight; the Knight of the Burning Dragon, with his enchanted shield; Knight of the Dragon; Luciabiaus, the devil; Mal Ostagier's man-eating bird; Marrien, the devil-spawned dog-headed centaur; the unnamed monster of the Green Meadow; the nameless monster that terrorized Queen Alemandine of the White City; Orguelleus the Fairy Knight; the Questing Beast; Papagustes, a gigantic serpent; the cudgel-headed monster Pen Palach; the warlike race of men, the Popelicans; the hag Ruel; the devil Sarant; Tericam the Impenetrable, Caradoc the Huge's brother; and Vulganus the demon.

Lives in a world where there is law enforcement and a government: more accurate to say, regarding Arthur et al., that they are the government and law enforcement, all at once.

Operates in a world in which crime/oppression/evil is clear-cut and obvious: the difference between good and evil is unquestioned in the Arthurian mythos.

Operates in a word in which law enforcement/the government is not capable of controlling or defeating crime/oppression/evil: in the Arthurian mythos the agents of the government—the knights of the Round Table—live a world of rampant crime, oppression, and evil, which they are tasked with and successful at defeating.

Operates under the assumption that law enforcement/the government is capable of holding and confining a criminal once they are apprehended: occasionally relevant in the Arthurian mythos, as when Guinevere imprisons the woman-abuser Akarins.

Operates under the assumption that vigilantism is welcome or at least tolerated by general society as well as law enforcement and the government: not true in the Arthurian mythos; the concept of the vigilante can hardly be said to be present in them when every knight is or will be an agent of the government.

Is finite and can be killed: certainly accurate of the knights.

Does not kill: the rules of the Round Table do not exactly forbid killing, but rather murder. (Malory's rules are explicit on this point.) Arthur's knights kill monsters and enemies in war, but give mercy when possible to other knights.

The cumulative effect of the Arthurian tales are the creation of a protosuperheroic universe, one in which individual knights, some very well known, may not meet every requirement for protosuperhero status, but, taken as a whole, the class of Arthurian knights do, ending up on the "greater" end of the protosuperhero spectrum. And the influence of the Arthurian corpus on superhero comics is extensive, needless to say.[81] It can't be said that superheroes began with Arthur et al.; they are part of the lineage that began with Enkidu. But Arthur and his knights are the most directly influential figures in this chapter, and the only ones whose motifs, tropes, and plot devices continue to be mined by modern comics writers.

Medieval Outlaws

The popular idea of the medieval outlaw—indeed, the archetypal form of it—is Robin Hood, and good yeoman (or gentleman) Robin is certainly the most influential medieval outlaw. But it must not be forgotten that for some centuries before the advent of the Robin Hood mythos there were tales told of medieval outlaws, and that these tales had currency and life—mythic power and resonance—concurrently with the tales of Robin Hood, well into the 17th or perhaps 18th century. If the stories of Earl Godwin et al. lack potency today, it is not because they were never powerful, but because they were succeeded by the urban outlaws, the likes of Moll Cutpurse and her rivals. The mythic figure never stays the same, but evolves over time and geography, accreting and eliminating individual aspects, taking on new source material in the form of historical figures, but always retaining core elements. The *latrones* influence the fictional portrayals of medieval outlaws; the medieval outlaws influence Robin Hood; Robin Hood influences Moll Cutpurse and her contemporaries; and Robin Hood and Moll Cutpurse influence the Costumed Avengers— and the Costumed Avengers become the superheroes.

In truth, there probably is no "beginning" for the character of the heroic outlaw. It's a universal character type, across time and geography,[82] and scholars in medieval French and German history could undoubtedly produce their own lists of heroic outlaws.[83] But as far as influencing the superhero, the relevant fictional medieval outlaws are English.

Historically first among these English noble outlaws was Earl Godwin, a historical figure of the first half of the 11th century. The fictional version of Godwin appears in the *Vita Ædwardi Regis qui apud Westmonasterurm*

Requiescit, which was composed in the 1060s and copied circa 1100. Earl Godwin's story—conflict between a heroic Saxon nobleman and corrupt Norman royal officials, false accusations, outlawry and banishment, hero's return, forgiveness by the king—introduced the standard noble outlaw plot and themes.

Following Godwin was Hereward the Wake, a historical outlaw of the late 11th century. The *Gesta Herwardi* (mid-12th century) introduces motifs and plot devices that were picked up by later stories, including the forest home, the band of merry fugitives, the deadliness with a bow, the use of disguise, and the appearance of the king as a means for Hereward's redemption.[84]

Following Hereward both in history and fiction was Eustache the Monk (ca. 1170–1217). History records Eustache Busquet as a French knight, then outlaw and pirate. In *The Romance of Eustache the Monk* (written between 1223 and 1284), Eustache is violent and often cruel and is an ambiguous, fascinating antihero. He is also a sorcerer who learns the black arts from the Devil himself in Toledo but then parts company acrimoniously with Lucifer, an anticipation of (and arguably influence on, given the life span and European scope of *The Romance of Eustache the Monk*) Faust and every modern Faustian sorcerer superhero.

Later influential tales of fictional outlaws included *Fouke Fitz Waryn* (late 13th century), *The Outlaw's Song of Trailbaston* (composed early in the 14th century), *The Tale of Gamelyn* (middle of the 14th century), *The Saga of Án BowBinder* (early 15th century), *The Acts and Deeds of Sir William Wallace* (1482?) and *Adam Bell, Clim of the Clough and William of Cloudesley* (1530s).

Like Robin Hood, these heroic outlaws are predecessors to the modern superhero, who largely, by virtue of their vigilantism, work outside the law, and break it in order to better enforce it. The heroic outlaws "pose the paradoxical problem of being outlaws, having committed real crimes, but they are admired and supported by the people. Their outlawry does not bring shame upon them, but instead proves them to be superior to their opponents, both in martial prowess and, most importantly, in moral integrity."[85]

This paradox lies at the heart of the modern superhero; without the examples of Earl Godwin et al., the modern superhero would lack historical justification for her actions, and be viewed with the same dubiousness that real-life vigilantes are.

Robin Hood

The single-most important protosuperhero of the premodern era—King Arthur et al. were important as a group and as a mythos rather than as individuals—Robin Hood is, for superheroes, the archetypal character, the "ur-vigilante."[86] His externals—the clothing/costume, the bow, the facial hair—have been lifted and used, to greater or lesser degrees, by superheroes since the beginning.[87] His internals—the code of ethics, his dual identity, his explicitly stated resistance to legal authority—have been similarly copied by modern superheroes, though they were not original with him and were taken in large parts from the medieval outlaws who preceded him, from Earl Godwin and Hereward the Wake and so on.

But like King Arthur, the character of "Robin Hood" evolved over a period of centuries and derived from a number of different sources, so that the current version of Robin Hood, what is influencing modern superheroes, is actually the culmination and evolution of everything that came before. Like King Arthur, Robin's historicity has been the subject of long debate by scholars and academics. As with King Arthur, there are a variety of fragments in the historical records that hint at but in no way prove the existence of a historical figure who was the "real" Robin Hood. From circa 1220 on there are "historical, topographical, quasi-biographical and literary"[88] references; from circa 1450 on there are ballads about him; from the late 15th century there are "plays, games, processions and charitable rituals"[89]; from the late 16th century there are dramas, masques, and light operas; from the early 19th century, novels, poetry, and poetic dramas. Robin as a Hobsbawmian social bandit active in the forest—"a rebel with a . . . retinue . . . causing disorder to the sober citizens"[90]—is a product of the 15th century; Robin as the wrongfully dispossessed-of-his-land, give-to-the-poor Earl of Huntington with Maid Marian by his side is a product of the 16th century; the full, "classic" story of Robin Hood, whose life and death are fully described, doesn't appear until the 19th century, with the version most known being the one Howard Pyle created in *The Merry Adventures of Robin Hood of Great Renown in Nottinghamshire* (1883).

So the following—the myth that influenced and influences superheroes—is not the original myth, but the culmination of many different iterations and mutations of it, over the course of several centuries.

Robin Hood and his band of Merry Men—which includes the massive Little John, the jovial Friar Tuck, the elegant Will Scarlet, the minstrel Alan-a-Dale, and Robin's love interest Maid Marian—live in Nottingham Forest, where they steal from the rich and give to the poor. Robin, the best archer in the land, is actually the Earl of Huntington, wrongfully dispossessed of his land and bearing a grudge against the local sheriff and bad King John, although Robin, like the rest of the land, waits in hope for good King Richard the Lionhearted to return from the Crusade to restore justice to England. Robin and his men have a number of adventures and exploits. Eventually King Richard returns and Robin is pardoned by the king and made a part of the king's retinue of loyalists. Robin Hood dies by being treacherously bled to death by a wicked prioress.

Although much of the Robin Hood megatext is not original to the Robin Hood stories—as mentioned, the Robin Hood megatext took a great deal from Earl Godwin et al.—Robin Hood's popularity meant that the values and tropes/motifs/plot devices of the megatext were specifically transmitted from the megatext to superheroes (via, of course, the heroic stories that appeared between the megatext's appearance and the debut of Superman in 1938). If we cannot credit the tellers of Robin Hood stories with originality in this regard, we nonetheless do have to credit them with being the source that superhero creators took from.

One aspect of the Robin Hood megatext that is influential on superhero fiction in a less obvious manner is what might be called Robin's conservatism. Just as superheroes are ultimately conservative, concerned with preserving or reinstating the status quo rather than trying to change the system itself,[91] so too is Robin Hood—ostensibly a rebel against legal authority in the person of the sheriff of Nottingham—in favor of the ultimate authority, King Richard. This reflects the sentiments of those listening to the Robin Hood ballads of the Middle Ages: "the illusions of the medieval English peasant that the king was really on their side, reflected in the Robin Hood ballads, show that their rebellious outlook was one of protest against immediately felt hardship. It was not critical of the established order."[92] Superheroes, like Robin Hood, can rebel against individually corrupt officials, but rarely if ever do they try to change the corporate capitalistic system itself. When they do, they are labeled "supervillains" and "terrorists."[93]

Conclusion

By 1500, the elements of the modern superhero were all in place, in a variety of different forms and in use by different characters, and some of these characters, including the Arthurian knights and Robin Hood, would prove to be influential (in some cases, heavily influential) on the heroes of the 16th and 17th centuries and, following them, superheroes in the 20th century.

Yet Enkidu remains an anomaly, not just in the ancient world but in the medieval one. The core superhero *heroenkonzept* that Coogan (2006) delineates in *Superhero*—mission, powers, identity, and costume—would not appear again for many centuries. What appeared instead were characters with individual parts of that core *heroenkonzept*, and those characters would be far more influential than Enkidu. Enkidu sadly must be considered a missed opportunity, a what-if. Looking ahead centuries, we can compare Enkidu to Tom Richmond, the detective of the pseudonymously authored novel *Richmond: Scenes in the Life of a Bow Street Runner* (1827), a proto–police procedural. Had it been noticed, and imitated, *Richmond* would be seen in the same light as Poe's "The Murders in the Rue Morgue," as one of the foundations of the mystery genre. But *Richmond* was not imitated, was not influential, and was quickly forgotten. It appeared in isolation and then disappeared the same way. So, too, with Enkidu, though to a lesser degree.

CHAPTER THREE

From 1500 to 1829

Why 1829? Because two events occurred that year that were symbolically important and serve as a useful dividing line between eras. The first event was the publication of Eugène François Vidocq's *Mémoires de Vidocq* (1829), a seismic event in how the French public viewed police work. The second was the passing in England of the Metropolitan Police Act and the formation of the Metropolitan Police Service, which formalized police work in London. The impact of the appearance of Vidocq's autohagiography and of organized, official policemen on protosuperheroic literature was not immediate; it would be another 20 years before the protosuperheroic policeman would appear. But the impact of both on the lineage of the protosuperhero would be considerable.

1500 seems as good an ending place as any for the previous chapter. Robin Hood was entering his classic stage, Arthuriana was well established, consumers had centuries of heroes to read about. What would follow over the next 300 years was a move away from the more uncomplicated heroism of King Arthur and later Robin Hood and toward more complicated figures, characters who are protosuperheroic to a greater or lesser degree but are more morally and ethically complex. If so much of Chapter 2 was laying the groundwork for the Übermensch—a character type notable by its absence, even in prototype form, in the years covered in this chapter—then 1500–1829 must be seen as producing the stuff out of which the Costumed Avenger was made.

But far more than in Chapter 2, the starting point for Chapter 3 should be seen as more of an open border than a closed one. Because of the nature of the character types covered in this chapter, I'll be jumping backward centuries to cover their beginnings before returning to the 16th or 17th or 18th or 19th centuries to cover their heydays. I was able to take a roughly linear approach in Chapter 2. Such an approach is not possible with the characters and character types mentioned in this chapter. On a macroscale I'm starting early in the 16th century and moving forward to the 19th, but on a microscale I'll be all over the place chronologically.

Orlando Furioso the Best Seller and Its Forerunners

Le Chanson de Roland and the entire metacycle of poems and *chansons de geste* about Charlemagne (see Chapter 2)—what became known as the "Matter of France"[1]—were as influential on the Continent as the "Matter of England," the Arthurian megatext, was in Britain. France became the leader of culture for the European countries, including Italy, by as early as the 13th century, and the non-French poets and song makers openly imitated French forms and used characters from the Charlemagne metacycle in their own works. These in turn led to a number of significant poems and prose works from Italian authors and for Italy to seize the crown of culture leader from France, so that "by the end of the 15th century, all of western Europe had begun to look on Italian culture with an ecstasy of admiration, and Italy was playing the role, as the leader of culture, that France had played earlier."[2] Ludovico Ariosto's *Orlando Furioso* (1516–1532) was the result of and culmination of these works, and with Edmund Spenser's *The Faerie Queene* (1596) set the standard for heroic poetry and fiction for decades, if not centuries. But both *Orlando Furioso* and *The Faerie Queene* had important predecessors.

The first of the significant influences on *Orlando Furioso* was the anonymously written poem *Orlando* (ca. 1400). About Roland (renamed "Orlando" by the Italians) and Renault de Montauban (see renamed "Rinaldo" by the Italians), *Orlando* also features the sorcerer Maugis (renamed "Malagigi") and Morgante, a Saracen giant who converts to Christianity. *Orlando* is about the quarrel between Orlando and Rinaldo's groups and the Christian fight against the Saracens, who in this case are Danish. Other giants appear, as do Meridiana the Amazon and various Saracen kings, and the poem ends midengagement, with the Saracens, who are besieging Paris with an army of 150,000, not yet defeated.

Various Italian writers continued to retell the Matter of France stories, but Luigi Pulci, in his epic poem *Morgante* (1478–1483), chose to duplicate the plot of *Orlando* and then to extend it. *Morgante* is not a work much studied in the Anglophone world, but it is one that, with Boiardo's *Orlando Innamorato*, was heavily influential on writers to follow, both well known (Rabeais, Cervantes, and Goethe)[3] and not-so-famous. As Frederick Artz puts it, "from Pulci and Boiardo, and their two great 16th-century successors, Ariosto and Tasso, the taste for romantic poems spread across

Europe."[4] In *Morgante*, Orlando, Rinaldo, Morgante, and Malagigi have a series of adventures across Europe. The adventures are occasionally semi-comic in tone—Morgante dies from a crab bite—but they become increasingly serious, and *Morgante* ends with Orlando's death at the Battle of Roncesvals.

Pulci and *Morgante* were in turn heavily influential on Matteo Maria Boiardo's poem *Orlando Innamorato* (1483–1495), in which the course of true love did never run smooth for Rinaldo and Angelica, the daughter of the king of Cataio (Cathay): Angelica falls in love with Rinaldo by drinking from the Stream of Love, while Rinaldo falls in hate with Angelica by drinking from the fountain of hate. Rinaldo and Orlando fight several times, once over Angelica, the sorcerer Malagigi becomes involved, Saracens invade, and Ruggiero (a Saracen knight) and the female knight Bradamante fall in love. The poem ends abruptly, with numerous matters unresolved.

Many authors picked up the story of *Orlando Innamorato*, turning out continuations with titles like *Innamoramento di Rinaldo da Monte Albano* and *Astolfo Innamorato*, but it wasn't until Ludovico Ariosto continued the story in *Orlando Furioso* (1516–1532) that a definite and generally accepted sequel to and completion of *Orlando Innamorato* appeared. (And in turn inspired another spate of sequels, with titles like *Rinaldo Furioso* and *Rodomonte Innamorato*.) *Orlando Furioso* was the first smash hit of the 16th century and was as popular in England as it was on the Continent.

In *Orlando Furioso*, Ariosto continues the story of Orlando's love for Angelica, which does not run smoothly: Angelica escapes from imprisonment and falls in love with a Saracen knight, Medoro, leading to Orlando going mad with despair and rampaging through Europe and Africa until the English knight Astolfo recovers Orlando's wits on the moon, which leads to Orlando falling out of love with Angelica. Meanwhile the Saracen king Agramante invades Europe and besieges Charlemagne in Paris. Orlando joins the fight against Agramante and kills him. Ariosto also continues the story of Ruggiero's love for Bradamante; Ruggiero is captured by the sorceress Alcina and has to be delivered from her magic island, while at the same time avoiding the spells of his foster father, the wizard Atlante. At length, Ruggiero converts to Christianity and marries Bradamante.

Orlando Furioso is notable for its influence; with *Faerie Queene* it was the archetypal story of heroes in the 16th century and for decades afterward, although Cervantes's *Don Quixote* (1605–1615) wickedly satirized both, and the heroic epic in general. But the Ariosto/Spenserian approach to epic heroism survived, so that 200 years after *Faerie Queene*'s debut, epic heroic quests still appeared: the anonymously written Gothic novel

The Rock of Modrec (1792) features Spenser's Archimago, a Spenserian quest, Spenserian heroes, and the use of Spenserian tropes, motifs, and plot developments, with *The Rock of Modrec's* hero, Sir Eltram, being a Gothicized Redcrosse Knight, one of the main heroes of *The Faerie Queene*.

But, influential though *Orlando Furioso* was, it and the epics leading up to it do not have protosuperheroes as their heroes. The heroes of *Orlando Furioso* et al. have distinctive attire and weapons and opponents, but they lack the selfless mission required of superheroes, being instead knights at religious war or being motivated primarily by the lure of glory or love. Orlando, Rinaldo, and the rest were archetypal heroes and influential on later heroes—and inarguably superhero fiction would not appear without the heroic epics of the 14th, 15th, and 16th centuries—but not protosuperheroes. At the most they are far down on the "lesser" end of the superheroic scale.

However, these epics did contain two superheroic archetypes in them—albeit not in the role of the lead characters. To address them, though, will require significant backtracking (and some flash forwarding).

Heroic Sorcerers and Heavenly Necromancers

The lineage of the heroic sorcerer protagonist is an ancient one, dating back to the third century BCE and Nectanebo II, running through the *Alexander Romance*, and flourishing with enchanter knights like Maugis and then, in the Arthurian megatext, Merlin. The character type of the heroic sorcerer would take a great leap forward beginning in the 16th century, though, both numerically and in terms of the character's complexity, although the end result, in the early 19th century, was the virtual disappearance of heroic sorcerers and their replacement with a character type that returned to the ambiguity of Nectanebo II in the *Alexander Romance* rather than the straightforward heroism of Maugis et al.

But during the 16th century the heroic sorcerer flourished, had momentum and vitality, and coexisted alongside the more ambiguous version, the Faustian sorcerer, for nearly a century. It's with the heroic sorcerer that we will begin—but this requires us initially to leap backward several centuries.

Merlin the Secondary

Merlin is a creation of the medieval era, of the creators of the Arthurian megatext, especially Geoffrey of Monmouth in his *Historia Regum Britanniae* (1130s), but Merlin's roots are different from those of most of the

Arthurian cast. Merlin is not the product of England or France, but of Dark Ages Wales. There, as "Myrddin," he appears in a variety of poems, beginning with the Arthurian taproot text[5] *Gododdin* (ca. 600) but frequenting a variety of Welsh poems over the next several centuries before emerging in the *Historia Regum Britanniae* and then the *Black Book of Carmarthen* (ca. 1250), and from there the Arthurian legendarium as a whole. But the Myrddin of Welsh legends is actually two different characters: one a bard of sorts, celebrating his own society against the Anglo-Saxon invaders and prophesying doom for them, and one a "conceivably historical nobleman whose new and terrible knowledge leads him to reject contemporary historic society in favor of nature and contemplation."[6]

This latter figure became a Welsh "wild man" and incrementally influenced the Arthurian Merlin, but it was the former, the patriotic prophet, that most influenced the Arthurian Merlin. However, what results is not a heroic sorcerer character, but a heroic supporting character. Merlin never becomes the protagonist; he is always there as a supplement to Arthur, an appendage, whether it is predicting his arrival, or teaching him, or assisting him in his conquests. Merlin's role changes—provider of wisdom up through Geoffrey of Monmouth, provider of advice from Geoffrey to Malory, provider of cleverness from Malory into the 18th century—but he is never what we would now think of as either a protagonist or even a heroic sorcerer. What Merlin contributed to the heroic sorcerer character was an alternative to wickedness. Magic and its practitioners were generally viewed as evil; Merlin, developing in parallel to Nectanebo II in the *Alexander Romance*, provided a different perspective on those who worked spells.[7]

Virgil the Necromancer

At the same time that the image of Merlin was developing in the English Arthurian sources, another kind of sorcerer figure was developing in Europe. Publius Vergilius Maro (70–19 BCE), better known as "Virgil," is ranked as one of Rome's greatest poets, having penned the *Aeneid*, among others. The impact of his oeuvre on learned society for centuries after his death fostered a great interest in the facts of Virgil's life, an interest that manifested itself in biographies of Virgil from as early as the fourth century and up through the Renaissance. However, from circa 1159 to the 14th centuries, these biographies took on a fantastic tone, so that the sage Virgil was replaced by the *magus* (wizard) Virgil:

> The Virgil of this tradition is a *magus* inasmuch as he is a benefactor of Naples, but also Rome, Mantua and others: his interventions free the

citizens from inclement weather, and from dangerous parasites such as leeches and flies, protect edible meat from contamination by vermin, establish impenetrable town walls, automaton statues, and enchanted gardens. Like the errant knights idealized in this period, Virgil too travels from city to city, and to him, also, significantly, erotic adventures are also attributed. He operates to the advantage of the communities by means of his knowledge, which is magical-scientific. But Virgil's is a white magic: only at a later stage, in the middle of the Renaissance, was black magic attributed to him, with Faust-like diabolic operations, but resolved (unlike those of Faust) entirely in Virgil's favor.[8]

The importance of the fictional Virgil is that, like Merlin, he presents an alternative to the wicked wizard of tradition: the white magician, who unlike Nectanebo II has no ambiguity about him. Even later, during the late 13th century, when Virgil becomes a necromancer in some of the romances and histories and biographies about him, he still remains more good than bad, flawed in human ways (his pursuit of other men's wives) rather than evil, but still "an essentially benevolent character who helps the underdog and is always ready to punish the wicked."[9] In the anonymously written *Les Faictz Merveilleux de Virgille* (1502–1518?), otherwise known as the "Virgilius *Romance*," Virgil becomes a full-fledged romance hero, even if he does conjure devils for his own purposes.

Too, Virgil presents a different appearance for the white magician. As Traister notes:

> The romance magician, who can be either male or female, is usually set apart from the other characters by some physical or spiritual peculiarity: Merlin is unnaturally hairy . . . Clinschor (in Wolfram von Eschenbach's *Parzival*) has been castrated; Morgan le Fay (*Gawain and the Green Knight*) and Cundrie (*Parzival*) are incredibly ugly.[10]

Not Virgil, though; he is ordinary looking, even handsome, even in *Les Faictz Merveilleux.*

Maugis/Malagigi and His Heirs

But Virgil, though certainly the protagonist of these "biographies" and a heroic character, is some distance from the more active heroes of the epics and romances. Virgil's power is used for good ends, but the results are relatively minor. It took another character to make the heroic sorcerer into a magical version of the knight or romance hero. As mentioned in Chapter 2, Maugis flourished in Europe beginning in the 13th century and in England via the *Renaut de Montauban* starting in the 14th century. Even more than the enchanter knights of the Arthurian megatext, Mabon and Menw and the rest, Maugis was the archetype of the active, noble sorcerer knight, the equivalent of a noble knightly hero but one that used magic in the place of or in addition to strength at arms.

Maugis became most famous for his exploits under another name, however: "Malagigi." Beginning with the anonymously written epic poem *Orlando* (ca. 1400), Maugis, as Malagigi, would become a central part of the Matter of France cycle, and would become a brother-in-arms to Roland (renamed "Orlando" by the Italians) and Renault de Montauban (renamed "Rinaldo"). *Orlando* is about Malagigi, Orlando, Rinaldo, and Morgante (a Saracen giant who converts to Christianity) and the fight between Orlando and Rinaldo's groups and the Christian war with the Saracens. Other giants appear, as does Meridiana the Amazon and various Saracen kings. Malagigi is active throughout *Orlando*, assisting Rinaldo (as he did in *Renaut de Montauban*) against both Orlando's side and the Saracens, particularly Creonta, the mother of giants and keeper of lions, "full of enchantments and possessed of many spirits"; Malagigi is "the only Christian whose arts suffice to foil Creonta" and ensure the release of Creonta's prisoner, Ganelon, Rinaldo's ally.[11]

Orlando ends midengagement, with the Saracens not yet defeated. Pulci's *Morgante* extends the plot of *Orlando*. *Morgante*, along with Boiardo's *Orlando Innamorato*, was heavily influential on writers to follow. As Frederick Artz puts it, "From Pulci and Boiardo, and their two great 16th-century successors, Ariosto and Tasso, the taste for romantic poems spread across Europe."[12] In *Morgante* Orlando, Rinaldo, and Morgante, a giant who becomes a loyal follower of Orlando, have a series of adventures across Europe. Throughout, Malagigi appears as a guide, protector, and sometime-savior of Orlando et al., "a good wizard who, through his powerful magic, is capable of foreseeing the future and of knowing the occult. If he wishes, he can even call on demons for assistance."[13] Malagigi plays a similar role in Matteo Maria Boiardo's *Orlando Innamorato* (1483–1495), which like *Orlando* ends *in media res*, and in Ludovico Ariosto's *Orlando Furioso* (1516–1532).

In *Orlando Furioso*, Malagigi is no longer alone in his role as the heroic sorcerer—he shares this position with others, including the ghost of Merlin. Following *Orlando Furioso*, the concept of the heroic sorcerer spread, so that readers saw the magic-using hermit and the good witch Melissa (and the converted sorceress Armida) in Torquato Tasso's *La Gerusalemme Liberata* (1581), Merlin *recidivus* in Spenser's *Faerie Queene* (1590–1596), and finally Prospero in Shakespeare's *Tempest* (1610–1611), who became (thanks to Shakespeare's fame) an iconic heroic sorcerer for generations afterward.

Admittedly, Prospero renounces his magic at the end of the play—a common enough trope in Renaissance plays about magicians—but he remains the hero of his play, the victor over the evil Sycorax's magics. "In *The Tempest*, as in most plays involving magical competitions, the triumph of a given side proves its moral superiority to the magic of the loser, thereby justifying the winner's magic."[14]

Even though the post-Shakespeare English audience would view magicians in more ambiguous ways, as we'll see, there was still room and support for positive portrayals of sorcerers:

> An Elizabethan audience could tolerate pacts and black magic without immediately condemning the character who engaged in them. Perhaps it was the ends of magic, not its means, that largely determined audience response. Magicians who used black magic for purely selfish purposes, to satisfy lust, to gain money or position, or to harm others, were condemned. But magicians who were supportive of the community or nation, who used their magic to restore order, to right wrongs, or to assist true love, were supported and seen as "good" no matter what the details of the magic they practiced.[15]

As a side note, one common motif of the good stage sorcerer, seen in plays like *Friar Bacon*, is his prophecy, "supportive of the king and his successors, affirms the political order. This has been a chief responsibility of good English magicians since Geoffrey of Monmouth first created Merlin."[16]

By the early 17th century the idea of "white magic" as a tool in the hands of a heroic (fictional) protagonist was firmly in place, although it would, under the increasing English focus on witchcraft and demonic possession in the Jacobean era and the rest of the 17th and 18th centuries, recede, and become something theoretically possible, but only in fiction of the past. What was left, during these years, was witchcraft, black magic, and the ambiguous, morally liminal sorcerer, enchanter, and magician, a character type from centuries before.

Michael Scot

Coexisting alongside the character concept of the heroic sorcerer was another one, not quite as old as Merlin or Virgil, but nonetheless predating the Renaissance and stretching back into the Middle Ages: the ambiguous enchanter, the antihero wizard. Barbara Traister, citing Barbara

Mowat, says that *"commedia dell'arte* scenarios, wizard legends, and classical portraits of witches and enchanters—as well as the nonliterary carnival juggler and illusionist—are background for Shakespeare's Prospero,"[17] but the same sources also fed into the more ethically liminal sorcerer characters of the time.

Magic was, naturally, of concern to the medieval church, and their position, unofficially only until the 13th century, officially for many years later, was that "magic was to be avoided by God-fearing men. God permitted magic partly to demonstrate, by its overthrow, his own miraculous powers, and partly as one of the pitfalls that appeared in the world as a result of original sin."[18] But the work of men like Albertus Magnus and Roger Bacon began to change that, confusing "magic" with "science," while a wide range of ordinary people practiced magic with few, if any regrets.[19] Overtly condemned, it was secretly (and not so secretly) practiced, and the view of magic was considerably more complicated and ambivalent than we might think.

Michael Scot (1175–ca. 1235) was of course a real person: a Scottish mathematician and scholar whose early life and career are relatively well documented, even if his eventual fate is unknown. But Scot had the misfortune to try to differentiate, in print, between permissible and impermissible magic—to distinguish astrology from more prohibited forms of magic and divination, and to argue that the former was not on the condemned list of 11 types of magic that Hugh of St. Victor had constructed in his *Didascalicon* (late 1130s).[20] For this, Scot gained a reputation as an actual evil sorcerer, a reputation permanently established when Dante placed Scot in the *Inferno* (1308–1320) in the Eighth Circle, Fourth Bolgia, the one reserved for sorcerers, astrologers, and false prophets: "That other one whose thighs are scarcely fleshed/was Michael Scot, who most assuredly/knew every trick of magic fraudulence."[21] Scot's name would become a byword for the ambiguous—verging on evil—enchanter, even if his real acts hardly qualified him for such and his own opinion of magic was ambivalent,[22] and he remained an icon of ambiguity even into the 19th century, when James Hogg featured him in *The Three Perils of Man* (1823).

John Dee

During the 16th century another real-life ambiguous sorcerer appeared. John Dee (1527–1608/1609) was in his lifetime a true Renaissance man—a mathematician, astrologer, astronomer, occult philosopher, and adviser to the Queen, in addition to a dedicated student of alchemy, divination, and magic. But after Dee staged a performance of Aristophanes's

Peace, in which Dee's mechanical beetle appeared to fly, rumors of Dee's dabbling in magic began, rumors which were to follow him throughout his lifetime. He was formally accused of using sorcery against Queen Mary, though he was acquitted by the Star Chamber in 1555, and as late as 1604 he was petitioning King James to clear his name of the taint of being a conjurer, but to no good: during and after his lifetime he was seen as the "arche coniurer, of this whole kingdom," rather than a philosopher who experimented, which is what he considered himself to be.[23]

Dee suffered from both a prejudice against magic and its users—despite the positive examples in romances and poetry and on stage, there was still widespread distrust of those who performed magic of any sort—and encouraged it, through the emphasis he placed on his studies and the heightening of his own persona, a persona that was still potent a generation after his death. If the degree to which Dee's contemporary reputation as a magus has perhaps been overblown,[24] it was nonetheless at least somewhat common, and became worse in the 17th century, with Dee's biographer agreeing with an earlier writer that Dee was "the sport, the laughing-stock and the prey of daemons."[25]

Dee served as a latest living example of the practitioner of the dark arts, a figure viewed with ambiguity and distrust by the ordinary Englishman and -woman.

Stage Magicians

Magicians began to routinely appear on English stages beginning in the 1570s, although there were earlier plays—now lost—that featured magicians, such as John Skelton's *The Nigramansir* (1504). Their portrayal was very much a mixed bag, ambiguous villains combined with ambiguous heroes, so that in the anonymously written *Clyomon and Clamydes* (ca. 1570) one of the two villainous enchanters, the masked, pseudonymous Subtill Shift, escapes the judgment and punishment that usually appends to such characters. In the anonymously written *The Rare Triumphs of Love and Fortune* (ca. 1582), the magician Bomelio is generally seen as a positive character. However, the connotations attached to his magic are ambiguous, to say the least: Bomelio's son burns his father's books, robbing Bomelio of his power, and the play refuses to take a stance on whether or not burning the books was the morally correct thing to do. Throughout this time period fictional magicians continued to be portrayed in largely equivocal fashion.

Of course, one reason for this ambiguity, apart from the audience's distrust of magicians, is the narrative difficulties that good magicians pose:

"Given a good magician with extraordinary powers, what opposition can be created for him that is not too easily toppled?"[26] The usual answer was to create an evil or morally ambiguous magician, such as the titular dueling magicians in Anthony Munday's *John a Kent and John a Cumber* (ca. 1587)[27] and Friar Bacon and the German magician Vandermast in Robert Greene's *Friar Bacon and Friar Bungay* (1588–1592) and *John of Boudreaux* (ca. 1592).[28]

Other playwrights simply moved the ambiguous sorcerer into the role of protagonist, as was the case with the anonymously written *The Merry Devil of Edmonton* (1602). The Merry Devil, a.k.a. Peter Fabell, has relatively muted magic, and insists that his magics are "no conjurations, nor such weighty spells/As tie the soul to their performancy,"[29] but Fabell is shown to have struck a deal with infernal spirits—a clear no-no for the Elizabethan audience. However, the play ends with Fabell tricking the demon and gaining seven more years of life. "The theological view that the magician who made a pact was damned was evidently not always applicable onstage."[30]

Faustus

Of course, the ultimate ambiguous sorcerous figure is Faust, both Marlowe's and Goethe's. This is more true of Goethe's than Marlowe's Faust, though.

The historical source for the Faust myth was Johann Georg Faust (1466–ca. 1539), a wandering German alchemist and magician about whom much has been written over the centuries, little with any basis in fact.[31] Suffice it to say that Faust was reputed to be a black magician in league with the Devil and claimed to be the greatest living master of necromancy, and that by 1587, when Johann Spies's *Historia von D. Johann Fausten, dem Weitbeschreyten Zauberer und Schwarzkünstler* was published, Faust's reputation as a "notorious black magician and desperate hellbrand"[32] was already well established. Spies's work, which painted Faust in the worst possible light—the title, "The History of Dr. Johann Faust, the Famous Magician and Black Artist" hints at where Spies intends to go with his book—credulously or cynically repeats the worst of the stories about Faust.[33] Naturally, the *Historia* was a best seller, widely translated and pirated.

A copy of the *Historia* made its way into the hands of English playwright Christopher Marlowe, and at some point—academics disagree on the date of composition, with many but by no means most accepting a 1592 date—Marlowe composed *The Tragical History of the Life and Death of*

Doctor Faustus. *Doctor Faustus* tells the story of Faust's learning necromancy, selling his soul to Lucifer (via his servant Mephistophilis) for power, frittering away his new powers on inconsequential practical jokes, and ultimately being condemned to Hell. Faust is the play's protagonist, and deliverer of soliloquies, and is meant to engage our sympathies. Which he does—but to the Elizabethan and Stuart audiences, a critical transformation takes place after Faust succumbs to the lure of the demonic pact—he becomes a witch, not a magician, a much more condemnable state: "the simplest distinction between a magician and a witch is that a magician coerces, attracts, or controls spirits but is never in their control, while a witch completely abandons himself to damned spirits, usually by some sort of pact or blood bond."[34] From a theological point of view, witches, by selling themselves, abandon the true faith, and reject it—a much more serious action than the sorcerers' use of magic. Faust before the pact is an ambiguous magician; afterward he is a literally damned witch, a distinction lost to later audiences, who viewed him as the archetypal ambiguous sorcerer.

Gothic Ambiguities

The heroic sorcerer would initially prove to be the more imitated of the two character types in 20th century popular fiction, especially in comic books, but the ambiguous sorcerer—who currently seems to be the predominant type of magician in superheroic fiction, including comic books[35]—flourished in the gap between *The Tempest* and *Action Comics* #1.

In the 200 years following *The Tempest*, evil sorcerers were more the norm than ambiguous ones, but starting in the middle of the 18th century and continuing through the Gothic era (broadly defined as 1764–1830) ambiguous sorcerers made a comeback and became more common than either heroic or evil magicians.

In real life, there was the example of the Comte de Saint Germain (1712?–1784). The Comte appeared, more or less out of nowhere, in Paris in 1748 and was quickly accepted into the circles of the rich, prestigious, and influential, including that of King Louis XV and Mme. de Pompadour. He became a diplomatic courier, practiced chemistry (or perhaps alchemy),[36] wrote a great deal of music and in general conducted himself like many another courtier and mountebank of the time. To distract attention from his own ambiguous background, he told fantastic stories about himself and encouraged rumors about his abilities and background, to the point that he was on the one hand known as the "Wonder Man of

Europe" but on the other hand rumored to be in league with the Devil—a reputation that would become widespread in the 19th century.

At the same time that Saint Germain was being compared to John Dee and other real life occultists, a series of ambiguous enchanters appeared in the popular literature of the era, Gothics and novels. William Beckford's *Vathek* (1786), with Horace Walpole's *The Castle of Otranto* (1764) the most influential of the early Gothics, presented a vulnerable-to-temptation bent-on-a-demonic-quest titular sorcerer as its Hero-Villain, the ambiguous protagonist (alternatively, the attractive antagonist) of the Gothic. Vathek presented a significant model for later Hero-Villains; Vathek's "devotion to evil comes to a focal point in his single, terrible eye that can maim or slay as Vathek wills. The fatal optic is one of Beckford's major contributions to the evolution of the Gothic villain."[37] Friedrich von Schiller's unfinished "Der Geisterseher: Eine Gesichte aus den Memoires des Graf en von O" (1787–1789) has in a significant role a supernatural Armenian who may be hero or villain—the unfinished text leaves it ambiguous and unclear what the Armenian's role truly is. Meg Merrilies, in Walter Scott's *Guy Mannering, or the Astrologer* (1815) a "harlot, thief, witch and gypsey [sic]"[38] is crucial in restoring the hero of the novel to his usurped estate. She is an unerring astrologer/prophet, but despite being a witch—which as mentioned above put her in the eternally condemned category two centuries before—is portrayed in mixed terms, verging on the positive. John Polidori's Count Filiberto Doni, from *Ernestus Berchtold* (1819), is more ambiguous, being a doomed sorcerer whose good intentions go awry through his own weakness.

Most influential of the Gothic era ambiguous sorcerers would be Goethe's Faust. Though what would later become known as the first half of *Faust* was published in German as *Faust: A Fragment* in 1790 and was somewhat read by English authors, it wasn't until the 1821 publication of an English translation that *Faust* had its greatest impact on English writers. *Faust: A Fragment* portrays the temptation of Faust by Mephistopheles, Faust's succumbing to temptation, and his ill-treatment of Gretchen and then his and Mephistopheles's flight as Gretchen is condemned to death and accepts her punishment. James Hogg's *The Three Perils of Man* (1823) brings back Michael Scot as a more Faustian character, a Hero-Villain who proclaims that his ambition is to be the Antichrist but who is, in proper Hero-Villain form, a man of great capabilities, and likable, who nonetheless cannot resist his passions. Obando, from William Child Green's *The Abbot of Montserrat* (1826), is a Faustian-inflected sorcerer, and even Ptolemy Horoscope, the voicebox for God in Richard Thomson's *Tales of an Antiquary* (1828) has Faustian elements.

As we'll see in Chapter 5, the ambiguous sorcerer would finally, in the mid-19th century, give way to more positive portrayals of enchanters.

Superheroines *Avant la Lettre*

The other influential character type from Ariosto's *Orlando Furioso* was the female knight. In *Orlando Furioso* the female knight was Bradamante, who was a model for Britomart in Spenser's *The Faerie Queene* as well as later comic book superheroines. But as with the heroic and ambiguous sorcerers, a consideration of female knights forces us to leap back substantially before *Orlando Furioso*, or even 1500, if we are accurately to trace its roots in the character.

The idea of a woman warrior is old, nearly as old as human civilization, with the Babylonian goddess Ishtar and the Ugaritic goddess Anat both being violent warrior-goddesses. The female version of the "wild man," the "wild woman," though popular in medieval art and literature, has its roots in the same ancient sources as the wild man,[39] and carried much the same symbolism for the medievals that the wild man did.[40] So there's no one starting point for the woman warrior, or in the modern era the superheroine. But there are characters who had an unusual amount of influence on characters who followed them, and this is certainly the case with medieval warrior women.

One superheroine prototype was the Amazon. Whatever their historical origins,[41] the Amazons made their literary debut in Homer's *Iliad* (eighth century BCE) as a nation of warriors, "equal to men" and adept at killing. To the Greeks, the Amazons were man-killers, but heroic, as heroic as the Greek heroes if not more so.[42] Aeschylus, Diodorus Siculus, Herodotus, and Tacitus all wrote of the Amazons, as flesh-eaters, horse-riding warriors, "women-men," and women-without-men.[43] (But, again, what the ancient Greeks considered heroic does not qualify as superheroic, and the Amazonian heroes, Penthesilia and Andromache and the rest, are counterparts to the Greek "heroes," not their moral superiors and certainly not possessed of a selfless mission.) Centuries later, the Amazons were seen by medieval European writers as essentially noble savages, commendable "for their ways of life, which though alien had much to recommend them—discipline and bravery . . . treatments of them consistently placed a greater emphasis on their similarities to European Christians than on their dissimilarities, and often concluded that God teaches men by showing us virtuous lives lived in contexts different from our own."[44]

Medieval *literati* got most of their information on the Amazons from Benoît de Sainte-Maure's *Le Roman de Troie* (ca. 1160), a reworking of the

Matter of Troy into a French epic. In *Le Roman de Troie* the Amazons' queen, Penthesilia goes to Troy in search of Hector, but finding him killed by the Greeks leads the Amazons to avenge Hector's and the Trojan deaths. Although Penthesilia is eventually hacked to death by a gang of Greeks, it is clear that she is noble Hector's female counterpart: "courageous, bold, beautiful and wise, of great valor and lineage, she was very esteemed and honored."[45] Penthesilia, and de Sainte-Maure's conception of the Amazons as both chaste and martially capable, were propagated by Guido de Colonne, who used *Le Roman de Troie* as the source of his *Historia Destructionis Troiae* (1287), "which then became the most popular vehicle for communicating the medieval tales of Troy . . . through both vernacular and Latin texts such as Benoît's and Guido's, the myth of the Amazon warriors contributed to debates about gender difference in Italy as well as the rest of Europe."[46] There were warrior women before Penthesilia, but she was the most famous of them and became the first great warrior woman of medieval literature, and the great-grandmother of the modern superheroine.[47]

The Early Female Knight

Meanwhile, as the image of Penthesilia and the Amazons was developing, another warrior woman character was developing in parallel: the female knight.

In the anonymously written *chanson de geste Aliscans* (ca. 1150), Guiborc, the sister of the song's protagonist, Rainourt, dons armor and leads the women of Orange in defending their city against the pagan forces; Guiborc does not fight as knights do, but throws rocks at the invaders from the city's towers. Guiborc, though hardly a female knight, at the least begins the tradition, if not invents the motif, of the female-knight-in-armor as a combatant. *Aliscans*, in turn, heavily influenced Wolfram von Eschenbach's unfinished poem *Willehalm* (ca. 1212), but in *Willehalm* Gyburc[48] defends Orange against the Saracens with a drawn sword, on the battlefield, just the male knights do.

In Wirnt von Gravenberc's *Wigalois* (ca. 1210/1215), a story about the titular Arthurian knight and son of Gawain, we meet Marine, whose grandfather is captured by the pagan King Roaz of Glois. Marine is thus inspired to take up arms and fight evil. She gathers around her 12 like-minded fighting woman and goes to war, serving featly as a virgin knight before dying in battle. In the *Roman de Silence* (first half of the 13th century), attributed to "Heldris de Cornuälle," the woman named Silence is raised as a boy so that she can escape the laws disallowing women from inheriting property. As a teenager she runs away from home and ends up at the king's court, where she poses as a knight. Chivalric adventures follow, including a tournament at which Silence defeats all challengers, and a war with England (during which she defeats a warrior compared to Alexander the Great),[49] and eventually she is sent to find Merlin; Silence succeeds and is married to the king.[50] In the *Vulgate Merlin* (1220–1235) when Avenable's father's lands are stolen from him, she travels to Julius Caesar's court and poses as the fighting man "Grisandoles." She is eventually knighted by Caesar and becomes his seneschal before Merlin exposes her gender, at which point Caesar marries her.

The organizational impulse was strong in the Middle Ages, and it was applied to fictional heroes as it was to so many other things. The Nine Worthies were formulated in the early 14th century; in response, the French poet Eustache Deschamps created the *"neuf preuses,"* the Nine Female Worthies who were the female counterparts to the Nine Worthies, in the ballad *Il est Temps de Faire La Paix* (1387) and the poem *Si Les Héros Revenaient sur Terre Ils Seraient Étonnés* (1396). The members of the Nine Female Worthies varied according to writer, with choices varying from Semiramis (the legendary wife of Assyrian king Ninus and his successor to the throne) to Penthesilia. The Nine Female Worthies became companions to the Nine Worthies in literature and art.

The two traditions of the Amazon and the female knight came together in Andrea da Barberino's prose epic *Aspramonte* (ca. 1415). A revamping of the Matter of France *chanson de geste Chanson d'Aspermont* (ca. 1180), *Aspramonte* has roughly the same characters, but Barberino added the character of Galaziella, the daughter of Penthesilia and a Saracen king Agolante. Uniquely (to this point) for the Italian epic, Galaziella "does not follow the longstanding literary model of the lady who encourages her love interest as she watches jousting matches from a balcony. Instead the warrior woman sighs in disappointment because she would like to participate and defeat the male contestants whose skills she can surpass."[51] Galaziella is wooed by a Saracen king, who gives her Durindarda, Charlemagne's former sword. In response Galaziella puts on a suit of armor and defeats a number of Saracens before being defeated by a Christian knight, converting to Christianity, and marrying him. Da Barberino then offers differing possibilities for Galaziella's fate: burned at the stake, imprisoned in Africa, escaped to Africa to become the hero of an African queendom, or dead in childbirth delivering twins.

16th- and 17th-Century Warrior Women

By the 16th century there was a long tradition of European female knights,[52] both in fiction and in real life.[53] *Orlando Furioso*'s Bradamante, however, was different—she was a main character in *Orlando Furioso*—arguably *the* main character, unlike her predecessors. The trail of influences on Bradamante is in some respects as lengthy as that of Orlando. The 14th and 15th century "Rinaldo da Montalbano" cycle of poems featured Braidamonte and Queen Laura, female knights both; *Orlando* (1400) has the warrior women Meridiana, Chiarella, and Antea; the anonymously written *Inamoramento de Carlo Magno* (1481) has a series of Saracen woman warriors who are literal giants; and Boiardo's *Orlando Innamorato* (1483–1495) has Luciana, the female knight. Boiardo in particular was an influence on Ariosto.

But Bradamante, as a protagonist whose story is central to the plot of *Orlando Furioso*, is different from those who came before. She was striking, combining martial capabilities with a love story, and she was influential. Alongside the character of Marfisa—another carryover from *Orlando Innamorato*, Marfisa is a Saracen warrior who eventually converts to Christianity and fights against the Saracens—Bradamante would provide a role model for the women warriors who followed her.[54] Marfisa, in *Orlando Furioso*, is "the first warrior maiden to have real character and to be allowed to keep her independence,"[55] but it was Bradamante who was allowed to combine romance and martial abilities, and it was Bradamante more than Marfisa who influenced later women warriors.[56]

A Spanish romance, written by Diego Ortunez de Calahorra and published in 1555, translated into English by Margaret Tyler in 1578 as *The Mirror of Princely Deeds and Knighthood*, proved to be exceedingly popular, initiating an English craze for Spanish chivalric romance. One of the most popular characters in *The Mirror* was the Amazon Claridiana, biological daughter of Penthesilia (and inheritor of her armor and, supposedly, her superior at arms) but in most ways the daughter of Bradamante. In Torquato Tasso's *La Gerusalemme Liberata* (1581), the story of the conquest of Jerusalem by the Crusaders in 1099 serves as the backdrop to the Bradamante-like Clorinda, another Saracen warrior woman who is killed in battle by a Christian knight, but not before converting to Christianity.[57]

The greatest character that Bradamante had an influence on was Britomart, in Spenser's *The Faerie Queene*. I'll summarize *The Faerie Queene*'s plot in the next section, but of importance here is *Faerie Queene*'s Britomart, the lady knight and the symbol of chastity. Like Bradamante, Britomart is one of the protagonists, not a secondary character like Clorinda or Claridiana, and her exploits and romance with Artegall take up much of *The Faerie Queene*. Britomart is a combination of martial skills and romantic yearnings (despite her role as the knight of chastity) who became, to reading audiences during and after Spenser's lifetime, representative of *The Faerie Queene* as a whole, much more so than the Redcrosse Knight,

the knight of holiness, or Sir Artegall, the knight of justice. Like Bradamante, Britomart became the archetypal woman warrior, not least because
of Spenser's dual emphasis on martial skill and chastity (a requirement for
the Elizabethan and Jacobean audiences), to the point that a British Navy
cutter was given her name during the Napoleonic War.

The female warriors who followed the Amazons and Bradamante and
Britomart over the next century were generally more pallid versions of
them, often taking their authors' obsession with chastity and portraying
the characters' subjugation to the exigencies of love but negating the original emphasis on their warrior's skills.[58] Shakespeare's Hippolyta, in *A
Midsummer Night's Dream* (1595?), though putatively an Amazon, is purely
a subject of the play's love plot, and represents "masculine anxiety over
England's anomalous rule by a woman."[59] Chastity is likewise a dominant concern for the women warriors of Margaret Cavendish's *Loves
Adventures and Deaths Banquet* (1662) and *Bell in Campo* (1662). Thomas
Killigrew, however, in his *Cicilia and Clorinda, or Love in Arms* (1663),
emphasizes his heroine Clorinda's warrior's skills as much as the concern
with love and chastity, and the Amazons of the Jacobean masques, such
as Ben Jonson's *Masque of Queens* (1609) personify female power to the
near-exclusion of the love plot, in a particularly transgressive and subversive (to male authority) fashion.[60]

Does this make Bradamante and Britomart and the Amazons protosuperheroines, however? Not in my view, any more than The Cid or Beowulf
were. Influential on later characters, certainly—without the Amazons
and without the lineage of warrior women that resulted in Britomart,
there would be no pulp heroines and there would be no Wonder Woman.
But, although these characters had some of the elements of the superhero
as listed in Chapter 1, from distinctive appearances to recognizable weapons to code names, none of them had them together in great numbers,
and none of them had the selfless mission that is the base requirement for
the superhero. Amazons were simply warriors, as was Bradamante; like
Bradamante, Britomart is driven by—one might even say obsessed with—
finding her destined husband. Britomart has the additional burden of
symbolizing chastity, and certainly Spenser gives Britomart sufficient
characterization that she becomes at least two-dimensional. But Britomart
never takes on the mission element. On the protosuperheroic scale, they
fall on the "lesser" end.

The Faerie Queene

It can fairly be said that the previous centuries' worth of *chansons de
geste* and romances and epic poems all culminated in Spenser's *Faerie*

Queene, generally acclaimed as not just Spenser's masterpiece but one of the greatest epics in the Anglophone world. *The Faerie Queene* is an advance on *Orlando Furioso* (one of Spenser's primary influences) thanks to its depth of allegory and lyrical language, and the influence of *The Faerie Queene* on later poets and writers is extensive. In the 20th century, C. S. Lewis's "Chronicles of Narnia" and his "Space Trilogy," and J. R. R. Tolkien's "Lord of the Rings" trilogy, owe Spenser much, as do modern fantasy writers in general—Spenser was "the first writer to create his own language to convey the distinct atmosphere of a fantasy world."[61] But superheroes as a genre do not owe Spenser a significant debt.

The Faerie Queene is an extensive allegory, about Queen Elizabeth I, about various virtues, about religion and politics and how to live a good life—as Spenser himself wrote in his letter to Sir Walter Raleigh, "the generall end therefore of all the booke is to fashion a gentleman or noble person in virtuous and gentle discipline."[62] Spenser originally intended to write 12 books, but died young, leaving only 6 completed, about holiness, temperance, chastity, friendship, justice, and courtesy. Holiness is represented by the Redcrosse Knight, temperance by Sir Guyon, chastity by the aforementioned Britomart, friendship by the relationship between Britomart and Artegall (her destined husband), justice by Artegall, and courtesy by Sir Calidore. The Redcrosse Knight fights allegorical monsters, Saracens, and enchanters before being married; Sir Guyon endures temptation in various forms and fights representations of the seven deadly sins and five vices; Britomart deals with the perils of love and chastity; Artegall pursues allegorical Irishmen, the enemies of justice; and Sir Calidore attempts to subdue the Blatant Beast, whose rumors and slanders are the enemy of Calidore's courtesy.

The Faerie Queene can be difficult reading, but it is colorful, exciting, multilayered, and surprisingly psychologically insightful, and it's no surprise that it was immediately acclaimed when published (despite its mock-archaic language) and has remained so to this day. Writers of epics following Spenser, most particularly John Milton with his *Paradise Lost* (1667), labored in its shadow. One would think that, epics being the precursors to modern heroic fiction, *The Faerie Queene* would therefore be notable for the influence it has on superheroes. Certainly, as Jason Tondro argues, there are substantial similarities between *The Faerie Queene* and modern superhero comics: "the symbols, tropes, and issues of *The Faerie Queene* are very familiar to readers of the superhero romance . . . a reader of superhero comics is secretly, perhaps even without his own knowledge, trained to be an excellent reader of Spenser."[63]

But *The Faerie Queene*, with a very few exceptions (Tondro notes Matt Wagner's use of Spenser in Wagner's *Mage*, 1984–1986), is more of a *general* influence on superheroes than a *direct* influence. *The Faerie Queene* stands as the preeminent example of the epic tradition that superheroes draw heavily upon, and as Tondro says, its symbols, tropes, and issues are common in superhero comics. But *The Faerie Queene* provided no archetypal characters for superheroes to model themselves upon; the Redcrosse Knight et al. are epic heroes but are on the "lesser" end of the protosuperheroic spectrum and don't vary in any significant way from their predecessors, the Arthurian knights and the Cid and so on. *The Faerie Queene* stands as an example of Art/High Culture whose halo of influence never quite extended into low culture, undoubtedly because of the difficulty of its language and the depth of its allegories. The producers of popular culture, the writers who made use of Arthur and Robin Hood and Long Meg and Moll Cutpurse in their ballads and chapbooks and plays, went with the easily understood rather than the difficult and dense. Art, in the form of *The Faerie Queene*, contributed some individual elements to the superhero tradition, but it was popular culture whose characters and plots were most commonly used by superhero writers and artists.

Descendants of Talos

One character from *The Faerie Queene* who has attracted a significant amount of scholarly and critical attention is Talus, Artegall's groom, "made of yron mould/ Immoveable, resistlesse, without end."[64] Talus would, as we'll see, become the model for nonflesh superheroes of all sorts, but, yet again, to properly treat him we need to leap back centuries and see where he came from.

The ancient Greeks ranked statuary highly among the arts; as was perhaps inevitable, the idea of mobile, conscious, even living statuary, and then human-shaped clockwork devices—automata—soon developed and appeared in the myths. The most significant of the mythological automata, though by no means the only one, is Talos of Crete. Greek mythology, as it does with so many other legendary figures, has varying origins for Talos, as for that matter do scholars studying Greek mythology. The most popular and longest-enduring of the myths involving Talos is that he was a "brazen" giant, constructed by Hephaestus—the *Argonautica* has it as follows:

> He was of the stock of bronze, of the men sprung from the ash-trees, the last left among the sons of the gods; and the son of Cronos gave him to Europa to be the warder of Crete and to stride round the island thrice a

day with his feet of bronze. Now in all the rest of his body and limbs was he fashioned of bronze and invulnerable; but beneath the sinew by his ankle was a blood-red vein; and this, with its issues of life and death, was covered by a thin skin.[65]

The job of Talos is to patrol Crete, enforcing its laws, and to throw rocks at those who would land there (alternatively, to make himself red hot and embrace strangers), especially pirates, something he fails at with the Argonauts thanks to Medea's spells. Talos is not the only robot of Greek myth—Hephaestus and Daedalus both construct numerous automata for various purposes—but he is the most significant one, being the only one concerned with the enforcement of law and order. But the question of whether or not Talos has agency and individual will is left ambiguous, leaving his status as a protosuperhero in doubt.[66]

Byzantium, inheritor to the classical tradition, would become the home of fantastic automata during the Eastern Empire's first several centuries:

> Though by the medieval period Latin and Arab literature had reworked the Greek legends and also imagined automata in connection with wondrous places, the origins of the trope are decidedly Hellenic. Ambassadors' accounts of the emperor's palace in Constantinople, for example, recount that emissaries were often startled by the roaring lion automata that surrounded the Byzantine throne of Solomon. Liutprand of Cremona reports in the tenth century that he was escorted to the Byzantine imperial palace and humbled before an elaborate mechanical throne on which the emperor himself sat when receiving official guests.[67]

Common in folktales and in romances were the tomb automata that were reputed to guard particularly valuable resting places; such automata "by one means or another, prevented the one who chanced to make his way thither, from carrying off any of their wealth."[68] One typical tomb automata is the golden archer guarding the warrior woman Camille's tomb in the *Roman d'Éneas* (ca. 1160): "The moment that a living person, metonymically referred to as 'breath,' enters her mausoleum, the archer springs into action, plunging the space into darkness and extinguishing the signifier of Camille's eternal spirit."[69] Another such appears in Thomas's *Tristan* (ca. 1170), in which Iseult's tomb is guarded by a statue of the giant Moldagog, who brandishes an iron club for use against intruders.[70]

More fantastic than the tomb automata were the mechanical knights who appeared in romance literature from the beginning of the 12th century onward.

In, for example, the *Roman de Troie* (circa 1160) we encounter four automata, two of which are female, and two of which are male. In the twelfth-century *Roman d'Alexandre*, the function of these figures was to act as guardians to a bridge, entrance, or gate of some sort. In *Lancelot* of the early thirteenth century, a series of mechanical knights are encountered, while in *Tristan* (circa 1220) the enchantress Morgan la Fée defends her castle with aid of copper knights. In the thirteenth-century *Huon de Bordeaux*, two copper men, armed with flails . . . guard a castle, and in the cycle of legends surrounding the ambiguous figure of Virgil the Necromancer brazen spearmen or archers have to be defeated by the questing hero.[71]

Of course, brazen guardians are inheritors of the idea of tomb automata—and as Truitt notes a common reason given for motive force of both tomb automata and brazen guardians is demonic possession[72]—but in the anonymously written *Gesta Romanorum* (ca. 1342) we see the idea of the automaton taken to another level in Virgil's creation of "a brazen horseman who scours the streets after curfew each evening, and slays all those who disobey the law by straying abroad."[73] Virgil's "brazen horseman," though still only an automaton (and fully automatic, rather than powered by demons), is now in the role of justice-keeper, hearkening back to Talos. Virgil is further credited, in an undated story ("Virgil, The Wicked Princess, and the Iron Man") whose collector nonetheless claims a medieval date for, with creating "a man of iron with golden locks, very beautiful to behold as a man, with sympathetic, pleasing air, one who conversed fluently and in a winning voice; and yet he was all of iron, and the spirit who was conjured into him was one without pity or mercy."[74] This "Iron Man" is sent after a poisoner and drags her to a cave where the ghosts of her victims wait for her; the ghosts force the poisoner to drink two goblets of poison, killing herself.[75]

But the idea of the artificial knight in the deliberately, consciously heroic role was a conceptual leap forward made by Edmund Spenser when he created Talus in *The Faerie Queene*, hearkening back to the Greek myths and displaying his debt to them by virtually duplicating Talos's name in Talus. Spenser created other automata in *The Faerie Queene*—Acrasia the sorceress, Munera the guardian of the castle—but Talus is the only heroic one—and quite a hero he is.

In *The Faerie Queene*, Astraea, the personification of justice, leaves the Earth, but before she does she "left her groome/An yron man, which did on her attend/Always to execute her stedfast doome,/And willed him with Artegall to wend,/And doe whatever thing he did intend."[76] Talus, this "yron man," serves Artegall as groom (or "squire" or "page" or "servant") in enforcing justice. Talus, in fact, comes to symbolically represent justice in its relentless, martial form; Talus is mechanical, like a blacksmith in its blows, rather than something more human.[77] Spenser never precisely describes what Talus looks like—he is simply an "yron man," "as swift as swallow in her flight,/And strong as Lyon in his Lordly might,"[78] invulnerable to harm and immune to spells. But the final impression left is of a literal "yron man," a being made of metal, missing Talos's heel vulnerability—an artificial, nonflesh sentient creature.

Moreover, his actions in *The Faerie Queene* are in assistance to Artegall in the cause of justice, and eventually as the conscience of Artegall, his moral guide and governor. In this role, Talus not only operates mechanically, but shows an independent will of his own, even displaying emotions—"did inly chill and quake"[79]—when Artegall is captured by the Amazons.

Talus is a being made wholly of metal, possessed of agency and his own personality, fulfilling a selfless mission, with a distinctive appearance and possessed of a unique weapon (his iron flail, a "strange weapon, never wont in warre.")[80] Talus, then, is the first superheroic android in heroic fiction, the precursor to characters like Robert Kanigher and Ross Andru's Metal Men (for DC), Gardner Fox and Dick Dillin's Red Tornado (for DC), and Roy Thomas, Stan Lee and John Buscema's Vision (for Marvel).[81]

Another type of artificial being to develop during this time appeared after Talus, and though originally not heroic would eventually become so. The word "golem" appears in Psalm 139, in the Hebrew sense of "embryo," but its current definition evolved from the kabbalistic *Book of Creation* (second century CE) and from medieval kabbalism, which portrayed the golem as a lower, imperfect form of creation and a living thing that could be made by man rather than God, though a living thing without a personality, a kind of animate empty husk. During the 16th and 17th centuries another version of the golem developed, derived from myths associated with Rabbi Elias Baalkschem of Chelm (?–1583) and Rabbi Löw (1512–1609) of Prague. In these legends, the Rabbi brings a golem to life to perform household tasks, but something goes wrong and the Rabbi is forced to destroy the golem. These legends would linger for quite some time, even filtering into the consciousness of educated non-Jews, before finally developing into something quite different.

Long Meg of Westminster

"Long Meg of Westminster" may never have existed. The stories of her being from Lancashire, working in a tavern, and serving in the army of

Henry VIII in the 1540s have no evidentiary basis, and Long Meg would certainly not be the first folk hero to have sprung purely from the people's imagination. But regardless of whether there was a flesh-and-blood woman who went by the name "Long Meg," the English of the 16th and 17th centuries believed in her reality, and made her into a folk heroine, in popular ballads, fiction, drama, and poetry.

In 1582, a pamphlet of her life was published. In 1590, a ballad about her, now lost, was licensed, and that same year appeared the anonymously written *The Life of Long Meg of Westminster*; no copies of the 1590 edition of *The Life of Long Meg* survive, but a 1620 biography by that title is extant and is likely the same text. In *The Life of Long Meg* the Amazonian protagonist, beginning as a 16-year-old, uses her size and strength and fighting skills to fight corruption and wickedness—and, yes, crime—on behalf of the poor and oppressed, rescuing penniless maidens from a usurious carrier, rescuing a poor debtor from a bailiff, casting down an arrogant nobleman in a fistfight, and—most important for our purposes— saving some Lancashire girls from robbery at the hands of two men. She beats the men into submission and makes them vow to never hurt woman, nor poor man, nor children, nor rob packmen nor carriers nor distressed persons. One exception she grants: rich farmers and country chuffs, who she directs the robber to focus their energies on. "Clearly, Meg is not only a figure of heroism but of righteousness triumphant."[82] Meg goes on to fight the French on the battlefield, marries, saves a young man from a cruel miller's anger, and, as an older woman, robs a crooked friar while disguised as a man.

Later writers cast her in less complimentary terms, although Thomas Heywood's *The Fair Maid of the West: Or, a Girl Worth Gold* (1631) has its cross-dressing, piratical heroine hold up Long Meg as an example to be striven for, but the favorable legend of Long Meg persisted well into the 19th century, with *The Life of Long Meg* being reprinted in 1805 and 1880. Her relevance to this history is as a protosuperheroine, with her more-than-normal strength, code name, costume (her male's attire), and her selfless activities, and if she lacks the specifically urban orientation of Moll Cutpurse, Long Meg nonetheless stands as the first *modern* protosuperheroine, the first inhabitant of the readers' and listeners' contemporary world. Long Meg isn't a knight or Amazon from centuries ago; she is a product of the modern world, and provided her readers and listeners with the idea that fighting evil and crime could take place in the modern world. Too, unlike the many cross-dressing warrior women of popular ballads of the 17th, 18th, and 19th centuries,[83] Long Meg is primarily an independent crime fighter rather than a soldier or sailor, with a heroic mission all her own. Her adoption by writers as an abuser of abusive and boastful, arrogant men, and her use as a role model for other fictional women warriors, obscured this side of her.

Moll Cutpurse

Mary Frith (ca. 1584–1659) was a remarkable woman. That so much of her life is obscured by stories about her (many circulating during her lifetime) and by later interpretations of her life, does not detract from how unusual she was. Purse-snatcher at 16, second-story woman at 25, crossdresser and "roaring girl" (the female version of the "roaring boy," who was known for public drinking, fighting, and petty crimes), part of London's female transvestite movement of the early 17th century, celebrity at 26, public figure for the rest of her life, licensed fence and familiar of the members of the underworld, inmate at the infamous Bethlehem Hospital for the insane—just the facts of her life make up a colorful litany of adventure. And that's not even taking into account the fictionalized versions of her life, beginning with T. Middleton and T. Dekker's play *The Roaring Girle; or, Moll Cut-Purse* (1611) and continuing up through the present, as each new generation of readers and scholars rediscover Frith's life and reinterpret and recast her for their own purposes.[84]

What is more relevant to this work is not the reality of Frith's life and career as a member of the *demimonde*, but her fictional self, the mythic "Moll Cutpurse." *The Roaring Girle* presents Frith—known to all the world as Moll Cutpurse—as a habitué of the underworld but not a member of it, and (more importantly) one who protects—violently, if need be—the honest and innocent from the tricks of the criminals. She dresses in men's clothes, carries a man's weapons, and smokes tobacco. *The Roaring Girle* was quite popular in its day, and the legend of Moll Cutpurse was added to in the anonymously written *The Life and Death of Mrs. Mary Frith, Commonly Called Mal Cutpurse* (1662), which turned her into "a royalist crossdressing Robin-hooder who eventually seeks redemption,"[85] a "popular outcast defending the poor and oppressed against rapacious lawyers."[86] This character, the Moll Cutpurse whose crimes are on behalf of a greater good, would become propagated further in Alexander Smith's *History of the Lives and Robberies of the Most Notorious Highwaymen* (1719), overshadowing for good the real Mary Frith's exploits and permanently solidifying the concept of Moll Cutpurse, Robin Hood–ing highwaywoman, a concept and character that lasted throughout the century.

Moll Cutpurse is of course a protosuperhero. She has the requisite fighting skills of every hero, a code name, and a dual identity (one she reluctantly accepts), but more importantly she has the heroic, selfless mission and a costume (her male clothing). Moreover, she is important in the history of the protosuperheroes because she marks the beginning of the transition of the protosuperhero from a hero of every environment to a specifically *urban* hero. Moll Cutpurse, like her real-life source Mary Frith, is a creature of the urban environment; though later authors like Smith would show her equally active in the countryside, Cutpurse is primarily known as an urban woman, active in the greatest city (by far) of the country and the largest city in Europe of the time. If the legend of Robin Hood popularized the concept of the costumed vigilante, Moll Cutpurse took the legend and brought it to the modern city, the location for the great majority of modern superheroes.

Heroic Highwaymen

Frith did not live to see *The Life and Death of Mrs. Mary Frith, Commonly Called Mal Cutpurse*, but she was alive in 1652 to see the royalist sympathizer George Fidge write several biographies of the highwayman James Hind (1616–1652), which portrayed Hind not as (or not just as) a robber and thief, but as a defender of royalism—in essence, a Robin Hood–like figure driven by hatred of the English Protectorate. These biographies began a trend toward "criminal biographies"[87] that would humanize criminals, often for political purposes. More relevant for our purposes here is how this trend would result, in the following century, in the presentation of criminals, especially highwaymen, not just as humans but as heroes.

The 18th century saw the rise of a new generation of legendary heroic highwaymen, modern Robin Hoods appropriate for the century. It was, in Eric Hobsbawm's words, "the golden age of bandit-heroes."[88] The reality of course was quite different. Although some, like the French Robert Mandrin, chiefly smuggled, which had the perception of being a victimless crime, and though some men really did prefer to rob from the rich (after all, they were the ones with the money), many of the other men were murderers first and social avengers second—"usually a very long way second"[89]—who preyed on the poor.

> Yet such was the need on the part of the rural poor to find a secular savior to give them hope of a promised land of plenty and social justice, that some very unpromising material was transfigured into heroic status . . . it was a period when pressure on rural communities from population growth was intense, when the state's control of the countryside was uncertain,

when physical communications were primitive, but when improvements in symbolic communications allowed the propagation of myths by word, image, and song. So it was also a period which saw the appearance of Stenka Razin (Russia), Juro Janosik (Slovakian part of Hungary), Angelo Duca, alias Angiolillo (Naples), Diego Corrientes (Spain), Robert Mandrin (France), Johannes Buckler, alias Schinderhannes (the Rhineland), "Rob Roy" MacGregor (Scotland), Matthias Weber, alias the Slicer (the Rhineland), Dick Turpin (England), and also a major revival of the cult of Robin Hood.[90]

A similar dynamic took place in urban environments, where gallows literature, which focused on the lives and to a lesser extent motivations of the criminals, humanized criminals. The inevitable follow-up to humanizing criminals was to turn some of them into heroes. "The intrepid cutthroat thirsting for social vengeance offered the next generation in particular an oneiric escape, far from the burdensome obligations and the repression of adolescent behavior forced on them by the prevailing morality."[91] For the urban middle class in particular, the stereotype fulfilled a political role:

> It sprang from a collective urban imaginary that was conscious of a major gulf between those who dominated and those who were subjected . . . a sign of dissatisfaction among the middling urban ranks. Wishing to differentiate themselves from the aristocracy and from the rich bourgeoisie who despised them and dominated urban life, they concocted these indomitable rebels as a way of dealing with their frustrations. They were also seeking, by endowing their mythical leader with a generosity that was often belied by the facts, to exorcize the fear of subversion associated with the unruly and dangerous rising generations.[92]

This mythmaking of rough men into heroic highwaymen—the modern Robin Hoods, the vigilantes for the newly urban world—began in the Continent later in the 17th century and in England and in France (which continued to heavily influence English popular culture) early in the 18th century. Figures like William Nevison (1639–1684), Claude Duval (1643–1670), Louis-Dominique Bourguignon, a.k.a. Cartouche (1693–1721), Jack Sheppard (1702–1724), Joseph "Blueskin" Blake (1700–1724), Jonathan Wild (1682?–1725) were a part of the first wave of heroic highwaymen; Tom King (?–1737), Dick Turpin (1705–1739), and Louis Mandrin (1725–1755) were a part of the second wave. During their lifetimes and afterward, ballads, popular legends, fictionalized biographies, and stage plays portrayed them as Robin Hood–like heroes, and these gave them reputations that they would not lose for a century or more, when popular novelists like William Harrison Ainsworth would immortalize them in novels like *Rookwood* (1834).

This association of the highwayman with a Robin Hood–like motivation for social justice heightened later in the 18th century when the *räuberroman*, or "robber novel," became popular. Essentially created by Friedrich Schiller's *Die Räuber* (1781), an incredibly popular and influential play with a protagonist, Karl von Moor, who robs from the rich, gives to the poor, rejects society's strictures, and embodies the heightened emotion of sensibility and the Sturm und Drang, the *räuberroman* created still another generation of heroic highwaymen, this one political in their specific rejection of society rather than just preying on elements of it. *Die Räuber* was fabulously influential, actually inspiring young German men to run off to the woods to live the life of noble banditry.[93] *Die Räuber* created the *räuberroman*; Christian Vulpius's *Rinaldo Rinaldini, der Räuberhauptmann* (1799–1801) accelerated the craze in England, and gave readers another heroic highwayman, the titular character, to idolize and imitate in further, specifically English novels. The craze lasted for a generation, and gave rise to books like Henry Siddons's *Reginal di Torby, or, The Twelve Robbers* (1803), in which "the stereotype of the admirable outlaw or Promethean rebel with a just cause against a criminal society appears in the character of Reginal di Torby, a noble criminal who turns against society's hollow values and allies himself with the 12 bandits."[94]

Masked Conspirators

The heroic highwaymen of the 17th and 18th centuries were presented as taking great care with their clothes and as being fashion plates, but, like Robin Hood, they kept their faces visible. The motif of the masked vigilante arose from a separate tradition, that of the political conspirators.

Although masks have likely always been a part of conspiracies and secret societies[95] the combination of the mask and secret conspiracy *and* a selfless mission, elements that make the masked men (and perhaps women) into protosuperheroes, is a more recent phenomenon. One could argue that the Vehm of Westphalia, rumored to have been in existence since the middle of the 13th century, or alternatively since Charlemagne's time, combined the selfless mission with the mask—certainly 19th century images of the Vehm presented them as operating while wearing unique hooded costumes.[96] The mission of the Vehm was to enforce justice in a lawless land:

The supreme authority of the Emperor had lost all influence in the country; the imperial assizes were no longer held; might and violence took the place of right and justice; the feudal lords tyrannized over the people; whoever dared, could. To seize the guilty, whoever they might be, to punish them before they were aware of the blow with which they were threatened, and thus to secure the chastisement of crime—such was the object of the Westphalian judges, and thus the existence of this secret society, the instrument of public vengeance, is amply justified, and the popular respect it enjoyed, and on which alone rested its authority, explained.[97]

But solid historical evidence of the Vehm's existence is hard to come by; they are much-discussed, but more as accepted history than in any reliable depth of detail. That rumors of them existed in the 18th century, however, is unassailable, and they were the main characters in at least one novel of the century, Christiane Naubert's historical novel *Herman von Unna* (1788), although this novel, appearing before Schiller's *Der Räuber* did in English, was not read in England and had no influence there. Similarly, Heinrich Zschokke's conspiracy Gothic *Der Schwarzen Brüder* (1791) was hugely popular and influential on the Continent but was never translated into English.[98]

However, what did appear in English was Karl Grosse's Gothic *Horrid Mysteries* (1796), which drew upon *Herman von Unna*, *Der Schwarzen Brüder*, Friedrich Schiller's "Der Geisterseher," and other Inquisition Gothics to create the *Geheimbundroman*, the secret society Gothic, which began to emerge in the late 1790s and continued to be popular as late as Edward Moore's *The Mysteries of Hungary* (1817). "In addition to the Inquisition itself, these malign fraternities appeared in Gothic fiction as sects of Freemasons, the Illuminati of Ingolstadt, the members of a cabalistic tribunal called the Vehmgericht, and sometimes as revolutionary or anarchist brotherhoods."[99]

The Vehm had influence on *Rinaldo Rinaldini*. So, too, did the stories of the Beati Paoli, the 18th-century Sicilian version of the Vehm, described at length in Heckethorn's *The Secret Societies of All Ages and Countries* but best described in D. H. Lawrence's *Sea and Sardinia* (1921):

The Blessed Pauls were a society for the protection of the poor. Their business was to track down and murder the oppressive rich. Ah, they were a wonderful, a splendid society. Were they, said I, a sort of camorra? Ah, on the contrary—here he lapsed into a tense voice—they hated the camorra. These, the Blest Pauls, were the powerful and terrible enemy of the Grand Camorra. For the Grand Camorra oppresses the poor. And therefore the Pauls track down in secret the leaders of the Grand Camorra, and assassinate them, or bring them to the fearful hooded tribunal which utters the dread verdict of the Beati Paoli. And when once the Beati Paoli have decreed a man's death—all over.[100]

Stories of the Beati Paoli were common throughout Europe during the 18th century,[101] so it comes as no surprise that the Beati Paoli, like the Vehm and like many other conspiratorial characters from contemporary European novels, show up in *Rinaldo Rinaldini*. Rinaldini is approached by "the Old Man of Fronteja," who attempts to recruit Rinaldini to join the "Black Judges in Secret," a conspiracy that grew "tired of the yoke of a tyrannical government" and "resolved to rule overselves," later trying to overthrow the Corsican government.[102] The Black Judges in secret, like the Vehm and the Beati Paoli, are hooded vigilantes. More unusually, the Old Man of Fronteja is a superpowered sorcerer, whose "Theosophist" and Rosicrucian training "unveiled the secrets of the Egyptians" and gave him various mystical abilities, including the power to summon visions of the future.[103] The Black Judges in Secret are protomasked killer vigilantes, the precursors to the Punisher (for Marvel) and Marv Wolfman and George Perez's Vigilante (for DC) and all the others, but the Old Man of Fronteja is the earliest version of the Rosicrucian Master, who as we'll see in Chapter 5 is one of the 19th century's supermen.

The Hero-Villain

The Gothic, as a genre, has its beginning in Horace Walpole's *The Castle of Otranto* (1764), but became truly influential with Ann Radcliffe's *The Mysteries of Udolpho* (1794), reigning for 25 years and peaking with Charles Maturin's *Melmoth the Wanderer* (1820). The most common male villain in the Gothic was the Hero-Villain, the antagonist of most Gothic novels but paradoxically the most attractive character to the readers in most of these novels.

Modeled on Satan, from John Milton's *Paradise Lost* (1667–1674), and heavily influenced by elements of the mid-18th century Cult of Sensibility, the Hero-Villain commits evil but is never purely evil. He is a mix of violent passions and uncontrollable impulses that he knows to be evil but cannot resist or overcome. He has great intellectual and physical gifts, great strength of character and will, but he uses them for evil ends. The Hero-Villain is attractive to the reader because of his passion and great abilities as well as for his temptation and suffering, but he is villainous because of his final surrender to evil. The Hero-Villain is tormented by his own dark urges at the same time that he torments others. To paraphrase master Gothicist Charles Maturin, the Hero-Villain is one who can apprehend the good, but is powerless to be it.

The Hero-Villain is the antagonist but he is also an antihero, and a model to the reader of the waste of potential and a lesson in what the inability to resist temptation and one's impulses can lead to. Common to the Gothics, the Hero-Villain survived well past the death of the Gothic and can be seen in a number of the significant post-Gothic novels, including Emily Brontë's *Wuthering Heights* (1847).

His relevance to this work lies in his liminal status as both Hero and Villain, opponent to a novel's hero or heroine but also the figure the reader roots for, and in the oversized impact his presence has, from his animal magnetism to the piercing glare that in Ann Radcliffe's words "seemed to penetrate, at a single glance, into the hearts of men and to read their secret thoughts; few persons could support their scrutiny or even endure to meet them twice."[104] Pale, handsome, physically mighty, with a scornful demeanor, the Hero-Villain is a kind of anticipation not just of the Byronic *homme fatale* but of a strain of the Übermensch of the 19th century, including Varney the Vampyre, and at a greater length every morally torn, emotionally tormented comic book superhero and antihero supervillain. Occasionally the Hero-Villain would become a masked adventurer or even a costumed vigilante, as in countless *räuber-romans*, like Edward Fitzball's *The Black Robber* (1819), in which the protagonist Ulrich St. Julien "exhibits the ambiguous moral traits of the Byronic hero, particularly Byron's Corsair, whose being is a strange compound of 'one virtue and a thousand crimes,'"[105] and displays this mix by attacking a monastery where Ulric's love was put to death and in turn slaughtering the monastery's abbot and putting the monastery to the torch.

The Venetian Batman

Schiller's *Der Räuber* was the landmark *räuberroman*. Heavily influenced by it, but an influential best seller in its own right, was Heinrich Zschokke's *Aballino der Große Bandit* (1794). Set in Venice, *Aballino* is about Count Rosalvo, who has taken on himself the onerous task of ridding Venice of conspirators, thugs, and assassins. He does this using two assumed identities: one is Flodoardo, a handsome, virtuous man who labors unceasingly to improve Venice; the other identity is Aballino, a huge, monstrous, and ugly outlaw. Ultimately Rosalvo succeeds in capturing and trapping all the criminals of Venice and turning them over to the friends and advisers of the Doge.

Abällino was immediately popular when it debuted, and it made Zschokke famous. It helped create the *räuberroman* craze in England at the turn of the 19th century and was so popular that an 1801 French version for the stage, and Matthew Lewis's loose adaptation of *Abällino*, *Rugantino: Or, the Bravo of Venice* (1805) were both hugely successful. The name "Abällino" even became, for a short time, slang for "bandit," and nearly every *räuberroman* written following Zschokke uses a Mediterranean background. The influence of *Abällino* on contemporary English writers is unquestionable, and one still finds mention of it in histories of literature written a century later.

What is not so often mentioned is that Count Rosalvo is an 18th-century version of the Costumed Avenger, the protosuperhero we will see much more of in the next chapter. One might even call Rosalvo a proto-Batman: Rosalvo uses disguise and his natural strength and skills to clean up the criminals, some of whom are exotic, of one particular city. This is his selfless mission: he is doing so regardless of personal cost because it is the right thing to do. And he functions in an urban environment, like Long Meg and Moll Cutpurse, but far more than either of them. Venice is *his* city, the city he is identified with, which he dominates and rules, much as Batman is identified with Gotham City and is ultimately its master. Rosalvo does not wear a cape and mask, instead wearing the disguises of Flodardo and Abällino, but both are as much a mask and disguise as Superman's is, or Bruce Wayne's is.

Moreover, this trope of the hidden master of a city, which was popular in the pulps and in the grittier forms of superhero comics, and which Batman is perhaps the archetypal form of, begins with *Abällino*.[106] The trope would come to fruition in the *romans feuilleton* in the 19th century, in the form of Edmond Dantès and Rodolphe von Gerolstein and Rocambole (see Chapter 4), but the source of it was *Abällino*, and Count Rosalvo.

Martinette de Beauvais

Women dressing as men so that they could enlist in the British military during the 18th century were exceptional and notable but not unprecedented. Women like Christian Davies, Catherine Lincken, Phoebe Hessel, Ann Mills, and, of course, Hannah Snell gained varying amounts of fame during the century for their military experiences. Similarly, women like Mary Hays, Margaret Corbin, and Deborah Sampson were active under fire for the Americans during the American Revolutionary War and became famous for it, and accounts of the fighting women of the French Revolution were "played up" in the American press.[107] Combined with the still-surviving stories about Long Meg and Moll Cutpurse, these real-life women presented a viable alternative—if one rejected by most men—to the "respectable," domestic women of the time. By the end of the century, women not only had the literary examples of women warriors to look to, they had real-life women to emulate.[108]

The epitome of this type of women warrior appeared in 1799, in Charles Brockden Brown's *Ormond; or the Secret Witness*. *Ormond* is an early American Gothic female *bildungsroman* about the perils that 16-year-old Constantia Dudley is subjected to by Ormond, an eavesdropper, mime, disguise artist, and murderer who puts all his skills to use toward the goal of seducing Constantia. Ormond, who is additionally a member of the Illuminati, served with the Russians in the war against the Turks, committing atrocities in the war. Once he is in the Americas, he rejects his mistress and pursues Constantia, eventually confronting her in a gloomy rural estate. Constantia stabs Ormond to death with her penknife.

A part of the novel is Constantia's friendship with Martinette de Beauvais, a forceful and self-reliant woman warrior, a veteran of the American and French Revolutions who has killed numerous men in battle. To do so, she dresses in men's clothing, an act she finds liberating: "I delighted to assume the male dress, to acquire skill at the sword, and dexterity in every boisterous exercise. The timidity that commonly attends women, gradually vanished. I felt as if imbued with a soul that was a stranger to the sexual distinction."[109] In her own words, "Danger . . . it is my element."[110]

De Beauvais, like some (but by no means all) women warriors of the 18th century, feels no shame over her actions, but glories in them, and in so doing deviates so severely from the gender norms of the day that she "serves neither as monster nor villain but as role model."[111] Interestingly, unlike the majority of the 18th century's cross-dressing women warriors, De Beauvais is "neither punished nor rebuked . . . Brown has her walk off possessed of her pride and self-confidence"[112]—a hearkening back to the happier fates of Long Meg and Moll Cutpurse, and a deliberate reversal on Brown's part of the fate that contemporary readers (gripped by what theorists call the "gender panic" of the late 18th century)[113] expected for De Beauvais.

Ormond is obscure today, and never inspired imitators, but the novel was consistently reprinted throughout the 19th and early 20th centuries, decades when Brockden Brown's fame was greater than it is today and his novels were required reading for students. Although never referenced directly by the authors of dime novels (during the 19th century) and pulps and comic books (during the 20th century), *Ormond* was undoubtedly read by them, and Martinette de Beauvais imprinted on their consciousnesses on some level. Alongside the many stories of women soldiers in the American Civil War—from 200 to 500 on both sides[114]—*Ormond* and Martinette de Beauvais presented later writers with models for dime novel and pulp heroines and comic book superheroines. Lady Jaguar developed out of the cowboy tradition and the novelette; the gun moll (a mainstay of the pulps) developed out of real-world 20th century female bandits and thieves and gang members; Domino Lady was the inheritor of the action/adventure heroine of the 20th century; but the superhuman superwoman and the female Costumed Avenger, like George Mandel's Woman in Red (for Standard, 1940–1945), are direct descendants of Martinette de Beauvais.

The Scottish Superman

Sir Walter Scott's *The Black Dwarf* (1816) was not one of Scott's most successful novels, with either critics (then or now) or the public. Scott himself disliked how he concluded the novel. But so popular was Scott and widespread was his work that *The Black Dwarf* was read with the rest of his novels for well over a century, if not as often as or with the affection of *Waverley* or *Ivanhoe* or any of Scott's most popular work. Curiously, though, literary critics (who generally look upon *The Black Dwarf* with contempt) have not given proper consideration to the titular character.

He is Sir Edward Mauley, a British nobleman of honorable lineage and position but a strikingly ugly four-foot-tall dwarf. He has the soul of a poet and longs for love, but he is mistreated and distrusted by the rest of humanity and deprived of the estates that are his due. Disgusted with himself, his family, and with all human society, Sir Edward takes to the wilds of Northumbria, making a home for himself in a dark cave surrounded by enormous boulders, and occasionally venturing out to help those who need him. The Northumbrians are afraid of him, not knowing his background, and see him as a figure of dread, "Elshender the Recluse" and "Canny Elshie the Black Dwarf." The plot of *The Black Dwarf* concerns the help Sir Edward gives to two young noblewomen. At the end of the novel Sir Edward kisses one of the noblewomen good-bye and disappears back into the English wilderness.

Significantly, Sir Edward not only is known by alternate identities, and does his best to help out innocents who are in trouble with the rebels, but he has superhuman strength, which is described as "preternatural" and "of Herculean powers."[115] No explanation is given for Sir Edward's strength— he has no origin story, and neither magic nor sorcery is used to explain how Sir Edward, a four-foot-tall dwarf, can single-handedly lift stones that two men working on their own can only shift with difficulty. Scott was influenced by Scottish folktales and what he claimed was a chilling encounter with an actual dwarf, but he came up with the idea of a superpower all on his own, and in *The Black Dwarf* presented it as a normal part of life, rather than the manifestation of something sinister or occult in nature.

Sir Edward, appearing near the end of the Gothic era, functions as a prototype for the Übermensch, albeit one that (though widely read during the century) was not copied during the 19th century. Sir Edward, though heroic in the story, has "the Byronic psychology of an intelligent, energetic but misshapen man,"[116] and the 19th-century authors of supermen heroes preferred their heroes less misanthropic and more uncomplicatedly heroic.

This Man, This Monster

Begun in 1816, finished in 1817, and published in 1818, Mary Shelley's *Frankenstein; or, The Modern Prometheus* was not initially a critical success, and, although it sold out, it was not reprinted. It wasn't until an 1823 stage version, *Presumption, or the Fate of Frankenstein*, that it gained popular acclaim and the concepts of the Victor Frankenstein, the erring creator, and the Creature, the towering but flawed creation, took hold in the popular imagination. A new edition was quickly brought out, and retellings of the story soon appeared as chapbooks and penny issues. Within a decade *Frankenstein* had "penetrated the public imagination, had become a story told, retold, and reinterpreted . . . most often the story warned against presumption, the prideful quest to create life and thereby overstep human bounds, but other versions spotlighted an innately innocent creature, turned monster by circumstances and society."[117]

The same was true of *Frankenstein* in the United States by the early 1830s, and in both countries *Frankenstein* and its protagonist and antagonist did not leave the public's consciousness for the rest of the century, or indeed in the 20th century.

Frankenstein is in the odd position of being influential on superheroes without featuring a heroic character. Victor Frankenstein, after all, ended up being the most influential fictional mad scientist of the 19th century (though there were a number of examples of mad scientists before and after his debut), and comic book mad scientists were largely modeled on him—as, to a lesser extent, have been superhero scientists in comic books. (The examples of Stan Lee, Larry Lieber, and Jack Kirby's Hank Pym, for Marvel, and Jerry Siegel and Jim Mooney's Brainiac-5, for DC, and their many experiments-gone-awry come to mind.) And Frankenstein's creation, the Creature, became a model for multiple character types: the scientifically created biological monster (in at least one later version, in 1849, the monster was portrayed as a literal "mechanical man with skill supreme"); the physically repulsive antihero (following on the Arthurian example of the knight, Acanor "the Ugly Hero"); and the innocent, put-upon naif of superhuman abilities and powers, as personified in the Hulk among others.[118]

More importantly, the Creature represented an influential example of one type of the Übermensch character that we'll follow in Chapter 5. There were many different supermen in 19th-century fiction, and we've already met some of their precursors: Talus, the Old Man from Fronteja, and Sir Edward, the Black Dwarf. Frankenstein's Creature differs from them as the product of science—a premise for superhero creation that would become increasingly common—and in what might be called his suite or portfolio of abilities, his superhuman intelligence and strength and speed and endurance, the greater-than-human package of powers that superheroes of various kinds, and their pulp precursors, would exhibit. The Creature is no superhero—he's clearly the villain of *Franken-stein*, even if his motivations give him greater recognizability and depth than most Gothic villains—but he created the mold, as it were, in which a number of the superheroes who would follow him were produced.

John Melmoth

A different kind of Übermensch appeared in Charles Maturin's *Mel-moth the Wanderer* (1820). *Melmoth the Wanderer* is a series of nested stories-within-stories that are ultimately about the efforts of the sorcerer John Melmoth to avoid eternal damnation. Melmoth sold his soul to Satan, but, when the Devil came to collect Melmoth's soul, Melmoth looked for an out, which Satan gave him: get someone else to pledge his or her soul to Satan in Melmoth's place. Melmoth tries repeatedly to lure someone else into doing this, but fails, and ultimately is taken by the Devil.

Melmoth the Wanderer was well received, critically and popularly, and, if it was the *dernier cri* of the Gothic proper, it represented a high note for the genre to go out on—*Melmoth the Wanderer* is usually seen as the great-est of the Gothic novels, not least because of its incorporation of all the major Gothic tropes, motifs, and plot types. Far and away the most attrac-tive, popular, and influential character in the novel is John Melmoth him-self, the doomed wanderer, seeker after knowledge, miserable but proud Hero-Villain. Melmoth became an updated version of the Faust figure, but one whose Devil-granted superhuman powers are more comic booky (so to speak), including the ability to call a firestorm down from the heavens. Melmoth has limited immortality, the Hero-Villain's penetrating gaze and overpowering presence, and the power of sorcery, making him a kind of Übermensch, albeit one we've already seen before. But, more than that, Melmoth, with his all-around set of skills and abilities and knowledge, is a precursor to a different sort of Übermensch, the Man of Extraordinary Capabilities, the Batman-like expert-at-everything. Melmoth is the ambiguous sorcerer of the medieval era updated, retaining his liminal, transgressive status and forbidden powers but now also bearing a set of abilities that others would appropriate, but for more selfless purposes than Melmoth was capable of.

Conclusion

By 1829, the Gothic novel was essentially dead, killed by Walter Scott and the rise of the historical novel. With the departure of the Gothic and the disappearance of the traditional Hero-Villain, as well as the departure of the *räuberroman*, the opportunities for protosuperheroes seemed to draw to an end. Scott's *The Black Dwarf* aside, there seemed to be little room in the historical romance genre for the kind of influential protosuperheroes that had appeared over the past couple of centuries. However, a new genre would arise, and with it new opportunities for heroic prototypes: crime fiction.

CHAPTER FOUR

Victorian Costumed Avengers

In this chapter I'll be covering the Costumed Avengers of the Victorian era, which I'm fudging a little bit to begin in 1830, but which ends with Queen Victoria's death in 1901. The reason for choosing this time period and these limits will, I hope, become clear: before 1830 there were proto-typical characters who had elements of the Costumed Avenger in them, but by 1901 the Costumed Avenger has become a fully distinctive character type, with obvious effects on later characters and on the superhero genre.

Moreover, the Victorian era is one in which the crime/mystery genre developed and came of age, and, as we'll see, the crime/mystery genre is densely intertwined with superheroes.

As I mentioned in Chapter 1, the Costumed Avengers wear costumes—which in this case I'm defining as a repeatedly worn, distinctive, and recognizable attire or piece of clothing or makeup or persona—while fighting evil or crime. Here, too, I'm fudging a little and accepting characters who regularly wear the same disguise, though again this is for reasons I hope will become clear.

Again, I'll be moving in a roughly chronological order. I may be required to leap forward or backward in order to properly cover a character type, but the general movement of the chapter is forward rather than sideways.

Masked Untermenschen: Threat or Menace

Class relations between rulers and ruled were tense through much of the 18th and 19th centuries. Even before the American and French Revolutions, the proletariat of Europe and America, much oppressed by laws designed to get the maximum amount of money out of them, were discontented, although the degree of discontent and the native responses to this discontent varied from location to location. Traditionally, one way in which this discontent was dealt with was through the pressure vent of carnival, as with the Feast of Fools and other celebrations that allowed the workers to safely express ill will toward the ruling classes.[1] At times, however, the pressure vent was overwhelmed, and workers took action in other ways, sometimes with interesting results.

In 1763, French administrators, desirous of rebuilding the French Navy following the failures of the Seven Years' War, began newly enforcing generation-old laws designed to boost timber production, get rid of corruption among forest managers, and improve policing in the forests. The proletariat responded poorly, especially in the Forêt de Chaut in the eastern province of Franche-Comté, where tensions between forest officials and local villagers were tense to begin with. In 1765, for two months, 200 locals, all men, put on disguises—the clothing of women, which earned them the name "demoiselles"—and held off officers and guards while funneling wood to their families for sale to manufacturers. This rebellion was eventually crushed by the arrival of a regiment of the king's army, who declined to engage the rebels in the woods but brutalized the local families until the demoiselles surrendered.

Although the demoiselles were defeated, their action did have an effect on the government, which agreed to alter the forestry laws to the benefit of the locals, and other forest villagers took note of what the demoiselles did and what they accomplished. In the Pyrenean department of the Ariège, the failed harvest of 1827 had a severe impact on upland villagers "dependent on buying grain in return for their livestock and already angered by the new forest code that closed state and communal forests to their sheep and goats. At the same time, owners of private forests were closing off access in defiance of ancient customary rights to fuel as wood became a valuable commodity to the expanding metallurgical industry."[2]

By October 1829, the private forests of Ariège were regularly invaded by a new generation of demoiselles (as they, too, called themselves), this set with blackened faces and sometimes masks and wearing flamboyant woman's clothing. "While such disguises no doubt prevented easy recognition by forest guards, they were also symbolic of 'a world turned upside down.' Like many southerners, Ariégeois celebrated Mardi Gras every year with an inversion of worldly restraints on sexuality, dress, obedience, food and drink: the popular justice of seizing forests was a carnivalesque moment symbolized in transvestism."[3]

The protests widened the following July, as not only were forests invaded again, but tax offices were raided and burned and forges destroyed. The "War of the Demoiselles" continued intensely until 1832 and intermittently until 1872.

While it's unclear how much detail (such as their attire and disguises) about the demoiselles of Ariège filtered into England and the United States, the War of the Demoiselles (like other peasant revolts of the time) did make it into the newspapers. We can't know how much influence the demoiselles in particular had on the Molly Maguires, of course, but the Maguires already had a tradition of transvestite vigilantism. The Maguires were an Irish secret society active in Ireland in the 18th and 19th centuries and in the United States in the 19th century. When active, they dressed up in women's clothing and blackened their faces.

Similar practices were common to nearly all Irish agrarian societies in the period 1760 to 1850. The Whiteboys (*na Buachaillí Bána*), for example, were so named because they wore white linen frocks over their clothes and white bands or handkerchiefs around their hats. At the same time, they apparently pledged allegiance to a mythical woman, Sieve Oultagh (from the Irish *Sadhbh Amhaltach*, or "Ghostly Sally"), whom they designated their queen. The Molly Maguires appear to have done much the same thing. Disguised as women when they went out at night, they dedicated themselves to a mythical woman who symbolized their struggle against injustice, whether sectarian, nationalist, or economic. The clothing was not just a means of disguise; it also served to endow these agrarian agitators with legitimacy, investing them as "the daughter of the disinterested agent of a higher authority," the "son" or "daughter" of Molly Maguire.[4]

In the United States, the Molly Maguires were a part of the mining industry in Pennsylvania from the mid-19th century, a time when labor conditions for coal miners were atrocious and routinely lethal and when mine owners treated miners as chattel. The Maguires quickly became involved in union activities and took part in vigilante actions against the police and mine owners who treated them so savagely. During the depression of the 1870s, the union, and the Maguires, were particularly active, leading to the owners bringing in agents of the Pinkerton Detective Agency, to vigilante activities deployed against mine owners and their representatives and by the Pinkertons and the mine owners against the miners, and to a strike, which was broken. Eventually the Maguires were infiltrated by the Pinkertons and the Maguire leaders put on trial and hanged in June 1877, destroying the Maguires in Pennsylvania.

The founding members of the Ku Klux Klan no doubt joined in the universal bourgeois scorn for the Molly Maguires, but the Klan, like the Mollies, found it convenient to disguise themselves for their vigilante activities, even if the Klan used white hoods and robes rather than cork black and women's clothes.[5] Founded in a judge's office in Pulaski, Tennessee, sometime in 1865 or 1866—different historians and early Klan members claim different dates for the Klan's establishment—the Klan (whose founding members were Southern gentlemen and not members of the working class) began with theatrical pranks (which included terrifying freed slaves) but soon moved on to more serious acts of terrorism. Their stated aims, however, were noble, as expressed in the principles laid down in 1866:

> To protect the weak, innocent, and defenseless from the indignities, wrongs, and outrage of the lawless, the violent and the brutal; to relieve the injured and oppressed, to succor the suffering, especially the widows and orphans of ex-Confederate soldiers; to protect the Constitution of the United States and its conformable laws, to protect the States and their people from invasion from any source, from unlawful seizure of person or property and from trial save by their peers and in conformity with the law of the land.[6]

That the Klan were racist terrorists from the start is indisputable; that "after 1867, it became a counterrevolutionary device to combat the Republican party and Congressional Reconstruction policy in the South"[7] is simply a historical fact. Strange, then, to include them in this book, in a history of the development of the superhero. But the sad (if not less than obvious) truth is that for many white Americans—from the South *and* the North—the Klan *were* costumed vigilante heroes, real-life Costumed Avengers, albeit without actual crimes to fight. The Klan was broken by force in 1871, but other groups with names like the "White Knights" and the "Red Shirts" took over for them, so that by the end of the century the South had a 35-year-long tradition of costumed vigilantism. As we'll see in Chapter 6, this tradition, and the rebirth of the Klan, played a part in the birth of the costumed superhero.

The Master Detectives

The mystery genre is usually held to have started in 1841, with Edgar Allan Poe's "The Murders in the Rue Morgue." Although largely accurate, this ignores the decades of protomysteries that preceded Poe, the Gothics, the German *kriminalgeschichte*, and the other works that had mystery and crime elements in them but did not—as Poe did—synthesize them into one text. Likewise, Poe is held to have created, in C. Auguste Dupin, the character of the consulting detective that Arthur Conan Doyle's Sherlock Holmes would later become the embodiment of—but this ignores the presence, in fiction and in reality, of the police detectives who solved crimes before Poe ever dreamed of Dupin.

Most of these detectives are obscurities, quickly forgotten about (if noticed at all), but one became internationally famous and is a known influence on Poe's Dupin.

In 1809, Eugène-François Vidocq (1775–1857), a French soldier who had spent time in jail for various crimes, volunteered himself to the police as a plainclothes agent. By 1811, Vidocq was training new agents, and, in 1812, he was put in command of the Brigade de la Sûreté, the security police of Paris. By 1824, Vidocq commanded dozens of detectives and was responsible for several important reforms in French police work. His work for the police gained him a reputation in France, and, in 1828 and 1829, he published his "autobiography," *Mémoires de Vidocq*, which made his name across the Continent, in Great Britain and in America. *Memoirs of Vidocq* is at least partially fictional and is greatly exaggerated, but despite (or perhaps because of) this it was hugely successful. Vidocq presents himself as the all-knowing master of every situation, intimately familiar with the customs of the underworld and surrounded by fools but nonetheless triumphing over criminals and seeing that justice is done. Vidocq's character in the *Memoirs* is self-congratulatory, boastful, and vain, but the French public was eager to believe that the Vidocq of the *Memoirs* was real, and Vidocq's name quickly became synonymous with brilliant police work.

The idea of the brilliant crime fighter was soon adopted by writers. Honoré de Balzac modeled his Monsieur Vautrin on Vidocq in the books of the *Comédie Humaine*, beginning with *Le Père Goriot* (1834–1835). Edgar Allan Poe followed the news from France and was familiar with Vidocq's achievements, and Poe's Chevalier Dupin is based in part on Vidocq as well as on Baron Pierre Charles François Dupin (1784–1883), a well-known French mathematician and politician.

But Dupin, who appeared in three stories in 1841, 1842, and 1844, is far more than a simple copy of Vidocq, and it is Poe's contributions to the character of the consulting detective—his personality and his methods— that made the character so influential. Like Vidocq, Dupin is brilliant. But where the Vidocq of the *Memoirs* is the daydream of a bored functionary, the Dupin of Poe's stories is a figure of essentially juvenile wish fulfillment. He is an aristocrat, calmly sure of his own superiority. Those who know him (his friends and the prefect of police) are in awe of him. Dupin is free of responsibilities: he has no family, no job, and (despite apparent poverty) no worries about bills. Dupin keeps his own hours and is free to voice his opinions without worrying about the consequences. He solves the hardest, most puzzling crimes with ease. Dupin could be an honored member of society but has voluntarily withdrawn from human contact. (Vidocq was involved in his surroundings and interacted daily with both police and criminals.) In Dupin's world, Dupin is the most important person. Later writers added to these qualities, humanizing the consulting detective character and making him more realistic, but the character patterns established by Poe have for the most part been maintained.

The influence of Vidocq and Dupin on the superhero genre is of course significant. Only Vidocq wore disguises, but both Vidocq and Dupin solved crimes and captured criminals, with crime prevention the primary role of many superheroes. What is most significant about both of them, at least as far as superhero comics are concerned, is that they were the first important and influential *personal* crime solvers, the first notable figures whose involvement with crime took place after the crime was committed and involved resolving the mystery rather than preventing further crimes from taking place, and were independent of their respective law enforcement groups. (Technically Vidocq is a member of the police in his autohagiography; practically speaking he is as independent as Dupin.)

Dupin seems on Poe's part to have been a response to the American lack of response to the British passage of the Metropolitan Police Act of 1829, which formalized and professionalized London policing and created a perception among ordinary Britons that at last an effective deterrent to crime had been created. Americans were not so fortunate. The first American police force, Philadelphia's, had only been established in 1833, eight years before Dupin's debut; the second police force was Boston's, established in 1838; and the third was New York's, which would not appear until 1845, the year after Dupin's final appearance.

> Crime was on the rise. There were no municipal police forces per se, only private "security firms" and groups of paid "watchmen" who were often as nefarious as the criminals they were paid to apprehend. Crime was a subject of much discussion in the papers . . . American cities were just beginning to formalize police operations and to employ the methods of "scientific" detective work, such as forensic analysis. The gutter press and the criminal element fed off each other: newspapers like the "penny dreadfuls" were awash in gruesome details of murders and rapt descriptions of barroom brawls and back-alley knife fights in the less seemly quarters of the nation's cities.[8]

For the British—the primary creators of mystery fiction in the Anglophone world in the 19th century—the Metropolitan Police Act and the creation of the bobby would lead to effective fictional policemen, in the form of the casebook detectives of the 1850s and 1860s and more famously Charles Dickens's Inspector Bucket (from *Bleak House*, 1852–1853) and Wilkie Collins's Sergeant Cuff (from *The Moonstone*, 1868). It wasn't until near the end of the century, when *fin-de-siècle* fears about crime rates reached new heights and the police had proven to be unable to solve high-profile crimes like the murders of Jack the Ripper, that British readers would seek order and justice in the form of a crime solver independent of the police: Arthur Conan Doyle's Sherlock Holmes.

But for Americans, who had to wait until the 1880s for all their major cities to have municipal police forces in place, there was no such comforting tradition of efficient official justice figures. Americans were forced to project their fears of crime and desires for swift and unerring justice to be done into fiction featuring independent crime solvers, like Nick Carter, rather than policemen. One can argue that this is why Americans essentially created the superhero whereas the British took to the superhero only gradually and grudgingly: not (just) because it was an American invention, and not (just) because the British are traditionally hierarchical and Americans are traditionally rebels, but because the British tradition of crime prevention and crime solving involves the government and the American tradition does not; it involves independents rather than officials.[9]

All this being said, Dupin is no protosuperhero, lacking much of a *heroenkonzept* or even the selfless motive of later fictional crime solvers like Holmes. "Dupin, in contrast, is a dilettante who takes on his 'cases' either for amusement—in 'The Purloined Letter,' it's to show off his skills in front of the nitwit police inspector—or to repay a favor—in 'The Rue Morgue,' the accused is a man who had 'done him a good turn' once before."[10]

Dupin is of great influence on later superheroes without being one of their number.

A Truly Dangerous Hero

Thomas De Quincey (1785–1859) was an English essayist and writer whose unsavory reputation rests largely on his opium addiction, which resulted in De Quincey writing *Confessions of an English Opium-Eater* (1821), the work that earned him fame, if not entirely of the sort he desired, and that he continues to be known by.

But De Quincey wrote widely, in a variety of forms, and if his fiction is today mostly forgotten it was not so obscure during his lifetime, nor for a long time afterward. One of these works is of particular interest for scholars of superheroes: *Klosterheim* (1832).

Klosterheim, set during the Thirty Years' War, is a Gothic novel: "Klosterheim . . . is an imaginary city groaning under the despotic occupation of a Protestant Landgrave who is determined to crush the religious rights of the citizens. A sordid atmosphere of religious terror and persecution like that found in the monastery shockers of the period hangs sullenly over the story."[11]

Fortunately for the people of Klosterheim, one man, the costumed "Masque," stands up to the Landgrave. "The Masque makes timely appearances, performing bold and occasionally supernatural deeds in behalf of the oppressed. He is also adept at unmasking and liquidating traitors, spies, and other political undesirables."[12] The Landgrave attempts to hunt him down, but fails, and after a number of other plot twists, including the requisite romantic plot, the Landgrave is deposed and dies of remorse and the Masque unveils himself as Prince Maximilian, a veteran of the war and rightful heir to Klosterheim, which at the end of the novel he rules.

The question of *Klosterheim*'s influence can (rightly) be raised here: Does a precursor count if nobody notices it? After all, *Klosterheim* is only an obscurity now. But, of course, *Klosterheim* was noticed; it was written about in *The Atlantic* in 1863, given substantial coverage in Alexander Japp's 1877 biography of De Quincey, read by Nathaniel Hawthorne to his son Julian, and used in literary criticism in the 1930s. *Klosterheim* was never a best seller, but it sold well enough for multiple editions to be issued during the 19th century. It may never have been read by the early superhero writers, but it made its way into the Zeitgeist no less than many of the other works included in this book did.

So the Masque must be counted among the Costumed Avengers of the 19th century. More importantly, he's an important precursor of two separate types of modern superhero. The first is the hidden master of the city, last seen with Count Rosalvo in *Abällino* and appearing more frequently, and memorably, in the next decade in the form of Rodolphe von Gerolstein and Edmond Dantès. The Masque takes his place in their company in the category of hidden urban ruler, the masked/costumed/disguised vigilante who is the true ruler of the city in which he operates. As the Masque tells the Landgrave in a note, "Landgrave, beware! henceforth not you, but I, govern in Klosterheim."[13] This is not a very long distance at all from Batman's dictatorship in Gotham City, or Daredevil's control of Hell's Kitchen.

The second type of modern superhero that the Masque anticipates is related to the first, but much rarer: the rebel, and it is here that the Masque is *truly* dangerous. The Masque not only declares himself as de facto ruler of Klosterheim, in opposition to the Landgrave, but the Masque sets out to actually depose the Landgrave and put himself in the Landgrave's place as the de jure ruler. That the Landgrave's reign is an unjust, oppressive one, and that the Masque is the true heir to the throne of Klosterheim, is ultimately beside the point. The Masque is a political rebel who works to overthrow the government *and succeeds*, with the author and the novel (and presumably the readers) cheering him on.

Comic book superheroes simply do not overthrow governments or even try to. Most superheroes, at least from Marvel and DC, are American, and their efforts are ultimately toward the end of preserving the status quo, the government, and the reigning system of corporate capitalism. A superhero may have liberal leanings, but his or her actions ultimately have conservative effects and consequences. Some heroes—the modern interpretation of Mort Weisinger and George Papp's Green Arrow (for DC), Steve Ditko's The Question (originally for Charlton, now at DC), Captain America (for Marvel during the 1970s)—question the system; DC's Anarky (created by Alan Grant and Norm Breyfogle) tries to go beyond questioning it; but only two superheroes actually became political dissidents and rebels: Alan Moore and David Lloyd's V, from *V for Vendetta* (1982–1985, 1988–1989)—and he is by any sane definition of the word a terrorist—and Alan Moore's 1980s interpretation of Mick Anglo's Marvelman (later renamed Miracleman).[14] The Masque, like V, employs violence against agents of the state in order to effect the government's overthrow and directs his energies toward that end.

This makes the Masque a very dangerous kind of superhero, indeed, and one that must be viewed as a kind of wasted opportunity. If more superheroes were true revolutionaries, superhero comics might look quite different indeed.

The Superhuman Superhero

Nathaniel Hawthorne's "The Gray Champion" (1835) is set in New England in 1689, at a time when King James II "sent a harsh and unprincipled soldier to take away our liberties and endanger our religion."[15] When British soldiers confront a crowd of natives who are afraid of what the soldiers intend to do, someone cries out "O Lord of Hosts . . . provide a Champion for thy people!"[16] The response is quick:

> Suddenly, there was seen the figure of an ancient man, who seemed to have emerged from among the people, and was walking by himself along the centre of the street, to confront the armed band. He wore the old Puritan dress, a dark cloak and a steeple-crowned hat, in the fashion of at least fifty years before, with a heavy sword upon his thigh, but a staff in his hand to assist the tremulous gait of age.[17]

The Champion confronts the British soldiers and their leader and drives them away with the threat, "Back, thou that wast a Governor, back! With this night thy power is ended—to-morrow, the prison!—back, lest I foretell the scaffold!"[18] When the soldiers are gone, the Champion disappears—literally—only to be seen again decades later, during the American Revolution: "His hour is one of darkness, and adversity, and peril. But should domestic tyranny oppress us, or the invader's step pollute our soil, still may the Gray Champion come."[19]

"The Gray Champion" was later reprinted in Hawthorne's collection *Twice-Told Tales* (1837), which made a minor kind of stir and gained Hawthorne a good reputation in New England. As Hawthorne's reputation grew, following the publication of *The Scarlet Letter* (1850), *Twice-Told Tales* was reprinted and gained more attention, with "The Gray Champion," as the first story in the collection, gaining its fair share of critical and readerly attention. We cannot be sure which 19th century authors read it, but Hawthorne was certainly widely read through the century, and "The Gray Champion" was written about by critics and other writers.

So we can say that "The Gray Champion" had a kind of influence on later writers. And, obviously, the Gray Champion is a Costumed Avenger, the first American one, and a kind of evolutionary leap forward on the "Angel of Hadley" folktale "The Gray Champion" was based on.[20] But what more than that is he? The first American superhuman superhero, for one: he combines the costume, the mission, the code name, and the superpower, in ways that no characters since the Arthurian epics had. He is not the first dual-identity Costumed Avenger, a character type that properly requires both identities to be established—and the Gray Champion's never is—for the Masque and *Aballino*'s Count Rosalvo got there before the Gray Champion did. But he is the first to be both Übermensch and Costumed Avenger. And thanks to Hawthorne's prominence and influence we can say that the Gray Champion was in all likelihood read by the dime novel writers who later created the Costumed Avengers that directly influenced the pulp and comics writers. As far as direct transmission of the concept of the Costumed Avenger Übermensch is concerned, the Gray Champion is the beginning of it in America.

The Dual-Identity Costumed Vigilante

Something was in the air in the 1830s. A reaction to a full generation of Gothic novels, perhaps, or the cumulative effect of centuries of heroic literature finally reaching a tipping point, but 1830 saw the demoiselles of Ariège, 1832 De Quincey's Masque, 1835 Hawthorne's Gray Champion, and then, in 1837, the publication of Robert Montgomery Byrd's *Nick of the Woods*, whose protagonist, although not the first dual-identity costumed vigilante of the 19th century, was the most influential of them.

In the mid-1700s Nathan Slaughter is an innocent Quaker living in the mountains of Pennsylvania with his wife, children, and mother. During an attack on Slaughter's family by a band of Shawnees, Nathan is scalped and his entire family is killed. This unbalances Nathan and he adopts a dual life. Around whites he is Nathan Slaughter, a gentle Quaker who, true to his religious beliefs, never takes up arms against the natives, even though this earns him the scorn and even hatred of the other white settlers. Nathan bears up under the gibes of the whites with as much dignity as he can manage and tries to be a good Quaker. However, when he is not around other whites he becomes another person: "Nick of the Woods," a.k.a. "Jibbenainosay," a.k.a. "Shawneewannaween." "Nick of the Woods" is derived from "Old Nick," a name for the Devil. "Jibbenainosay" is taken from the "Injun gabble" for "Spirit that walks."[21] And "Shawneewannaween" is taken from the Shawnee for "Howl of the Shawnees," because "of his keeping them ever a howling."[22] As Nick of the Woods, Nathan slaughters every Indian he runs across, and always leaves them with a tomahawk cloven skull and the shape of a cross carved in their chest. Nick of the Woods never allows a witness to live, so that to the Indians of the frontier Nick of the Woods is an invisible, evil creature. Nick takes a particular pleasure in hunting down and massacring the Shawnees. *Nick of the Woods* is the story of Nick's encounter with a group of white settlers in Kentucky and his vengeance, after years of searching, on the particular Shawnee chief responsible for the death of Nick's family.

Byrd wrote *Nick of the Woods* as a reaction to James Fenimore Cooper's "Leatherstocking" novels, which Byrd saw as dangerously misguided, even offensive, in their quasipositive portrayal of Native Americans. Byrd's response, to Cooper's novels and especially the character of Natty "Hawkeye" Bumppo, was to create Nick of the Woods, the embodiment of Byrd's opposition to Native Americans and all they stood for. Byrd was influenced by earlier "Indian Killer" novels—novels in which the lead character becomes a murderous avenger acting out his homicidal vengeance on Native Americans—and perhaps by previous dual-identity characters such as the Masque or the protagonists of the Gothic. What Byrd created, though, was the first major dual-identity costumed vigilante, a character with two well-delineated identities who fights crime or evil while wearing a disguise. *Nick of the Woods* was hugely influential, remaining in print for a century and being widely imitated in the novelettes and frontier novels of the 1840s and 1850s and in the dime novels of the 1860s and 1870s.

Nick of the Woods is also, of course, a prototype for the dual-identity killer vigilante of the pulps and the comics, a specifically American version of the Black Judges in Secret from Vulpius's *Rinaldo Rinaldini*, with American concerns and American tactics. If Hawthorne's "Gray Champion" was the modern American source for the Costumed Avenger Übermensch, Byrd's *Nick of the Woods* was the modern American source for the darker, grimmer, more morally compromised version of same. One can't imagine superheroes without the "Gray Champion" having provided superheroes' forebears a model to work off of; and one can't imagine mass murdering Costumed Avengers like Henry Steeger, R. T. M. Scott, and Norvell Page's The Spider (from the pulps), the Punisher, and Roy Thomas, Len Wein, John Romita Sr., and Herb Trimpe's Wolverine (for Marvel), without Nick of the Woods.[23]

A second dual-identity costumed vigilante appeared a few years later, in Paul Féval's *Le Loup Blanc* (1843), a historical novel set in Brittany a century before. About the quest of the rightful lord of Brittany to regain his lands and title, *Le Loup Blanc* also features an amiable albino, Jean Blanc, who pretends to be a humble charcoal burner while at the same time fighting the French as the White Wolf, leader of a band of outlaws. All the outlaws wear masks of wolf skin; but Blanc wears a wolf's head as a hood and mask. Féval was popular in France and *Le Loup Blanc* was read by many French writers who would later create dual-identity costumed vigilantes of their own, but despite several English translations published in the 19th century *Le Loup Blanc* had no discernible influence in the United Kingdom or in the United States. (Conversely, *Nick of the Woods* was not translated into French, and Féval would not have known about it.)

The Hidden Master

Although the hidden master of the city, the unofficial but de facto urban ruler, had appeared in fiction before the 1840s, the French *romans feuilleton* produced the archetypal versions of the character, the ones most influential on comic book superheroes.

Romans feuilleton were the precursors to modern serial fiction, but with some differences:

> Novels that are read in installments are known as *romans-feuilletons*. The word *feuilleton* (leaf) originally referred to the lower, detachable section of a French daily newspaper. As news communication was unreliable, alternative material was published below the feuilleton line. At first the fill-in material consisted of indexes, literary and dramatic criticism, and short tales. Gradually, however, episodic fiction took over the space, and for about 15 years in the mid-19th century the feuilleton dominated French literature and literature worldwide. *Roman-feuilleton* became a generic, and usually derogatory, term for light literature.[24]

Those 15 years were from 1836 to 1851, a relatively short period for a genre to last, but during those 15 years two major works of French literature appeared that would prove to be of great importance to superhero comics: Eugène Sue's *Les Mystères de Paris* (1842–1843) and Alexandre Dumas *père's Le Comte de Monte Cristo* (1844–1845). The first would firmly create the hidden master character type. The latter will be dealt with in the next section.

Les Mystères de Paris is about Rodolphe von Gerolstein, the Grand Duke of the small German state of Gerolstein, and his adventures in Paris. Cut off from his fortune and name by his father and forced into exile, Rodolphe moves to Paris and becomes the de facto master of the city. Rodolphe and his friend and servant Walter "Murph" Murphy roam the streets and sewers of Paris in disguise, fighting crime and learning the secrets of the city and its underworld. Rodolphe lives a double life, as the toast of Paris society and as the scourge of the underworld. Rodolphe is not so much a punisher of thieves as someone who helps all the good, poor people he runs across, although he does blackmail an evil lawyer into using his criminally gotten money to establish worthy charities.

Le Comte de Monte Cristo is usually given more academic and critical attention than *Les Mystères de Paris*, with Edmond Dantès being given more credit for influence than Rodolphe von Gerolstein. This is not, however, entirely proper. It was *Les Mystères de Paris*, after all, that went on to be the best-selling European novel of the 19th century. It was staggeringly successful, being translated into 10 different languages by 1844 and appearing across the United Kingdom and in the United States. Over the next five years hundreds of imitations were written, about cities as various as Berlin, San Francisco, and Fitchburg, Massachusetts.

The influence of Eugène Sue on other writers should not be underestimated. Sue created, through his Paris, the archetypal version of the city in need of a hidden master,[25] and created, in the character of Gerolstein, the hidden urban ruler, the one true king—but in disguise—of the city. Gerolstein dominates his city, prevents evil from being done, defeats a variety of exceptional villains with names like "The Schoolmaster," "The Stabber," and "The Owl," directly or indirectly controls the actions of and secures the lives and safety of dozens if not hundreds or thousands of men and women. Gerolstein is a stout fighter when called upon, but is consumed by compassion more than by vengeance. His function is to provide an effective de facto ruler to a city whose de jure ruler(s) are hapless or helpless or corrupt. He uses disguise to present different identities to the world. If Nick of the Woods is, as comics writer Michael Lopez is reputed to have phrased it, "Batman in buckskin," Rodolphe von Gerolstein is Batman in breeches, the unofficial, hidden monarch[26] of Paris—in Eco's words, "judge and executioner, benefactor and reformer without the law."[27] And uncountable readers internationally, including in England and the United States, were exposed to this character type via *Les Mystères de Paris*, which took the fame and reach of Zschokke's *Aballino*—the first version of the hidden urban master—and multiplied it.[28]

The Man of Extraordinary Capabilities

Rodolphe von Gerolstein is also a Man of Extraordinary Capabilities, though the protagonist of *Le Comte to Monte Cristo* would come to eclipse him in that regard.

Le Comte de Monte Cristo should be familiar enough to my readers that only a short plot summary is required. The novel is about Edmond Dantès, a humble sailor who is framed for a crime and jailed. He languishes in prison for 14 years, but by accident meets the Abbé Faria, who educates Dantès and tells him the location of a great treasure. Dantès escapes from prison, collects the treasure, and wreaks a lengthy revenge against the men who framed him and had him jailed.

Le Comte de Monte Cristo was an immediate best seller, if not an international smash hit on the level of *Les Mystères de Paris*. That *Monte Cristo*'s fame and influence have lasted, while *Les Mystères de Paris*'s has not, has as much to do with the vagaries of publishing as it does with the relative styles and merits of Dumas and Sue. That *Monte Cristo* won the eventual war of influence between the two does not mean that *Les Mystères de Paris* did not win any number of battles. But *Monte Cristo* remains internationally famous, widely read by young and old around the world, and influential on any number of writers, while *Les Mystères de Paris* is not.

But with regard to superheroes and their development, the two should be considered separately. As described, *Les Mystères de Paris* established in permanent fashion the protosuperhero as hidden urban ruler. Rodolphe von Gerolstein is also a Man of Extraordinary Capabilities, although it is Edmond Dantès who would become the archetype in that regard.

The Man of Extraordinary Capabilities is, essentially, the man (less often, a woman) who is good at everything, who excels at whatever the story requires him to, whose skills are the superior to everyone regardless of who "everyone" is and what skills might be in question. Numerous pulp characters, such as Henry W. Ralston, John Nanovic, and Lester Dent's Doc Savage, fall into this category. So, too, with many comic book superheroes, such as the omnicapable Batman, who has been described, like Eratosthenes, as "second best in the world at everything."[29] This character came from the *romans feuilleton* and Rodolphe von Gerolstein and Edmond Dantès.

The Man of Extraordinary Capabilities is what Umberto Eco actually claims for Dantès in Eco's introduction to *Le Comte de Monte Cristo*. Eco uses the word "superman," but it is clear that he means something other than Siegel and Shuster's creation:

> And over everything towers the supreme topos of the serialization: the Superman. But unlike Sue and all the other craftsmen who have tried their hand at this classic instance of the popular novel, Dumas aims for a disconnected and breathless psychology of the superman, showing him to us as torn between a vertiginous omnipotence (by reason of money and knowledge) and a terror of his own privileged role, in short, tormented by doubt and lulled by the awareness that his omnipotence is born of suffering. Whereby, as a new archetype imbued with a superior strength, the Count of Monte Cristo is also a Christ, duly diabolic, who falls into the tomb of the Chateau d'If, a sacrificial victim of human malice and, in the thunderbolt of the treasure's rediscovery after centuries, rises again to judge the living and the dead, without once forgetting that he is the son of man.[30]

Dantès is not a Superman prototype, but a Batman prototype. Dantès is omnicompetent and omnicapable, master of every situation by virtue of his money, knowledge, and skills—just like Batman et al. They are all Men of Extraordinary Capabilities, and they got that from Rodolphe von Gerolstein and from Edmond Dantès.

The First Series Heroes

Edgar Allan Poe is commonly credited with having invented the mystery genre with his "C. Auguste Dupin" stories, a claim that as mentioned should come with some qualifiers but is generally true. One thing that Poe does *not* get enough credit for, from critics or readers, is his creation of the open-ended series hero. Dupin appears in three stories, "The Murders in the Rue Morgue" (1841), "The Mystery of Marie Rogêt" (1842), and "The Purloined Letter" (1844), but none of the stories hint at an ending for Dupin. "The Purloined Letter" ends with Dupin still in his apartment, still solving mysteries with the help of the narrator—still stuck in the second act of his life, past his origin (never explained by Poe, of course) but far from the end of his story, his death.

This was, of course, a significant change in the way that a series hero was treated. Traditionally, and by this I mean not just in antiquity but in the centuries leading up to the 19th, characters who appeared in multiple stories had first, second, and third acts—their deaths were described, their endings laid out. It was customary, practically *required*, to describe how a hero in a series of stories ended his or her life. Epics and romances told the entire lives of heroes, and the unauthorized sequels to them—which were in essence the first serializations—worked within the previously established constraints of those lives. *Romans feuilleton*, which were in essence extremely long serials later published in book form, had definite endings.

Not for Poe, however, who created the idea of the hero of the second act—the dynamic later adopted by virtually every author of heroic series fiction, dime novel, pulp, comic books, and novel series—what Umberto Eco describes as the breaking down of "the concept of time . . . the stories develop in a kind of oneiric climate . . . where what has happened before and what has happened after appear extremely hazy."[31] Eco was speaking of the relationship of the Superman comic book stories to time, but it was Poe who created this idea. But Poe was not the author, nor Dupin the character, who was primarily responsible for transmitting this idea to later generations of writers and readers. Credit for that must be given to the authors of and characters in the British casebook novels, a genre of mystery fiction that started in 1849, when the "Recollections of a Police Officer" series began in *Chambers' Edinburgh Journal*. This series, written by the pseudonymous "Waters" and starring a detective named "Thomas Waters," was immediately popular, and numerous imitators followed, both in England and in America, where the casebook collections were popular and frequently reprinted. The casebook mysteries flourished over the next two decades, acting as a lower-class counterpart to the sensation novel and not disappearing until after the demise of the sensation genre in the early 1870s.

The casebook mysteries can be thought of as precursors to modern police procedurals. The casebooks are partially or entirely fictional portrayals of police work, usually told in the first person, with a significant amount of accurate details of contemporary policing and a focus on realistic plots and characters. The authors of casebook mystery series—who seem not to have known about Poe's mysteries—took their inspiration from different sources, and their use of series characters was after all no different, in some respects, from the *feuilleton* authors' use of series characters. But the casebook authors had the happy idea to choose the eternal-second-act dynamic for their heroes. In doing so the casebook novels essentially established the mystery novel series form.

The casebook detectives are street-level detectives who make use of disguise in a limited, realistic way. Realism was the abiding rule for the casebook detectives, in fact; rarely did fantastic elements enter into the stories. The criminals did not have flashy sobriquets or colorful personalities; they were grim, depressing, brutal, and entirely too close for comfort to what the casebook readers saw on a daily basis. The detectives who pursued them were similarly much more mimetic than fantastic. So the detectives don't really count as Costumed Avengers, despite the use of disguise.

But the casebook detectives were extremely influential on the Costumed Avengers to come. The names of the casebook authors were used as pseudonyms by dime novel detective authors and were chosen because the dime novel writers and publishers knew that their audience would be aware of the casebook characters and would associate the dime novel detectives with those characters. By the 1860s the casebook genre was the dominant one among American dime novel mystery writers, with American authors openly aping British writers—and these American writers would go on to create the Costumed Avengers of the dime novels, who were open-ended series characters like the casebook heroes and like Poe's Dupin. The dime novel heroes of the second act would go on to heavily influence the pulp heroes, who were similarly second act heroes, and they would in turn influence the comic book superheroes.

Spring-Heeled Jack

The London urban legend of Spring-Heeled Jack began at the end of 1837, with supposed attacks on women being caused by a burning-eyed "devil" who when pursued would literally leap over houses and get away. The legend was picked up by newspapers early in 1838, which portrayed him as attempting to assault two young women. From there, the legend spread, with Spring-Heeled Jack becoming a genuine urban legend in a relatively short time and even becoming a stage character, though always a monster.[32]

But, in 1863, Alfred Coates—"journalist, playwright, and penny dreadful hack"[33]—repurposed Spring-Heeled Jack. In the penny dreadful *Spring-heel'd Jack: The Terror of London a Romance of the Nineteenth Century* (1863–1867), Spring-Heeled Jack became a hero, a nobleman who put on the disguise for entertainment and ended up helping other people. In his own words: "You donned the mask and cloak for fun and adventure, that you might afford your mischievous mind the gratification of frightening people out of their wits; but instead you find yourself acting the part of the Good Samaritan on all sides—serving by kindness, rather than killing by fear."[34]

Coates's Spring-Heeled Jack is not only a Costumed Avenger, but thanks to the springs in his boots and the design of his cape he is capable of leaps far into the air and gliding that approaches flying. This does not make him an Übermensch—the superhuman accomplishments come from his costume rather than from any physical abilities he possesses—but does make him the first protosuperhero with a costume that provides him with a superpower, a trope later used by Marvel's Iron Man among many others.

Coates's *Spring-heel'd Jack: The Terror of London a Romance of the Nineteenth Century* inspired stage productions in 1863 and 1868 that also portrayed Jack as a hero, rather than a villain, a dynamic that would continue throughout the century and into the next.

Coates's Spring-Heeled Jack was, via the many productions that imitated Coates, influential on the idea of the dual-identity costumed vigilante. Coates's Spring-Heeled Jack is hated and feared in his costumed form, but, in his civilian disguise as "the Marquis," he is loved by all. Coates's *Spring-heel'd Jack* also takes from the casebook series heroes the idea of an open-ended hero; *Spring-heel'd Jack* ends with Jack jumping into the sea to avoid capture, with no third act ending appearing. Coates's Spring-Heeled Jack updated the dual-identity costumed vigilante that *Nick of the Woods* had popularized but that had previously appeared in Zschokke's *Aballino* and De Quincey's *Klosterheim*, made him modern and urban, and modified and modernized the character for a new generation of authors and readers, and shifted his focus from politics to fighting the evil deeds of a single man.

The Man of Extraordinary Capabilities Redux

Edmond Dantès, and the Man of Extraordinary Capabilities character type, had spent nearly 20 years filtering through the Zeitgeist when the French author Ponson du Terrail published the *roman feuilleton La*

Résurrection de Rocambole (1865–1866), the fifth of Terrail's "Rocambole" novels. The first three Rocambole novels had covered the rise in power of Rocambole, a brilliant, scheming, wicked criminal who anticipates Pierre Souvestre and Marcel Allain's Fantômas in his ruthless, amoral, conscienceless approach to theft and murder. But at the end of the third novel, *Les Exploits de Rocambole* (1858–1859), Rocambole is captured, his face is burned with acid, and he is sent to a hard labor camp in Toulon. Terrail's fourth book in the series, *Les Chevaliers du Clair de Lune* (1860–1862), brought back Rocambole in a *Comte de Monte Cristo*–like story of redemption, but reduced him to a plotter and schemer rather than an active hero, and Terrail's fans reacted negatively to it. So in the fifth book in the series Terrail began again, pretending *Les Chevaliers du Clair de Lune* hadn't happened and having Rocambole escape from the hard labor camp, experience an epiphany, and become a force for good.

Over the remainder of the novel and the next four novels, published until Terrail's death in 1871, Rocambole becomes a crime-fighting Man of Extraordinary Capabilities, active in Paris, in India against the Thugs, and in London as the "Man in Grey." Although not translated into English, Terrail's novels were hugely popular in France, earning him the title "king of the *roman feuilleton*" and donating the word "rocambolesque" to the French language.

The importance of Rocambole is twofold. First, he was the first Man of Extraordinary Capabilities whose brief and focus were fighting a variety of criminals over a series of books rather than taking revenge (as with Edmond Dantès) or asserting urban rulership (as with Rodolphe von Gerolstein). Second, he was the first major protosuperhero to assemble a team of talented assistants, from every class of society and with a variety of talents, to aid him in the fight against crime. Ponson du Terrail wasn't the first author to do this; Mary Elizabeth Braddon, in her detective novel *Three Times Dead* (1860), the first English murder mystery,[35] surrounded her detective, Joseph Peters (the first disabled detective in a murder mystery) with a gang of assistants, the "Cheerful Cherokees," who were as diverse and talented as Rocambole's team. But Terrail, because his widespread readership, was the more influential of the two to do so, and the idea of a hero with a gang of capable assistants, which shows up throughout the pulps (in Walter Gibson's Shadow stories and in Doc Savage stories, to name just two) and the comics (The Batman Family), begins with Terrail and Rocambole.

As Terrail's *La Résurrection de Rocambole* was being published in France, *The Dead Letter* was appearing in serial from and then as a novel later in 1866. *The Dead Letter* was written by "Seeley Regester," the pseudonym of Mrs. Metta Victoria Fuller Victor, and was the first full length American detective novel. A murder mystery, *The Dead Letter* features as a private detective Mr. Burton, an independently wealthy amateur detective who, out of personal convictions, investigates crimes. Burton is extremely capable as a detective and as a person, being well schooled in many areas of crime solving, including breaking ciphers. He is an expert at "chirography," or handwriting analysis, "reading men and women from a specimen of their handwriting."[36] He has a magnetic gaze that seems to look directly into others' souls, a gaze straight from the Gothic Hero-Villain. He is good at following others, unseen. And he is sensitive to atmosphere, always knowing when he is in the presence of evil men and women.

In addition to his all-around excellence and skills, Burton further has an almost superhuman skill at deduction:

> The more he called into play the peculiar faculties of his mind, which made him so successful a hunter on the paths of the guilty, the more marvelous became their development. He was like an Indian on the trail of his enemy, the bent grass, the broken twig, the evanescent dew which, to the uninitiated, were "trifles light as air," to him were "proofs strong as Holy Writ."
>
> In this work he was actuated by no pernicious motives. Upright and humane, with a generous heart which pitied the innocent injured, his conscience would allow him no rest if he permitted crime, which he could see walking where others could not, to flourish unmolested in the sunshine made for better uses.[37]

Burton is the first Man of Extraordinary Capabilities who is *specifically* a crime fighter rather than a kind of adventurer/crime fighter as was the case with Rocambole.

Penny Vigilantes

Cheap fiction during the Gothic era appeared in "chapbooks," flimsy pamphlets ranging from 8 to 72 pages long. Chapbooks contained everything from advice books to traditional fairy tales to abridgments of popular novels, especially of Gothic novels.

The Gothic era ended roughly in 1830, and the chapbook was replaced by the "penny blood." Changes in educational methods and a new demand for literate workers led to an increase in literacy among the working classes, and changes in technology made printing less expensive. These two developments led to a boom in cheap fiction for the working classes.

The penny blood were pamphlets, 8 or 16 pages long, that were issued weekly.[38] They

> told stories of adventure, initially of pirates and highwaymen, later concentrating on crime and detection . . . at first the bloods copied popular cheap fiction's love of late 18th-century gothic tales, the more sensational the better . . . Later, after highwaymen and then evil aristocrats fell out of fashion, penny-bloods found even more success with stories of true crimes, especially murders . . . Soon, however, it was the pursuers, not the murderers, who took centre-stage.[39]

By the 1860s, when the pursuers were at the center of the story, the penny blood was known as the "penny dreadful," and was in full flower, printing a wide variety of stories, some quite racy indeed—the bloods and dreadfuls were in many ways the inheritor of the Gothic tradition, including the inclusion of sexually explicit (for the era and medium) material. The moral panic and crackdown of the early 1870s, which hadn't taken place yet, led to a restriction in what was published in the dreadfuls. The 1860s were the high point for the dreadful, just as it was for the sensation genre of novels that were the dreadfuls' middle- and upper-class counterpart. And, perhaps in imitation of Spring-Heeled Jack or perhaps simply using the same tropes that had appeared throughout the century, Costumed Avengers began appearing.

The two most significant appeared in the anonymously written *The Skeleton Horseman; or, The Shadow of Death* (1866–1867) and the anonymously written *The Skeleton Crew; or, Wildfire Ned* (1867). Both dreadfuls were heavily influenced by the Gothic, making use of numerous Gothic tropes and motifs, but the plots hearkened back to the heroic highwayman stories. *The Skeleton Horseman*, set in Restoration England, involves the conflict between a band of costumed highwaymen, the Skeleton Crew, and their leader, the costumed Skeleton Horseman, and a "rich and powerful brotherhood," the Black Band, led by the vile abuser of women Lord Glendore. Allies of the Skeleton Crew are the masked highwaymen the Red Hand and his crew, the Red Avengers, among whose friends is Claude Duval. Allies of the Black Band are King Charles the II and his men. After numerous plot twists and complications Lord Glendore and the Black Band are defeated and the highwaymen and Nell Gwynne (later to be the King's mistress) live happily ever after.

Wildfire Ned, set in the 17th century during the heyday of the Duke of Buckingham, is about a young man's attempt to regain his inheritance. Immortal devilish pirates going by the name "the Skeleton Crew" appear, only to eventually be opposed by thief takers from London and "the Red Man," "a man in armour, glittering from head to foot in polished steel," who has supernatural powers.[40] The usual penny dreadful plot twists follow, though justice naturally triumphs in the end.

The Skeleton Horseman and *Wildfire Ned* had no direct influence on American authors; there was no American distribution of either, and although American publishers often "borrowed" British publishers' publications, neither dreadful was subject to such borrowing. But British writers, like Alfred S. Burrage, author of the influential 1904 *Spring-Heeled Jack Library*, did—Burrage was in fact the author of the notorious dreadful *Sweeney Todd, the Demon Barber of Fleet Street* (1878) and was well aware of his competitors among the periodicals. If *The Skeleton Horseman* and *Wildfire Ned* only contributed to the Costumed Avenger Zeitgeist as it communicated itself to America, both dreadfuls can be said to have had a more direct influence on the 1904 Spring-Heeled Jack, who did appear in the United States.

Dime Vigilantes

Meanwhile, in the United States, a counterpart to the penny dreadfuls was appearing. In the 1830s and 1840s publishers had issued weekly paper-bound stories, "novelettes," in newspaper form. They were usually adventure stories but often offered serial reprints of the latest popular British novels. The market expanded, and publishers began commissioning new works. In 1860, the publisher Beadle and Adams began publishing a novelette, *Beadle's Dime Novels*, which included sensational adventure plots, and soon other publishers followed suit.

> The proliferation of paper-covered fiction in the latter part of the nineteenth century turned the brand-named "dime novel" into a generic term for any work of fiction in paper covers, no matter what the cover price. Other formats appeared in the following decades. The "libraries" (later known as "weeklies") and the paper-covered novels of 200 to 300 pages were also dime novels although they did not externally resemble the original Beadles.[41]

Originally the dime novels were frontier and Western stories in imitation of James Fenimore Cooper, but soon enough other genres became popular, including mystery/detective fiction. The genre did not cohere in American novel publishing until the late 1870s, when writers like Anna Katherine Green became best sellers and solidified the form, but the dime novel writers had the example of casebook detective novels and casebook series detectives to imitate, as well as the real-life rise in private detective agencies following the end of the Civil War to draw inspiration from. So, when Harlan Halsey began his "Old Sleuth" stories in 1872, Halsey was initiating a form in America with both real-life and fictional predecessors.

Old Sleuth, who ended up appearing in over 50 stories over the next 19 years, is Harry Loveland, a private detective in New York City. Although he's from the upper classes and is cultured and well educated, speaking French and German fluently, the crimes he solves range from the Gothic to the dime novel to the sensation novel in inspiration and the criminals he apprehends are everything from upper-class poisoners to scheming Romanies to Indian Thugs. He is assisted by a younger man, Young Badger, and on other occasions by other dime novel detectives, including Old Electricity, the Lightning Detective, and the Gypsy Detective.[42] Old Sleuth is notable for two main reasons, his superhuman strength and his skill at disguise, which is exceptional and a regular part of the Old Sleuth stories, thus making him the first dime novel series Costumed Avenger.

Old Sleuth was the first recurring, serialized dime novel detective and was sufficiently popular that for a generation the phrase "Old Sleuth" was identified with fictional detectives. The first "Old Sleuth" story is one of the earliest written uses of the word "sleuth" for detective. Halsey shortened the previous existing phrase, "sleuth hound," and Halsey's usage stuck and became popular. Influenced by Halsey's creation, other dime novel detectives who used disguises as a regular part of their repertoire began appearing, so that the disguise-heavy Costumed Avenger became a heavy part of the dime novels' rotation of characters, and a character type that American readers and future writers were regularly exposed to.

Cowboy Vigilantes

The rise in the popularity of dime novel detectives led to detective dime novels assuming more of the market share for dime novels, at the expense of Western and frontier dime novels; Westerns were 36 percent of the market in 1874 but only 18 percent in 1884. As this was taking place, however, a curious dynamic was occurring: the masked frontier outlaw was becoming popular.

The real-life backdrop to this was the ongoing conflict between workers and management, with strikes by Pennsylvania coal miners in 1873 and 1874 and by railway workers in 1877 turning violent and being bloodily repressed by management. Relations between labor and capital were extremely bitter nationwide, with the liberal and conservative media slinging venomous rhetoric at each other. While this was taking place,

Frank and Jesse James were gaining fame as bank robbers and being touted by the liberal press as the modern inheritors of the Robin Hood and heroic highwaymen tradition, to the point that one Missouri editor fabricated a letter from the James Gang and signed it "Jack Shepherd, Dick Turpin, Claude Duval."[43]

The dime novels responded to this, perhaps surprisingly, by siding with the liberal media and creating sympathetic masked cowboy outlaws, the American frontier version of the heroic highwaymen. The first masked outlaw was Edward L. Wheeler's Deadwood Dick, who appeared in 34 stories from 1877 to 1885. Dick—real name Edward "Ned" Harris—was originally from the East but was driven West through the connivance of an evil banker, who arranges for the deaths of Harris's foster parents and then swindles Harris and his sister out of their share of the family wealth. Left with no other alternative except starvation, Harris is forced to lead the life of a highwayman. He gathers around him a gang of bandits and becomes the infamous "Deadwood Dick." He leads an exciting and violent life of adventure, but he longs to leave behind outlawry and become a settled man with a wife, children, and home. He is never successful in this, however, for events conspire against him, he is often betrayed by his friends, and the women who accept his marriage proposals usually die.

The major difference between Wheeler's Deadwood Dick stories and those of previous heroic highwaymen were the specific politics of the stories and of the new breed outlaws. The new breed were made into versions of the *räuberroman* hero. The cause of their outlawry was corrupt businessmen who had the support of the law. The new breed of outlaw heroes no longer preyed on the average inhabitant of the frontier. The victims of their robberies were members of the upper classes, usually Eastern, and when communities were threatened, the identity of the community was defined as working class, and the enemies of the community were exploitive capitalists like stockbrokers and financiers who were evil not through what they did but through what they were. Officials who represented business and the financial establishment were automatically both corrupt and the enemy of the outlaw hero, who fought them but defended the poor and the working class.

The James Brothers got the masked outlaw treatment in 1881, and with Deadwood Dick were the two most popular outlaw characters to appear in the dime novels in the 1870s and 1880s. Led by these two, the outlaw hero character became so successful so quickly that the dominant narrative model for the dime novel Western changed, from James Fenimore Cooper–like stories to those of the outlaw hero, a state of affairs that lasted well into the 1880s, at which point a moral panic ensued over the politics of the dime novels and government censors got involved and forced the cancellation of heroic outlaw frontier pulps; those that didn't get canceled had their politics castrated by the dime novel's publishers.

The "safe" counterpart to the masked outlaw was Buffalo Bill. The Buffalo Bill stories had begun appearing in a dime novel in 1869, but for the first 10 years the fictional Buffalo Bill's adventures were closely tethered to reality and based on the actions of the historical Buffalo Bill Cody. Beginning in 1879, however, his character changed, as did the contents of his stories, becoming more fantastic, more romantic (in the old sense), and more responsive to the most prominent contemporary trend in frontier dime novels, the masked frontier vigilante. Buffalo Bill became a frontier vigilante, always clad in the same buckskin outfit—his costume—but now a member of the upper class, an early version of the *parfait knight* cowboy that Owen Wister would later perfect in *The Virginian* (1902). His vigilante actions are safe, never threatening the status quo, and he becomes a man whose opponents never indicted the system through their existence, as had been the case with Deadwood Dick's and the James Brothers' enemies. When Buffalo Bill defeated a corrupt official the audience was reassured that the official was an anomaly, not the norm, and when Buffalo Bill helped union members the striking union men would happily place themselves back in the power of their employers. Ingraham's Buffalo Bill reinforced the status quo, with Bill himself correcting matters on behalf of the establishment, rather than acting as its opponent.

Buffalo Bill's tenure as the Costumed Avenger safe for corporate lackeys and the middle and upper classes would run for hundreds of issues, through 1912.

Lady Detectives

Male detectives were not the only ones to be featured prominently in the dime novels. Women detectives appeared there as well, less frequently but given the same pride of place in dime novels when they did so. In these stories the dime novel authors were not just adding to detective literature, as they did with male detectives; they were updating the figure of the action/adventure heroine and laying the groundwork for the superheroine.

Throughout much of the 19th century, Charles Brockden Brown's Martinette de Beauvais was the biggest fictional role model of modern action/adventure heroines. Nineteenth century fiction certainly had a large number of female protagonists, but relatively few of them were willful and independent-minded, and of those the great majority ended up at a bad end (like Becky Sharp, from Thackeray's *Vanity Fair* [1850], and Lydia Gwilt, from Wilkie Collins's *Armadale* [1864–1866]) or were safely married off (like Jane Eyre, from Charlotte Brontë's *Jane Eyre* [1847]). Moreover, there was little room in 19th-century adventurous fiction for women in any role except as wives.

The dime novels changed that, primarily through their popularization of detective fiction. There were female detectives or female protodetectives before the dime novel, whether informal (like E. T. A. Hoffmann's Mademoiselle de Scudéry, in "Das Fraulein von Scuderi" [1819]) or formal (like Mrs. L., in William Burton's "The Secret Cell" [1837]). There were even female amateur detectives as protagonists in protomystery novels, as with Susan Hopley in Catherine Crowe's *Adventures of Susan Hopley, or Circumstantial Evidence* (1841). When the casebook novels became popular in the 1850s and 1860s, authors began using female detectives as protagonists, as with "G," in Andrew Forrester Jr.'s *The Female Detective* (1864) and with Mrs. Paschal, in William Stephens Hayward's *Revelations of a Lady Detective* (1864).

But these were unusual characters, rare examples of women detectives in a predominantly male field. In the dime novels, however, women detectives were not common, but not so seldom appearing as to be extraordinary. The trend began with Harlan P. Halsey's Kate Goelet, in "The Lady Detective" (*Fireside Companion*, 1880) and continued through the next several years. These detectives were independent, skilled, courageous, capable in a fight, and usually dressed in men's clothing, just as Martinette de Beauvais had been and just as real-life women detectives were doing.[44] Within a few years, women detectives were comparatively common in mainstream detective literature, with many of them similarly cross-dressing. While this was taking place, three decades of physical education programs for women had produced thousands of women with unusual strength, women who would join the Physical Culture movement or simply take up hobbies like bicycling, weight lifting, and fencing. The groundwork for the comic book superheroine was being laid by these women.

Lady Jaguar

Cowboy heroines were never as popular as cowboy heroes as protagonists for dime novels. More often the women in dime novels were friends, love interests, or enemies to the main character, as was the case with Calamity Jane and Deadwood Dick. But the cowboy heroine was not unknown, either, going back at least to Charles Averill's novelette *The*

Mexican Ranchero; or, The Maid of the Chapparal (1847), with its Mexican heroine, Buena Rejon, acting as a noble outlaw queen (this, well in advance of Deadwood Dick and the James Brothers).

But in 1882 William H. Manning took the next step. Influenced by the frontier Costumed Avengers that were in vogue at the time, he wrote "Lady Jaguar, the Robber Queen. A Romance of the Black Chaparral," about Doña Luisa Villena, a Mexican noblewoman forced into what she thinks is a marriage to a cruel local bandit who killed her father. In response, Doña Luisa and her brother Juan become the costumed and masked outlaws "Lady Jaguar" and "El Alacran," preying on travelers (including Americans) while searching for the means to avenge themselves on Doña Luisa's husband. Juan maintains his alternate identity as a wealthy Mexican landowner while Doña Luisa heads up their gang.

"Lady Jaguar, the Robber Queen" appeared in *Beadle's New York Dime Library*, one of the most popular of the dime novels. The story's influence is debatable, but given the *New York Dime Library*'s readership the story was undoubtedly read widely. It provided readers and future writers with a Costumed Avenger who is a heroic highwaywoman—Lady Jaguar's gang robs from the rich and gives to the poor—while wearing an actual bodysuit costume and mask, in proper superheroine form, and is a woman. Lady Jaguar anticipates the superheroines to come and provided a model for them, although the idea of allowing her independence at the end of her story was too transgressive a notion for Manning, who ends up marrying Lady Jaguar off to an American and making her into a "proper" woman. The idea of an ongoing series about an independent cowgirl heroine was too much for the conservative Western/frontier audience, unlike those reading mysteries, who were already reading about independent female detectives in series fiction.

The Man in the Black Cloak

Perhaps more influential, in a very direct sense, is the titular character from Francis Doughty's "The Man in the Black Cloak" (1886). A detective story heavily influenced both by dime novel traditions and the tropes and motifs of the Gothic, "The Man in the Black Cloak" is a typical dime novel story in many ways, except for the Man in the Black Cloak, a Costumed Avenger "draped in a long, black cloak, now thrown widely open in front, revealing a man's head, with fiery eyes, surmounting a skeleton frame of white, grisly bone."[45] Earlier, he is described as "wearing a low slouched hat and enveloped in a long black cloak which reached to his feet."[46] The Man in the Black Cloak's behavior—his creeping around the city, appearing and disappearing as necessary, and working behind the scenes to right a wrong—is typical of Gothic and dime novel heroes but it and the Man in the Black Cloak's appearance—slouched hat, protruding nose, burning eyes—are also typical of the Walter Gibson's pulp crime fighter the Shadow, who also shares with the Man in the Black Cloak the slouch hat and black cape.

Although there is no direct evidence that Gibson read "The Man in the Black Cloak,"[47] Gibson was familiar with the dime novels, once referring in print to "the home of a celebrated detective named Nick Carter, the horse-and-buggy crime doctor of his day."[48] It is possible that Gibson, as child, had read "The Man in the Black Cloak" and remembered the image of the title character when he was creating the Shadow. And, of course, the content and iconography of the Shadow were heavily influential on Bill Finger and Bob Kane when they created Batman.

Nick Carter

Dime novel series detectives had been meanwhile appearing with regularity, most notably William I. James Jr.'s Old Cap. Collier (beginning in 1883) and Francis Doughty's Old King Brady (beginning in 1885). Like Old Sleuth, Old Cap. Collier and Old King Brady were a large part of the lineage of the Übermensch dime novel detective. But they were also popular series detectives, establishing to the satisfaction of the publishers that series detectives were not only possible but profitable. Publishers had known this to be true about series about cowboy heroes for years, but mysteries were a more dubious field.[49]

No preceding character had prepared the publishers or the audience for Nick Carter, however. Created by Ormond G. Smith and John Russell Coryell and debuting in 1886, Carter was almost immediately popular and became a cash cow for publisher Street & Smith, eventually appearing in over 4,000 stories in dime novels, movies, radio shows, pulps, comic strips, and comic books through 1955.[50] Carter was multiply influential, simply by virtue of his longevity—he was the iconic dime novel detective through the life span of the dime novels and was successful as a pulp character for years—and because of the content of his stories.

Carter was a dime novel Übermensch—the archetypal dime novel Übermensch, which I cover in greater detail in Chapter 5. Carter was a Costumed Avenger, a master of disguise and regularly used it, especially creating a few recurring alternate identities he assumed, such as "Old Thunderbolt." He was a Man of Extraordinary Capabilities, both physically and mentally, only focused on solving crimes and an expert in every conceivable subject that might have to do with crime solving. He was even, to a large degree, the hidden master of his city, albeit one famous to both citizens and criminals.

Numerous dime novel detectives were modeled on him. Carter's influence extended beyond his immediate contemporaries, however. Many aspects of the Carter stories are models for later pulp characters. Carter's origin is remarkably similar to Doc Savage's, and several elements of Carter's approach to detecting, from the guises to the separate identity maintained at another office to the band of agents, were also used by the Shadow. Carter uses a number of gadgets, including superexplosives, which several pulp characters would later use, including Lester Dent's Click Rush, the Gadget Man. Doc Savage, the Shadow, and Click Rush were all published by Street & Smith, the publisher of Nick Carter's adventures.

The corpus of Carter stories in fact are taproot texts for superhero comics, a number of whose elements came from Carter:

- The origin. Not only is Nick raised from birth to be a great man and a great detective, but his first case involves solving the murder of his father, Old Sim. Nick Carter was the first detective of ongoing serial fiction to have an actual origin story. Before Carter, story paper and dime novel detectives were simply professionals who were good at their job. After Carter, a colorful origin became necessary to distinguish a dime novel detective from the rest of the pack, and the tragic elements of Carter's origin story have been imitated in countless superhero comics.

- Continuity and "Marvel Time." The Nick Carter stories essentially established the tendency of ongoing series to acknowledge the years and in many cases decades of stories that had preceded them, and even referred to previous events on a semiregular basis. Time passed in the universe of Nick Carter, albeit slowly and sometimes inconsistently, so that some characters would age quickly and others, like Nick, slowly, but time did pass. (This adjusted process of time's passing is known in comics as "Marvel Time.") The most prominent example of this attention to continuity is Nick Carter's wife, Ethel, who appeared in the first storyline and was a semiregular for 15 years before being killed by one of Nick's enemies. This death was referred to in passing several times over the years. Nick's adopted son, Chick Carter, also had a wife murdered by one of Nick's enemies. Chick married again, and his son grew up and eventually joined Nick's agency. Students from Nick's school for detectives appeared for years as Nick's assistants. And when some of Carter's enemies died, their brothers or sons would appear, years later, to attempt to avenge their fathers or siblings.

- Cross-genre fluidity. The Nick Carter series was the first to treat genre boundaries as inconveniences rather than as limits to be obeyed. The Nick

Carter stories were ostensibly detective stories, but Carter also discovered lost races in the Tibetan Himalayas, in Nepal, and in the Andes. Carter traveled in time, fought pirates, defeated zeppelin pirates, wrestled killer octopi on the ocean's floor, overthrew Aryan superhumans who ruled a lost city with "vibrational science," and fought white Amazons in Bolivia.

- Finally, the Nick Carter stories were the first to give its hero a rogues' gallery. Every superhero with a memorable array of villains has Carter to thank. Carter's archenemy was the sociopathic vivisector Doctor Quartz, who preceded Professor Moriarty by over two years and is the first major recurring villain in popular crime fiction. Many of Carter's enemies were beautiful, capable, and homicidal women, characters with names like Zanoni the Woman Wizard, Scylla the Sea Robber, Zelma the Female Fiend, Princess Olga, tiger chief of the Russian Nihilists, the Bird of Paradise, Diana the Arch Demon, and Inez Navarro, the Beautiful Demon. Others were Codman the Poisoner, Ordway the Unaccountable Crook, Prince Sang Tu of the Yellow Tong, Madge Morley, the Dangerous Woman, Praxatel of the Iron Arm (the first cyborg of the dime novels), and Gustave Rogler, a genius of crime, comparable to Professor Moriarty, and a man who left a symbol of vengeance, a purple spot, on the foreheads of his victims.

John Amend-All

Robert Louis Stevenson's *The Black Arrow* was originally published as a serial in 1883, with hardcover publication being delayed five years. *The Black Arrow*—not among Stevenson's best-known or best-loved novels— is an adventurous tale of peasant and outlaw vengeance against an evil nobleman and his retainers during the time of the War of the Roses. The antagonist is Sir Daniel Brackley, a self-serving, avaricious traitor knight responsible for giving the orders for various atrocities, including the death of the protagonist's father. "John Amend-All" is the pseudonym of Ellis Duckworth, who organizes the fellowship of the Black Arrow to avenge the wrongs done to him and his friends and to break the frame that Brackley's men placed on him for the death of the novel's protagonist's father. Duckworth, as John Amend-All, leads the Black Arrow Fellowship, who use black arrows to kill their enemies. He further creates a poem to proclaim the forthcoming death of Brackley and his men.

The question of *The Black Arrow*'s influence is a fair one: Did it appear in isolation, or did it have some influence on what followed? *The Black Arrow*, as mentioned, appeared as a serial in 1883 and as a novel in 1888, and although the novel was not reprinted in the United Kingdom until 1894 and the United States until 1895, thereafter it was continually in print. Although never the most famous of Stevenson's work, nor the best received with critics, nor the best selling (as a novel; as an 1887 newspaper serial in the United States it was quite popular), it nonetheless sold well and was well liked enough among adolescents to spawn numerous American high school plays based on it.

So *The Black Arrow* was ever-present in the marketplace and popular among adolescents, and a case can be made for its influence on the more notable Costumed Avenger novels and stories that followed it. John Amend-All is of course a Costumed Avenger and protosuperhero. His mission is debatably heroic, although tending more toward vengeance than justice. Otherwise, the John Amend-All meets several of the criteria for the superhero laid down in Chapter 1: an unusual origin story (framed and driven to the outlaw's life by Brackley and his men), a distinctive weapon (the black arrows), a codename (John Amend-All), a dual identity (John Amend-All's real identity is Ellis Duckworth), and a world in which law and order has failed and vigilantism is welcome. John Amend-All kills, but other than that he meets most of the criteria for the superhero or at least the protosuperhero.

John Amend-All is in many ways a copy of Robin Hood, of course, and *The Black Arrow* appeared as a serial in the same year as *The Merry Adventures of Robin Hood of Great Renown in Nottinghamshire*, the novel by author and illustrator Howard Pyle, which compiled various episodes from the legends of Robin Hood and made a coherent narrative out of them. *The Merry Adventures of Robin Hood* solidified Robin Hood's image as a medieval outlaw and hero for children's books, and later Costumed Avenger heroes like the Scarlet Pimpernel and Zorro owe a debt of inspiration to Pyle's Robin Hood. But John Amend-All, aimed at adults rather than children (as had been the case with *The Merry Adventures of Robin Hood*), had a similar inspirational effect on later Costumed Avengers—perhaps less (if only because the original, Robin Hood, is always going to be a more potent influence than a copy like John Amend-All), but still significant, thanks to *The Black Arrow*'s existence in the marketplace and the consciousness of readers.

Conclusion

By the turn of the 20th century, the Costumed Avenger was no innovation, but a long-established character type, one that (thanks to the dime novel detectives, especially Nick Carter) was showing unexpectedly enduring creative and financial strength. When the pulps (which actually began in 1896) looked for models of successful characters to imitate, it would be to the dime novels, and the dime novel Costumed Avengers.

Meanwhile, the Übermensch had been developing in parallel.

CHAPTER FIVE

Victorian Supermen

The development during the Victorian era of the Übermensch as a protagonist was slow in coming, the anomalous example of Gray Champion excepted. The supermen of Chapter 3 were influential, but far more influential on the producers and consumers of popular culture was the Gothic and its characters, and the most significant and usually the most attractive character in any Gothic was its villain, who was usually a superpowered Hero-Villain—attractive despite themselves, morally liminal, and certainly the focus of the reader's gaze, but ultimately the villain of each text rather than the hero. The association of superpowers with the Gothic Hero-Villain would remain a strong one, and it would take decades before writers of popular literature began producing uncomplicated heroes with superhuman powers. Until then, the only characters to have them would be monsters, villains, artificial beings, and sorcerers—outsiders, all. For 50 years after the Gothics ended, the supermen and superwomen of Victorian heroic fiction would be outsiders—not outsiders whose stories were of their slow reintegration into society, but permanent outsiders, for whom society reintegration into society is simply not possible. And for the Victorians, to be a permanent outsider who never would be or could be reintegrated into society was largely to be an enemy of society.

Monsters

As we've seen in previous chapters, the *idea* of superpowers of various kinds is an old one. Setting aside those mortals, like Enkidu, who got their powers directly from the gods, there are any number of pre-Victorian characters with superhuman abilities, with a relatively large number of them appearing during the 18th and early 19th centuries.

But authors of heroic fiction during the first half of the Victorian era were generally shy of portraying humans with superhuman abilities; the fashionable literary genres most often used by writers during these years, the historical novel, the domestic novel, and the Sensation novel, encouraged mimetic realism over the use of *fantastika*, and authors of heroic fiction, though writing in their own vein, were as vulnerable to the fashionable literary trends as any other author, and imitated their more respected colleagues.

Whatever the reason, monsters and villains rather than heroes were for 50 years most often the possessors of superhuman abilities. This had the virtue of making the authors' quite human heroes and heroines seem more heroic in comparison when they overcame their superhuman enemies. It also tied the idea of superhuman abilities to outsiders and enemies of society, so that, where once the reason for avoiding superhuman heroes might have been in obedience to fashionable literary trends, later on the idea of a mortal hero facing off against a superhuman enemy became a tradition in heroic fiction, especially British heroic fiction.

Throughout much of the century, the most famous and influential characters with superhuman abilities were monsters and villains. This had two long-term effects on heroic fiction. The first was that it set up the mortal-hero/superhuman-enemy dynamic that would be common in the pulps and early in comic books' Golden Age (1935–1949). Many of the pulp heroes and early comic book superheroes had no powers but often or routinely clashed with villains with various superhuman powers—again, allowing the creators to emphasize their human heroes' heroism when they triumphed over their more powerful opponents.

The second effect, however, was to make the idea of superhuman abilities and powers an essential part of heroic fiction. Superhumanly powered protagonists and antagonists, before the Victorian era, were influential but relatively rare, especially by comparison with Costumed Avengers. But during the Victorian years, characters with superhuman abilities, the supermen, became regular occurrences, even though they were the antagonists, not the protagonists. It took only a small leap in logic and inspiration for contemporary and later writers to begin applying the concept of the Übermensch and of superhuman powers to their own characters. The roots of the Übermensch go far back, as we've seen, but the trunk of the Übermensch family tree lies in the monsters and villains of the Victorian age.

I already covered Mary Shelley's *Frankenstein* (1818) in Chapter 3, and described some of the Creature's influence on later supercharacters: as a being created by science rather than nature and as the scientifically engineered physically superior being, which Shelley calls "a new species."[1]

Shelley here was drawing upon contemporary understanding of racial science, most specifically the racial theories propounded by Johann Friedrich Blumenbach in 1775, who

> developed the analytical concept of race to classify the specific varieties or sub-groups within the human species. As both Nicholas Hudson and Ivan Hannaford have demonstrated, the concept of race as a stable, transnational, biological or genetic category was not widely available before the late eighteenth century. In 1775, Blumenbach—following Renaissance and Linnaean theories of the four humors—identified *four* races of men: Caucasian . . . Mongolian, American, and Ethiopian.[2]

Shelley, friends with one of Blumenbach's most ardent disciples, would have been well aware of this (literally) racist categorization scheme. What Shelley created, in Frankenstein's Creature, was a *new* race, an Asian race that is actually physically superior to Caucasians (the highest race in Blumenbach's schema). The Creature has yellow skin, long black hair, dun-colored eyes, and is first seen crossing the steppes of Russia and Tartary, all signifiers to Shelley's audience of the Creature being a Mongolian or Asian in Blumenbach's schema.[3]

Post-Darwin and his *On the Origin of Species* (1859), this concept of the new race would become, literally, what Shelley described as "a new species," something higher and better than *Homo sapiens*, something with human body parts but altered through alchemy/science into something different than humanity. Although this concept of a new, artificially created superior race would be used sparingly in the 19th century, in the 20th century in the pulps and especially in the comic books it would come into full flower.

In the iconic trio of monster types, Frankenstein's Creature can be counted as a zombie, although he is neither a Romeroesque shambler nor a Danny Boyle-esque runner, and is closer to a golem than he is to the traditional idea of a zombie. The second iconic monster type, and by far the most popular monster type of the Victorian age, was the vampire. Folkloric reports of Eastern European vampires returning from the dead were common in London in the 17th and 18th centuries, following the introduction of the term "vampire" into the English language in 1732. Even though educated men and women dismissed vampires as fictional by the turn of the 19th century, the folklore, of the savage living dead returned from the grave to suck the blood of the living, was widely disseminated. It wasn't until 1819 that the modern vampire—suave, educated, emphatically not a snarling beast—would appear, in John Polidori's "The Vampyre." About the visitation upon London of a newcomer, Lord

Ruthven, the narrator's friendship with him, and the eventual revelation that Ruthven is a vampire, "The Vampyre" essentially created modern horror fiction. Polidori, heavily influenced by the Gothics, made his vampiric monster into a Gothic Hero-Villain modeled on Lord Byron, a cultured creature of the cities rather than a slavering monster of tradition and folklore. "The Vampyre" gave to vampire lore the vampire's mesmerizing gaze (a part, recall, of the Gothic Hero-Villain), the vampire's healing and rejuvenation by moonlight, and changed the monster into something that reflected the times in which the monster's story was written: Ruthven is a jaded, cynical, amoral aristocrat of the 1810s, of the early British Regency, rather than the slavering corpse-fiend of folklore.

Théophile Gautier's "La Morte Amoureuse" (1836), about a tragic love affair between a mortal man and a vampiress, made the vampire sympathetic (a first in vampire stories) as well as (vaguely) alluded to the variety of supernatural powers that vampires possessed. James Malcolm Rymer's *Varney the Vampyre* (1845–1847) returned the vampire to the Polidoriesque Gothic Hero-Villain, but added an element of tragedy to it that Lord Ruthven lacked[4] as well as, for the first time, superhuman strength in addition to functional immortality and rejuvenation by moonlight. Sheridan Le Fanu's "Carmilla" (1871–1872), the first lesbian vampire story, confirmed the vampire's superhuman strength and added shape changing to the vampire's list of powers. And Bram Stoker's *Dracula* (1897), via the popularity of its stage and screen adaptations, made the vampire into the archetypal Victorian monster.

As with the Creature in Frankenstein, the fictional examples of vampires of the Victorian age propagated the concept of the superpowered character, adding to it the elements of the Gothic Hero-Villain, the specifically folkloric origin of the Übermensch and their powers, and the concept of the *package* of diverse powers linked together through theme, rather than through base physicality (as with the superstrength/superspeed/superendurance trio). Vampire superheroes are few: J. M. DeMatteis's Andrew Bennett (for DC) and Marv Wolfman and Gene Colan's Blade and Hannibal King (both for Marvel) are the most prominent ones. But the concept of the package or set of bodily powers of diverse kinds that the Übermensch possesses and uses begins with the Victorian vampires and with Lord Ruthven.

The last of the three great monster types is the werewolf. A protowerewolf appears in Charles Maturin's historical novel *The Albigenses* (1824), but the character only acts in a wolflike manner, with no physical transformation—though he advises, "trust not my human skin—*the hairs grow inward*, and I am a wolf within—a man outward only."[5] It wasn't until Frederick Marryat's Flying Dutchman novel, *The Phantom Ship* (1839), with its "The White Wolf of the Hartz Mountain" section, that the modern werewolf myth began. Marryat was the first to portray the wolf as a beautiful young woman, and added the idea that the wounded werewolf transforms into its true human form after death. George Reynolds's *Wagner the Wehr-Wolf* (1846–1847), a full-fledged werewolf novel, was heavily influenced by Marryat but added the feature that the transformation from human to wolf was a painful one. And Clemence Housman's "The Were-Wolf" (1891) added a femme fatale element to the werewolf's human form and generally emphasized the superhuman strength and endurance of the werewolf, whether in human or wolf form.

More broadly, though, werewolves are a lupine variation on the doppelgänger, which appeared throughout the century; it was a common motif in the Gothics and became a stock device in supernatural stories during the 19th century. However, the emphasis on the doppelgänger existing bodily within the protagonist was stressed in the werewolf stories but came to the fore in Robert Louis Stevenson's *The Strange Case of Dr. Jekyll and Mr. Hyde* (1886). Admittedly, Stevenson's doppelgänger character, Edward Hyde, gains no superpowers from his transformation; he is actually shorter, if more apelike, than Henry Jekyll. What *Dr. Jekyll and Mr. Hyde* did do, though, because of its popularity, was to propagate the concept of the doppelgänger-in-the-same-body, which when matched with the ideas of the werewolf transformation easily led to the idea of the transformation of a hero from his or her mortal body to a superhuman one. This is a basic wish fulfillment idea, that one could physically change into an Übermensch at will, but the doppelgängers of the 19th century, particularly the werewolf stories, reified this, until it became a basic trope of superheroes.[6]

Superhumanly powered monsters were popular in the 19th century, and thanks to stage productions and movies became much more so during the 20th, but by then the idea of the Übermensch and their powers had shifted from monster to mortal.

Villains

Monsters were not the only superhumanly powered characters to provide inspiration for creators when it came to applying powers to human characters. Villains with superhuman abilities were a somewhat regular occurrence during the Victorian age, and earlier.

Sketching a history of action/adventure literature is beyond the scope of this book. But, briefly, the English literature during the Enlightenment had no formal counterpart to the German *ritterroman* ("knight novel"), *räuberroman* ("robber novel"), and *schauerroman* ("shudder novel"). English literature had chapbooks, plays, and ballads, and, of course, translations of genre novels from France, Germany, and Spain, but nothing native, especially nothing with well-defined villain characters. It wasn't until the advent of the Gothic novel in the second half of the 18th century that action/adventure genre and the villain character as we now think of them began appearing in English. The one exception to this rule was the English craze for Arabian Nights–style adventures, which began with the translation of *The Thousand and One Nights* by Antoine Galland during the first two decades of the 18th century. This translation created the enthusiasm among Western readers for Arabian fantasies, which eventually gave rise to William Beckford's *Vathek*. It also gave the West the figure of the evil Arabian Vizier, a character type that would reappear in different Arabian fantasies throughout the 18th century. One notable one is Thomas-Simon Gueullette's *Aventures Merveilleuses du Mandarin Fum-Hoam* (1723). Fum-Hoam, an evil Chinese Mandarin, is the novel's protagonist. He has a range of magical powers, including flight and shape-shifting, and can be seen as a precursor to and influence on Vathek himself.

But most villains during the Gothic and Victorian eras did not have sets of abilities in the Fum-Hoam fashion to make use of. They had the attributes of the Hero-Villain—his presence, his stunning gaze—and, if they were lucky, one additional power, which they made use of to the best of their abilities.

For example, ventriloquism, in the 18th century, was seen not as a vocal trick but rather as a genuine power, so that Carwin, the Hero-Villain in Charles Brockden Brown's *Wieland; or, The Transformation* (1798), has ventriloquism in addition to his powerful gaze. Carwin was in turn influential on Mrs. Isaacs's *Ariel; or, the Invisible Monitor* (1801), with the heroic Rosaline's vocal powers (carefully explained in scientific terms), and on the Black Spirit, from George Lipscomb's Gothic novel *The Grey Friar and the Black Spirit of the Wye* (1810). *The Grey Friar* features a ventriloquist outlaw who out of a combination of capriciousness, high-mindedness, and amorality assumes two identities: the Grey Friar, a holy do-gooder, and the Black Spirit of the Wye, an evil creature out of legend. The outlaw is not a genuine dual-identity costumed vigilante, however, because the Black Spirit is much closer to the outlaw's true personality, and his pose as the Grey Friar is just that.

Again, what is important here is not so much the individual ability being shown—ventriloquism being a secondary or tertiary ability for those comic book characters who have it, such as Superman—as the fact that superhuman powers appear and are shown in a sober manner and not as something aberrant or transgressive, but as something relatively ordinary people could possess.

Superstrength was relatively frequently shown among the Übermensch antagonists. As one of the most common (and least imaginative) superpowers, it was an easy choice for writers to make when drawing up a character, and of course writers had the examples from legend and of Walter Scott's Black Dwarf to inspire them. Victor Hugo's first novel, *Han d'Islande* (1823), features as the titular character the fearsome outlaw Hans, a superhumanly strong dwarf who carries out a scheme of vengeance and uses his strength to kill. George Lippard's notorious porno-Gothic novel *The Quaker City; or, the Monks of Monk Hall* (1844–1845) has two main villains: the immortal alchemist-sorcerer Ravoni, and the Devil Bug, the grotesquely ugly, superhumanly strong bouncer of Monk's Hall. In Charles Averill's *The Mexican Ranchero* (1847), the novelette that stars Lady Jaguar (see Chapter 4), one of the villains is "Montano the monster," a Mexican "half breed" who is ugly enough to be compared with an "ourang outang" and has superhuman strength. And Nick Carter's archenemy from 1891 onward was the vivisector Dr. Quartz, who while anticipating the sociopathic genius archvillains of the 20th- and 21st centuries—Dr. Quartz is very much Thomas Harris's Hannibal Lecter, except for Quartz's dime novel origins—has the superstrength of a dime novel villain. (Or hero, as we'll see.)

The second half of the 19th century, with the dual rise in the interest in occultism and the mystic, and science, led to authors taking a different approach to their superpowered villains. H. Rider Haggard's Ayesha, from *She: A History of Adventure* (1886–1887), is an African demigoddess with an array of occult (or magic—their cause and source are never explained) powers. The titular character in Richard Marsh's *The Beetle* (1897) can magically shape change as well as practice mesmerism and mind control. And Guy Boothby's Pharos, in *Pharos the Egyptian* (1899), is an Egyptian sorcerer of various abilities and powers. Science as a source of superpowers, as in H. G. Wells's *The Invisible Man* (1897), was relatively rare, although it would be picked up much more often in the 20th century.

The rise of serial heroic fiction—in the dime novels, in the pulps, and then in comics—later in the century would temporarily halt the production of superpowered villains. The majority of heroes in serial heroic fiction were human rather than superhuman, and the authors of their stories made their opponents similarly human, whether from editorial dictate or consumer expectation. The dime novel supermen generally (with a few notable exceptions, like Dr. Quartz) faced evil humans, not evil super-men, and this trend extended to the pulp heroes and then the superheroes of the first phase of comics' Golden Age. Doc Savage, The Shadow, The Spider—their opponents were colorful and varied, but generally mortal, and it took many years for the average superhero's opponent to regularly be superpowered and more powerful than the hero him- or herself. Power creep—the tendency in writers to make every villain more superhumanly powered than the hero, then to gradually power up the hero, and then to make the villains even more powerful—was a product of the modern era, not the 19th century, the pulp era, or comics' Golden Age.

The Gray Champion

As described in Chapter 4, Nathaniel Hawthorne's "The Gray Cham-pion" (1835) is about the appearance of a Costumed Avenger in Boston in 1689 and his dispersal of a group of inimical British troops. As men-tioned, the titular character is the first American superhuman superhero, the first character to combine the Costumed Avenger and the Über-mensch, if not the dual-identity aspect of the dual-identity costumed vigi-lante character.

The Gray Champion was not widely imitated; there was no flood of costumed superhumans appearing in print after 1835. In one respect, he appeared in isolation and is more of a secluded harbinger of what was to become common in the 20th century than he was the direct grandfather of costumed superhumans. Coogan considers him the "starting point" for the "dual-identity avenger vigilante" character type,[7] and Gavaler describes him as "America's first superhero."[8] True to a very limited degree (although, again, the Gray Champion has no alternate identity and so can't be described as a "dual-identity" character),[9] but given the lack of direct communication of the concept from the Gray Champion to succes-sors, the Gray Champion is more akin to the aforementioned Tom Rich-mond, detective hero of *Richmond: Scenes in the Life of a Bow Street Runner.* Had Tom Richmond been noticed, and imitated, he would be seen in the same light as Poe's Chevalier Dupin, as one of the founding fathers of detective fiction. But *Richmond* was not imitated, was not influential, and was quickly forgotten. It appeared in isolation and then disappeared the same way, only being noticed more than a century later. So too with the Gray Champion and the concept of the costumed superhuman vigilante, the Costumed Avenger Übermensch.

What I would argue, though, is that the Gray Champion helped trans-mit the concept of the superhumanly powered hero, absent the costume (and his Puritan outfit counts as a kind of costume). Hawthorne's popularity after his death ensured that *Twice-Told Tales*, the short story collection that contains "The Gray Champion," was widely in print in the 1860s and early 1870s. "The Gray Champion" is the first story in the collection, and was widely read and held up as one of Hawthorne's best stories at this time—which not coincidentally is when the superhumanly powered dime novel detectives were coming into being, in the person of Old Sleuth. This chapter argues that the *idea* of superpowers was common in the 19th century, in various forms and in various character types. It does not require a particularly strenuous leap of logic to suppose that Harlan Halsey—who as a former director of the Brooklyn Education Board would have been well aware of the reading lists for students—had the example of the Gray Champion somewhere in the back of his mind when creating Old Sleuth.

At a greater chronological remove, The Gray Champion could still have been influencing writers of superhumans in the 1930s. Hawthorne's *Twice-Told Tales* remained required reading for high school seniors in many states in the 1930s, and the writer and anthologist Edward O'Brien included "The Gray Champion" in his *Short Story Case Book* (1935), an anthology of short stories meant for the use of high school students in literary analysis—students who would in a few years be graduating from high school and writing comics. Harlan Halsey may well have had the Gray Champion in mind in creating Old Sleuth; so, too, the many creators of superheroes during the Golden Age.

Artificial Beings

Golems, as mentioned in Chapter 3, were already in the educated public's mind as a concept by the 19th century, but authors began adding to this concept, and that of the robot/android/automata, during the Victorian era and giving them a protosuperheroic gloss.

Jane Loudon's *The Mummy! A Tale of the Twenty-Second Century* (1827), an early work of feminist science fiction heavily influenced by both *Frankenstein* and the Gothics, is set in the future, as the title indicates. In this future "automaton judges and lawyers who are operated by clockwork"[10] maintain the justice system. No clockwork policemen are mentioned (though automaton prison guards are shown), but their presence is inevitable, given the automata who make up the rest of the justice system. Coming at a time when the public's conception of what law enforcement was changing—as noted previously, the Metropolitan Police Act of 1829 established the Metropolitan Police in London, replacing the previously

shambolic system of constables and watchmen with a professional, organized force—Webb's clockwork justice system was a logical conception
and anticipation, even if clockwork or artificial heroes were not a part of
The Mummy! and, despite changes in how society viewed automata,[11] did
not make their way into heroic fiction for decades.

A particular version of the golem story was beginning to appear in
print at this time. This version, centered on Prague and events familiar to
and of specific relevance to German-speaking Jews, involved Rabbi Löw
creating a golem to carry water and help with other household chores, but
the Rabbi had to interrupt the Friday evening ritual to destroy the golem
but was neither harmed nor killed by the golem. The first written mention
of the Prague golem appeared in 1834, in Ludwig Philippson's "Der Golem
und die Ehebrecherin." Of note is the fact that before destruction, the
golem functions in a mystery-solving and vigilante role: "whereas the
poem's Jewish community responds with religious lamentations to a fatal
epidemic among the ghetto's children, Löw's golem is sent out to find the
source of this misfortune, an adulterous woman."[12]

In Ludwig Tieck's "Die Vogelscheuche" (1835) a leather scarecrow is
animated and given human flesh (though it remains a scarecrow) by an
elf-comet. The scarecrow is possessed by the philosophy of the Aufklärung
(the Enlightenment) and begins solving mysteries with the aid of his "second sight," defends bourgeois values by establishing an Illuminati-like
secret society, and eventually marries the daughter of his maker, all the
while proclaiming that he remains an artificial being. Tieck's work was
widely available and read in Great Britain and the United States, and the
idea of the artificial being as vigilante may have been given momentum
specifically by "Die Vogelscheuche."

The story of the golem continued to make its way through Eastern
European Jewish communities, but new ideas, inspired by the Enlightenment and a growing Jewish awareness of the need for self-defense, were
being added to the story. In the collection of Hebrew legends, *Die Galerie
des Sippurim* (1846):

> The role of the Golem is reversed, and related very closely to the Jewish
> problem. According to the new tradition, the Mah'Aral created the Golem
> during the anti-Jewish pogroms to defend Jews against accusations of rit-
> ual murder that were being brought against them. The Golem plays the
> role of hero and protector of the ghetto, of saviour and Messiah even, and,
> as such, it can perform miracles.[13]

This protosuperheroic version of the golem was further propagated and
made familiar to English audiences in Friedrich Hebbel's libretto for
Anton Rubinstein's musical drama, *Ein Steinwurf* (1858).

In 1884, the pseudonymous "Don Quichotte" wrote "The Artificial Man. A Semi-Scientific Story," in which the narrator meets a man

> who claims to be an artificial human being. He was reared, he says, in a bell jar and is nourished by chemicals inserted into his stomach, which contains the gastric juices of a calf. To prove his claim the stranger lifts off the top of his head and removes his brain . . . the artificial man contends that he is the man of the future, who will take the place of present-day man; but he, in turn, will be supplanted by more vigorous types. Evolution thus moves in a perpetual cycle.[14]

Quichotte's Artificial Man is an entirely passive observer and recounter of his story, but the implication is clear, that a new generation of artificial men will soon arrive, and among them will be vigilantes.

In 1888, Arthur Machen's *The Chronicle of Clemendy* appeared, containing the story "How the Folk of Abergavenny Were Pestered by an Accursed Knight." In the story, a Freemason's mark, deliberately placed on a clockwork knight, gives the knight—known to the townsfolk of Abergavenny as "Sir Jenkin Thomas"—life. Sir Jenkin chooses to leave his post on the town's clock tower and hunt down local wrongdoers, miscreants, and adulterous monks. He is caught, tried for witchcraft, and burned, of course, but before he dies he has provided the townfolk of Abergavenny, and the readers, with an example of an artificial being vigilante, similar to Virgil's "brazen horseman" but with agency.

By the 1890s, the golem story, in the hands of Eastern European writers, was gaining international fame as a symbol of a self-recognized need of the Jews for protection—the golem was now an official vigilante and warrior. In Yitshok Leyb Peretz's "The Golem" (1893), Rabbi Löw

> creates the golem to face an impending attack on the Prague ghetto. Three days later, the city is filled with corpses as the golem indiscriminately slaughters all Gentiles, and soon there will be no non-Jew left to light the fire and extinguish the lamps on the Sabbath. Thus Löw lays the golem to rest, and to this day it lies in the attic of the synagogue, waiting to be awakened.[15]

Eight years later, in 1901, Sholem Aleichem's "Der Golem" was published, wherein the golem plays a similar role:

> Upon hearing of a new anti-Jewish decree threatening more bloodshed in the ghetto, Aleichem's Rabbi Löw decides to make a golem. He sends the caretaker of the synagogue to fetch clay, forms a crude figure from it, and animates it with an amulet. The golem positions itself at the bridge outside

the ghetto and throws those Gentiles with evil intentions toward the Jews into the Moldau River, which is soon heaving with corpses.[16]

These two stories are representative of the new Jewish interpretation of the golem, as an automaton with will, agency, and most of all with a killer vigilante attitude. This interpretation, unconsciously imitating that of Spenser's Talus, would color later writers' approaches to how fictional artificial beings would be betrayed.

Rosicrucians and Theosophists

In the early 17th century, a group of European individuals began espousing certain esoteric beliefs through their scientific writings. These individuals, most of whom were moral and religious reformers, later became known as the Rosenkreuzer, or the Society of Rosicrucians, although there is no evidence that they ever met as a group. Their beliefs combined mysticism, alchemy, and the sciences. During the 18th century, various European groups and societies began to claim possession of Rosicrucian secrets and knowledge and/or descent from the Society of Rosicrucians.

Theosophy is a broad set of philosophical and mystic beliefs that became popular in the last quarter of the 19th century, starting in 1875 when Helena Blavatsky and Henry Olcott founded the Theosophical Society. Roughly, Theosophy argues that: God is infinite, unknowable by humans, and the source of all matter and spirit; reincarnation and karma govern spiritual growth; and that all human souls are a part of the universal soul.

These two sets of beliefs, and the legends that grew up around them, were commonly used as the source of occult powers for a variety of characters throughout the 19th century, although for the first 40 years these powers were relegated to the possession of antiheroes and villains.

William Godwin's Gothic novel *St. Leon. A Tale of the Sixteenth Century* (1799) is about Reginald St. Leon, a noble Frenchman, who is shown the secrets of making gold and the elixir of life by a grateful Rosicrucian. Neither brings St. Leon happiness, and eventually St. Leon is forced to become a kind of Wandering Jew figure.

As mentioned in Chapter 3, the Old Man of Fronteja, from Christian Vulpius's *Rinaldo Rinaldini, der Räuberhauptmann* (1799–1801), is a super-powered sorcerer, whose "theosophist" and Rosicrucian training "unveiled the secrets of the Egyptians" and gave him various mystical abilities, including the power to summon visions of the future. The idea of sorcery was common to the Gothics and the *räuberromans*, but not so common was the Theosophical and Rosicrucian source for it.

Percy Shelley's *St. Irvyne: or, The Rosicrucian* (1811) has as its central figure "a colossal and enigmatic figure with an air of the fallen archangel about him. His inordinate curiosity and Rosicrucian affiliations have led him to possess the secret formula of ever-lasting life but such knowledge has failed to yield eternal bliss and power."[17]

In Honoré de Balzac's Gothic novel *Le Centenaire, ou les Deux Beringheld* (1822), a Napoleonic general encounters a 400-year-old man, the Centenarian who learned from the Rosicrucians the secret of eternal life as well as various other superhuman powers, which unfortunately derive from draining the life essence from other people. The Centenarian is a kind of Wandering Jew character, but with superhuman abilities, driven to right wrongs, save the good, and kill the wicked, but at the cost of various human lives drained.

But the real leap in the use of Theosophy and Rosicrucianism began when Lord Bulwer-Lytton wrote *Zanoni* (1842), an occult love story that incorporates mysticism, occult fantasy, and horror. *Zanoni* is the first major British work of occult fantasy in the 19th century and the novel that, along with Bulwer-Lytton's *A Strange Story*, helped establish the genre of occult fantasy in the English language. *Zanoni* features the titular Chaldean sorcerer, who gained immortality and other magical powers through the writings of the Rosicrucians, and tries to use his powers to protect his wife and child from the plague and the French Revolution. Bulwer-Lytton would return to the Rosicrucian sorcerer character type in "The Haunted and the Haunters" (1859), one of the landmark haunted house stories of the 19th century, and in *A Strange Story* (1861–1862), which with *Zanoni* made the occult fantasy genre into a definite literary type for writers and readers. Bulwer-Lytton, a groundbreaker here as elsewhere,[18] began the process of making the Rosicrucian/theosophist sorcerer a hero, skipping past the entire tradition of Faust and the ambiguous sorcerer to show a more heroic magician. At the same time, in the character of Zanoni Bulwer-Lytton created the iconic sorcerer who dooms themselves by making use of powers beyond human understanding.

Heavily influenced by Bulwer-Lytton was Rosa Praed. In her *The Brother of the Shadow* (1886), two dueling theosophist sorcerers fight for the soul of a woman. *The Brother of the Shadow* is one of the earliest works to feature what would become a reliable cliché in 20th century science fiction and occult fantasy: the hidden masters of Tibet/India/Central Asia, whose secret knowledge and superhuman psychic/mystic abilities are far beyond those of mortal men. The hidden masters labor to bring enlightenment to the world as well as defeat the evil forces that plague humanity, especially the hidden masters' corrupt but powerful opposites. This is a basic tenet of Theosophy, and via Theosophy this notion influenced a large number of genre writers, who put the cliché of the hidden masters (often called things like "The Nine Unknown" or "The White Lodge") in their fiction.

William Oliver Greener's *Rufin's Legacy: A Theosophical Romance* (1892) features another Theosophical sorcerer, this one a freelance agent for the Russian secret police. And Emeric Hulme-Beaman's *Ozmar the Mystic* (1896) and *The Prince's Diamond* (1898) ends the century and the Victorian era with a Theosophist Übermensch detective, who uses his various mental abilities, including telepathy and teleportation, to help others and to solve crimes, in what are standard adventure novels except for the fact that Ozmar has a suite of mental powers and uses them as, in effect, a vigilante.

Rosicrucians and theosophists would still appear as supermen heroes in the 20th century—Hereward Carrington's Dr. Payson Alden from 1916 is a notable one—but the increasing antipathy with which both groups were held during the 1920s and 1930s by mainstream opinion makers[19] meant that the influential (on popular culture) elements of Rosicrucian and Theosophical thought had to be taken out of their original context and independently presented. As mentioned, the idea of hidden masters in Tibet with advanced wisdom and technology was a basic tenet of Theosophy, but when it became incorporated into the pulps in the 1920s and the comics in the 1930s and 1940s the rest of Theosophy's teachings were nowhere to be found, and the hidden Tibetan masters (when they were given dialogue at all) were carefully written to be generic rather than Theosophical.

Dime Novel Supermen

The first break from the century's tendency toward making supermen into outsiders, whether monsters, villains, or adherents of unusual faiths like Rosicrucianism or Theosophy, took place in America, not Great Britain. As mentioned in Chapter 4, the American dime novel developed out of the American "novelette" but was heavily influenced by the British casebook novel, with Harlan Halsey's Old Sleuth, who debuted in 1872, being a groundbreaking character in American series literature but significantly modeled on the British casebook detectives.

As mentioned, Old Sleuth was the first recurring, serialized dime novel detective and was sufficiently popular that for a generation the phrase "Old Sleuth" was identified with fictional detectives. In many ways he established the stereotype that would prevail for the next 14 years, until Nick Carter made his debut. And Old Sleuth was an Übermensch, possessed of superstrength, "able to throw grown men around like pillows."[20] The cause of these superpowers is never addressed, although it is implied that Old Sleuth's moral superiority—he neither smokes nor drinks nor ever entertains unchivalrous thoughts about women—have something to do with it.

Old Sleuth as serialized detective hero was an idea taken from the casebook novels. Old Sleuth as an Übermensch hero—not a monster, not a villain, not a sorcerer, not even an outsider of any kind, Old Sleuth is a member of the upper classes, and in the Victorian fashion his being a detective did not make him into an outsider[21]—may have been taken from Hawthorne's "The Gray Champion" or from farther back, from the Book of Judges and the story of Samson.

Whatever the source of his superpowers, Old Sleuth was popular enough to inspire imitators. The first major, successful one was William I. James's Old Cap. Collier, who appeared in at least 34 stories between 1883 and 1898. A New York City detective like Old Sleuth, albeit a young man dressing up like an old man (unlike the actually elderly Old Sleuth), Old Cap. Collier was portrayed on covers to resemble Old Sleuth. Collier is similarly a master of disguise and is extraordinarily strong, capable of holding a burly thug over his head with one hand and of throwing men 30 feet with ease. Unlike Old Sleuth, however, Old Cap. Collier smokes and drinks and gambles, and no Galahad-like purity is responsible for Collier's superstrength.

Two years later, Francis Doughty created Old King Brady, who appeared in around 830 stories in four magazines from 1885 to 1912. Doughty, a successful dime novelist, used the rough outlines of previous dime novel detectives, but made an effort to make Brady unique:

> Old King Brady does no theorizing from slender clews. He wields no magnifying glass. False whiskers seldom disguise his strong features. He is a poor shot, and cannot even swim. He proceeds in a common way, just as a real detective would, with plenty of leg work, a bit of good old Irish luck, and a liberal use of stool-pigeons. When captured by the villains, and in dire peril of his life, he does not defy the scoundrels in high sounding dime novel dialogue. Indeed, he begs for his life, often in pretty abject terms, too.[22]

Although Doughty emphasizes that Brady is only human, and accomplishes things thanks to legwork and common sense and ordinary detective work, Brady is an Übermensch nonetheless, equipped with a "mystic" or "intuitive" gift, supposedly a part of his Irish heritage, which he finds highly useful in solving crimes.

Up through 1886, Old Sleuth had been the archetypal dime novel detective, but the arrival of Nick Carter changed all that. I described in Chapter 4 Carter's long-term effect on dime novel detectives and pulp characters and superheroes, but it deserves emphasizing that Carter was not only a Man of Extraordinary Capabilities, and a hidden master of his city, but also an Übermensch. "Giants were like children in his grasp. He could fell an ox with one blow of his small, compact fist . . . he could lift a horse with ease . . . while a heavy man is seated in the saddle . . . he can place four packs of playing cards together, and tear them in halves between his thumbs and fingers."[23]

This ability was initially explained as arising from the intense training that Carter's father, Old Sim Carter, put Carter through during his childhood; later, Carter's friendship with Eugen Sandow adds to the explanation for Carter's superstrength.

As was usually the case with dime novel and pulp supermen—the Shadow and Doc Savage are two prominent examples of this—the later stories in the Nick Carter corpus underplayed Carter's superstrength, so that by the 1940s Carter is a purely human private detective. But for at least 30 years, well into the pulp era, Carter remained an Übermensch, and an influential example for other characters to imitate.[24]

Psychic Heroes

Interest in investigating what we would now call psychic issues began developing in the early 19th century; more relevantly, *methods* for communicating investigations of psychic issues and occurrences began developing, with literary and philosophical societies being founded whose purpose was to communicate recent scientific discoveries to the middle class, which fed the general hunger for scientific information. Independently wealthy gentlemen and gentlewomen began working as scientists, in a variety of fields. One such was Samuel Hibbert, whose work in geology became secondary to his *Sketches of the Philosophy of Apparitions, or, an Attempt to Trace Such Illusions to Their Physical Causes* (1824), a landmark work of parapsychological investigation into ghost apparitions, visions, near-death experiences, and other psychic occurrences. Widely read in its day, it earned a response 23 years later from Catharine Crowe, whose *The Night Side of Nature* (1848), a collection of ghost and poltergeist experiences, was designed as a rebuke to Hibbert, who Crowe felt was too skeptical. *The Night Side of Nature* was reprinted numerous times in the late 1840s and 1850s and helped to foster an interest and belief in the reality of psychic occurrences and abilities—a belief that was generated by a middle class with time on its hands, a growing interest in science, and an understandable interest in fates of the too-soon-departed.

As the concept of occult powers and magic in the hands of a protagonist became more common, via Bulwer-Lytton and the occult fantasy novels, so too did the idea of psychic powers.[25] By 1882, when the Society of Psychical Research was founded in London, psychic powers were just one of the suite of abilities a protagonist or antagonist could be expected to wield. Occasionally they were used as a plot device by an author in need of a plot shortcut, as in Villiers de l'Isle Adam's *L'Ève Future* (1883), or to make a point about humanity's evolutionary end point, as in Louis Boussenard's *Dix Mille Ans dans un Bloc de Glace* (1889). Sometimes they were used to emphasize the alienness of a character, whether literally, as in Reverend Wladyslaw Lach-Szyrma's "Aleriel" stories (1860s–1893) and in Ritson and Stanley Stewart's *The Professor's Last Experiment* (1888), or figuratively and racially, as with the Tibetan Agarthans of Joseph Alexandre Saint-Yves's *Mission de l'Inde en Europe, Mission de l'Europe en Asie* (1885).

But more often they became part of the heroic toolbox. In Edward Heron-Allen and Selina Delaro's *The Princess Daphne* (1888), the doomed hero Paul du Peyral wields mesmerism and psychic projection in an effort to prove that mesmerism works, and later to bolster his lover's failing health. In George Griffith's *The Angel of the Revolution* (1893), the heroic rebel Natas uses his psychic mesmerism to aid the rise in power of his anarchist organization, Terror.[26] Most significantly, in Alexander Reynolds's "The Mystery of Djara Singh" (1897) a police chief hires a professional "spiritualist" to psychically spy on and apprehend a Tibetan thief who used his psychic ability to steal large amounts of money from various New York City banks. (The resulting psychic duel ends badly for the spiritualist.) "The Mystery of Djara Singh" anticipates the psychic detective/occult detective genre of stories—the Prichards' "Flaxman Low" stories did not make their debut until the following January, and the first psychically powered occult detective, Algernon Blackwood's Doctor Silence, would not appear until 1908—and presented readers and writers with an action hero whose abilities were psychic, not physical.

Interestingly, while psychic abilities became a part of the heroic toolbox in the 1880s and 1890s, and became a basic aspect of 20th century occult detectives, psychic abilities were generally avoided by later writers of ordinary pulp heroes and were rarely used during the Golden Age as an explanation for a superhero's superhuman abilities.[27] Psychic topics were of great interest to many people in the 1920s, but at the same time men like Harry Houdini famously spent their time debunking supposed psychics and spiritualists, so that by the 1930s psychic topics had become disreputable and not suitable as a source for a clean-cut hero's powers.

Science Fiction Supermen

Late in the century, the new genre of science fiction began presenting superhumans as heroes to readers. While critics usually trace the beginning of the genre of science fiction to Mary Shelley's *Frankenstein* in 1818, the genre didn't cohere until much later. Science fiction stories and novels were written consistently from 1832 on; science fiction was given a variety of descriptive labels in the 1840s, 1850s, and 1860s, and a general consciousness that science fiction was a distinct, separate genre of fiction had developed during these decades. But it was not until 1871, with the dual publication of Lord Bulwer-Lytton's *The Coming Race* and George Chesney's "The Battle of Dorking," that science fiction, as a marketing genre in America and Great Britain, developed.

In *The Coming Race* the narrator discovers a subterranean civilization of biologically and technologically advanced beings, the "Ana" or "Vril-ya." Their civilization is a Utopia, and they are generally peaceful, but on a few occasions they use violence, including hunting down atavistic subterranean monsters and even warring on other expansionist underground cultures and races. The Vril-ya take their name from the "vril," a "unity in natural energetic agencies," an all-purpose electric-magnetic-galvanic energy that is capable of destroying almost anything but that the Vril-ya can control and use to power their civilization. The narrator of *The Coming Race* falls in love with one of the Vril-ya, but the Vril-ya cannot tolerate the idea of their civilization being sullied by one of their own marrying a lesser being, and ultimately the narrator is forced to flee back to the surface world.

The Coming Race is "an ideal society written with several purposes: demonstrating the sterility of perfection, the possible achievements of future science, the implications of social trends in Western civilization, and, as secondary matters, satire on Darwinism and American democracy."[28]

The *point* of *The Coming Race* is, as Bleiler says, to satirize some of the conclusions of Darwinism and evolution; but the *means* used are the creation of a race of supermen and superwomen (with the Vril-ya women actually being the superior of the Vril-ya men), and the Vril-ya are taken quite seriously and not satirically, both by the narrator of *The Coming Race* and by Bulwer-Lytton himself. Sir Francis Galton hadn't coined the word "eugenics" yet—he didn't do so until 1883—but Bulwer-Lytton incorporated the theme of eugenics into *The Coming Race*, and produced the

Vril-ya, who are longer lived and physically and intellectually superior to humanity.

The Coming Race, along with Chesney's "The Battle of Dorking," caused quite a stir among readers, writers, and publishers, with similar works of what is now known as "science fiction" appearing in the United States and Great Britain. The rise in production of Anglophone science fiction led to a shift in emphasis. Science fiction went from something predominantly European—more works of science fiction were produced in France from 1860 to April 30, 1871, than in the United States and the United Kingdom combined—to something dominated by Anglophones, both writers and audience. (The number of English-language translations of European works of science fiction roughly quadrupled from 1870 to 1880.) The increased output led to an increase in coverage by reviewers, but also by critics. Jules Verne gave the genre of science fiction critical respectability later in the 1870s with his "Voyages Extraordinaires" novels but it was Bulwer-Lytton who did it earlier in the decade. *The Coming Race* was initially published anonymously, but its true author was widely known, and Bulwer-Lytton's status as one of the most esteemed novelists of the time lent science fiction a respectability among critics it had not previously possessed.

This effect was felt in the United States, where the production of science fiction increased. One of these novels was Edward Payson Jackson's *A Demigod. A Novel* (1886). Published at roughly the same time as Nick Carter's debut, the protagonist of *A Demigod*, Hector Vyr, is a Carteresque Übermensch. The product of a eugenics program that began in the 17th century, Vyr is "evolved from ordinary humanity by a long-continued program of artificial selection, aided by auspicious fortune . . . Vyr is incredibly handsome, unbelievably powerful, a genius mentally, and with reflexes so fast that he can seemingly dodge bullets. He is also the soul of honor."[29]

In *A Demigod* Vyr rescues two kidnapped Americans in Greece, falls in love with one of them, and after various plot complications marries her. *A Demigod* was published to critical acclaim and popular success, being reprinted at least twice and selling well both in the United States and in England, and it is not out of the realm of possibility that Ormond Smith and John Russell Coryell, the creators of Nick Carter, were influenced by the portrayal of Vyr in *A Demigod*, or that *A Demigod*, as a science fiction best seller of the day, had a longer-term effect on other writers and readers than we would today suppose, given the obscurity into which *A Demigod* has currently fallen.[30]

Two years later, in Great Britain, another novel, Joseph Nicholson's *Thoth. A Romance*, appeared. *Thoth* is a Lost Race novel involving a high-tech Egyptian city-state, founded around 2500 BCE by Thoth the First, and how in 435 BCE an Athenian woman brings about its downfall. "One of the major science-fiction novels of the nineteenth century,"[31] *Thoth* has, among many other things, genetic engineering and eugenics as its themes, with the result, the inhabitants of Thoth's city, being physically superior superhumans thanks to a program of selective breeding. *Thoth* was influenced by *The Coming Race* rather than *A Demigod*, but the end result was the same: the fictional presentation of a race of supermen. Like *A Demigod*, *Thoth* was popular in both the United States and Great Britain, running to four editions and being reprinted in Germany in 1913 and 1920,[32] and helped contribute—indirectly, to the Zeitgeist, if not directly, to authors—to the popularity of the concept of the race of supermen.

The trend toward science fiction authors making use of supermen during the late Victorian era culminated in the titular character of Luther Marshall's *Thomas Boobig* (1895):

> An sf novel depicting—perhaps for the first time—a genuine Superman, the eponymous Boobig who is born of natural size but soon grows into a mental and physical giant . . . his great good temper seems to ensure that his influence on his native California as a Paul Bunyan–like entrepreneur are beneficial; but he disappears into a bottomless cavern.[33]

Thomas Boobig was not a best seller in the United States, nor even particularly well known following publication, so no argument of its influence can be made. But its titular Übermensch is typical of the supermen trend in science fiction and presages the flood of science fiction supermen to come in the 20th century. Moreover, *Thomas Boobig* for the first time portrays a modern Übermensch who turns his superhuman abilities toward doing good. Boobig's motives are selfless, and his superhuman abilities are turned toward helping others rather than benefiting himself. Boobig has no costume and fights no crime, but, in other respects, especially his selfless motivation, he counts as a protosuperhero and ends up in the middle part of the superheroic spectrum. Had more notice been taken of him, the science fiction heroes who followed him might have been quite different.

Conclusion

Compared to the Costumed Avengers of the Victorian era, the supermen and superwomen of 1830–1901 were scattered and disunified. The direct lines of descent of concepts and characters that can be seen in Chapter 4 were mostly missing when it came to supermen and super-women, whose creations seem mostly to have occurred in isolation rather than as a direct result of what came before. Nonetheless, the comic book superheroes of the 20th century owe much to the supermen and super-women of the 19th century, for numerous concepts that became common in the 20th century had their beginnings in the 19th.

CHAPTER SIX

Costumed Avengers, 1901–1938

Through the Victorian era and the first 38 years of the 20th century protosuperheroes fell into one of two categories: the Costumed Avenger, and the Übermensch. The Costumed Avenger was the more distinctive of the two types and the better developed by 1901, and to outside observers the best-known protosuperheroes of the 1901–1938 years are Costumed Avengers, giving rise to the idea that there was a more or less direct line of influence from the Scarlet Pimpernel to Zorro to Batman.

But the truth is more complicated. Not only were there multiple influences on the comic book Costumed Avengers, but the Costumed Avengers of the 1901–1938 years—what I'm calling "the pulp era"—manifested themselves in some unusual places, with unusual consequences.

The Carter Effect

As mentioned in Chapter 4, Nick Carter's influence was considerable, extending beyond dime novels and pulps into superhero comics themselves. The tropes and dynamics described in Chapter 4 implanted themselves into serial heroic fiction and stayed there. This was especially true during the last five years of the 19th century and the first 15 years of the 20th century, the Golden Age of the Nick Carter stories, the time when Frederick van Rensselaer Dey was writing the great majority of the Nick Carter stories and when the stories had the most variety of imaginative concepts and characters, and when the Carter continuity most fully developed.[1]

Carter's effect was as Übermensch, Man of Extraordinary Capabilities, and Costumed Avenger. Carter did not wear a costume, as such, although he regularly used a limited set of alternate identities who always wore the same outfits. But Carter's attire, as portrayed on the covers of the many dime novels in which he appeared, was unvarying: Always the same style of suit coat and pants, always the same high-necked shirt and dark tie. This outfit became Carter's trademark, the one by which he could always be recognized—in other words, a suit as a costume. This visual brand spread to other dime novel detectives, who appeared on the covers of their dime novels similarly attired. Carter, in other words, created a "look," one that was widely imitated for a generation.

Carter, of course, was imitated in more than just visuals. Carter was the second-most imitated fictional hero internationally during his Golden Age, after Sherlock Holmes, and numerous American and international characters took their conceptual as well as visual cues from Carter. Typical of these imitations was Frederick W. Davis's Felix Boyd, who appeared from 1904 to 1908. Boyd is a New York City private detective, in manner modeled on Sherlock Holmes, but in approach to detection most influenced by Nick Carter. Boyd carries two revolvers and shows no compunctions about using them, and his enemies—street-level thugs, vicious murderers, and amoral blackmailers—are closer to Carter's than Holmes's. Boyd's Moriarty is the Big Finger, an "obscure genius of crime . . . a man of power, of vast criminal resources, a man to be feared, and a man whose misdirected genius one cannot but respect."[2] Boyd pursues the Finger and clashes with him for 24 stories before finally defeating him. After breaking up the Big Finger's operations Boyd begins roaming across New York City, solving crimes and fighting criminals both domestic and international.

Boyd, in particular, is notable because his 48 magazine appearances were in *The Popular Magazine*, a solidly middle-of-the-road, middle-class pulp magazine (as opposed to the less respectable dime novels that were Carter's main venue), and because five collections of Felix Boyd short stories were published bound together, as books—again, a more respectable format than Carter's dime novels. The comic books largely took their cues from the pulps, and the pulps, until 1919, took their cues from both the dime novels and book publishing—and the pulp detectives took their cues from Nick Carter. To a surprisingly large degree the Costumed Avenger detectives of the first 15 years of the pulp era were living in the shadow of Nick Carter and openly aping him.

Immigrants and Foreign Influences

Superheroes are for the most part an American invention, even if their roots lie abroad. Some of these immigrant roots, some of these foreign influences on the superhero, are not particularly old and can be found in the 20th century, not the 19th.

American popular culture has never been purely American, of course. American authors and publishers have long been influenced to varying degrees by foreign concepts and authors and texts. But in the late 19th and early 20th centuries the Atlantic Ocean became a particularly porous border, as foreign influences flooded the United States.

In series hero publishing, the most famous example—the most overt example—took place in 1906, when the demand for Nick Carter and Sexton Blake stories was so fierce that Street & Smith, the publisher of Nick Carter, came to an agreement with Amalgamated Press, the British owners of Sexton Blake: each company would allow the other to rewrite the stories of their most popular hero. This led to duplicated stories and the occasional bleed over from one corpus of stories to another, as when, in 1906, Nick acquired a Cuban bloodhound named Pedro, just like Blake's bloodhound.

For a number of years Carter and Blake developed in parallel, influencing each other, before Blake ultimately pulled away and became his own (internationally famous and influential) character.[3] Carter's influence, as I have argued, is significant; a part of that is due to Sexton Blake and his authors.

At times, the influences were primarily directed outwardly from America. Eugène Villiod (?–?), head of a French private detective agency and author of several books on true crime and criminology, asked the artist and graphic designer Leonetto Cappiello in 1913 to design an ad for the Villiod detective agency. Cappiello responded by drawing a masked and caped sleuth in the American style,[4] an image that Villiod would use in advertisements for over a decade and that would be the cover image for the anonymously written French pulp *Mémoires de Villiod, Détective Privé* (1921), which (greatly) fictionalized Villiod's exploits. Cappiello's image in turn became influential on French images of fictional and real private detectives—a case where art influenced life, which was then further imitated by both art and life, a series of influences and imitations that began with the American Costumed Avenger.

At other times, the influences were from abroad, with American creators taking inspiration from foreign texts. The prime example of this took place in 1904. Spring-Heeled Jack had appeared as a hero in various British texts through the latter half of the 19th century,[5] but in 1904, British publisher Aldine Publishing Company took the next step. Aldine had begun in 1887 by publishing abridged reprints of American dime novels, but in 1901 they "embarked on a programme of 'libraries,' resuscitating British outlaws and highwaymen popular half a century before."[6] As part of this program of new story papers, Aldine published *The Spring-Heeled Jack Library* in 1904. Written by Alfred S. Burrage, *The Spring-Heeled Jack Library* is set in 1803, after Napoleon has conquered Europe. It begins with Bertram Wraydon, a lieutenant in the British Army and the handsome young heir to £10,000 a year, who is framed for treason by his evil half brother Hubert Sedgefield. Before he can be executed, Wraydon escapes and sets out to avenge himself by the expedient of dressing up in a costume and terrorizing Sedgefield and his lackeys. Wraydon establishes a secret headquarters, a crypt in a graveyard, and uses that as his base. In costume, Wraydon looks like this: "It was that of a man wearing a tight fitting tunic, slashed in front with white, as though his ribs were laid bare. But whoever dreamed of a man taking such leaps, or looked up such eyes as gleamed from the demoniacal head upon which sat a tight fitting cap surmounted with a feather."[7]

Wraydon goes on to fight Napoleon's agents, but the series ends before Wraydon can reclaim his inheritance and properly punish his half brother. As Spring-Heeled Jack, Wraydon can leap 30 feet or more into the air and his touch delivers electric shocks. When he kills a man he carves an "S" into the victim's forehead. In combat, he carries pistols in both hands.

Crucially, Aldine briefly succeeded in getting an American distributor for *The Spring-Heeled Jack Library* before the firm ran into financial difficulties in 1906.

The Burrage Spring-Heeled Jack was not, contra Coogan, "the first dual-identity crime-fighter in the English language"[8]; Count Rosalvo, in the very popular 1805 English translation of Zschokke's *Abällino*, got there first. Nor is the Burrage Spring-Heeled Jack the first urban crime fighter; Long Meg and Moll Cutpurse were doing that 250 years before, and on a more general crime-fighting mission than the Burrage Spring-Heeled Jack, who is primarily focused on his half brother, his half brother's lackeys, and on the agents of Napoleon. But the Burrage Spring-Heeled Jack is the first character published in the modern era to incorporate the dual identities, the costume, the secret headquarters, and the selfless mission. Moreover, the Burrage Spring-Heeled Jack had superpowers, making him one of the first dual-identity Costumed Avenger supermen. And thanks to the American distribution of *The Spring-Heeled Jack Library* American readers and writers got to read and be influenced by him.

The Lupins

The heroic highwaymen of the 17th and first half of 18th centuries gave way to the gentlemen thieves of the second half of the 18th century and the 19th century, in both real life and in fiction.

The gentleman thief is the man of society, of good breeding and good manners, who enriches himself, or simply earns his daily wage, through crime, all while carrying himself in a high style and dressing in the most au courant fashion. The most influential of the historical 18th-century gentlemen thieves was George Barrington (1755–1804). He was taught how to pickpocket by his theatrical mentor in Ireland, and only avoided arrest in 1773 by moving to England, where he took up thieving in the theater foyers and pleasure gardens of London. Barrington worked alone and in disguise, and for almost 14 years had a successful and profitable criminal career. Many of his thefts became famous, but the most notorious was his pickpocketing of the diamond snuffbox of Russian Prince Orloff in Covent Garden in 1775. During this time period Barrington was arrested 14 times, but his eloquence and gentlemanly carriage so impressed the courts that he was forced to serve only three short prison terms. Barrington became a favorite of the press, who called him "the Prince of Pickpockets." Unfortunately, press coverage of Barrington, including court transcripts and accurate engravings of his face, made him too familiar to his intended victims, and his career as a successful thief was over by 1790. Before his death, however, Barrington's portrait was painted by Sir William Beechey, his caricature appeared on a commercially produced mug, and at the turn of the 19th century he was, in popular songs, melodramas, and fiction, the archetypal gentleman thief.

By the end of the 19th century the most successful professional criminals acted like their 17th and 18th century counterparts had, living as flamboyantly and expensively as any of the *haut ton*. Adam Worth, the model for Doyle's Professor Moriarty . . . had a yacht with a crew of 20 men. "Baron" Maximillian Shinburn, Worth's rival, tried to outdo Worth in everything, including sartorial excellence. Charles Becker, "the king of forgers," lived a genteel life while performing acts of forging brilliance. These men were known as "silk hat and kid glove" criminals because of their lifestyles and those they associated with, and served as the real-life models for the fictional gentlemen thieves of the time.

These fictional gentlemen thieves began with Grant Allen's "Colonel Clay" stories (1896–1897) and Guy Boothby's "Simon Carne" stories (1897–1900), but neither gained a fraction of the fame of E. W. Hornung's A. J. Raffles (1899–1909) or Maurice Leblanc's Arsène Lupin (1905–1939). Though Raffles is the better known of the pair in Anglophone countries, it was Arsène Lupin who created the standard for gentlemen thieves in the 20th century, and it was Lupin who was widely imitated in the popular literature of Europe, Asia, and Central and South America, to the point that the modern archetype deserves to be named after him.

The reason for the inclusion of the Lupins here is that, like Nick Carter, the Lupins had a standard uniform: Raffles with his evening wear, Lupin with his tuxedo, top hat, cape and monocle. Imitators of both used this uniform for their own characters—who, like Raffles and Lupin, and the heroic highwaymen before them, were of often dubious morality but could be relied upon to do the right thing in the end, even if their means for getting there were illegal—as would be the case with the more directly influential Scarlet Pimpernel. The Lupins, and their costumes and justice-over-the-law approach, would influence the early comic book superheroes, even if none of the early superheroes were master thieves. (Raffles did appear in a George Klein–drawn story in Marvel's *All-Winners Comics* #8 [cover date Spring 1942–1943] as a reformed master thief who helps the superhero the Whizzer break two officials out of a locked vault.)

The Scarlet Pimpernel

The Scarlet Pimpernel is an important character in the history of superheroes. Because of the character's fame, he took concepts that had previously been at a lower level of the public's consciousness and thrust them to the forefront. But it is important to delineate what the Pimpernel novels did, and what they did not do.

The Pimpernel was created by the Baroness Emmuska Orczy for the stage, and his initial appearance was in an extremely successful West End play in 1905. Spurred by the success of the play, publishers in Great Britain and the United States rushed to put out Orczy's Pimpernel novel, *The Scarlet Pimpernel* (1905), which was eventually followed by 13 more Pimpernel novels and short story collections through 1940.

The Pimpernel is Sir Percy Blakeney, one of the richest men in England during the years of the French Revolution. Blakeney is a silly, brainless fop, a "nincompoop," an utter twit. He's languid, logorrheic, and a ninny. At least, that's his cover. In the disguise of the Scarlet Pimpernel, Blakeney is a brave, dashing hero who specializes in rescuing the imperiled French aristocrats from their sentences of death-by-guillotine, often from Paris and under the noses and eyes of the French guards.

Sequels to *The Scarlet Pimpernel* followed in 1906, 1908, and 1913, by which time the Pimpernel was a distinct heroic type in popular heroic fiction, and attracting imitators, even far abroad.[9]

But exactly what heroic type the Pimpernel is requires some exploration.

The Pimpernel does not wear a costume, although his consistent use of disguise places him in the Costumed Avenger category. The Pimpernel is not in the dual-identity crime-fighting tradition; Coogan's placement of him in this category[10] is incorrect. The Pimpernel doesn't fight crime. The Pimpernel's specific mission is to rescue French aristocrats from the clutches of the French Revolutionary government and from the guillotine to which they are sentenced. No crime is fought, except in the moral/metaphorical sense. If anything, the Pimpernel is committing an act of war against an immoral foreign government, one to whom his own government is on extremely hostile terms. The Pimpernel is a kind of freelance government agent (he has the tacit support and encouragement of the Prince of Wales) enacting his own government's foreign policy on hostile soil.

Nor is the Pimpernel a modern character. Orczy's novels are historical adventures, rather than set in the modern day. (Orczy created the Pimpernel in 1903, before the publication of Burrage's *The Spring-Heeled Jack Library*, so any question of Burrage's influence on Orczy is moot.) The influence of the Pimpernel and Orczy on superheroes did not extend to creating an enthusiasm for historical heroes. Moreover, the portrayal of the Pimpernel is a nostalgic's view of what Englishness once was, and of the glories of fighting for English imperialism while abroad—neither of which value modern American superheroes have ever embraced.

Nor is the Pimpernel the first hero with a secret identity and the precursor to subsequent literary creations such as Don Diego de la Vega (Zorro) and Bruce Wayne (Batman). This is a common theory, appearing even in the Scarlet Pimpernel's Wikipedia entry. But there were influential heroes with secret identities, like Stevenson's Black Arrow, before Orczy created the Scarlet Pimpernel in 1903 (the year of the Pimpernel's creation; it would be two years before he came to life on stage and in print); the character type of the "hero with a secret identity" was already a well-worn cliché by then. Orczy may have given momentum to the concept through the fame of the Pimpernel, but that was all; the Pimpernel is *a* precursor to Zorro and the Batman, not *the* precursor.

No, the Pimpernel's influence, and what he and Orczy deserve recognition for, is something that has become peculiar to superhero comics. Laura Mulvey famously wrote, in her essay "Visual Pleasure and Narrative Cinema," about the "male gaze," the way that, in film, the camera puts the audience into the perspective of a heterosexual male, and more generally how the visual arts are structured around a masculine viewer: "woman as image, man as bearer of the look."[11] Texts about superheroes and protosuperheroes, whether Costumed Avengers or supermen, tend to have what might be called the "fan's gaze," the structuring of the text so that the focus of the text is on the protosuperheroes, the object of the viewer's—the fan's—gaze, to the exclusion of other characters.[12] Protosuperhero and superhero texts pander to the fan's gaze in the manner in which plots, dialogue, and character arcs are developed; the text becomes about the fan's relationship with the heroic character.

Traditionally, in dual-identity superheroic fiction, the text is structured to focus equally on the alternate identity and on the heroic identity. In Zschokke's *Aballino*, the fan's gaze is turned equally on Count Rosalvo and on the Flodardo/Aballino identities. In *Spring-Heeled Jack Library* as much time is spent on Bertram Wraydon as on Spring-Heeled Jack. In modern comics, writers do their best to direct the fan's gaze to Bruce Wayne and Clark Kent and Tony Stark as much as possible, rather than Batman and Superman and Iron Man. But what Orczy did in the Scarlet Pimpernel texts was to increase the textual importance of the heroic character, and to focus the fan's gaze on him, at the expense of the alternate identity, so that even when the Pimpernel's civilian identity, Percy Blakeney, is on the page or screen, he still lies under the shadow of the Pimpernel, and the fan's gaze remains directed on the Pimpernel.

In essence, Orczy was the first to make the civilian identity of the hero the alternate identity of the hero, and to manipulate the fan's gaze to support this authorial emphasis. The Scarlet Pimpernel is the real identity; Percy Blakeney is just a disguise that the Pimpernel wears when he's not at work. Fans of superheroes will recognize this dynamic as being the source of endless fan and critical arguments: Is Bruce Wayne or the Batman the real character? Is Superman really Superman when he wakes up in the morning, and is Clark Kent just a disguise he puts on to get through the day? Orczy started this dynamic with her shifting of the fan's gaze on to the Pimpernel at the expense of Blakeney, something that had not been the case with earlier dual-identity heroic characters.

The Klan

The Ku Klux Klan, as an organization, had essentially disappeared by 1905, having been broken by government legislation and federal action in 1871. Other organizations with names like the "White Knights" and the "Red Shirts" had taken their place, however, and increased the degree and kind of terror inflicted on African Americans over the next three and a half decades, so that, in 1905 alone, 57 African Americans were lynched in the United States. By 1905, the Southern part of the United States had a decades-long tradition of violent costumed terrorism.

At the same time, however, sociocultural dynamics were working against these Klan-like organizations and those carrying out the lynchings. Reconstruction, despite great resistance, made gains in bettering the positions of African Americans. Notable black Americans ate at the White House (Booker T. Washington, in 1901), published books calling for agitation (W. E. B. Du Bois, *The Souls of Black Folk*, in 1903), and founded black civil rights movements (the Niagara Movement, in 1905). Culturally, Northern whites continued to drive home the point that the South was in the wrong during the Civil War, with plays like Harriet Beecher Stowe's *Uncle Tom's Cabin* touring the United States.

It was a performance of *Uncle Tom's Cabin* that inspired North Carolinian minister and lecturer Thomas F. Dixon Jr. to begin writing. Dixon was horrified at the play's portrayal of Southerners and slavery, and set out to present a counternarrative. His first novel, *The Leopard's Spots* (1902), had Northern carpetbaggers and freed slaves as villains and members of the Ku Klux Klan as heroes. Dixon repeated this with *The Clansmen* (1905), which heightened the villainy of the freed slaves and the heroism of the Klan, who are the only protectors of helpless Southerners. *The Clansmen* was hugely popular both as a play and as a novel—it was the fourth best-selling novel in the United States in 1905—and served as the source for D. W. Griffith's 1915 film *Birth of a Nation*, which led to the rebirth of the Ku Klux Klan.

Dixon's Clansmen were the Costumed Avenger counterparts to Orczy's Scarlet Pimpernel and to Spring-Heeled Jack.

> When hunting for superhero ground zero, many scholars point to Orczy's Scarlet Pimpernel mostly because of McCulley's Zorro imitation, which in turn influenced Finger's Batman . . .
>
> Dixon's 1905 historical novel . . . is a more convincing predecessor. His homicidal Klansmen are the first twentieth-century dual-identity costumed heroes in American lit. Like other superheroes, they keep their alter egos a secret and carry their costumes with them ("easily folded within a blanket and kept under the saddle in a crowd without discovery"). They change "in the woods," the nineteenth-century equivalent of Clark Kent's phone booth ("It required less than two minutes to remove the saddles, place the disguises, and remount"). Their powers, while a product of their numbers and organization, border on the supernatural (their "ghostlike shadowy columns" rode "through the ten townships of the country and successfully disarmed every negro before day without the loss of a life").[13]

And Dixon's Clansmen were twice influential—first in 1905 with Dixon's best-selling book, and then in 1915 with Griffith's best-selling film. The early writers of superhero comics—and indeed most of the writers of Costumed Avengers in the pulps—loathed the Klan, and the Klan in fact was routinely an enemy to be fought in the pulps and in early superhero comics—but the writers were nonetheless influenced by Dixon's and Griffith's Klan portrayal of the Klansmen as dual identity Costumed Avengers.

Films

By 1916, film was a mature medium, with movie stars and star directors, dominant studios, smash hits, go-to formats, and its own set of tropes, motifs, and clichés. Perhaps the most financially successful film format of the time was the film serial (also known as "chapter plays"). And by 1916 costumed characters were beginning to appear in film serials; Louis Feuillade's very successful *Fantômas* was released in the United States that year. Film audiences were ready for their own Costumed Avenger, and screenwriter Charles Goddard and director George Seitz obliged with the film serial *The Iron Claw* (1916), starring the Laughing Mask, a hooded crime fighter who battles the wicked Legar, a.k.a. Iron Claw, an arsonist who likes to set fires with his ray gun. Years before Iron Claw had stolen a young girl, Margery, from her father, Enoch Golden, who had once seared the Iron Claw's face with hot irons and crushed his hand. In the years following Iron Claw taught the girl how to be a criminal. The Laughing Mask succeeds in defeating Iron Claw and saving the girl from a life of crime. The Laughing Mask is eventually revealed to be Enoch himself.

Critically and financially successful, *The Iron Claw* was soon followed by Louis Feuillade and Arthur Bernède's *Judex* (1917, released in the United States in 1919) and *La Nouvelle Mission de Judex* (1918, not released in the United States). Judex is the oldest son of the Trémeuse family. He was raised by his mother to avenge the injuries done to their family by the evil banker Favraux. Judex eventually gains revenge on Favraux. In *The New Mission of Judex,* Judex takes on the "Rafle aux Secrets," a criminal organization that specializes in the theft of high-tech inventions and whose chief is a powerful hypnotist. Judex is a master of disguise and has an underground, cliffside headquarters with an early form of television in it. While fighting crime, Judex wears a slouch hat and a dark cloak and makes use of hypnotic abilities. Judex also commands an organization of circus folk and low-life apaches who help him in his war on Favraux. (The similarities between Judex and the Shadow are interesting but likely coincidental.)

These were followed by Eugene B. Lewis, H. C. Warnack, and Elmer Clifton's *The Eagle* (1918). After John Gregory's mother dies of a broken heart, due to the Gregory family's fortune having been stolen from them by a mining company, Gregory becomes "the Eagle," a masked thief preying on the mining company. Gregory is eventually captured and convicted for a murder he did not commit, but he is finally freed thanks to the efforts of Lucy, the girl that he loves.[14]

And with the end of the war and the great outpouring of popular culture that took place in 1919, films about Costumed Avengers became a part of the medium, so that the 1920 *The Mark of Zorro* (like the Johnston McCulley story serial it was based upon) was popular and influential without being groundbreaking.

Films about Costumed Avengers, though today the most popular and financially successful medium for stories about Costumed Avengers, have traditionally been reflections of what was going on in other media, rather than being content drivers themselves. This was especially true in early Hollywood. The success of Costumed Avenger films reflected popular trends elsewhere, in other media, rather than driving them, so that superhero films didn't begin appearing until the 1940s, well after comic books had proven to be extremely popular. The popularity of Hollywood films has always given the creators of genre fiction an inferiority complex, but Hollywood needs to be seen more as a staggeringly successful parasite than some kind of monstrous predator.

Zorro

As with the Scarlet Pimpernel, it's important to delineate what Johnson McCulley did, with Zorro, and what he did not do.

First, the basics. Zorro was created by Johnston McCulley and appeared in 81 stories and 2 short story collections from 1919 through 1951. Zorro is Don Diego de la Vega, an aristocrat of Spanish descent in California in the early years of the 19th century. Almost all those who know de la Vega believe he is a foppish coward, but in reality this is only a pose. When necessary he will put on a black mask and become Zorro, "the fox," to challenge wicked Mexican and American men and to see that right is done and wrong is defeated.

The first Zorro serial, "The Curse of Capistrano," was hugely popular in *All-Story Weekly* and the film rights were quickly grabbed by Douglas Fairbanks and filmed as *The Mark of Zorro* (1920), which was also enormously popular. Further serials and novellas intermittently followed—McCulley had not intended Zorro to be an ongoing character and as a working pulp writer was busy creating other characters and writing other serials and stories (see below)—through the 1920s, 1930s, and 1940s.

McCulley's work, in print and in film form, were influential, both in the United States and worldwide.[15] Zorro was specifically influential on superhero comics: "Fairbanks' costume pictures—particularly . . . *The Mark of Zorro* . . . inspired Superman's costume . . . Fairbanks served as a general model for Batman and as a specific inspiration for both the Boy Wonder Robin's name and costume."[16] "Batman co-creator Bill Finger was six when *The Mark of Zorro* stormed theaters. He included stills of the masked and swashbuckling Fairbanks in the scripts he handed Bob Kane."[17]

So it must be conceded that Zorro was a *direct* influence and inspiration on the early superhero comics and their creators.

But, again, neither McCulley nor Zorro created anything new. Zorro was not McCulley's first masked character: his Black Star (17 stories from 1916), a masked gentleman thief (though lacking the Lupin's insouciance and Robin Hood–like ways), was a minor success for McCulley. Zorro was not the first dual-identity crime fighter. (He protects the oppressed through Robin Hood–style tactics, but one cannot accurately say he fights crime, except as a rare occurrence in later serials or movies.) Zorro's film costume was not original, being likely heavily influenced by a similarly costumed cowboy vigilante in the Aubrey M. Kennedy film *The Masked Rider* (1919). The foppish pose of Don Diego de la Vega was influenced by both Sir Percy Blakeney's foppish pose in *The Scarlet Pimpernel* and by the other fops of popular fiction and film during the 1900s and 1910s.[18] Like the Scarlet Pimpernel, Zorro is a historical hero, rather than a modern one, and active in the countryside rather than in an urban setting.

So Zorro does not get marks for originality or creativity, even if his influence is undeniable. The most that can be said for McCulley and Zorro is that the increased popularity of film in 1920[19] gave the heroic concepts of Zorro, via *The Mark of Zorro*, momentum and distribution that they otherwise lacked—Zorro was a direct influence on early superhero comics and their creators, as mentioned, but it was the film rather than McCulley's print original that was the inspiration. More broadly, Zorro's enormous popularity and influence, despite being the culmination of preexisting, less popular elements rather than something radical and new, might be explained in the phrase of writer Charles Fort: "A tree can not find out, as it were, how to blossom, until comes blossom-time. A social growth cannot find out the use of steam engines, until comes steam-engine-time."[20] 1919 and 1920 were Costumed Avenger–time, time for realistic wish fulfillment characters to appear to take readers and viewers minds off their problems and the uncertainties of a rapidly changing world. McCulley was the one lucky enough to publish Zorro at the beginning of Costumed Avenger–time.

The Pulps

Pulp magazines, named for the wood pulp paper they were printed on, grew out of the dime novels. The pulps began when *Argosy* went to an all-fiction format in 1896, but for the first 20 years of the pulp format's existence, it was outnumbered on the market by dime novels. In 1918, there were the same number of dime novels being published, 22, as there were pulps; it wasn't until 1919 that there were more pulp magazines being published—30—than dime novels—21.

The traditional outsider's view of the pulps is that it was full of costumed vigilantes, and that these Costumed Avengers were a primary influence on the development of the comic book superhero. This is true, as far as it goes, but it is primarily true of the 1930s, the heyday of the pulp Costumed Avenger, characters like the Shadow, Doc Savage, the Spider, and D. L. Champion's Phantom Detective. During the first 20 years of the pulps' existence, however, Costumed Avengers were not to be found. It wasn't until 1920 that one appeared in the pulps.

The situation of the pulps in 1920 was one of fragmentation. The pulps had begun as general interest magazines but had quickly developed pulps devoted to special interests or one genre: railway pulps beginning in 1906, general adventure in 1910, "spicy" (pornographic) pulps in 1912, romance pulps in 1913, mystery and detective pulps in 1915, and the first Western pulp in 1919. The post–World War I surge in interest in the pulps helped accelerate this.

Not only were pulps specializing, so too were writers. Johnston McCulley was one of these. A working professional writer after World War I, he had already created seven series characters by 1920, including Zorro, the Black Star, and the morbidly obese master criminal the Spider. Perhaps inspired by the success of Zorro, he decided to begin creating modern, crime-fighting Costumed Avengers, beginning with the John Flatchley, "the Thunderbolt." Flatchley is 30 years old and has a taste for excitement; he is athletic, strong, handsome, and the scion of wealth and society. Before World War I, Flatchley had been a big game hunter and had trekked to the North Pole. During World War I, Flatchley was an air ace and won metals for bravery under fire. But when Flatchley returns from armed service he discovers that his massive inheritance, the $200,000 he was due to receive from his uncle's estate, is gone as the result of his uncle's dealings with six crooked financiers, the Big Six. Flatchley is outraged that these men, the Big Six, could get so rich off of widows and orphans (literally—"You are thieves who robbed widows and orphans")[21] without anything being done about it. Flatchley puts on a black hood (slits cut for eyes, yellow lightning bolt pained on the forehead) and becomes The Thunderbolt, a masked crusader who will right wrongs, steal all the money from the Big Six and return it to its rightful owners.

McCulley followed the Thunderbolt up with the Man in Purple, in 1921, a heroic purple-costumed Lupin; with the Crimson Clown in 1926, a clown-costumed Robin Hood; with the vengeance-driven Mongoose in 1932; with the Zorroesque Whirlwind in 1933; and with the cop-turned Robin Hood the Green Ghost in 1934.

During the 1930s other writers got into the act, influenced by McCulley and then the quartet of the Shadow, Doc Savage, the Spider, and the Phantom Detective: there was the pseudonymously written Hawk (hawk-masked Robin Hood) in 1930, Erle Stanley Gardner's crime-solving Patent Leather Kid (1930–1934), Perley Poore Sheehan's costumed undertaker Doctor Coffin (1932–1933); Frederick C. Davis's protosuperhero the Moon Man (1933–1937); the pseudonymously written Bat (1934–1935)[22]; Erle Stanley Gardner's grim crime-fighting Man in the Silver Mask (1935); and Alan Hathway's rogue cop The Whisperer (1936–1942).

Comic books were the successors to the pulps, as the pulps were the successors to the dime novels. There was significant overlap between the pulps and the comics, as there was between the dime novels and the pulps: 1941, the year when Captain America made his debut (fabulously successfully) and when *Captain Marvel Adventures* was selling a million issues a year, was also the year of the highest number of pulps being published (264 total pulps, with 1804 total issues published).[23] Pulps and comics coexisted successfully for 15 years, throughout the war and the postwar surge in pulp publishing. So comics developed in parallel to the pulps at the same time that they were being influenced by them. In superhero comics, these influences were major, involving the use of concepts, motifs, tropes, character types, plot devices, and story lines that first appeared in the pulps.

Sometimes the influence was overt: comic book writers were not above taking character concepts from other media and using them in superhero comics. So Robert O. Erisman and Newt Alfred's The 3Xs, for Timely/Marvel in 1940, was a near-note-perfect lift of Carlton E. Morse's Jack, Doc, and Reggie from the radio show *I Love a Mystery* (1939–1952), and numerous comic book magicians, like Fred Guardineer's Zatara, for DC from 1939, were copies of Mandrake the Magician and Chandu, and the Batman took the key moment of his origin from the Bat.

Sometimes the influence was less overt, but heavy nonetheless. One of the innovations of superhero comics was supplementary material at the back of comics. In *Superman*, this meant articles on the types of kryptonite and the culture of Krypton and maps of Krypton. The cumulative effect was to create the first fully developed fictional world in ongoing superhero comics. Supplementary material, and the fleshed-out fictional worlds, are commonplace in superhero comics now, but they were new when Mort Weisinger, *Superman*'s editor, did it. Mort Weisinger took this concept, of additional extrastory supplementary textual material, from the pulp *Captain Future* (1940–1944), where he had conceived of and edited a column, "The Worlds of Captain Future," which had contained similar supplementary material. Again, this concept is common now in comic books and in other media, but it first appeared in the pulps.

Westerns

The Western genre was ascendant in 1921. The publications of Owen Wister's *The Virginian* (1902), B. M. Bower's *Chip, of the Flying U* (1907), and Zane Grey's *Riders of the Purple Sage* (1912) had led to an upswing in the popularity of the genre, and Westerns had become the fourth-most popular film genre. Westerns were no longer the province of the dime novels; they were best sellers, both in print and on the screen.

However, the popularity of the genre was not being reflected in radio shows or in serial magazines. There were no Western dime novels left, and only one Western pulp, *Western Story Magazine* was being published, and that was only two years old. General interest and adventure pulps printed stories about cowboys and cowgirls, even series about recurring characters—Clarence E. Mulford's Hopalong Cassidy had appeared in two dozen stories in a variety pulps by 1921, and Bower's "Flying U Ranch" characters had appeared in 44 stories in *The Popular Magazine* by this point—but magazine publishers were shy of investing serious resources into the genre.

However, the tropes, motifs, and plot devices of the Western were already well in place by 1921, and creators of Westerns were already looking for new things to introduce into the genre. Drawing on the dime novel tradition of masked cowboys—*New Buffalo Bill Weekly* had ended only two years before, at issue #356—creators of Westerns introduced a new type of cowboy, the fully costumed vigilante cowboy, now Costumed Avengers in practice as well as form.

Richard E. Norman wrote and directed *The Crimson Skull* (1921). Bob Calem is the African American foreman of a ranch in the peaceful black town of Boley, Oklahoma. Unfortunately, Boley is terrorized by the outlaw "the Skull" and his band of "Terrors," so Bob and the Law and Order League take on the outlaws. Bob does so by infiltrating them and then attacking them while wearing a skeleton costume.

The Crimson Skull was a small-scale film,[24] and it is highly unlikely that Frederick Faust (better known as "Max Brand") had *The Crimson Skull* in mind or had even heard of it when he created Jim Curry, in *Western Story Magazine* in 1922. Jim Curry's father (also named Jim Curry) was a giant of enormous enthusiasms and tempers, "one of those fellows who had never grown up."[25] His wife died and he let his son raise himself, with the result that the son grew to be as indolent and careless as his father, and as skillful with the gun. When the father accidentally kills a man, the Curry home is attacked by a posse. Curry Senior is killed, but Curry Junior escapes and goes on the run. He becomes the Robin Hood–like Red Devil to avenge his father's death by stealing from those who did Curry Senior wrong.

These two types of cowboy Costumed Avengers—crime-fighting vigilantes, and Robin Hoods—were the dominant types of Costumed Avengers in Western fiction through the 1920s. The 1930s would see the crime-fighting vigilantes become dominant, first with Fran Striker and George Trendle's Lone Ranger (on radio from 1933, in film from 1938) and then Oscar Schisgall's Masked Rider (in pulps and novels from 1934).

In 1938, Westerns were the most popular genre of pulp magazine being published, with 21 percent of all titles and 22 percent of all issues.[26] Their popularity affected comics both overtly, in the types of characters who appeared in superhero comics,[27] and, more subtly, as one of the sources of the Costumed Avenger character type.

Nonstandard Sources

By the mid-1920s the concept of the heroic Costumed Avenger was showing up in a variety of places that wouldn't ordinarily host them.

Sigmund Romberg's 1926 operetta and later play *The Desert Song* features one. Pierre Birabeau is the son of a general in the French Foreign Legion. His father and the other Legionnaires see Birabeau as a bungler and a coward who was driven mad or stupid by the blow of a venal general—Pierre had tried to stop the French's campaign of terror in Morocco and was beaten by the general for his troubles. But in reality Pierre is the dreaded Red Shadow, a masked marauder who leads the Berber tribes of the Rif Mountains against the French in Morocco. Birabeau hates "the cruelty that was disgracing France"[28] and tries to free the Moroccans. The Red Shadow is a friend to the poor as well as to his band of Riffs, and the people of Morocco would rather die than betray the Shadow. The Riffs feel this way as well, and "have sworn that when the law is wrong, we will right it, by force."[29] Most of the Riffs believe that the Red Shadow is a Muslim Riff, like them, but Sid el-Kar, the Shadow's lieutenant among the Riffs, knows the Shadow's real identity.

The 1932 radio serial *The Scorpion* had as its protagonist a crime-fighting Costumed Avenger. By 1934 even the science fiction pulps were getting into the act. In 1934 and 1935 *Astounding Stories*, perhaps the foremost science fiction pulp of its time, Nat Schachner wrote two stories a Costumed Avenger, "Redmask." In the 55th century there are four major cities in America, one fascist, one communist, one feudal, and one democratic. Plaguing all four cities is the outlaw Redmask, so-called because he wears a red fishbowl helmet that conceals his identity. Redmask flies an enormous, invisible airship and bothers the rulers of each city. He is actually Stephen Halleck, the jester in the court of the feudal world. At the end of the story Redmask forces the three unsavory cities to participate in a food airlift to the democratic city. In the sequel the Purple Emperor, a Yellow Peril, is succeeding in his plans to conquer the world. He has airships and ray guns powered by the magnetic field of the Earth, and even Redmask's ship can be detected by the Emperor's ships. But the new Redmask, the son of Stephen Halleck, succeeds in destroying the enemy fleet.

These nonstandard sources were in all likelihood not influential on the writers of superhero comics, who had more prominent sources to draw upon.[30] They do indicate, however, how widespread the concept of the Costumed Avenger had become.

Killer Vigilantes

Arguably the most contentious inclusion in this book are the killer vigilantes. Coogan, in discussing the Punisher, places the Punisher in the "aggressor formula" and therefore "out of the center of the superhero formula."[31] Gavaler spends an entire chapter, entitled "Thou Shalt Not Kill," debating the issue. Endless Usenet and online message board threads and blog posts argue the matter. But if the question of superhero definitions is reduced to a fuzzy spectrum rather than a binary "is/is not" equation, however, the contention can be removed, the heroes defined as less superheroic than non–killer vigilantes are (as opposed to not superheroic at all), and the killer vigilante superheroes like the Punisher can be placed in their historical context.

The early 1930s were years when the national crime rate peaked after many years' increase, the violence brought on by Prohibition-funded organized crime being one among many other factors. The common perception—a perception that matched reality—was that the cities were lawless affairs dominated by criminals who took a Wild West approach to settling differences between them. Naturally, pulp fiction writers responded to this in the only way possible: by projecting their frustrations and fears into fictional form, where they could be neatly handled by wish fulfillment figures.

Pulp heroes had never been squeamish about violence, and the rise of the hard-boiled detective character—debuting in Carroll John Daly's "Race Williams" in 1923, but becoming typified with Dashiell Hammett's Continental Op from 1923 on, and Hammett's Sam Spade from 1929 on—had led to a coarsening of the mystery pulps and an authorial willingness, even eagerness, to use violence and killing as the preferred method to solve crimes. But the early 1930s saw a new attitude toward heroic violence. Daly's first Vee Brown story was published in 1932; Brown is a quick-draw private detective with an extremely high body count to his name. A month later, the first Costumed Avenger killer vigilante appeared, D. L. Champion's Mister Death. Mister Death is James Quincy Gilmore. Years ago a horrified Gilmore discovered his father's body in his study. His father was killed to prevent him from exposing the members of the "Murder Club," a group of nine rich socialites who murdered for pleasure and for greed. Gilmore, at that time a 24-year-old Yale graduate and former gridiron star, was left an orphan and the heir to his father's fortune. To the eyes of the world he remained James Gilmore, a bored socialite playboy of Newkirk City. In secret, he trained himself and became Mister Death, the man who deals death to those who deserve it. As Mister Death he dresses all in black, from his mask to his cloak and gloves. His methods are lethal, as the members of the Murder Club soon discover. After Mister Death strikes, he leaves a small white card on the body of his victims; on the card are the words "Alias Mister Death." These are the words that soon put all of Newkirk City into a nervous, fear-filled uproar. After all nine members of the Murder Club have been killed, Mr. Death supposedly dies in a plane crash. Gilmore actually bails out at the last moment and then begins traveling around the world, trying to forget. Unfortunately, he discovers that Newkirk City is actually riddled with graft and evil, and so he returns to work.

Two months after that, the first cowboy Costumed Avenger killer vigilante appeared, Guy Maynard's Señor Red Mask. Tom Goodwin is the owner of the Bar G Ranch in the American Southwest. During a bandit raid on the ranch Tom's father is killed, so Tom puts on a costume—black with a red velvet mask and silver spurs—and becomes "Señor Red Mask" to hunt down his father's killers. When he finds them, he kills them and leaves behind a sprig of sagebrush on the bodies. To further his quest and gather information he adopts a second persona, that of "El Muchaco," a poor Mexican youth who wanders from town to town, playing catchy Mexican songs on a battered guitar.

The floodgates opened, and Costumed Avenger killer vigilantes would become common. The embodiment of this urge—which continued long after the end of Prohibition in 1933 led to a marked reduction in violent crime—was the Spider, who is dealt with below.

The influence of writer- and reader-sanctioned murder would permanently stain the pulps, across genres, with a willingness, even eagerness, to settle matters with the gun rather than the fist being one of the medium's most prominent traits. The very early appearances of superheroes in the comics, bearing the traces of the pulps as they did, reflect this: in Superman's first appearance he threatens to kill criminals—a threat the text and art make clear he would carry through on—and in Batman's early appearances he is simply lethal, even machine-gunning a truck from the Batplane in *Batman* #1 (cover date Spring 1940, on sale date April 24, 1940).

Air Aces

It was predictable that publishers would seize on the popularity of aviation and create a series of specialist pulps. In 1927, there were specialist pulps for railway adventure, pornography, romance, mystery and detective fiction, Westerns, sports fiction, science fiction, and weird/supernatural fiction. Why not aviation? Especially "why not?" in 1927, following the May flight of Charles Lindbergh to Paris, which caused an American frenzy for aerial fiction. In August, 1927, the first aviation pulp, *Air Stories*, debuted, followed by 8 more aviation pulps in 1928, and 10 in 1929, and by 1930 there were as many aviation pulps being published as there were romance pulps.

But 1930 was the high point for the genre, and by 1932 the pulp medium itself was beginning to feel the effects of the Depression: only 170 pulps were published, with a total of 1517 issues, the fewest titles since 1929 and the fewest issues since 1928.[32] Publishers were eager to do anything unusual and out of the ordinary to boost sales, and given how well Costumed Avengers were doing in other genres, why not try to combine the Costumed Avenger with the air adventure genre?

Enter Harold Cruickshank's Red Eagle. Captain Ted Blair is "The Red Eagle," a masked air ace in World War I. He is a redheaded, steel-gray-eyed, handsome, scarred intelligence agent of G-2. He leads the "Eagle Brood" of the 44th Squadron: Lt. Sam Martin, Monty Rider, Spud Fallon, and Babe Deakin, who are "big-chested sky-scrapers who feared nothing except the tongue-lashing from their leader."[33] Blair flies a Spad decorated with rampant red eagles, has as a catchphrase "You can only die once," and is opposed by Baron von Bleutz.

Less than a year later, and appearing the same month as the Spider, came Arthur J. Burks's Black Falcon. Evan Post is a first lieutenant in the U.S. Air Force during World War I. Post is fast and "reptile-like" as a pilot, and has "hawk-like eyes, black and grim," but he has a "Quaker conscience" and dislikes killing, especially those who can't fight back.[34] This is why, if at all possible, he shoots down elite German pilots rather than recon planes. Despite his hatred of war, when he puts on a "black helm" and flies his Spad, which bears the insignia of a black falcon, he becomes "an emotionless striker like the hammer of Thor."[35] He flies with nine other pilots, the "Condors."

Throughout the 1930s, similar Costumed Avengers appeared in the air adventure pulps, and when the last of the air adventure pups were canceled in 1939, the concept of the Costumed Avenger air ace transferred to other adventure pulps, as it did to superhero comics, with early pilot characters like Paul Lauretta's American Ace (for Timely from 1939) and Bob Jenney's Masked Pilot (for Dell from 1939) being the norm for comic book superhero pilots rather than the exception.

The Fabulous Four

One of the many genres of pulp magazines during the 1930s was the hero pulp, a pulp that focused on the exploits of a particular hero. Better remembered now than the more popular and successful genres of the era,[36] the hero pulps were rarely as well written as the other pulps and never as critically accepted as the other pulps, but they inspired a fervent fan base and reflected a hunger for Costumed Avengers of the crime-fighting type.

The hero pulps actually began in radio. Street & Smith, one of the largest publishers of pulp magazines, relied heavily on its mystery and detective pulps, but had been challenged throughout the decade by the "true crime" pulps of its competitors.[37] After one of these competitors, McFadden, had success with a radio version of a true crime pulp, Street & Smith decided to venture into radio. The result was *Detective Story Hour*, which adapted stories from Street & Smith's *Detective Story Magazine* and, innovatively, had a mysterious figure announce the show through a filter microphone. This announcer figure was "The Shadow."

The Detective Story Hour was immediately popular on its July 31, 1930, debut, but even more popular was the Shadow, and fans began demanding pulps starring the Shadow. Street & Smith was happy to oblige, publishing *The Shadow* #1 in April 1931, written by Walter B. Gibson. The radio Shadow and the pulp Shadow are different characters. The radio Shadow is the Superhuman Lamont Cranston, "wealthy young man about town who, years ago in the Orient, learned the hypnotic power to cloud men's minds so they could not see him."[38] The pulp Shadow is Kent Allard, a World War I aviator and adventurer who uses the Lamont Cranston identity to keep an eye on Inspector Joe Cardona, the Shadow's would-be police nemesis. Likewise, the pulp Shadow did not initially have the ability to make himself invisible to others. The pulp Shadow does have the cloak and hat and twin .45 automatics and the girasole ring. He's also a master of disguise, maintaining a number of alternate identities to help his fight in crime.

A year later, Ned Pines Publications brought out a competitor, the Phantom Detective, created and written by Leo Margulies and D. L. Champion. The Phantom Detective is Richard Curtis Van Loan, who gained a taste for adventure during World War I and then became a rootless veteran when he returned to the big city. He is challenged by his friend Frank Havens, the publisher of the *New York Clarion*, to solve a case that the police cannot. Van Loan does and discovers that he has a talent for crime fighting. But he does not immediately put on his trademark tuxedo and mask costume and jump in against the bad guys. He begins learning everything he can and trains himself to be an expert in crime detection, disguise, criminal psychology, hand-to-hand combat, and anything else that will help him as a costumed vigilante. When he has learned all he can, he goes to work. He builds a secret "crime laboratory" that he uses as his headquarters in the war against evil. In the lab he has all the latest equipment and science that can be used against criminals.

Street & Smith's response, a month later, was Henry Ralston, John Nanovic, and Lester Dent's Doc Savage. He is a "man of superhuman strength and Protéan genius, whose life is dedicated to the destruction of evildoers."[39] Clark Savage was raised by his widower father to be the perfect human and was taught by a series of experts in every field ranging from "Indian *fakirs* to Yale physicists, from circus acrobats to jungle trackers."[40] He was especially trained in surgery and became the world's best surgeon (hence his nickname of "Doc"). His headquarters and home is his Fortress of Solitude, a superfortress located on a desolate island in the far north, beyond the Arctic Circle. The fortress serves as a place for Savage to periodically retire to, to meditate and invent—for Savage is a master of advanced science and has created a variety of technologically advanced equipment and weapons, including miniature grenades, gas-filled glass balls, infrared goggles, and special high explosives. When not in use, the equipment is kept in the fortress, as are special creations too dangerous to be used.

Six months later, Popular Publications—Street & Smith's main competitor—brought out the Spider, created by Henry Steeger, R. T. M. Scott, and Norvell Page. Richard Wentworth, a millionaire playboy and philanthropist. Wentworth is a veteran of World War I and has a great hatred for evil. He hates it so much that every night he puts on a frightening outfit, with long white hair, sallow skin, a hunchback and fangs, and prowls the city, "ruthless and terrible," guns in hand, killing all those who broke the law. His trademark is the brand left by his cigarette lighter on the foreheads of murdered criminals; the brand is a red spider with tensed legs and poison fangs, and is instantly recognizable.

These four were quickly followed by other hero pulps, so that by 1938, the year of Superman's debut, there were 12 hero pulps on the market.

The impact of these four heroes was considerable. They were the highest-profile Costumed Avengers since the Ku Klux Klan of *Birth of a Nation*, 20 years previously, and thanks to the cover art on their pulps all four were consistently shown in the same outfits, month after month, thereby equating "costumed" with "crime fighter" in the public's mind.[41] Aspects of the individual heroes were taken by the more prominent comic book superheroes: the Shadow's slouch hat and mask and cape look were duplicated by pulp-style comic book superheroes like Gardner Fox and Bert Christman's Sandman (for DC) and Jim Chambers's Crimson Avenger (for DC), various elements of the Shadow were used by Bill Finger and Bob Kane when creating Batman, Doc Savage's "Fortress of Solitude" was taken by Superman, and the Phantom Detective's Man of Extraordinary Capabilities *shtick* was taken by major characters like Batman and minor characters like Charles Wojtkoski's Challenger (for Marvel) and Charles Reizenstein and Hal Sharp's Mr. Terrific (for DC). Because of the prominence of these four heroes, well-worn genre clichés like the alternate identity and the sidekick were treated as if they were something new and were adopted by comic book superheroes.

In a larger sense, the hero pulps, as led by the Shadow, the Phantom Detective, Doc Savage, and the Spider, created the open-ended heroes-versus-villains dynamic of superhero comics. This dynamic was not unique to the hero pulps, of course; they had been the premise of the hero dime novels of the 19th century, most prominently in the Nick Carter corpus of stories. Too, as mentioned in Chapter 4, Nick Carter was the first hero to possess a rogues' gallery of distinctive villains; the writers of the Shadow et al. were happy to pilfer that idea from the Nick Carter stories and to run with it.[42]

Comic Strips

The success of the Costumed Avenger pulp characters led to similar characters in other media, specifically comic strips. The 1920s and 1930s were the Golden Age of adventure comic strips, with Roy Crane's "Captain Easy" (from 1924), Don Moore and Alex Raymond's "Flash Gordon" (from 1929), Milton Caniff and Noel Sickles's "Scorchy Smith" (from 1933),[43] and Caniff's "Terry and the Pirates" (from 1934) being standout examples of the form. But until the appearance of the pulp Costumed Avengers the typical comic strip hero didn't wear a costume or uniform.

Lee Falk, with "Mandrake the Magician" (from 1934), helped change that. Mandrake set the archetype for comic strip and comic book magicians for decades. The fictional Mandrake is modeled on the famous stage magician Leon Mandrake (1911–1993) and is drawn to match him. The fictional Mandrake wears a tuxedo, tails, top hat, and opera cape. At first he is an actual magician, capable of casting real spells, but not long after his debut Mandrake was changed to a stage magician who is very skilled at hypnotism, so that he doesn't perform any actual magic, he only makes people think he did. His background is never delved into in any great detail; it is eventually revealed that he has done an apprenticeship in Tibet and has an evil twin, Derek, and a younger sister, Lenore.

This was followed a year later by Mel Graff's Phantom Magician, in the comic strip "The Adventures of Patsy." Patsy is a moppet whose adventures begin in the kingdom of Ods Bodkins before shifting to the real world. Patsy and her uncle Phil move to Hollywood, where she becomes an actress and begins having the usual adventures, getting involved in the fight against crime, kidnappers, hijackers, escaped cons, and the like, traveling to the South Seas and the North Pole and other places. One of Patsy's early friends is the Phantom Magician. He can perform a number of magical deeds, including turning invisible, and is the first Costumed Avenger Übermensch in comic strips.

And a year after that came Lee Falk's The Phantom. He is "the ghost-who-walks," the latest in a long line of warriors for truth and justice. Originally the Phantom's name was Christopher Standish, a British citizen whose headquarters were in India, but in the 1940s he was remade into Kit Walker, an American whose headquarters were in the remote African jungle nation of Bangalla. The tradition of the Phantom began in the 16th century when Captain Kit Walker is killed in a pirate raid. His son Kit is the only survivor of the raid and washes ashore on Bangalla, where he is rescued by a group of Bandar pygmies. Walker swears an oath on the skull of the pirate who had killed his father that he and his descendants will fight pirates and evil men around the world. Ever since then the men and women of the Walker family have put on the costume of the Phantom and struck fear into the hearts of wrongdoers. The current Phantom, Kit Walker, is the 22nd Walker to bear the name. He operates from a skull-shaped cave deep in the jungles of Bangalla and is assisted by the Jungle Patrol, a group of native Africans who help enforce the peace. Walker is also helped by Guran, the leader of the Bandar pygmies, by Walker's gray wolf Devil, and by his girlfriend, the explorer Diana Palmer.

The daily circulation of the major newspapers in 1938 was in the hundreds of thousands, with the largest papers approaching a half-million issues, giving these comic strips a cultural reach that the early producers of superhero comics could only envy. Too,

> most of the first wave of comics books from 1934 to 1938 used reprinted comic strips. The aim in these first comic books was simply to repurpose comic strips to a new medium to squeeze additional profit from proven properties . . . the success of these reprint books was once again demonstrated by *Famous Funnies* in the first half of 1938. The Audit Bureau of Circulation had *Famous Funnies* with an average monthly circulation of around four hundred thousand.[44]

The producers of early superhero comics were well aware of the presence of Costumed Avengers in successful comic strips, and modeled their characters on those Costumed Avengers.

Domino Lady

After a decade in abeyance, female leads were once again appearing in the pulps in the mid-1930s. Cowgirl heroines, following the dime novel cowgirl heroines and the popularity of cowgirl films during the 1910s, were a notable part of the Western pulps during the 1930s. Female detectives were leads in series from the beginning of the pulps, and by the mid-1930s there were even female hard-boiled detectives, like Cleve Adams's Violet McDade (from 1935). Even science fiction pulps, the most backward genre in terms of gender issues,[45] had female protagonists, like Arthur K. Barnes's galactic big game hunter Gerry Carlyle (from 1937). Not surprisingly, the hero pulps tentatively followed suit, with the anonymously created[46] Domino Lady in 1936. Ellen Patrick is the daughter of one of the most feared politicians in California. Patrick's father is assassinated by a group of political rivals. Patrick swears vengeance and puts on a backless halter dress and a black domino mask and begins robbing her father's murderers. She keeps a small portion of the proceeds for herself and turns the rest over to charity.

Domino Lady did not inspire imitators in the pulps. Her home pulps, *Saucy Romantic Adventures* and *Mystery Adventure Magazine*, were short lived with low circulation. She only appeared in six stories. And she was not influential in the comics. None of the early superheroines, with the possible exception of Ken Fitch and Bernard Baily's Miss X (from 1940, for DC), were modeled on the Domino Lady, and the archetypal superheroine of the Golden Age—influential in theme if not in concept or particulars—was William Marston and Harry Peter's Wonder Woman, who did not appear until the late fall of 1941 (cover date December 1941), years after Domino Lady's last appearance.

Domino Lady is not the start of the Costumed Avenger superheroine tradition in comics; she is an obscure evolutionary predecessor, not unlike Spring-Heeled Jack as an Übermensch. What the Domino Lady is instead is the culmination of the dime novel and pulp tradition of action/adventure detective heroines. In the first decade of the 20th century, the major dime novel detectives added women agents to their core groups of characters: Alice Montgomery for Old King Brady, and several for Nick Carter, including Adelina de Mendoza (later wife to Carter's first kid sidekick Patsy Murphy), Cora Chickering (cousin to Carter's second kid sidekick Chick Carter), Ida Jones (a student at Carter's "detective academy"), and Nellie Carter, Nick Carter's cousin. The quartet of major pulp heroes had female sidekicks as well: the Shadow had Margo Lane, the Phantom Detective had Muriel Havens, the Spider had Nita van Sloan, and most famously Doc Savage had Pat Savage. The Domino Lady is a part of this lineage, merely costumed.[47]

Domino Lady was not the last of this type of character, in the pulps or the comics, and is exceptional only because of her costume. This type of character would appear numerous times in the early comics, some of them (Charles Flanders's Sandra of the Secret Service, for DC, 1935–1940, Dick Ryan's Dale Daring, for DC, 1936–1939) even dressing in men's clothing and overlapping substantially with the era of the superheroine. These detective heroines and adventuresses, in the line of Moll Frith and Martinette de Beauvais, were the prototypes for the superheroines, but once the superheroines began appearing the detective heroines and adventuresses began disappearing, just as detective heroes and adventurers were elbowed aside in comic books by superheroes.

Conclusion

By the time Superman debuted, the Costumed Avenger was almost a cliché, so common had it become in various media and genres. Superman would of course meld the Costumed Avenger and Übermensch traditions together and start the costumed superhuman superhero tradition, but he had decades of Costumed Avengers before him, influencing him. As with the 19th century, the 20th century Costumed Avengers had a direct through line that influenced Superman's creation. Not so the supermen and superwomen of the 20th century.

CHAPTER SEVEN

Supermen, 1901–1938

Victorian Holdovers

Queen Victoria's death, on January 22, 1901, and the succession to president of Theodore Roosevelt on September 14, 1901, were historical and cultural turning points for Great Britain and the United States. Victoria was succeeded by King Edward VII, ushering in the Edwardian era in England, and Roosevelt was the highest-profile and most successful politician and activist of the Progressive Era in the United States. Much of what followed, culturally and especially in literature, would not have been possible in the previous decade. This is especially true of fantastic literature and the manifestations of the supermen that appeared over the next 10 years.

But eras rarely end or begin neatly, and as is usually the case, the first decade of the 1900s was haunted by Victorian concepts and characters. Eugenics, of course, would be a recurring theme among creators of the supermen, and although the eugenics movement was given new life in the 1900s it began in the 1880s. Suffrage for women, discontent among the laboring classes, and growing discord between the races—all carried over from the 1890s into the 1900s. In popular literature, science fiction, mysteries, and the Western continued to grow in popularity.

Most crucially to the Übermensch, two of the major superman detectives appeared and flourished during this time period. The adventures of Old King Brady, New York policeman with a mystic intuition, appeared from 1885 through 1912. And 1901–1915 were the Golden Age of Nick Carter, the superstrong Übermensch consulting detective. It wouldn't be until 1910 that an Übermensch vigilante appeared who significantly differed from the archetype that Carter embodied; before then, the influence of Carter was sizable.

Physical Culture and Eugen Sandow

One of the most significant holdovers from the late Victorian era was the Physical Culture movement, which would reach its peak in the 1900s and then slowly diminish through the 1910s and 1920s. The Physical Culture movement sprang from British fears of physical degeneracy on the part of the British working class, fears that were widespread throughout the Victorian era. Two separate social movements grew in response to this fear: "muscular Christianity," whose proponents believed in *mens sana in corpore sano*, a sound mind in a sound body, and "New Athleticism," which attempted to use sports to instill character, manliness, and modesty. Despite these movements many Britons during the 1860s and 1870s became convinced that the average British soldier was physically weaker than his predecessors. Fears that the empire was in decline were commonplace, increasing numbers of men were found to be physically invalid for military service, and it was commonly believed that the infant mortality rate was skyrocketing. Most Britons believed that the British race was decaying and in danger of becoming decadent.

A response to these fears was the Physical Culture movement, which emphasized cultivating the self in mind and body to become a better Christian and to reverse the trend toward racial decay. The Physical Culture movement de-emphasized the games of New Athleticism and instead promoted gymnastics and weight lifting.

The most famous advocate for Physical Culture was the first globally famous bodybuilder, Eugen Sandow (1867–1925). By 1897, Sandow was famous across the United States as a bodybuilder, an icon of muscle and strength, and had even appeared in a four-minute kinetoscope short film, "Sandow, the Modern Hercules." That year he began what he thought of as his true mission, reforming the bodies of humanity, and toward that end he opened the Institute of Physical Culture in London. The institute was immediately successful, and in two years fitness was a national craze in both the United States (then gripped by fears of racial nervous exhaustion) and the United Kingdom.

In 1898, he founded *Sandow's Magazine of Physical Culture*, which combined articles on health and bodybuilding with fiction. Imitations of *Sandow's Magazine* followed, but it was *Sandow's Magazine* that remained the leader in the Physical Culture field. Sandow provided a model for other bodybuilder/entrepreneurs to follow, including Bernarr Macfadden, who went on to found Macfadden Publications.

During the 19th-century carnival strongmen routinely compared themselves to Heracles, Atlas, and other figures from Greek myth and performed feats of supposedly superhuman strength. These feats were deceit and fraud, and this fraud was one of the things that the young Sandow had worked to discredit. But with Physical Culture at its peak, strongmen began combining actual feats of strength with traditional circus trickery and advertised themselves as "superhuman."

> The rhetoric, from Sandow, Macfadden, and other Physical Culture proponents, used phrases like "perfect manhood and womanhood," "idealized form of the human body," and "peak of human development." Those attempting to surpass Sandow used rhetoric like "first of a new breed of man," "forerunner of the next stage of human development," "a man of legendary, not human, strength," "a human being of supernatural powers," and, simply, "superhuman."[1]

The association between bodybuilding and superhumanity was repeatedly made in popular fiction, and the craze for Physical Culture led to a surge in bodybuilder superhumans in popular fiction. Sandow himself appeared as a character in dime novels as early as 1894, and by 1899 *Sandow's Magazine* was regularly running fiction starring superhumanly strong bodybuilder characters. There had been heroic characters with superhuman strength before Sandow, including Old Sleuth, Old Cap. Collier, and Nick Carter. But the bodybuilder superhuman was popular in the best-selling Physical Culture magazines, and other magazine publishers were quick to imitate *Sandow's Magazine* and to capitalize on the popularity of Sandow and the Physical Culture movement by creating more superhuman bodybuilders.

Until 1918, the end of World War I, numerous characters possessed of superhuman strength appeared in popular fiction who were either explicitly bodybuilders and Physical Culture devotees or whose iconography and personality implicitly made them such to their audiences. The titular hero of the 1902 comic strip "Hugo Hercules," for example, is capable of lifting elephants and stopping runaway carriages simply by grabbing them. He is never explicitly described as being a Physical Culture devotee, but every contemporary reader, seeing Hercules's dress and manner, knew where Hercules's strength came from. Hercules was "the first positive presentation of a heroic superman in comics"[2] but was purely a product of the Physical Culture movement and was no different from the heroic superstrong bodybuilders of *Sandow's Magazine* and the other Physical Culture magazines.

Not long after "Hugo Hercules," Physical Culture magazines began printing stories about Physical Culture heroes and heroines that went beyond mere crime fighting. In John Russell Coryell's "The Weird and Wonderful Story of Another World," *Physical Culture* (Oct. 1905–Sept. 1906), the protagonist Tyman Currio flies to Jupiter and discovers that it is not only Earth-like in atmosphere but that it is also inhabited by a race of humanoids who are physically and mentally superior to humans. Currio befriends one of them, Bel, and she tells him of their civilization. In the distant past they had mastered advanced technology, but they are believers in vegetarianism, nudity, physical exercise, returning to nature, and political anarchism. Currio, a meat-eating human, comes off rather badly in comparison to them, and when he falls in love with Bel and tries to impress her by shooting a bird, she knocks him out with a punch and tears apart his rifle with her bare hands. She returns to Earth with Currio to act as a missionary and then abandons him, telling him that she can do her work better without him.

Bel was not the first superwoman of the 20th century, but she was the first to have the superhuman body/superhuman intelligence package, and was the first truly dangerous superwoman rebel, akin to de Quincey's Masque but set in the modern day. Compared to Bel, Wonder Woman's threat to bring peace to man's world is pallid indeed.

The Physical Culture craze faded by the start of World War I and became associated in the public's mind with fascism in the late 1920s and early 1930s—part of the 1920s backlash against supermen and superhuman abilities in general—but by then the ideas of Physical Culture as a source of superpowers, and of superhumans wearing strongman-style tights, were well-embedded into the Zeitgeist.[3]

Origin Stories

The supermen's superpowers, during the Victorian era, had been of a relatively limited variety: strength and endurance, magic, and psychic. And it wasn't until Nick Carter that writers began to feel the need to explain the powers' cause through what we now think of as an origin story.

With the start of the 20th century the idea of the superpower began to change, so that writers began imagining characters with superhuman abilities beyond strength—and always attaching origin stories to them.

In H. G. Wells's "The New Accelerator" (1901), Professor Gibberne creates a drug that "stimulates all round, that wakes you up for a time from the crown of your head to the tip of your great toe, and makes you go two—or even three to everybody else's one,"[4] resulting in Gibberne and the story's narrator gaining Flash-like superspeed. Harold Begbie's

Andrew Latter (from 1904) gets his dream traveling abilities simply by following a psychologist's theory. And Thomas Hanshew's face-changing Hamilton Cleek (from 1910) gets his superpowers from his mother having played with a rubber toy while pregnant.

The variety of superpowers displayed during the pre-Superman decades of the 20th century would grow as the years passed, although body enhancement (strength, agility, endurance) and psychic abilities would remain the most common. Likewise, the number of origin stories would begin to increase—but unlike Nick Carter (and Frankenstein's Creature before him) the origin story would not always be either traumatic or tragic, or have to be. Tragedy and trauma would be central to comic book superhero origin stories—as Hatfield, Heer, and Worcester write about superheroes' origin stories, "to read origin stories about destroyed worlds, murdered parents, genetic mutations, and mysterious power-giving wizards is to realize the degree to which the superhero genre is about transformation, about identity, about difference, and about the tension between psychological rigidity and a flexible and fluid sense of human nature."[5]

But the supermen stories of the pre-Superman years often offered an alternative to these traumatic origins, even if the writers of Golden Age comic books ultimately declined to make use of this alternative.

Mysteries

The new century also saw a development in another genre, mysteries, which had to this point largely been free of supermen and superhuman elements and abilities.

Detective and mystery fiction was a very popular genre by 1902. Arthur Conan Doyle's Sherlock Holmes had been "dead" for eight years—his return in "The Adventure of the Empty House" did not take place until 1903—but the genre's popularity had continued undiminished, with other detective characters performing as more than adequate substitutes.

Interestingly, though, detective fiction in 1902 was still playing out a basic social conflict that had taken place over the second half of the 19th century in Great Britain and the United States: the conflict between spiritualism and the scientific impulse. The vogue in detective fiction at the time was for the "scientific detective," the Holmes-like detective who applied logic and science to the task of solving crimes and catching criminals. This vogue reflected "yet another characteristic of modernity: the emergence of the intellectual professions as new repositories of social power."[6]

This emergence was countered by the rise in enthusiasm for spiritualism and its attendant effects, which included psychic phenomena. And while the Holmesian scientific detective would be in vogue for a generation, the psychically powered Übermensch as detective would be a recurring character in detective magazines and novels.

It all began with L. T. Meade and Robert Eustace's Diana Marburg in 1902: "I am a palmist by profession. Occult phenomena, spiritualism, clairvoyance, and many other strange mysteries of the unseen world, have, from my earliest years, excited my keen interest."[7] She studied under Reichenbach and Mesmer before becoming a professional thought reader and palmist on Maddox Street in London. She has psychic abilities that manifest themselves through palm reading, and she uses these abilities to foretell the future and solve crimes.

However, despite beginning with a female detective, and involving spiritualism—what was perceived as a female interest in Victorian and Edwardian times—psychic powers soon became the province of male detectives.[8] Samuel Gardenhire's consulting detective Le Droit Conners (1905–1906), modeled on Sherlock Holmes, is a "supersensitive" who forms his conclusions first, based on his intuition, and then works backward to discover the evidence to confirm his conclusions. Conners's mental powers are implied to come from his Native American mother, who gave birth to him while being partially eaten alive by wolves.

At the same time, though, appeared Harold Begbie's Andrew Latter (1904), who is an ordinary Englishman who follows a Dutch psychologist's theory of dreams and gives himself the ability to travel in time and space when he dreams. Latter uses this ability to first solve the mystery of the murder of his friend and then to spy on mysterious women he sees and to discover why a man hates a cat so much, and why the cat eventually murders him.

By the end of the decade, when detectives were possessed of superhuman abilities, like Frank Howel Evans's Jules Poiret[9] (from 1909) and his "superhuman intelligence," the psychic element was removed from it, and other reasons (if any) were given for the detective having superhuman abilities, as in Ernest Bramah's Max Carrados stories and novels (from 1913). When Wynn "Max" Carrados was a young man he developed amaurosis as the result of a riding accident and eventually became blind. In reaction to this, in the words of Bramah, "so far from crippling his interests in life or his energies, it has merely impelled him to develop those senses unused. Thus you will understand that while he may be at a disadvantage while you are at an advantage, he is at an advantage while you are at a disadvantage."[10]

His other senses are heightened, and he uses them to become a detective. He is capable of Sherlock Holmes–like deductions about those around him: he can read newspaper headlines with the touch of a fingers, can recognize a friend he has not been in the company of for over 20 years simply by the sound of his voice, can smell a false mustache, and on at least one occasion, win a shoot-out. He can even sense good and bad "emanations."

However, as the popularity of detective fiction continued to rise, the popularity of superhuman detectives diminished. Fops and brilliant (though mortal) consulting detectives became more common than superhuman detectives, and during the 1920s, a decade that generally discouraged the presentation of fictional supermen and superwomen, hard-boiled detectives, portrayed as being quite mortal, indeed, became the vogue.

Yellow Perils

The anti-Asian stereotype of the "Yellow Peril" was made commonplace in the 20th century, but the modern incarnation of it has its roots in the 18th and 19th centuries. Beginning with Thomas-Simon Gueullette's Fum-Hoam, the villains—especially the Gothic Hero-Villains—of the 18th and 19th century had racial aspects hinting at Eastern or Asian origins. Later in the 19th century, historical and cultural trends in the United States such as the growth of Chinese immigration and the rise of white nativism led to a rise in anti-Chinese sentiment that manifested itself in fiction in the form of Yellow Peril masterminds.

Beginning in the 1880s, American writers began portraying individual Chinese master villains as drug pushers (Emma Dawson's Tseng-ko-lin-ch'in, 1880), as sinister doctors (Ellen Sargent's Doctor Ping, 1882), as pirate-inventors (the pseudonymously created Kiang Ho, 1892), as superhuman sorcerers and rulers in China (Robert Chambers's Yue-Laou, 1896), as military leaders bent on conquering the West (M. P. Shiel's Doctor Yen How, 1898), and as urban crime lords living in America (C. W. Doyle's Quong Lung, 1897).

The 20th century continued this trend. The archetypal Yellow Peril is Sax Rohmer's Fu Manchu, but Yellow Perils appeared during the 1900s before him, adding the superhuman ability of mesmerism to the stereotype that Fu Manchu would later exhibit. One typical Yellow Peril of these years was Joyce Vincent's Amarbal, from *The Celestial Hand* (1903). Amarbal is a Mongolian "Akkad" of high education whose driving ambition is to lead the Mongolians to "universal dominion." To achieve this goal he assembles an army of Mongolians and criminals from around the world, a navy of hundreds of ships, and a fleet of technologically advanced airships. He also has a variety of psychic powers, including the abilities to project his image and kill with terror from a distance.

Fu Manchu, though, would combine all the previous major aspects of the Yellow Perils—sexual threat, crime lord, threat to the West, military leader—into one villainous package. Fu Manchu is an elderly Chinese doctor and scholar who has been scheming toward power since the reign of the Empress Dowager in the 19th century. He is distantly related to the Manchu Dynasty and tried to strengthen the dynasty and limit Western influence in China through a series of abductions and assassinations. After the fall of the Manchu Dynasty he broadened his war against the West, using the Si Fan to strike against his enemies and the enemies of China. In Fu Manchu's words, his ultimate goal is to

> restore the lost glories of China—my China. When your Western civiliza-
> tion, as you are pleased to term it, has exterminated itself, when from the
> air you have bombed to destruction your palaces and your cathedrals,
> when in your blindness you have permitted machines to obliterate human-
> ity, I shall arise. I shall survey the smoking ashes which once were Eng-
> land, the ruins that were France, the red dust of Germany, the distant fire
> that was the great United States. Then I shall laugh. My hour at last![11]

Fu Manchu is a Chinese patriot whose plans are all aimed at strengthen-ing China and weakening its enemies. He is the leader of the Si Fan, a secret international society of murderers that consists of Chinese Tongs, Indian Phansigars and Thuggees, Burmese dacoits, Syrian Hashishin, and Sea-Dyaks of Borneo, among other Asian groups. In addition to the Si Fan, Fu Manchu has an unmatched knowledge of both Eastern and West-ern medicine, a knowledge he uses to create poisons, gases, and drugs for his plans. He makes use of non-Western creatures for his killings, from scorpions to adders to an Abyssinian half-man, half-baboon. He also has an almost supernatural ability to hypnotize. Although in the later novels Fu Manchu personally operates around the world, in the early novels his headquarters are in Limehouse, England.

Fu Manchu would establish the archetype so firmly beginning in 1912 that nearly every Yellow Peril villain following him would be written in imitation of him.[12]

The importance of the Yellow Peril villain to the superhero lies in their omnipresence throughout the 1910s, 1920s, and 1930s, almost always with the same mesmerist (and occasionally other) abilities of the Über-mensch Fu Manchu. As perhaps the most common type of foe for pulp heroes to fight, the Yellow Peril presented the hero or heroine's evil oppo-site, their Jungian shadow aspect, a sociopolitical threat toward every-thing the hero stood for while at the same time a brother to them.[13] The Yellow Peril's traits were in some respect necessary to define the hero; without a Yellow Peril archenemy the hero did not reach the highest levels of the heroic archetype. Yellow Perils were necessary, thematically, to pulp and superhero stories, and the Übermensch aspect of the Yellow Perils was necessary thematically to the character, and therefore to the superhero.

Lost Races and Utopias

Lost Races and Utopias were common during the 19th century, having their roots in the popular literature of the 17th and 18th centuries, with Jonathan Swift's *Gulliver's Travels* (1726) being the first significant Lost Race tale[14] and Francis Bacon's *New Atlantis* (1626) being the first signifi-cant nonsatirical Utopia. "Lost Race" is used here indistinguishably from "Lost World," both representing "lands, continents, Islands, or regions Underground . . . which . . . come equipped with one or more indigenous races ripe for First Contact and perhaps displaying interesting quirks for the student of Anthropology."[15]

One interesting wrinkle that the Lost Races and Utopias of later in the 19th century added to their subgenres was the notion of the members of the Lost Races and inhabitants of the Utopias having advanced science at their disposal, and possibly even being superhuman themselves. This began with Bulwer-Lytton's *The Coming Race* (1871), whose Utopian inhabitants not only wielded the ur-power "vril" but were themselves superhuman, but fully flowered during the 20th century, influenced by the rise in science fiction, the growing enthusiasm for Utopias, and espe-cially the interest in all things Eastern and the association—fostered by Theosophists—of Tibet with higher wisdom and associative superhuman powers.

John Macmillan Brown, writing under the name "Godfrey Sweven," attracted a fair amount of critical and popular attention for his Utopia *Riallaro* (1901), and inspired a number of other authors, including the pseudonymous "Aston Forrest," whose *The Extraordinary Islanders* was published in 1903. *The Extraordinary Islanders* is a combination of imagi-nary voyage and Lost World fiction, about (among other things) the ultra-rational Rectinians, who are supermen with superhuman intellects and abilities. Alfred Lawson's *Born Again* (1904) features a superwoman, the last survivor of a race that died over 4,000 years ago, who has psychic abilities and is generally physically and mentally superior to ordinary humans. Three years after that, Frederic van Rensselaer Dey had Nick Carter confront first a Lost Race of Amazonian superwomen in the Andes and then a race of blond white Nepalese supermen who have "control of the life force (vitic energy)."[16]

Other authors picked up this theme, and especially the association of the East with superhuman abilities, and used them. A typical later use is Henry Carew's *The Vampires of the Andes* (1925), in which the narrator encounters a global secret society, dating back to Atlantis, with headquarters in the Andes, and ends up marrying a woman of the secret society, "and together they will produce the next evolutionary step in mankind."[17]

The significance of Lost Race and Utopia fiction to comic book superheroes was that they provided authors with an additional source of the superhuman abilities, a handy alternative to eugenics/science or magic. The tradition of white men going to a Lost Race and being the exceptional person there, or going to a Utopia and being irrevocably changed and made superior by it, was an old one, even by the turn of the 20th century; the addition of those white men gaining superhuman abilities via the Lost Races or the Utopias was merely a version of the metaphor-made-flesh.

Will Eisner and Lou Fine's Flame (for Fox from 1939), Bill Everett's Amazing Man (for Centaur from 1939), Klaus Nordling's Thin Man (for Marvel from 1940) . . . the number of early superheroes who gain superhuman abilities from Lost Races and Utopias, especially in the East, is sizable. There are also those heroes, like Joe Simon and Louis Cazeneuve's Red Raven (for Marvel from 1940), Basil Wolverton's Rockman (for Marvel from 1941), and most notably Stan Lee and Jack Kirby's Inhumans (for Marvel from 1965) who are members of the Lost Race. This trend became common enough that Planetary Romance heroes like John Carter were actually an innovative alternative to Lost Race heroes and their dynamic of acquired superpowers.

Evolutionary Predecessors

As described in Chapter 6, Alfred Burrage's Spring-Heeled Jack was the first 20th century Costumed Avenger to incorporate the dual identities, the costume, the secret headquarters, and the selfless mission. Burrage's Spring-Heeled Jack also had a superpower: the ability to deliver electric shocks with a touch.

The publisher of Burrage's Spring-Heeled Jack, the Aldine Publishing Company, briefly had an American distributor for *The Spring-Heeled Jack*

Library, and it's possible that future writers of stories involving superhuman Costumed Avengers read some of Burrage's stories and were inspired by them.

Possible, yes, but unlikely. As Coogan says, Burrage's Spring-Heeled Jack "did not inspire imitation and repetition necessary to initiate a genre, so he is not the founding figure of the superhero genre . . . instead, his adventures stand as an intriguing anomaly."[18]

Less anomalous, and representing the effect of the Scarlet Pimpernel, is the focus of the fan's gaze in *The Spring-Heeled Jack Library*. The emphasis of the series is on Spring-Heeled Jack's dual identity, the relationship between Bertram Wraydon and his costumed persona. As the series progresses, Spring-Heeled Jack's Übermensch ability is de-emphasized as surplus to requirements, until it disappears in the final issues.[19]

Spring-Heeled Jack stands as an isolated predecessor in the evolution of the superhero genre, an oddity that, though springing out of previous developments, did not inspire further imitations or repetition, as Coogan notes. Robert Chambers's William Manners (from 1907) is another such. Manners is an upper-class American ninny who finds it too difficult to quit smoking and finally consigns himself to the care of the famous Doctor Duncan. Doctor Duncan cures Manners of smoking, through the "absent treatment," which consists of Duncan "worked a sort of mental rabbit's foot" on Manners,[20] thus removing the mental and physical need for tobacco from Manners's mind and body. Manners decides to see if he can perform the "absent treatment" on other people. He can. Manners's new ability of mind control works, and he bestows/inflicts new convictions and urges on both friends and acquaintances.

An Übermensch who appeared in the pages of the *Saturday Evening Post*, one of the foremost "slicks" (the higher-class alternatives to the pulps) of the day, Manners would not be imitated, and the *Post* would not again print fiction featuring an Übermensch until 1924.

Still another isolated predecessor in the superhero genre is George Arthur Gray's Wolf-Devil, from the film serial *Queen of the Northwoods* (1929). The Wolf-Devil wears a wolf costume, complete with wolf mask, and has an unnatural control over wolves. He attempts to destroy all the whites in northern Canada, but the RCMP is there to stop him. The Wolf-Devil is not just a Costumed Avenger Übermensch, but also the first superpowered costumed supervillain in Anglophone literature—this, in 1929, at a time when costumed superpowered superheroes were still a comparative rarity. The first superpowered costumed supervillains, Bill Everett's The Great Question (fighting Amazing Man in Centaur's *Amazing Man Comics* #5, September 1939) and Bill Finger and Bob Kane's vampire The Monk (fighting Batman in *Detective Comics* #31, September 1939), wouldn't appear for another decade. The Wolf-Devil, like Spring-Heeled Jack, was simply ahead of his time—in Coogan's words "an intriguing anomaly."

Science Fiction's Supermen

By 1904, science fiction, as a genre, was well developed. Hugo Gernsback didn't coin the phrase "scientifiction," which would later become "science fiction," until 1915,[21] but the decade 1895–1904 had seen the publication of H. G. Wells's *Time Machine* (1895), Wells's *The Island of Dr. Moreau* (1896), Wells's *The Invisible Man* (1897), Wells's *War of the Worlds* (1897), Garret Serviss's *Edison's Conquest of Mars* (1898), Fred T. Jane's *The Violet Flame* (1899), H. G. Wells's *When the Sleeper Wakes* (1899), George Griffith's *A Honeymoon in Space* (1901), and Wells's *The First Men in the Moon* (1901)—best sellers, and a stream of works that cumulatively convinced fans and critics of the novels (and the many science fiction short stories published during these years) that science fiction, whether known as "scientific romance" or "imaginative fiction" or under the other labels of the time, was a discrete, popular, functioning genre of fiction.

This would remain the case through the 1910s and into the 1920s, so that the publication of *Amazing Stories* in 1926, which is generally seen as the start of modern science fiction, was only an acceleration of the genre rather than the start of it.

So those writers of science fiction novels about supermen during the 1900s, 1910s, and 1920s knew what genre they were working in as well as what tradition—that of the supermen—they were publishing in. Luther Marshall's *Thomas Boobig* was less than a decade old, and *Thomas Boobig* had had predecessors.

Interestingly, though, the authors of the science fiction supermen novels took a different approach to the subjects of their books than their predecessors, their contemporaries, or the writers who followed them.

In H. G. Wells's *The Food of the Gods* (1904), a scientist creates a super-food that, when given to children, allows them to grow to 40 feet in height and to develop intellects to match. *The Food of the Gods* follows their growth and their final unamiable divorce from ordinary humanity. In Edith Nesbit's "The Third Drug" (1908) a man on the run is given mental abilities through a scientist's experiment. M. P. Shiel's *The Isle of Lies* (1909) is about the development of an child into the greatest intellect and athlete possible—"the highest human feat, a peerless being"—toward the end of translating a stele.[22] The child, when grown, attempts to raise money to launch an artificial moon around the Earth and hints at ultimately planning to rule the world.

In J. D. Beresford's *The Hampdenshire Wonder* (1911) a five-year-old child has such a vast superintellect (and the stunning gaze of the Gothic Hero-Villain) and such a depth of knowledge that he disquiets those he looks at and is capable of verbally demolishing the beliefs of those he deigns to speak to (which are few; the boy is incapable of communicating in an ordinary fashion with regular human beings). "Though unbelievably intelligent, he is inhuman and alien in emotional development, and in some respects is more helpless than an ordinary child."[23] Ultimately, the child is killed by a local curate.

In E. V. Odle's *The Clockwork Man* (1923) the titular cyborg travels to the present day from 8,000 years in the future; he is the product of "makers," a race of supermen who use the clockwork men for their incomprehensible games. Guy Dent's *The Emperor of the If* (1926) a scientist creates a disembodied brain-in-a-jar with such vast mental powers that it is capable of rewriting reality itself. And in Muriel Jaeger's *The Man with Six Senses* (1927), a sickly young man has the mental abilities to see the molecular composition of objects and the patterns of electromagnetic fields, but his abilities end up destroying him, mentally and physically.

In each of these works the superman or superwoman assumes a much different set of responsibilities than those taken up by supermen and superwomen from genres other than science fiction. In these works the superhumans are either passive and acted upon rather than active agents ("The Third Drug," *Hampdenshire Wonder*, *Clockwork Man*, *Man with Six Senses*) or bypass lesser matters to attempt to change society or rule the country or the world (*Food of the Gods*, *Isle of Lies*, *Emperor of If*). None of them take what might be thought of as a dime novel or pulp or comic book approach to crime and evil and confront individual representatives of both.

One reason for this may be the fact that all the authors of these works were British (though the works had American editions). The 20th-century British approach to heroic fiction had a distinctive air of separation from the more direct and aggressive American methods, from the "cosy catastrophe" approach to end-of-the-world scenarios (as distinct from the more American one-man-takes-on-the-world) to the more refined, hands-off style of Arthur Conan Doyle's Sherlock Holmes and the various armchair detectives (compared to the brutal and quite physical American hard-boiled detectives).[24] British science fiction before World War I was heavily influenced by Wells and his sociopolitical concerns, but after 1918 "the bitter disenchantment left by the war lasted far longer than the fighting"[25] and made British science fiction a hostile environment for even mildly adventurous science fiction. So, too, with the British approach to the Übermensch, which though springing from previous treatments of the Übermensch, and though distributed (through American editions of these books) in the United States, proved not to be influential on the comic book superheroes, or American authors of science fiction.

Philip Wylie's *Gladiator* stands as a kind of rebuke to the British approach.

Occult Detectives

Horror and mystery have been linked together from before the works of Poe, but it wasn't until the 1860s—specifically, with J. S. Le Fanu's "Green Tea" (1869)—that the horror mystery combination truly began. In "Green Tea," and in Le Fanu's short story collection *In a Glass Darkly*, Le Fanu's detective, Dr. Martin Hesselius, tries to use specialist knowledge to solve crimes with psychic or occult elements, making him into the first occult detective.

It is the occult detective who became the central figure in horror mysteries for the next 60 years. In the 25 years following *In a Glass Darkly*, the occult detective would slowly become more commonly used in crime fiction, but only using what might be called the Scooby Doo approach to occult crime: the supernatural is ultimately revealed to have purely materialistic causes. Typical of this approach, and best known of the Scooby Doo occult detectives, is L. T. Meade's John Bell, who appeared in a series of stories in 1897 and 1898. Bell, a Holmesian consulting detective, is called upon to deal with mysteries that seem to involve the psychic phenomena, but in each case he catches those responsible for the crimes: always men, never spirits. Meade's prominence as a detective writer gave John Bell a higher profile than many other, lesser-known Scooby Doo occult detectives.

But even as the Bell stories were appearing, the trend in occult detective fiction was shifting toward the supernatural and away from the rational. Alexander Reynolds's "The Mystery of Djara Singh" began this trend, Hesketh and Kate Prichard continued it with their Flaxman Low stories, and in 1908 Algernon Blackwood published *John Silence, Physician Extraordinary*. The titular character is a medical doctor who is far more interested in investigating psychic and occult phenomena. Toward this goal he put himself through five years of "long and severe training, at once physical, mental and spiritual."[26] It gave him psychic abilities, usually undefined but of the sort that allow him to cast off evil mesmeric influences.

Three years later, Max Rittenberg began his Dr. Xavier Wycherley stories. Wycherley is a professional psychologist who is on occasion called in to solve inheritance cases and the like. Wycherley has an additional advantage: he is a psychic sensitive. Wycherley's powers include mental healing and the ability to perceive the emotions that make up each person's "mental aura." Wycherley can increase his perception of this aura by putting himself into a light hypnotic sleep, to draw on his subconscious impressions and conclusions, or by injecting himself with "pyridye-novocaine." Wycherley's own aura is a fiery one and he is full of personal magnetism—on meeting him one is compelled to confess things to him. His ability to read auras and his psychoanalytical skills make him a formidable investigator.

And in 1912 J. U. Giesy began his Semi-Dual stories. Prince Abduel Omar of Persia, is, variously, an astrologer, a mystic, a telepath, and a psychologist. Prince Omar is known as "Semi-Dual" because of his habit of solving problems "by dual solutions—one material for material minds—the other occult, for those who cared to sense a deeper something back of the philosophic lessons interwoven in the narrative."[27] His primary tool for solving solutions is astrology, at which he is both talented and completely accurate. He is a fervent believer in the "many other esoteric angles of thought and the application of higher laws of force"[28] and that astrology can be used to precisely predict a person's actions. Based on the time of birth, Semi-Dual can accurately predict what a person will do and when she or he will do it.

Numerous other occult detectives appeared over the following decade, with the occult detective genre dwindling in popularity only in the mid-1920s and being replaced a few years later with the more ordinary (and not usually superhuman) heroes of the "weird menace" pulps.

The influence of the occult detective on superhero comics runs through the lineage of similar characters, which range from Jerry Siegel and Joe Shuster's Doctor Occult (for DC, from 1935) to John Broome and Carmine Infantino's Phantom Stranger (for DC, from 1952) to Alan Moore and Steve Bissette's John Constantine (for DC, from 1985), and in the use of horror in comics, from the Lovecraftian opponents fought by Charles Voight's Dr. Styx (for Prize, from 1945) to the more ordinary horrors facing Marilyn Mercer and Jerry Grandenetti's Dr. Drew (for Fiction House, from 1949). Horror was a common interest in Hollywood films in the 1910s, 1920s, and 1930s, but cinematic horror always focused the fan's gaze on the monsters and villains, rendering the heroes of such films one- or at best two-dimensional secondary characters. Written horror, by comparison, either gave equal emphasis to the heroes and the monsters (as in the weird menace pulps) or directed the fan's gaze to the heroes (as in occult detective pulps). Superhero horror comics traditionally have taken the latter approach.

Artificial Supermen

Continuing with the 19th century use of artificial supermen was L. Frank Baum, who in *Ozma of Oz* (1907) presented Tik-Tok, a round copper mechanical man who is wound up with three keys, one each for thinking, motion, and speech. Tik-Tok assists and protects Dorothy throughout the novel and later appears in an Oz play and film and further Oz books. Tik-Tok, though hardly the first robot in science fiction,[29] or even the first robot with agency, was nonetheless the first artificial superman in the 20th century, and the first to take on an active, physically beneficial role since the golem of the 1840s and 1850s.

Not long after came another early treatment of the artificial being as a literal übermensch, in Filippo Tommaso Marinetti's *Mafarka the Futurist* (1909), in which a North African warlord, depressed by the death of his brother, has a vision of bringing to life a son, Gazourmah, "a gigantic winged automaton, animated by both high technology and magic."[30] Gazourmah is a higher, better being: "Nature herself tries to bring him down with her elements out of fear and jealousy of his power and beauty, but just as his father has predicted, Gazourmah proves invincible as he dominates the sky in the fullness of his glory."[31]

One prominent example of the vigilante artificial being, this one influenced by the principles of the Physical Culture movement as well as by the new "muscle Jew" movement,[32] took place in 1917, when Chajim Bloch lightly altered Yudl Rosenberg's Yiddish collection of stories, *Niflaot Maharal* (1909), and published the stories under his own name in the *Österreichische Wochenschrift*. The stories were published in book form two years later and translated into English in 1925 as *Prager Golem*, not going out of print for the rest of the century. Rosenberg/Bloch "underplays the golem's destructive element and instead heightens its protective properties. The golem may be hero of the action, however, it is shown as a warrior upholding justice for the Jews rather than an automaton that has spun out of control."[33] His lift of Rosenberg quite successful, Bloch followed his book up with a new set of stories about the Chelm golem, entitled *Israel der Gotteskämpfer* (1920), supposedly about the golem of Rabbi Eliyahu of Chelm. Bloch's Eliyahu

> makes his golem in response to increasing hostility against the Jews of Poland, where abductions and sexual violence against Jewish women are the order of the day, as are murder and blood libel accusations. Salvation

from this condition, Bloch's Chelm golem suggests, must come from a Jew-ish warrior type based in ancient Jewish tradition and contrasting with the vulnerable and feminized diaspora Jew.[34]

During the 1920s, the golem's new image as a "muscle Jew" creature was well received and well distributed in Yiddish-language popular literature (the more commonly consumed literature of Jews of the time).

At the same time, the modern conception of robots was appearing, thanks to the work of Karel Čapek, whose 1920 play, *R.U.R.: Rossum's Universal Robots*, introduced to the world the word "robot" and greatly propagated the idea of artificial beings (which in *Rossum's Universal Robots*'s case are made out of synthetic organic material) with will and agency. *Rossum's Universal Robots* debuted as a play in America in 1922 and was translated as a book into English in 1923, leading to the adoption of robots in American science fiction. During the 1920s and early 1930s the pulps and the slicks, the two most common sources of science fiction at the time, were ambivalent in their portrayal of robots, but by the early 1930s their portrayal had changed. In Neil R. Jones's Professor Jameson stories (from 1931) human and alien minds are implanted into immortal cyborg and robot bodies, and the alien robots in Eando Binder's "The Robot Aliens" (1935) are well meaning.

The comic books of the Golden Age were filled with a surprising num-ber of robots, androids, and artificial beings, from Carl Burgos's Human Torch (for Marvel, from 1939) to Burgos's Iron Skull (for Centaur, from 1939) to Daniel Peters's Dynamic Man (for Marvel, from 1940) to Burgos's White Streak/Manowar (for Novelty Press, from 1940) to Dick Briefer's Frankenstein (for Prize, from 1940). Though obviously influenced by the trend toward heroic robots in the science fiction of the late 1930s and early 1940s, the writers of these early superhero comics were working off both the Talus tradition and the golem tradition, with the many Jewish writers of superhero comics, including Jerry Siegel (cocreator of Super-man), Joe Shuster (cocreator of Superman), Bill Finger (cocreator of Bat-man), Bob Kane (cocreator of Batman), Jack Kirby (cocreator of Captain America), and Stan Lee (cocreator of Spider-Man), recapitulating the golem legend in a new form and medium.

The Men of 40 Faces

Through 1910, Nick Carter's example was the main one that pulp and dime novel supermen of his particular type—the aggressive, crime-solving independent superhuman vigilante—followed. Carter had been the dominant type, and the modern master of his city, for over 20 years and had become an archetype, if not a cliché. With the rise in pulps (13 published in 1910, 5 more than in 1909) and the rise in interest in action/ adventure detective characters, it was to be expected that authors wanting to be successful and create a character whose appearances would be demanded by the audience would try not only to duplicate Carter's success but also strike out in new directions.

Thomas Hanshew succeeded, with his character Hamilton Cleek. Hanshew described Cleek in this way:

> The biggest and boldest criminal the police had ever had to cope with, the almost supernatural genius of crime, who defied all systems, laughed at all laws, mocked at all the Vidocqs, and Dupins, and Sherlock Holmeses, whether amateur or professional, French or English, German or American, that ever had been or ever could be pitted against him, and who, for sheer devilry, for diabolical ingenuity and for colossal impudence, had not met his match in all the universe.
>
> Who or what he really was, whence he came . . . no man knew and no man might ever hope to know unless he himself chose to reveal it. In his many encounters with the police he had assumed the speech, the characteristics, and, indeed, the facial attributes of each in turn, and assumed them with an ease and a perfection that were simply marvelous, and had gained for him the sobriquet of "Forty Faces" among the police, and of "The Vanishing Cracksman" among the scribes and reporters of newspaperdom.[35]

Cleek has the Übermensch ability to change his facial features because while pregnant Cleek's mother played with a rubber-faced toy, and this somehow affected Cleek, giving him the ability to rearrange the features of his face into anything he wishes.

Cleek, though beginning as a Lupin, quickly becomes a consulting detective and puts his superhuman ability to work fighting evil and solving crimes. Cleek was an immediate success, appearing in 18 stories and serials over the next three years as well as a film serial, George Lessey's *The Chronicles of Cleek* (1913–1914).

Cleek's minor influence was in the creating of the face-changing superpower, one later adopted by Elsa Barker's Dexter Drake (from 1925), Donald Wandrei's Man with the Molten Face (from 1937) and more notably the Avenger (from 1939) and used at various times by every stretching hero from Jack Cole's Plastic Man (for Quality, from 1939) to John Broome and Carmine Infantino's Elongated Man (for DC, from 1960) to Stan Lee and Jack Kirby's Mr. Fantastic (for Marvel, from 1961). Every time a pulp or comic hero uses their superpower(s) to change their face, they are hearkening back to Hamilton Cleek.

More broadly and influentially, though, Cleek represented the first major diversion from the Nick Carter stereotype. Cleek is an Übermensch vigilante, like Carter, but with a significantly different power, one that Hanshew drew the fan's gaze to far more often than the authors of the Carter stories, particularly Frederic van Rensselaer Dey, did to Carter's strength. Cleek is no Costumed Avenger—his power leads him to wear the opposite of a regular costume or disguise—but he is an Übermensch and urban adventurer who in essence becomes the master of his city, as Carter was of his. Too, Cleek was one of the major open-ended heroes of the time—Hanshew consistently wrote his adventures so that, like Carter before him, Cleek was stuck in the perpetual second act—and one whose popularity allowed him to appear in multiple magazines, across publishers, but in a popular pulp rather than in a dime novel, as had been the case with Carter. This established the cross-magazine, cross-publisher vigilante hero as a type (a trend that later pulp and comic publishers were not eager to embrace, for obvious reasons), but also as a popular alternative to the straight-laced, law-upholding Carter. Cleek retained many traces of his Lupin origin and fought for morality rather than the law—a character trait that numerous later heroes would inherit from him.

John Carter

Edgar Rice Burroughs's John Carter, first appearing in "Under the Moons of Mars" in 1912, was an immediate hit with readers and with publishers, leading to a number of sequels over the next 30 years and creating a series only a little less popular than Burroughs's most famous creation, the Tarzan books. Carter is a Civil War veteran (for the Confederacy) who is transported by mysterious means to Mars, which has less gravity than Earth, thus giving the athletic Carter superhuman strength and agility. On Mars, or "Barsoom" as its inhabitants call it, Carter encounters a literally colorful variety of aliens, from the warlike, four-armed Green Martians to the religious fanatic White Martians. Carter finds adventure, falls in love with a Red Martian, Princess Dejah Thoris, and becomes an intimate and comrade-in-arms of the leaders of Mars.

Burroughs is generally given a significant amount of credit for his creation of Carter. Coogan writes that "With John Carter . . . Edgar Rice Burroughs created the first wholly positive SF superman and the model for science fiction heroes of the next few decades."[36] Junot Díaz writes that

"John Carter was also one of our first recognizable superhumans, and there is little doubt that his extraordinary physical feats inspired Superman's creators."[37] Critics generally count Burroughs's Barsoom stories as the start of the "planetary romance" genre—adventure stories and novels set on other (usually primitive) planets.

These claims need qualifying. This is not to diminish Burroughs's achievements with the Barsoom stories; he was certainly responsible for *popularizing* the planetary romance genre in prose science fiction—a significant predecessor, Edwin Arnold's *Lieut. Gullivar Jones: His Vacation* (1905) did not attract a great deal of attention—and especially the idea of humans going to another planet and thereby gaining superhuman abilities[38]—an idea often used in planetary romance stories and novels and in comics, in Malcolm Kildale's Auro stories (for Fiction House, from 1940), among others.

But Burroughs was not a trailblazer, more of a snapper-up and developer of unconsidered trifles.

Interplanetary romance in the 20th century involves humans traveling to other planets and having adventures among the alien primitives there. But this is merely an inversion—and a predictable one—of the 19th century subgenre of aliens with superhuman abilities traveling to Earth and adventuring here, among the primitive humans. Zarah, in Charles Rowcroft's *The Triumph of Woman* (1848), has advanced technology and the power to change metals to gold. The Reverend Wladislaw Lach-Szyrma's Aleriel, who appeared in stories and novels from the 1860s through 1893, is an immortal winged Venusian alien, ethically superior and sinless compared to mere humans, who travels around Earth (and the other planets in the solar system). The "Marsman" of the pseudonymously written *The Professor's Last Experiment* (1888) is telepathic. Representatives of two superior alien races in Robert Potter's *The Germ Growers* (1892) use Earth as the battlefield for their proxy war. This trend can be seen in early 20th-century science fiction, as in John Russell Coryell's "The Weird and Wonderful Story of Another World," but also in comics, beginning with Superman and G. Ellerbrock and William Kent's Martan the Martian Man (from 1939, for Dell) and continuing through Grieg Chapian's Jupiter (for Prize, from 1940) and Joseph Samachson and Joe Certa's Martian Manhunter (for DC, from 1955).

What Burroughs did, predictably given his character and tastes, was to simply reverse this plot and make the human the hero and the Übermensch, so that the politics, morals, and allegories of the 19th century alien visitation novels (which after all are no more than 19th-century science fictional treatments of classical and medieval Christian stories about visitors from Heaven) would be overwritten by aggressive, id-heavy science fantasy full of nude women and nonwhite races who inevitably fall beneath the sword or gun or fists of a white man—a genre with great appeal to the juvenile (and juvenile at heart and in mind) white readers (and viewers) of science fiction, past and present.[39]

Victorian science fiction had no lack of stories in which humans travel to the Moon or to another planet, from John Munro's "A Message to Mars" (1895, as a novel 1897) to H. G. Wells's *First Men in the Moon* (1901). But the alien civilizations visited in these stories and novels were superior to human civilizations, morally and/or technologically. Again, Burroughs simply took this plot, and more broadly the plot of numerous Lost World and Hollow Earth novels, and replaced those elements less complimentary to juvenile American men with themes, tropes, and motifs that would be more flattering to them.

From a genre development point of view, the rise of Planetary Romance stories (which would become much more common in the 1920s and 1930s with the appearance and growth of the science fiction pulps) was matched by a decline in Lost World and Hollow Earth stories and novels, with other planets becoming the source of superpowers, as opposed to Lost Worlds or Hollow Earths being the venue in which ordinary humans can be supermen. There was still the occasional use of the Lost World or Hollow Earth in this manner, as in Frank Thomas's Chuck Hardy stories (for Centaur, from 1939) but more common were other planets.

Cinematic Supermen

The years just preceding World War I were ones of increasing interest in and production of films. In 1910, 85 films were made; in 1911, when most movie studios made their move to Southern California and Hollywood studios were established, 214 films were made; in 1912, 366 films were made; and, in 1913, 662 films were made.[40] The vast majority of these were dramas, comedies, and romances, but an increasing number of action/adventure, detective/mystery, and science fiction and fantasy films were also being made. And, as is usually the case, Hollywood copied what was successful in other media and made use of it themselves, which in this case were men and women with superpowers—the supermen and superwomen.

It began in 1912, with Colin Campbell's two short films about the Sherlock Holmesian Professor Locksley, *The Hypnotic Detective* (1912) and *The Stolen Treaty* (1913). Locksley is an English consulting detective whose ability at hypnosis is superhuman. Locksley is Watsoned by Dr. Pelham and reenacts Arthur Conan Doyle's "The Adventure of the Norwood Builder" in *The Hypnotic Detective* and Doyle's "The Naval Treaty" in *The Stolen Treaty*.

1914 saw three films with superhumans. Daniel Goodman and Lloyd Lonergan's *Zudora* featured Hassam Ali, a Hindu mystic of vague and undefined mystical powers, including the ability to light fires with his gaze from several miles' distance. George Melford's *The Invisible Power* featured Major Dean, a U.S. Army surgeon who has psychic abilities, including the power to read minds, and uses these abilities to lure a beautiful young woman away from her work in a low dance hall and to protect her from the owner of the dance hall. And Cecil Hepworth's *The Basilisk* featured Basil Reska, a vile villain who uses his mind control powers to put a beautiful woman in his control. His plans are ultimately foiled by the appearance of the film's titular serpent.

Over the next 10 years, 13 films would appear featuring men and women with superhuman abilities. Most of these men and women were the heroes and heroines of their films and used their powers for good. Compared to the total output of films in these years, one or two superhero films per year is a small number. But as a percentage of all the science fiction films produced during those years, the number of superhero films was much greater. However, the 1920s prejudice against superhumans put an end to the trend of superhero films, and supermen and superwomen would disappear from films until 1940, when James Horne's *Shadow*, Ford Beebe and Ray Taylor's *Green Hornet*, and William Witney and John English's *Mysterious Doctor Satan* all appeared.

The Night Wind

In 1913, Frederic van Rensselaer Dey was still churning out Nick Carter stories but apparently resented the comparatively small amount of money he was getting from Street & Smith, the owner of Nick Carter, for Dey began putting more effort into writing stories under his pseudonym of "Varick Vanardy." Dey, as "Vanardy," pitched and sold stories to pulps—*The Cavalier, All-Story Weekly*, and later *Detective Story Magazine*—which paid writers far better than what dime novel authors were getting. One of Dey's stories introduced Bingham Harvard, the Night Wind. Bingham Harvard is a bank clerk wrongly accused of theft. However, Harvard does not go quietly into custody and becomes a fugitive instead. The police pursue him, only to discover their mistake as Harvard begins preying on them. Harvard, called "the Night Wind" by the police for his elusiveness, does not kill the police, but he is quite content to break their limbs. He finds this easy to do, as he is at least five times stronger than a normal man. The police finally call in Kate Maxwell (later Maxwilton), a nurse turned police detective, to capture Harvard. She becomes convinced he's innocent, they fall in love, and together they escape from Gotham after marrying. They eventually return to the States, and after various harum-scarums and to-dos over various story arcs corrupt police and bank staff are uncovered, Harvard's good name restored, and Harvard and his wife live happily ever after.

The Night Wind would appear in four story serials in all (collected and published as novels each time) from 1913 to 1919.

The Night Wind is not, as Gavaler puts it, "the first 'extra-man,'"[41] but he was the first significant 20th-century Übermensch to straddle the ethical line between hero and villain and lean toward the villain side. Hamilton Cleek—who by this time had appeared in 17 short stories, serials, and novels and was still going strong—straddled the line but always made sure he was on the right side of it. Not so for the Night Wind. In this respect the Night Wind is not only the child of Nick Carter—for, as mentioned, the Night Wind was the creation of Frederic van Rensselaer Dey, the primary author for over 20 years of the Nick Carter stories, and has Carter's superstrength, albeit to a far greater degree—but also of the Lupins. The sympathies of the reader are supposed to be with the Night Wind at all times; the preferred inscribed narrative of Dey's stories is that the Night Wind is the hero, despite the fact that he is using his superhuman abilities for personal goals—to restore his reputation—rather than toward some selfless goal. This is in line with the Lupin stories of the 1910s.

Significantly, the Night Wind's superhuman ability, the combination of far-greater-than-human strength and agility, would essentially disappear from nonscience fiction pulps for a decade after the last Night Wind serial in 1919, not returning until Philip Wylie gave Hugo Danner a similar power set—this, despite the loving fan's gaze directed at the Night Wind's feats of strength. Far more typical of the supermen following the appearance of the Night Wind were heroes like Hereward Carrington's Dr. Payson Alden, from 1916. Alden is the fiancé of Myra Maynard. After her father's death Maynard inherits a packet of papers from him. The papers incriminate a group of hooded Rosicrucians who live in an underground city (Maynard's father had been a member), and the Rosicrucians attack her through vampires, malign spirits, and walking trees. Fortunately for Maynard, Dr. Alden is a master of the occult as well as a brilliant scientist, and when the Rosicrucians send fire spirits to set Maynard's house on fire, Dr. Alden summons up water elementals to put the fire out.

Witchcraft, thought transference, astral projection, and vampirism appear before Maynard and Dr. Alden get their happy ending.

Another typical superhuman hero was William Le Queux's John Durston, from 1917. He is a revolutionary educator and is acclaimed by the papers to be "the greatest authority on the psychology of crime in the world." He also practices a kind of mind control, through the manipulation of colors from the "chromatic centre of ideation," which he puts to good use in solving crimes and catching spies.[42]

The heroes of the postwar environment were similarly powered. Although these texts would keep the fan's gaze firmly on the heroes' powers, as the Night Wind stories did, the texts succumbed to the post–World War I discouragement of aggressive, physical superabilities and more generally of superhuman abilities altogether. Action/adventure pulps and mercenary stories and stories of down-and-dirty physical conflict, lovingly described, were on the rise, but neither writers, publishers, nor readers wanted the heroes of such stories to be superhuman.

Superwomen

Feminism, in the form of campaigns to get women the right to vote—women's suffrage—was a household issue in the United States by the start of World War I. Victorian women's suffrage movements had developed into canny political organizations that were effective both at lobbying and at public relations, and several individual states had already given women the right to vote. Women's suffrage was a national issue. Those working in favor of it were the "New Women," the generation of independent women who were living out the theories of economic, political, and sexual liberation and freedom that previous generations had mainly theorized about.

New Women fiction—written by New Women and featuring New Women main characters—had been around for a generation, and even begun filtering into genre fiction, with characters like Grant Allen's detective Lois Cayley (from 1898) and Robert Barr's journalist Jennie Baxter (1899) providing examples for later writers to follow. Inevitably, some of these characters became superwomen.

In George Allan England's "The Fatal Gift" (1915), two physicians "have worked out fantastic techniques for plastic surgery, and they plan to make 'Alexandra,' a wealthy Russian woman, into the utmost of female beauty."[43] The result is not just a beautiful woman, but an immortal one.

In 1917, John Charles Beecham created Koyala, a half-white, half-Indonesian woman who hates the Dutch colonists of the Netherlands East Indies and the white visitors to the islands. She wants them all to die: "When the last white man spills his heart on the coral shore and the wrongs done Chawatangi's daughter, my mother, have been avenged, then Koyala will join the *Hanu Token* that call her."[44] The *Hanu Token* are the spirits that sometimes possess Koyala, speak through her, and tell her hidden things.

1918 saw three superwomen. Frank Clark and Norris Shannon created Shirley Bowman, for the film *The Magic Eye*. Bowman has clairvoyance, and uses her visions to rescue her father from drowning and her mother from an unscrupulous shipping agent. F. Tennyson Jesse began a series of stories about Solange Fontáine. Fontaine is the daughter of a French scientist and an Englishwoman. Fontaine lives in Paris and works as an assistant in her father's police laboratory. Fontaine is an expert chemist, but uses her instincts and the psychic visions she receives in her dreams to solve crimes.

And George D. Baker created Mary Manners for the film *In Judgment Of.* She is the descendant of a Romany (Gypsy) family and has inherited from them the ability to read minds. When Manners, a debutante, is rescued from robbers by Dr. John O'Neil, the two become friends. This causes friction between Manners and her fiancé Robert Brainard, which is made worse by the revelation that O'Neil is Robert's stepbrother. Robert's father, Judge Brainard, is blackmailed with this information, but the Judge kills the blackmailer. O'Neil is arrested for the crime, but Manners uses her abilities to discover the truth and Judge Brainard, knowing that Manners knows the truth, admits to the crime. But according to the jury Judge Brainard acted in self-defense and is acquitted of the crime, and Manners and O'Neil marry.

This trend toward using superwomen in fiction and film ceased in 1920, a decade hostile to superhumans of both sexes. Not coincidentally, so did the trend toward using women as protagonists in nonromance fiction and film. For most of the next decade, in fact, action/adventure genres—adventure, Westerns, detective/mystery, and science fiction—tended to avoid using women in anything but the love interest role. There were a few notable exceptions—Charles W. Tyler's "Blue Jean Billy" stories, about an oceangoing female Robin Hood (from 1918); Archibald Thomas Pechey's "Adjusters" short stories and novels (from 1922) have Daphne Wrayne, society girl and amateur detective; and Agatha Christie's "Tommy & Tuppence Beresford" short stories and novels (from 1922) have Tuppence as a crime-solving nurse and wife—but to a significant degree female leads before 1920 outnumbered female leads after 1920 by roughly 10:1.

The 1920s are generally seen as a time of liberation-in-action for women, with "flappers," the 1920s version of the Victorian New Woman, flouting social and sexual norms and living independent lives, but it was also a time when the real gains of women during the 1910s were being rolled back:

> Just as women had won the right to vote and a handful of state legislatures had granted women jury duty and passed equal-pay laws, another counter-assault on feminism began. The U.S. War Department, with the aid of the American Legion and the Daughters of the American Revolution, incited a red-baiting campaign against women's rights leaders. Feminists like Charlotte Perkins Gilman suddenly found they couldn't get their writings published . . . the media maligned suffragists; magazine writers advised that feminism was "destructive of women's happiness"; popular novels attacked "career women"; clergymen railed against "the evils of woman's revolt"; scholars charged feminism with fueling divorce and infertility . . . post-feminist sentiments first surfaced, not in the 1980s media, but in the 1920s press. Under this barrage, membership in feminist organizations soon plummeted, and the remaining women's groups hastened to denounce the Equal Rights Amendment or simply converted themselves to social clubs. "Ex-feminists" began issuing their confessions.[45]

This "counterassault on feminism" manifested itself, in genre fiction, by the relatively abrupt removal—again, with a few exceptions—of female protagonists from fiction and film, including superwomen. Their absence would last through the decade, although in the late 1920s that would begin to change, with the appearance of Agatha Christie's Miss Marple in 1927 and Katherine Brocklebank's Border Service agent Tex in 1928. The 1930s, however, would see a return to the form of the 1900s and 1910s. H. Bedford-Jones's mesmerist Mme. Vanderdonk (1933), Constance May Evans's clairvoyant Pam Wayne (1935), Jessie Douglas Kerruish's psychic occult detective Luna Bartendale (1936), Watt Dell's superhumanly strong Olga Mesmer (1937–1938, and the first superhuman superwoman in a comic strip), John Russell Fearn's superhumanly strong and resilient Golden Amazon (1939–1960), Watt Dell's superhumanly strong Vera Ray (1940–1943)—these and other superwomen appeared in the pulps and in novels in the 1930s, in some cases (like Olga Mesmer's and Vera Ray's) repeatedly, so that when the female superheroes of the comics appeared, they had the models of the superwomen of the 1930s to draw upon.

Westerns

American frontier fiction, especially the Western, has always been perceived as a conservative and even reactionary genre, its borders and limits set not just geographically and chronologically but racially and thematically. Although this perception is largely true, there have always been exceptions to this, so that within the Western, from the very beginning, there have been subversive and even radical elements.

Before the development of the Western in the middle of the 19th century, there was frontier fiction, and frontier fiction not only gave the reader the (ultraconservative, Indian-killer) character of Nick of the Woods, but also numerous works in which the authors portrayed a surprising amount of sympathy with poor Mexicans and native Mexicans (as opposed to the Mexican ruling elite, who were seen as an oppressive class responsible for the Mexican-American War). During the 1870s, when the Western had become the dominant form of frontier fiction, a repeating theme was the corruption of the upper classes and the defense of the poor and working classes by the cowboy hero. Owen Wister's *The Virginian* (1901–1902), generally seen as the first modern Western, has a nuanced take on masculinity and a significant homoerotic subtext, to the point that the narrator says, of the Virginian, "The Virginian looked at her with such a smile that, had I been a woman, it would have made me his to do what he pleased with on the spot."[46] And the dime novel Buffalo Bill had a Chinese sidekick, Lung Hi, portrayed in positive (if stereotypical) terms—this, at a time when government legislation in the form of Immigration and Naturalization Acts were aimed at preventing Asians from emigrating to the United States.

Writers of Westerns in the 20th century did not usually display the same progressivity on sexual issues, but continued to push at the borders of the genre in other ways. In 1918, Frederick Faust, under the pseudonym of Max Brand, inserted *fantastika*[47] into the Western when he began writing the adventures of Dan Barry. Barry is the "Pan of the Desert," an orphan of mysterious origin who is adopted by Joe Cumberland, a rancher in the "mountain-desert" of the American Southwest. Barry grows up to become a rather strange man, short, slim, and almost feminine, with an uncanny (literally) rapport with animals; he is always accompanied by a wolf named Black Bart and by a horse named Satan. When Cumberland first sees Barry, the boy is following a flight of geese and apparently whistling to them. This gives rise to Barry's nickname: "Whistlin' Dan."

Unfortunately, the generally conservative approach of the pulps in the 1920s toward innovation meant that writers, though heavily influenced by Faust's style and work ethic, did not choose Dan Barry to imitate and did not produce further supermen. Although Westerns were popular during the 1920s, rising from 3 percent of the total market in 1920 to 13 percent of the total market (second-highest genre) in 1930,[48] Western plots and characters tended to be on the conservative side, with the presence of *fantastika* being limited to the appearance of Lost Races. It wasn't until 1929—an important year, as we'll see—that border-pushing returned: in Paul Ellsworth Triem's "Ting-a-Ling" stories (from 1929), about a Chinese immigrant cowboy hero; in the anonymously written 1933 "Hawk of the Plains" series that combined Westerns with science fiction; and, finally, a return to supermen in the character of Thomas Ernest Mount's Silver Trent, written before the debut of Superman in *Action Comics* #1 (published in April 1938), but debuting a few months afterward. Trent is sometimes called the "Rio Robin Hood" and is known as "El Halcon de la Sierra," "The Great Hawk of the Sierras," because of his superhuman night vision, which he uses to fight against his enemy, El Diablo.

Eugenics and the Backlash

By the 1920s the eugenics movement was well established in the United States and taken seriously as a cause by intellectuals and a group of outspoken scientists. The mass of Americans, though soured on the more extreme suggestions for achieving the eugenic paradise its proponents dreamed of, still supported the movement's goals; while "negative eugenics," the coercive sterilization, institutionalization, and dehumanization of neighbors and family members, was not something that most Americans could support, they still felt that its ideals and ends were correct. The intelligentsia were meanwhile fervently embracing it, as were social reformers.[49]

Responding to the widespread concern with producing better babies, healthier families, and a fitter, stronger race, public intellectuals began producing serious works—nongenre works, works of fiction that were intended to be taken seriously by other intellectuals, not just the public—that played with the idea of the Übermensch. George Bernard Shaw's play *Back to Methuselah* (published in 1921) describes a future in which men have discovered the secret of living to be 300 years old, a secret that also gives them superhuman mental and physical abilities. *Back to Methuselah* was taken very seriously by leading journals and thinkers, and the issues it raised were debated at length. H. G. Wells—at this point an enormously influential figure—responded with *Men Like Gods* (1922–1923), a novel in which present-day humans are transported to a Utopia located in a parallel universe. The inhabitants of the Utopia are physical supermen with telepathic abilities.

Supermen and superwomen became much less common in the pulps, slicks, novels, and films of the 1920s than they had been in previous decades, although they were hardly unknown. Albert Smith's flying, phasing, invisible Dr. De Brutel (film, 1920); John Grey and Arthur Reeve's telepathic mesmerist Robert Dupont (film, 1920); George Seitz and Frank Leon Smith's teleporting Phantom (film, 1920); Norbert Jacques's telepathic mesmerist Dr. Mabuse (films from 1921); George Seitz and Frank Leon Smith's mesmerist Dr. Santro (1921); Dion Fortune's occult detective Dr. Taverner (stories, from 1922); Finis Fox and Milford Howard's telepathic Dr. Godfrey (film, 1923); Clarence Budington Kelland's magic "Still Face" (print serial, 1924, film 1927); Elsa Barker's Dexter Drake (from 1925); and Victor Rousseau Emmanuel's occult detective Dr. Martinus (stories from 1926)—all these were superhuman, though note that 7 of the preceding 10 appear in the first three years of the decade, 7 of them were in film rather than in print, and 5 of those 10 were villains.

But an examination of the popular genre fiction of the 1920s and the leading newspapers and magazines of the decade shows that the Übermensch was largely considered to be a subject for debate and sober consideration rather than just another product of popular culture. Eugenics, and the production of real-life supermen, were discussed at the highest public levels, in the pages of the *New York Times* (whose Editor of Science would inveigh against it in 1928, warning that eugenics would "establish an artificial aristocracy, which, like all aristocracies, would seek to perpetuate itself"),[50] *Harper's Weekly*, *Atlantic Monthly*, *Saturday Evening Post*, and *Time* magazine. Consciously or unconsciously, the producers of popular culture generally refrained from creating, publishing, and distributing texts with supermen in them, and left the making of supermen to real life, in which "Better Babies" contests were common and the Supreme Court, in its 1927 *Buck v. Bell* case, made eugenical sterilization the law of the land.[51]

Other, broad sociopolitical currents and trends were also discouraging the casual fictional use of supermen in the role of heroes.

Although the iconic clash over evolution took place in 1925 with the Scopes trial, the battle between religious fundamentalists and believers in science on the subject of evolution had been carried out since the beginning of World War I, and had intensified after the end of the war. The basic objection that fundamentalists had was that Darwin's denial of religious miracles and the supernatural left, in the words of prominent anti-evolutionist William Jennings Bryan, "the Bible a story book without binding authority on the conscience of man."[52] Less often articulated by fundamentalists, but an unavoidable conclusion given Darwin's theories, was evolution's rebuke to the religious belief that man was God's ultimate

creation—that man was made by God in His own image—and the consequent idea in evolutionary theory that some other, higher, better race
would eventually supersede humanity. Fictional supermen—new races,
like Frankenstein's creature had been—were an unpleasant and unwelcome reminder of this notion, and while fundamentalists were not usually the ones writing (or reading) *fantastika*, their displeasure with the
idea of humanity being superseded seeped into the Zeitgeist and affected
even the nonreligious.

Darwin, of course, was not the only significant figure who had voiced
the notion of humanity's being replaced by a successor. Friedrich
Nietzsche, in his *Also Sprach Zarathustra* (1883–1891), famously wrote "I
teach you the superman. Man is something that is to be surpassed."[53]
Nietzsche's idea of the "superman" was not of a superhumanly *powered*
being—the Übermensch described in this book—so much as one of a
higher *moral* and *aesthetic* order of being than ordinary men and women.
But many Americans (as shown in the newspaper and magazine articles
of the decade that discussed Nietzsche) blurred this distinction and con-
ferred the offense taken at the latter concept, Nietzsche's original, to
offense taken at the former concept, the product of popular fiction rather
than philosophy.

For many Americans, including the less religiously inclined, superhuman heroes were objectionable (and to be avoided) on other grounds.
Many white Americans had a positive view of eugenics' aims at creating
better white people, but were simultaneously hostile toward and afraid of
advanced technology and science and modernity itself, both the products
of it and the producers of it, including industrialization, bureaucracy, and
mass-produced culture, and the superhuman action hero was one of the
products of advanced science and cultural modernity. Educated secular
Americans turned toward a celebration of the "primitive" in the arts, and
away from the concepts created in mass-produced low art, like superhuman action hero texts.

Last, the idea of a higher being than humanity, physically and intellectually superior, likely represented one shock too many to the psyches of
creators and the reading and viewing public. Consider: for much of the
decade Americans were still emotionally reeling from the costs of World
War I and the losses of the influenza epidemic. Extreme right-wing governments appeared across the world, while at home wild irresponsibility
(in the form of the stock market, out-of-control spending, soaring divorce
rates, and disturbing changes in youth morality) seemed the norm. Future
shock, in the form of rapidly advancing technology, had set in: the appearance of the Model T, the appearance of talking cinema, the rise in air

travel from an oddity to a common occurrence, the rise in medical technology (like adhesive bandages and penicillin)—all these things had to contribute to a basic feeling of instability on the part of creators and consumers. Having astronomer Percival Lowell begin the decade by speculating that there was an intellectually and technologically superior race of Martians watching the Earth[54]—that humanity was not, after all, either alone in the solar system or the most advanced species in it—would have been touching Americans hard on a sensitive spot. The sentiment against superior beings—supermen, in the case of popular fiction and film—must have been widespread.

Spawn of the Depression

The United States entered a recession in August 1929, two months before the stock market crashed—a recession the crash made far worse. The first round of stock failures did not take place until the following September, and the second round of bank failures did not take place until May 1931, but the word "depression" was used in newspapers within days of the crash, the rise in unemployment had already begun during the recession and surged following the stock market crash, and consumer confidence and consumption also immediately declined. From the point of view of the average American, the economic bad times began in August 1929 and just kept going.

There were several responses to this by the creators and producers of popular culture. One of them was to give consumers ever-more-incredible stories. There was an increase in *fantastika* in film, from 11 films (out of 1486) in 1929 to 42 films (out of 1524) in 1933.[55] In the pulps, both general and science fiction, the amount of *fantastika* being published increased yearly throughout the decade.[56] Overt, extreme wish fulfillment texts suddenly became popular again, after a decade of being unwelcome; worries about appropriate behavior for courting men and women were replaced by worries about being able to pay for food, and those doing the worrying needed increasingly vivid escapist literature and film. And influential and high-profile supermen began appearing regularly again for the first time in a decade.

E. C. "Elzie" Segar's comic strip "Thimble Theater" had been appearing since 1919, with Segar introducing Popeye the Sailor only in January 1929. Over a period of a few months Popeye took over the strip, which was renamed "Thimble Theater, Starring Popeye." By June it was established that Popeye got superpowers by rubbing the head of the magic Whiffle Hen—Popeye is able to shrug off being shot 16 times and was able to knock men out with one blow—but as a regular occurrence the exhibition of Popeye's superhuman abilities did not begin until the fall of 1929, after the beginning of the Depression.[57]

The following June, Philip Wylie's *Gladiator* was published, featuring Hugo Danner. Danner is the son of Abednego Danner, a scientist who wants to produce a superman. To do so Danner gives a special serum to his son, Hugo, who grows up to be superhumanly strong, fast, and tough. Hugo is capable of leaping 40 feet in the air, of lifting cars, of bending steel with his hands, and of ignoring everything short of an exploding artillery shell.

Gladiator, and Hugo Danner, are important in the history of superheroes because of their influence on Superman. Jerry Siegel, cocreator of Superman, read *Gladiator* in 1932 and reviewed it in his fanzine *Science Fiction*, although Siegel would later downplay the influence of *Gladiator* on the creation of Superman. (There's no evidence that Ralston, Nanovic, and Dent, the creators of Doc Savage, read *Gladiator* before creating Doc Savage, but another of Wylie's novels, *The Savage Gentleman* (1932), about a physical Übermensch raised in isolation, has some interesting parallels with the Doc Savage stories.) Hugo Danner's strength, agility, and endurance were more exaggerated versions of what Popeye had, and Danner's aggressive brutality was a marked change from the more refined, less physical approach of 20 years of superhumans since the Night Wind—and Danner's strength and physical approach would be duplicated by Siegel and Shuster in the Superman stories.

But, as with the Scarlet Pimpernel and Zorro, Hugo Danner and *Gladiator*'s place in the lineage of the superhero needs qualifying. *Gladiator* was directly influential on Siegel and the inventors of Doc Savage, but Danner did not invent the concept of the physical superman. As mentioned, Popeye precedes him, and in the February 1930 issue of the science fiction pulp *Astounding Stories* Sophie Wenzel Ellis's "Creatures of the Light" appeared, in which a hunchbacked scientist, Dr. Emil Mundson, creates an Übermensch:

> Adam, a superman of incredible mental ability and physical perfection. He is one of Mundson's creations, and it was his giant intellect that created the solar sphere that Mundson flies. Adam also is telepathic and has the power to disappear, entering the fourth dimension (time), a few moments ahead of the present. He does this by mental power. Adam has also perfected a death ray. Amiability, however, is not a strength of the future race, for Adam is power mad and intends to take over the world. He also wants the human female Athalia, whom Mundson has reared . . . Eve, Adam's female counterpart. Just as perfect as Adam, she is the most advanced of the superpeople in the Antarctic oasis.[58]

Wylie, of course, would never have stooped to allow himself to be influenced by Popeye or by a story appearing in *Astounding Stories*: "Wylie mocked junk culture, mocked yellow journalism and Bernarr MacFadden and narcissistic bodybuilders, and he'd surely have mocked *Amazing Stories* if he'd bothered to notice it."[59] But Wylie was, however unconsciously, drawing upon the Zeitgeist's desire for escapism and for supermen as well as a decade's worth of debate about supermen on the highest cultural and intellectual levels.

Soon thereafter came Sewell B. Wright's "From the Ocean's Depths" (*Astounding Stories*, March 1930) and "Into the Ocean's Depths" (*Astounding Stories*, May 1930), starring Warren Mercer, a wealthy inventor and explorer and diver who finds a mermaid near his estate in Florida. Mercer has invented a form of telepathy that he uses to communicate with the mermaid, and he learns about their culture. A year later, Jane Littell began her Pussy Fane stories. Fane is a beautiful escort ("party girl") for the Pauline Whiting Entertainment Agency, letting herself be used as arm candy by men who want a pretty girl by their side for an evening. And Fane is more than just pretty: she's beautiful, with blonde hair and green eyes. But she's a little screwed up, as well. She grew up in a circus, among the big cats, "and then, because someone said, within her hearing for the hundredth time that she wasn't human, that she was more than half cat herself, that she even reeked with that acrid, pungent odor of the cats, she had walked from the circus without a penny or shred of baggage."[60] She continues to fear that "the strong jungle odor of the cats would cling to her for life," and regularly douses herself in the strongest perfume she knows. But the athleticism she learned in the circus, and the superhuman strength that she was born with—"any sudden need always found her possessed of the strength of twenty men"—help her in times of peril.[61]

Pussy Fane appeared in *Underworld Romances*, a short-lived attempt to merge the crime and romance pulp genres, and it's hardly likely that any of the later producers of superwomen or supermen read the stories in which she appeared. But Pussy Fane embodied the readers' desire for physically larger-than-life characters during the Depression, a desire that also produced Hugo Danner.

Pulp Supermen

Following the debut of *Gladiator*, which attracted enough attention to gain a positive review in *American Mercury*, more active, aggressive supermen began to appear in the pulps. The air aces pulps, which at the time were beginning to make use of Costumed Avenger heroes, similarly began making use of supermen, beginning with Donald Keyhoe's Philip Strange stories in *Flying Aces* from August 1931. Strange is the "phantom ace of G.2.," an agent of American military intelligence. During World War I, he fights against the Germans, specifically targeting their Mad Scientists and Evil Surgeons, killing them on the ground and in the skies. Strange is aided in this by his mental powers, for which he gained the nickname "the Brain Devil." Strange has ESP, clairvoyance, and various other mental powers that he can call upon as the plot requires it.

Similarly powered heroes would follow in the air ace pulps, so that even late in the genre's lifetime, Keyhoe could get 34 stories published, from 1936, about a similar hero, Richard Knight, who was blinded fighting the Germans during World War I. Through undescribed means he regains his sight and gains the power to see at night, and becomes Secret Agent "Q" for the American government, fighting Yellow Peril Japanese spies in China, Lost Races, and dinosaurs.

Other pulp genres would similarly begin using supermen. In the science fiction pulps, no less than editor John Campbell, whose philosophy of fiction was that it should show the consequences of scientific development in terms of how society changed—a thoughtful philosophy antithetical to the shallow superhero comics of the Golden Age—indulged in supermen fiction with his 1934 Aarn Munro stories, about a 21st-century native of Jupiter. That planet's high gravity leads to Munro having strength and agility far beyond those of humans from Earth. He also has a superhuman brain and is capable of solving in hours the problems of antigravity, infallible meteor shields, and traveling at faster-than-light speeds.

The ostensibly espionage/adventure-oriented pulp *Secret Agent X* hosted Frederick C. Davis's Ravenwood stories, about a psychic occult detective, in 1936, who says of himself "the realities of Oriental mysticism are incredible to the modern Occidental mind, but fortunately I am of both worlds. I devote myself to investigating strange crimes because the unknown ways of Siva–Siva, the attribute of destruction in the system of Yoga—is a challenge I must meet."[62] His powers allow him to get psychic impressions off of objects, as well as be vaguely clairvoyant and have other abilities as the plot requires.

Even the semipornographic *Spicy Mystery Stories* got into the act in 1935, 1936, and 1937, with Robert Leslie Bellem's Dr. Zarkov. He is the "Surgeon of Souls," a superhuman being (he may not even be human) who has the ability to travel in time and space and to warp reality. He uses these abilities to appear to those who are at moral crossroads, offering to cure them of the "cancerous tumors" (lust, envy, hate, etc.) in their souls and to guide them to a righteous course of living.

There was also Watt Dell's Olga Mesmer (1937–1938). The scientist Mesmer saves a mysterious amnesiac woman, Margot, from death at the hands of a knife-wielding murderer. Margot's eyes have a supernaturally enchanting quality, so Mesmer marries her and subjects her to various experiments, including a "soluble X-ray." The effects leave Margot bed-ridden, with bandages over her eyes. Mesmer celebrates by throwing a party in the next room. Margot overhears one, tears the bandages from her eyes, and sees through the walls into the room. She turns her gaze on Mesmer, killing him, and then gives birth to her daughter, Olga, and dies. Olga inherits her mother's ability and as an adult has both X-ray vision and superhuman strength, which she uses to prevent crime.

After the Shadow began displaying his ability to cloud men's minds so they could not see him, the detective pulps began joining in the use of Übermensch detectives. Wyatt Blassingame's John Smith, from 1937, in *Detective Tales* is a wealthy, well-known private detective in New Orleans. He was blinded while in college and spent 10 years without sight, during which time he developed his other senses to a superhuman level. An operation restored his sight, and since then he has used all of his senses to investigate crime, many of which, as befits New Orleans, have Gothic overtones.

A late attempt at a hero pulp also followed, in Paul Chadwick's *Captain Hazzard Magazine* (cover date May 1938, on sale date February 1938). The titular hero is modeled on Doc Savage and is a master of technology and advanced science, as well as an "ace adventurer, conqueror of fear, and master of modern science."[63] He also has enhanced senses. As a child Hazzard lost his sight, and to compensate he developed his other senses to the human peak. He also developed limited telepathy and the ability to project his thoughts across long distances. An operation restores his eyesight, and Hazzard is inspired to use his new good fortune to help others.

By April 1938, when Superman debuted, the pulps could be said to be providing enough supermen that the superhero comics were in large part imitating them, rather than providing something new.

Outside the Pulps

Creators outside the pulps were similarly following the supermen trend, inspired by the public's Depression-fueled need for larger-than-life characters. Harry Earnshaw's radio program *Chandu the Magician* (1932; it would inspire an eponymous movie later that year) featured two super-humans. Chandu, née Frank Chandler, is a secret agent for the American government. He went to Tibet and India and stayed there for three years, learning hypnosis and the various mystic and occult "arts of the *yogi*." He then returned back home and began a war on crime and evil, using his powers against wickedness (although his "magic" is "impotent in the face of blind fear").[64]

Vera Oldham's Omar debuted in *Chandu the Magician* and in 1935 was the lead in his own radio program, *Omar the Wizard of Persia*. On *Chandu the Magician,* Omar appears as a mystic who had learned the secrets of the East from the same *yogi* who taught Chandu. In *Omar the Mystic* Omar takes center stage, fighting a variety of supernatural evils with the assistance of the lovely Zaidda and Omar's Watson, the American jewel dealer Henry Mason. Omar's leitmotif is the ringing of eerie bells, which signifies Omar's presence or interest in events. Omar also passes on cryptic warnings: "wise men bar the door against a howling wolf," "beware, the heart of a woman is weak," "the black wings of death . . . their shadow cast," and so on.[65]

The trend expanded to the world of children's books, beginning with Harold Sherman's four-book "Tahara Adventure" series, from 1933. Young explorer Dick, while adventuring in the Sahara, discovers a Lost Race of blue-eyed Aryans at a Stone Age–level of civilization. He befriends them, and a group of treehouse-dwelling missing link ape-men, and discovers that he is the reincarnation of the lost race's greatest mystic, "Tahara." With a couple of members of each group, and accompanied by the Indian mystic Mahatma Sikandar, Dick (now calling himself "Tahara") journeys into the jungles of Africa, where he goes in search of the lost treasures of King Solomon and the lost lore of Queen of Sheba. As time passes, Tahara's mental powers grow, and eventually Tahara fulfills the prophesies about his fate in battles with immortals from a hidden city in the Yucatan jungles to the ruins of an Aztec fortress.

The trend even returned to mystery novels, in Gilderoy Davison's Mister Brent novels, from 1935. He has a kind of telepathy, which means he can receive impressions of other people's thoughts when they come within a few feet. It, and his skills as a thief and killer, is used by him to steal and to strike at humanity, which Brent hates. Unfortunately for Brent, he is mad, suffers from black outs, and lacks the ability not just to be introspective but even to remember much beyond a few days. He is actually an alternate personality of Tony Rockleston, the son of an eminent diplomat.

In Constance May Evans's Pam Wayne mystery stories, from 1935, Pam Wayne is a young Englishwoman who uses her extraordinary ability to see through walls to solve crimes and help England against its hostile enemies.

In Howard Higgin's 1936 film *The Invisible Ray*, Janos Rukh is a scientist who convinces several of his colleagues and supporters to accompany him on an expedition to Africa, to study an ancient meteorite. Rukh discovers that the meteorite is radioactive and exposes himself to it. One of the scientists on the trip, Dr. Benet, creates an antidote that saves Rukh from death by radiation poisoning, but Rukh is left with the ability to kill others simply by touching them.

By the time the Shadow returned to the radio, in 1937—his original series had been canceled in 1935 due to Street & Smith's insistence that the radio host be replaced by the vigilante of the pulps—and began displaying his ability to cloud men's minds so they could not see him, he was simply part of a trend.

Conclusion

By the time Superman made his first appearance, there were a panoply of supermen and superwomen in the pulps and the slicks, on the radio, and in novels. None of them combined the elements of the Costumed Avenger and the Übermensch the way that Superman did, but those supermen and superwomen already in existence cumulatively presented readers with all the elements of superheroes as listed in Chapter 1. What was required—and it can be fairly stated that if Siegel and Shuster didn't invent Superman then someone else would have—was a new medium to host these new figures.

CHAPTER EIGHT

Comics' Early Years

The first comic book published in the United States was created by a Swiss cartoonist, Rodolphe Töpffer, in 1837 for a Swiss audience, and was only published in the United States in 1842, as *The Adventures of Mr. Obadiah Oldbuck*. The 1870s saw the rise in humorous cartoons in magazines for adults and children. The 1880s saw the appearance of hardbound books reproducing humorous drawings. But it wasn't until the 1890s that comic strips—series of drawn panels that cumulatively told a story—came to be.

The New Medium

Comic strips developed out of the 19th-century newspaper cartoons. In 1892, William Randolph Hearst owned the *San Francisco Examiner*, and his cartoonist, Jimmy Swinnerton, customarily drew little bears to accompany the newspaper's weather section. Eventually Swinnerton turned the bears into a regular feature, "The Little Bears," what we would now recognize as a comic strip, arguably the first such in American newspapers. In 1895, when Hearst moved to New York City and acquired the *New York Journal*, he brought Swinnerton with him, and Swinnerton began the strip "The Little Tigers." The 1895 move began a bitter competition for circulation with Joseph Pulitzer's *New York World*. As part of the competition, Hearst stole Richard F. Outcault from the *World*, and Outcault began producing "The Yellow Kid," the first color comic strip for newspapers, for the *Journal*. "The Yellow Kid" became an instant hit and cultural phenomenon.

Comic strips flourished over the next 30 years, so that in 1929 a number of comic strips of high quality were being published in newspapers, including Don Moore and Alex Raymond's "Flash Gordon" and Harold Gray's "Little Orphan Annie." Dell Publishing, at the time a magazine publisher, including pulps, issued *The Funnies*, a 16-page newspaper insert made up of original comic strips. *The Funnies* ran for 36 weekly issues, through October 1930, before ceasing publication, but it did lay the groundwork for Gulf Oil Company's *Gulf Comic Weekly*, a four-page tabloid featuring original strips, for Eastern Color *Print's Funnies on Parade*, a similar tabloid-format collection of comic strips (these licensed rather than original), and for *Famous Funnies: A Carnival of Comics*, another collection of licensed comic strips, but this time in what we now recognize as the comic book format. *Famous Funnies* was the first American comic book.

Famous Funnies was a one-shot, given away (or sold, no one is sure which) through Woolworth's department store chain, but in 1934 Eastern Color followed up with an ongoing comic book, also titled *Famous Funnies*, which quickly became a hit and a cash cow for its publisher and inspired several imitators.

Prologue to Superman

In the fall of 1934, Malcolm Wheeler-Nicholson, a writer for the pulps and for self-published work, founded National Allied Publications and began publishing a comic book, *New Fun* (cover date February 1935). *New Fun* was Wheeler-Nicholson's response to the success of *Famous Funnies* and its imitators, his attempt to cash in on the new medium. Finding that all the rights to the popular newspaper comic strips were signed away, however, Wheeler-Nicholson commissioned original work from writers and artists (writing five of the features himself), so that *New Fun* was the first American comic book with all-new material.

Although *New Fun* was not an immediate success—Wheeler-Nicholson continually struggled with finances during these years—Wheeler-Nicholson added a second comic book, *New Comics*, 10 months later (cover date December 1935), and a third, *Detective Comics* (cover date March 1937, on sale date February 10, 1937). By April 1938, the month of Superman's debut, there were 22 comics being published from 11 publishers, with more comics appearing on a seemingly monthly basis. However, the great majority of these comics remained comic strip reprints or originals.

So the period of years before Superman's appearance needs to be viewed very much as prologue to what is currently seen as the Golden Age of comics, both generically and from a business standpoint. In terms of the comic book business, comic strips, whether original or (preferably) reprints, remained the best investment. Superman's appearance changed that, as we'll see, but not immediately.

Table 1   Number of New Strips in Comic Books from 1935–December 7, 1941 Based on Cover Dates

	1935	1936	1937	1938	1939	1940	1941*	1942
Adventure	8	9	8	12	25	58	26	2
Artificial					2	6	2	1
Costumed Avenger		2	3	6	9	72	110	14
Cowboy	3	1	9	4	7	19	4	5
Crime	1	11	20	14	34	78	40	5
History	3			3	4	5	3	
Jungle		2		1	2	15	3	
Pilot	2		1	1	9	43	21	
Pirate			1	1	1	2	2	
SF	2	1	2	3	11	48	10	2
Spy	1	1	3	2	10	19	27	1
Supermen	1	2	1	1	35	158	115	9
Villain					2	10	3	
War					3	19	23	5

*Last three months of 1941 have a 1942 cover date.

The content of *New Fun* and *New Comics* in 1935 reflects the best-selling pulps of the day, especially *Argosy* and *Adventure*, with their emphasis on straightforward adventure strips. 1935 was the second year of the pulps' boom period, which ran from 1934 to 1941, but the quickest growing genres—Westerns, spicy, and detective—were not necessarily the best selling, and Wheeler-Nicholson, in *New Fun* and *New Comics*, was imitating what was selling and popular, not what was growing, with his emphasis on adventure strips. The relatively heavy use of science fiction in 1935 may seem curious, as science fiction pulps in 1935 commanded 4 percent of the pulps market[1] and were only 2 percent of all films made during that year,[2] but Ken Fitch (the writer of the two science fiction strips in *New Fun* and *New Comics*) was clearly influenced by the popularity of, among others, the "Flash Gordon" and Philip Nowlan's and Dick Calkins's "Buck Rogers" comic strips, with Fitch's "Don Drake" comic being particularly obvious in its "Flash Gordon" tendencies.

1936 was the first year when comics began to explore what this new medium was capable of, increasing the number of genres that were appearing in the comics and trying out new or previously ignored genres. By 1937, the number of Costumed Avengers increased to five and the number of supermen to three.

But in April 1938, the month of Superman's debut in *Action Comics* #1 (cover date June 1938), there were still only two characters of significance to what would become the superhero genre.

The first was George E. Brenner's The Clock. Brian O'Brien, a former All-American fullback and champion polo player, is outraged at the widespread crime in the city, so he retires from his job as District Attorney and devotes his time to crime fighting, making criminals' time run out as the Clock. (The police hate him for this.) He is helped by a young woman named Butch and a former boxer named Pug. He has no superpowers but is in great shape and is an excellent fighter. The criminals he fights are usually ordinary gangsters and Nazis, but there is also the occasional Mad Scientist and superhuman (like the massive, bullet-proof idiot Stuporman).

The Clock is the first Costumed Avenger in the comics. His debut was in the Comics Magazine Company's *Funny Pages* (cover date November 1936), so that by the time Superman came along the Clock had been appearing for 18 months. The Clock is an ordinary man wearing a three-piece suit and a mask covering his face, visually similar in many ways to the masked heroes of the pulps, albeit more crude and primitive.[3] This was also true of the writing on the Clock's strip, although he lasted for eight years and 86 appearances in all. It can't be said that the Clock was influential on other characters, for there were no imitations of the Clock— he was purely a product of the pulp line of Costumed Avengers, a line many other comic Costumed Avengers would draw from. But the Clock deserves recognition as the first comic book Costumed Avenger, even if he was not otherwise distinctive in any way.

The second significant character was Jerry Siegel and Joe Shuster's Doctor Occult. During the Golden Age this nameless private eye was a costumed agent of the mystic Seven. And then he was a ghost. He is assisted by his girlfriend Rose and his butler Jenkins. He has a number of mystic powers, including teleportation, invisibility, hypnosis, telekinesis, and the ability to cast illusions. He also has the spell-breaking and spell-casting amulet, the Symbol of the Seven. He combats vampires, a Mad Scientist zombie master, and the alien sorcerer Koth.

Doctor Occult is an occult detective, but his superpowers make him the first Übermensch in the comic books. He debuted in DC's *New Fun* (October 1935) and had appeared 18 times by the time Superman first appeared. Crudely written and drawn, Doctor Occult's adventures were nonetheless imaginative *fantastika* by the standards of the comics of the time, if no more than average for the usual pulp occult detectives. Like the Clock, Doctor Occult had no imitators; those few occult detectives in the Golden Age comics tended to choose other characters to imitate. And Doctor Occult's final appearance in the Golden Age was in April 1938, so he lacked even longevity to set him apart. Nonetheless, as the first Übermensch in the comic books he deserves special attention.

However, both the Clock and Doctor Occult were just two characters among many in April 1938, appearing in a variety of comics. The medium was still developing its parameters, still figuring out what its consumers wanted (adventure and crime strips), and most important still searching for that first undeniable hit, the thing that would set the medium apart from comic strips and radio and movies and fiction.

That thing would, of course, be Superman.

The Last Son of Krypton

Jerry Siegel and Joe Shuster had actually created Superman years before, in 1933, as a would-be world dominator villain for a story in their fanzine *Science Fiction*. After that, they tried to sell a heroic proto-Superman (not yet costumed) as a premise for a comic book, then as a newspaper comic strip, without luck. The two continued to try to sell work to comic book publishers, eventually succeeding at DC Comics and producing strips featuring detective and adventure characters and Dr. Occult, but it wasn't until late 1937 that the unsold Superman story was picked up by DC Comics and published in *Action Comics* #1 (cover date June 1938, on sale date April 18, 1938).

The influences on Superman were numerous. The ones that Siegel and Shuster admitted to included Baroness Orczy's Scarlet Pimpernel (for his dual identity), Edgar Rice Burroughs's Tarzan (as a general action hero), and E. C. Segar's Popeye (for his superstrength)[4]; others, that Siegel and Shuster denied, perhaps out of ego or from fear of copyright infringement lawsuits, were Doc Savage and Philip Wylie's Hugo Danner.

The end result was Kal-El, the last son of Krypton, sent from that dying planet by his biological parents. He landed on Earth and was raised by a good couple, the Kents, to fight for truth, justice, and the American way. He is a newspaper reporter when not fighting crime and supercriminals. He cannot fly, but he can perform miles-long jumps, he is nearly invulnerable and has superstrength, superspeed, and heat vision.

Superman was the first significant merging of the Costumed Avenger and the Übermensch types; previous supermen had worn types of costumes, but those had on the whole been either uniforms or standard sets of clothing. Superman was the first major combination of the two.[5] Superman also merged genres, combining science fiction and crime-fighting action/adventure in ways that were uncommon. Further, Super-man, as a superhuman alien come to Earth, was a reversal of the Edgar Rice Burroughs's John Carter type and a reversion to the Victorian superhuman-alien-visiting-Earth story line. And the strips, through basic, had an undeniable energy and wish fulfillment aspect to them. Little sur-prise, then, that Superman should eventually prove to be popular.

Interestingly, though, Superman's popularity was uneven at first. The character was, according to anecdotes, immediately popular with chil-dren, and the first issue of *Action Comics* sold out. But sales of the follow-ing issues, which did not have Superman on their cover, did not sizably increase, and the sales of *Action Comics* could not be said to leap forward significantly until Superman's fourth appearance. Superman didn't have an appreciable effect on other characters, inside DC or outside, for six months. Too, Superman doesn't appear on the cover of *Action Comics* until six months after his debut, and for the first year of his existence he only appeared once per issue, sharing space with detectives, cowboys, and magicians. Superman was immediately *appealing* to readers, but it took several months for that appeal to translate into sales in an appreciable way. (Although, as has often been noted, when the appeal did translate into sales, it did so in a huge way: "At a time when most comic book titles sold between 200,000 and 400,000 copies per issue, each issue of *Action Comics* [featuring one Superman story each] regularly sold about 900,000 copies per month.")[6]

His appeal during this early period deserves analysis. The stories make an effort to shy away from Superman's science fictional origins and to embrace crime fighting, which at 26 percent of all comic book stories published in 1938 were a far more popular genre than the superhero stories in which Superman was appearing. These stories are much closer to Hugo Danner than to Doc Savage: Superman stops a wife beater and scares a corrupt Senator; stops rebellion-fomenting munitions manufac-turers; saves a group of miners from a wicked mine owner; impersonates a football player to help a college football team; stops the collapse of a dam; and saves Lois Lane's life from criminal boxing manager. All this, at a time when Doc Savage is fighting his archenemy John Sunlight as well as the Giggling Ghost and the Devil on the Moon, the Shadow is fighting The Hand, the Golden Vulture, and Shiwan Khan, and the Spi-der is fighting the Grey Horde, the Emperor from Hell, and the Black Legions.

Clearly, the appeal of Superman during these early months—when he was gathering popularity and making *Action Comics* into an undeniable hit for DC Comics—was not in the villains. Pulps cost the same as the comics, and you got more reading material and better reading material for your money. Why did readers flock to Superman rather than spend money on the pulps?

Perhaps it was the primal appeal to children and something as simple as the colorful costume against the modestly colored backgrounds. Perhaps it was the simpler wish fulfillment aspect of Superman's powers, which were simpler in ways that the more complicated supermen of other media could not achieve. (The limited space of comic books were in this respect an advantage for Siegel and Shuster rather than a disadvantage.) Or perhaps it was the aforementioned embrace of realistic crimes that needed fighting and the avoidance of the unrealistic foes of other Costumed Avengers and supermen—the Superman stories might almost be called mimetic wish fulfillment, so much are they real-crime oriented.[7]

Eleven Months of Silence and Echoes

The 11-month period following Superman's debut—April 1938 through February 1939, for comics cover date June 1938 through April 1939—were comparatively quiet. DC brought out *Adventure Comics* in August (cover date November). Earlier in the year, comics company Comics Magazine Company had been acquired by Joseph Hardie and renamed Centaur Publishing, and in April Centaur launched *Keen Detective Funnies* (cover date July), and in May Centaur launched *Amazing Mystery Funnies* (cover date August). And, slowly, DC and Centaur began debuting new superheroes.

As of February 1939, there were 14 superheroes in the comics. Ten of them were Costumed Avengers: Paul Gustavson's the Arrow, the Clock, Sven Elven's Cosmo the Phantom of Disguise, Jim Chambers's Crimson Avenger and Wing, Jack Kirby's Crimson Rider, George Filchock's Ermine, Jim Chambers's Masked Ranger, A. L. Peterson's Phantom Rider, and Edward Ellis's Red Avenger. Five were supermen: Doctor Occult, Fred Guardineer's Zatara, Bill Ely's Nadir, Homer Fleming's Sandor, and Superman.

But the influences on these characters were from other sources than Superman. The Arrow was a cross between the Costumed Avenger pulp heroes and Douglas Fairbanks's Robin Hood. Cosmo the Phantom of Disguise was modeled on Leslie Charteris's The Saint. The Crimson Avenger was modeled on the Shadow, Wing on the ethnic sidekicks of pulp heroes. The Crimson Rider, the Masked Ranger, and the Phantom Rider were modeled on Fran Striker and George Trendle's Lone Ranger. The Ermine was modeled on Nick of the Woods. The Red Avenger was modeled on Zorro. Nadir was modeled on Chandu the Magician, Sandor was modeled on Tarzan, and Zatara was modeled on Mandrake the Magician.

Despite Superman's rising popularity—his daily newspaper comic strip launched on January 16, 1939—the writers and editors at DC and at Centaur were not rushing to imitate him. Again, this was due to the relative popularity of other genres. Superman remained *sui generis*, but exactly what kind he was the only one of, other creators were having a hard time getting a handle on, nor was anyone else having any luck in duplicating his success.

Matters would soon become much more complicated.

Four Months of Chill

Late in the fall of 1938, Victor Fox, the accountant for DC Comics, had seen the profits that DC was making from *Action Comics* and broke away from DC to form his own company, Fox Features Syndicate. Reportedly he told the head of a comics-producing studio,[8] "I want another Superman," and the studio dutifully delivered to Fox the Superman-like Wonder Man, created by Will Eisner. Fred Carson is a radio engineer who likes to travel on his vacations. He's in Tibet when a yogi gives him a magic ring to fight for "humanity and justice." This gives him the powers of superstrength, performing miles-long leaps, and repelling bullets. He uses these abilities to stop a war and feed the hungry as "Wonder Man."

Wonder Man appeared in Fox's *Wonder Comics* (cover date May 1939), and immediately provoked a response from DC: *Detective Comics, Inc. v. Bruns Publications, Inc.*, brought on March 15, 1939, with DC alleging that Fox infringed on DC's Superman copyright with Wonder Man. The case was only settled on April 29, 1940, with a complete victory for DC,[9] but the effect of the case was immediate: Wonder Man disappeared, and the next issue of *Wonder Comics* (cover date June 1939) featured other characters, including a superhero magician, Yarko the Great.

March, April, May, and June 1939—the months in which issues with the cover dates May, June, July, and August 1939 appeared—would seem to have been good months for comics. In March, Bob Kane and Bill Finger's Batman appeared in DC's *Detective Comics*; in May, Fox Features brought out a new comic, *Wonderworld Comics*, featuring an Übermensch, Will Eisner and Lou Fine's The Flame, who had vaguely defined plot powers of flame that were both un-Superman-like and yet obviously superhuman; and in June DC debuted the comic *Superman*, Fox brought out a third comics, *Mystery Men Comics*, with two superhuman superheroes, Will Eisner and Charles Nicholas's superstrong Blue Beetle and Walter Frehm's plot-device-powered Green Mask, and a new comics publisher, Quality, brought out *Smash Comics*, with its own set of superhuman heroes. At the end of August one would have thought superhero comics were on the rise: 4 publishers (Centaur, DC, Fox, and Quality) and 14 new Costumed Avengers and supermen.

Yet seen from a modern perspective, a definite chill seems to lie over the industry during these four months as a result of DC's lawsuit. Superman remains the standout success of the industry during these four months, with his own newspaper comic strip and his own comic book (the first dedicated to just one character). One would think, given how rabidly imitative the comics industry was, even in mid-1939—even then few of the characters were wholly original, most being modeled on other characters and character types—that there would have been a rush to copy Superman and attempt to capitalize on his success. But there was not, with the superhuman superheroes of these months being obvious attempts to strike out in different directions, away from Superman. If, as Victor Fox is reported to have said to Will Eisner, he "wanted more characters like Superman—well, not exactly like Superman, but whatever the law would allow,"[10] that does not seem to have been what he got.

A Fantastic Seven Months

This began to change in August 1939, the month of several debuts: Centaur's *Amazing Man Comics*, Marvel Comics (then called "Timely Comics") and its *Marvel Comics*, and Brookwood Comics' *Speed Comics*. *Amazing Man Comics* was the first of these three, and the most important. It was the first non-DC comic to lead with a "Man" hero since the Wonder Man lawsuit—DC had published Finger and Kane's Batman and Gardner Fox and Bert Christman's Sandman, but Centaur, Fox, and Quality, DC's three competitors, had declined to make a "Man" hero, deciding that the risk of another lawsuit was too much, even though calling a superhero "Man" was an obvious creative and marketing hook. *Amazing Man Comics* was the first comic from one of DC's competitors to imitate DC's *Superman* and publish a comic book specifically about one character, rather than something broader and designed to be exciting (Fox's *Wonderworld Comics*, Quality's *Smash Comics*). And Centaur, in the character of Bill Everett's Amazing Man, had its Superman character, its Übermensch superhero figurehead; Amazing Man would last until early 1942, when Centaur (which suffered from poor distribution) folded.

Most important, *Amazing Man Comics* was the first comic from a publisher that was specifically devoted to superheroes in general. DC's *Superman*, which had debuted three months earlier, in May, was an overtly superheroic comic, but it was devoted to Superman rather than superheroes. *Amazing Man Comics* had two stories about Amazing Man, but more importantly had stories about Tarpe Mills's Cat Man,[11] Carl Burgos's Iron Skull, John Kolb's Minimidget, and Martin Filchock's Mighty Man, superheroes all. Of *Amazing Man Comics'* 11 stories, 6 featured superheroes—the first non-*Superman* majority-superhero comic book, and a declaration by Centaur of business confidence in the superhero genre. Previously new comics had featured a variety of heroes, but Centaur was now going all-in with superheroes, gambling (successfully) that the consumers' interest in superheroes was both broad and deep enough to sustain a majority-superhero comic that wasn't from DC. This business model would quickly be imitated by other comics publishers and become the dominant model in superhero comics.

Marvel's *Marvel Comics* #1, appearing three weeks later, was an immediate success; its first print run was for 80,000 copies, its second print run a month later for 800,000 (by comparison, *Superman* #1 had three print runs of 500,000 copies, 250,000 copies, and 150,000 copies). Like *Amazing Man Comics* #1, *Marvel Comics* #1 was majority-superhero, and featured two characters, Carl Burgos's Human Torch and Bill Everett's Sub-Mariner, who would become two of Marvel's three headline superheroes and would go on to star in comics of their own. For a fledgling publisher[12] Marvel had done very well out of the gate.

Brookwood Comics and its *Speed Comics* were not similarly successful—*Speed Comics* would be Brookwood's only comic, and it would fold the following summer after only 11 issues—but in August and September 1939 the owners of Brookwood, and more importantly its competitors, could not have known that, and in short order, over a few weeks' time, MLJ Magazines debuted with *Blue Ribbon Comics*, Fox capitalized on the popularity of the Blue Beetle by giving him his own comic, Worth Carnahan debuted with *Champion Comics*, Marvel Lev Gleason debuted with *Silver Streak Comics*, Marvel resumed publishing *Marvel Comics* under a new title, Marvel issued a second comic, DC gave Gardner Fox and Harry Lampert's The Flash his own comic, and MLJ issued a second title.

A few weeks after that, four more publishers debuted: Novelty, Standard, Fawcett, and Prize, and heavyweight magazine publisher Street & Smith began publishing its own line of comics based on its popular pulp and radio characters. Over the course of seven months, 10 new publishers entered the comics industry, and established publishers like DC brought out new comic titles as well, so that 23 titles in all debuted over these seven months—all, it hardly needs adding, done from the calculation that comics were a profitable field to expand and invest in. This was an emphatically correct calculation.

As can be seen, the failure rate of these books was quite low, with those ending in the first half of 1942 being canceled because of the effect of the

Table 2   Comics Debuting during the August 1939–February 1940 Period

Title	Number of Issues	Start Date (cover)	End Date (cover)
Amazing Man	22	Sept. 1939	Jan. 1942
Marvel Comics	1	Oct. 1939	Oct. 1939
Speed Comics	44*	Oct. 1939	Jan./Feb. 1947
Champion Comicss	10	Oct. 1939	Aug. 1940
Blue Ribbon Comics	22	Nov. 1939	Mar. 1942
Blue Beetle	40	Winter 1940	Aug. 1950
Fantastic Comics	23	Dec. 1939	Nov. 1941
Marvel Mystery	90	Dec. 1939	June 1949
Silver Streak Comics	23	Dec. 1939	ca. Nov. 1946
Daring Mystery	8	Jan. 1940	Jan. 1942
Flash Comics	104	Jan. 1940	Feb. 1949
Pep Comics	136	Jan. 1940	Dec. 1959
Science Comics	8	Feb. 1940	Sept. 1940
Target Comics	105	Feb. 1940	Aug./Sept. 1949
Thrilling Comics	80	Feb. 1940	Apr. 1951
Whiz Comics	155	Feb. 1940	June 1953
Zip Comics	47	Feb. 1940	Summer 1944
Batman Comics	ongoing	Spring 1940	ongoing
Master Comics	133	Mar. 1940	Apr. 1953
Mystic Comics	10	Mar. 1940	Aug. 1942
Prize Comics	68	Mar. 1940	Feb./Mar. 1948
Shadow Comics	101	Mar. 1940	Aug. 1949

*Speed Comics had two incarnations: its first, published by Brookwood, for 11 issues (cover dates October 1939–August 1940); and its second, after being acquired by Harvey, for an additional 33 issues (cover dates March 1941–January/February 1947). As far as the fans were concerned, the two comics were essentially the same, which is why I'm considering them so here.

war rather than because of a lack of consumer interest and bad sales. By the end of January 1940, the end of these seven months, the comics market was roaring, and publishers were convinced that the industry was a healthy new market to exploit. It was significant that Street & Smith entered the lists in January 1940, with *Shadow Comics*. Street & Smith was one of the most successful pulp publishers at that time, publishing best-selling pulps like *Street & Smith's Love Story Magazine* and *Street & Smith's Western Story*, but it had begun discontinuing its less successful pulps in 1937 as a way to diversify its business. Expanding into the comics market was a part of this business strategy, done for purely financial reasons rather than out of any idea that art could be produced in this new medium.

There were other notable firsts during this time period. Bill Parker and C. C. Beck's Captain Marvel debuted in Fawcett's *Whiz Comics*; Captain Marvel would go on to become the most popular and best-selling superhero of the Golden Age (and the most open imitation of Superman on the market). The first superpowered superheroine appeared: John Kolb's Ritty, the female partner of Minimidget (for Centaur in *Amazing Comics'* September 1939 issue). The first two lead superwomen debuted, C. A. Winter's Camilla (for Fiction House in *Jungle Comics'* January 1940 issue) and Fletcher Hanks's Fantomah (for Fiction House in *Jungle Comics'* February 1940 issue). The first patriotic superhero appeared: Harry Shorten and Irv Novick's The Shield (for MLJ Magazines' *Pep Comics'* January 1940 issue).

The first person of color superhero was Bill Ely's "prince of India" Nadir, who had debuted in DC's *New Adventure Comics'* July 1937 issue, but his last appearance was in *New Adventure's* September 1938 issue, before the seven months of progress had begun. A second person of color superhero appeared debuted during these seven months: Art Pinajian's Native American Übermensch Red Man (for Centaur). While superhero comics were a largely white affair during the Golden Age, there were a number of superheroes of color during this time—74, including sidekicks—and the adventures of Red Man, portrayed as unstereotypically as possible for the time period, set the tone for the superheroes of color who followed him.

The trend toward artificial superheroes picked up steam. George Brenner's Bozo the Iron Man (for Quality) had debuted in *Smash Comics'* August 1939 issue; he was followed by Carl Burgos's Iron Skull (for Centaur, September 1939), Carl Burgos's Human Torch (for Marvel, October 1940), Steve Dahlman's Electro (for Marvel, February 1940), Carl Burgos's White Streak (for Novelty, February 1940), Will Harr, Jack Binder, and

E. C. Stoner's Flexo the Rubber Man (for Marvel, March 1940), and Daniel Peters's Dynamic Man (for Marvel, March 1940).

Finally, these seven months are when writers and artists truly began to flex their imaginations and exploit the artistic possibilities inherent in this new medium. The first truly different superhero had been Malcolm Kildale's Speed Centaur, for Centaur (*Amazing Mystery Funnies*, August 1939). Speed Centaur is a member of a race of centaurs living in the Arctic. Unfortunately, an earthquake destroys Speed's race and their city. He is the only survivor but is rescued by a trapper named Norton. Norton raises Speed, who studies hard, "showing signs of supernatural powers of thought and strength." Norton becomes an old man, after having raised Speed to "hate evil and crime. That's to be your mission in life—crusading against crime!"[13] Speed makes his way to "the city of rackets" and saves the life of "Reel" McCoy, a reporter for the Daily Views. Speed goes on to fight crime. His adventures vary: in one, he travels to his home city and discovers it inhabited by an insane "king" who puts Speed through various dangerous tests. In another, he fights *kaiju*-sized insects produced by a German Mad Scientist. In another, Speed and Reel find a cave that sends them both back in time. And in another a sea monster is battled. Speed is a centaur and has superstrength and endurance.

But Speed Centaur was in the minority for his time period. However, in the fall of 1939 *fantastika* suddenly became the dominant mode for superhero stories. A new editorial team, Whitney Ellsworth, Mort Weisinger, and Jack Schiff, took over Superman's adventures in both *Action Comics* and *Superman* and made Superman's adventure wholeheartedly science fictional. Other publishers went similarly imaginative with their heroes. There was Frank Thomas's The Eye, for Centaur (*Keen Detective Funnies*, December 1939):

> "I am the Eye! The Eye!—to whom time and distance are nothing—who bares man's thoughts and pierces his conscience! The Eye's powers are limitless—his vengeance terrible!" "The Eye!—Symbol of the haunting voice of Man's inner conscience. Time or distance means nothing to the Eye, as he wreaks his terrible vengeance in all four corners of the world!!"[14]

The Eye is a giant, flying eyeball which shoots rays from its pupil and hunts down criminals. He is assisted by ordinary human Jack Barrister, who the Eye advises on which criminals to pursue and who acts as the Eye's legman. The Eye knows and sees all, but it needs a human to solve the crimes and occasionally carry out an execution, and that's what Barrister does.

There was Bill Everett's Sub-Mariner. The Sub-Mariner is the child of an American ship captain and Fen, an Atlantean woman. The pair marry, but when American ships blast through the ice sheets of the Arctic and destroy most of Fen's people, she deserts the captain and raises her son, Namor, to hate surface dwellers. When he turns 20, he goes on a rampage against surface dwellers. But eventually he mellows and begins fighting the Axis powers for the Allies, teaming up with Captain America and the Human Torch. Sub-Mariner has superstrength, can fly via the wings on his ankles, and can live underwater indefinitely. He fights Germans, Japanese, the Human Torch, man-eating monsters, Mad Scientists, the Mad Artists, the Flying Dutchman, the Nazi agent the Python, and the mad genius the Iron Brain.

And there was Norman Modell and Lionel March's Tulpa of Tsang, for Sun Publications (*Colossus Comics*, March 1940). "In faraway Tibet a few of the holiest Lamas are said to possess strange mystical powers. By employing an age old secret of concentration they can actually will unto being Tulpas or phantoms of themselves. Such a lama was Tsang."[15] He gets involved with Nazis and Bart London, an Allied intelligence officer.

Writers, artists, and publishers were turning out entertaining bizarreries and artistic grotesques alongside ordinary (clichéd) heroes; singular talents like Fletcher Hanks and Basil Wolverton were getting regular work; new superheroes were unpredictably different from what had come before. The imaginative promise of the new medium was finally being fulfilled.

The Boom of 1940

In 1940 the economic promise of the new medium also seemed to be fulfilled. Forty-one new titles debuted during the calendar year, with the resulting rise in total number of stories published seen in Table 8.3.

This reflected the state of the economy, which had rebounded from the recession of 1937–1938, as (among other factors) the U.S. money stock started to rise again and gold and capital from war-torn (and therefore economically unstable) Europe continued to flood the comparatively safe and stable United States. The real Gross National Product was growing at a rate of over 10 percent per year, and the economy, despite high unemployment, was in a solid recovery phase—industrial production and real income were both increasing. After May 1940, when the Germans attacked the Low Countries and then France, Britain and its remaining allies began placing large-scale orders for war material in the United States, boosting production, employment, and personal income, while the U.S. government began expanding its defense program.

Table 3   **Number of Strips by Genre, 1939–March 1942* Based on Cover Dates**

	1939	%	1940	%	1941	%	1942	%
Adventure	275	24.5	529	12.4	401	8.4	81	6.5
Artificial	11	1.0	68	1.6	59	1.2	5	0.4
Costumed Avenger	125	11.1	569	13.3	891	18.7	315	25.2
Cowboy	41	3.65	133	3.1	97	2.0	25	1.8
Crime	293	26.1	553	13.0	517	10.9	118	9.4
Historical	16	1.4	36	0.8	29	0.6	0	0
Jungle	13	1.2	116	2.7	121	2.5	19	1.5
Pilot	54	4.8	287	6.7	361	7.6	83	6.6
Pirate	19	1.7	29	0.7	27	0.6	6	0.5
Science Fiction	45	4	324	7.6	171	3.6	29	2.3
Spy	91	8.1	222	5.2	258	5.4	60	4.8
Superhero	127	11.3	1162	27.2	1582	33.2	443	35.4
Villain	9	0.8	83	1.9	53	1.1	10	0.8
War	5	0.4	157	3.7	194	4.1	58	4.6
Total	1124		4268		4761		1250	

*March 1942 was the cover date for comics issued in December 1941.

Interestingly, this economic boom, so visible in comic books, was not felt in comic books' two main competitors, the pulps (where the total number of issues published declined by 8 percent compared to 1939, to the lowest total since 1934)[16] and the movies (where the total number of movies made decreased by 4 percent compared to 1939 and by 10 percent compared to 1938).[17] There are easily traceable reasons for these declines: in movies, the decline in films made reflects in part the relative flatness in movie attendance figures; the decline in pulps appearing on newsstands reflects declining advertising revenue for the pulps. (Rising circulation numbers meant that publishers were trying to charge more for ads, but many advertisers could no longer afford to pay these higher prices, leading to flat revenue streams.) But it must be considered that the boom in the comic book industry was fueled by money that would in previous years have been spent on films and pulps but was now being spent on comic books. Comic books were not only becoming hugely profitable, they were having an actual effect on other industries, something unimaginable even three years before.

In the comics themselves, the editors and publishers stuck with what was most unique and popular about the comics—superheroes—at the cost of other genres. Westerns and detective stories were the most popular pulp genres in 1940, and drama, comedies, romance, and Westerns were the most popular film genres in 1940, but, as seen in Table 8.3, 40.5 percent of all comic book stories in 1940 were superhero, while Westerns were at 3 percent of all stories published and crime at 13 percent, down 13 percent from the year before. The only other genres to experience any notable sort of growth in the comics were science fiction (the sixth most popular genre of pulp in 1940) and war (obviously reflecting worry over what was happening in Europe).

Interestingly, while the number of Costumed Avengers stories increased by 2 percent compared to 1939, the number of supermen stories increased by 16 percent, after years of being markedly fewer than Costumed Avengers. Editors and publishers, seeing the great popularity not only of Superman but of Captain Marvel and the Human Torch and the Sub-Mariner and the other superhuman superheroes, were demanding stories about them from the writers and artists far more often than they did stories of Costumed Avengers. Superhumanly powered superheroes were the vogue, and the large majority of the newest popular superheroes were supermen, not Costumed Avengers.

Captain Marvel and Superman remained the most popular characters in comic books in 1940, but a third figure was added to them at the end of the year: Joe Simon and Jack Kirby's Captain America (for Marvel's *Captain America Comics* #1, cover date March 1941, on sale date December 20, 1940). Puny Steve Rogers, outraged at the actions of the Germans and Japanese, attempts to enlist in the Army but is rejected because he is "too frail." He begs to be accepted and is taken instead by General Chester Phillips, who hands him over to Professor Reinstein, who gives Rogers a serum that turns him into a superman—a "super agent" for the U.S. government. Rogers puts on a costume and busts crime and Axis attempts at evil wherever he finds them. In his civilian identity he is a private at Camp Lehigh. He is partnered with Bucky and is a member of the All-Winners Squad. He has no superpowers but is in the best physical shape humanly possible, is an excellent fighter, and has a shield that he uses both defensively and offensively.

Captain America wasn't the first patriotic superhero—that was the Shield, who had appeared in November 1939. Captain America wasn't the second patriotic superhero: that was Emil Gershwin's Eagle (for Fox), who had appeared in January 1940. But Captain America was by far the most popular of the patriotic superheroes, making *Captain America Comics* into Marvel's best-selling comic and inspiring 11 imitators from other publishers by the end of 1941.

Another major development was the advent of the kid sidekick, which began with Bill Finger, Bob Kane, and Jerry Robinson's Robin for DC, debuting in *Detective Comics* (cover date April 1940, on sale date March 1940). Dick Grayson, a child acrobat, watches in horror as his parents are killed through the work of a gangster. The Batman is on the trail of the gangster, and makes the child his helper and legal ward, and together they bring down the gangster. Robin becomes Batman's sidekick; he has no powers but is trained by the Batman and is a skilled fighter and acrobat. He also has a neat utility belt.

Robin wasn't the first sidekick to a comic book superhero: that was Wing, the sidekick of the Crimson Avenger, who had debuted in *Detective Comics* #20 (cover date October 1938). Robin wasn't the first juvenile sidekick; that was Art Pinajian's The Kid, sidekick to Red Man (for Centaur, cover date October 1939—also the second Übermensch superhero of color). But Robin was far and away the most popular superhero sidekick and inspired numerous imitators from other publishers within two years, to the point that new superheroes were almost required to have kid sidekicks.

The appearance of Robin had another effect on comics beyond essentially inventing the role of the kid sidekick. Batman at this point was a major character for DC, popular enough to earn his own title, *Batman*, a month after Robin's debut. But Batman's stories up to Robin's debut were dark even by comic book standards; the month before Robin's debut, Batman had stopped a man from being tortured to death. The writer and editor of *Batman* were worried that the Batman stories were too dark and intense for the children who were presumably the main purchasers of comic books. So Robin was invented. The effect of Robin was to humanize the Batman himself and to almost immediately lighten the Batman stories and make them more similar in tone to the stories of DC's other superheroes.

This created an opportunity for other publishers to take advantage of. It's not that there were no grim and intense superhero stories on the market in 1940; DC was publishing the stories of Jerry Siegel and Bernard Baily's The Spectre from the end of December 1939, and the stories of Gardner Fox and Howard Sherman's Doctor Fate from March 1940, and both characters appeared in dark horror series. But the great majority of the superheroes for DC—still the industry leader in 1940—were closer to Superman in tone than to what the Batman had been.

But the Batman as he had been—wading through a dark world of twisted murderers—had been popular with readers, and now there wasn't a major hero to fill that gap. So darker, more lethally violent heroes began appearing, including Jack Cole's The Comet for MLJ (debuting the previous November, but truly becoming popular in 1940), Manning de Villeneuve Lee's The Scarlet Seal (for Quality), Emile Schurmacher and Ed Kressy's The Scorpion (for Hillman), Paul Gustavson's The Spider (for Quality), and Klaus Nordling's Thin Man (for Marvel). This trend would increase in 1941, with the Comet giving way to George Storm's The Hangman (from May 1941 for MLJ), the most lethal of all the killer vigilantes of comic books' Golden Age.

Amid the flood of new characters in 1940, several of which went on to have very long careers, indeed, three stand out for various reasons.

There was Dick Briefer's Frankenstein, debuting in *Prize Comics* (for Prize, cover date December 1940). Briefer's Frankenstein, a creature of vast strength stitched together from corpses, is actually a gentle soul who consorts with ghouls, ghosts, and goblins in a series of humorous adventures. Occasionally he fights a costumed hero named Bulldog Denny. Eventually his stories turn serious, and Frankenstein becomes a creature of wrath and vengeance.

This comic book version of Mary Shelley's character debuted in the fall of 1940 and lasted until 1954—a very long career for a character from a third-tier comic book publisher like Prize. More importantly, its combination of adventure, humor, and later horror was virtually unique among superhero comics, and done with an unusual amount of skill, wit, and artistic success.

There was Jack Binder's Daredevil, debuting in *Silver Streak Comics* #6 (cover date September 1940), for Lev Gleason. Bart Hill is orphaned as a child by crooks who killed his father. They also torture Bart, branding a boomerang-shaped scar into his chest. This renders Bart mute. He swears on his parents' grave that he will avenge them, and so puts himself in top shape and trains himself to be a master of the boomerang. He then goes out and fights crime, and eventually he regains his voice. He is assisted by his girlfriend, Tonia, and by the youth gang known as the Little Wise Guys. Daredevil has no superpowers but is an outstanding hand-to-hand fighter and acrobat, and is, as mentioned, a master of the boomerang. His archenemy is the Claw, but there are Nazis to be fought, Mad Scientists, the Deadly Dozen, Wolf Carson (a wolf with a human brain), the Ghoul, Reve Venge (the Phantom of Notre Dame), and Crepto, the imbecile with the strength of 15 men, as well as ordinary criminals.

Daredevil's last appearance was in 1951, 11 years after his debut and 2 years after the unofficial end of comics' Golden Age, which was a more than respectable run for a character from a third-tier comics publisher. The Daredevil stories were most notable for the ongoing clashes between Daredevil and his archenemy, the Yellow Peril archvillain The Claw, clashes that made both Daredevil and the Claw, and the books they appeared in, quite popular and one of the great ongoing sagas (not resolved until the Claw's death in 1945) of comics' Golden Age.

There was also Will Eisner's The Spirit. Denny Colt, a criminologist, is battling with the evil Dr. Cobra when he is drenched in Cobra's formula, which is intended to put all of Central City in a coma. Colt is rendered senseless and believed dead, so he is buried in Wildwood Cemetery. He appears at the doorstep of Police Commissioner Dolan two days later, explaining that he'd only been in suspended animation. He decides to remain dead and fight crime as the costumed Spirit. His girlfriend is Ellen Dolan, and his assistant is Ebony White. He has no superpowers but is really, really, really tough. His villains range from the master criminal the Octopus to numerous femmes fatales, from the siren Lorelei Rox to Silk Satin, who eventually reforms and works as a spy for the British government, to weapons smuggler Sand Saref, to P'Gell, an internationally wanted spy who becomes the Spirit's Loving Enemy.

The Spirit was created by Will Eisner for a tabloid-sized insert for newspapers and debuted in June 1940, not making it to comic books until 1942, but he lasted until 1950 in the comics and 1952 in the newspapers. More importantly, the Spirit was the most artistically successful superhero of the Golden Age, written and drawn by Will Eisner (and later Eisner assistants like Jules Feiffer) with a remarkable amount of skill and imagination.

Finally, the first intracompany superhero crossover took place. Crossovers—meetings between characters from different texts—were by this time a tradition in popular culture, with those first meetings between Old Sleuth and other dime novel detectives having been duplicated by crossovers in the pulps, especially the very popular Western pulps of Street & Smith. But it was not until 1940 that comic book publishers' fictional universes had enough ongoing, popular characters to begin crossing them over.

The first such crossover was created by Will Harr and Edd Ashe and appeared in MLJ's *Top-Notch Comics* #5 (cover date May 1940, on sale date March 1940), in which the Harr and Ashe's Wizard teamed up with two other MLJ characters, Harr and Ashe's Midshipman and Harry Shorten and Irv Novick's The Shield. This crossover lasted for only one issue and did not particularly catch the readers' imaginations. However, the next crossover did. A month later, in Marvel's *Marvel Mystery Comics* #8, a crossover began between Bill Everett's Human Torch and Carl Burgos's Sub-Mariner—a crossover that started the long tradition/cliché of superheroes fighting when they first meet before becoming friends. The Human Torch-Sub-Mariner crossover lasted for three months and was popular with the readers.

Seven months later, on November 22, 1940, DC published *All-Star Comics* #3, a landmark issue in superhero comics. The issue starred the Justice Society of America, the creation of writer Gardner Fox and editor Sheldon Mayer. The Justice Society of America, or JSA, was formed first by a group of heroes sitting around shooting the bull, and later formed to fight threats. The JSA's membership consisted of the Atom, Batman, Dr. Fate, Dr. Mid-Nite, the Flash, Green Lantern, Hawkman, Hourman, Johnny Thunder, Mr. Terrific, Red Tornado, Sandman, Spectre, Superman, Wildcat, and Wonder Woman.

The Justice Society of America was comics' first superhero team and appeared in the first comic dedicated to ongoing team-ups between heroes. Although other companies in the Golden Age were slow to try to duplicate the success of the Justice Society of America—Harvey's unnamed team of superheroes only appeared once, in 1942, Fawcett's Crime Crusaders Club only appeared once, in 1943, and Marvel's All-Winners Squad did not appear until 1946—the superhero team would become a standard of comic books in the 1960s and remain so through the modern day.

1941

Aspects of the economy continued to improve in 1941—industrial production, money stock, income, and the gross national product all increased throughout the year—but wholesale prices rose dramatically, as did tax rates, and unemployment remained high. While the country's economy as a neutral during a time of war was on the whole solid, the advent of the Lend Lease program in March meant that the U.S. government was paying for war material to be shipped abroad, rather than the British government, as had been the case the previous year. Making matters worse was the perceived state of affairs of the war in Europe, with all of Europe (with the exception of Great Britain) conquered by Germany and the Soviet Union seeming to face a never-ending series of defeats throughout the course of the second half of the year. Great Britain seemed to stand alone, and Americans were asking when, not if, the United States would be drawn into the war.

There was a similar instability in magazine publishing. Mainstream magazine publishing was undergoing a boom period, with circulation gains for the 26 leading consumer magazines all up by at least 10 percent. But in the pulps matters were considerably less rosy. As was the case in 1940, increased circulation meant increased prices for advertisements, which meant that fewer companies could afford to buy ads, which led to rising costs but flat revenue streams. The major magazines could weather this situation, but the pulp publishers, who often had a much lower profit margin, could not.

This resulted, in the pulps (comics' closest analogue), in 1941 being the year of the absolute high point in the number of pulp titles while at the same time being the lowest point in seven years for the number of issues published per title.[18] Publishers were increasingly throwing new pulps onto the market while at the same time canceling them more quickly than ever before, or publishing them less frequently through the year. Major pulps were subject to this, *All Story Love Stories, Argosy, Clues, Dime Mystery Magazine, Double Detective,* and *G-8* among them. The leading publisher of the "spicy" pulps, Detinuer, went out of business because of a decline in the "spicy" market.[19] Fawcett stopped publishing pulps altogether to concentrate on comics. And the government threatened legal action against the publishers of the more extreme horror pulps, forcing the publishers to cancel them or modify their content.

Films, likewise, were down 10 percent in output from 1940.[20] In all, comics' competing media were suffering from weakness and instability, largely due to external factors, which should have meant that comics could capitalize. And in some respects they did—49 new titles were published through the year, with an increase of 41 percent in the number of stories told over 1940. However, most of this increase happened in the last three months of the year, with the comics cover date January, February, and March 1942. The increase over the first nine months of the year in the number of stories was considerably less.

Superhero stories took up 52 percent of all stories in comic books for the first nine months of 1941, and 61 percent of all stories for the last three months of 1941. Western stories, so popular in the pulps and films—they were the most popular type of pulp on the market in 1941 and the fourth most popular type of film that year—were stuck in a permanent decline in the comics. Crime stories, the second most popular type pulp, were also declining. War stories were the only genre that saw any sort of positive increase. Essentially, comic books, once so friendly to a range of diverse genres, were becoming dominated by superheroes.

Those superheroes took an aggressive turn in 1941. *Superman* and *Captain Marvel Adventures* continued to be best sellers, and both told relatively innocent and innocuous stories, but *Captain America Comics* was also a best seller in 1941, and its stories were aggressively anti-Japanese and anti-German, with sadistic enemies like the German Red Skull and the Japanese Fang, the "Arch-Fiend of the Orient," prominently featured. Superhero comics as a whole took a pro-intervention-in-the-war turn, a more advanced position than the average American (who was in favor of limited U.S. aid to the Allies but not intervention) took. Quality's *Military Comics* (cover date August, on sale date May) featured the very popular Black-hawks, created by Will Eisner, Bob Powell, and Chuck Cuidera. A young Polish fighter pilot takes on the German Butcher Squadron during the German invasion of Poland and shoots most of them down but is gunned down in the end. He survives the crash and goes to his parents' farm, only to find them already killed by the Germans. He vows bloody destruction for the Germans and puts together both his own airplane as well as a crack team of international pilots. He and they become the dreaded Blackhawks, among the greatest of the pilots of the Golden Age. The Blackhawks are Blackhawk, the French Andre, the Polish Stanislaus, the Dutch Hendrickson, the Norwegian Olaf, the Chinese Chop-Chop, the Russian Boris, the Polish Zeg, and the Texan Chuck. Their opponents range from ordinary German and Japanese pilots to femmes fatales (including the Black Tigress, the Black Widow, the Cobra, the communist Hitla, and Satana) to the Scavengers of Doom to Genghis Khan II to Mad Doctor Baroc (and his Z Bomb Menace) to the Thunderer and his storm machine.

Also appearing in *Military Comics* in 1941 was a less popular but even more representative (of the general tenor of superhero comics during the year) character, The Sniper, created by Ted Udall. "Men call me the Sniper ... a hunter of men ... and it is true! But the only men I hunt are those similar in action to the beasts of the jungle ... cold, ruthless slayers! Men who have committed acts of such brutal violence."[21] This nameless character is a sharpshooter fighting the Germans in Occupied Europe.

Other popular new characters were less overtly militaristic and less anti-Axis but as proextreme (for comics) violence. Richard Hughes and Dave Gabrielson's Black Terror (for Standard) debuted in *Exciting Comics* #9 (cover date May 1941, on sale date March). Bob Benton, mild-mannered pharmacist, is the victim of a protection racket. Irritated, he invents a formula of "formic ethers" that gives him superstrength and limited invulnerability, which he uses to fight crime and the Axis powers. He often only knocks out criminals, but is notable among Golden Age heroes for the degree to which he kills his enemies, either by hand or with a machine gun in each hand. The Black Terror has enemies ranging from Nazis to Mad Scientists like Thorg (he of the "million dollar death ray"), the hypnotic femme fatale Lady Serpent, and the Japanese scientist Hanura and his "electro-hypnotizer," which is used to assassinate American generals and admirals.

Although the Black Terror fought ordinary criminals (as opposed to Japanese or Germans) during his first year, he still exhibited the violence that would later become his trademark. At the same end of the provi-olence spectrum was George Storm's Hangman (for MLJ). College boy Bob Dickering is forced to watch, horrified, as his big brother John, a.k.a. The Comet, gets killed rescuing him. Bob, furious, vows that he will kill his brother's murderers and all the enemies of justice and humanity. He puts on a costume ("Criminals are all cowards at heart, so my first task will be to find a uniform that will take advantage of this!")[22] and becomes the Hangman, one of the killingest of the Golden Age's killer vigilantes. He has no superpowers but is good in a fight, knows how to use a noose, and uses a light to project the outline of a noose on to walls, just to shake up the bad guys. His girlfriend and sidekick is Thelma Gordon, formerly John's girlfriend. He fights ordinary criminals and Axis agents, name criminals like the Jackal, the Walrus, the Executioner, Mother Goose, and the Clockmaker of Death, a Tyrannosaurus Rex found in a remote section of Africa, and especially the Axis's top agent, Captain Swastika.

Even William Marston and Harry Peter's Wonder Woman (for DC), who debuted in *All-Star Comics* #8 (cover date December 1941/January 1942, on sale date October 1941) and whose adventures during the Golden Age were often uniquely (for comics) fabular rather than attempting mimesis in its treatment of crime and costumed opponents, was fighting Nazi opponents in her third appearance, *Sensation Comics* #2 (cover date February 1942, on sale date December 2, 1941—five days before the attack at Pearl Harbor brought the United States into World War II).

Wonder Woman was immediately popular, getting her own comic book series within nine months of her debut, but it cannot be said that her appearance led to an influx of superheroines following her or in imitation of her. In fact, of the 102 superheroines of comics' Golden Age, only 9 appeared within a year of Wonder Woman's debut. Nor was Wonder Woman the first superheroine—as mentioned, that was Will Eisner and S. M. Iger's Sheena—or the second or third—39 superheroines, Costumed Avengers and superwomen, preceded Wonder Woman or debuted in the same month that she did. Nor was Wonder Woman even DC's first superheroine; that was Ken Fitch and Bernard Baily's Miss X (from *Action Comics* #26, cover date July 1940, on sale date May 1940). But Wonder Woman was the highest-profile superheroine to date and became the iconic superheroine of the Golden Age, retaining her own title through the 1950s (at a time when only Batman and Superman had their own comics) and eventually becoming the archetypal superheroine in all of comics.[23]

The other development of significance in the superhero comics of 1941 was the debut of Otto Binder and Charles Nicholas's Young Allies (for Marvel, in *Young Allies* #1, cover date Summer 1941, on sale date July 10, 1941). The Young Allies are a kid gang brought together by Bucky and Toro to help fight crime when Bucky and Toro aren't busy helping Captain America and the Human Torch. The Allies are, in addition to Bucky and Toro, Knuckles (the Brooklyn tough guy), Tubby (the fat kid), Jeff (the bookworm) and Whitewash Jones (the racist stereotype). They primarily fight Axis agents: the Red Skull, Agent Zero, the Monk, the Black Talon, the Khan, the Owl, and so on. There are also ordinary gangsters and name criminals like the Doll-Devil, the Python, and the Mad Fiend of Horror Castle.

The Young Allies were the first kid gang in superhero comics, a type of group that would quickly become popular and would show surprising longevity. The Young Allies weren't the first kid gang in comics; Bob Kane's "Rusty and His Pals," from DC's *New Adventure Comics* (cover date May 1938), featured a kid gang. But the Young Allies were the first kid gang to be the lead characters in the strip, and soon the other major comic book companies were imitating them, making kid gangs the lead in features or making them into heroes' sidekicks. The kid gang concept was a popular one with readers and continued to appear throughout the war, and it had such longevity that in 1951, two years after the death of comics' Golden Age, when Lev Gleason finally phased out Daredevil, they replaced him in his own comic with the Little Wise Guys, who had been Daredevil's sidekicks since 1942.

Conclusion

In previous chapters, I applied the elements listed in Chapter 1 to various protosuperheroes, ranking them on the superheroic continuum. The following is a list of how the five major characters of the first wave of superhero comics would rank.

- The **unusual origin story**. Batman (the violent death of his parents); Captain America (the application of the supersoldier serum and death of his creator); Captain Marvel (transformation by the wizard Shazam from a newsboy to an Übermensch); Superman (with his birth on another planet and arrival on Earth); Wonder Woman (emissary from the Amazons). The great majority of heroes during the pre–World War II Golden Age had an unusual origin of one kind of another, something especially true for the major heroes of this period, and one of the influences of Nick Carter (via the pulps) on superheroes.

- The **superpower**. Captain Marvel (flight, strength, speed, endurance); Superman (flight, strength, speed, endurance); Wonder Woman (strength, speed, endurance). As the Golden Age progressed increasing numbers of superhuman (as opposed to mere Costumed Avenger) heroes appeared (as seen in Tables 8.1–8.3); the trend, before the beginning of the war, was for more superhumanly powered heroes and fewer Costumed Avengers. But there were notable exceptions, including Captain America (created late in 1940), the Hangman (created in spring 1941), and Alfred Harvey and Al Gabriele's Black Cat (created in summer 1941 for Harvey).

- **Extraordinary Skills and Abilities**. Batman (everything); Captain America (fighting). As a rule during these years the fan's gaze lingered on the super-men's superpowers; it was only mortal heroes—Costumed Avengers—who were shown to have extraordinary skills and abilities.

- **Extraordinary Technology**. Batman (Batmobile); Wonder Woman (Invisible Jet).

- **Distinctive Weapon**. Batman (batarangs); Captain America (shield); Wonder Woman (bracelets, tiara, and lasso). As a general rule during these years the more powerful an Übermensch was the less they relied upon weapons.

- **Distinctive Appearance**. Batman (costume); Captain America (costume); Captain Marvel (costume); Superman (costume); Wonder Woman (costume). Following Superman's debut it was industry standard for superheroes to wear brightly colored costumes. Costumed Avengers who had previously worn pulp-style outfits, like the Crimson Avenger and the Sandman (both visually modeled on the Shadow), traded in their outfits for superhero-style costumes.

- **Code name**. Batman; Captain America; Captain Marvel; Superman; Wonder Woman. From the beginning code names were a part of superhero comics. Heroes who fought crime under their own names, like Bob Byrd and Ben Thompson's jungle hero Ka-Zar (for Marvel), and sorcerer Nadir, were comparative rarities and were largely modeled on preexisting genre heroes rather than being the product of the nascent superhero genre.

- **Dual Identity**. Batman (Bruce Wayne); Captain America (Steve Rogers); Captain Marvel (Billy Batson); Superman (Clark Kent); Wonder Woman (Diana Prince). As with code names, superheroes without a secret identity were few and for the most part drew on the traditions of other genres.

- **Heroic mission**. Batman (fight crime); Captain America (defend the country against its enemies); Captain Marvel (fight evil); Superman (fight crime);

Wonder Woman (bring peace to man's world). In the early years of super-hero comics heroes without a heroic mission did not exist.

- **Extraordinary opponents**. Batman (Joker, Penguin, Catwoman, etc.); Captain America (Red Skull, Unholy Legion, Ringmaster, etc.); Captain Marvel (Dr. Sivana and his family). In the prewar issues Superman's opponents (with the exception of the mad scientist, the Ultra Humanite), and Wonder Woman's opponents were mortal and ordinary.

- **Lives in a world where there is law enforcement and a government**. True for the five major heroes and indeed the vast majority of superheroes; only Jungle Hero superheroes and the rare historical superhero work in law- and government-free zones.

- **Operates in a world in which crime/oppression/evil is clear-cut and obvious**. True for the five major heroes and every other superhero during the prewar years. Moral ambiguity was no more welcome in superhero comics than it had been in the pulps or the dime novels.

- **Operates in a world in which law enforcement/the government is not capable of controlling or defeating crime/oppression/evil**. True for the five major heroes and every other superhero during the prewar years, though largely as a result of narrative necessity rather than as a social statement.

- **Operates under the assumption that law enforcement/the government is capable of holding and confining a criminal once they are apprehended**. True for the five major heroes and every other superhero during the prewar years.

- **Operates under the assumption that vigilantism is welcome or at least tolerated by general society as well as law enforcement and the government**. True for the five major heroes and every other superhero during the prewar years.

- **Is finite and can be killed**. Batman; Captain America; Wonder Woman. Neither Captain Marvel nor Superman are mortals in the comics of the prewar years.

- **Does not kill**. Captain Marvel; Superman; Wonder Woman. Both Batman (until the appearance of Robin, as mentioned above) and Captain America were not hesitant about killing their enemies during the prewar years. When the war began, Batman was accompanied by Robin and using less lethal means against enemies, but Captain America, now fighting German and Japanese soldiers, become more lethal. As mentioned above, killer vigilantes like the Black Terror were in the minority but by no means unknown.

CHAPTER NINE

Ages upon Ages

In this chapter, I will be discussing the history of superhero comics after the events of December 7, 1941, a history that can be usefully defined as consisting of six periods, or in the commonly accepted critical and fan terminology, "ages:" the Golden Age, the Atomic Age, the Silver Age, the Bronze Age, the Modern Age, and the Metamodern Age. These ages do not end or begin neatly; while there are distinct events that begin each age and in some cases end them, there is also bleed over (sometimes significant) between the ages. Nonetheless, the years (if not the names) of most of these ages are generally accepted.[1]

During these ages the superhero no longer evolves in form; the Übermensch and the Costumed Avenger are set, and superheroes almost entirely fall into one of those two categories. However, the *content* of the superhero—the ethos of the character type, their typical personality, their generic outlines—does continue to develop, so that the superhero, taken as a whole, can be said to have recognizable characteristics specific to each particular age.

The Golden Age: 1935–1949

As mentioned previously, the Golden Age runs from 1935, the beginning of superhero comics, to 1949. As with the other ages of comics, however, the end of the Golden Age is a fuzzy border rather than a distinct line of demarcation. The reason for this is that the transition from the Golden Age to the Atomic Age took place over the course of several years, from 1946 to 1953, and 1949 is the rough midpoint of this transition, as well as the year with the most cancellations of titles or changes in format and genre.

The effect of World War II on superhero comic books was initially positive. Government paper restrictions on publishers did not take hold until after 1943, and before then the increase in defense spending meant that many families were suddenly relatively flush with money, which meant larger allowances for children and teenagers to spend on comic books.

> In early 1942 *Publishers Weekly* and *Business Week* both reported that some 15 million comic books were sold each month. Moreover, publishers assumed a generous "pass-along value" of five readers per comic book. By December 1943, monthly comic book sales had climbed to 25 million copies. As many as 125 different titles could be found at newsstands every month. Retail sales of comic books in 1943 added up to nearly $30 million.[2]

But superheroes were a fad during the Golden Age rather than something longer lasting, and fads inevitably end. Even as early as 1942 the warning signs for the superhero genre could be seen. Of the 113 titles that debuted in 1942, 76 were nonsuperhero. Comic book publishers, new and old, attempted to exploit the market in new ways by pushing genres like humor and "funny animal" that had not been exploited prewar, and these genres became increasingly popular as the war progressed. By 1946 only 4 of the top 10 best-selling comics were superhero, and in 1947 sales for superhero comics dropped precipitously, with industry-leader *Captain Marvel* losing 2.5 million in sales between 1946 and 1947. The Golden Age ended with superhero comics disappearing from the newsstands and being replaced by romance, crime, Western, cartoon tie-in, and religious comics, all of which sold far better than superhero comics.

However, while this was taking place superheroes were beginning to appear and become popular in other media, perhaps even more so than they were in the comics, in a kind of precursor to what took place in the 2010s in films. In some cases, the superheroes were used for parodic purposes, as in Walter Karig's satire of government bureaucracy, *Zotz!* (1947). For the most part, however, the supermen and superwomen were portrayed in a straightforward, heroic fashion, as in A. E. Van Vogt's *Slan* (originally published in the pulp *Astounding Science-Fiction* in 1940, published as a hardcover in 1946) and Jack Williamson's *Darker Than You Think* (originally published in the pulp *Unknown* in 1940, published as a hardcover in 1948). By the end of the Golden Age the superhero character had a certain amount of cultural traction outside of comic books, although superheroes were still primarily appearing in the cultural ghetto of science fiction novels and films rather than in mainstream vehicles.

During the 1942–1949 period the character of the superhero went through two separate phases, both reactive against current events. The first phase, during the 1942–1945 years, was largely propagandistic, with the heroes reacting to the war by promoting patriotic virtues such as hating the enemy and buying war bonds. By 1942 the majority of the patriotically themed and patriotically costumed superheroes had already appeared—only four of them debuted after the events of December 7, 1941—but the degree to which overt patriotism appeared in the superhero stories was greatly increasing, and superheroes began fighting German villains rather than villains from Germanic-sounding countries, as had commonly been the case in superhero comics before America's entrance into the war.[3]

The second phase, during the 1946–1949 years, portrayed superheroes as reacting against postwar developments. Crime, especially urban crime, was a central cultural concern for the country's thought leaders, with concerned and even panicked articles about it regularly appearing in newspapers and magazines like *Time*. The reality was that the actual crime rate fluctuated during these years. According to the FBI's *Uniform Crime Reports*, in 1946 there was a 13 percent increase in crime.[4] In 1947, crime went up 7.5 percent in rural areas, but went down 2.3 percent in urban areas.[5] In 1948, crime went up 3.8 percent in rural areas but went down 1.8 percent in urban areas.[6] In 1949 crime went up 7.6 percent in rural areas and went up 2.7 percent in urban areas.[7] But, as is often the case, the public's primary concern (or what the comic book publishers thought was the public's primary concern) was at variance with the facts. So ordinary, realistic crime became a recurring theme in comics. Superhero comics began eliminating supervillains as the main opponents for superheroes and instead focused on mundane criminals, like the juvenile delinquent street gangs the Justice Society of America famously fought in *All-Star Comics* #40 (cover date April–May 1948).

Comic books' reactions to the advent of atomic power were less uniform. For some comic book writers, atomic power was a mere excuse to increase the power of a character (as occurred with Bill O'Connor, Ben Flinton, and Leonard Sansone's Atom, for DC Comics, who gained atomic strength in *Flash Comics* #98, cover date August 1948), or to create an atom-themed character, such as Charles Voight's Atomic Man (for Prize Publications, late 1945), Ken Crossen and Jerry Robinson's Atoman (for Spark Publications, early 1946), and Robert Peterson and Mort Lawrence's Atomic Thunderbolt (for Regor, early 1946).

But for other comic book writers and companies, atomic power was taken seriously, whether as a neutral, as in the Wayne Boring cover to

Action Comics #101 (cover date October 1946), or as an outright threat, as in the famous Otto Binder–written Captain Marvel story of nuclear apocalypse, "The Atomic War," in *Captain Marvel Adventures* #66 (cover date October 1946). Captain Marvel, nearly alone among superheroes in confronting social issues after the war, often dealt with atomic issues, both emphasizing its peaceful uses while at the same time starring in cautionary tales of what would happen if atomic power got into the wrong hands, or if there was some kind of atomic accident.

As mentioned, the sales of superhero comics declined precipitously after the war, and by 1949 comic book companies had mostly abandoned superheroes for other genres. The question of why the craze for superheroes ended so abruptly deserves some examination (though as we'll see the premise of this question is debatable).

For some critics, the reason that superheroes were suddenly much less popular with the public was the change in opponents brought about by the end of the war:

> The most obvious casualty of peace suffered by the superheroes was the disappearance of such satisfying villains as the Nazis and the Japanese. After four years of fighting spies, saboteurs, and all the soldiers of Germany and Japan, comic book heroes had to turn to more prosaic villains like common criminals and street thugs—certainly not as exciting as despicable Axis agents.[8]

Another reason given is a supposed sudden distaste for the fantastic and an enthusiasm for the ordinary and mundane. As C. C. Beck (cocreator of Captain Marvel) said, "Then the war ended. As for the comic book heroes and heroines, they had nothing to do. They had become so humanized that they could no longer fly around, chase outlandish villains, or fight impossible monsters as they once had done; nobody believed in that fairy tale stuff any more."[9] Supporting this argument is the fact that there was a general depowering of fictional superhuman characters: 75 percent of the superhumans outside the comic books either lost their powers, had them fade away without explanation, or got married and abandoned using their superhuman abilities,[10] while superpowered superheroes in the comics disappeared/were canceled at a greater rate than nonsuperpowered superheroes.

Murray, in *Champions of the Oppressed*, takes a more cynical view, seeing superheroes during the war as primarily vectors for prowar propaganda, and consequently unneeded after the war.[11]

Some writers claim that the postwar economic climate was to blame. The nation's economy was generally positive during the 1946–1949 period. There were large numbers of newly discharged servicemen and women out of work in 1946, but unemployment numbers declined over the next three years as the national economy grew. According to these writers, the growing number of jobs meant that men and women had better things to do than read superhero comic books. As C. C. Beck said, "Gone were the huge sales of comic books to soldiers and sailors everywhere and to children of war industry workers who had been making big wages. Out of uniform, young men and women had to find jobs; they had no time to sit around reading comic books any more."[12]

Other writers charge that what might be called the spirit of the age had a deleterious effect on the very idea of superheroes. The social causes and injustices that superheroes had fought for and against before World War II, and the existential/ontological threats to America that superheroes had fought against during World War II, were gone, or seemed to be, seemingly leaving the superheroes nothing to fight for. "Superheroes animated by the crusading spirit of the New Deal and World War II seemed directionless and even irrelevant now that those victories had been won. In a vague sense, the decline of the superhero reflected a postwar public mood that had grown conservative and weary of reform."[13]

Supporting this position was the irrelevancy of superheroes generated by the comics themselves, as industry leader DC changed the direction of the superheroes away from righting social wrongs. "Once the leader in producing comic books relevant to contemporary issues, DC Comics adopted a postwar editorial direction that increasingly de-emphasized social commentary in favor of lighthearted juvenile fantasy."[14]

William Savage ascribes superheroes' postwar fall from favor to two factors:

> By 1946 or 1947 readers, whether they were children or belonged to the older audience built by the war, were jaded by the redundant deeds of redundant heroes. The costumed types, pale copies of Superman and Batman to begin with, had exhausted the dramatic possibilities of the medium as well as of their individual personae by having done, in four action-packed years, everything that anyone could imagine them doing. By the end of the war, comic-book heroes had been pushed to all manner of improbable pastimes, including tearing Axis tanks in half and leaping from one aircraft to another in the middle of a dogfight. Such foolishness continued for awhile . . . but it was simply too much for readers to bear, and comic book sales plummeted.[15]

All of the preceding had a cumulative effect on the genre as a whole, which can be read as a sort of "thinning," as described by John Clute:

> Fantasy tales can be described, in part, as fables of recovery. What is being regained may be (a) the primal Story that the surface tale struggles to rearticulate, (b) the True Name, or home, of the protagonist, (c) the health of the Land ... through a process of Healing, or indeed (d) the actual location of the land itself ... But, although it is true most fantasy stories finish—and tend to end in a Eucatastrophe—it is also true that the happy endings of much fantasy derive from the notion that this is a restoration, that before the written story started there was a diminishment.
>
> Even in High Fantasy—which tends to be ringfenced from time's arrow—the Secondary World is almost constantly under some threat of lessening, a threat frequently accompanied by mourning ... and/or a sense of Wrongness. In the structurally complete fantasy, thinning can be seen as a reduction of the healthy Land to a Parody of itself, and the thinning agent—ultimately, in most instances, the Dark Lord—can be seen as inflicting this damage upon the land out of envy.[16]

In this interpretation, the Land is the superhero genre itself, and the diminishment and Wrongness are the lessening and weakening of the genre. The postwar era, and in a broader sense the post–December 7, 1941 years, were an ongoing thinning of the superhero genre. Numerous characters and comics were canceled. Many of those who survived were depowered to a lesser or greater degree. The fantasy trappings of superhero stories—the "outlandish villains" and "impossible monsters" Beck spoke of—were slowly taken away and replaced with the grime and grit and tawdry mundanity of ordinary criminals. The innocence of the genre—the simplistic story premises, the uncomplicated villains, the childlike idea that killing a villain is the same as defeating villainy, the distance between the world of the superheroes and the real world— was largely lost. The joy of invention and creation—the explosion of ideas and concepts that accompanied the 1935–1941 years of superhero comics—was gone, as the great creators, returning from service, went into other genres.[17]

But this still leaves open the question of the cause of superheroes' thinning. There was no single agent, no Dark Lord responsible (although Fredric Wertham qualifies as the Dark Lord of the Atomic Age). The audience didn't lose its taste for superheroes-qua-superheroes in the late Golden and Atomic Ages. Superhumans continued to be popular in prose science fiction and in film through the end of the Golden Age. This popularity casts doubt on the premise that superheroes themselves were to blame. Benton may be partially correct that the mundane villains of superhero comics had something to do with the downturn in sales—but comics like the Captain Marvel family of comics from Fawcett that featured fantastic villains suffered from declining sales alongside comics with ordinary villains. Too, crime comics, whose criminals were ordinary and mundane, were popular. Ordinary villains in superhero comics may have contributed to the decline in superhero comics' popularity, but were certainly not a primary cause of it.

Beck's theory about a loss of audience taste for the fantastic is not borne out by the facts, either. The audience was happy to consume the fantastic in prose and in movies during the 1946–1949 period. Prose science fiction rose in popularity after the war, and there were a number of films and cartoons released during the time period. Series characters were depowered in comics, comic strips, pulps, and magazines, but this depowering was not a universal constant.

The other theories fail in light of the skyrocketing popularity of comics as a medium after the war and the presence of superheroes in other media.

Perhaps it is ultimately more accurate to say that the audience was weary of superheroes in comics because of the limitations that comic books imposed on superhero stories. Other genres—crime, romance, Westerns—could be neatly told in 12-page chunks (the standard length of stories in comic books at this time). But the enemies superheroes were expected to grapple with, the societal conditions superheroes were expected to fix, the enemies of the state superheroes were expected to foil, were all too complex in real life to be neatly disposed of in 12 pages. Superheroes, in other words, could handle complexity at length, in prose and in film, and be enjoyed and consumed by audiences in those formats, but not in the 12 pages each hero and team were allowed in comic books. Iconic superheroes—Superman, Batman, Wonder Woman—were partially immune to this by virtue of the power of their archetypal, even mythic natures, but everyone else was not.

As Clute points out, thinning is rarely the end, or eternal, in fantasy stories: "Thinning may be kept at bay, generally by dyking it: physically through a polder of some sort, within which a toughened reality can be maintained through constant vigilance; promissorily through knowledge that somewhere a Sleeper Under the Hill awaits the call to restore to the world the savour of spring."[18] As we'll see, the polder that dyked the thinning through postwar Golden Age and the Atomic Age were Superman, Batman, and Wonder Woman, and the Sleeper Under the Hill who restored to the world of superheroes the savor of spring in the Silver Age was actually three men: the trio of Stan Lee, Jack Kirby, and Steve Ditko.

The Atomic Age: 1949–1956

The Atomic Age of comics[19] ran from 1949 to 1956: the former date being the unofficial end of superhero comics' Golden Age, thanks to the prominent heroes and comics canceled that year, and the latter date being the year in which DC Comics brought back The Flash (and in doing so started the Silver Age) in the Robert Kanigher and Carmine Infantino *Showcase* #4 (cover date October–November 1956).

During the 1949–1954 period, despite controversies—about comics' content and its effects on juvenile delinquents, about whether the act of reading comics led to the corruption of young people's character—the comics industry as a whole was at its most successful.

> By conservative estimates, about 300 comic book titles published in 1950 generated an annual industry revenue of $41 million. In 1953 over 650 titles grossed $90 million. Average monthly circulation had grown from 17 million in 1940 to nearly 70 million by 1953. Some estimates put the monthly figure close to 100 million. *Publishers Weekly* reported that the American public in 1953 spent over $1 billion on comic books. Surveys suggested that over 90 percent of boys and girls under eighteen read them, and 25 percent of high school graduates admitted to reading them as well. Comic books also remained the literature of choice for American G.I.s. Between 1950 and 1954 the comic book industry reached its zenith in audience and sales.[20]

Not coincidentally, this was the era when there were the fewest superheroes in comics.[21] At DC, *Flash* and *Green Lantern* had been canceled in 1949; in 1951 *All Star Comics* (home of the Justice Society of America) became *All-Star Western*. At Marvel, *The Human Torch* and *The Sub-Mariner* were canceled in 1949, the same year that *Marvel Mystery Comics* became a horror comic. *Captain America Comics* was canceled in 1949, surviving until 1950 as *Captain America's Weird Tales*. Fawcett's big four—*Whiz Comics*, *Master Comics*, *Captain Marvel Adventures*, and *The Marvel Family*—lasted the longest, but they, too, were all gone by 1954. Most of the superhero comics to continue publication during the Atomic Age were at DC: *Action Comics*, *Adventure Comics*, *Detective Comics*, *Batman*, *Superboy*, *Superman*, *Wonder Woman*, and *World's Finest Comics*—and of those, *Action Comics* and *Detective Comics* were anthologies, not majority-superhero comics.

DC was not the sole publisher of superheroes during this time span. Charles Biro's Crimebuster, for Lev Gleason, appeared regularly until 1955 in *Boy Comics*. Alfred Harvey and Al Gabriele's Black Cat, for Harvey, appeared regularly throughout the period in *Black Cat*. Kin Platt's Super-mouse, for Standard, appeared continuously throughout the period, in *Coo Coo Comics* and *Supermouse*, as did Mighty Mouse, in *Mighty Mouse* (for Marvel) and in various titles for St. John. Al Fago's Atomic Mouse appeared continuously from 1953–1956 in *Atomic Mouse* (for Charlton).[22]

So the Atomic Age, despite the great overall success that the comics industry was enjoying, was a fallow period for superheroes, especially compared to the Silver Age that succeeded it. And yet, there were super-heroes active during it, within comics and without. DC's iconic trio, Superman, Batman, and Wonder Woman, were all active and popular; less popular, but appearing continuously through the period, were Aqua-man, Green Arrow, and Superboy, with Johnny Quick and the Vigilante appearing regularly until 1954. Too, DC regularly published stories fea-turing science fictional superheroes, including Virgil Finlay's Tommy Tomorrow (appearing continuously throughout the period), John Broome and Carmine Infantino's Captain Comet (1951–1954), Robert Kanigher and Carmine Infantino's Knights of the Galaxy (1951–1952), and Otto Binder and Howard Sherman's Space Cabbie (from 1954).[23]

For its part, Marvel brought back Captain America, the Human Torch, and the Sub-Mariner during the Atomic Age, first in *Young Men* #24 (cover date December 1953) and then in *Captain America* for 3 issues in 1954, in *Sub-Mariner Comics* for 10 issues in 1954 and 1955, and *Human Torch* for 3 issues in 1954. Marvel also brought back the Ken Bald and Syd Shores character Namora as the Sub-Mariner's sidekick during this time, retriev-ing an obscure superheroine from comic book limbo and introducing her to a new audience.

The publisher Farrell brought back the obscure Golden Age hero Black Cobra and gave him his own self-titled comic for three issues in 1954 and 1955; they did the same with Samson and Wonder Boy in the pages of *Samson* for three issues in 1955. Charlton irregularly reprinted Blue Beetle stories during 1953 and 1954.

And, occasionally during the Atomic Age, new superheroes made their debut:

- Art Pinajian's Zip-Jet appeared for two issues from St. John in 1953.
- Standard's Freddy Frog appeared in eight stories from 1951–1954.
- Avon's Super Pup appeared in five stories in 1954.
- Mike Sekowsky's Captain Flash appeared in Sterling's *Captain Flash* #1–4 (1954–1955).
- Hy Fleishman's Crimson Avenger, for Premier, appeared in nine stories in 1954 and 1955.

- Jerry Siegel's Invisible Boy, for St. John, appeared in *Approved Comics* #2 (March 1954).

- Paul Newman and Dick Ayer's Avenger (not to be confused with the pulp character of the same name), for Magazine Enterprises, in *The Avenger* #1 (cover date February–March 1955).

- Jack Kirby and Joe Simon's Fighting American, for Headline Publications, in *Fighting American* #1 (cover date April–May 1954). *Fighting American* lasted for seven issues, through 1955.

- Bob Powell's Strongman, for Magazine Enterprises, in *Strongman* #1 (cover-date March–April 1955). *Strongman* lasted for four issues, through 1955.

- Later that year, DC introduced a new superhero, Joe Samachson and Joe Certa's Martian Manhunter (in *Detective Comics* #225, cover date November 1955).

However, the Martian Manhunter was the only one of these new heroes to be long lasting, appearing in an unbroken streak of issues through the end of the Atomic Age and well into the Silver Age.

As can be seen, then, the Atomic Age was a bad time for superheroes, especially compared to other comics' genres, but not a period entirely without life. Some heroes appeared throughout the period, others were introduced or reintroduced. The superhero genre was in a coma, but not dead during the 1949–1956 time period.

This coma—a carry-over from the 1946–1949 period of the Golden Age—was maintained for a few reasons. During the late Golden Age superheroes had been in need of a general cause. The Germans and Japanese had been the über-enemies of superheroes before and during the war, but there was no similar character type or nationality for superheroes after the war. Ordinary crimes and ordinary criminals lacked the allure and sales power of spies, supervillains, and superpowered Axis men and women. But matters for superheroes changed somewhat with the gradual realization that the Soviet Union was an active enemy of the United States. For a time, in the years before the Korean War, superheroes engaged in a kind of containment policy of their own, bringing in Communist-themed villains. "By the early 1950s, when the Cold War pervaded all aspects of American life, comic book makers in search of relevant material increasingly turned to anticommunist stories."[24]

One might think that superheroes would take advantage of this, especially during the Korean War years (1950–1953). This did not prove to be the case in superhero comics. In part this was because of the small number of superheroes being published—quite the reverse of the situation during World War II—but largely it was due to a lack of corporate willingness to use the heroes in this way.

> DC Comics and Fawcett were the only publishers at that time still produc-
> ing superhero titles of any commercial significance. The DC characters
> remained conspicuously aloof from the war, as they did from most politi-
> cal concerns during the 1950s. Fawcett's superheroes, in commercial
> decline since the end of World War II, had more to gain and less to lose by
> going to Korea ... but the intervention of Fawcett's superheroes did noth-
> ing to reverse their slide in the marketplace.[25]

After the Korean War the Cold War remained, hotter than ever, and most
of those superheroes on the market, especially Marvel's revived trio of
Captain America, the Human Torch, and the Sub-Mariner, were finally
enlisted into the fight against communism. But none of the anti-Communist
superheroes of the Atomic Age were financially successful. "They were old
fashioned, and audiences were not particularly captivated by such fear-
mongering, and the strangely up-beat imagery of troops slaughtering
North Korean troops was at odds with the frustrating war of attrition
described in news reports."[26] An anticommunist attitude was not enough
to make children and adults buy comics with superheroes in them, especially considering those comics' aesthetic and artistic inferiority compared to the superior work being done in other genres.[27]

Too, superheroes, with the self-confidence and self-assurance inscribed
into their very beings as well as their stories, were out of step with the
tenor of the age, when the basic American assumptions of masculinity
seemed to be questioned, thanks to Dr. Spock's *Baby and Child Care*
(1946), with its statement that fathers should have minimal input into
the raising of children, and Alfred Kinsey's 1948 *Sexual Behavior in the
Human Male*, which stated that more than a third of American men had
had a homosexual experience and half of married American men had
cheated on their wives. As well, the atomic bomb had had an effect on
American men:

> To the extent that comic books mirrored society, they were treating, how-
> ever elliptically, prevalent concerns over the condition of American males.
> One could not, in those days, articulate the notion that perhaps the Bomb
> had brought on a degree of psychological impotence by denying that final
> assault on Japan and lulling people into complacency with the idea that
> conventional war was a thing of the past, negating the long-held image of
> man-the-protector, man-the-hunter.[28]

Other genres repeated these concerns, which superheroes were at odds
with and particularly unsuited to deal with. It might be said that the
problem with superheroes during the Atomic Age was not so much that

there weren't attractive villains to grapple with so much as that the problems of society were ones that superheroes were ill-suited to defeat. Superman could punch supervillains, but masculine insecurity and the threat
of atomic warfare were two foes that could neither be punched nor ultimately defeated by superheroes.

Superheroes were generally out of step with contemporary concerns
during the Atomic Age. DC was more concerned with building up fantastic mythoi in their superhero stories than in portraying real life. Atlas (as
Marvel was known during the 1950s) was stuck on fanatical anti-
Communism—certainly a common sentiment in the mid-1950s, but the
simplistic victories over Communism portrayed in the comics were at
odds with and seemed childish next to the messy reality of atomic spying
and the Korean War that most Americans were familiar with during the
1950s. Fawcett's comics, largely still the same in content and style, were
exhibiting a late period decadence. Generally comics ignored contemporary concerns and went their own way, maintaining a universe of a unique
and peculiar ethos regardless of its irrelevance to consumers.

The single most significant event to take place during the Atomic Age,
as far as the medium of comic books as a whole was concerned, was the
publication of Fredric Wertham's *Seduction of the Innocent* (1954), the culmination of 15 years of comics-bashing by parents and literary critics and
a decade of statements, by Wertham, about the supposedly dangerous
effects of comics on children. By 1948, Wertham had become a leading
spokesman against comics, describing them as a central cause of juvenile
delinquency, and for the next six years he regularly condemned comics,
in print and as an expert witness before state legislatures. But it was
Seduction of the Innocent, a sweeping indictment of the comic book industry, which had the greatest impact. Despite its many flaws,[29] *Seduction of
the Innocent* prompted the Senate Subcommittee to Investigate Juvenile
Delinquency to investigate the comic book industry. The results of these
hearings were significant: "For months the comic book industry reeled in
a state of crisis. Increasing pressure from civic groups, wholesalers, and
retailers as well as government officials at all levels compelled publishers
to act before they were acted upon."[30] The industry's response in September 1954 was to form the Comics Magazine Association of America
(CMAA), which quickly established the Comics Code, a de facto code of
censorship for all comics. The effect of the CMAA, the Comics Code, and
the repression of comics that weren't sanitized enough for concerned parents, was to drive 18 publishers from comics between 1954 and 1956,
reducing the number of comic book titles published from around 650 in
1954 to around 300 in 1956. However, Duncan and Smith note that, of

these lost publishers, "Most . . . were recent startups that had tried to capitalize on the very trends that the Code banned."[31] By the end of 1955 monthly sales of comic books were halved, dropping from 80 million to 40 million, and, by 1958, 24 of the original 29 publishers of the CMAA had stopped making comics.

The effect of the Code on superhero comics was twofold. Although the primary targets of the CMAA and the Comics Code were horror, crime, and romance comics, and although the content of superhero comics during the mid-1950s was innocuous and unobjectionable, the institution of the Comics Code still had a significant effect on the sales of superhero comics. Regardless of genre, comics' sales suffered after the Senate Subcommittee hearings and the adoption of the Code, and even DC's superhero comics were not immune to this. (The sole exception was the Superman family of comics, which continued to sell around a million copies per issue, thanks largely to the popularity of the *Adventures of Superman* TV show, 1953–1957).

The second effect of the Code on superhero comics was not so immediate but was longer lasting. Television, available only to a minority of households at the beginning of the decade, was becoming increasingly popular and increasingly widespread, with over two-thirds of American households owning a television in 1955. Free, and full of an increasing number of programs appealing to children and teenagers, television posed a direct threat to other media, who found themselves losing their audiences to television. To counter this, movies changed their content: Hollywood produced more epics, more films with "realistic" subject matter, and highlighted their stars' sex appeal. Superhero comics, however, could not take these steps because of the existence of the Code, which straitjacketed the comics into stories whose content could only appeal to the children and young juveniles who had abandoned comics for television. This state of affairs continued years into the Silver Age, ending only with the appearance of Marvel's Fantastic Four in 1961.

Another event, far less publicized, also had a pronounced impact on superhero comics. In 1955, the American News Company, which distributed more than half of the comic books in circulation, was left the business of national magazine distribution after settling an antitrust lawsuit with the Justice Department over monopolistic practices. In 1957, American News Company abruptly went out of business. This severely impacted the magazine industry in general and the comics business in particular. Publishers Lev Gleason, Fawcett, and Quality all went out of business, and Atlas (the name by which Marvel Comics was known in the 1950s) was forced to switch distributors to one owned by National Periodical

Publications, the owner of DC Comics. This resulted in Atlas being limited in its publishing output for the next 10 years, and DC being left in the position of the heavyweight of comics.

Superhero comics as a whole existed on the margins of the comics industry during the Atomic Age. Entertaining and inventive work was being done with the Superman and Batman mythos and in the funny animal comics, but as far as the comics industry in general was concerned, superheroes were an afterthought. This state of affairs would continue into the Silver Age for several years.

The Silver Age: 1956–1970

Compared to the Atomic Age, the Silver Age of comics was a complex and busy period, full of achievements for the two major companies, Marvel and DC. Unlike the Atomic Age, the starting point of the Silver Age is generally agreed upon, the end point less so.

The beginning of the Silver Age was the appearance of the new Flash, created by Robert Kanigher and Carmine Infantino and debuting in DC's *Showcase* #4 (cover date September–October 1956). The end point of the Silver Age is still a matter of some debate for comics scholars, although the majority place the end in 1970, when Mort Weisinger retired from editing the Superman comics and Jack Kirby left Marvel to join DC. As we'll see, though, there were earlier occurrences and trends that signaled the end of the Silver Age. It can be argued that the transition between the Silver Age and the Bronze Age took place between 1968 and 1973, and 1970 is the midpoint of the transition, just as 1949 was the midpoint of the transition between the Golden and the Atomic Ages.

Thematically and symbolically, the appearance of the new Flash (named after and influenced by the Golden Age Flash) signified the rebirth of the superhero genre, with debuts by Otto Binder and Al Plastino's Legion of Super-Heroes (in *Adventure Comics* #247, cover date April 1958), John Broome and Gil Kane's Green Lantern (in *Showcase* #22, cover date September–October 1959), Gardner Fox and Mike Sekowsky's Justice League of America (in *Brave and the Bold* #28, cover date February–March 1960), Gardner Fox and Joe Kubert's Hawkman (in *Brave and the Bold* #34, cover date February–March 1961), and Gardner Fox and Gil Kane's Atom (in *Showcase* #34, cover date September–October 1961) following, albeit spaced out over several years' time—DC was by no means eager to embrace new superheroes unless their sales justified their existence, and the only new superhero to experience significant popularity was the Green Lantern.

The success of these characters and of the Justice League of America inspired imitators: Joe Simon and Jack Kirby's Private Strong and The Fly for Archie (June and August 1959), and Joe Gill and Steve Ditko's Captain Atom for Charlton (March 1960). But the most important imitator was at what was in the late 1950s and early 1960s a minor comics company: Marvel Comics. Martin Goodman, Marvel's publisher, ordered Stan Lee (editor at Marvel) to create a superteam to rival the Justice League. Lee and Jack Kirby created the Fantastic Four in *Fantastic Four* #1 (cover date November 1961), beginning Marvel's involvement in superheroes after several years away from them.[32]

Likewise, while there were trends before 1970 that meant the end of what had come before, Weisinger's retirement from the Superman comics and Jack Kirby's departure from Marvel were symbolically important. These departures deprived both DC and Marvel of heavily influential, arguably even dominant[33] artistic personalities, greatly contributing to a fragmenting of what had been nearly monolithic states of affairs at both companies.

Given the quite different histories of Marvel and DC during these years, the events of the Silver Age cannot be neatly broken down into universally applicable phases or eras. Instead, there are multiple different phases, each applying to a different aspect of the Silver Age.

The first five years of the Silver Age, the 1956–1961 period, are the easiest to describe. The five-year period between the Flash's debut and the debut of the Fantastic Four were clearly DC's, both in terms of aesthetic/artistic momentum and in terms of sales (which, thanks to the restrictive agreement Marvel had signed with its distributor, were Marvel's all-time low point). During this time period Marvel was limping along with 16 comics, published only every other month, the best of which sold less than a fifth of what DC's best-selling comic sold, and none of which had superheroes in them. (Marvel's usual fare at this time were anthology books like *Tales of Suspense* and *Tales to Astonish*, Westerns like *Kid Colt Outlaw* and *Rawhide Kid*, and romances like *Love Romances*.)

DC, meanwhile, had as its five best-selling comics *Superman*, *Superboy*, *Batman*, *Superman's Pal Jimmy Olsen*, and *World's Finest Comics*—all superhero. More importantly as far as the comics themselves were concerned, the Superman and Batman comics were constantly adding to the Superman and Batman megatexts and mythoi, and publishing inventive stories that were a central part of DC's Silver Age.[34] What was taking place with the Flash, the Green Lantern, Hawkman, the Atom, and the Justice League was creative and would later become important to DC, but the

Superman and Batman comics were much more important to DC during this time period.

But at the same time, the 1956–1961 phase was for Marvel the period when Stan Lee and a variety of artists, most notably Jack Kirby and Steve Ditko, began playing with the themes, in the Westerns, science fiction, and weird adventure stories, that they would later so successfully make use of in their superhero comics. The science fiction stories were responses to the anxieties of the atomic age, with Jack Kirby's rampaging monsters standing in for fears of what nuclear power and unchecked technology would produce. In contrast, DC consistently promoted atomic power as clean and as a product of scientific progress, and technology as being the key to world peace. Steve Ditko's alienated and neurotic characters were a response to dissatisfaction with the limits of 1950s social life. Western heroes, in the Marvel stories, became misunderstood outcasts, just as Spider-Man and the X-Men would be. Kirby's monsters were the direct ancestors of the Hulk and the Thing, and Ditko's desperate and paranoid characters would later appear as men in need of help from Dr. Strange, or as would-be assailants of Daredevil. Financially and artistically, DC was Marvel's superior during this time period, but Marvel was laying the groundwork for its later successes.

The 1961–1970 period of the Silver Age is most usefully broken down into two- and three-year chunks.

From 1961–1963, Lee et al. debuted new characters and experimented with what superheroes could be. This was a period of rapid change and experimentation, from content (ranging from characterization to costumes) to plot and story formula to the format of the comics themselves. The year 1961 saw the introduction of the Fantastic Four, whose squabbling and flawed, even tragic characters were a marked change from the uniformly positive characters that DC was presenting. And 1962 saw the debut of Lee and Steve Ditko's Spider-Man, Lee, Larry Lieber, and Kirby's Thor, and Lee and Kirby's Hulk. In 1963, Iron Man and Lee and Kirby's X-Men first appeared, as well as Lee and Kirby's Avengers, Marvel's counterpart to the Justice League.

DC, meanwhile, was content to cruise along, turning out stories that were similar across the board, regardless of who the main character was, and outselling Marvel by a sizable margin. In 1961, 13 of the top 20 comics sold were DC's, with Marvel's best, *Tales to Astonish*, coming in at 41st place and selling less than a quarter the issues of DC's best, *Superman*; in 1963, with DC retaining its grip at the top and middle of the sales chart, Marvel's best-selling comic was *Rawhide Kid*, again at less than a quarter of what *Superman* was selling. It was during this period that DC made the editorial decision to emphasize its superheroes at the cost of other genres. Superheroes were proving to be successful and profitable—driven by the audience realization that superhero comics could show them things that television and movies could not—and DC decided to capitalize upon this—although only upon the characters and comics they had already created, rather than any new ones—as Gabilliet notes, "after the summer of 1961, DC ceased to introduce notable new characters for a long time."[35]

The news was not entirely good for DC during the 1961–1963 period, however. In 1961 comics publishers began raising prices from 10 cents to 12 cents, but Dell mistakenly raised theirs to 15 cents, leading to a significant drop in sales for Dell comics and a consequent surge in sales for DC's superhero comics. But, in 1962, the price increase became the industry norm, leading to a widespread, cross company decrease in sales numbers.

From 1963–1964, Marvel underwent what Pierre Comtois calls the "era of consolidation," when

> Lee considered what had already been accomplished and began a conscious effort to adapt the new style not only to existing titles, but to new ones specifically created for that purpose. And so, it was during these years of consolidation that Lee and his stable of artists . . . began to actively exploit the disparate elements that had defined the nascent, but increasingly popular Marvel style and to deliberately weave them into a coherent "universe."[36]

Marvel resurrected Captain America and introduced Stan Lee and Bill Everett's Daredevil in 1964.

The fourth phase was the 1965–1968 years, when Marvel's comics hit their Silver Age high point aesthetically and artistically.

> In the grandiose years to be considered here, with the foundation of the Marvel style in place, Lee would pursue a deliberate spirit of humanism, adapting his comics to the spirit of the times . . . which resulted in comics written and conceptualized in such a way as to appeal to adults as well as children . . . Marvel was now able to take its readers either to the ends of the universe in cosmos-spanning adventures or to the streets of New York City to experience the anguish of drug abuse, racism, and environmental pollution.[37]

During the 1961–1968 period the status quo between DC and Marvel changed for good, financially and artistically. As mentioned, in 1961 13 of the top 20 comics sold were DC's, with Marvel's best only appearing at number 41. In 1968, 10 of the top 20 comics sold were DC's, with Marvel placing only 2 in the top 20. However, beginning in 1966 Marvel's total sales surpassed DC's, and by 1968 Marvel's total sales were a third again higher than DC's. DC still ruled the top of the sales charts, but Marvel owned the middle of the charts.[38]

This time period saw outside forces positively affect sales. In 1966, the *Batman* television show almost doubled sales for the *Batman* comic book, with humor, romance, Westerns, and war comics' sales plummeting and being cannibalized by superhero comics.[39] By 1967, Marvel's success at branding itself as the comics company for today's youth, not just through the content of its comics but through the salesmanship of Stan Lee himself, had broadened Marvel's appeal far beyond what superhero comics companies were used to. Marvel comics were popular at colleges, both among college students and in the classes themselves as required reading. Stan Lee began doing college lectures, and magazines like *Esquire* began writing articles about Marvel's superheroes.

More important than sales and branding were the revolutionary innovations Marvel brought to superhero comics. For the first 10 years of the Silver Age, DC outsold Marvel by an appreciable sum, but this did not create a situation in which Marvel, eager for sales, imitated DC. Rather, Marvel began carrying out a series of innovations in content and production, innovations that were at first scorned by DC, then clumsily aped by them, and finally fully imitated by them.

Marvel's production innovation is the easiest to describe. Before the Silver Age, comics were produced script first. The script would be written, and then the artist would draw the art to match the script. But Stan Lee implemented what became known as the "Marvel style," in which a story's writer would plot the story and then turn it over to the artist, who would draw the art but in doing so create the story beats and breaks, essentially scripting the story. The writer would get the art back and then add dialogue to each panel. This change in the way that stories were produced—a method that DC refused to imitate—meant that an artist's skill at visual storytelling became as important to the final result as the writer's plot and words, and that in many cases it was visuals rather than words that drove the story. Marvel had the good fortune, for much of the Silver Age, to employ artists who were masterful storytellers—men like Jack Kirby and Steve Ditko—with the end result being that the stories were augmented by the artists in enormously positive ways.

But Marvel's most significant and longest-lasting innovation lay in the change in characterization that it brought to comics—the fact of the change itself, and the ways in which the characters changed.

Before *Fantastic Four* #1, during the 1956–1961 phase of the Silver Age, superheroes' characters were, by default, all the same. DC's superheroes, from Superman to Wonder Woman, all had roughly the same personality, reacted to events in the same way, and all had the same beliefs. The DC desire for a "house style" of characters imposed a uniformity on the characters, despite the characters existing in different lines or families of comics, edited by different individuals. Stan Lee, in *Fantastic Four* #1, changed all of that, giving his characters individual personalities, an innovation he would continue to practice throughout the Silver Age. The Thing wasn't like the Hulk; Mister Fantastic wasn't like Iron Man; Spider-Man wasn't like the Human Torch. In the development of the superhero genre, this innovation was crucial in creating characters and stories with two and sometimes three dimensions, which were necessary for the genre to reach maturity.

The ways in which the characters changed were even more revolutionary. DC's heroes were authoritarian in character and concept. They were authority figures, whether formally (as scientists, pilots, policemen, police scientists, or deputized members of police forces) or informally (Superman). They were solidly in favor of established authority. They emphasized responsibility to the community over individualism. They embodied what Bradford Wright calls "a blandly optimistic consensus vision of America premised on the virtues of anticommunism, corporatism, domesticity, and middle-class social aspirations. This was the consensus ... that DC championed."[40]

Marvel's heroes, however—beginning with the Fantastic Four and continuing throughout the Silver Age—were the opposites of DC's characters. They epitomized individualism (although they remained heroes, never shirking their ultimate responsibilities to their communities). They rejected consensus and conformity. They were usually alienated from society and felt themselves to be men and women apart. They were the products of tragic beginnings, but unlike DC's characters the Marvel superheroes were never allowed to forget the tragedies that birthed them. They had uneasy relationships with the public, who often turned on them. They had uneasy relationships with the forces of authority. They lived in "the world outside your window," in the phrase commonly credited to Stan Lee—meaning they lived in real places like New York City, the deserts of the American Southwest, and Westchester County, unlike the fictional locales of DC, Gotham City, Metropolis, Central City, and so on. They interacted with real people, whether that meant appearances by major politicians like Nikita Khruschev and John F. Kennedy Jr., or simply the appearance of African Americans as secondary or tertiary characters or even passers-by.

Even Marvel's villains were granted two dimensions, leaving them villainous but flawed in recognizable and understandable ways. Marvel's heroes, villains, and stories were often ambiguous, and ambiguity was an entirely new concept in superhero comics.

Too, real-world issues began appearing in Marvel's superhero comics—issues like drug abuse, racism, and environmental pollution, issues that DC didn't begin to tackle until the "relevant" phase that began with the Denny O'Neil and Neal Adams issues of *Green Lantern* in 1968. To an increasing degree, these issues, and ones like the Vietnam War, the hippy movement, and the rise in feminism and black activism, appeared as the decade passed. The African American Gabe Jones dealt with racism and discrimination in Stan Lee and Jack Kirby's *Sgt. Fury and His Howling Commandos* #6 (cover date March 1964), a few months before the passage of the Civil Rights Act of that year. The Avengers fought the Sons of the Serpent, an overt Ku Klux Klan stand-in, in Stan Lee and Don Heck's *Avengers* #32 (cover date September 1966). The Black Panther made his debut in Lee and Kirby's *Fantastic Four* #52 (cover date July 1966), the year after Malcolm X's assassination and the year in which the "black power" movement began to form. Thor confronted hippies in Lee and Kirby's *Thor* #154 (cover date July 1968), the year after the Summer of Love and the year before Woodstock. Daredevil performed for the troops in Vietnam and befriended a blind African American veteran in Stan Lee and Gene Colan's *Daredevil* #47 (cover date December 1968). Late in the decade, Marvel "further exaggerated the disaffection of its superheroes by setting their adventures in the increasingly violent cultural upheavals of the late 1960s."[41] In 1969, Marvel introduced the Falcon, cocreated by Stan Lee and Gene Colan, in *Captain America* #117 (cover date September 1969); the Falcon was the first African American superhero. And throughout the period, via his editorials in the "Stan's Soapbox" column, Stan Lee "lectured readers on the evils of racism, the problems of war and peace, pollution, drugs, and even religion."[42]

Spider-Man in particular was a radical change. As the Silver Age progressed, he aged, graduating from high school and going to college—and aging a character in such a way had never been seen before in superhero comics. The emphasis on subplots involving his character, and the development of his character, made Peter Parker the subject of superhero comics' first soap opera, and the first character to be as interesting as his costumed alter ego. Spider-Man—teenaged, flawed, brooding, and constantly suffering from bad luck—became the new superheroic archetype, effectively replacing the flawless, unintrospective, mature adult Superman as the most popular archetype in comics.

In one respect Marvel's heroes were not so different from DC's: Marvel's heroes were staunch anti-Communists and patriots, just as DC's were. But for most of the Silver Age DC's heroes ignored Communism and did not acknowledge the Cold War, while Marvel's heroes were Cold Warriors, ardently or reluctantly—again, Marvel reacting to the contemporary concerns of the "world outside your window" while DC's heroes essentially lived in an enclosed cocoon. Marvel's anti-Communism was reached by way of its devotion to individualism: "The veneration of individualism in the Marvel Cold War story generates a logic to the ideology of the books. Because the core value is defined as liberty, the central evil of the communist system is its trampling of individual freedoms."[43] Marvel's heroes were the products of the Cold War, from the Fantastic Four hijacking a rocket in order to beat the Communists into space, to the Hulk being born out of a weapons experiment gone wrong—a "gamma bomb" explosion sabotaged by a Soviet agent—to Iron Man's alter ego Tony Stark being a weapons manufacturer. Too, Marvel's heroes regularly fought Communist opponents, far more often than DC's Silver Age heroes did.

Last, Marvel created the modern comic book universe by regularly showing its heroes existing side-by-side with other heroes, by crossing heroes over into other heroes' titles, by acknowledging the events of one comic in another comic, and in essence creating a collective narrative. DC had done these things in a scattershot fashion—Batman and Superman regularly teamed up in the pages of *World's Finest,* Aquaman showed up in *Superman's Girl Friend, Lois Lane* #12 (cover date October 1959), and the establishment of the Justice League of America—but never as a deliberate editorial measure. Given the different lines/families of comics at DC during the Silver Age, each overseen by a different editor, such an editorial measure would have been impossible. Given the great success DC continued to have with the Superman and Batman family of comics, most likely such a move would have been seen as unnecessary by DC editors. But the weaving together of many different characters into one cumulative universe became the industry norm after Stan Lee began the practice at Marvel, and DC eventually began imitating Marvel in this regard.

DC was, of course, not ignorant of what was taking place at Marvel. For much of the decade DC had little but scorn for Marvel, both because of its biggest titles' comparatively lackluster sales and because of Marvel's use of antiheroes as protagonists, something DC felt was inappropriate for children's literature. Nor was DC willing to take the chances Marvel did with characterization and content, both because as the frontrunner it didn't feel the need to and because it was unwilling to take the risks that the underdog Marvel was willing to take. And DC had pride in their own product; the writing was competent (if rarely inspired) and lived up to the requirements that DC posed the writers, and the art—particularly Gil Kane's and Carmine Infantino's—was slick and professional, especially compared to the cruder Jack Kirby and Steve Ditko.

The 1968–1970 years were filled with change for Marvel and DC, positive in some respects but significantly negative in others. In 1968, Marvel negotiated a new deal with its distributor, allowing it to publish numerous new monthly titles and finally capitalize in a larger way on its new popularity. That same year Gold Key became the first publisher to raise all its comics' prices to 15 cents. In 1969, other publishers followed suit, leading to a major drop in sales for DC and a lesser drop for Marvel, the first of many years in a row of declining sales.

Other disruptions were less visible to outsiders. The year 1968 saw the first faltering of the Marvel machine, and what in retrospect are obvious signs of the end of the Silver Age began appearing. Pierre Comtois calls 1968 the beginning of Marvel's "Twilight Years": "By 1968, Marvel Comics had reached its zenith in terms of its development and sheer creative power. Soon after came an expansion of the company's line of titles and a commensurate dilution of the talent that had made its first years great."[44] That year Marvel publisher Martin Goodman sold Marvel Comics and the rest of his publishing holdings to the Perfect Film and Chemical Corporation, though Goodman remained as publisher. Marvel was free to publish as many comics as it liked, but the market for superhero comics was suddenly flat, leading Goodman to try to cut costs and boost sales, in turn leading to new (for Marvel) decrees: from Goodman, a ban on the trappings of science fiction and ongoing story lines; and from Stan Lee, the infamous directive that "Marvel's stories should only have 'the illusion of change,' that the characters should never evolve too much, lest their portrayals conflict with what licensees had planned for other media."[45]

Also, 1968 saw the beginning of the end of the Silver Age for DC. DC Comics merged with the Kinney National conglomerate. DC ended its decentralized editorial system, where individual editors had their own fiefdoms—the Superman family of books, the Batman family of books, the science fiction family of books—but there was no overall supervision of all of DC's comics, as there was at Marvel under Stan Lee. This changed in 1968, as Carmine Infantino became DC's editorial director and was charged by DC with revitalizing its line. Infantino began hiring artists and writers away from other companies and directed a revamp of traditional characters, including Batman (who returned to his grim hardboiled roots), Wonder Woman (who was depowered and made glam and hip), Green Arrow (who was politically radicalized), and Superman.

Aware of both their second place position in sales compared to Marvel and of Steve Ditko's great discontentment with Marvel Comics in general and Stan Lee in particular, DC (via Infantino) hired Ditko to begin producing Marvel-style characters and comics for them. The results—*Hawk and Dove*, *Beware the Creeper*—were different from anything DC was producing at that time, but were not successful with readers and were canceled within a year's time. Much more successful were Neal Adams's "Deadman" stories, which had begun in *Strange Adventures* in late 1967 but drew the most attention in 1968. Adams's run on *Strange Adventures* was hugely successful, and although the comic was one of DC's weird adventure comics, rather than a straightforward superhero title, it nonetheless gave DC editorial and DC's fans an alternative vision of comics for DC.

The year 1969 furthered the process of change for DC. Denny O'Neil and Neal Adams did a run on *Green Lantern* that "immersed its superheroes in the social and political issues of the times: racism, poverty, political corruption, the 'generation gap,' the plight of Native Americans, pollution, overpopulation, and religious cults."[46] Between those and the one-sided political debates between ardent leftist Green Arrow and dull establishment square Green Lantern, the series was attention-grabbing, foregrounding the issues in a way that not even Marvel's comics had attempted. The series attracted significant media attention, with articles in the *New York Times*, *Wall Street Journal*, and *Newsweek*, although *Green Lantern*'s sales continued to decline.

The retirement of Mort Weisinger and Jack Kirby's leaving Marvel for DC had a powerful impact on their respective companies, but each was merely representative of the larger trends at work.

Ultimately, the story of comics' Silver Age is one of rebirth, of the genre of superheroes, and then adolescence, maturity, and senescence. What came next would be less glorious, and in many ways considerably different from what had come before.

The Bronze Age: 1970–1985

Many critics (though not all) see the beginning point of the Bronze Age of superhero comics as 1970, with the retirement of Mort Weisinger and the departure of Jack Kirby from Marvel. The generally agreed-upon ending point of the Bronze Age of superhero comics is the 1984–1985 period: Marvel published its limited series, *Secret Wars*, in 1984, and DC published its limited series, *Crisis on Infinite Earths*, from 1984–1985. In between these two points was largely a bland and inartistic set of years for superhero comics, in which the creativity that had characterized it during the Silver Age was to be found in other genres and during which superhero comics as a genre no longer progressed but turned inward and began feeding upon itself.

The Bronze Age, for superheroes, is most marked by that last aspect. The pushing outward against the limitations of genre and medium and the Comics Code, the tendency toward experimentation and boundary-pushing, the progress in areas from characterization to plot development, all departed. For the first time formula was more important than originality, and superhero comics began relying upon what had been successful in the past rather than trying further generic evolution and experimentation. This example of what sociologist Todd Gitlin, in writing about network television in *Inside Prime Time,* called "recombinant culture,"[47] or a culture and corporate environment in which companies rely upon recycled material and formulas to produce cheap content, led to particularly uninspired results in the superhero comics. The emphasis changed from being revolutionary to maintaining the status quo.

In part this was due to editorial dictates—foremost among them, Stan Lee's notorious "illusion of change" statement. But this was also due to a new generation of writers and artists replacing the older creators, men like Stan Lee (who stepped away from active scripting in 1970) and Jack Kirby, men who had approached superhero comics as a profession and brought professional sensibilities to the job. What replaced them were fans, writers, and artists who had grown up with superhero comics and loved the genre and were happy to write and draw comics within the genre's boundaries, rather than pushing at them.

Gabilliet goes further:

> This decade proved problematic for the large publishers. They had to cope with dropping revenue, increasingly rebellious employees, and a society in permanent change necessitating a permanent evolution in the contents of their magazines. The unquestionable creative originality of several high-profile creators ... originated a perceptible change in readers' attitudes, as more and more of them purchased comic books not because of the character(s) featured in them but because of the artist(s) who had drawn them.[48]

Superheroes, in other words, were in the doldrums during the Bronze Age, creatively as well as financially. Characters did not progress or change; adherence to continuity became an incestuous devotion to it; and with the exception of the "relevancy" period stories became about fights rather than about characters or intricate plots.

The first third of the Bronze Age, the 1970–1975 period, saw a number of trends develop. Foremost among them was the trend toward "relevancy," of publishing stories in which the superheroes dealt with pressing social or political issues. Although as mentioned Marvel had been publishing stories with these elements in a rather low-key fashion through much of the 1960s, the O'Neil/Adams *Green Lantern* issues—which ran *Green Lantern* #76–89 (cover dates April 1970 through April–May 1972)—foregrounded the issues and made them the point of each script. Despite media attention to the "relevancy" comics, they sold poorly, and the "relevancy" period ended at DC in 1973, but continued at Marvel until 1974, with the "Secret Empire" story line, which culminated in *Captain America* #175 (cover date July 1974) with a stand-in for President Nixon committing suicide in front of Captain America. The high point of the "relevancy" issues—where could one go after a story line in which the president himself is shown to be a supervillain?—the "Secret Empire" stories gave way to mundane superhero stories from both Marvel and DC. "By the middle of the 1970s readers and creators alike seemed to have concluded that crusades to bring about a more just society had taken superheroes too far from their basic appeal as escapist entertainment. Comic book makers interpreted declining sales as a signal that superheroes ought to spend less time proselytizing and more time punching."[49]

One aspect of the relevancy trend was the increasing inclusion of people of color and women in superhero comics. Although these attempts at racial and sexual equality were, as Paul Lopes puts it, "halfhearted,"[50] they were at least steps in the right direction, however halting. Marvel had introduced the African American superhero the Falcon in 1969. In 1970, Marvel introduced its first costumed Native American hero, Red Wolf, created by Roy Thomas and John Buscema and debuting in *Avengers* #80 (cover date September 1970). That same year DC introduced its first African American superhero, Robert Kanigher and Nick Cardy's Mal Duncan, in *Teen Titans* #26 (cover date March–April 1970). In 1972 Marvel introduced the blaxploitation-inspired Luke Cage, Power Man, created by Archie Goodwin, John Romita Sr., and George Tuska, and gave him his own comics: *Luke Cage, Hero for Hire* (cover date June 1972). In 1973, the Black Panther was given his own series in *Jungle Action* (cover date for #5 July 1973). In 1974, the Asian hero Shang-Chi, created by Steve Englehart, Al Milgrom, and Jim Starlin the year before, was given his own series, *Master of Kung Fu* (cover date for #1 April 1974). DC would not give an African American hero a title until Tony Isabella and Trevor von Eeden's Black Lightning, in *Black Lightning* #1 (cover date April 1977). However, superhero comics remained nearly entirely white, with superheroes of color appearing in the margins or in their own poorly promoted comics rather than in the best-selling comics of the time.

Marvel and DC's attempts to grapple with the feminist revolution were as halfhearted as their attempts to include people of color in their comics. Both companies had featured female heroes throughout the Silver Age, beginning with Wonder Woman and Lee and Kirby's Invisible Girl (a founding member of the Fantastic Four), but the characterization of those superheroines was hardly on par with that of their male counterparts, being predominantly stereotypes rather than two- and three-dimensional as the male superheroes were. The situation in the 1970s improved only marginally through the decade. New characters of the early 1970s—Roy Thomas and John Buscema's Thundra, Gerry Conway and Jim Mooney's Man-Killer, Roy Thomas and John Buscema's Lady Liberators (all for Marvel)—were caricatures of female libbers. At DC, the response to the feminist revolution was to depower Wonder Woman and have her open a flower store and learn judo, a state of affairs that lasted throughout the early 1970s. In 1972, Marvel launched three comics that attempted to give their female leads three-dimensional, nonstereotyped characters, but none of the three—Roy Thomas and Linda Fite's *The Cat*, Jean Thomas and Win Mortimer's *Night Nurse*, Carole Seuling and Steve Gerber's *Shanna, the She-Devil*—lasted more than five issues. By the end of the decade Marvel and DC had four titles featuring superheroines and were regularly including superheroines in other titles. The companies' eventual, positive reaction to the feminist revolution only took place after the 1979 defeat of the Equal Rights Amendment and during an era when feminism, like the black rights movement, had given way to political anomie.

As mentioned, the superhero comics had no forward momentum in the first half of the 1970s, being stuck feeding upon themselves and recycling the past rather than trying to innovate and expand. In part this was due to the aforementioned influx of fan writers as opposed to professionals. It was also due to bad editorial leadership: DC's editor in chief, Carmine Infantino, was an uninspired leader. At Marvel, Stan Lee stepped away from active day-to-day editorial management in 1970, and from 1970–1977 Marvel went through six editors in chief, leading to a significant loss of editorial direction, too many comics with reprinted material, too many missed deadlines, and a generally fannish (as opposed to professional) approach to the work by the writers. Superhero comics weren't entirely a wasteland during the first half of the 1970s—Jack Kirby's "Fourth World" series of comics (1970–1973) for DC were a high point, with Kirby being allowed to write as well as illustrate, leading to some of his best, most imaginative and energetic work—but compared to what had come before most superhero comics were clichéd and flat. As Pierre Comtois puts it, "Humor became stale, formula trumped originality, and elements such as characterization and realism began to fade."[51]

Of course, writers of superhero comics during the first half of the 1970s could hardly have felt that they had the full confidence of their editorial and business masters. Their response to the sudden flattening of the comic book market at the end of the 1960s and the beginning of the 1970s was to move away from superhero comics, even though those were the stories that had enjoyed mass-market popularity only a few years before. Arguably, the decision makers at DC and Marvel, and in their parent companies, felt that superheroes were only a fad whose time had come and gone. Whatever the reason, during this time DC canceled most of its superhero titles other than those starring Superman and Batman, while Marvel canceled weaker-selling titles such as *Dr. Strange*, *Sub-Mariner*, and the *X-Men*.

What replaced them was Marvel and DC's attempt to expand into other genres, after having spent the Silver Age concentrating on superhero comics to the exclusion of their other, once-successful nonsuperheroic comics. Marvel and DC began publishing romance, Western, horror, and monster comics (such as Roy Thomas's and Gene Colan's *Tomb of Dracula*, from cover date April 1972, and Len Wein's *Swamp Thing*, from cover date October–November 1972), and adaptations of pulp heroes' adventures, and sword and sorcery comics (such as Roy Thomas's *Conan the Barbarian*, from cover date October 1970). Marvel, under the name "Curtis Magazines,"[52] began publishing a series of black-and-white comics magazines (magazines as opposed to comic books, and because they were magazines they were not subject to the Comics Code) that were explorations of nonsuperhero genres. As an attempt to diversify their publishing lines, these attempts by Marvel and DC were worthy. As attempts to capitalize on then-trendy and popular genres in other media, they were canny. As art, many of these new comics had all the originality, inventiveness, experimentation, and energy that the superhero comics of the time lacked. But as business ventures, viewed coldly through the lens of the bottom line, these comics were for the most part failures, being outsold to a significant degree by the superhero comics of both companies. By 1975, Marvel and DC had reverted to producing predominantly superhero titles.

Perhaps the most significant new trend in superhero comics during the 1970–1975 period was the growth in what would later be called the "direct market." Traditionally comics were sold by the comic book companies to proxies—drugstores, supermarkets, and newsstands—who would then sell the comics alongside other magazines. But the flat sales of the late 1960s had given way to declining sales in the early 1970s, and the traditional venues for comics—the drugstores, supermarkets, and newsstands—were taking a cold look at comics and beginning to order fewer of them, on the grounds that newsstands would make more money selling magazines for a dollar or more rather than comics for 25 cents.

The response to this, by comic book fans and comic book convention organizers, was to develop the direct market. These men (rarely, women) opened comic book specialty stores (a practice that had begun on a much smaller scale in the 1960s) and began buying comics directly from independent distributors like Phil Seuling's Sea Gate Distributors, founded in 1972 as the first specifically comic book distributor. The economic effect of the direct market for comics was small at first, but would become significant by the end of the decade.

The 1975–1985 period was in some respects tumultuous for Marvel and DC. The most unsettling event of the period was the "DC Implosion" in 1978. Sales of superhero comics had remained on a downward slide through the 1970s. Marvel and DC's response was to saturate the market with an ever-increasing number of comics, as a way to keep their profits steady. The result was that overall circulation numbers slightly increased for Marvel over the decade and slightly decreased for DC. But the saturation strategy was one that could not be maintained indefinitely, and in 1978 the crash came, caused by notably poor sales the previous winter (the result of winter storms that had disrupted distribution and hampered consumer spending), ongoing economic inflation and recession, and the increased cost of both paper and printing, which led to declining profitability and declining readership numbers. DC responded in June 1978 by laying off numerous staff members and canceling approximately 40 percent of its titles. Marvel similarly shrank its line, down to 32 titles.

These efforts to save money did not work, as Marvel's and DC's cumulative sales continued falling, so that by 1981 Marvel's sales were at 4.75 million and DC's at 2.75 million, down from 7.5 million and 4.5 million in mid-1977. The traditional distribution system was failing faster than ever, and the newsstands were jettisoning comics faster than ever, again due to the lack of profit comics produced compared to more expensive magazines.

However, the situation was by no means hopeless for Marvel and DC during the 1975–1980 phase. Other genres besides superheroes were increasingly popular, especially sword and sorcery. Marvel and DC had notable successes putting out comic books based on popular movies (*Star Wars*), television shows (*Battlestar Galactica*), and even toys (*Rom, Micronauts*). The rise in the direct market—Marvel made 1.5 million in direct market sales in 1976 and 3.5 million in 1979—pointed at a potential new direction for the comics business to go in. In 1979, legal actions resulting from Phil Seuling's arrangement with comics published led to a surge in new comics distributors, which in turn spurred a boom in new comic book stores. Most importantly for Marvel and DC, both companies were making a greatly increasing amount of money from licensed products. By 1979, Marvel was making more money from licensed products than from the comics themselves, and in 1980 only a third of DC's total revenue came from comics. Too, an increasing number of media properties were based on comics, including television shows *Superfriends* (1973, 1977–1979, 1981), *Wonder Woman* (1975–1979), and *The Incredible Hulk* (1977–1982) and movies *Superman* (1978) and *Superman II* (1980).

The year 1981 was the low point for both Marvel and DC in terms of sales. After that, Marvel's sales rebounded and rapidly grew through the early 1980s, while DC's finally stabilized and remained flat instead of declining, as had been the case since the mid-1960s. In part, this was due to the ascension of Jim Shooter to editor in chief of Marvel in 1978. Shooter imposed his personal editorial vision on the comics—the first editor in chief to successfully do so at Marvel since Stan Lee's departure—and brought about renewed professionalism and attention to deadlines. A larger part of the success was the comics themselves, which featured several long-lasting writer/artist teams of unusual quality, including Chris Claremont and John Byrne's *X-Men* (1977–1981) (the best-selling title in the industry during this time period, and one that, undoubtedly due to its strong female characters, had an unusually large following of female fans), Frank Miller's *Daredevil* (1979–1983), Marv Wolfman and George Perez's *New Teen Titans* (1980–1985), and John Byrne's *Fantastic Four* (1981–1986).

Perhaps coincidentally, the comics of these years featured a pronounced turn toward violence—pronounced, and excessive compared to what had come before. Superhero comics have always relied on violence to solve problems, but the superhero comics of the 1975–1985 period, thanks to the 1971 liberalization of the Comics Code and perhaps in imitation of the increasingly violent movies of the 1970s, used violence artistically and as a part of characterization rather than merely as plot complication and resolution. The revamped (and quite popular) X-Men from 1975 forward had Wolverine, a hero with lethal claws and a lethal temper. Frank Miller's *Daredevil* (from *Daredevil* #165, cover date July 1980), one of the most cinematic and influential titles of the era, relied heavily upon violence. So did the Doug Moench/Bill Sienkiewicz *Moon Knight* (from 1980 forward) and Claremont and Miller's *Wolverine* miniseries (cover dates September–December 1982). The Punisher, reintroduced in Miller's *Daredevil*

#181–184 (cover dates April–July 1982), was a remarkably lethal vigilante, though in Miller's portrayal an antihero rather than a villainous right-wing foil to Marvel's more liberal heroes. DC's Vigilante, created in 1983 by George Perez and Marv Wolfman, was DC's answer to the Punisher.

Superhero comics as a whole have almost always been reactive, and eager to capitalize upon whatever was popular in other genres and other media, but this was particularly so in the 1975–1985 period. Marvel responded to the mid-1970s craze for martial arts by putting out the black-and-white comics magazine *Deadly Hands of Kung Fu* (1974–1977). Several years late, Marvel and writer Steve Gerber responded to a variety of comics' genres by putting out the satirical superhero comic *Howard the Duck* (1976–1979). The novelist Robert Mayer responded to superhero comics by writing *Superfolks* (1977), the first "literary" approach to super-heroes. DC responded to the popularity of the X-Men by introducing the "new" Teen Titans in Marv Wolfman and George Perez's *New Teen Titans* (beginning with issue #1, cover date November 1980). Comic book pub-lisher Archie reacted to the increasing popularity of superhero comics in the early 1980s by reentering the superhero publishing field in 1983, although the attempt failed by 1985.

And the two miniseries that ended the Bronze Age, Marvel's *Secret Wars* and DC's *Crisis on Infinite Earths*, were ultimately reactions to exter-nal phenomenon. *Secret Wars* (written by Jim Shooter and drawn by Mike Zeck), which lasted from early 1984 to early 1985, was created as a reac-tion to interest from toy manufacturer Mattel, who was interested in pro-ducing licensed action figures of Marvel superheroes, but only if Marvel produced a series that would heighten interest in the action figures. And *Crisis on Infinite Earths* (written by Marv Wolfman and drawn by George Perez), which lasted from early 1985 to early 1986, was a response to the perceived antipathy of fans toward the complexity and convoluted (and at times internally inconsistent) continuity of the DC universe.

Thematically, *Secret Wars* spelled the end of the Bronze Age for Marvel, symbolically ending the recursive, recombinant trend in favor of some-thing more shallow and nakedly commercial. *Crisis on Infinite Earths* ended the Bronze Age for DC by destroying (inside the comics) the previ-ous 50 years of continuity and stories in favor of a clean slate of heroes and stories, reinvented and unencumbered by the past.

The Modern Age: 1986–2001

Three of the previous four ages of superhero comics occurred in roughly 15-year periods: the Golden Age (1935–1949), the Silver Age (1956–1970), and the Bronze Age (1970–1985). Following this pattern, the next age of comics would last from 1985 or 1986 to 2000 or 2001. 1986 had three separate comics miniseries—the Steven Grant and Mike Zeck *Punisher*, the Alan Moore and Dave Gibbons *Watchmen*, and the Frank Miller *Batman: The Dark Knight*—which together heavily influenced the majority of the superhero comics over the next 15 years. The end point of this period is, as with some of the other comics ages, not one single event but a multiyear transitional period, beginning in 1999 with the launching of the "Marvel Knights" line of comics and ending with the events of September 11, 2001. Labels for this time period vary, with "Iron Age" being a popular choice—iron being a darker, harder metal, which reflects the comics of this age. I'm choosing "The Modern Age" because of the Modernist tendencies of the writers of this age, which I think better reflects the character of the period than yet another choice from the hackneyed metal-themed naming trend.

The Modern Age was a period of great highs and lows for the comics companies, as the boom-or-bust tendencies of the comic book market returned in full force. For the first few years of the Modern Age Marvel remained the undisputed industry leader, with the X-Men family of comics being the best-selling comics franchise. But in 1992 many of the top creators at Marvel left to form Image Comics, beginning an economic tailspin for Marvel. After Image's founding, DC's sales began slowly to increase, and DC matched Marvel in market share in 1998 and, for the first time in over 30 years, DC took the lead from Marvel in 1999, holding it through 2001.

The comics business as a whole was remarkably unstable during the Modern Age. At the start of the Modern Age, half of Marvel's sales were via the direct market, a number that grew to 70 percent in two years. This number was key to reassuring the comics companies and their investors that the comic book business had a future. Thanks to the direct market, and thanks to the business approach to editing of Jim Shooter, the value of individual comics began to increase, and older issues of comics, especially those with nominal landmarks in them (first appearances of characters or writers or artists, characters' deaths, and so on), began to shoot up in value. The number of comic book stores soared, while Marvel's and DC's corporate policies meant that there were an ever-decreasing number of distributors controlling all comics sales. In the early 1990s comics sales were at their highest point in generations; Chris Claremont and Jim Lee's *X-Men* #1 (cover date October 1991) sold over eight million copies, the all-time record for best-selling comic, and in 1993 comics as a whole was a billion dollar business. Superheroes were so popular that writers George

R. R. Martin and Melinda Snodgrass were able to edit a prose anthology series about a new universe of superheroes, the *Wild Card* series, between 1987 and 1993, totaling 12 volumes in all.

Unfortunately, the comics bubble burst beginning in 1993. The companies were putting out too many comics and increasing the prices of them too rapidly. Gimmicks designed to boost sales, such as DC's "Death of Superman" story line in 1992, temporarily boosted sales but disillusioned speculators who believed the issues of these gimmick story lines would be valuable—which did not prove to be the case, as Marvel and DC were printing large numbers of each issue. Printing costs were increasing above the ability of the comics companies to match. There were too many new comic shops trying to take advantage of the high sales. And Marvel Comics' corporate owners made a series of disastrous business decisions, including buying a distributor, Heroes World, and refusing to sell issues through any other distributor, and buying other noncomics businesses, which were often overvalued or in financial trouble. The end result was that Marvel Comics was forced to file for bankruptcy in early 1997, although Marvel was able to continue selling comics under new terms. (Marvel itself was profitable during this time period, but its owners' spending spree on other companies leveraged Marvel into enormous debt.) Sales began declining, so that by 2001 the comics industry was less than half of what it had been in 1993.

In terms of content, superhero comics became more reactive to societal trends than they had been in years.

Crime increased nationally from 1985 to 1990, with specific increases in violent crime, property crime, murder, rape, robbery, and aggravated assault. The overall violent crime rate rose unabated from 1983 to 1993. America's response was to "get tough" on crime, in the words of Ronald Reagan, beginning the "war on drugs," the era of "three strikes," and the loss of judicial discretion in applying sentences to convicted criminals. The numbers of incarcerated people in the United States increased from roughly 500,000 in 1996 to 1.4 million in 2002. Generally, America became acutely conscious of crime and wished for a panacea to end it.

Comics' response to this was to make many of their superheroes extraordinarily violent antiheroes. The three 1986 miniseries that began the Modern Age—*Batman: The Dark Knight, Watchmen,* and *The Punisher*— are generally seen as the cause of this trend.

The later years of the Bronze Age, as mentioned above, had seen an increase in the use of violence in superhero comics and an increase in the violence of the superheroes themselves. But the three miniseries of 1985– 1986 irrevocably altered the situation. *The Punisher* presented the titular character not as the violent right-wing foil for the left-leaning heroes, as had originally been the case, nor as merely a lethal vigilante, as had been the case in his appearances in *Daredevil* during the late Bronze Age; *The Punisher* series, for the first time in Marvel's history,[53] presented a serial killer (albeit of criminals) as the protagonist of a comic. *The Punisher*, with its realistic setting and its array of realistic violent criminals, organized crime figures, and corrupt politicians, presented an amoral universe in which the ruthlessly lethal "morality" of the Punisher was a positive thing, and the Punisher an undeniable hero. The Punisher had a number of the elements of the superhero described in Chapter 1, but the universe he operated in was a far cry from the universe of most Marvel comics. Rather than correct the universe (and the Punisher himself) to make it more in line with the traditional Marvel universe, the writers and artists of the Punisher were emboldened by the sales of *The Punisher* and its sequel series to maintain the Punisher's universe as something that could somehow coexist with the Marvel universe at large.

Batman: The Dark Knight (1986), a story of an aging Batman in a decrepit future battling a broken down society and a variety of murderous opponents, sold enormously well and garnered positive reviews from a number of sources, including *Time* magazine. The series was told with bravura and assurance, and instantly worked as a corrective to lingering impressions of Batman as the campy protagonist of the 1966 *Batman* television show. But the object lessons that other writers took from *Batman: The Dark Knight* were neither the skill with which writer/artist Frank Miller told the story nor the method in which Miller had reimagined Batman and his universe, but instead the seedy depiction of the Gotham City setting and the grim, humorless portrayal of a Batman who, though never killing his opponents, was happy to cripple them—a distinct change from previous portrayals of Batman.

Watchmen was the best comic of the three. It was a best seller and was critically acclaimed, to the point where it appeared on *Time*'s 2005 "All-Time 100 Greatest Novels" list. *Watchmen* was a series of startling complexity and depth, then and now the ultimate in comics' attempts to show what superheroes would be like in the real world. However, what the comics industry took from *Watchmen* was not the idea that comics should be written like literature, as writer Alan Moore succeeded in doing, but that *Watchmen*'s realistic-seeming violence and deconstruction of superheroes' two-dimensional characterization were things worth imitating.

The cumulative result of all three series was for both Marvel and DC to produce a wave of deconstructive comics full of what Bradford Wright calls "Miller's brand of morally complex and ruthless superheroes."[54]

Superheroes acquired brooding personalities, even those who had generally been positive and optimistic before Miller and Moore. So-called "street level" heroes[55] acquired lethal edges, both traditional heroes like Green Arrow (whose usual trick arrows gave way at this time to ordinary arrows that were razor sharp and dealt serious, often lethal wounds) and new heroes like Denny O'Neil and Joe Quesada's Batman-substitute Azrael. A level of violence previously unimaginable became the norm, and within a few years both Marvel and DC were putting out enough brooding and merciless vigilantes for the character type to become a cliché. Worse, the complexity that Miller and Moore had put into *Batman: The Dark Knight* and *Watchmen* were ignored as unimportant to comics' success; those comics that succeeded *Watchmen* and *Batman: The Dark Knight* and were most influenced by them were particularly shallow by comparison.

The Modern Age was not an unrelieved wasteland for superhero comics, though—quite the reverse. The Modern Age is largely viewed negatively by many comics fans, who dub these years "the Iron Age" and "the Dark Age." And many of the comics of these years were instantly forgettable and no better than mediocre, even by comparison with Bronze Age comics. But throughout the Modern Age there were superhero series and writer/artist runs on comic books that were of high quality. A brief list of superheroic high points of the Modern Age would include: *Watchmen, Batman: The Dark Knight,* Mike Baron and Steve Rude's *Nexus* (1985–1991), Grant Morrison and Chas Truog's *Animal Man* (1988–1990), Neil Gaiman's *Sandman* (1989–1996), Grant Morrison and Richard Case's *Doom Patrol* (1989–1993), James Robinson and Tony Harris's *Starman* (1994–2001), Kurt Busiek and Alex Ross's *Marvels* (1994), Kurt Busiek and Brent Anderson's *Kurt Busiek's Astro City* (1995–present), Warren Ellis and Tom Raney's *Stormwatch* (1996–1998), Mark Waid and Alex Ross's *Kingdom Come* (1996), and Garth Ennis and John McCrea's *Hitman* (1996–2001). Most of these comics hold up well today.

These comics had several things in common that contributed to the series' and runs' overall excellence. The first was that these comics were not a central part of their publishers' superhero universes, so that the comics' creators did not have to be concerned with the ongoing continuity of those universes and the negative, violent developments in them. Essentially, these comics took place in their own self-contained universes, with for the most part nominal ties to "mainstream" continuity. Some of these comics—*Watchmen, Nexus, Kurt Busiek's Astro City*—took place in their own isolated universes. Others—*Batman: The Dark Knight, Marvels, Kingdom Come*—though published by Marvel and DC, took place in the past or the future. The remainder had limited ties to continuity, with the events of *Animal Man, Doom Patrol, Sandman, Starman,* and *Stormwatch* taking place at the same time as the other comics of their respective universes, but in virtually self-contained pockets separate from the rest of their respective universes. In every case the creators of these comics operated with virtual impunity, which allowed the creators the freedom to tell whatever stories they wanted without fear of consequences or repercussions. Freed from the burden of continuity and paying attention to what the rest of their companies were publishing, these comics' creators could focus on achieving more artistic goals.

The second was that few of these comics were intended to be ongoing concerns. All of these comics but one, *Kurt Busiek's Astro City,* were conceived of as limited in scope, with a limited number of story lines and overarching plots with predetermined beginnings, middles, and ends. Superhero comics, as a capitalist enterprise, are required by the market and by audience demand to be stuck eternally in the second act of characters' lives, so that creators are not allowed to solve ongoing problems or bring to a resolution or conclusion any of the major issues of their characters' lives. But these comics of the Modern Age, being conceived of as limited in scope and duration, included third acts, and in so doing gave their creators the freedom to finish stories, as mature works of art do.

The third was that these stories were ultimately about other things besides cops-and-robbers and catch-the-supervillain (the staple plot of superhero comics). *Watchmen* was about what the real world would look like if it had superheroes in it; *Kurt Busiek's Astro City* was about what real people would be like in a superheroic world. *Nexus* was about the morality of vengeance versus justice. *Sandman* was about the power of fiction. *Starman* was a loving, leisurely amble through the side streets of DC Comics' history; *Marvels* was a shorter, more intensified trip down the thoroughfare of Marvel Comics' history. *Stormwatch* was about *realpolitik* and power, political and superheroic. *Kingdom Come* was a recapitulation of what was best about DC's superheroes, in response to years of comics scorning traditional superheroic morality. And *Hitman* was a buddy comic with superheroic trappings. Being able to write about other themes, many of which were new to superhero comics, gave the creators of these comics an artistic freedom that ordinary superhero creators lacked.

One final aspect of the superheroes of the Modern Age is worth noting: the Modernist approach of many of their creators, and the Modernist comics that resulted. Modernism is in this case defined as a radical break with traditional practices by creators who felt that those practices, and the stories that resulted from them, were insufficient to deal with the problems of the contemporary environment. Modernism brings with it a discontinuity from the past and a rejection of traditional values and assumptions. And Modernism is a reaction against the literary movements of Realism and Naturalism.

Modernism appeared in Modern Age comics in a number of ways: by subverting the distinctions between "high" and "low" art, through the artistic ambitions and success of *Watchmen*; formally, as with *Watchmen's* intricate structure and characterization, *Animal Man's* use of metafiction, and *Doom Patrol's* surrealism and structural experimentation; as a reaction to traditional superheroic morality, in *Nexus's* protagonist, who executes the guilty regardless of their legal status; as a reaction to the political assumptions of traditional superheroics, in *Stormwatch's* presentation of its protagonists fighting a group of superhumans who attempt to bring about an anarchist Utopia; in its psychological realism, as "a revolt that employs realism in the service of remaking a medium known for irrealistic genres,"[56] in the careful characterization of *Watchmen, Starman, Kurt Busiek's Astro City, Marvels,* and *Hitman*; and, later in the Modern Age, by its reconstructionist tendencies, jettisoning the traditional practices and methods and ethos of the Bronze Age—the prevailing tendencies of the Modern Age—and embracing the ethos of the Golden and Silver Age, in *Marvels'* and *Kingdom Come's* loving wallow in the heroes and heroic moralities of the past.

While the transition from the Modern Age to what followed it took place over the course of several years, three events in particular stand out: the "Marvel Knights" initiative at Marvel, which began in late 1998 and encouraged writers and artists to rethink traditional characters and comics and reenvision them for the modern era; Marvel's "Ultimate" line of comics, which began with Brian Bendis and Mark Bagley's *Ultimate Spider-Man* #1 (cover date October 2000) and which created a new, contemporary universe of Marvel superheroes; and the events of September 11, 2001, which brought politics back to superhero comics.

The Metamodern Age: 2001–2015

Comics' ages run for roughly 15 years each, and the 1998–2001 period saw the ending of the Modern Age, leaving the 2001–2015 period to succeed it. The question of what to label this age is a difficult one, especially in light of the fact that many comics critics and fans see the Modern Age as not really having ended. But I believe the appropriate name for the 2001–2015 span of years is the Metamodern Age.

Metamodernism is, as Vermeulen and van den Akker put it, "characterized by the oscillation between a typically modern commitment and a markedly postmodern detachment,"[57] "between a modern enthusiasm and a postmodern irony, between hope and melancholy, between naiveté and knowingness, empathy and apathy, unity and plurality, totality and fragmentation, purity and ambiguity."[58] Vermuelen and van den Akker describe various aspects of metamodernism: "performatism ... the willful self-deceit to believe in—or identify with, or solve—something in spite of itself";[59] "an attitude that says, *I know that the art I'm creating may seem silly, even stupid, or that it might have been done before, but that doesn't mean this isn't serious*";[60] "romantic conceptualism," which replaces postmodernism's rational calculation with affective sentimentalism, so that "if the postmodern deconstructs ... Romantic Conceptualism is concerned with reconstruction";[61] an "attempt to restore, to the cynical reality of adults, a childlike naivety";[62] and "an emergent neoromantic sensibility."[63]

Superhero comics never went through a postmodernist period. Postmodernism, after all, is a negative reaction to Modernism and its traits, its grand narratives and Utopianism, its functionalism and formal purism. Postmodernism's attributes—nihilism, sarcasm, deconstructionism—are not only nonstarters for a capitalist commercial enterprise like superhero comics, but they are at odds with the ethos of superheroes and superhero universes. But several creators made use of postmodern approaches and methods in creating superhero stories in comic books, especially during the Modern Age, and the books of the Metamodern Age are largely a reaction to them, as well as to the postmodernism of the culture at large.

Metamodernism, with its emphasis on the reconstruction and renewal of meaning and enthusiasm, is an accurate description of the superheroes of the 2001–2015 period, although the roots of it are to be found as early as 1996, with *Kingdom Come* and *Kurt Busiek's Astro City*. The Modern Age's deconstruction, and its questioning of the motivations of superheroes, was countered by the reconstructionism of the Metamodern Age, with its reassertion of the fact of superheroes' heroism. Amoral protagonists were replaced by men and women with truly heroic characters, as in Grant Morrison and Frank Quitely's *All-Star Superman* (2005–2006). The hyperviolence of the Modern Age was replaced by heroic restraint and a respect for all lives, even those of criminals, as in *Kurt Busiek's Astro City* (1996–present). The nihilism of the Modern Age was replaced by a cynical hopefulness, as in Warren Ellis and John Cassady's *Planetary* (1999–2009) and Matt Fraction and David Aja's *Hawkeye* (2012–2014). The derisive humor of the Modern Age—the comics written by creators who laugh at superhero comics and their absurdities—was replaced by a kind of humor that, while still cutting, ultimately laughs with superhero comics rather than at them, as in Warren Ellis and Stuart Immonen's *Nextwave: Agents of H.A.T.E.* (2006–2007) and in Ryan North and Erica Henderson's *The Unbeatable Squirrel Girl* (2015–present).

The comics of the Metamodern Age are in continual negotiation between commitment and detachment, but tend toward commitment, and choose enthusiasm over irony and hope over melancholy, as in Mark Waid and Chris Samnee's *Daredevil* (2011–2015). What Vermuelen and van den Akker called the "attitude that says, *I know that the art I'm creating may seem silly ... but that doesn't mean this isn't serious*"[64] appears in Kieron Gillen and Jamie McKelvie's *Young Avengers* (2013–2014). The restoration of naive enthusiasm in the face of cynical realism can be seen in Grant Morrison's *Seven Soldiers* series (2005–2006), with its modern take on epic superhero storytelling.

The business of comics grew slowly from 2001–2008, aided by the appearance of trade paperback reprints in book stores, by rising revenues from licensed merchandise, and especially by profits from movies. The 2008 "Great Recession" had a sizable impact on comics, as it did on other industries, but by 2014 comics had recovered, again helped by merchandise and film revenues. Money lost to digital piracy—a new problem for the industry, one that arose during this period as a result of the globalization of the Internet—were more than replaced by revenue from bookstores.

One aspect of the changing business world of comics did have a direct impact on superhero comics. Image Comics was created in 1992 by a group of high-profile creators who intended their new company to be a place where writers and artists would own the copyrights of the characters they created (unlike at Marvel and DC). This had previously been attempted in 1974–1975 with Atlas Comics, the comic company founded by Martin Goodman after Goodman left Marvel, but Atlas Comics' output did not find favor with the audience of the time, and Atlas folded 18 months after its debut. However, Image Comics was far more successful than Atlas Comics had been, and Image had a number of successful and long-running series. Throughout the Modern and Metamodern Ages Image was the #3 comics publisher in the market, after Marvel and DC.

During the Metamodern Age Image consistently and successfully promoted itself to comics creators as a viable alternative to Marvel and DC: viable financially (as Image's comics sold well, relatively speaking), viable from a rights perspective, and viable creatively (as Image allowed things like explicit violence, sex, and profanity that were not allowed to be shown in mainstream superhero comics). An increasing number of creators, many the best in the industry, took advantage of this opportunity—and similar ones given to it by Vertigo Comics, an imprint of DC Comics that offered much the same terms as Image's—to create characters and comics at Image, Vertigo, and other rights-offering comic book companies.

The result of Image's existence and success, and that of its imitators, was to convince creators that nonsuperhero comics were economically viable, and to convince the comic-buying audience that nonsuperhero comics could be of high quality. During the Metamodern Age many of the industry's most talented creators refrained from creating new characters and comics for Marvel and DC and published those projects closest to their hearts through Image, Vertigo, and other companies, or through Marvel and DC but with the arrangement that the creators would own their own copyrights.

Consequently, a list of the best comics of the late Modern Age and the Metamodern Age would include a number of comics and graphic novels— arguably, the majority of the best comics—which were of genres other than superheroes. A brief list of these would include Gilbert and Jaime Hernandez's magical realist/contemporary life *Love and Rockets* (1982– present), Grant Morrison's science fiction adventure *The Invisibles* (1994– 2000), Garth Ennis and Steve Dillon's horror Western *Preacher* (1995–2000), Carla Speed McNeil's anthropological science fictional *Finder* (1996–present), Terry Moore's romance *Strangers in Paradise* (1997– 2007), Warren Ellis and Darick Robertson's science fictional *Transmetropolitan* (1997–2002), Alan Moore and Kevin O'Neill's literary fantasia *League of Extraordinary Gentlemen* (1999–present), Brian Azzarello and Eduardo Risso's hard-boiled *100 Bullets* (1999–2009), Marjane Satrapi's biographical *Persepolis* (2000–2003), Grant Morrison and Frank Quitely's science fictional *We3* (2005), Matt Fraction and Gabriel Bá's science fictional *Casanova* (2006–2015), Ed Brubaker and Sean Phillips's noir *Criminal* (2006–present), Alison Bechdel's biographical *Fun Home* (2006), Kieron Gillen and Jamie McKelvie's contemporary fantasy *Phonogram* (2006–2015), Jason Aaron and R. M. Guera's contemporary Western noir *Scalped* (2007–2012), David Mazzucchelli's contemporary life *Asterios Polyp* (2009), Matt Kindt's science fictional espionage *Mind Mgmt* (2012– present), Brian K. Vaughan and Fiona Staples's science fictional *Saga* (2012–present), Matt Fraction and Chip Zdarsky's comic fantasy *Sex Criminals* (2013–present), Kelly Sue DeConnick and Valentine DeLandro's science fictional *Bitch Planet* (2014–present), and Kieron Gillen and Jamie McKelvie's contemporary fantasy *The Wicked and the Divine* (2014– present).[65] While Marvel dominated the best-sellers list for most of the Metamodern Age, the most creative and artistic work of the age was done away from Marvel and away from the superhero genre.

Besides the prevalence of talented creators taking their passion projects to publishers besides Marvel and DC, another trend hurt superhero comics during the Metamodern Age. Both Marvel and DC made crossover "events" a yearly part of their publishing program. For decades the two companies have placed heightened importance on story lines that crossed over from one comic strip or issue to another. Although the practice began with comic company MLJ in 1940, Marvel quickly imitated it to much greater acclaim with the Human Torch–Sub-Mariner crossover in the pages of *Marvel Mystery Comics*. When superheroes became popular again in the Silver Age, both DC and Marvel made use of the crossover, beginning (with DC) in 1964 with the "Zatanna's Search" story line and (with Marvel) in 1965 with the "Quest for Krang" story line.

However, beginning in the Modern Age, with DC's "Crisis on Infinite Earths" story line (1985) and Marvel's "Secret Wars II" story line (1985–1986), the crossover event became more intrusive. The comics taking part in the story line were forced to set aside the story lines their creators were producing in favor of the crossover event's story line. Crossover events like these, which forced creators to interrupt their own stories to tell the stories conceived of by editors and other creators, were relatively rare at Marvel through the 1990s, but were common at DC during that decade. However, during the Metamodern Age, these intrusive, interrupting crossover events became yearly occurrences at both Marvel and DC.

This practice, driven largely by the increased sales that the crossover events brought about, had a markedly negative effect on superhero comics. Year-long stories and extended subplots were no longer possible, due to the requirement that creators write someone else's story for one to three months at a time, and creators no longer had control over their own stories. Crossover events like DC's "Flashpoint" (2011) and Marvel's "Secret Wars" (2015–2016) ended their respective universes and forced some or many creators to write and draw their characters in altered or entirely new ways—all at the instigation (and insistence) of the company's editorial staff. Needless to say, these constant interruptions do not foster good art and impose restrictions on comics that hamper creators' ability to produce the best stories possible.

This is not to say that the entirety of both comics' superhero lines were in thrall to editorial dictates and whims during the Metamodern Age. Individually excellent series like Ryan North and Erica Henderson's *The Unbeatable Squirrel Girl* (2015–present) (a perfect example of the Metamodern "childlike naivety") and G. Willow Wilson and Adrian Alphona's *Ms. Marvel* (2015–present) (a challenge to superhero comics' grand narrative of white male Christian superheroes, but a reconstructive, restorative effort of superheroic fiction rather than a deconstructive destruction of them) were published and thrived despite being a part of the editor-heavy Marvel universe. Grant Morrison achieved excellence with his run on the various Batman comics from 2007–2013, despite laboring under the constraints of DC's editorial regime. But as a whole superhero comics were more than ever under the control of editorial and the business end of comics' companies, and out of the control of the creators.

Those looking for hope in superhero comics had reason to find it there at the end of the Metamodern Age. The very best superhero comics published in 2014 and 2015 could stand comparison with the best of any age. But those pessimistic about superhero comics had good reason to be, as the majority of superhero comics were inferior as art, recalling the worst of the Bronze and the Modern Ages.

CHAPTER TEN

Television and Film

Just as superheroes, in various forms, have been popular throughout the history of popular culture, so too have they been a popular subject in television and film. As noted in Chapter 6, films with superhero characters began appearing in the 1910s, so that by the 1930s they were no longer oddities. The superhero films mentioned in Chapter 6—*The Iron Claw* (1916), *Judex* (1917), *The Eagle* (1918), *The Mark of Zorro* (1920)— portrayed Costumed Avengers, rather than supermen, a situation that continued in the 1930s, when superhero serials based on pulp characters began appearing. The Lynn Shores and Al Martin film *The Shadow Strikes* (1937), based on the radio and pulp superman, portrayed the Shadow as a Costumed Avenger rather than as a character with the power to cloud men's minds. The James Horne, Ray Taylor, Robert Kent, and George Plympton film *The Spider's Web* (1938), based on the pulp Costumed Avenger, similarly eschewed the portrayal of superpowers, albeit in the portrayal of the Spider's enemies, a departure from the Spider's pulp stories.

It wasn't until the early 1940s, after superheroes had proved their popularity and commercial viability in comic books, that filmmakers began portraying actual supermen in films. Officially licensed Superman cartoons, produced by Fleischer Studios, appeared from 1941 to 1943 and were popular, though expensive to make. The 1940 *Green Hornet* film, directed by Ford Beebe and Ray Taylor and written by George Plympton and Basil Dickey, is in a sense a holdover from the 1930s, being about the popular radio Costumed Avenger and inspiring the use of the Green Hornet in comics, rather than vice versa. And the John English, William Witney, Franklin Adreon, and Ronald Davidson serial *The Mysterious Doctor*

Satan (1940) was originally intended to be a Superman film. However, DC Comics decided they didn't want Republic Pictures to make a Superman film, so Republic, via John English et al., remade *The Mysterious Doctor Satan* into a Costumed Avenger superhero film starring the original hero the Copperhead.

Supermen in films began with the Fleischer Superman cartoons, which started a trend that continued for several decades. Due to the limitations of Hollywood special effects, the Fleischer Superman cartoons, and the Terrytoons Studio's Mighty Mouse cartoons of the 1940s (which began in 1942 with the Eddie Donnelly and John Foster short *Mouse of Tomorrow*) were more faithful to superhero comics in their portrayal of superheroes performing superhuman feats. The superhero cartoons of the 1940s were not in direct competition with the superhero live action films and serials of the 1940s, being generally aimed at a younger audience (not, however, the case with the Fleischer Superman cartoons, which were intended for adult audiences), but they were more superheroic both in spirit and in the recapitulation of what made superhero comics so popular. By contrast, the live-action superhero films and serials of the 1940s, beginning with the John English, William Witney, Ronald Davidson, and Norman Hall *Adventures of Captain Marvel* (1941), were aimed at adult audiences but were generally less "comic-booky" and de-emphasized the superheroes' superhuman abilities. The result was not quite the creation of Costumed Avengers with the familiar names of supermen, but something close to that. It wasn't until the Spencer Gordon Bennet, Thomas Carr, George Plympton, and Joseph Poland *Superman* (1948) serial, which animated its flying sequences, that superhero films fully embraced what might be called the "superheroness" of its characters and premise.

Interestingly, the late 1940s and the early and mid-1950s were periods when film audiences were happy to see superhero serials, films, and cartoons, despite being unwilling to buy them in comic book form. The Bennet et al. *Superman* (1948) was a success. So too were the Spencer Gordon Bennet and George Plympton serial *Batman and Robin* (1949), the Bennet and Plympton *Atom Man vs. Superman* (1950), and the Lee Sholem and Robert Maxwell *Superman and the Mole-Men* (1951), with the latter being a trial balloon for the even more successful TV series *The Adventures of Superman* (1952–1958)—which was popular with audiences even in the years immediately following the imposition of the Comics Code, when superheroes were at their lowest point. The special effects on these films were primitive by modern standards but effective within the context of their era, and offered audiences superhero thrills that were not generally available in the comics.[1]

The mid- and late-1950s would see the beginning of the superhero genre of films in both Mexico and Japan, though their influence on American superhero filmmakers and films was negligible.

The 1960s began with the George Blair *The Adventures of Superboy* (1961), what had in 1959 been intended to be a spin-off from *The Adventures of Superman*. But *The Adventures of Superboy* pilot never led to a series pick-up, and only one episode was broadcast. It wasn't until 1964 that the next major superhero series would appear: W. Watts Bigger and Chad Strover's animated series *Underdog* (1964–1967). *Underdog* was the product of the superhero craze of the mid-1960s. Interestingly, it was the first major media superhero (as opposed to print superhero) to be wholly original and not based on a licensed property since *Mysterious Doctor Satan* in 1940. Most significantly, though, *Underdog* was the first superhero series, in film or in print, to approach superheroes in a parodic and satiric way since Sheldon Mayer's "Red Tornado" strip (1940–1944) and Jack Kirby and Joe Simon's *Fighting American* (1954–1955). *Underdog* anticipated the William Dozier–produced *Batman* TV series (1966–1968), E. Nelson Bridwell and Mike Sekowsky's *Inferior Five* (for DC, 1967–1968), and Stan Lee's *Not Brand Echh* (for Marvel, 1967–1969), and approached superheroes with a cynical, humorous eye at a time when superheroes were increasingly popular thanks to Marvel's increased-realism-and-increased-characterization approach. The influence of *Underdog* on *Batman* was likely minute, but the 1960s vein of superhero parody, satire, and camp, which thanks to the popularity of *Batman* had a sizable influence on other superhero cartoons and films of the late 1960s as well as on the *Batman* comic book for a few years, ultimately began with *Underdog* rather than *Batman*.

The 10 years after the *Batman* television show were a period in which superheroes were largely confined to cartoons like *Super Friends* (1973, 1977–1979, 1981) or to low-budget productions intended solely for children, like *Shazam!* (1974–1977) and *Isis* (1975–1976). The exceptions— Harve Bennett and Martin Caidin's *Six Million Dollar Man* (1973–1978) and *Bionic Woman* (1976–1978), the Douglas Cramer and Wilfred Baumes–produced *Wonder Woman* (1975–1979), and the Kenneth Johnson *The Incredible Hulk* (1978–1982)—were television shows broadcast in prime time for adult audiences, but were the superhero equivalent of what John Clute calls "technothrillers,"[2] and downplayed as much as possible each show's fantastic and superheroic elements.

What changed this trend was the Richard Donner and Mario Puzo *Superman* (1978), the first film in a generation to present superheroes in a serious, adult fashion using state-of-the-art special effects. *Superman* was not only a box office success but a critical success as well. Thanks to *Superman* film audiences of all ages were prepared to accept a serious, adult treatment of superheroes—and thanks to *Superman*'s box office success filmmakers were prepared to make films with serious, adult treatments of superheroes.

The 1980s continued this trend and were the decade in which commercially viable superhero films became yearly occurrences. The Richard Lester and Mario Puzo *Superman II* (1980), the Stephen J. Cannell television series *The Greatest American Hero* (1981–1983), the Wes Craven *Swamp Thing* (1982), the Richard Lester and David Newman *Superman III* (1983), the Paul Verhoeven and Edward Neumeier *RoboCop* (1987), the Gary Goddard and David Odell *Masters of the Universe* (1987), the Ilya and Alexander Salkind television series *Superboy* (1988–1992), and the Tim Burton and Sam Hamm *Batman* (1989) were all made with large budgets and intended for large audiences and were taken seriously by filmmakers, actors, and critics alike. That most of them were artistically middling or worse was largely irrelevant to those producing and consuming the television series and films, and throughout the decade superhero films and television series were considered the same as science fiction and fantasy films and television series: genre fare, for good and bad.

This state of affairs did not change in the 1990s. The major superhero films and television series of the decade, including the Danny Bilson and Paul de Meo *Flash* (1990–1991), the Andy Heyward, Benjamin Melniker, and Michael Uslan *Swamp Thing* (1990–1991), the Joe Johnston and Danny Bilson *Rocketeer* (1991), the Larry Houston and Will Meugniot *X-Men: The Animated Series* (1992–1997), the Chuck Russell and Michael Fallon *Mask* (1994), the Alex Proyas and David Schow *Crow* (1994), the Russell Mulcahy and David Koepp *Shadow* (1994), the Deborah Joy LeVine *Lois & Clark: The New Adventures of Superman* (1993–1997), the Stephen Norrington and David Goyer *Blade* (1998), and the Kinka Usher and Neil Cuthbert *Mystery Men* (1999), were run-of-the mill lowbrow fare, and with three exceptions the superhero genre was no better or worse off by the end of the decade than it was at the start of the 1980s.

Those three exceptions, however, are worth noting. The Bruce Timm and Paul Dini *Batman: The Animated Series* (1994–1995) was thematically complex, visually sophisticated, and critically acclaimed, and in contrast to contemporary treatments of superheroes stood as evidence that superheroes could be done in a serious, mature manner, and that animated superheroes needn't automatically be less sophisticated than live-action superheroes. Ben Edlund's *The Tick* (1994–1996) and Craig McCracken's *Powerpuff Girls* (1998–2005), despite their simple animation, were both intelligently written and appealed as much to adults (for the unexpectedly sly humor) as to children. Both *The Tick* and *Powerpuff Girls* handled super-heroics smartly and proved to audiences and creators alike that superhero comedies needn't be simple.

The 2000s were the decade in which superhero films became commercial juggernauts. The Bryan Singer and David Hayter *X-Men* (2000) began the decade as a critical and popular hit. Unusually for a superhero movie, *X-Men* featured highly respected actors, and their performances and the sober, serious plot—free of the labored whimsy of so many superhero films of the 1990s—set the tone for superhero films to come and conditioned audiences to expect more from superhero films. The M. Night Shyamalan *Unbreakable* (2000) was a throwback to the superhero films of the 1970s, taking the Clutean "technothriller" approach to superheroics while grounding everything else in a gritty world of solemn, humorless performances. *Unbreakable* was not advertised as a superhero film, but even if it had been it would not have been a commercial success (although critics thought better of the film than audiences did), as it would have run against audience expectations of what a superhero film could and should have been in the year 2000.

The Sam Raimi and David Koepp *Spider-Man* (2002) continued the trend of high-quality superhero films, telling Spider-Man's origin story with heart, humor, solid performances, and a good screenplay. Critics approved, and audiences responded in huge numbers; the film's domestic gross was over $400 million, a record for superhero films and sudden, undeniable evidence to the movie industry that superhero films could not just be profitable, but could function as tent-pole films (movies that prop up a studio's finances and enable the studio to fund a range of products and films as well as the studio's less profitable projects and films). The Bryan Singer and Michael Dougherty *X-Men II* (2003), the best of the *X-Men* films, was another critical and box office success, albeit not on the scale of *Spider-Man*.

Spider-Man and the two *X-Men* movies were largely responsible for the sea change of opinion of superhero films—not just the audience's opinion, but also critics', actors', directors', and producers' opinions. The three films proved that superhero films—like every other genre of film—had room for realistic and even moving performances by esteemed actors, could be taken on by respectable and respected directors without losing their position in Hollywood, could provide solid, colorful, and respectable entertainment to audiences, and could be not just commercially viable, but potential blockbusters. The next two critically successful superhero projects proved that they could scale hitherto-undreamed-of heights.

Brad Bird's *The Incredibles* (2004), though primarily aimed at children, was highly entertaining to adults, thanks to its adroit mixing of comedy, action, and family matters. In some respects a satire of comic book clichés, *The Incredibles* nonetheless played most of the superheroics straight, to great effect, and thanks to good voice performances and a highly intelligent script the film won not just a Hugo (the science fiction community's award) but an Academy Award as well.

The Michael Dante DiMartino and Bryan Konietzko *Avatar: The Last Airbender* (2005–2008), an animated television series on a children's network, was ostensibly a fantasy set in another world, but by any sober definition the main characters are superheroes and the events superheroic. Beloved by audiences, critically acclaimed, and a multiple award winner (including an Emmy and Peabody), *Avatar: The Last Airbender* stands as the most successful superhero television series, before or since. Unlike *Batman: The Animated Series*, *Avatar* was not restricted to one story per episode, instead telling one overarching story over the course of four seasons, which allowed it an unprecedented (for superhero television) opportunity for characterization and storytelling, an opportunity *Avatar* took full advantage of.

Most of the superhero television series and films of the next few years were competent at best and mediocre at worst, ranging from the Bryan Singer and Michael Dougherty *Superman Returns* (2006) to the Tim Kring television series *Heroes* (2006–2010). But although critics were largely indifferent to them, for the most part even the worst of these films were commercially successful.

2008 saw the next phase of superhero movies begin, with the Christopher Nolan and Jonathan Nolan *The Dark Knight* and the Jon Favreau, Mark Fergus, and Hawk Ostby *Iron Man*. *The Dark Knight* took in over $1 billion worldwide, *Iron Man* bringing in $585 million. Each film was highly successful with critics. Each film had smart scripts and standout performances; Heath Ledger, from *Dark Knight*, received an Academy Award for his performance as the Joker. And each film's audience, critical, and financial reception altered what all involved could and would expect from superhero films. After *The Dark Knight* and *Iron Man*, audiences no longer expected to be just entertained; superhero movies were now major cinematic events, the kind that studios began advertising the year before and that entertainment companies' calendars were built around. Studios now expected superhero films to be not just tent-pole movies but blockbusters that would bring in hundreds of millions of dollars worldwide, the sort of money previously reserved for record-holders like *Titanic*, *Avatar*, and the *Star Wars* and *Lord of the Rings* films. The mark for a certified blockbuster had been $200 million; now, thanks to *Dark Knight* and *Iron Man*, the goal to be reached—the goal expected to be reached by industry figures—was the half a billion dollars mark.

And even that goal was a dynamic rather than a static one, thanks to the increasing importance of the global moviegoing public. Peter Berg and Vince Gilligan's *Hancock* (2008) took in $227 million domestically—an undeniably positive amount—and $397 million globally, and *Hancock* was a completely original film, not a film about a licensed, preexisting property. Jon Favreau and Justin Theroux's *Iron Man 2* (2010) earned $312 million domestically and $311 million globally. Kenneth Branagh and Ashley Miller's *Thor* (2011) earned $181 million domestically and $268 million globally. And Joe Johnston and Christopher Markus's *Captain America: The First Avenger* (2011) earned $177 million domestically and $193 million globally.

The international moviegoing public became a priority for movie producers, who began including more internationally oriented material and non-American characters in their movies. The most important aspect of superhero films during this time period, however, was the gradual construction of the "Marvel Cinematic Universe," the dynamic by which *Iron Man* and *Thor* and *Captain America: The First Avenger* all existed in the same fictional universe, and all contained references to Marvel comics or to the events or personages of other Marvel Cinematic Universe films. The culmination of this dynamic was Joss Whedon's *The Avengers* (2012), which brought together in one film the heroes from the previous Marvel cinematic universe's films: the Hulk, Iron Man, Thor, and Captain America. The script was intelligently written, the effects state-of-the-art, and the acting professional, and the result was a film that took in $623 million domestically and $896 million internationally.

The Marvel Cinematic Universe dominated superhero films of the 2010s. There were certainly other financially successful superhero films during this time period: Christopher Nolan's *Dark Knight Rises* (2012) earned over $1 billion dollars, Zack Snyder and David S. Goyer's *Man of Steel* (2013) earned over $660 million, and Zack Snyder and David S. Goyer's *Batman v. Superman: Dawn of Justice* (2016) earned over $863 million. Yet none of these other films won the critical approval that the Marvel Cinematic Universe films did, and the competing Cinematic Universes of the time period—the X-Men Cinematic Universe (produced by 20th Century Fox), the Spider-Man Cinematic Universe (produced by Columbia Pictures), the Fantastic Four Cinematic Universe (produced by 20th Century Fox), and especially the DC Extended Universe (produced by Warner Brothers)—were neither financially nor critically as successful as the Marvel Cinematic Universe, nor engendered the same amount of fervor and affection from moviegoers and superhero fans.

The prevailing trend in superhero films, then, is similar to that of superhero comics: toward the dominance of two groups. As of spring 2016, there are 25 superhero films scheduled from 2016–2020. Eleven of them are part of the Marvel Cinematic Universe, 10 of them are part of the DC Extended Universe. There is always the possibility that an independent film with original (unlicensed) characters, like Josh Trank and Max Landis's *Chronicle* (2012), which grossed $127 million worldwide on a $12 million dollar budget, will do well, but the lion's share of the attention and room and profits will continue to be consumed by Marvel and DC.

The business of superhero movies is largely positive for the comic book companies, with superhero films bringing in hundreds of millions of dollars in revenue, so that it can be said that the films financially support the comics. But the movies are less positive for the comic books, which are forced to react to the movies rather than influence them. Superhero comics, as described in Chapter 9, are largely editorially driven rather than being wholly created by writers and artists. Business considerations, such as an unwillingness to deviate too much from film portrayals, likewise influence the stories.

Epilogue

According to the traditional dating scheme of comics' Ages, a new Age began in 2016. It's too early to name the Age; the Age's common traits and aspects and tendencies will not become apparent for years, a few if not many. All that any observer of superhero comics can do is look at the present and try to judge what the genre's future will be.

I write this in the fall of 2016, when the major superhero movie of the year, *Captain America: Civil War*, took in $1.15 billion dollars globally—not quite the $1.5 billion dollars taken in globally by *Avengers: Age of Ultron*, but still enough to make it the 19th most profitable film of all time. There are 11 ongoing television shows about superheroes (and that's not counting cartoons), and my eight-year-old son and his classmates know more superhero trivia than I do. A Google search for the word "superhero" brings up 126,000,000 hits, with 223,000,000 hits for "Superman," 399,000,000 hits for "Batman," and 108,000,000 hits for "Spider-Man." An Amazon.com search for "superhero" brings up 540,000 products to buy, from onesies for toddlers to more, ahem, adult products. Superheroes have conquered the pop culture world. Those of us bullied and mocked in decades past for our affection and enthusiasm for superheroes can at last rest easy. We won the war between geeks and jocks.

But at what price, victory? To quote Plutarch's *Life of Pyrrhus*, "Pyrrhus replied to one that gave him joy of his victory that one other such would utterly undo him."[1] Superheroes are now the dominant wish fulfillment figures in popular culture—which is splendid. Isn't it?

I wonder. The massively successful superheroes we see now are some distance from the superheroes I knew growing up in the 1970s—they kill their enemies now, and they don't maintain friendships with each other. The common relationship between superheroes now seems to be bickering distrust, at best. The best comics today are better written and drawn than the comics of my youth were, and access to them has never been easier, but the deliberately maintained innocence of the superheroes of my youth is long gone and has been replaced by what is too often a ghastly combination of post-9/11 ruthlessness and postmodern, even nihilistic, cynicism. The price superheroes paid for conquering all media has been high, indeed.

I try to comfort myself by looking for signs of progress in the industry, evidence that superheroes aren't stuck in some kind of permanent down-cycle of mediocrity and worse. Truly innovative stories continue to be told by skilled men and women (when their editors let them). Marvel's *Secret Wars* (2015–2016) has seemed to revitalize Marvel, leading to an unusually high number of series of good quality, and DC's "Rebirth" movement has the potential to do the same for DC's comics. The new Age that began in 2016 seems in many ways promising. Superheroines and characters of color have a higher profile than ever before. Thor is now a woman, one of the Captains America is now an African American, Iron Man is a teen-aged African American woman, and the Marvel superheroes with the most enthusiastic fan bases are Kelly Sue DeConnick and Dexter Soy's version of Captain Marvel (a woman) and G. Willow Wilson and Adrian Alphona's Ms. Marvel (a.k.a. Kamala Khan, a Pakistani American Muslim). LGBT fans have more LGBT characters than ever before to look up to. The grand narrative of superheroes being white males is dead and has been replaced by diversity—for the better, needless to say.

And yet in so many ways the comic book industry seems stuck in the 1930s and 1940s, an observation possible now that (thanks to social media) there is an unprecedented amount of industry transparency. The hiring of women and people of color for either creative or editorial positions continues to be a rare occasion. Sexual harassment seems de rigueur in the industry, and sexual harassers in positions of power are protected rather than driven out of the industry. Writers and artists have to work very long hours indeed to earn a livable wage (although this, of course, can be traced back to the general, nationwide flattening of compensation that began in the 1970s and continues to this day). Glad-handing mediocrities are published while much more talented individuals beg for jobs or leave the industry in disgust. While comic book sales dwindle, Marvel and DC seem to be addicted to yearly events—stunt stories—that temporarily boost sales while forcing writers and artists to kowtow to the editors in charge of the events and that do nothing to allow those writers and artists to create actual art in their own comics. The general impression of superhero comics as a medium is that it is a severed frog's leg through which increasing amounts of electricity (the yearly events) have to be pumped in order to make it twitch even slightly. The best work in comics is done outside of the superhero genre, away from Marvel and DC. Both companies will undoubtedly continue to publish superhero comics for the foreseeable future, but only because those comics are idea farms for superhero television shows and movies—a far cry from the comparatively idyllic period of the 1960s and even the 1970s. And, as mentioned, the characters themselves are often not moral paragons, or even particularly likable.

Mais où sont les neiges d'antan? This process of coarsening, degradation, and dwindling, of fading away from a previous ideal state, is a common enough dynamic in pop culture genres, and by striking the *ubi sunt* note I'm really no different from mystery fans of the 1920s and 1930s comparing the hard-boiled detectives to the more genteel crime solvers of the 1890s, 1900s, and 1910s, or science fiction fans in the 1960s and 1970s complaining about the New Wave with invidious comparisons to the science fiction of the 1940s and 1950s. (Or, for that matter, music fans of the 1970s complaining about punk rock.) Genres evolve, inevitably, and the character types in them do as well, and those who complain about that evolution inevitably end up looking like dinosaurs balefully eyeing those scampering young mammals and muttering about the good old days.

Superheroes will continue to evolve, and older fans like me will continue to find ourselves in a position of having to (in writer Warren Ellis's phrase) change or die. So be it. I just wish I could say that I was more hopeful about what those changes will bring.

Appendix

Perhaps the most frustrating aspect of writing this book is that its goal, the tracing of the idea and reality of the superhero throughout the history of popular culture, imposed various restraints against which I repeatedly chafed. Had I written a different kind of book, I often told myself, or if I had only broadened my remit a little, I might have been able to include a great deal of information that I had to leave out.

One type of information I could not in good conscience leave out is the existence of international (non-U.S., non-U.K.) protosuperheroes—Costumed Avengers and supermen whose only crime was that they were influenced by the protosuperheroes of this book rather than influencing them. That there was considerable popular culture commerce between the Anglophone sphere and the rest of the world, in both directions, is undeniable, but when it comes to the subject matter of this book—protosuperheroes, Costumed Avengers, and supermen—the sad truth is that the Anglophone sphere led, for the most part, and the rest of the world followed.

But that doesn't mean there was a lack of protosuperheroes outside the Anglophone word before the appearance of Superman. Quite the contrary! As the following list shows, the *idea* of the protosuperhero is a universal one.

Ace of Spades. Created by Nagendra Majumdar. From the Indian film *Kalina Ekka* (1930). Costumed Avenger; a masked anti-British gentleman bandit.

Alraune. Created by Hans Heinz Ewers. From the German novel *Alraune. Die Geschichte eines lebenden Wesens* (1911). Übermensch; occult femme fatale.

Atalanta. Created by Robert Kraft. From the German pulp *Atalanta* (1904–1905). Übermensch; superhuman adventurer.

Audreses. Created by Raimondo Scotti and Renee de Liot. From the Italian film *L'Atleta Fantasma* (1919). Costumed Avenger; a masked, bare-chested crime fighter.

Aztocs. Created by Ignacio Muñoz and Cecil V. Law. From the Mexican comic strip "Aztoc, La Ciudad Perdida" (1936–1937). Übermensch; superhuman Lost Race Aztec warriors.

Black Bandit. Created by Raja Sandow. From the Indian film *Chalak Chor* (1936). Costumed Avenger; a masked female vigilante modeled on Zorro.

Black Cloak. Created by Zheng Zhengqiu. From the Chinese film *Heiyi Nüxia* (1928). Costumed Avenger; a masked female vigilante martial artist.

Black Jack. Created by Karl Schneider. From the German film *Der Schwarze Jack* (1919). Costumed Avenger; masked cowboy vigilante.

Black Mask (I). Created by Luang Sārānupraphan. From the Thai serial "Phrāe Dam" (1922–1923). Costumed Avenger; masked vigilante.

Black Mask (II). Created by Niubó Melchor. From the Spanish pulp *Mascara Negra* (1935?). Costumed Avenger; masked vigilante in 17th-century Europe.

Black Rider. Created by W. Baxter Rugles and Riera Rojas. From the Spanish comic strip "Peter Jones en el Valle del Infierno" (1935–1936?). Costumed Avenger; masked cowboy vigilante.

Bokulmoon. From the Indian novel *Mumtaz Damsaz* (1909). Übermensch; evil wizard.

Bon, Carlos and Marcos. Created by José Canellas Casals and Francisco Darnis. From the Spanish pulp *Los Vampiros del Aire* (1933–1934). Costumed Avengers; vigilantes using Iron Man–like flying suits.

Brown, Billy. From the Danish pulp *Billy Brown. Den Frygtelige Hypnotisør* (1909). Übermensch; hypnotic master detective.

Cagliostro. Created by Vicente Huidobro. From the Chilean serial "Cagliostro" (1921–1922). Übermensch; occult historical figure.

Captain Mors. From the German pulp *Der Luftpirat und sein Lenkbares Luftschiff* (1908–1911). Costumed Avenger; masked science fiction hero.

Captain Storm. Created by Emilio Salgari. From the Italian novels *Capitan Tempesta* (1905) and *Il Leone di Damasco* (1910). Costumed Avenger; female knight active during the Third Crusade.

Carson, Dr. From the Danish pulp *Dr. Carson* (1926). Übermensch; hypnotic master detective.

Cat's Eye. Created by Guido Bassi. From the Italian novel *La Maschera Rossa* (1910). Costumed Avenger; masked consulting detective.

Charro Negro. Created by Adolfo Ruiz. From the Mexican comic strip "El Charro Negro" (1936–1937?). Costumed Avenger; masked Mexican cowboy vigilante.

Chibisuke. Created by Mitsuyo Seo. From the Japanese film *Issunboshi Chibisuke Monogatari* (1935). Übermensch; magically powered female Buddhist monk.

Chucho el Roto. Based on the historical swindler and bandit Jesús Arriaga (1858–1894). From comic strips of the 1930s. Costumed Avenger; masked Mexican Robin Hood.

Cossack. From the Spanish pulp *El Cosaco Enmascarado. El Defensor de los Debiles* (1933?). Costumed Avenger; masked Cossack vigilante.

Cruz Diablo. Created by Vicente Oroná and Fernando de Fuentes. From the Mexican film *Cruz Diablo* (1934). Costumed Avenger; masked Mexican cowboy vigilante.

Daring Damsel. Created by Saqi. From the Indian film *Azad Abla* (1933). Costumed Avenger; female masked vigilante.

Daxo. Created by Henri Rainaldy. From the Moroccan novel *Daxo* (1934). Übermensch; psychic science fiction vigilante.

Deccan Queen. Created by Mehboob Khan. From the Indian film *Deccan Queen* (1936). Costumed Avenger; female costumed vigilante.

Delorme, Lucien. Created by Francois-Edmond Gautier de Teramond. From the French novel *L'Homme Qui Voit a Travers les Murailles* (1914). Übermensch; psychic detective.

Detective Nobody. Created by Robert Kraft. From the German pulp *Detektiv Nobody's Erlebnisse und Reiseabenteuer* (1904–1906). Costumed Avenger; masked detective adventurer.

Drude. Created by Aleksandr Grin. From the Russian novel *Blistaiushchii mir* (1923). Übermensch; flying peasant.

Dubrosvky, Alexander. Created by Alexander Pushkin. From the Russian novel Дубровский (*Dubrovsky*). Costumed Avenger; a masked Robin Hood type.

Dyenis, Dr. Created by Jorge Cardeña Álvarez and Juan José Segura. From the Mexican film *El Superloco*. Übermensch; psychic mad scientist.

Eagle Eye. Created by J. Nowee. From the Dutch comic book *Arendsoog* (1935–1938). Übermensch; superhuman cowboy.

Fascinax. From the French pulp *Fascinax* (1921). Übermensch; psychic vigilante.

Félifax. Created by Paul Féval *fils* and Henri Allorge. From the French novel *Félifax* (1929). Übermensch; superhuman Tarzan type.

Frankenstein. Created by Francisco Casillas and Alfonso Tirado. From the Mexican comic strip "Frankenstein" (1937–1938). Übermensch; superhuman wandering vigilante.

Future Germans. Created by Richard Hagen. From the German novel *Der Brennende Kontinent* (1927). Übermensch; superhuman science fiction adventurers.

Gagaklodra. Crated by Njoo Cheong Seng. From the Indonesian story "Penjakit Tjinta" (1930). Übermensch; superhuman master thief and vigilante.

Garibaldi. From the Russian serial novel *Garibal'di. Korvavye Prikliucheniaa Groznogo Atamana Razboinikov* (1902–1903). Costumed Avenger; masked Robin Hood type.

Golden Mask. From the Japanese *kamishibai* (stories for children told by wandering performers) *Golden Mask* (early 1930s). Costumed Avenger Übermensch. Superpowered costumed vigilante.

Hansa. Created by J. B. H. Wadia. From the Indian film *Hurricane Hansa* (1937). Costumed Avenger; masked female vigilante.

Herne, Robert. Created by Hans Brennert and Friede Köhne. From the German film *Algol—Tragödie der Macht* (1920). Übermensch; superhuman vigilante.

El Hidalgo. Created by Jean Martet. From the Spanish novel *El Vengador Hidalgo Don Cristóbal* (1930). Costumed Avenger; costumed vigilante.

Hind Kesari. Created by H. E. Khatib and J. B. H. Wadia. From the Indian film *Hind Kesari* (1932). Costumed Avenger; costumed Robin Hood type.

Hodomur. Created by Ege Tilms. From the Belgian novel *Hodomur, L'Homme de l'Infini* (1934). Übermensch; superhuman science fiction hero.

Hunterwali. Created by Homi Wadia. From the Indian film *Hunterwali* (1935). Costumed Avenger; masked Robin Hood type.

Hypnos, Tom. From the German pulp *Tom Hypnos, der König der Geheimwissenschaften* (1921). Übermensch; hypnotic adventurer.

Invisible Man (I). Created by Yeoryios Tsoukalás. From the Greek novel *The Invisible Man* (1930). Übermensch; superhuman pirate.

Invisible Man (II). Created by Hemendra Kumar Ray. From the Indian novel *Adrishya Manush* (1935). Übermensch; superhuman modeled on H. G. Wells's Invisible Man.

Judex. Created by Arthur Bernède and Louis Feuillade. From the French film serials *Judex* (1917) and *The New Mission of Judex* (1918). Costumed Avenger; costumed vigilante.

Jumelia. Created by Panchkori Dey. From the Indian novel *Mayabi* (1902). Übermensch; magic *femme fatale*.

Kachinskiy. Created by Aleksandr Beliayev. From the Russian novel *Vlastelin Mira* (1929). Übermensch; psychic adventurer.

King, William. Created by Fernando Bellini. From the Italian pulp *William King, il Re Degli Avventurieri* (1931). Costumed Avenger; masked master thief and Robin Hood type.

Klara. Created by Rudolf Presber. From the German film *Die Hexe von Endor* (1932). Übermensch; witch.

Klingsor, Loke. Created by Robert Kraft. From the German pulp *Loke Klingsor, Der Mann Mit Der Teufelsagen* (1927). Übermensch; hypnotic vigilante.

Kram. From the Spanish pulp *Kram. El Hipnotizador* (1930?). Übermensch; hypnotic adventurer modeled on Sâr Dubnotal.

Kurama Tengu. Created by Osaragi Jirō. From Japanese story serials, novels, and movies, beginning with the story "Kurama Tengu" (1923). Costumed Avenger; masked, costumed samurai vigilante.

Lion Man. Created by J. B. H. Wadia. From the Indian film *Sinh Garjana* (1932). Costumed Avenger; costumed vigilante.

Lubineski. Created by Jacques Presser. From the Dutch pulp *Onder Hypnose* (1921–1922). Übermensch; hypnotist.

Magician. From the Spanish pulp *El Tesoro Magico* (1923?). Übermensch; wizard.

Masked Cavalier. Created by Anand Prasad Kapur. From the Indian film *Bhedi Sawar* (1929). Costumed Avenger; costumed vigilante.

Masked Rider. Created by Vithaldas Panchotia. From the Indian film *Gaibi Sawar* (1930). Costumed Avenger; masked gentleman bandit.

Masked Terror. Created by Nanubhai Desai. From the Indian film *Kala Pahad* (1927). Costumed Avenger; masked gentleman bandit.

Minnalkodi. Created by K. Amarnath. From the Indian film *Minnalkodi* (1923?). Costumed Avenger; masked killer vigilante and Robin Hood type.

Mister Nothing. Created by Louis Boussenard. From the French story "Monsieur Rien" (1907). Übermensch; invisible man.

Momotarō. From the Japanese film *Omochabako Shiriizu Daisanway: Ehon 1936* (1934). Übermensch; superhuman adventurer.

Morgan, Phil. From the German pulp *Phil Morgan—Der Herr der Welt* (1920–1922). Übermensch; superhuman adventurer.

Morgan, Ralph. Created by V. I. Kryzhanovskaia. From the Russian novel *The Elixir of Long Life* (1909). Übermensch; superhuman adventurer.

Neera. Created by R. S. Choudhury. From the Indian film *Neera* (1926). Übermensch; occult adventurer.

Nelson, Jack. Created by Joe Morris. From the German pulp *Jack Nelson vom Tric-Trac-Tric* (1925–1926). Costumed Avenger; costumed science fiction vigilante.

Ninja Boy. From Japanese *kamishibai* (stories for children told by wandering performers) (early 1930s). Costumed Avenger; costumed vigilante.

Ninja Woman. From Japanese *kamishibai* (stories for children told by wandering performers) (early 1930s). Costumed Avenger; costumed vigilante.

Nyctalope. Created by Jean de la Hire. From the French novel *L'Homme Qui Peut Vivre dans l'Eau* (1908). Übermensch; superhuman adventurer.

Ōgon Batto. Created by Takeo Nagamatsu and Ichiro Suzuki. From Japanese *kamishibai* (stories for children told by wandering performers) (1930–1938). Costumed Avenger Übermensch; superpowered costumed vigilante.

Phantom. Created by Saqi. From the Indian film *Abad Chor* (1933). Costumed Avenger; masked vigilante based on Zorro.

Phantom X. From the Spanish pulp *El Fantasma X* (1927?). Costumed Avenger; costumed vigilante.

Prince of Gamma. From Japanese *kamishibai* (stories for children told by wandering performers) (early 1930s). Costumed Avenger Übermensch; superpowered costumed vigilante.

Princess Radost. Created by Pavel Nikolaevich Krasnov. From the Russian novel *Za chertopolokhom* (1922). Übermensch; psychic.

Psychic Detective. Created by Jacques Presser. From the Dutch pulp *De Avonturen van de Man met Het Zesde Zintuig* (1922–1923). Übermensch; psychic detective.

Purple Hood. Created by Rokuhei Susukita. From the Japanese film *Murasaki-Zuken: Ukiyo Eshi* (1923). Costumed Avenger; costumed vigilante.

El Rajo. Created by Emilio Fancelli. From the Italian pulp *El Rajo. Il Cavaliere Misterioso del Messico* (1931–1932). Costumed Avenger; masked vigilante modeled on Zorro.

Rakshita. Created by Ahmed H. Essa. From the Indian film *Dilruba Daku* (1933). Costumed Avenger; masked vigilante modeled on Zorro.

Red Archer. Created by Sundarao Nadkarni. From the Indian film *Teer-e-Qatil* (1931). Costumed Avenger; masked vigilante.

Red Mask. From the Spanish pulp *La Mascara Roja* (1930–1931?). Costumed Avenger; masked vigilante.

Rolf, Jens. Created by Karl Müller-Malberg. From the German pulp *Jens Rolfs Mystisch Abenteuerliche Erlebnisse* (1922–1923). Übermensch; occult detective.

Rollon, Joe. Created by Jean de la Hire. From the French novel *Joe Rollon, L'Autre Homme Invisible* (1919). Übermensch; invisible man.

Sâr Dubnotal. From the German dime novel *Sâr Dubnotal* (1909). Übermensch; Rosicrucian psychic detective.

Sarutobi Sasuke. From a Japanese novel (1913). Übermensch; superhuman samurai.

Strongman. From the Russian serial novel *Russkii Bogatyr'* (1909). Übermensch; superhuman adventurer.

Swordsman. Created by Zayya. From the Burmese novel *Mya Lay Shwe Dar Bo* (1920). Costumed Avenger; costumed vigilante modeled on the Scarlet Pimpernel.

Three Vigilantes. Created by Walther Kabel. From the German pulp *Die Drei von der Feme* (1933). Costumed Avengers; masked vigilantes.

Thunderbolt. Created by J. B. H. Wadia. From the Indian film *Diler Daku* (1931). Costumed Avenger; masked vigilante modeled on Zorro.

Unknown Ally. From the Italian pulp *L'Alleato Sconosciuto* (1908). Costumed Avenger; masked vigilante.

Vantolio. Created by J. B. H. Wadia. From the Indian film *Vantolio* (1933). Costumed Avenger; masked vigilante modeled on Zorro.

Wan, Mack. Created by José Canellas Casals and Marc Farell. From the Spanish comic *Mack Wan. El Invencible* (1933–1934). Costumed Avenger; costumed vigilante modeled on Edmond Dantès.

Wilson, Bob. From the French pulp *Extraits des Dossier de Bob Wilson, le Célèbre Détective* (1920–1921). Costumed Avenger; masked master detective.

Zalor. Created by Ignacio Munoz and Cecil V. Law. From the Mexican comic strip "Zalor el Hijo de la Bruja" (1936–1937). Übermensch; occult adventurer.

Zigomar. From the Japanese film *Shin Jigoma Daitantei* (1912). Costumed Avenger; costumed master thief and detective.

Notes

Introduction

1. Peter M. Coogan, *Superhero: The Secret Origin of a Genre* (Austin, TX: MonkeyBrain, 2006), iii.
2. Ibid., iv.

Chapter 1

1. Otto Rank, *The Myth of the Birth of the Hero: A Psychological Interpretation of Mythology*, translated by Drs. F. Robbins and Smith Ely Jelliffe (New York: The Journal of Nervous and Mental Disease Publishing Company, 1914), 61. Originally published as *Der Mythus von der Geburt des Helden: Versuch einer psychologischen Mythendeutung*, 1909.
2. Baron Raglan, *The Hero: A Study in Tradition, Myth, and Drama* (1956; repr., Westport, CT: Greenwood Press, 1975), 174–175.
3. Joseph Campbell, *The Hero with a Thousand Faces* (1949; repr., Princeton, NJ: Princeton University Press, 1972), 30.
4. Campbell, *The Hero with a Thousand Faces*, 245–246.
5. An argument can be made that a third demand keeps superheroes in an eternal second act: a flaw in the genre itself, or at least the common execution of it. Superheroes, both characters and what passes for the genre they appear in, are flexible enough to tell practically any story, regardless of genre; comics, as a medium, are no more limited in what stories can be told in it than any other medium. To quote the coinage of Belgian artist Maurice de Bevere and editor Yvan Delporte, comics are the "ninth art," a medium that takes parts of prose and the visual arts and creates something unique. The medium can do anything that any other art can do. Superheroes, as a genre of comics—the dominant genre now, though that has not always been the case, as I describe in Chapter 9—should have that freedom. But too often this is not the case, and badly flawed art is produced, with heroes caught in mid–second act, never able to

embrace the maturity of the third act, and finality. Perhaps superhero comics' origin, as fodder for children, infects the genre to the point of altering its creators' art—perhaps superhero comics are ultimately not only for children, but they also embody a child's point of view of the world, one that does not accept or understand the basic realities of the world—death, marriage, becoming a parent, and so on. Campbell, in describing the hero's life, wrote, "At the return threshold the transcendental powers must remain behind," but the great majority of superheroes never do that—never relinquish their powers and embrace true adulthood. The epic cycle stops before it properly should end. Perhaps, then, it is not just the marketplace and the demands of the consumer that keep most superheroes trapped in the eternal second act, but the origin of superhero comics themselves.

6. Learned Hand, *Detective Comics, Inc. v. Bruns Publications, Inc.* 111 F.2d 432 (2nd Cir., Apr. 29, 1940). This case is better known as "*Superman v. Wonderman*," the seminal early copyright-infringement suit of superhero comics. Hand did not define superheroes as a class, but described DC's Superman and Fox Publications' Wonder Man as having superpowers and costumes and as being "the champion of the oppressed." From Hand's legal description most modern definitions of the superhero seem to flow.

7. Peter M. Coogan, *Superhero: The Secret Origin of a Genre* (Austin, TX: MonkeyBrain, 2006), 31.

8. Ibid., 32.

9. Ibid., 33.

10. Robin Rosenberg and Peter Coogan, *What Is a Superhero?* (Oxford: Oxford University Press, 2013), 43.

11. Ibid., 133.

12. Ibid., 89.

13. Ibid., 125.

14. Chris Gavaler, *On the Origin of Superheroes: From the Big Bang to Action Comics, Issue 1* (Iowa City, IA: University of Iowa, 2015), 4.

15. I am indebted to my friend, the author Cherie Priest for this approach. In 2012, when asked about the definition of the literary subgenre of steampunk, she wrote, "I don't believe in steampunk as a binary. I see it as more like a spectrum." Cherie Priest, e-mail message to the author, January 17, 2012.

16. Gregory Mobley, *Samson and the Liminal Hero in the Ancient Near East* (New York: T & T Clark, 2006), 13.

17. Gavaler, *On the Origin of Superheroes: From the Big Bang to Action Comics, Issue 1*, 26.

18. Which is why *Paradise Lost* does not appear in these pages except mentioned in passing: it has no mortal heroes with the exception of Adam, who lacks any superheroic quality. In addition, there is the small matter of the lack of influence of *Paradise Lost* on heroic fiction in general. Truthfully, *Paradise Lost*'s main influence, the character model it provided for later superhero writers, was Lucifer, a central role model for the Gothic Hero-Villains covered in Chapter 3.

19. "If superior in *kind* both to other men and to the environment of other men, the hero is a divine being, and the story about him will be a *myth* . . . if superior in *degree* to other men and to his environment, the hero is the typical hero of *romance*, whose actions are marvelous but who is himself identified as a human being . . . if superior in degree to other men but not to his natural environment, the hero is a leader . . . of the *high mimetic* mode." Northrop Frye, *Anatomy of Criticism: Four Essays* (Princeton: Princeton University Press, 1971), 33–34. Frye is obviously still quite useful in discussing types of fiction, and Coogan wisely applies his theory of modes to the various types of superheroes. Coogan, *Superhero: The Secret Origin of a Genre*, 49. But Frye's applicability decreases when we venture into more basic definitions of the genre itself.

20. Jacques Derrida and Avitall Ronell, "The Law of Genre," *Critical Inquiry* 7, no. 1 (1980), 57.

21. Derrida and Ronell, "The Law of Genre," 65.

22. Coogan, *Superhero: The Secret Origin of a Genre*, 52.

23. James Nicoll, "The King's English." In rec.arts.sf-lovers (Usenet newsgroup), May 5, 1990. Internet.

Chapter 2

1. But read Rollin's "Beowulf to Batman: The Epic Hero and Pop Culture," helpfully reprinted in Charles Hatfield, Jeet Heer, and Kent Worcester's *The Superhero Reader* (Jackson: University of Mississippi, 2013), if you need reminding.

2. A. R. George, *The Epic of Gilgamesh: The Babylonian Epic Poem and Other Texts in Akkadian and Sumerian* (London: Penguin, 2003), 2.

3. Ibid., 3.

4. Ibid., 5.

5. Ibid., 8.

6. Ibid., 1.

7. Ibid., 2.

8. Ibid., 2.

9. Ibid., xxxvii.

10. And as a Mesopotamian he has darker skin than Caucasians. It bears emphasis, in the current environment of racism and xenophobia toward those of Middle Eastern descent: the first superhero was not a white man. As we'll see, there is a partially submerged tradition of people of color as protosuperheroes throughout the history of heroic fiction, leading up to Bill Ely's Nadir and Art Pinajian's Red Man, the first two superheroes of color in the comics (with Nadir predating Superman by almost a year).

11. John L. Foster, *Ancient Egyptian Literature: An Anthology* (Austin, TX: University of Texas, 2001), 97.

12. Steve Vinson, "The Accent's on Evil: Ancient Egyptian 'Melodrama' and the Problem of Genre," *Journal of the American Research Center in Egypt* 41 (2004), 33–35.

13. Foster, *Ancient Egyptian Literature: An Anthology*, 124.

14. Ibid., 124–128.

15. Victor Harold Matthews and Don C. Benjamin, *Old Testament Parallels: Laws and Stories from the Ancient Near East* (New York: Paulist, 1991), 137.

16. See Gregory Mobley, *Samson and the Liminal Hero in the Ancient Near East* (New York: T & T Clark, 2006), 4, for a discussion of Wolfgang Richter's chronological locating of the hero stories in Judges.

17. Gregory Mobley, "The Wild Man in the Bible and the Ancient Near East," *Journal of Biblical Literature* 116, no. 2 (1997), 220.

18. Looking ahead, we can see the influence of the wild man on medieval and Renaissance art and culture (Shakespeare's Caliban) and iterations of the wild man in Arthurian myth (Lancelot when he loses his mind, the Green Knight, Tristan in the woods) and in modern superhero comics (Stan Lee and Jack Kirby's Hulk; Roy Thomas, Len Wein, John Romita Sr., and Herb Trimpe's Wolverine). Enkidu is the original version of the wild man, which makes the wild man the first superheroic archetype.

19. Mobley, "The Wild Man in the Bible and the Ancient Near East," 226–228.

20. Jgs 3:31.

21. Mobley, *Samson and the Liminal Hero in the Ancient Near East*, 21.

22. Jgs 13:5.

23. Mobley, *Samson and the Liminal Hero in the Ancient Near East*, 115.

24. Ibid., 115.

25. The critical formulation about the classic Western goes something like this: on the frontier the barbarians can only be defeated through the use of the gun; but the hero who uses the gun is a barbarian; therefore, there is no room in society for the hero once the barbarians are defeated. The classic examples of this are A. B. Guthrie Jr. and George Stevens's *Shane* (1953), John Ford and Frank Nugent's *The Searchers* (1956), and James Warner, Bellah Willis Goldbeck, and John Ford's *The Man Who Shot Liberty Valence* (1962), but numerous other examples come to mind. As with Samson, so with the classic cowboy: there is no room for the society they build once it is built. Not so with superheroes, perhaps because their use of violence is traditionally nonlethal—when they turn lethal, as the killer vigilante superheroes (like the Punisher) do, the old rules apply, and they become doomed outsiders.

26. Ian Rutherford, "Mythology of the Black Land: Greek Myths and Egyptian Origins." In *A Companion to Greek Mythology*, edited by Ken Dowden and Niall Livingston (Chichester, West Sussex: Wiley-Blackwell, 2011), 461.

27. Foster, *Ancient Egyptian Literature: An Anthology*, 96–99.

28. M. L. West, *The East Face of Helicon: West Asiatic Elements in Greek Poetry and Myth* (Oxford: Clarendon, 1997), 339–401.

29. Allen's "The Indo-European Background to Greek Mythology" (see citation below) intriguingly argues for an Indo-European protomythology and ties between the roots of Greek mythology and Hindu religion, which leads the interested reader into an investigation of the Indian heroic stories—this protomythology of the fourth millennium BCE is the only time period in which

Indian heroes might be said to be influential on the concept of the Western hero—but what the reader finds are epic heroes, not protosuperheroes. Nicholas J. Allen, "The Indo-European Background to Greek Mythology." In *A Companion to Greek Mythology*, edited by Ken Dowden and Niall Livingston (Chichester, West Sussex: Wiley-Blackwell, 2011), 341–356. And Lincoln's "The Indo-European Cattle-Raiding Myth" describes a particular myth of the proto-Indo-Europeans, about the hero, "Trito" ("the Third"), and his battle against a three-headed serpentine monster and the winning of back of cattle stolen from him by the monster. Bruce Lincoln, "The Indo-European Cattle-Raiding Myth," *History of Religions* 16, no. 1 (1976), 58. But Trito is ultimately an epic hero, not a protosuperhero; Trito lacks the elements of the protosuperhero, although Lincoln notes that Trito is retrieving the stolen cattle rather than stealing it, and further Trito uses "open force to regain his stock, in contrast to what must have been regarded as the despicable stealth of the tricephal." Lincoln, "The Indo-European Cattle-Raiding Myth," 64. But ultimately the myth of Trito as Lincoln tells it is a justification for the Indo-European invasion and taking of lands from the preexisting aboriginals and the raiding of their herds of cattle; Trito is no protosuperhero of a selfless mission and extraordinary abilities, simply an epic hero with an extraordinary opponent. Enkidu's status as the great-grandfather of superheroes remains unchallenged.

30. M. I. Finley, *The World of Odysseus* (New York: New York Review, 2002), 20.

31. William Blake Tyrrell and Frieda S. Brown, *Athenian Myths and Institutions: Words in Action* (New York: Oxford University Press, 1991), 48.

32. Pindar and Charles Augustus Maude Fennell, *Pindar: The Nemean and Isthmian Odes: With Notes Explanatory and Critical, Intro., and Introductory Essays* (Cambridge: Cambridge University Press, 1883), 23.

33. It's worth noting that, as with so much else in Greek myth, there wasn't a universality about Prometheus as the individual who gave fire to humanity. According to Pausanias (ca. 110–180 CE), there was a poem, the *Phoronis*, in which the first man, Phoroneus, introduced fire. Ken Dowden, "Telling the Mythology: From Hesiod to the Fifth Century." In *A Companion to Greek Mythology*, edited by Ken Dowden and Niall Livingston (Chichester, West Sussex: Wiley-Blackwell, 2011), 54.

34. L. J. Engels, "Hector." In *A Dictionary of Medieval Heroes: Characters in Medieval Narrative Traditions and Their Afterlife in Literature, Theatre, and the Visual Arts*, edited by W. P. Gerritsen, A. G. Van Melle, and Tanis M. Guest (Woodbridge, Suffolk, UK: Boydell, 1998), 145.

35. Martin Braun, *History and Romance in Graeco-Oriental Literature* (Oxford: B. Blackwell, 1938), 22.

36. Ibid., 22.

37. B. E. Perry, "The Egyptian Legend of Nectanebus," *Transactions and Proceedings of the American Philological Association* 97 (1966), 329.

38. Braun, *History and Romance in Graeco-Oriental Literature*, 23.

39. It has been persuasively argued that Aeneas is not just an epic hero but also a prominent example of the "one just man" who survives the wholesale catastrophic destruction. Uta-napishti, the one just man of his world, survives

the flood in *The Epic of Gilgamesh*; Lot survives the destruction of Sodom and Gomorrah in the Bible, in Genesis 18–19, by being the sole righteous man in the city; and Baucis and Philemon survive the world-destroying flood in Ovid's *Metamorphosis* (8 CE) due to the hospitality they offered to Zeus and Hermes. Aeneas is in this tradition. Bruce Louden, "Aeneas in the Iliad: The One Just Man," Paper presented at the 102nd Annual Meeting of the Classical Association of the Middle West and South, Gainesville, FL, April 2006. But note that this is a passive attribute rather than an active (and superheroic) one; the gods and the Greeks spare Aeneas rather than Aeneas being an active participant in his own survival.

40. L. J. Engels, "Aeneas." In *A Dictionary of Medieval Heroes: Characters in Medieval Narrative Traditions and Their Afterlife in Literature, Theatre, and the Visual Arts*, edited by W. P. Gerritsen, A. G. Van Melle, and Tanis M. Guest (Woodbridge, Suffolk, UK: Boydell, 1998), 9–10.

41. Brent Shaw, "Bandits in the Roman Empire," *Past and Present* 105 (1984), 4.

42. Ibid., 9.

43. Thomas Grünewald, *Bandits in the Roman Empire: Myth and Reality* (London: Routledge, 2004), 14–32.

44. E. J. Hobsbawm, *Bandits* (1969; reprint, New York: New Press, 2000), 20.

45. Jack Winkler, "Lollianos and the Desperadoes," *The Journal of Hellenic Studies* 100 (1980), 176.

46. Ian Rutherford, "The Genealogy of the Boukoloi: How Greek Literature Appropriated an Egyptian Narrative-Motif," *The Journal of Hellenistic Studies* 120 (2000), 109–113.

47. Shaw, "Bandits in the Roman Empire," 44–45.

48. Grünewald, *Bandits in the Roman Empire: Myth and Reality*, 110–126.

49. Cassius Dio and Earnest Cary, *Dio's Roman History IX* (London: William Heinemann Ltd., 1905), 259.

50. Shaw, "Bandits in the Roman Empire," 46–47.

51. See, for example, Arrian's account of the capture of the Malli citadel, in which Alexander is first up the walls of the citadel, cuts down numerous attackers before being impaled by an arrow, yet still gets up and walks to his tent in order to rally his frightened men. (Peter Green has a splendid recounting of this on pp. 418–423 of *Alexander of Macedon, 356–323 B.C.: A Historical Biography* [Berkeley: University of California Press, 1991]).

52. Richard Stoneman, *Alexander the Great: A Life in Legend* (New Haven: Yale University Press, 2008), 9.

53. Ibid., 20.

54. Pseudo-Callisthenes and Albert Mugrdich Wolohojian, *The Romance of Alexander the Great by Pseudo-Callisthenes* (New York: Columbia University Press, 1969), 113.

55. Ibid., 113.

56. John Andrew Boyle, "The Alexander Romance in the East and West," *Bulletin of the John Rylands Library* 60 (1977), 13–27.

57. L. J. Engels, "Alexander the Great." In *A Dictionary of Medieval Heroes: Characters in Medieval Narrative Traditions and Their Afterlife in Literature, Theatre, and the Visual Arts*, edited by W. P. Gerritsen, A. G. Van Melle, and Tanis M. Guest (Woodbridge, Suffolk, UK: Boydell, 1998), 15–16.

58. It can be argued that Alexander was more influential than I've given him credit for in one particular regard. Alexander was popular across cultures, powerful, distinctive, and seen as an exemplar (if a flawed one) of the good guy—not one culture's good guy, but multiple cultures' hero. This mutability—unintended by the authors of *The Alexander Romance*, needless to say, but an attribute of Alexander that accreted to him over time—which starts with the assumption that Alexander is a hero and then builds the case for it, rather than vice versa, as usually was the case with premodern heroes, can be seen in certain iconic heroes of the modern era, like Superman. Most major heroes covered in this book begin with a set personality; writers of Superman, like those who added to the *Alexander Romance*, begin with the assumption that their subject is the hero and then build the attributes and personality to fulfill that role. The Alexander of the *Romance* is mutable over time, always being the hero but taking on different attributes and traits, depending on the creator and reader/listener/viewer. The same can be said of Superman and Nick Carter and certain other archetypal heroes of the modern age, whose authors take their cues, however unconsciously, from Pseudo-Callisthenes.

59. Robert E. Bjork and Anita Obermeier, "Date, Provenance, Author, Audiences." In *A Beowulf Handbook*, edited by Robert E. Bjork and John D. Niles (Lincoln: University of Nebraska, 1997), 13–34.

60. R. D. Fulk, *The Beowulf Manuscript: Complete Texts; and The Fight at Finnsburg* (Cambridge, MA: Harvard University Press, 2010), 295.

61. Ibid., xviii.

62. Henk Aertsen, "Beowulf." In *A Dictionary of Medieval Heroes: Characters in Medieval Narrative Traditions and Their Afterlife in Literature, Theatre, and the Visual Arts*, edited by W. P. Gerritsen, A. G. Van Melle, and Tanis M. Guest (Woodbridge, Suffolk, UK: Boydell, 1998), 58.

63. Comic book fans will object to this statement on the grounds that there have been superhero deaths that were final and brought a third act quality to that superhero's life, beginning with the death of Jack Cole's Comet in Harry Shorten and George Storm's "The Origin of the Hangman" in *Pep Comics* #17, July 1941. But the reversible state of death in superhero comics is a sadly common cliché; every superhero who dies gets brought back eventually, whether because a writer thinks it's a good idea or because the fans (or the editors) demand it.

64. Edward B. Irving Jr., "Christian and Pagan Elements." In *Beowulf*, edited by Harold Bloom (New York: Chelsea House, 2007), 124.

65. Aertsen, "Beowulf," 59.

66. Neidorf's "Beowulf before *Beowulf*" contains an interesting onomastic analysis of the usage and disappearance of heroic Anglo-Saxon names. Neidorf's conclusion is that the use of the name "Biuuulf" "offers strong evidence for the

existence of Beowulf legends before the year 700." Leonard Neidorf, "Beowulf before *Beowulf*: Anglo-Saxon Anthroponymy and Heroic Legend," *The Review of English Studies* 64, no. 266 (2013), 554.

67. Robert L. Harrison, *The Song of Roland* (New York: Signet Classic, 2012), 1.

68. Ibid., 9.

69. Ibid., 12.

70. Ibid., 36; Gerard J. Brault, *The Song of Roland* (University Park: Pennsylvania State University Press, 1978), passim.

71. C. Hogetoorn, "Fierabras." In *A Dictionary of Medieval Heroes: Characters in Medieval Narrative Traditions and Their Afterlife in Literature, Theatre, and the Visual Arts*, edited by W. P. Gerritsen, A. G. Van Melle, and Tanis M. Guest (Woodbridge, Suffolk, UK: Boydell, 1998), 104.

72. Bruce's "Arthurian Name Dictionary" contains a good list of knights of color in the Arthurian mythos. Christopher Bruce, *Christopher Bruce's Arthurian Name Dictionary*, http://gorddcymru.org/twilight/camelot/bruce_dictionary/index.htm. For a broader treatment of examples of people of color in medieval literature and art, see the "People of Color in European Art History," Tumblr at http://medievalpoc.tumblr.com/. Accessed October 3, 2016.

73. R. J. Resoort, "Robert the Devil." In *A Dictionary of Medieval Heroes: Characters in Medieval Narrative Traditions and Their Afterlife in Literature, Theatre, and the Visual Arts*, edited by W. P. Gerritsen, A. G. Van Melle, and Tanis M. Guest (Woodbridge, Suffolk, UK: Boydell, 1998), 222.

74. R. A. Fletcher, *The Quest for El Cid* (New York: Knopf, 1990), 185.

75. Ibid., 194.

76. Although it is possible that Gardner Fox and Sheldon Mayer, who created the first comic book superteam, DC Comics' Justice Society of America, in *All-Star Comics* #3 (cover date Winter 1940-1941, on sale date November 22, 1940), had in mind Carolyn Wells's "Society of Infallible Detectives" stories (1905–1917) or the massive dime novel character team-up of Ralph Smith's "Frank Merriwell vs. Fred Fearnot" (*Frank Reade Library*, September–December 1928), rather than Arthur's Round Table of knights. But the Justice Society of America's round table of heroes, as seen on the cover of *All-Star Comics* #3 (drawn by Everett Hibbard), points toward the Arthurian influence being foremost.

77. The preceding scants, more than any other character or historical figure in this book, the reality of the development of Arthurian myth, for which I can only apologize and claim the restrictions of limited available space. Those curious should search out Mike Ashley's *Mammoth Book of King Arthur* (New York: Carroll & Graf, 2005) for a much more thorough examination.

78. Christopher Bruce, "Arthur," *Christopher Bruce's Arthurian Name Dictionary*, http://gorddcymru.org/twilight/camelot/bruce_dictionary/index_a.htm.

79. Christopher Bruce, "Twelve Rules of the Round Table," *Christopher Bruce's Arthurian Name Dictionary*, http://gorddcymru.org/twilight/camelot/bruce_dictionary/index_t.htm.

80. Christopher Bruce, "Round Table," *Christopher Bruce's Arthurian Name Dictionary*, http://gorddcymru.org/twilight/camelot/bruce_dictionary/index_r.htm.

81. The curious should begin with Jason Tondro's *Superheroes of the Round Table: Comics Connections to Medieval and Renaissance Literature* (Jefferson, NC: McFarland, 2011).

82. E. J. Hobsbawm, *Bandits* (1969; reprint, New York: New Press, 2000), passim.

83. Such a list might perhaps culminate in the stories of the noble German pirate Klaus Störtebecker (?–1401), whose staying power in Europe was such that as late as 1909 he was the hero of a 60-issue pulp series, *Klaus Störtebecker, Der Gefürchtete Herrscher der Meere* (Berliner Verlagshaus), in Germany.

84. Thomas H. Ohlgren, *Medieval Outlaws: Ten Tales in Modern English* (Thrupp, Stroud, Gloucestershire: Sutton Pub., 1998), xvii.

85. Ibid., xxiv.

86. Gavaler, *On the Origin of Superheroes: From the Big Bang to Action Comics, Issue 1*, 239.

87. The Robin Hood–like Arrow, first of the archer superheroes, was created by Paul Gustavson and appeared from 1938–1941, beginning with *Funny Pages* 2.10 (cover date September 1938), which came out only three months after Superman's debut. Later archer superheroes, like Stan Lee and Don Heck's Hawkeye (for Marvel) and Mort Weisinger and George Papp's Green Arrow (for DC), openly imitated Robin Hood, with the 1969 Neal Adams redesign of Green Arrow being a near-duplicate of Errol Flynn's Robin Hood and the 1987 Mike Grell redesign being more historically accurate but still quite close to Flynn's Robin. Other superheroes, like Superman and Robin, took as models Douglas Fairbanks's Robin Hood. Coogan, *Superhero: The Secret Origin of a Genre*, 124.

88. Stephen Knight, *Robin Hood: A Complete Study of the English Outlaw* (Oxford: Blackwell, 1994), 7.

89. Ibid., 8.

90. Ibid., 25.

91. This is a position of some debate within the superhero community. Coogan, *Superhero: The Secret Origin of a Genre*, 202–203, agrees with me, as do Robin S. Rosenberg and Jennifer Canzoneri, in *The Psychology of Superheroes: An Unauthorized Exploration* (Dallas, TX: BenBella, 2008), and Terrence R. Wandtke, in *The Meaning of Superhero Comic Books* (Jefferson, NC: McFarland, 2012), among others. Fans usually take the opposite position.

92. R. H. Hilton, "The Origins of Robin Hood." In *Robin Hood: An Anthology of Scholarship and Criticism*, edited by Stephen Knight (Woodbridge, Suffolk: D. S. Brewer, 1999), 209.

93. In the entire history of superhero comics, only two anti-corporate-capitalist costumed characters have been treated as heroes rather than villains: Alan Grant and Norm Breyfogle's Anarky (for DC Comics), originally a Batman foe before being given his own limited series in 1997 and 1999, and Marvelman (later renamed Miracleman), originally created by Mick Anglo in 1954 as

a British version of Bill Parker and C. C. Beck's Captain Marvel, but reinterpreted in 1982 by Alan Moore in a deconstructionist series that culminates in Marvelman/Miracleman imposing a Utopian society (one free of the constraints of money, naturally) on the world.

Chapter 3

1. The "Matter of France," classified as such in the 12th century, is the phrase for all the romances about Charlemagne and his knights—the Charlemagne megatext, the French version of the Arthurian megatext, which was known as the "Matter of Britain." The Matter of France megatext included many other *chansons de geste* and epic poems besides the *Song of Roland*—W. P. Gerritsen, A. G. Van Melle, and Tanis M. Guest's *A Dictionary of Medieval Heroes: Characters in Medieval Narrative Traditions and Their Afterlife in Literature, Theatre, and the Visual Arts* (Woodbridge, Suffolk, UK: Boydell, 1998) is a particularly good introduction to them—and was thematically about, among other things, the conflict—martial, religious, and moral—between French Christianity and the Saracens on the one hand, and the individual's fight against despotism on the other.

2. Frederick Binkerd Artz, *The Mind of the Middle Ages, A.D. 200–1500: An Historical Survey* (Chicago: University of Chicago, 1980), 354.

3. Luigi Pulci and Joseph Tusiani, *Morgante: The Epic Adventures of Orlando and His Giant Friend Morgante* (Bloomington: Indiana University Press, 1998), xi.

4. Artz, *The Mind of the Middle Ages, A.D. 200–1500: An Historical Survey*, 354.

5. I'm stealing this phrase from John Clute. In his and Richard Grant's *Encyclopedia of Fantasy*, Clute applies the term to seminal works in the history of the fantasy genre:

> The notion of the TT seems necessary—or at least desirable—for at least two reasons. The first is that a Water Margin of not easily definable intentions marks what we may now read as an irreversible impulse towards fantasy over the last decades of the 18th century, and it seems advisable to have a blanket term available to use in order to distinguish relevant texts composed or written before those we can legitimately call fantasy. The second is that, because almost any form of tale written before the rise of the mimetic novel could be retroactively conceived as ur- or proto-fantasy, it seems highly convenient to apply to works from this Ocean of Story a term—i.e., "taproot"—which emphasizes the *heightened* significance of the text mentioned. When we refer to a text as a TT, in other words, we describe one that contains a certain mix of ingredients and stands out for various reasons—not excepting quality. (John Clute, "Taproot Text," *Encyclopedia of Fantasy* [New York: St. Martin's Press, 1997], 921)

6. Stephen Knight, *Merlin: Knowledge and Power through the Ages* (Ithaca: Cornell University Press, 2009), 7.

7. The Biblical magi who visited the Christ child were also placed in such a support role. They provided a positive portrayal of wizards, something that

medieval and Renaissance "writers against magic were always rather embarrassed about . . . and developed numerous ingenious ways of getting around the problem." Barbara Howard Traister, *Heavenly Necromancers: The Magician in English Renaissance Drama* (Columbia: University of Missouri, 1984), 4. But they were observers and worshippers rather than active participants in the story.

8. Fabio Stok, "Virgil between the Middle Ages and the Renaissance," *International Journal of the Classical Tradition* 1, no. 2 (1994), 19.

9. Juliette Wood, "Virgil and Taliesin: The Concept of the Magician in Medieval Folklore," *Folklore* 94, no. 1 (1983), 94–95.

10. Traister, *Heavenly Necromancers: The Magician in English Renaissance Drama*, 21–22.

11. William Wistar Comfort, "The Saracens in Epic Italian Poetry," *PMLA* 59, no. 4 (1944), 896.

12. Artz, *The Mind of the Middle Ages, A.D. 200–1500: An Historical Survey*, 354.

13. Pulci and Tusiani, *Morgante: The Epic Adventures of Orlando and His Giant Friend Morgante*, 779.

14. Traister, *Heavenly Necromancers: The Magician in English Renaissance Drama*, 126.

15. Ibid., 53.

16. Ibid., 75. Obviously, one can say the same about superheroes: their job is to reinforce and if necessary reinstate the status quo, not question it and by no means to disturb it.

17. Ibid., 1.

18. Ibid., 2–3.

19. Richard Kieckhefer, *Magic in the Middle Ages* (Cambridge: Cambridge University Press, 2000), 56–57.

20. Philip C. Almond, *The Devil: A New Biography* (Ithaca, NY: Cornell University Press, 2014), 82–83.

21. Dante Aligheri and Mark Musa, *The Divine Comedy: Volume 1: Inferno* (New York: Penguin, 2002), 254.

22. Richard Kay, "The Spare Ribs of Dante's Michael Scot," *Dante Studies, with the Annual Report of the Dante Society* 103 (1985), 7.

23. Traister, *Heavenly Necromancers: The Magician in English Renaissance Drama*, 19.

24. William H. Sherman's *John Dee: The Politics of Reading and Writing in the English Renaissance* (Amherst, MA: University of Massachusetts Press, 1995) makes a strong argument for Dee's reputation, in his lifetime, being somewhat or substantially different from what later historians have described.

25. John Dee and Gerald Suster, *John Dee: Essential Readings* (Berkeley, CA: North Atlantic, 2003), 12.

26. Traister, *Heavenly Necromancers: The Magician in English Renaissance Drama*, 43.

27. And, as has often been the case, the morally ambiguous counterpart to the hero proved to be the more appealing and interesting to the audience.

28. Greene's Friar Bacon is presented as the English rival to the German Vandermast, and a victor over him in the clash of nations, and therefore the hero of the piece. So the audience would likely have perceived him. But *Friar Bacon and*

Friar Bungay, and to a lesser extent *John of Bourdeaux*, present a problematic read-ing of Bacon as a straightforward hero—Bacon's victory over Vandermast "is nationalistic, not moral." Traister, *Heavenly Necromancers: The Magician in English Renaissance Drama*, 126. Moreover, Bacon is a necromancer who is willing to use his magic to further one character's lust for another, and even uses his magic to kill. In fact, there has been considerable scholarly debate about the nature and personality of Bacon. Bacon is the nominal hero but can just as easily be said to be an ambiguous antiheroic sorcerer.

29. Hugh Walker, *The Merry Devil of Edmonton: A Comedy* (London: J. M. Dent, 1897), 65.

30. Traister, *Heavenly Necromancers: The Magician in English Renaissance Drama*, 53.

31. Leo Ruickbie's *Faustus: The Life and Times of a Renaissance Magician* (Stroud, Gloucestershire, UK: The History Press, 2011) would seem to be the best recent work to consult to figure out what was real and what was not about Johann Georg Faust's life and legend.

32. Hogel's *Chronica*, quoted in Ruickbie, *Faustus: The Life and Times of a Renais-sance Magician*, 77.

33. With the sole exception of Faust's homosexuality or bisexuality, which apparently Faust was notorious for being; Couliano quotes the records of the city council of Nuremberg, which calls Faust "*Doctor fausto dem groszen Sodomiten und Nigromantico*, To Doctor Faust, the great sodomite and necromancer." Ioan P. Couliano, "Dr. Faust, Great Sodomite and Necromancer," *Revue de l'histoire des religions* 207, no. 3 (1990), 274. A curious exclusion, though as Couliano points out the author's purpose was to frighten the masses, but to do so "he had to be careful enough to leave some room for identification of the man in the street with Faust himself. Making a homosexual of the latter, who was actually famous for being such, would have endangered that message." Couliano, "Dr. Faust, Great Sodomite and Necromancer," 274.

34. Traister, *Heavenly Necromancers: The Magician in English Renaissance Drama*, 90.

35. In the Golden Age (1938–1949) and Silver Age (1956–1970) of superhero comics, sorcerers and magicians were almost entirely noble in personality, emu-lating Maugis. In the Golden Age, the enchanter heroes were mostly naked imita-tions of Harry Earnshaw's Chandu the Magician (1932–1933, 1948–1950) and Lee Falk's Mandrake the Magician (1934–present); in the Silver Age, magician heroes were influenced by different role models. But all of them remained nearly entirely positive. It wasn't until the Modern Age (1985–2001) of comic books that superhero sorcerers, like superheroes themselves, began to darken and become more complex and "realistic," so that today (2016) the ambiguous sorcerer is prevalent. Alan Moore, Stephen Bissette, and John Totleben's John Constantine (for DC) is far more popular than Dr. Fate, and even Dr. Strange—the foremost of the sorcerer heroes of Marvel and DC—is far more ambiguous than he once was.

36. The Comte Saint-Germain is a particularly nebulous figure, with much written about him, little of it reliable. The best "modern" source of information about him remains Isabel Cooper-Oakley's *The Comte de St. Germain* (Blauvelt, NY: R. Steiner Publications) and that was first published in 1912.

37. Frederick S. Frank, *The First Gothics: A Critical Guide to the English Gothic Novel* (New York: Garland Publishing, 1987), 24.

38. Walter Scott and Peter Garside, *Guy Mannering* (Edinburgh: Edinburgh University Press, 1999), 15.

39. Mobley, "The Wild Man in the Bible and the Ancient Near East," 217.

40. Timothy Husband and Gloria Gilmore-House, *The Wild Man: Medieval Myth and Symbolism* (New York: Metropolitan Museum of Art, 1980), 1–17.

41. Adrienne Mayor's *The Amazons: Lives and Legends of Warrior Women across the Ancient World* (Princeton, NJ: Princeton University Press, 2014) is a well-documented argument in favor of a Scythian origin for the Amazons, 2,500 years before Homer. If so, and Mayor's case is a convincing one, the "true" Amazons predate *Gilgamesh* by a millennia or more, and whatever legendary heroes and heroines they believed in would be the first superheroes, not Enkidu. But the Scythian heroes and heroines are lost to us, while Enkidu survived and influenced his followers. So the first superhero remains Enkidu.

42. Mayor, *The Amazons: Lives and Legends of Warrior Women Across the Ancient World*, 26–28.

43. Régis Boyer, "Virile Women." In *Companion to Literary Myths: Heroes and Archetypes*, edited by Pierre Brunel (London: Routledge, 1992), 1160–1161.

44. John Friedman, *The Monstrous Races in Medieval Art and Thought* (Syracuse, NY: Syracuse University Press, 2000), 165.

45. Juliann Vitullo, "Contained Conflict: Wild Men and Warrior Women in the Early Italian Epics," *Annali d'italianistica* 12 (1994), 47.

46. Ibid., 48.

47. The first great comic book superheroine was Wonder Woman (first appearance: *All-Star Comics* #8, cover dated Winter 1940–1941, on sale date November 22, 1940), and she was explicitly an Amazon. But she was the 40th superheroine, not the first; the first comic book superheroine was Will Eisner and S. M. Iger's Sheena (first appearance *Jumbo Comics* #1, cover dated September 1938, on sale date July 12, 1938), and the first superpowered superheroine was John Kolb's Ritty (first appearance *Amazing-Man Comics* #5, cover dated September 1939, on sale date August 11, 1939), the female companion to the superhero Minimidget.

48. Interestingly, both Guiborc and Gyburc are Saracen by birth, although Christian by conversion. For those keeping track at home, that means the first person-of-color warrior women appeared before Malory's *Le Morte d'Arthur*. Not only is the tradition of knights of color an old one, so too is the tradition of superheroines of color.

49. Lorraine Kochanske Stock, "'Arms and the (Wo)man' in Medieval Romance: The Gendered Arming of Female Warriors in the 'Roman d'Eneas' and Heldris's 'Roman de Silence,'" *Arthuriana* 5, no. 4 (1995), 73.

50. Christopher Bruce, "Silence," *Arthurian Name Dictionary*, accessed October 3, 2016, http://gorddcymru.org/twilight/camelot/bruce_dictionary/index_s.htm.

51. Vitullo, "Contained Conflict: Wild Men and Warrior Women in the Early Italian Epics," 49.

52. For the completists: I didn't mention, on the grounds that it would be repetitive, the competitors in *Li Tournoiement as Dames* (1261), Formoso (Galaziella's daughter) from the sequel to *Aspramonte* (late 15th century), or for that matter Joan of Arc (ca. 1412–1431), not to mention Bradiamonte from *Historia di Bradiamonte Sorella di Rinaldo* (1489).

53. See, for example, Helen Solterer, "Figures of Female Militancy in Medieval France," *Signs: Journal of Women in Culture and Society* 16.3 (1991), 535–537, and McLaughlin: "but if medieval writers consistently associated the warrior role with masculinity, their attitude towards women who assumed that role changed over the course of the period. Before the end of the 11th century, chroniclers generally noted the activities of women warriors with little comment." Megan McLaughlin, "The Woman Warrior: Gender, Warfare and Society in Medieval Europe," *Women's Studies* 17 (1990), 194. Interestingly, Lillian S. Robinson, in *Monstrous Regiment: The Lady Knight in Sixteenth-Century Epic* (New York: Garland Publishing, 1985) argues that it was additionally a growing consciousness of the different brands of statecraft that led to the rise in appearance of women warriors in epic romance, while Patricia Labalme, in *Beyond Their Sex: Learned Women of the European Past* (New York: New York University Press, 1980) argues that it was a reaction to the growing number of women scholars of the era.

54. Bradamante is also one of the early examples of a woman knight, disguised as a man, becoming the object of another woman's affection, what Terry Castle, in *The Literature of Lesbianism*, calls "'accidental' or 'disguised' female homosexuality." Terry Castle, *The Literature of Lesbianism* (New York: Columbia University Press, 2003), 59. Castle usefully points out that one of Ariosto's sources for *Orlando Furioso* might have been the anonymously written *chanson de geste Huon de Bourdeaux* (ca. 1225), which has a similar scene with the disguised female knight Ide.

55. Margaret Tomalin, *The Fortunes of the Warrior Heroine in Italian Literature: An Index of Emancipation* (Ravenna: Longo Editore, 1982), 16.

56. Tomalin, in "Bradamante and Marfisa," argues that Ariosto ultimately renders Bradamante as a comic figure and Marfisa, "although she is seen in comic situations, has become a credible person, positive, clear-headed, and well-integrated"—that it is Marfisa who "is perfectly content as a virago" and Bradamante who, though both warrior and lover, succumbs to "hysteria" at the destined loss of her independence. Margaret Tomalin, "Bradamante and Marfisa: An Analysis of the 'Guerriere' of the 'Orlando Furioso,'" *The Modern Language Review* 71, no. 3 (1976), 540. If so, and Tomalin makes a good case, then we can theorize that Bradamante was the influential one, rather than Marfisa, because later authors feared unapologetic warrior women like Marfisa and would portray them as partially comic characters, to be mocked as Bradamante is.

57. The conversion of a heathen woman warrior to the True Faith is a motif in medieval and Renaissance Christian literature, as shown. Interestingly, the same is true of Classical Arabic literature. One example of many takes place in "The Story of 'Umar an-Nu'mân," one of the stories of the *Arabian Nights*, when the

invincible female knight Princess Abrîza converts to Islam out of love for the Muslim Prince Sharkân. As Remke Kruk demonstrates, there are numerous warrior woman like Abrîza in Arabic and related literature. Remke Kruk, "Warrior Women in Arabic Popular Romance: Qannâ a bint Muzâ im and Other Valiant Ladies. Part One," *Journal of Arabic Literature* 24, no. 3 (November 1993), 213–230. And as Robert Irwin notes there was substantial plundering of Arabic literature by the authors of medieval European popular literature, and that at least the frame story of *Arabian Nights* was known in medieval literature by the 14th century, with echoes of some parts of *Nights* in *Orlando Furioso* itself. Robert Irwin, *The Arabian Nights: A Companion* (London: I. B. Tauris, 2004), 98. It is certainly possible that Ariosto's portrayal of Bradamante was influenced on some level by the *Nights*' portrayal of Abrîza and the other warrior women in the stories that make up *Nights*.

58. Wright's "Amazons in Elizabethan Literature" makes clear the contradictory ways in which the English of the Elizabethan and Jacobean years viewed the historical Amazons, as everything from monstrously cruel to "aswell in private, as in publicke vertue." Celeste Turner Wright, "The Amazons in Elizabethan Literature," *Studies in Philology* 37, no. 3 (1940), 442. Little surprise, then, that creators of new Amazons in those years chose to emphasize the most harmless aspects of the Amazons at the expense of the dangerous, whether physically (martial ability) or socially (the Amazons having been representative of female rule and used since Christine de Pisan's *The Boke of the Cyte of Ladyes* (ca. 1407) as arguments for and historical justifications of female emancipation).

Of course, as Wright points out, "one reason for such vehemence against fighting-women was doubtless the roughness and immodesty of such Roaring Girls as London actually knew." Wright, "The Amazons in Elizabethan Literature," 448. The Elizabethan and Jacobean writers dealt with their fear of real-life women by making them harmless in fiction and on stage—not a long distance from the way in which male comic book writers have treated women in comic books, through the repellant modern phenomenon of "fridging" a female character—subjecting them to death, rape, depowering, crippling, turning evil, maiming, etc., as a means of providing motivation to a male character. Gail Simone, *Women in Refrigerators*, accessed October 3, 2016, http://lby3.com/wir/. Thankfully, fridging is missing from Elizabethan and Jacobean texts.

59. Karen L. Raber, "Warrior Women in the Plays of Cavendish and Killigrew," *Studies in English Literature, 1500–1900* 40, no. 3 (2000), 413.

60. Kathryn Schwarz, "Amazon Reflections in the Jacobean Queen's Masque," *Studies in English Literature, 1500–1900* 35, no. 2 (1995), 293.

61. Gary Westfahl, "Edmund Spenser." In *The Encyclopedia of Fantasy,* edited by John Clute and John Grant (New York: St. Martin's Press, 1997), 889–890.

62. Edmund Spenser and Thomas P. Roche Jr., *The Faerie Queene* (London: Penguin, 1987), 15.

63. Jason Tondro, *Superheroes of the Round Table: Comics Connections to Medieval and Renaissance Literature* (Jefferson, NC: McFarland, 2011), 48–50.

64. Spenser and Roche Jr., *The Faerie Queene*, 730.

65. Apollonius Rhodius and William H. Race, *Argonautica (Loeb Classical Library)* (Cambridge, MA: Harvard University Press, 2008), 130.

66. Plato the Spoilsport, in his *Minos* (ca. 345 BCE)—which admittedly might not even be Plato's—had to go ahead and rationalize the whole thing, making Talos a mortal rather than a robot: "For Talos made a circuit three times a year through the villages and guarded the laws in them, having laws written down on bronze tablets, for which reason he was called the 'bronze man.'" Plato and W. R. M. Lamb, *Plato in Twelve Volumes*, reprint of the 1925 edition, Perseus Digital Library, accessed October 3, 2016, http://www.perseus.tufts.edu/hopper/text?do c=Perseus:text:1999.01.0180:text=Minos:section=320c&highlight=talos. Fortunately, the *Argonautica*'s version has proven to be the more widespread and the longer lasting.

67. Megan Moore, *Exchanges in Exoticism: Cross-cultural Marriage and the Making of the Mediterranean in Old French Romance* (Toronto: University of Toronto Press, 2014), 61.

68. M. B. Ogle, "The Perilous Bridge and Human Automata," *Modern Language Notes* 35, no. 3 (1920), 131.

69. E. R. Truitt, *Medieval Robots: Mechanism, Magic, Nature, and Art* (Philadelphia: University of Pennsylvania Press, 2015), 104.

70. J. Douglas Bruce, "Human Automata in Classical Tradition and Mediaeval Romance," *Modern Philology* 10, no. 4 (1913), 518.

71. Jonathan Sawday, *Engines of the Imagination: Renaissance Culture and the Rise of the Machine* (London: Routledge, 2007), 193.

72. Truitt, *Medieval Robots: Mechanism, Magic, Nature, and Art*, 58–60.

73. John Webster Spargo, *Virgil the Necromancer: Studies in Virgilian Legends* (Cambridge, MA: Harvard University Press, 1934), 124.

74. Charles Godfrey Leland, *The Unpublished Legends of Virgil* (New York: Macmillan, 1900), 152.

75. Had Leland, the collector/editor of *The Unpublished Legends of Virgil*, from which "Virgil, the Wicked Princess, and the Iron Man" comes, been able to provide any kind of historical source for the story, any kind of proof that the story was indeed of medieval origin, then "Virgil, the Wicked Princess, and the Iron Man" would indeed deserve credit as the origin of the artificial justice-dealer, the automaton superhero. But Leland is deliberately ambiguous about where he gathered his stories from, even claiming that "they were gathered . . . chiefly among witches or fortune-tellers." Leland, *The Unpublished Legends of Virgil*, xiii. Given that the veracity of Leland's sources has been disputed before, and the similarity of the "Iron Man" of this story to Spenser's Talus, I can only conclude that *if* Leland actually found a native Italian source for "Virgil, the Wicked Princess, and the Iron Man," and didn't make it up himself, then the source was drawing upon memories of Spenser to create a new Virgil legend, rather than repeating one that was legitimately medieval (or older) in origin.

76. Spenser and Roche Jr., *The Faerie Queene*, 730.

77. The number of critics who have argued over what Talus represents is extensive, and readers are virtually invited by Spenser and the critical apparatus around *The Faerie Queene* to pick a side, any side, when it comes to Talus. One intriguing argument is that Spenser was working out his guilt over having taken part in the suppression of the Irish rebellion by having Artegall as the "idealistic justification of violence" against the rebels and Talus as the "image of effective violence against the rebellion." Lynsey McCulloch, "Antique Myth, Early Modern Mechanism: The Secret History of Spenser's Iron Man." In *The Automaton in English Renaissance Literature*, edited by Wendy Beth Hyman (Farnham, Surrey: Ashgate, 2011), 66.

78. Spenser and Roche, Jr., *The Faerie Queene*, 732.

79. Ibid., 790.

80. Ibid., 771.

81. Talus's ontological status—human/metal hybrid? Cyborg? Animated statuary? Robot?—is, like so much else about Talus, a subject of dispute. Lynsey McCulloch calls him a "cyborg," although this is, I think, because this allows her to bring in the work of theorist Donna Haraway and to discuss Talus as a "border figure." Lynsey McCulloch, "Antique Myth, Early Modern Mechanism: The Secret History of Spenser's Iron Man," 69. I disagree; I think the text of the *Faerie Queene* makes clear that there is nothing biological about him—he lacks even Talos's fleshy weakness, the vein in his heel—and that he is as completely artificial as the animated statuary of the inhabitants of the Bower of Bliss in Book II. This makes Talus a human-shaped robot—an android—rather than a part-metal, part-flesh creature—the cyborg McCulloch labels him.

82. Patricia Gartenberg, "An Elizabethan Wonder Woman: The Life and Fortunes of Long Meg of Westminster," *The Journal of Popular Culture* 17, no. 3 (1983), 51.

83. Simon Shepherd makes the point that "we have met before the woman who tames a braggart male's sexual aspirations by physical punishment. We have met before the sudden, theatrical, release of long female hair. These are the archetypal attributes of the warrior woman." Simon Shepherd, *Amazons and Warrior Women: Varieties of Feminism in Seventeenth-Century Drama* (New York: St. Martin's, 1981), 70. As Shepherd goes on to explain, the story of Long Meg predated Spenser's *Faerie Queene* by eight years and may—only "may"—have been influenced by Italian epics; rather, Long Meg is part of the English tradition of fictional warrior women and real women posing as warriors in warriors' garb, the foremost example of which was Queen Elizabeth's visit to Tilbury in August 1588 to encourage the English troops to resist the Spanish Armada. During the visit, Elizabeth was dressed as an Amazon queen, complete with truncheon, gauntlet, and gorget. Shepherd, *Amazons and Warrior Women: Varieties of Feminism in Seventeenth-Century Drama*, 22. Shepherd emphasizes Long Meg's experience in the campaign against the French, and casts her experience fighting crime and evil as "a form of lower-class resistance against the dominant order of society." Shepherd, *Amazons and Warrior Women: Varieties of Feminism in Seventeenth-Century Drama*, 73. This aspect does not in any way preclude Long Meg being a protosuperhero.

Dianne Dugaw's *Warrior Women and Popular Balladry, 1650–1850* (Chicago: University of Chicago Press, 1996) is revelatory with regard to the sheer number of cross-dressing women warriors who appeared in the ballads of the 17th, 18th, and 19th century. Women dressed as men and going to war were popular subjects for the British of those centuries—for the Americans less so, but to a still significant degree—and what Dugaw calls the "Female Warrior" was a recognizable character type (even a cliché) in British and American popular culture during those centuries. It should come as no surprise, therefore, that superheroines appeared not long after superheroes—women warriors in costumes were a part of the Zeitgeist. But, as mentioned, the cross-dressing women warriors of the popular ballads were soldiers and sailors rather than crime fighters, and lacked the heroic mission that is necessary for protosuperheroes and protosuperheroines.

84. Some modern novelists, like Ellen Galford, in *Moll Cutpurse, Her True History: A Novel* (Ithaca, NY: Firebrand, 1985), claim Frith as a lesbian—an assertion that can't be proven or disproven, given the ambiguity around Frith's sexual life, and a statement that, like a lot of other critical claims, says more about the author and the tenor of the times than it does about the subject addressed. A more considered judgment is made by Terry Castle, in *The Literature of Lesbianism*: "of Frith's amorous inclinations we know nothing, though her masculine tastes and apparent antipathy to marriage suggest a possibly unorthodox sexual makeup." Terry Castle, *The Literature of Lesbianism* (New York: Columbia University Press, 2003), 155.

85. Bryan Reynolds and Janna Segal, "The Reckoning of Moll Cutpurse: A Transversal Enterprise." In *Rogues and Early Modern English Culture*, edited by Craig Dionne and Steve Mentz (Ann Arbor: University of Michigan, 2004), 77.

86. Gustav Ungerer, "Mary Frith, Alias Moll Cutpurse, in Life and Literature," *Shakespeare Studies* 28 (2000), 46.

87. See Lincoln B. Faller's *Turned to Account: The Forms and Functions of Criminal Biography in Late Seventeenth- and Early Eighteenth-Century England* (Cambridge: Cambridge University Press, 1987) for more on this.

88. E. J. Hobsbawm, *Bandits* (1969; reprint, New York: New Press, 2000), 127.

89. T. C. W. Blanning, *The Pursuit of Glory: Europe, 1648–1815* (New York: Viking, 2007), 176.

90. Ibid., 176–177.

91. Robert Muchembled and Jean Birrell, *A History of Violence: From the End of the Middle Ages to the Present* (Cambridge, UK: Polity, 2012), 256.

92. Ibid., 256–257.

93. Jess Nevins, *The Encyclopedia of Fantastic Victoriana* (Austin, TX: Monkeybrain, 2004), 596.

94. Frank, *The First Gothics: A Critical Guide to the English Gothic Novel*, 359.

95. The ancient Greek worshippers of Dionysus in Athens wore masks during ceremonial rites and celebrations, and, of course, Greek actors had a variety of masks at hand. It doesn't take too much of a leap of imagination to picture Greek conspirators plotting while masked.

96. Levi's *Histoire de la Magie* (1860) describes the Vehm as "masked and wearing black vestures." Eliphas Levi and Arthur Edward Waite, *The History of Magic: Including a Clear and Precise Exposition of Its Procedure, Its Rites and Its Mysteries* (Cambridge: Cambridge University Press, 2013), 253.

97. Charles William Heckethorn's *The Secret Societies of All Ages and Countries* (London: Richard Bentley and Son, 1875), 150.

98. Interestingly, Zschokke's *Die Schwarzen Brüder* (his first novel) "ends with a vision of Europe in the 23rd century, its prosperity secured by the philanthropic Black Brothers." Patrick Bridgwater, *German Gothic Novel in Anglo-German Perspective* (New York: Rodopi, 2013), 465. One of a number of science fiction novels appearing in late 18th-century Germany, *Die Schwarzen Brüder* and its science fictional companions never appeared in English but nonetheless deserve closer examination than they currently have received for possible influence on English authors. Mary Shelley "is said to have read little German" but had "easy access to German Gothics" via her husband. Bridgwater, *German Gothic Novel in Anglo-German Perpsective*, 474. Shelley's *Frankenstein*, it can be argued, owes much to a number German authors. Could Jane Loudon have read *Die Schwarzen Brüder*, or Julius von Voss's *Ini: Ein Roman aus dem 21. Jahrhunder* (1810), before writing *The Mummy!: Or a Tale of the Twenty-Second Century* (1827)?

99. Frank, *The First Gothics: A Critical Guide to the English Gothic Novel*, 130.

100. D. H. Lawrence, *Sea and Sardinia* (Cambridge: Cambridge University Press, 2002), 188.

101. The Beati Paoli, as a specifically Italian creation, had enough longevity that they were still appearing as Costumed Avengers in fiction serials and novels in the 1930s in Italy.

102. Christian Vulpius, *The Life, Surprising Adventures, and Most Remarkable Escapes of Rinaldo Rinaldini, Captain of a Banditti of Robbers* (London: Ann Lemoine, 1801), 122–123.

103. Ibid., 47.

104. Ann Radcliffe, *The Italian; or, The Confessional of the Black Penitents; a Romance* (London: T. Cadell and W. Davies, 1811), 69–70.

105. Frank, *The First Gothics: A Critical Guide to the English Gothic Novel*, 14.

106. Arguably Harun al-Rashid, in the 10th-century Arab stories that later appeared in *The Thousand and One Nights*, and Duke Vincentio, in Shakespeare's *Measure for Measure* (1604), with their practice of roaming their cities at night in disguise, are predecessors to the modern hidden master.

107. Paul Lewis, "Attaining Masculinity: Charles Brockden Brown and the Women Warriors of the 1790s," *Early American Literature* 40, no. 1 (2005), 53.

108. Julie Wheelwright's *Amazons and Military Maids: Women Who Dressed as Men in Pursuit of Life, Liberty and Happiness* (London: Pandora, 1989) is a good introduction to the history of modern cross-dressing women warriors.

109. Charles Brockden Brown, *Ormond; or, the Secret Witness* (New York: American Book Company, 1937), 167.

110. Ibid., 170.

111. Paul Lewis, "Attaining Masculinity: Charles Brockden Brown and the Women Warriors of the 1790s," 40.

112. Ibid., 46.

113. As Dror Wahrman shows, the "topos of the female knight or warrior" was long-standing, going back to the beginning of the 18th century. Dror Wahrman, "Percy's Prologue: From Gender Play to Gender Panic in Eighteenth-Century England," *Past & Present* 159 (May 1998), 119. Near the end of the century there was a backlash against the woman warrior—more specifically, her use of men's clothing, which had the practical effect of making gender boundaries seem like something that could be violated simply by putting on a pair of breeches. By the end of the century, "gender collapsed into sex; no longer given the leeway of cultural play, gender categories were now widely expected to mirror the presumed rigidity and stability of sexual ones." Dror Wahrman, "Percy's Prologue: From Gender Play to Gender Panic in Eighteenth-Century England," 156. Even the active, willful, independent heroines of the Gothics were still obedient to gender categories, with women like Victoria de Loredani, in Charlotte Dacre's transgressive Gothic *Zofloya; Or, The Moor* (1806) being remarkable by their rarity. It is this trend which Martinette de Beauvais bucked.

114. Stephanie Bryant, "America's Amazons: Women Soldiers of the American Civil War," *History in the Making*, 14, accessed October 3, 2016, https://historyitm .files.wordpress.com/2013/08/bryant.pdf.

115. Sir Walter Scott, *The Black Dwarf* (London: William Blackwood, 1816), 79.

116. James Reed, *Sir Walter Scott: Landscape and Locality* (London: A&C Black, 2014), 100.

117. Susan Tyler Hitchcock, *Frankenstein: A Cultural History* (New York: W. W. Norton, 2007), 93.

118. Stan Lee directly claimed Frankenstein as a direct inspiration for the Hulk. Coogan, *Superhero: The Secret Origin of a Genre*, 40.

Chapter 4

1. Mikhail Bakhtin's *Rabelais and His World* (Bloomington, IN: Indiana University Press, 1984) is, of course, the starting point for studies of this "carnivalesque" cultural dynamic. Jacqueline Howard's *Reading Gothic Fiction: A Bakhtinian Approach* (Oxford: Clarendon, 1994) is a good starting place for those interested in applying Bakhtinian theory to the Gothic novel.

2. Peter McPhee, *A Social History of France, 1789–1914* (New York: Palgrave Macmillan, 2004), 157.

3. Ibid., 157.

4. Kevin Kenny, *Making Sense of the Molly Maguires* (New York: Oxford University Press, 1998), 22.

5. While superheroes generally wear some form of distinctive outfit—usually a full-body costume—cross-dressing is comparatively rare, more common with women characters wearing men's clothing (like Tarpe Mill's Miss

Fury, for Marvel, Sean Catherine Derek, Laren Bright, and Mitch Brian's Renee Montoya in her guise as The Question, for DC, Dan Curtis Johnson and J. H. Williams III's Cameron Chase, for DC, and Warren Ellis and Tom Raney's Jenny Sparks, for Wildstorm) than men wearing women's clothing (the only two examples of which are Tarpe Mills's Cat Man, for Centaur, and Art Pinaji-an's Madam Fatal, for Quality). This, of course, hearkens back to the many heroic women of Renaissance prose fiction and epics, Amazons and warrior women alike, who wear men's clothing so they can adventure—an imposture that began, in the early works, so that the woman could get out of the house, "risk sexual adventure, get rescued, tempt men, or prove their own virtue." Helen Hackett, "Suffering Saints or Ladies Errant?? Women Who Travel for Love in Renaissance Prose Fiction," *The Yearbook of English Studies* 41, no. 1 (2011), 126. This eventually became a means by which women, through "a disturbing active virginity," could preserve their chastity but also recoup their own sexuality. Helen Hackett, "Suffering Saints or Ladies Errant?? Women Who Travel for Love in Renaissance Prose Fiction," 128. "Virginity ceases to denote submission and begins to denote revolt." Richard Halpern, "Puritanism and Maenadism in *A Mask*." In *Rewriting the Renaissance: The Discourses of Sexual Difference in Early Modern Europe*, edited by Margaret W. Ferguson, Maureen Quilligan, and Nancy J. Vickers (Chicago: University of Chicago Press, 1986), 94. Virginity thereby became "simultaneously . . . menaced and menacing." Helen Hackett, "Suffering Saints or Ladies Errant?? Women Who Travel for Love in Renaissance Prose Fiction," 128.

6. Chester L. Quarles, *The Ku Klux Klan and Related American Racialist and Antisemitic Organizations: A History and Analysis* (Jefferson, NC: McFarland, 1999), 34.

7. Ibid., 37.

8. James M. Hutchisson, *Poe* (Jackson: University of Mississippi, 2005), 114.

9. This is the perception, of course, rather than the reality. Official miscarriages of justice are as old a British tradition as the bobbies, and it can be argued that Dickens's famous 1850 and 1851 puff-pieces in *Household Words* about the new breed of British detective—which particularly lionized Inspector Charles Frederick Field, the model for *Bleak House*'s Inspector Bucket—were propaganda designed to cover up what the men and women of the street knew to be so: that British policemen of the time were more concerned with closing cases rather than finding those responsible for the crimes.

For Americans, conversely, the perception that independents are the best at enforcing justice and preventing and solving crime likely comes from the Southern tradition of slave patrols, which began in the late 18th century—the first formal slave patrol was in the Carolina colonies in 1704—and evolved into anti-freedmen vigilante groups working out of police departments in the South in the post–Civil War era and as late as the 1930s.

10. Hutchisson, *Poe*, 115.

11. Frank, *The First Gothics: A Critical Guide to the English Gothic Novel*, 92.

12. Ibid., 92.

13. Thomas De Quincey, *Klosterheim: Or, The Masque* (Boston: Whittemore, Niles, and Hall, 1855), 144.

14. Arguably, the Superman analogue The High, from Warren Ellis and Tom Raney's run on Wildstorm's *Stormwatch* (1996–1997), and The High's team of superhumans, should be included here. They are the antagonists of Stormwatch, and commit violence to achieve their goal—but their goal is a techno-Utopia, and the preferred inscribed narrative of *Stormwatch* is that Stormwatch is actually wrong to oppose them.

15. Nathaniel Hawthorne, "The Gray Champion," *Twice-Told Tales* (Boston: Fields, Osgood, 1871), 13.

16. Ibid., 18.

17. Ibid., 19.

18. Ibid., 22.

19. Ibid., 24.

20. Quoting Coogan, "the Angel of Hadley, General William Goffe, who in 1675 is reported to have suddenly appeared, rallied the inhabitants of Hadley, Massachusetts, and led them against an Indian attack during the King Philip's War, and then vanished." Coogan, *Superhero: The Secret Origin of a Genre*, 150. Goffe was a regicide (he was one of 59 signatories to King Charles I's death warrant in 1649) in hiding in New England, being protected by Increase Mather among others. Legend has it that Goffe appeared, rallied the militia in the town of Hadley, Massachusetts., and led them to victory against the more numerous Wampanoags before disappearing. Nineteenth century historians debunked the story, although at least one 20th century historian has revisited the story of the Angel of Hadley and concluded that it is at least possible that something similar to the legend took place and that it was covered up by Goffe's protectors.

From a broader perspective, the "Angel of Hadley" story, like "The Gray Champion" itself, falls into the category of stories about revenant avengers, the kind covered by E300–E510 in Stith Thompson's *Motif-Index of Folk-Literature* (Bloomington, IN: Indiana University Press, 1955–1958). "The Gray Champion" stands apart from similar myths because of its specifically American orientation and its position as the point from which folktales about revenant avengers transitioned into popular literature about Costumed Avengers. As mentioned in this chapter and in Chapter 5, "The Gray Champion" was in all likelihood influential on later writers of heroic literature, especially the dime novels but not excepting superhero comic books, because of Hawthorne's fame and because of the story's position as the lead story in *Twice-Told Tales*. (The Gray Champion most obviously stands as a model for Kurt Busiek and Brent Anderson's Old Soldier in *Kurt Busiek's Astro City*.)

21. Robert Montgomery Byrd, *Nick of the Woods* (London: Richard Bentley, 1837), 63.

22. Ibid., 64.

23. It should be noted that Thomas de Quincey, in his Gothic revenge fantasy "The Avenger" (1838), takes the killer vigilante plot of *Nick of the Woods* and

transplants it into the modern era, setting his story in a university town in 1816. "The Avenger" is about a Jewish man who avenges the murder of his family members by methodically killing, years later, those responsible, who by that time are elderly, well-respected burghers. As Chaplin points out in "De Quincey's Gothic Innovations," de Quincey's story "implicitly calls into question a newly emerging political discourse of progress, rights, and hospitality." Sue Chaplin, "De Quincey's Gothic Innovations: 'The Avenger', 1838," *Romanticism* 17, no. 3 (2011), 323. This discourse has become an unstated assumption about the law and the possibility of juridical correctness in our time, an assumption that the Punisher and the other killer vigilantes question through their actions.

Slavoj Žižek, in *Violence*, differentiates between "subjective violence," which is "experienced as such against the background of a non-violent zero level," and "objective violence," which is the systemic violence "inherent to this 'normal' state of affairs." Slavoj Žižek, *Violence* (London: Picador, 2008), 2. Objective violence is what governments arrogate to themselves to carry out; killer vigilantes like the Punisher question this arrogation and take the role of wielder-of-violence for themselves. Maximilian, de Quincey's titular Avenger, provides an early example of this, set at a time when the law functions much as it does in superhero comics, unlike *Nick of the Woods* and its frontier setting.

But this book is about the influence of authors and characters on the lineage of superheroes, and "The Avenger" cannot be claimed to have much, being obscure even upon publication. De Quincey's famous essay "On Murder" was far more influential on detective fiction, and through that on superhero fiction. Maximilian is a Punisher-like serial killer, but the Punisher et al. come from the killer vigilante tradition begun by Nick of the Woods.

24. Toni Johnson-Woods, "Roman-Feuilleton." In *Encyclopedia of the Novel*, edited by Paul E. Schellinger, Christopher Hudson, and Marijke Rijsberman (Chicago: Fitzroy Dearborn, 1998), 1108.

25. Appearing in the United States very soon after Sue's *Mystères* began was George Lippard's infamous porno-Gothic *The Quaker City; or, the Monks of Monk Hall* (1844–1845), what Stephen Knight calls "both the first response to Sue's initiative outside France and also the first Amerian fiction to deal in detail with the complexity and corruptions of the modern city." Stephen Knight, *The Mysteries of the Cities: Urban Crime Fiction in the Nineteenth Century* (Jefferson, NC: McFarland, 2011), 132. Lippard, like Sue, portrayed his city—Philadelphia—as an environment in need of a ruler, a one true king. But unlike Sue, Lippard does not give the reader hope in the form of a Rodolphe character. For Lippard, the city was an unrelievedly negative space, a Bad Place similar to the haunted castles of numerous Gothics, a place where nothing good can ever happen except a merciful, peaceful death.

It is notable that the French author invented the hidden urban ruler for the city in distress, while the American author chose to portray the city as a place not only without a king but undeserving of one, and incapable of being saved by anything short of an apocalyptic cleansing by fire. Virtually every later American author of urban fiction would choose the French author to be influenced by rather than the American—a rare case in which a French author's influence on superhero comics is significantly greater than their American counterpart's. But *The Quaker City*, despite being aesthetically superior to the many American knockoffs of Sue's *Mystères* and despite being one of the first American best sellers (27 editions of *The Quaker City* were issued through 1850, with total sales approaching 200,000), was not influential on later authors, and Sue, via the imitations of *Mystères*, was. Knight, *The Mysteries of the Cities: Urban Crime Fiction in the Nineteenth Century*, 133. Sue offered a simpler template to use than Lippard, and Sue gave the reader (and imitators and future writers of heroic serial fiction) a memorable hero to make use of and model their own heroes upon, while Lippard offered only another memorable villain. The Devil-Bug, the central figure of *The Quaker City*, is what Knight calls "an almost meticulous reversal of Rodolphe." Knight, *The Mysteries of the Cities: Urban Crime Fiction in the Nineteenth Century*, 134. Devil-Bug is a fascinating study in how to construct a post-1830 Gothic villain, but he is hardly suitable as a figure to build a heroic tale around, while Rodolphe is. Likewise, Lippard's Philadelphia may have been an American location in real life, but writers (and readers) preferred (and prefer) their cities to be portrayed with the potential for hopeful transformation, as Sue portrayed Paris and that Lippard refused to portray Philadelphia as having.

26. John Clute and Richard Grant's *Encyclopedia of Fantasy* uses the phrase "hidden monarch" in a slightly different—though relevant here—fashion:

> When King Richard returns incognito from exile and unveils himself to Robin Hood, a monarch who had been hidden is recognized, and the Land is healed. But Richard already *is* a monarch, and knows he is. As a Plot Device or Topos in fantasy, the HM motif commonly follows a somewhat different pattern: the HM is a youngster who does not know his (less frequently her) identity or destiny . . .
>
> Most HMs are Ugly Ducklings when first met; Wart in *The Sword in the Stone* is certainly one. They are children occupying a lowly position in the world; they are badly dressed; they are mocked; they have unappeasable longings for some other state, but their Bondage—their immolation in the wrong identity—seems unloosenable, often having been imposed by Magic at the behest of a jealous Dark Lord . . .
>
> The wish-fulfilment function of the HM device is obvious. An HM is a figure easy for young readers to identify with. But his function is wider than that in some texts, where his ascension to the throne carries a promise of profound transformation, a confirmation of Healing—a healing function which may in fact be literal. (John Clute, "Hidden Monarch," *Encyclopedia of Fantasy*, 466)

The Hidden Monarch trope is a familiar one from the Gothics; the "external Gothic" is concerned with the home: the lineage and patrimony of the hero, his disinheritance by the villain, and the revelation of the hero's true identity and the restoration of his estate. Often the home is not just a castle, but—as in De Quincey's *Klosterheim*—a city or kingdom. Rodolphe von Gerolstein is a traditional Hidden Monarch in that he returns to Gerolstein to claim his throne after his hero's journey in disguise. In superhero comics, however, that are stuck in a perpetual second act because of the demands of the audience and the exigencies of the capitalist publishing system, the Hidden Monarch never unveils himself or herself, never comes into his or her kingdom, never *officially* rules. Batman and Daredevil are forced into perpetual secrecy in their rulership. Only superhero comics set in the future, like Mark Waid and Alex Ross's *Kingdom Come* (1996, for DC), or comics whose storylines are designed to have short-lived and reversible consequences, like Brian Bendis's run on *Daredevil* (2001–2005), are allowed to change this dynamic. All other comics with urban superhero rulers are Hidden Monarchs.

27. Umberto Eco, *The Role of the Reader: Explorations in the Semiotics of Texts* (Bloomington, IN: Indiana University Press, 1994), 131.

28. Now is as good a time as any to address Italian cultural theorist Antonio Gramsci's claim that *Les Mysteres de Paris* provides a model for the behavior of the Italian Fascists of the 20th century. Quoting from Gramsci's writing in *Selections from Cultural Writings* (1985), Steve Jones summarizes:

> Gramsci sees a clear relationship between the text's narrative drive and the behaviour of the Fascists. This, he writes, "is the romantic setting in which the fascist mentality is formed" (Gramsci 1985: 346n). Just as Mussolini imposed a Caesarist solution to the weakness of Italian social democracy, so Prince Rodolphe is a Caesarist figure who "paralyses" the class struggle. *The Mysteries of Paris* and similar texts both produce and mimic fascism since they share its "unbalanced imagination, quivering of heroic fury [and] psychological restlessness." Like fascism, this adventure fiction is both nostalgic and committed to a violent reordering of society. (Steve Jones, *Antonio Gramsci* [London: Routledge, 2006], 105)

This is true to a limited degree—certainly of heroic characters who are Hidden Monarchs in the Clutean sense, as *Abällino*'s Count Rosalvo and De Quincey's Masque and Rodolphe are. But critics need to be careful of extending this claim, of a commitment to a "violent reordering of society," to superhero comics. The hidden masters, Batman and Daredevil and so on, have *already* reordered society to their liking; their Fascist impulses are limited to wanting to hold on to what they already have, as ruling Gotham or Hell's Kitchen is already almost too much for them to bear, and extending their rule to other cities or even parts of their own city is—as they acknowledge—beyond their capabilities. The vast majority of superheroes, however, don't want to *reorder* society, but want to defend the current order. Superman is ultimately a defender of the status quo, a conservative—but not a Fascist, not someone in favor of changing the way things are. Superman et al. may be desperately lacking politically from a left/liberal/progressive point of view, but they are not Fascists.

29. J. L. Heilbron, "Geometry," in *The Oxford Guide to the History of Physics and Astronomy*, edited by John L. Heilbron (Oxford: Oxford University Press, 2005), 131.

30. Alexandre Dumas, Umberto Eco, and Peter Washington, *The Count of Monte Cristo* (New York: Knopf, 2009), xiv.

31. Eco, *The Role of the Reader: Explorations in the Semiotics of Texts*, 113–114.

32. See John Adcock, "Spring-Heeled Jack in Popular Culture, 1838–2005," *Yesterday's Papers*, and Mike Dash, "Spring-heeled Jack: To Victorian Bugaboo from Suburban Ghost," *Mike Dash*, accessed October 3, 2016, http://mikedash .com/extras/forteana/shj-about/, for more complete histories of Spring-Heeled Jack's career.

33. Adcock, "Spring-Heeled Jack in Popular Culture, 1838–2005."

34. Alfred Coates, *Spring-heel'd Jack: the Terror of London a Romance of the Nineteenth Century*, quoted in Jess Nevins, *The Encyclopedia of Fantastic Victoriana* (Austin, TX: MonkeyBrain: 2005), 821.

35. Obviously a large claim, but consider: *Three Times Dead* (later released as *The Trail of the Serpent*) is a murder mystery. It is explicitly a murder mystery, rather than a satire of the law, as Dickens's *Bleak House* was, or the story of an inheritance lost and regained, as Lord Bulwer-Lytton's *Night and Morning* (1841) and R. D. Blackmore's *Clara Vaughan* (1854) were. *Three Times Dead* places the crime and its solution at the center of the plot, rather than relegating them to secondary status. *Three Times Dead* is not a whodunit; the reader is aware from the beginning who is responsible for the crime. Rather, *Three Times Dead* is about a crime, those involved with the crime, the aftermath of the crime, and the resolution of the crime. Previous novels—protomysteries all—had used these individual elements. Only *Three Times Dead* synthesized them into a whole.

36. Metta Victoria Victor, *The Dead Letter* (Createspace, 2014), 143.

37. Ibid., 45.

38. Not to give away the narrative twists here, but it bears emphasizing: chapbooks became penny bloods. Dime novels inherited the weekly issuance method from the penny bloods. The pulps imitated the dime novels. And comic books imitated the pulps. The commercial model of cheap fiction for sale on the same day every week, week after week, year 'round, goes back over nearly 200 years—as do the exigencies of a weekly or monthly demand for creativity leading to writer and artist burnout. And, for that matter, publishers of these periodicals growing rich off the work of writers and artists who later starve to death—as Frederic van Rensselaer Dey (author of the stories of Nick Carter's golden age) did.

39. Judith Flanders, "Penny Dreadfuls," *Discovering Literature: Romantics and Victorians*, accessed October 3, 2016, https://www.bl.uk/romantics-and-victorians /articles/penny-dreadfuls.

40. Anonymous and Christopher Banham, *The Skeleton Crew, Or, Wildfire Ned* (Brighton, UK: Victorian Secrets, 2015), 38.

41. J. Randolph Cox, *The Dime Novel Companion: A Source Book* (Westport, CT: Greenwood, 2000), xiii–xiv.

42. In a modest way Harlan Halsey, via Old Sleuth, created the multicharacter fictional universe via these crossovers with other series characters. The crossover—the appearance of one character in another character's text—was hardly a new concept; the Greeks had done it (with Jason and the Argonauts), Balzac had done it (in his *La Comédie Humaine* cycle of novels), and various American authors had done it in novels (such as Mary Cowden Clarke's *Kit Bam's Adventures,* 1849, in which the titular retired sailor tells stories of his encounters with characters from Greek myth, the Arabian Nights, *Othello, The Tempest,* "The Rime of the Ancient Mariner," and *Frankenstein*). But Halsey was the first to use an ongoing, open-ended series character in this way, anticipating the pulp universes of Street & Smith's Western pulps and then the superhero universes of Marvel, DC, and Fawcett.

43. Graham Seal, *The Outlaw Legend: A Cultural Tradition in Britain, America, and Australia* (Cambridge, UK: Cambridge University Press, 1996), 96.

44. Women began working as floor detectives in New York City department stores in 1866, were employed as Pinkerton agents in the late 1860s, were used as unofficial police agents in the early 1870s, and became common as private detectives in the 1880s. These women commonly wore men's clothing as disguises on cases, with some of them dressing like men even in their offices.

45. "The Man in the Black Cloak, or, In Search of the John Street Jewels," *The Boys of New York; a paper for Young Americans* 11, no. 569 (New York: Frank Tousey, 1886), 11.

46. Ibid., 4.

47. Joseph L. Rainone's Introduction to *The Man in the Black Cloak, or, In Search of the John Street Jewels* (Baldwin, NY: Almond Press, 2009) makes a convincing argument by way of the weight of indirect evidence that Gibson was aware of Doughty's work and used the Man in the Black Cloak as a model for the Shadow.

48. Walter B. Gibson, "The Whispering Eyes," *The Shadow* 55, no. 1 (New York: Street and Smith, 1949), 32.

49. While detective stories were quite popular in the dime novels in the 1880s—17 percent of all dime novel titles were mysteries in 1879, 24 percent in 1884, and 24 percent in 1889—the mystery genre was in a peculiar position in the mid-1880s. Anna Katherine Green's *The Leavenworth Case* (1878), arguably the first American best-selling novel, had established the mystery as respectable reading for middle-class adults, but *The Leavenworth Mystery* and the work of Metta Victor had, if anything, made the detective novel and the series detective *too* respectable—both were marketed to the middle and upper classes, unlike the dime novels—so that dime novel publishers had reason to question whether their lower-class audience would be interested in what the middle-class audience was consuming.

50. The two reinventions of Nick Carter, in the 1960s as a James Bond lift, and then in the 1970s as the mass-murderer "the Killmaster," were desecrations of the original Nick Carter and are essentially separate characters from the dime novel detective.

Chapter 5

1. Mary Shelley, D. L. Macdonald, and Kathleen Scherf, *Frankenstein: The Original 1818 Text* (Calgary: Broadview Press, 1999), 82.

2. Anne K. Mellor, "*Frankenstein*, Racial Science, and the Yellow Peril," *Nineteenth Century Concepts* 23 (2001), 4.

3. Ibid., 2–3.

4. Varney is the most emotionally complex monster character of 19th-century English literature, and the cumulative effect of *Varney the Vampyre* on the reader is of a sneaking sympathy for the tragic Varney, who loathes his own cursed un-life and tries repeatedly (failing each time) to end his own existence. *Varney*, the first vampire novel in the English language, may be one of the two best-known penny dreadfuls, but it has a dire reputation, one that it does not deserve. The famous line from the 1931 film of *Dracula*, "to die, to be *really* dead, that must be glorious!" and the sentiments behind it—sentiments common to much modern vampire fiction—ultimately come from *Varney the Vampyre*.

5. Charles Maturin, *The Albigenses, A Romance* (London: Hurst, Robinson and Co., 1824), 263.

6. Billy Batson changes into Captain Marvel by saying "Shazam;" Ben Grimm, at various times in his superhero career, can change into the Thing by wishing it so; Bruce Banner turns into the Hulk through rage; and so on. In a broader sense, any comic book change scene, where the protagonist transforms from their mundane self into their superself—Clark Kent ripping off his shirt in the phone booth, Bruce Wayne changing into the Batsuit, etc.—owes a great deal to the symbolic transformation of the *doppelgänger* and the werewolf.

7. Coogan, *Superhero: The Secret Origin of a Genre*, 149.

8. Gavaler, *On the Origin of Superheroes: From the Big Bang to Action Comics, Issue 1*, 59.

9. And technically the Gray Champion does not even seem to be human, but rather a spirit of some kind: recall that "should domestic tyranny oppress us, or the invader's step pollute our soil, still may the Gray Champion come." Nathaniel Hawthorne, "The Gray Champion," *Twice-Told Tales* (Boston: Fields, Osgood, 1871), 24. This suggests that he is some form of patriotic spirit or ghost, a new Angel of Hadley, or a Sleeping King/king under the mountain/King Arthur type of character, rather than an ordinary human. If the Gray Champion isn't mortal, he can hardly be called a superhuman or even a superhero.

10. E. F. Bleiler and Richard Bleiler, *Science-Fiction, the Early Years: A Full Description of More Than 3,000 Science-Fiction Stories from Earliest Times to the Appearance of the Genre Magazines in 1930: With Author, Title, and Motif Indexes* (Kent, OH: Kent State University Press, 1990), 792.

11. John Tresch, writing about the new machines and techniques for measuring, displaying, and harnessing energy during the 1810s, 1820s, and 1830s, says that

historians of science have recently associated these techniques with an emerging scientific ideology of "mechanical objectivity," in which automatic machines were valued because they removed the effects of human error and idiosyncrasy; such devices have been seen as weapons in the ever-renewed campaign to purify knowledge of bias, metaphysical error, and superstition. (John Tresch, "The Machine Awakens: The Science and Politics of the Fantastic Automaton," *French Historical Studies* 34, no. 1 [2011], 95)

Webb's *The Mummy!* and its clockwork justice system can be seen as a manifestation of "mechanical objectivity." Intriguingly, this ideology communicated itself remarkably slowly to law enforcement in England and the United States—the Germans had their *polizeiwissenschaft* from the early 18th century, but it took the English and Americans decades to begin to grapple with this position, and police hostility to "mechanical objectivity" remains common to this day. Perhaps not surprisingly, clockwork/robot/automata police were absent from 19th-century heroic or imaginative fiction.

12. Cathy S. Gelbin, *The Golem Returns: From German Romantic Literature to Global Jewish Culture, 1808–2008* (Ann Arbor: University of Michigan, 2011), 45.

13. Catherine Mathière, "The Golem," in *Companion to Literary Myths: Heroes and Archetypes*, edited by Pierre Brunel (London: Routledge, 1992), 473.

14. Bleiler and Bleiler, *Science Fiction: The Early Years,* 199.

15. Gelbin, *The Golem Returns: From German Romantic Literature to Global Jewish Culture, 1808–2008*, 71.

16. Ibid., 73.

17. Frederick S. Frank, *The First Gothics: A Critical Guide to the English Gothic Novel* (New York: Garland Publishing, 1987), 353.

18. In the words of John Sutherland, the *eminence grise* of Victorian criticism: "It is not easy to sum up Bulwer-Lytton's achievement. He was overvalued in his own day, and has been under-valued by posterity. He can plausibly claim to be the father of the English detective novel, science fiction, the fantasy novel, the thriller, and the domestic realism novel." John Sutherland, *The Longman Companion to Victorian Fiction* (Harlow, England: Pearson Longman, 2009), 394.

19. The delicate position of pulp and comic book publishers in the 1920s and 1930s deserves consideration. Publishers generally had long memories for things like government crackdowns and the imposition of government censorship, both of which happened in the 1880s after a moral panic ensued over the leftist politics of the dime novels and would happen again in the 1930s when the "weird menace" pulps grew too explicit. Publishers were not interested in experiencing that all over again, or any kind of government interference, which likely would have taken place had pulp and comic book writers been as willing to mouth Rosicrucian and theosophist propaganda as the Victorians had been. Further complicating matters for pulp and comic book publishers—who as we'll see in Chapter 8 were often the same—were their ties to the underground pornography industry (whether directly or through the "spicy" pulps) and to organized crime. See Gerard Jones's *Men of Tomorrow: Geeks, Gangsters, and the Birth of the Comic Book* (New York: Basic, 2004) for more on this. Pulp and comic book

publishers usually made money, but likely were continually looking over their shoulders, waiting for the hand of a policeman to fall on them, as they did so. So those publishers were usually quick to repeat whatever the received wisdom of mainstream opinion makers was, as a way to avoid drawing attention to themselves. There were exceptions, but they are disappointingly few.

20. Harlan Halsey's "Old Sleuth, the Detective; or, The Bay Ridge Mystery," *Fireside Companion* 241 (June 10, 1872), 1.

21. To an experienced reader of mysteries and detective novels it is notable the degree to which 19th-century detectives are incorporated into society despite being crime solvers. Vidocq and Dupin were outsiders to their societies because of their personalities, not because they solved crime, and the decades' worth of detectives who followed them were comfortably ensconced in the bosoms of their societies rather than being regarded, by other characters, by authors, or by readers, as somehow being apart from society. It's really only with Arthur Conan Doyle's Sherlock Holmes that readers were presented with the detective as a Mircea Eliade–like shaman, above and separate from the society he heals, and it wasn't until the hard-boiled detectives of the 1920s and 1930s that detectives became (urban) frontier characters who suffered from the same rules as the (Western) frontier crime fighters—that barbarians can only be fought by taking up the gun, but that only barbarians take up the gun, and that society has no room for barbarians—and became permanent outsiders to society.

22. Francis Doughty, "Old King Brady the Sleuth-Hound," *New York Detective Library* 241 (November 14, 1885), 1.

23. John Coryell, "The Old Detective's Pupil; or, The Mysterious Crime of Madison Square." *New York Weekly* 41, no. 46 (1886), 1.

24. The Night Wind is rightfully credited as an influential pulp character; both Coogan and Galaver privilege his role in the continuity of superheroes. Coogan, *Superhero: The Secret Origin of a Genre,* 135–136; Gavaler, *On the Origin of Superheroes: From the Big Bang to Action Comics, Issue 1,* 153. But the Night Wind was created by Frederic van Rennselaer Dey, who spent the majority of his writing life working on Nick Carter stories, and the Night Wind (whose strength is superhuman, like Carter's) should be seen as Nick Carter 2.0 rather than as an "anomaly," as Coogan puts it, or as a character without precedent.

25. E. F. Bleiler's *The Guide to Supernatural Fiction* (Kent, OH: Kent State University Press, 1983), a magisterial guide to the supernatural fiction of the 19th and early 20th centuries, lists dozens of examples of psychic phenomena in the literature of the era, from the Ability To Kill Psychically to Teleportation, Telekinesis, in its Motif Index.

26. Within the preferred inscribed narrative of *The Angel of the Revolution,* however, Natas and Terror are the *good guys,* and the governments of the world, including England's, are the villains. *The Angel of the Revolution* was ahead of its time in a number of ways.

27. Louis Golden's Eternal Brain (for Marvel), G. Ellerbrock and William Kent's Martan the Marvel Man and his wife Vana (for Dell), Russ Lanford's

Merzah the Mystic (for Marvel), Leonard Sansone's Mystico (for Standard), C. C. Beck's Radar (for Fawcett), Basil Wolverton's Spacehawk (for Novelty), Maurice Kashuba's Supermind's Son (for Dell), and Steve Jussen's Zardi (for Centaur) are the only psychic superheroes of the Golden Age—nine of the 380+ superheroes listed in *The Encyclopedia of Golden Age Superheroes*, and a much lower rate of occurrence than can be seen in modern superheroes, where psychic abilities are comparatively common. Jess Nevins, *The Encyclopedia of Golden Age Superheroes*, accessed October 3, 2016, http://jessnevins.com/encyclopedia /characterlist.html.

28. Bleiler and Bleiler, *Science Fiction: The Early Years*, 92.

29. Ibid., 387.

30. The sources of the iconic 20th-century action heroes have been researched by scholars for many years, so that we know, for example, the contents of Edgar Rice Burroughs's library (see *The Personal Library Collection of Edgar Rice Burroughs* Web site, at http://www.erbzine.com/dan/, accessed on October 3, 2016) and the adult reading habits of Lester Dent (creator of Doc Savage) and Walter Gibson (creator of the Shadow). Considerably less time and effort have been spent on the *childhood* reading habits of these authors. We can never know what Burroughs, Dent, Gibson, and the other authors of iconic 20th-century heroes read as children, what caught their imagination and inspired them, what works and characters stuck with them and influenced them, consciously or unconsciously, when they were conceiving the characters they would be most remembered for. This book is about the influences that led up to the creation of the modern superhero. I can't definitively state that Vyr, or even Nick Carter, were *directly* influential on early comic book writers, simply because I don't know what those writers read as children. The most I can say is that given the longevity of Carter and the best-selling status of Jackson's *A Demigod*, we can theorize that they were read by Burroughs et al., in addition to having entered the Zeitgeist.

31. Bleiler and Bleiler, *Science Fiction: The Early Years*, 546.

32. German authors have done yeomen's work in tracing the Fascist strains and portrayals of Fascist supermen in German science fiction during 1900s, 1910s, 1920s and 1930s—see, for example, Heinz Galle's *Sun Koh, der Erbe von Atlantis und Andere Deutsche Supermänner* (Zurich: SSI, 2003)—but the influence of imported, translated non-German science fiction that might have influenced the German authors of Fascist science fiction has not received quite so much scrutiny. I do not say that Nicholson's *Thoth* is Fascist science fiction, but certainly it has elements that would appeal to Fascist authors of science fiction, and it is quite conceivable that Edmund Kiss, the author of the "Ases" tetralogy (1930–1939) of science fiction—the best-known works of science fiction produced in Hitler's Germany—and Paul Alfred Müller-Murnau, the creator of Sun Koh, the Nazi Doc Savage, read and were influenced by *Thoth*.

33. John Clute, "Marshall, Luther," *Science Fiction Encyclopedia*, http://www .sf-encyclopedia.com/entry/marshall_luther.

Chapter 6

1. Carter appeared in over 4,000 stories in all, from 1886 through 1955, with a discernible ongoing continuity. The only thing that keeps fans and academics from referring to the "Nick Carter Universe" with the same frequency and respect as they do the "Marvel Universe" and the "DC Universe" is the regrettable obscurity into which Carter has fallen, and the difficulty with which the Carter stories are found and read.

2. Frederick W. Davis, "Below the Dead Line," *Magnet Library* 428 (January 4, 1906), 4.

3. Sexton Blake's importance, internationally, cannot be understated. Blake's Golden Age—1919–1934—neatly follows Carter's and matches the period in which series hero fiction was ballooning internationally. The first great period of international series hero fiction was 1905–1914, when Sherlock Holmes was the most imitated character internationally, followed by Nick Carter; the second great period was 1919–1934, when Blake replaced Carter and for some years eclipsed Holmes as the most imitated character. Blake's dominance in the British story papers was far greater than Carter's in the American dime novels. And the imagination, color, and rogues' gallery of the Blake corpus is nearly a match for that of the Nick Carter corpus. Sexton Blake and Nick Carter are counterparts and equals; that Blake is dismissed as the "schoolboy's Sherlock Holmes" is snobbery and little more. Like Carter, he deserves much better from scholars and readers.

4. Margaret Cohen incorrectly describes Villiod's outfit as "a Fantomas outfit," referring to Pierre Souvestre and Marcel Allain's murderous "genius of evil," Fantômas. Margaret Cohen, *Profane Illumination: Walter Benjamin and the Paris of Surrealist Revolution* (Berkeley: University of California Press, 1995), 75. Cohen errs; Fantômas famously wears a top hat, domino mask, and tuxedo, while Villiod is clad in a half-face mask, not a domino, wears a waist coat and evening wear, over which is worn a knee-length cape.

5. John Adcock, "Spring-Heeled Jack in Popular Culture, 1838–2005," *Yesterday's Papers*, accessed October 3, 2016, http://john-adcock.blogspot.com/2015/10/spring-heeled-jack-in-popular-culture.html.

6. Kevin Carpenter, "Robin Hood in Boys' Weeklies to 1914," in *Popular Children's Literature in Britain*, edited by Julia Briggs, Dennis Butts, and Matthew Orville Grenby (Aldershot, England: Ashgate, 2008), 58.

7. Alfred S. Burrage, *The Spring-Heeled Jack Library* #1, quoted in Jess Nevins, *The Encyclopedia of Pulp Heroes* (Hornsea, U.K.: P.S. Publishing, 2016), 1232–1233.

8. Peter M. Coogan, *Superhero: The Secret Origin of a Genre* (Austin, TX: MonkeyBrain, 2006), 154.

9. The Burmese author Zayya's *Mya Lay Shwe Dar Bo* (1920) features a Burmese Scarlet Pimpernel active in the Rangoon of the late 1910s. It is highly unlikely Orczy ever heard of her Burmese imitator, unfortunately.

10. Coogan, *Superhero: The Secret Origin of a Genre*, 147.

11. Laura Mulvey, "Visual Pleasure and Narrative Cinema," *Screen* 16, no. 3 (1975), 12.

12. In writing about the male gaze and its exclusion of women, Mulvey devastatingly quotes film director Budd Boetticher: "What counts is what the heroine provokes, or rather what she represents. She is the one, or rather the love or fear she inspires in the hero, or else the concern he feels for her, who makes him act the way he does. In herself the woman has not the slightest importance." Mulvey, "Visual Pleasure and Narrative Cinema," 13. In a way the same is true in superhero texts: all that matters is the superhero. Other characters are there to provoke or inspire the hero; in themselves these other characters have not the slightest importance. There is something innately Fascist to superhero fiction and film, even if the superheroes and comic book plots and writers are vaguely moderate-left politically.

13. Chris Gavaler, *On the Origin of Superheroes: From the Big Bang to Action Comics, Issue 1* (Iowa City, IA: University of Iowa, 2015), 179.

14. Nevins, *The Encyclopedia of Pulp Heroes*, 438.

15. Foreign imitations of Zorro include the English El Caballero (serial by Alec G. Pearson, 1919–1920), the Indian Thunderbolt (film by J. B. H. Wadia, 1931), the Italian El Rajo (pulp by Emilio Fancelli, 1931–1932), the Indian Phantom (film by Saqi, 1933), the Indian Rakshita (film by Ahmed H. Essa, 1933), the Indian Vantolio (film by J. B. H. Wadia, 1933), the Indian Black Bandit (film, 1936), the American Eagle (film, 1936), the Mexican El Alacrán (comic strip by Alfonso Tirado, 1939–1941), the Chinese Yi Zhimei (film by Ren Pengnian, 1940), the Spanish El Coyote (pulp by José Mallorqui, 1943–1953), and the Spanish Black Knight (pulp by Guillermo Sánchez Boix, 1945).

16. Coogan, *Superhero: The Secret Origin of a Genre*, 124.

17. Gavaler, *On the Origin of Superheroes: From the Big Bang to Action Comics, Issue 1*, 61.

18. Nevins's *The Encyclopedia of Pulp Heroes* lists 10 fop heroes from those two decades, including two—Roger Verbeck (the Black Star's foe) and Terry Trimble—created by McCulley before he created Zorro.

19. 2086 films were released in 1918, 2223 in 1919, and 2528 were released in 1920. Internet Movie Database, accessed October 3, 2016, http://www.imdb.com. The film industry was beginning its rise into a national obsession due to postwar changes in production, distribution, and exhibition.

20. Charles Fort, *Lo!* (New York: Cosimo Classics, 2006), 34.

21. Johnston McCulley, "The Big Six," *Detective Story Magazine* 34, no. 4 (September 7, 1920), 7.

22. One suspect for the Bat's author is Johnston McCulley. If so—and Will Murray persuasively argues the case in his Introduction to *The Bat Strikes Again and Again!* (Will Murray, 2009)—Bill Finger and Bob Kane doubly owe McCulley, not just for the costume but for Bruce Wayne's moment of inspiration. The Bat is Dawson Clade, who resolves to fight crime:

> He must become a figure of sinister import to all of these people. A strange Nemesis that would eventually become a legendary terror to all of crimedom . . . he glanced at the oil lamp burning on a table. Then he swung

around, suddenly tense. In the shadows above his head there came a slithering, flapping sort of sound.

Clade leaped back instinctively as something brushed past his cheek. Again the flapping of wings—a weird rustling sound. Terror overcame him for an instant as something brushed against his hair, caught in a tangled lock. Something that seemed unspeakably evil.

He reached up, tore at it with fingers that had suddenly grown frantic. He flung the thing aside. As he did so he saw that it was a bat. An insectivorous mammal, with its wings formed by a membrane stretched between the tiny elongated fingers, legs and tail.

As the creature hovered above the lamp for an instant it cast a huge shadow upon the cabin wall.

"That's it!" exclaimed Clade aloud. "I'll call myself 'The Bat!'" (C. K. M. Scanlon, *The Bat Strikes Again and Again!* [Will Murray, 2009], 15–16)

This sequence was lifted by Finger and Kane from the Bat's debut story in *Popular Detective* for use in the Batman's first appearance.

23. Jess Nevins, *The Pulps* (Tomball TX: Jess Nevins, 2012), 65.

24. Small-scale in terms of its production—it was made in Jacksonville, Florida, by an independent filmmaker rather than in one of the major cities by a name director—and in terms of its distribution and reception. *The Crimson Skull*'s distribution and reception were undoubtedly affected by the fact that the film was made up of African American actors and actresses. Bob Calem, in his skeleton costume, was not only the first cowboy Costumed Avenger in film, he was the first African American superhero, appearing four decades and more before Jack Kirby and Stan Lee's Black Panther at Marvel.

25. Max Brand, "Jim Curry's Compromise," *Western Story Magazine* 24, no. 6 (April 1, 1922), 1.

26. Nevins, *The Pulps*, 59.

27. Western comics actually preceded superhero comics, with *Western Picture Stories* (Comics Magazine Company, 1937), *Star Ranger* (Centaur, from 1937), and *Western Action Thrillers* (Dell, 1937) all appearing before *Action Comics* #1, the comic book that featured Superman's debut. And Western heroes, many of them Costumed Avengers, appeared in superhero comics from the beginning: DC's *Action Comics* #1 had the adventures of Homer Fleming's Chuck Dawson, DC's *Detective Comics* #1 had the adventures of Homer Fleming's Buck Marshall, Timely/Marvel's *Marvel Comics* #1 had the adventures of Al Anders's Masked Raider (a Costumed Avenger), and Fawcett's *Whiz Comics* #2 (the series' first issue) had the adventures of Bill Parker and Pete Costanza's Golden Arrow (a Costumed Avenger).

28. Sigmund Romberg, Otto Harbach, Oscar Hammerstein II, and Frank Mandel, *The Desert Song: A Musical Play in Two Acts* (New York: S. French, 1959), 11.

29. Ibid., 17

30. Even by 1938, the year of Superman's debut, science fiction only consisted of 3 percent of the entire pulp market. Nevins, *The Pulps*, 59. Too, the

range of influence of short-lived obscurities like *The Scorpion* and geographically limited works like *The Desert Song* was minor.

31. Coogan, *Superhero: The Secret Origin of a Genre*, 54.

32. Nevins, *The Pulps*, 33–45.

33. Harold F. Cruickshank, "The Gray Phantom," *Battle Birds* 2, no. 1 (April 1933), 82.

34. Arthur J. Burks, "The Black Falcon," *Sky Fighters* 3, no. 1 (October 1933), 10.

35. Ibid., 12.

36. It bears emphasizing that the hero pulps, like the science fiction pulps, made up only a small part of the pulp universe. Throughout the 1930s, detective, romance and Western pulps were by far the most popular genres, with hero pulps and science fiction pulps never making up more than 9 percent of the genre. Nevins, *The Pulps*, 39–63. The critical and fan emphasis on hero pulps and science fiction pulps is an example of focusing on one species of plant while ignoring the forest all around and is yet another example of genre bias among scholars and writers who should be bias-free.

37. The true crime pulps rose in popularity throughout the 1930s, so that, in 1938, the year of Superman's debut, true crime pulps were the fifth most popular genre of pulp—ahead of sports, hero, aviation, and science fiction. Nevins, *The Pulps*, 59. Sadly, true crime pulps are not studied by scholars; an appropriate analysis of their contents remains to be written.

38. Quoted in Nevins, *The Encyclopedia of Pulp Heroes*, 1177.

39. Lester Dent, "The Man of Bronze," *Doc Savage* 1, no. 1 (March 1933), 3.

40. Ibid., 4.

41. The Shadow's distinctive slouch hat and cape did not appear on the cover of his pulp until the December 1931 issue of *The Shadow Detective Monthly*. The Phantom Detective's trademark tuxedo, top hat, and domino mask were present from the start. The Spider's mask, fedora, and cape first appeared on the cover of the March 1934 issue of *The Spider*, while the look that most people associate with Doc Savage, the close-cropped widow's peak and torn shirt, was actually the product of James Bama's illustrations for Doc Savage novel reprints in the 1960s. On the cover of his pulps Doc Savage was consistently illustrated with longer, wavier hair, untorn white oxfords, and heightened bronzed skin. All four characters' appearances were as standardized as that of any costumed comic book superhero.

42. The idea of the reappearing *villain* was also taken from the pulps—and, again, from Nick Carter, who had not just generational villains—the Professor Moriarty–like Livingston Carruthers and later his brothers Morris and Maitland, and then Livingston's son, Livingston Carruthers Jr.—but reappearing villains—Doctor Quartz and a continuity among villains—Doctor Quartz's school for criminals produced a number of villains who later showed up to plague Nick Carter, most notably Zanoni the Woman Wizard. The Nick Carter stories also produced fiction's first cyborg villain, Praxatel of the Iron Arm. Again, the Nick Carter corpus was the taproot text for so much of the hero pulps and superhero comics.

43. "Scorchy Smith" was created by John Terry and first appeared in 1930, but it first reached undeniable greatness under Caniff and Sickles starting in 1933.

44. Paul Douglas Lopes, *Demanding Respect: The Evolution of the American Comic Book* (Philadelphia: Temple University Press, 2009), 18.

45. Compared to the science fiction pulps, the romance pulps were exemplars of gender progressivism and advanced feminist thought—but then, the best-selling romance pulp (and the best-selling pulp of them all), *Street & Smith's Love Story Magazine*, was edited by a woman, Daisy Bacon, an accomplished editor and writer whose sympathies for women's issues and rights was far greater than comparative cavemen like Hugo Gernsback and John W. Campbell.

46. The Domino Lady stories were credited to "Lars Anderson," but "Lars Anderson" was a house-name for *Saucy Romantic Adventures'* publisher, Fiction Magazines. The true author of the Domino Lady stories remains unknown.

47. It deserves emphasizing, though, that the very fact of Domino Lady's existence is notable. It is true that the Domino Lady was the latest in the line of action/adventure heroines, and in fact the 20th-century inheritor of the tradition of the costumed heroine, which as shown goes back through Martinette de Beauvais and Moll Cutpurse to the female knights of the Middle Ages. But consider the context and the times in which Domino Lady and the later comic book superheroines existed. The end of the 19th century and the beginning of the 20th century had seen a substantial gender panic break out among men:

> During the 1880s and 1890s various discourses—occult, literary, scientific, psychological, and technological—converge to inaugurate shifting models of permeability and suggestibility of the individual's mind and body. The 1890s is also the decade in which these selfsame anxieties erupt in crises around sexuality. Sexual and gender panic manifests itself in representative figures such as the New Woman and the dandy, in public scandals such as the Oscar Wilde trials, and in the reification of medicalizing, pathologizing, and criminalizing discourses around homosexuality. Deep and far-reaching anxieties about the stability of the traditional grounds of gender and sexuality pervade *fin de siècle* culture. (Madhudya Sinha, "Masculinity Under Siege: Gender, Empire, and Knowledge in Late Victorian Literature" [PhD diss., University of Cincinatti, 2009], 15)

The backlash to all of the preceding would repeat in the 1920s after women achieved the vote, as Faludi covers in *Backlash*. At the same time, the way women were supposed to look was being revised by men, so that ordinary women were suddenly deemed "fat," a label that was going to apply to most women, suddenly freed from the corset and displaying a natural amount of belly: "In order to contain, or at least assuage, the gender panic which accompanied this de-legitimation of Victorian gender classifications, impossibly high standards of thinness for women emerged." Heather Jane Sykes, *Queer Bodies: Sexualities, Genders, & Fatness in Physical Education* (New York: Peter Lang, 2011), 55. In the 1920s this resulted in a wave of diet books for women, driving home the point that the average woman was unfit and fat and needed to change—and certainly wasn't capable of having heroic adventures.

So Domino Lady, and all the comic book superheroines that followed her, had substantial cultural inertia to overcome simply to exist, much less to thrive.

Chapter 7

1. Jess Nevins, "Those Who Cannot Remember Doc Savage Are Condemned to Repeat Him," Paper presented at the Biopolitics of Popular Culture Seminar, Irving, CA, December 2009.

2. Peter M. Coogan, *Superhero: The Secret Origin of a Genre* (Austin, TX: MonkeyBrain, 2006), 165.

3. This is one reason among many that Thomas Andrae's article "From Menace to Messiah" falls down. Andrae did not perform sufficient research before writing the article, and assertions like "the superman theme did not really catch on until the early thirties" are incorrect. Thomas Andrae, "From Menace to Messiah: the Prehistory of the Superman in Science Fiction Literature," *Discourse* 2 (1980), 87. As this chapter shows, supermen were common, and approved of, in the 1900s and 1910s. Andrae's argument about the reasons for Superman's popularity in the 1930s has some merit, but his analysis of what came before Superman, and the supposed hostility toward the supermen, does not.

4. H. G. Wells, "The New Accelerator." In *Twelve Stories and a Dream* (Auckland, NZ: Floating Press, 2011), 123–124.

5. Charles Hatfield, Jeet Heer, and Kent Worcester, *The Superhero Reader* (Jackson: University of Mississippi, 2013), 3.

6. Martin A. Kayman, "The Short Story from Poe to Chesterton." In *The Cambridge Companion to Crime Fiction*, edited by Martin Priestman (Cambridge: Cambridge University Press, 2003), 46.

7. L. T. Meade and Robert Eustace, "The Dead Hand," *Pearson's Magazine* 7, no. 2 (1902), 177.

8. Women detectives were not unknown at this time, in fiction or in real life, but as is usually the case with mystery fiction and mystery writers, what began from the pen of a woman, featuring a female character, was quickly co-opted by men for male characters.

9. Poiret is an interesting case, with a number of similarities to Agatha Christie's Hercule Poirot, so much so that unconscious duplication has been (convincingly) alleged by a number of critics and scholars.

10. Ernest Bramah, *The Eyes of Max Carrados* (Hertfordshire: Wordsworth, 2013), ix.

11. Sax Rohmer, "Fu Manchu." In *Meet the Detective*, edited by H. C. McNeile, A. E. W. Mason, and Cecil Madden (London: G. Allen & Unwin, 1935), 66.

12. Nevins's *The Encyclopedia of Pulp Heroes* lists over 250 Yellow Peril characters following Fu Manchu's debut in 1912 through 1945; a rough estimate is that 90 percent of them are closely modeled on Fu Manchu.

13. Warren Ellis and John Cassaday's *Planetary* (1999–2009), an intelligent exploration and celebration of traditional popular culture archetypes—especially those of the pulps and superhero comics—and in many ways the evolutionary successor to the pulps, makes explicit what the traditional white hero-versus-Yellow Peril character clashes had always implied in this confrontation between Axel Brass, the Doc Savage analogue, and Hark, the Fu Manchu analogue:

> Here was a man of equal control—the very pinnacle of the ingenuity of the East, contained in this tall, frightening figure. Hark had been the terror of the Occident since the turn of the century, bedeviling first Britannia, and then America itself . . .
>
> "Damn it, Hark! We're not your enemy! America doesn't hate you! It just doesn't understand you!" (Warren Ellis and John Cassaday, *Planetary: All over the World, and Other Stories* [La Jolla, CA: WildStorm/DC Comics, 2000], 117)

The logical next step is for someone to write an encounter between a white hero and a Yellow Peril that proceeds as does Philip Jose Farmer's *A Feast Unknown* (1969), in which the charged (if sublimated) homoerotics of the white-hero-versus-Yellow-Peril clash become overt and pornographically developed.

14. Although David Langford's point is well-taken that

> the famous eighteenth-century precursors of the theme . . . should not perhaps be termed lost-race tales because . . . there was still a sense that vast tracts of Earth remained unexplored and that marvels could still be expected somewhere over the horizon. Only in a mostly known world does the presence of a forgotten people inhabiting a kind of Pocket Universe generate its special sf piquancy. (David Langford, "Lost Races," *Science Fiction Encyclopedia*, http://www.sf-encyclopedia.com/entry/lost_races)

15. Ibid.

16. Bleiler and Bleiler, *Science Fiction: The Early Years*, 124.

17. Ibid., 121.

18. Coogan, *Superhero: The Secret Origin of a Genre*, 177.

19. A similar phasing out of superpowers in pulp characters would take place in the late 1930s, 1940s and 1950s—Doc Savage, Philip Strange, Henry Ralston, Lester Dent, Walter Gibson and Paul Ernst's the Avenger, Russell Stamm's Invisible Scarlet O'Neill, and Norman Daniels's Black Bat would all lose their superpowers or have them severely de-emphasized in their respective stories—but was largely due to the backlash against Physical Culture and its ties to Fascism. This trend anticipated and then paralleled the post–World War II decline of superhero comics in favor of crime, Western, romance, and other more "realistic" genres of popular culture.

20. Robert W. Chambers, "Diana's Chase," *Saturday Evening Post* 179, no. 4 (June 8, 1907), 3.

21. Gernsback *defined* "scientifiction" in the first issue of *Amazing Stories* (April 1926), and used *Amazing Stories* to try to popularize the term, but Gernsback's *invention* of the word was in the January 1916 issue of *Electrical Experimenter.*

22. M. P. Shiel, *The Isle of Lies* (London: T. Werner Laurie, 1909), 34.

23. Bleiler and Bleiler, *Science-Fiction: The Early Years*, 58.

24. Nick Carter, for all his detective skills, solved crimes as much by his fists and guns as by his wits and learning. Sexton Blake used his fists comparatively sparingly.

25. Brian Stableford, "Science Fiction before Genre." In *The Cambridge Companion to Science Fiction*, edited by Edward James and Farah Mendlesohn (Cambridge, U.K.: Cambridge University Press, 2003), 27.

26. Algernon Blackwood, *John Silence, Physician Extraordinary* (Boston: John W. Luce & Co., 1909), 3.

27. William J. Clark, "The Occult Detector by J. U. Giesy and Junius B. Smith," *Xenophile* 2, no. 5 (September 1975), 55, quoted in Robert Sampson, *Yesterday's Faces: Strange Days* (Bowling Green, OH: Bowling Green University Popular Press, 1984), 81.

28. J. U. Giesy and Junius Smith, "The Occult Detector," *The Cavalier* 12, no. 3 (February 17, 1912), 444.

29. In addition to the artificial beings listed in Chapter 5, there had been several decades of agencyless automatons, artificial beings, and robots in science fiction. From the clockwork dancer of E. T. A. Hoffmann's "Der Sandman" (1816) to the man-shaped steam engines of Edward S. Ellis's *Steam Man of the Prairies* (1868) and successive Edisonades's creations to Eve in Villiers de L'Isle-Adams's *Eve of the Future* (1886), the 19th century was full of artificial beings who were clockwork or steam-driven automata, but lacked intellect, will, and agency.

30. Minsoo Kang, *Sublime Dreams of Living Machines: The Automaton in the European Imagination* (Cambridge, MA: Harvard University Press, 2011), 256.

31. Ibid., 247.

32. Muscular Judaism was a 20th-century response to the traditional stereotype of male Jews as physically inferior and sickly and to the perception that the Jewish people themselves were ailing and in need of physical and cultural revival. The "muscle Jews" cultivated both mind and body, to produce Jews of obvious physical strength and agility, to the point that European Jews were regularly well represented at the Olympic Games. Todd Samuel Peterson's *Muscular Judaism: The Jewish Body and the Politics of Regeneration* (London: Routledge, 2007) is a strong introduction to the subject.

33. Cathy S. Gelbin, *The Golem Returns: From German Romantic Literature to Global Jewish Culture, 1808–2008* (Ann Arbor: University of Michigan, 2011), 92.

34. Ibid., 94.

35. Thomas L. Hanshew, *Cleek: The Man of Forty Faces* (New York: Cassell & Co., 1913), 6–7.

36. Coogan, *Superhero: The Secret Origin of a Genre*, 135.

37. Junot Diaz, quoted in Gavaler, *On the Origin of Superheroes: From the Big Bang to Action Comics, Issue 1*, 119.

38. Carter was in one respect an Übermensch before he went to Mars: as he says in the opening of *A Princess of Mars*,

> I am a very old man; how old I do not know. Possibly I am a hundred, possibly more but I cannot tell because I have never aged as other men, nor do I remember any childhood. So far as I can recollect I have always been a man, a man of about thirty. I appear today as I did forty years and more ago. (Edgar Rice Burroughs, *A Princess of Mars* [New York: Grosset & Dunlap, 1917], 1)

Burroughs did not return to this plot device in later "Barsoom" stories, however.

39. If, as science fiction fan Peter Graham once said, the Golden Age of science fiction is 12, then Burroughs's Barsoom books should be read then, and not afterward. Read as adults, the Barsoom books are notable not so much for their invention or storytelling (which, admittedly, are high in the early books) as for their unconsciously or subconsciously inserted content, what they say about not just Burroughs but about the readers of science fantasy in the 1910s and 1920s—about the tendency toward facile racism, literally juvenile sexism, and the urge to escape "Progressive Era" America.

40. Internet Movie Database, http://www.imdb.com.

41. Gavaler, *On the Origin of Superheroes: From the Big Bang to Action Comics, Issue 1*, 153.

42. William Le Queux, *The Rainbow Mystery* (London: Hodder & Stoughton, 1920), quoted in Nevins, *The Encyclopedia of Pulp Heroes*, 434.

43. Bleiler and Bleiler, *Science Fiction: The Early Years*, 226.

44. John Charles Beecham, "The Argus Pheasant," *All-Story Weekly* 67, no. 3 (February 3, 1917), 355.

45. Susan Faludi, *Backlash: The Undeclared War against American Women* (New York: Crown, 1991), 49–50.

46. Owen Wister, *The Virginian: A Horseman of the Plains* (London: Macmillan, 1902), 251.

47. I'm using this here in the sense that John Clute does in his critical writings, to cover fantastic literature as a whole, including but not limited to science fiction, fantasy, fantastic horror, and all their various subgenres.

48. Nevins, *The Pulps*, 18–39.

49. Edwin Black, *War against the Weak: Eugenics and America's Campaign to Create a Master Race* (Washington, DC: Dialog Press, 2012), 125.

50. Waldemare Kaempffert, *New York Times* (1928), quoted in Gavaler, *On the Origin of Superheroes: From the Big Bang to Action Comics, Issue 1*, 149.

51. Buck v. Bell, 274 U.S. 200 (1927). It can be argued that the white American obsession with race in the 1910s and especially the 1920s, not only with breeding a better, higher race of "Nordics" but with controlling the birth rate of

inferior immigrant races and with killing off the mentally and morally unfit, betrays a deep insecurity about not just the status of the "white race" but with the ability of whites to triumph in any kind of final contest of the races. If whites were truly so insecure about the fitness of the white race—and everything about the 1910s and 1920s suggests that whites were so insecure as to be paranoid about and obsessed with the subject—then an additional reason for an aversion to fictional supermen becomes clear: the Übermensch, no matter how benign his actions were portrayed in fiction, was not a figure of hope for white readers, but a figure of fear. The Übermensch, for race-obsessed whites, would not aid them, but replace them—and, on some level of consciousness that whites would not or could not admit to themselves, whites were convinced that the Übermensch would treat whites as whites had treated other races.

52. Edward B. Davis, "Science and Religious Fundamentalism in the 1920s," *American Scientist* 93, no. 3 (2005), 255

53. The original passage is "Ich lehre euch den Übermenschen. Der Mensch ist Etwas, das überwunden werden soll. Was habt ihr gethan, ihn zu überwinden?" Differences in translation are common—"overcome" is used in place of "surpassed"—but a surprisingly large number of translators choose "overman" rather than "superman" on the grounds that "the comic book associations called to mind by 'superman' and superheroes generally tend to reflect negatively, and frivolously, on the term superhuman." Friedrich Nietzsche, Adrian del Caro, and Robert Pippin, *Thus Spoke Zarathustra* (Cambridge: Cambridge University Press, 2006), 5. I've chosen "superman" rather than "overman" due to the pith, recognizability, and overall accuracy of "superman" as opposed to "overman."

54. Arnold D. Prince, "Life on Our Distant Neighbor Is 'Grand, Intense, Formidable,' Says M. Perrier," *New York Tribune* (February 1920).

55. Internet Movie Database, http://www.imdb.com.

56. Jess Nevins, "Pulp Science Fiction." In *The Oxford Handbook of Science Fiction*, edited by Rob Latham (Oxford: Oxford University Press, 2014), 97–98.

57. The link between spinach and superstrength in the Popeye stories was not made until 1931, with the spinach-fueled transformation into a superstrong Übermensch not taking place on a regular basis until the Max Fleischer Popeye cartoons (from 1933).

58. E. F. Bleiler, *Science-Fiction: The Gernsback Years: A Complete Coverage of the Genre Magazines . . . from 1926 through 1936* (Kent, OH: Kent State University Press, 1998), 104.

59. Gerard Jones, *Men of Tomorrow: Geeks, Gangsters, and the Birth of the Comic Book* (New York: Basic, 2004), 79.

60. Jane Littell, "Party Girl," *Underworld Romances* 1, no. 1 (1931), 50.

61. Ibid., 61.

62. Frederick C. Davis, "Murder Shrine," *Secret Agent X* 8, no. 2 (March 1936), 88.

63. Paul Chadwick, "Python Men of the Lost City," *Captain Hazzard Magazine* 1, no. 1 (May 1938), 10.

64. John Dunning, *On the Air: The Encyclopedia of Old-Time Radio* (Oxford: Oxford University Press, 1998), 148.

65. Ibid., 512.

Chapter 8

1. Jess Nevins, *The Pulps* (Tomball, TX: Jess Nevins, 2012), 53.

2. Internet Movie Database, http://www.imdb.com.

3. It should go without saying that the writing and art of the pre–*Action Comics* #1 comics, and indeed the great majority of the pre–December 7, 1941, comics, was crude and primitive, cranked out on a deadline by men and women whose main concern was a quick buck and not Art of any kind. Most of the pulps had a much higher standard of quality for their stories, and only a handful of the best comic stories of the Golden Age can compare to the best pulp stories. Which is not to say that the best comic stories of the Golden Age are without their charms; some of them are indeed quite well executed and well drawn, and some of the comic book artists of this time—Jack Cole, Reed Crandall, Will Eisner, Lou Fine, Jack Kirby, Mort Meskin, Mac Raboy, and Jerry Robinson, among others—would have flourished in any time period. We can only bemoan the fact that the stories they illustrated were usually so poorly written.

4. Mike Benton, *Superhero Comics of the Golden Age: The Illustrated History* (Dallas, TX: Taylor Publishing, 1992), 12.

5. Siegel and Shuster's Doctor Occult had actually gone through a brief period—four issues of *More Fun*, cover dated October 1936–January 1937, in which he wore a costume and flew. As Mike Benton writes of this period, "Dr. Occult could have been the understudy for Superman . . . Siegel and Shuster had hoped that this early attempt to sneak in a Superman prototype might open the way for their cherished creation. It did not." Mike Benton, *Superhero Comics of the Golden Age: The Illustrated History*, 16.

6. Bradford W. Wright, *Comic Book Nation: The Transformation of Youth Culture in America* (Baltimore, MD: Johns Hopkins University Press, 2003), 13.

7. Also deserving of consideration regarding the initial appeal of Superman: his direct and in some ways brutal vigilante activity against these realistic crimes and criminals. Superman is a noble outsider acting violently against evil insiders, in the tradition of the Hobsbawmian social bandit, the *latrones*, and Robin Hood et al., and the social bandit, in reality and in fiction, has always held a great appeal for civilians.

8. The process for producing comics in the Golden Age often involved artists' studios or "shops," independently producing (writing, drawing, and lettering) comic book stories or even entire issues and selling them to the publishers. The smaller comic book publishers in particular did not have writers and artists on staff, and instead acquired the material they ended up publishing through the artists' studios. "Comic book stories were turned out in an assembly-line fashion." Mike Benton, *Superhero Comics of the Golden Age: The Illustrated History*, 21.

This left publishers in the position, once the stories and issues were delivered from the artists' studios, of only having to "turn the finished pages of drawings over to his engraver and plate makers and then his printers." Mike Benton, *Superhero Comics of the Golden Age: The Illustrated History*, 22.

9. Rightfully so. The broad outlines of Wonder Man are substantially different from Superman, but the particulars of Wonder Man's lone appearance have substantial similarities to stories in which Superman appeared. As the judge in the case, Learned Hand, wrote, "We think it plain that the defendants have used more than general types and ideas and have appropriated the pictorial and literary details embodied in the complainant's copyrights." Learned Hand, *Detective Comics, Inc. v. Bruns Publications, Inc.* 111 F.2d 432.

10. Mike Benton, *Superhero Comics of the Golden Age: The Illustrated History*, 22.

11. Cat Man only appeared twice, but is of note for being comics' first transvestite hero, continuing the tradition of the demoiselles of Ariège and the Molly Maguires.

12. Martin Goodman, the owner of Marvel Comics, was a publisher of pulps during the 1930s, having entered magazine publishing in 1929 and begun publishing his own pulps early in 1933. Goodman's pulp company, which had four lines of pulps under the umbrella name "Red Circle," was only ever middling successful, and when Goodman was told in the summer of 1939 about the production costs versus cover price of comics he undoubtedly felt that his money was better spent in the new industry of comics rather than in pulp publishing, where he was a third-rater.

13. Malcolm Kildale, "Speed Centaur," *Amazing Mystery Funnies* 2, no. 8 (August 1939), 4.

14. Frank Thomas, "The Eye Sees," *Keen Detective Funnies* 2, no. 12 (December 1939), 52.

15. Norman Modell and Lionel March, "The Gold of Garlok," *Colossus Comics* 1 (1940), 39.

16. Nevins, *The Pulps*, 51–63.

17. Internet Movie Database, http://www.imdb.com.

18. Nevins, *The Pulps*, 65.

19. "Spicy" pulps, the pulp equivalent of soft-core pornography, constituted a major part of the pulp market for a number of years: in 1924, 30 percent of the pulp titles were "spicy," 16 percent in 1929, 28 percent in 1934, and 14 percent in 1939. Nevins, *The Pulps*, 25 ff. But the market for "spicy" pulps weakened once World War II began, because of the rise of comics (which diluted the pulp market generally) and the influx of Canadian and European pornography (directed at the United States by Germany, which had not been the case before the war; Germany had been a prime consumer and importer of Belgian pornography before World War II began, but became an exporter and director of other countries' exports after conquering Europe). In 1941 the "spicy" pulps were only 6 percent of the market and were stuck in a permanent decline. Nevins, *The Pulps*, 65.

20. Internet Movie Database, http://www.imdb.com.

21. Ted Udall, "Enter the Sniper," *Military Comics* 5 (December 1941), 12.

22. Harry Shorten and George Storm, "The Origin of the Hangman," *Pep Comics* 17 (July 1941), 27.

23. Again, though, one must not overstate Wonder Woman's significance in the comic book marketplace. Wonder Woman was iconic, true, but as mentioned 39 Costumed Avengers and superwomen preceded her, and only 9 superheroines appeared in the year after her debut. Too, consider the marketplace in which Wonder Woman appeared. Of those 39 superheroes, 22 of them were still appearing in the comics the month that Wonder Woman debuted, and several of those—Eisner and Iger's Sheena (for Fiction House), C. A. Winter's Camilla (for Fiction House), Gardner F. Fox and Dennis Neville's Hawkgirl (for DC), Fletcher Hanks's Fantomah (for Fiction House), Al Carreno's Bulletgirl (for Fawcett), Alfred Harvey and Al Gabriele's Black Cat (for Harvey), and Arthur Peddy's Phantom Lady (for Quality)—were significant, even major superheroines, and some of those—Sheena, Camilla, Black Cat, Phantom Lady—lasted into the Atomic Age. Wonder Woman became iconic and archetypal, but she had significant company.

Chapter 9

1. Note, however, that the ages of superhero comics and the ages of the comic book medium itself differ, in some cases substantially, because the *genre* of superheroes and the *medium* of comic books are two different things, and at times *very* different things. (This distinction is often ignored by critics of comic books, who fixate on superhero comics to the exclusion of other genres.) The Golden Age of superhero comics, for example, is about the rise, dominance, and fall of the superhero genre, which as I describe in this chapter is generally seen as being in the 1935–1949 period. (Some critics, however, place the end of the Golden Age as late as 1953). But a history of comic books as a medium would likely describe a first age as existing from 1935–1942 and a second, much longer age, as beginning in 1942 (when as mentioned above the vast number of new comics were not superhero) and ending in 1964 (the last month in which the majority of the best-selling comics were not superhero). During this 1942–1964 period superheroes were not the best-selling genre of comics, and were far behind crime, horror, Western, romance, funny animal, and humor comics.

Duncan and Smith usefully provide their own ages for the comic book medium as a whole: the Era of Invention (1842–1897), when the characteristics of comics as an art form and medium were being established; the Era of Proliferation (1934–1938), when superheroes became associated with comics; the Era of Diversification (1940–1947), when other genres became established in the comics; the Era of Retrenchment (1952–1954), when comics were forced to respond to restraints placed upon it; the Era of Connection (1956–1962), when the antihero became an established character type; the Era of Independence (1958–1968), when the alternative and small press comics emerged, creating an alternative to the mainstream; the Era of Ambition (1979–1986), when creators began putting out artistically ambitious works; and the Era of Reiteration (1986–1994), when mainstream publishers catered to the specialized audience of superhero comic book collectors. Randy Duncan and Matthew J. Smith, *The Power of Comics: History, Form, and Culture* (New York: Continuum, 2009), 23–24.

Gabilliet conversely has the ages as 1842–1936 ("from comics to comic books"), 1936–1940 ("the beginnings of an industry"), 1940–1945 ("comic books at war"), 1945–1954 ("the apogee and the fall"), 1955–1962 ("decline and rebirth"), 1963–1969 ("the age of innovation"), 1969–1979 ("research and development by trial and error"), 1980–1993 ("the recovery of the 1980s"), and 1993–2005 ("the end of a century and the beginning of a new century"). Jean-Paul Gabilliet, Jean-Paul, Bart Beaty, and Nick Nguyen, *Of Comics and Men: A Cultural History of American Comic Books* (Jackson, MS: University of Mississippi, 2010), v.

What I'm calling the Metamodern Age of superhero comics, the 2001–2015 span of years, is a time period that for the medium of comic books would better be called "the Digital Age," reflecting the great impact of the Internet and electronic media on comics. Were I to write a history of comics as a medium, I would likely describe the Digital Age as 2001–2010 and 2010–present as the Mosaic Age, when creators like Raina Telgemeier and Ed Brubaker (and artist partner Sean Philips), comics like *Lumberjanes* (by Shannon Watters, Grace Ellis and Noelle Stevenson), *Saga* (by Brian K. Vaughan and Fiona Staples), and *Sex Criminals* (by Matt Fraction and Chip Zdarsky), and companies like Image and Boom! were successful (financially as well as aesthetically) while having nothing at all to do with superheroes, and when the greatest cultural momentum and cachet seem to be with nonsuperhero comics.

2. Wright, *Comic Book Nation: The Transformation of Youth Culture in America*, 31.

3. This hesitancy to directly name Germany was more common with some companies than with others. Timely was anti-Hitler almost from the start, with Captain America famously punching Hitler in the face on the cover of *Captain America Comics* #1 (cover date March 1941, on sale date December 12, 1940) and Nazis being portrayed as villains as early as Timely's second issue, *Marvel Mystery Comics* #2 (cover date December 1939, on sale date October 13, 1939). Other companies, such as All-American Publications (initially a sister company to DC, later merged with them) were slower to name the Germans directly, using the aforementioned Teutonic-sounding substitutes. This hesitancy arose not out of pro-German sympathies but out of a desire to stay out of the war engulfing Europe or, in the case of MLJ, out of a greater suspicion of the Russians than of the Germans. This isolationism vanished as soon as Germany declared war on the United States, of course.

Superhero comics did not have a similar hesitancy when it came to the Japanese, who were named as villains in stories appearing months before the attack on Pearl Harbor, and, in the case of Gill Fox and Lou Fine's Uncle Sam story in *National Comics* #18 (cover date December 1941), were shown to actually bomb Pearl Harbor months before December 7, 1941. Superhero comics, like most

American popular culture of the war years, promoted an anti-Japanese animus that was racial in nature, a hatred feeding off of decades-old anti-Asian and specifically anti-Japanese sentiment in the United States. This tradition of toxic anti-Japanese hatred was given additional weight and venom during the war, so that superhero comics "spent a great deal of time visualizing Japanese defeat and humiliation, always in a manner drawing attention to racial and cultural differences and supposed inferiority." Christopher Murray, *Champions of the Oppressed? Superhero Comics, Popular Culture, and Propaganda in America during World War II* (Cresskill, NJ: Hampton, 2011), 218. Superhero comics visualized German defeat and humiliation as well, but not with the same degree of race hate.

4. Federal Bureau of Investigation, *Uniform Crime Reports for the United States* (Washington, DC: U.S. Department of Justice, 1947), 1.

5. Federal Bureau of Investigation, *Uniform Crime Reports for the United States* (Washington, DC: U.S. Department of Justice, 1948), 1.

6. Federal Bureau of Investigation, *Uniform Crime Reports for the United States* (Washington, DC: U.S. Department of Justice, 1949), 1

7. Federal Bureau of Investigation, *Uniform Crime Reports for the United States* (Washington, DC: U.S. Department of Justice, 1950), 1.

8. Benton, *Superhero Comics of the Golden Age: The Illustrated History*, 58–59.

9. Quoted in Benton, *Superhero Comics of the Golden Age: The Illustrated History*, 58.

10. Nevins, "Those Who Cannot Remember Doc Savage Are Condemned to Repeat Him."

11. Murray, *Champions of the Oppressed? Superhero Comics, Popular Culture, and Propaganda in America during World War II*, 237.

12. Quoted in Benton, *Superhero Comics of the Golden Age: The Illustrated History*, 58.

13. Wright, *Comic Book Nation: The Transformation of Youth Culture in America*, 59.

14. Ibid., 59.

15. William W. Savage, *Commies, Cowboys, and Jungle Queens: Comic Books and America, 1945–1954* (Middletown, CT: Wesleyan University Press, 1990), 12. It must be said, however, that superheroes were not too much to bear in the science fiction of the time, nor—as we'll see in Chapter 10—in the animated cartoons or live-action films of the era. Savage's disdain for superheroes leads him partially astray here.

16. John Clute, "Thinning," *Encyclopedia of Fantasy*, 942.

17. Exceptions to this include Will Eisner's work on The Spirit and Jack Cole's work on Plastic Man, the former doing consistently inventive work with both content and form, the latter channeling his joyful genius for unusual visuals into the stories themselves. Binder and Beck's Captain Marvel continued to be playful and innocent as well as inventive. And under Mort Weisinger's editorial direction Superman developed its classical science fantasy mythology. But more typical was Jack Kirby, who had spent the early war years drawing Captain America but spent the postwar years doing kid gang and romance comics.

18. John Clute, "Thinning," *Encyclopedia of Fantasy*, 943.

19. The very act of giving the 1949–1956 span of years a label is in some respects controversial, as critics and scholars continue to debate whether these eight years can be said to constitute a discrete era. Those opposed to giving this time period a proper "Age" label argue that most comic ages last 15 to 20 years, not 8; that there were too few superhero comics, and superheroes, published during this time period for it to deserve an "Age" label of its own; and that the superheroes and superhero comics of the time period lack a cohesive theme that would earn them an "Age" label. Wikipedia does not give the 1949–1956 period an "Age" label, instead calling it an "interregnum." Wright's *Comic Book Nation* deals with the medium as a whole rather than focusing on superheroes, and in so doing eschews the entire "Golden"/"Silver"/"Bronze" naming pattern. Tim Bryant, in the "Ages of Comics" entry in Booker's *Encyclopedia of Comic Books and Graphic Novels*, writes that "this period is best understood as a transition to the Silver Age of comics, which was characterized by increased public scrutiny of comics and further refinement of generic conventions." Tim Bryant, "Ages of Comics." In *Encyclopedia of Comic Books and Graphic Novels*, edited by M. Keith Booker (Santa Barbara, CA: Greenwood, 2010), 12–13.

On the other hand, the *Overstreet Comic Book Price Guide* uses the label "The Atom Age." Robert M. Overstreet, *Official Overstreet Comic Book Price Guide* (Timonium, MD: Gemstone Publishing, 1999), 37. So does Shirrel Rhoades in *A Complete History of American Comic Books*. Shirrel Rhoades, *A Complete History of American Comic Books* (New York: Peter Lang, 2008), 15. I'm using a variant of that. I believe that the eight-year span of 1949–1956 does have enough unique characteristics to label it an "Age;" that the absence of many superheroes and superhero comics is itself indicative of the time period having traits and attributes; and that the concern with the atomic bomb and the prospect of nuclear war were common enough in popular culture that the time period deserves the label "the Atomic Age" rather than "the Interregnum" or "the Transition" or anything like that.

20. Wright, *Comic Book Nation: The Transformation of Youth Culture in America*, 155. However, Gabilliet qualifies this, noting that the economic peak of the industry was 1952, not 1954, and that the comic book market was actually a

> switchback market since 1945: continuous increase of print runs until 1948 was succeeded by a two-year drop. Circulation shot up dramatically in 1951 and 1952 before falling back abruptly to the 1950 level in 1953 and hitting bottom in 1954, when circulation was back to the 1945 level. From the following year, print runs increased again and leveled off around values close to those of 1946 throughout the 1960s. (Jean-Paul Gabilliet, Jean-Paul, Bart Beaty, and Nick Nguyen, *Of Comics and Men: A Cultural History of American Comic Books*, 47)

21. The Atomic Age was the period of the greatest generic diversity for comic books, when the widest range of comic books were available to the public, and

when the greatest number of comic book publishers existed. It was the time of the medium's greatest sales. It was *not* a time when superheroes and superhero publishers dominated the market. The obvious lesson was that comics as an industry and as a medium flourished best when it offered a range of products, not just one type. This was a lesson later ignored by Marvel and DC.

22. The argument can be made that, per capita, funny animal superheroes were not only the most successful type of superhero of the Atomic Age, but that they defied the trends dominating nonfunny animal superheroes during the Atomic Age. They weren't grim and gritty, they didn't have mundane, ordinary opponents, they had regularly appearing supervillains, the stories were joyfully inventive—in many ways, they were the funny animal equivalent of Superman, albeit without the intricate mythology that Mort Weisinger constructed around Superman during the Atomic Age. Unfortunately, the genre of funny animal comics—a genre older than superhero comics, thanks to the presence of Mickey Mouse, Dip and Duck, and the Frog Pond Ferry in various pre-1935 comics, and "the most prevalent genre during the period of 1940–1945," Jean-Paul Gabilliet, Jean-Paul, Bart Beaty, and Nick Nguyen, *Of Comics and Men: A Cultural History of American Comic Books*, 25—is the least studied of all genres of comics, despite being an important part (economically if in no other way) of the development of the medium. No significant work of length has been done on them, and most critical works on the history of comic books mention them only in passing or focus solely on the one or two best-known funny animal characters or creators. More study at much greater length is clearly needed.

23. Like the label "the Atomic Age," the description of Tommy Tomorrow, the Knights of the Galaxy, and Space Cabbie as superheroes is at least debatable. None seem to pass the intuitive sniff test for superheroes. Nonetheless, applying the 17 superheroic elements described in Chapter 1 to Tommy Tomorrow, the Knights, and Space Cabbie does lead to the conclusion that they are on the superhero scale, albeit in the middle rather than on the end of Superman et al.

24. Wright, *Comic Book Nation: The Transformation of Youth Culture in America*, 111.

25. Ibid., 111.

26. Christopher Murray, "Cold War." In *Encyclopedia of Comic Books and Graphic Novels*, edited by M. Keith Booker (Santa Barbara, CA: Greenwood, 2010), 107.

27. This bears emphasis. The best superhero comics of the Atomic Age do not stand comparison, as written text or drawn art, with the best romance, Western, crime, or horror comics. Superhero comics of this time were written for children, while other genres were written for adults, with resulting aesthetic and artistic superiority for the nonsuperhero stories.

28. Savage, *Commies, Cowboys, and Jungle Queens: Comic Books and America, 1945–1954*, 52.

29. The curious are directed to Carol L. Tilley's "Seducing the Innocent: Fredric Wertham and the Falsifications That Helped Condemn Comics," a thorough savaging of the many ways in which Wertham "manipulated, overstated, compromised,

and fabricated evidence . . . for rhetorical gain." Carol L. Tilley, "Seducing the Innocent: Fredric Werthamm and the Falsifications That Helped Condemn Comics," *Information & Culture: A Journal of History* 47, no. 4 (2012), 383.

30. Wright, *Comic Book Nation: The Transformation of Youth Culture in America*, 172.

31. Randy Duncan and Matthew J. Smith, *The Power of Comics: History, Form, and Culture* (New York: Continuum, 2009), 40.

32. A notable precursor to the Fantastic Four at Marvel was Stan Lee and Steve Ditko's Dr. Droom, who debuted in *Amazing Adventures* #1 (cover date June 1961) and appeared in the next five issues of *Amazing Adventures*. Strictly speaking, Dr. Droom is Marvel's first Silver Age superhero, even if his adventures were of the weird menace genre rather than the more straightforwardly superhero genre of Droom's counterparts at DC. But despite his repeated appearances Droom was never intended to be an ongoing hero in the same vein as his DC counterparts; Stan Lee would later describe Droom as a "one-shot thing." Roy Thomas, "Stan Lee's Amazing Marvel Interview!" *Alter Ego* 104 (2011), 21. The Fantastic Four were intended to be ongoing heroes. Nor did Droom inspire any imitators, although he was eventually reformatted by Lee into Dr. Strange. Ultimately Droom stands as a what-if character rather than as a solid member of Marvel's Silver Age, similar to the relationship that Tom Richmond has to mystery fiction.

33. Few would argue with the idea that Mort Weisinger was the dominant editorial personality at DC Comics during the Silver Age, even with Julie Schwarz and Jack Schiff also working at DC as editors at this time. Weisinger, after all, was the editor of the best-selling line of comics DC had to offer, the Superman family of books. But the question of where to place Jack Kirby in the history of Marvel Comics is not so clear-cut, and is in fact considerably fraught. Stan Lee and Jack Kirby worked together as a writer–artist team during Marvel's Silver Age, producing some of the company's best (and best-selling) stories during this time period—this much everyone agrees upon. What each contributed to the partnership and the final product, the comics themselves, is not agreed-upon, and is the subject of much debate, which among fans and online is usually fractious and ill-tempered. Sean Howe, author of the to-date definitive history of Marvel Comics, *Marvel Comics: The Untold Story*, tends toward the Kirby camp. Pierre Comtois, in *Marvel Comics in the 1960s*, is firmly in the Lee camp, while Fred Van Lente, in *The Comic Book History of Comics*, tends toward the Kirby camp. I believe that each contributed elements that the other creator lacked, so that the stories and characters they worked together on were stronger, more creative, and more aesthetically and artistically successful than the stories and characters they worked alone on. This opinion is not a popular one with the Kirby and Lee zealots, needless to say.

34. The editorial and marketplace restrictions placed on the Superman and Batman stories were extreme, and these resulted in the Superman and Batman stories of the era being in many ways crude and primitive, especially compared to what Stan Lee and Jack Kirby would produce at Marvel in a few years' time.

But the Superman and Batman stories of the 1956–1961 era have their own charms: innocence, joy, colorfulness, and creativity and inventiveness, on display every month without fail. P. G. Wodehouse's "Jeeves and Wooster" stories are wonderful despite the Wodehouse-imposed requirement that the status quo be reset at the end of every story. The Superman and Batman stories of DC's Silver Age should be regarded in the same light.

35. Gabilliet, Beaty, and Nguyen, *Of Comics and Men: A Cultural History of American Comic Books,* 57.

36. Pierre Comtois, *Marvel Comics in the 1960s: An Issue-by-Issue Field Guide to a Pop Culture Phenomenon* (Raleigh, NC: TwoMorrows, 2009), 57.

37. Ibid., 95–96.

38. It's worth noting that while DC had the best-selling superhero comics through this period, other companies also appeared at the top of the sales charts. In 1961, Dell had three comics—*Uncle Scrooge* (best-selling comic that year), *Tarzan,* and *Turok, Son of Stone*—in the top 20, and Archie had 4 comics—*Archie, Betty and Veronica, Archie Giant Series,* and *Pep Comics*—in the top 20—and none of them were superhero comics. In 1966, Archie, Catholic Guild, and Gold Key had comics in the top 20. In 1969, *Archie* was the best-selling comic book, and Archie and Gold Key had 8 comics in the top 20. The Silver Age is largely the story of superhero comics, but there were other companies and genres who were quite successful throughout the Age.

39. Marvel and DC were the dominant publishers of superhero comics throughout the Silver Age, but there were a number of other comic book publishers who tried to capitalize upon the success of Marvel and DC's superhero comics and especially that of the 1966 Batman television show. Over two dozen publishers, including industry heavyweight Archie, Dell, and Harvey, published hundreds of stories of superheroes, some comedic and parodic, many others in open imitation of either DC or Marvel. Few of these stories were of aesthetic or artistic worth, and few of the superheroes made any sort of lasting impact, but they presented an alternative (on rare occasions, particularly interesting ones) to the DC and Marvel heroes and comics. Archie even went so far as to put superheroes on the cover of their Archie family of comics—*Archie, Archie's Girls Betty and Veronica, Archie's Pals 'n' Gals, Josie, Jughead*—in a series of 1966 and 1967 issues whose contents did not reflect their cover and were decidedly nonsuperheroic.

40. Wright, *Comic Book Nation: The Transformation of Youth Culture in America,* 184.

41. Ibid., 230.

42. Comtois, *Marvel Comics in the 1960s: An Issue-by-Issue Field Guide to a Pop Culture Phenomenon,* 207.

43. Matthew J. Costello, *Secret Identity Crisis: Comic Books and the Unmasking of Cold War America* (New York: Continuum, 2009), 67.

44. Pierre Comtois, *Marvel Comics in the 1970s: An Issue-by-Issue Field Guide to a Pop Culture Phenomenon* (Raleigh, NC: TwoMorrows, 2011), 6.

45. Sean Howe, *Marvel Comics: The Untold Story* (New York: Harper, 2012), 101.

46. Wright, *Comic Book Nation: The Transformation of Youth Culture in America,* 227.

47. Todd Gitlin, *Inside Prime Time* (Berkeley: University of California Press, 2000), 63.

48. Gabilliet, Beaty, and Nguyen, *Of Comics and Men: A Cultural History of American Comic Books*, 73.

49. Wright, *Comic Book Nation: The Transformation of Youth Culture in America*, 245.

50. Lopes, *Demanding Respect: The Evolution of the American Comic Book*, 69.

51. Comtois, *Marvel Comics in the 1970s: An Issue-by-Issue Field Guide to a Pop Culture Phenomenon*, 8.

52. Martin Goodman, Marvel's publisher, had a long tradition of publishing magazines and comics under a bewildering variety of company names. He'd begun this in the 1930s, as a publisher of the pulps, and continued it up through the 1970s.

53. Unusually for DC, they had anticipated the trend of violent antihero protagonists with the Marv Wolfman–written series *The Vigilante* (from cover date November 1983). But *The Vigilante* only lasted 50 issues, through cover date February 1988, and was never able to successfully capitalize on the audience's taste for violent heroes, largely due to Wolfman's ambivalent approach to the characterization of the Vigilante and the morality of his actions. Ambivalence, in the Modern Age of violent-hero comics, was something that happened to other comics.

54. Wright, *Comic Book Nation: The Transformation of Youth Culture in America*, 273.

55. "Street level" to differentiate them from "sky level" heroes and teams like Superman, Thor, the Avengers, and the Justice League, who flew and dealt with large-scale menaces and threats, unlike the street-level heroes who were supposedly lower-powered and dealt with street crime. The unity of comic book universes—the idea that the Punisher, Daredevil, and Spider-Man were active in the same comic book universe as superpowered heroes like Thor and Iron Man—began to break down at this time, leading to the "Marvel Universe" becoming de facto two separate universes, one low powered and one high powered.

56. Andrew Hoberek, *Considering Watchmen: Poetics, Property, Politics* (New Brunswick, NJ: Rutgers University Press, 2014), 75.

57. Timotheus Vermeulen and Robin Van Den Akker, "Notes on Metamodernism," *Journal of Aesthetics and Culture* 2 (2010), 2.

58. Ibid., 5–6.

59. Ibid., 6.

60. Ibid., 7.

61. Ibid., 7.

62. Ibid., 7.

63. Ibid., 8.

64. Ibid., 7.

65. Robert Kirkman and Tony Moore's *The Walking Dead* (2003–present) and Brian K. Vaughan and Pia Guerra's *Y: The Last Man* (2002–2008) were both best sellers and influential but did not possess the aesthetic qualities of those comics listed here.

Chapter 10

1. It's worth noting that the superhero stories appearing in the cartoons, serials, films, and television episodes of the 1950s were radically different from the stories appearing in the comics. The Superman and Batman stories were becoming increasingly fantastic, continually adding science fictional and fantasy elements to the Superman and Batman mythoi; to a lesser extent the same was true of the Green Arrow and Aquaman stories that DC published during the 1950s. (Wonder Woman's stories had always been fantastic.) At the same time, what was appearing on the big and small screens was essentially mimetic except for the inclusion of the superhero himself and one or two fantastic devices. This was not due to audience bias against stories with fantastic underpinnings; the 1950s were a time of popularity for science fiction, both on screen and in print.

2. Clute defines "technothriller" as

> a tale which, though it often makes use of sf devices, in fact occupies an undisplaced, essentially mundane narrative world, one that—during the years when technothrillers were most popular, from the 1950s to the 1970s—was commonly seen through a Cold War lens. Though usually taking place in the present day, technothrillers may be set in the Near Future and invoke Technologies beyond the capacities of the present moment, but they differ from sf in two important respects. First, like the unknown in Horror novels, science in the technothriller is either inherently threatening or worshipfully (and fetishistically) exploited. Second, a typical technothriller plot evokes a technological scenario whose world-transforming implications are left unexamined or evaded, often through the use of plots in which a potential sf Novum is reduced to a McGuffin. Thus the sf element, though common enough, tends not to be presented in a sophisticated or analytic way. (John Clute, "Technothriller," *Science Fiction Encyclopedia*, http://www.sf-encyclopedia.com/entry/technothriller)

A similar dynamic took place in the superheroic television shows of the 1968–1977 period. The fantastic science of *Six Million Dollar Man* and *Bionic Woman* and the magical, fantastical elements of *Wonder Woman* were for the most part downplayed or ignored in favor of routine, mimetic adventure scenarios. Even those exceptions—aliens and a bionic sasquatch in *Six Million Dollar Man*, aliens and sentient computers in *Wonder Woman*, fembots and Bigfoot in *Bionic Woman*—and their "world-transforming implications are left unexamined or evaded," as Clute puts it.

Epilogue

1. Plutarch, *Plutarch: Lives of the Noble Grecians and Romans* (Oxford: Benediction Classics, 2015), 537.

Selected Bibliography

As might expected with a work of this sort, many books and articles were consulted during the writing process, many more than could reasonably be listed here. So the following is intended to be a starting place—not the final destination—for those interested in the subjects covered. One could reasonably fill an entire bibliography with modern Arthuriana, for example; the works given here are places to start on each character or subject, rather than anything intended to be the last word on that character or subject.

Primary Sources

Aaron, Jason, and R. M. Guera. *Scalped Deluxe Edition Book One*. New York: DC / Vertigo, 2015.

"Ace Spy-Smasher." *Black Cobra* 1 (October–November 1954): 1–7.

The Adventures of Captain Marvel. Directed by John English and William Witney. 1941. Santa Monica, CA: Artisan Home Entertainment, 2003. DVD.

Adventures of Superman: Season 1. Directed by Lee Sholem. 1952. Burbank, CA: Warner Home Video, 2006. DVD.

Aeschylus. *The Prometheus Trilogy*. Translated by Ruth F. Birnbaum and Harold F. Birnbaum Lawrence, KS: Coronado Press, 1978.

Ainsworth, William Harrison. *Rookwood*. New York: E. P. Dutton, 1931.

Aligheri, Dante. *The Divine Comedy Volume 1: Inferno*. Translated by Mark Musa. New York: Penguin, 2002.

Allen, Grant. "The Adventure of the Cantankerous Old Lady." *The Strand Magazine* 15.87 (March 1898): 320–330.

Anders, Al. "Origin of the Masked Raider." *Marvel Comics* 1 (October 1939): 38–45.

Anderson, Lars. "The Domino Lady Collects." *Saucy Romantic Adventures* 1.1 (May 1936): 91–102.

Ariosto, Ludovico. *Orlando Furioso*. Translated by Guido Waldman. Oxford: Oxford University Press, 2008.

Armitage, Simon, trans. *Sir Gawain and the Green Knight*. New York: W. W. Norton, 2008.

Arnold, Edwin. *Lt. Gullivar Jones, His Vacation*. 1905. Reprint, New York: Arno Press, 1975.

Avallone, Michael, and Valerie Moolman. *Run, Spy, Run*. New York: Award Books, 1964.

Avatar: The Last Airbender; The Complete Series. 2005–2008. Hollywood, CA: Paramount, 2015. DVD.

The Avengers. Directed by Joss Whedon. 2012. Burbank, CA: Walt Disney Home Entertainment, 2012. DVD.

Averill, Charles E. *The Mexican Ranchero: Or, The Maid of the Chapparal: A Romance of the Mexican War*. Boston: F. Gleason, 1847.

Ayers, Dick. "The Fog Robbers." *The Avenger* 1 (February–March 1955): 1–8.

Azzarello, Brian, and Eduardo Risso. *100 Bullets Book One*. New York: DC / Vertigo, 2014.

Bacon, Francis. *Essays and New Atlantis*. Edited by Gordon Sherman Haight. New York: W. J. Black, 1942.

Baker, Matt. "Dangerous Desperadoes." *Samson* 12 (April 1955): 16–20.

Balzac, Honoré de. *The Centenarian: Or, The Two Beringhelds*. Middletown, CT: Wesleyan University Press, 2005.

Balzac, Honoré de. *Père Goriot, and Eugénie Grandet*. New York: Modern Library, 1950.

Banham, Christopher, ed. *The Skeleton Crew: Or, Wildfire Ned*. Brighton, U.K.: Victorian Secrets, 2015.

Bard, Phil. "The Man Who Demanded Death." *Master Comics* 41 (August 1943): 19–31.

Barker, Elsa. "The Mystery of Cabin 135." *The Red Book Magazine* 46.2 (December 1925): 79–83.

Baron, Mike, and Steve Rude. *Nexus Omnibus Volume 1*. Milwaukie, OR: Dark Horse, 2012.

Barr, Robert. *Jennie Baxter, Journalist*. Toronto: Copp, Clark, 1899.

Bates, Paul A. *Faust: Sources, Works, Criticism*. New York: Harcourt, Brace & World, 1969.

Batman. Directed by Tim Burton. 1989. Burbank, CA: Warner Home Video, 2009. DVD.

Batman: The Animated Series, Volume One. 1992–1995. Burbank, CA: Warner Home Video, 2005. DVD.

Batman: The Complete Television Series. 1966–1968. Burbank, CA: Warner Home Video, 2014. DVD.

Batman and Robin: The Complete 1949 Movie Serial Collection. Directed by Spencer Gordon Bennet. 1949. Culver City, CA: Sony Pictures Home Entertainment, 2005. DVD.

Batman v. Superman: Dawn of Justice. Directed by Zack Snyder. Burbank, CA: Warner Home Video, 2016. DVD.

Battefield, Ken. "The Electric Curtain." *Samson* 12 (April 1955): 2–8.

Baum, L. Frank. *Ozma of Oz: A Record of Her Adventures with Dorothy Gale of Kansas . . .* Chicago: The Reilly & Britton Company, 1907.

Bechdel, Alison. *Fun Home: A Family Tragicomic.* Boston, MA: Mariner Books, 2007.

Beck, C. C. "Radar, the International Policeman." *Captain Marvel Adventures* 35 (May 1944): 2–13.

Beckford, William, and Thomas Keymer. *Vathek.* Oxford: Oxford University Press, 2013.

Bedford-Jones, H. "The Evil Eye of Bali." *Detective Fiction Weekly* 79.4 (October 7, 1933): 50–59.

Beecham, John Charles. "The Argus Pheasant." *All-Story Weekly* 67.3 (February 3, 1917): 353–378.

Beecham, John Charles. "A Daughter of Borneo." *All-Story Weekly* 100.3 (August 16, 1919): 353–377.

Begbie, Harold. "The Amazing Adventures of Andrew Latter." *The London Magazine* 12.71 (June 1906): 508–512.

Bellem, Robert Leslie. "The Executioner." *Spicy Mystery Stories* 1.4 (August 1935): 4–15.

Beresford, J. D. *The Hampdenshire Wonder.* 1911. Reprint, London: Eyre & Spottiswoode, 1948.

Bernstein, Robert, and Kurt Schaffenberger. "The Mermaid from Metropolis!" *Superman's Girl Friend, Lois Lane* 12 (October 1959): 1–9.

Binder, Otto, and C. C. Beck. "The Atomic War." *Captain Marvel Adventures* 66 (October 1946): 2–12.

Binder, Otto, and Charles Nicholas. "The Coming of Agent Zero." *Young Allies* 1 (Summer 1941): 2–10.

Binder, Otto, and Al Plastino. "The Legion of Super-Heroes." *Adventure Comics* 247 (April 1958): 1–12.

Binder, Otto, and Howard Sherman. "Space Taxi." *Mystery in Space* 21 (August–September 1954): 14–19.

Binder, Eando. "The Robot Aliens." *Wonder Stories* 6.9 (February 1935): 1032–1057.

Bionic Woman: The Complete Series. 1976–1978. Los Angeles, CA: Universal Studios Home Entertainment, 2015. DVD.

Blackmore, R. D. *Clara Vaughan.* London: Sampson Low, Marston, 1886.

Blackwood, Algernon. *John Silence, Physician Extraordinary.* Boston: John W. Luce, 1909.

Blade. Directed by Stephen Norrington. 1998. Los Angeles, CA: New Line Home Video, 2006. DVD.

Blassingame, Wyatt. "He Kills in Darkness." *Detective Tales* 6.3 (June 1937): 60–70.

Bloch, Chajim. *Der Prager Golem.* Vienna: The Golem, 1925.

Boiardo, Matteo Maria. *Orlando Innamorato [Orlando in Love].* Translated by Charles Stanley Ross. West Lafayette, IN: Parlor Press, 2004.

Boothby, Guy Newell. *Pharos the Egyptian*. London: Ward, Lock, 1899.

Boussenard, Louis. *10,000 Ans Dans Un Bloc de Glace*. Paris: C. Marpon et E. Flammarion, 1890.

Braddon, M. E. *The Trail of the Serpent*. 1879. Reprint edited by Chris Willis, New York: Modern Library, 2003.

Bramah, Ernest. *The Eyes of Max Carrados*. Hertfordshire: Wordsworth, 2013.

Brand, Max. "Jim Curry's Compromise." *Western Story Magazine* 24.6 (April 1, 1922): 1–34.

Brand, Max. "The Untamed." *All-Story Weekly* 91.3 (December 7, 1918): 353–370.

Branscombe, Eugene. "Child or Demon—Which?" *Ghost Stories* 1.4 (October 1926): 24–26.

Brault, Gerard J. *The Song of Roland*. University Park: Pennsylvania State University Press, 1978.

Brenner, George E. "The Clock Strikes." *Funny Pages* 1.6 (November 1936): 27–28.

Brenner, George E. "Iron Monster at Large Again." *Smash Comics* 1 (August 1939): 58–64.

Bridwell, E. Nelson, and Mike Sekowsky. "Five Characters in Search of a Plot!" *The Inferior Five* 1 (March–April 1967): 2–23.

Briefer, Dick. "New Adventures of Frankenstein." *Prize Comics* 1.7 (December 1940): 22–29.

Brocklebank, Katherine. "Bracelets." *Black Mask* 11.10 (December 1928): 86–94.

Brontë, Charlotte. *Jane Eyre*. New York: Knopf, 1991.

Brontë, Emily. *Wuthering Heights*. New York: Random House, 1943.

Broome, John, and Carmine Infantino. "The Mystery of the Elongated Man." *The Flash* 112 (April–May 1960): 1–13.

Broome, John, and Carmine Infantino. "The Origin of Captain Comet!" *Strange Adventures* 9 (June 1951): 2–11.

Broome, John, and Gil Kane. "SOS Green Lantern." *Showcase* 22 (September–October 1959): 1–6.

Broome, John, and Arthur F. Peddy. "The Plight of a Nation." *All-Star Comics* 40 (April–May 1948): 1–12.

Brown, Charles Brockden. *Ormond: Or, The Secret Witness*. New York: American Book Company, 1937.

Brown, Charles Brockden. *Three Gothic novels: Wieland or, the Transformation; Arthur Mervyn or, Memoirs of the Year 1793; Edgar Huntly or, Memoirs of a Sleep-walker*. New York: Literary Classics of the United States, 1998.

Brown, J. Macmillan Brown. *Riallaro, the Archipelago of Exiles*. London: H. Milford, 1931.

Brubaker, Ed, and Sean Phillips. *Criminal, Deluxe Edition*. New York: Marvel, 2009.

"Buffalo Bill's Heathen Pard: Or, Lung Hi on the Warpath." *Buffalo Bill Stories* 240 (December 16, 1905): 1–32.

Burgos, Carl. "But Terry, I Tell You I Need Another $10,000!" *Amazing-Man Comics* 5 (September 1939): 20–26.

Burgos, Carl. "The Coming of Manowar." *Target Comics* 1.1 (February 1940): 9–14.

Burgos, Carl. "The Origin of the Human Torch." *Marvel Comics* 1.1 (October 1939): 2–17.

Burks, Arthur J. "The Black Falcon." *Sky Fighters* 3.1 (October 1933): 10–48.

Burrage, Alfred S. *Spring-Heeled Jack Library* 1.1 (1904): 1–24.

Burroughs, Edgar Rice. *A Princess of Mars.* New York: Grosset & Dunlap, 1917.

Burton, William E. *The Baronet's Daughter, and the Secret Cell!* Boston: Henry L. Williams, 1845.

Busiek, Kurt, and Brent Anderson. *Astro City: Life in the Big City.* New York: DC Comics, 2011.

Busiek, Kurt, and Alex Ross. *Marvels.* New York: Marvel, 2010.

Byrd, Robert Montgomery. *Nick of the Woods.* London: Richard Bentley, 1837.

Byrne, John. "Back to the Basics!" *Fantastic Four* 232 (July 1981): 1–22.

Campell, John W., Jr. "The Mightiest Machine." *Astounding Stories* 14.4 (December 1934): 10–30.

Capek, Karel. *R.U.R. (Rossum's Universal Robots): A Fantastic Melodrama.* Garden City, NY: Doubleday, Page, 1923.

Captain America: The First Avenger. Directed by Joe Johnston. 2011. Burbank, CA: Buena Vista Home Entertainment, 2013. DVD.

Carew, Henry. *The Vampires of the Andes.* 1925. Reprint, New York: Arno Press, 1978.

Carreno, Al. "The Origin of Bulletgirl." *Master Comics* 13 (April 1941): 1–9.

Cavendish, Margaret. *The Convent of Pleasure and Other Plays.* Edited by Anne Shaver. Baltimore, MD: Johns Hopkins University Press, 1999.

Chadwick, Paul. "Python Men of the Lost City." *Captain Hazzard Magazine* 1.1 (May 1938): 10–60.

Chambers, Jim. "Block Buster." *Detective Comics* 20 (October 1938): 39–44.

Chambers, Jim. "The Night Raiders." *More Fun Comics* 36 (October 1938): 1–6.

Chambers, Robert W. "Diana's Chase." *Saturday Evening Post* 179.4 (June 8, 1907): 3–6, 26.

Chambers, Robert W. *The Maker of Moons.* Freeport, NY: Books for Libraries Press, 1969.

Chambers, Robert W. "The Mischief Maker: Diana's Chase." *Saturday Evening Post* 179.4 (June 9, 1907): 3–5.

Champion, D. L. "Alias Mr. Death." *Thrilling Detective* 1.4 (February 1932): 95–111.

Champion, D. L. "The Emperor of Death." *The Phantom Detective* 1.1 (February 1933): 8–105.

Chapian, Grieg. "Jupiter's Mission to Earth." *Prize Comics* 1.1 (March 1940): 24–31.

Chapman, Hank, and Russ Heath. "The Return of…the Human Torch." *Young Men* 24 (December 1953): 1–9.

Charteris, Leslie. *Meet the Tiger.* London: Ward, Lock, 1928.

Christie, Agatha. *The Mysterious Affair at Styles: A Detective Story.* London: John Lane Company, 1920.

Christie, Agatha. *The Secret Adversary.* New York: Dodd, Mead, 1922.

Christie, Agatha. "The Tuesday Night Club." *The Royal Magazine* 57.350 (December 1927): 1–8.

Chronicle. Directed by Josh Trank. 2012. Century City, CA: 20th Century Fox, 2012. DVD.

Claremont, Chris, and John Byrne. "Armageddon Now!" *The X-Men* 108 (December 1977): 1–17.

Claremont, Chris, and Frank Miller. *Wolverine.* New York: Marvel, 2009.

Clarke, Mary Cowden. *Kit Bam's Adventures: Or, The Yarns of an Old Mariner.* Boston: Ticknor and Fields, 1856.

Coates, Alfred. *Spring-Heel'd Jack: The Terror of London; A Romance of the Nineteenth Century.* London, 1867.

Cody, Stone. "Guns of the Damned." *The Western Raider* 1.1 (August–September 1938): 4–65.

Cole, Jack. "The Coming of the Comet." *Pep Comics* 1 (January 1940): 11–17.

Cole, Jack. "The Origin of Plastic Man." *Police Comics* 1 (August 1941): 32–37.

Collins, Wilkie. *Armadale.* New York: Dover Publications, 1977.

Collins, Wilkie. *The Moonstone.* New York: Knopf, 1992.

Conway, Gerry, and Jim Mooney. "The Man-Killer Moves at Midnight!" *Marvel Team-Up* 8 (April 1973): 1–20.

Conway, Gerry, Roy Thomas, and Gene Colan. "Dracula." *Tomb of Dracula* 1 (April 1972): 1–25.

Cooke, David C., and Charles J. Mazoujian. "Death-Bird Squadron." *Marvel Mystery Comics* 2 (December 1939): 52–53.

Coryell, John. "The Old Detective's Pupil: Or, The Mysterious Crime of Madison Square." *New York Weekly* 41.46 (1886): 1–8.

Crossen, Ken, and Jerry Robinson. "The Making of the Mightiest Man." *Atoman Comics* 1 (February 1946): 1–15.

The Crow. Directed by Alex Proyas. 1994. Santa Monica, CA: Miramax Lionsgate, 2012. DVD.

Crowe, Catherine. *The Night Side of Nature: Or, Ghosts and Ghost Seers.* London: George Routledge & Sons, 1882.

Crowe, Catherine. *Susan Hopley: Or, the Adventures of a Maid-Servant.* Edinburgh: William Tait, 1842.

Cruickshank, Harold F. "The Red Eagle." *Battle Birds* 1.1 (December 1932): 61–74.

Dacre, Charlotte. *Zofloya: Or, the Moor, A Romance of the Fifteenth Century, Etc.* London: Longman, Hurst, Rees & Orme, 1806.

Dahlman, Steve. "Prof. Philo Zog, Mechanical Wizard . . ." *Marvel Mystery Comics* 4 (February 1940): 42–49.

Daly, Carroll John. "The Crime Machine." *Dime Detective Magazine* 1.3 (January 1932): 82–93.

The Dark Knight. Directed by Christopher Nolan. 2008. Burbank, CA: Warner Home Video, 2008. DVD.

The Dark Knight Rises. Directed by Christopher Nolan. 2012. Burbank, CA: Warner Home Video, 2012. DVD.

Davis, Frederick C. "Murder Shrine." *Secret Agent X* 8.2 (March 1936): 85–107.

Davis, Frederick W. "Below the Dead Line." *Magnet Library* 428 (January 4, 1906): 1–8.

Davison, Gilderoy. *The Mysterious Mr. Brent.* London: Herbert Jenkins, 1935.

Dawson, Emma. *An Itinerant House and Other Stories.* San Francisco, CA: William Doxey, 1897.

De Cornuälle, Heldris, and Sarah Roche-Mahdi. *Silence: A Thirteenth-Century French Romance.* East Lansing, MI: Colleagues Press, 1992.

De Quincey, Thomas. *Klosterheim: Or, The Masque.* Boston: Whittemore, Niles, and Hall, 1855.

De L'Isle-Adam, Villiers. *Eve of the Future.* Lawrence, KS: Coronado, 1981.

De Villeneuve Lee, Manning. "Origin of the Scarlet Seal." *Smash Comics* 16 (November 1940): 22–26.

DeConnick, Kelly Sue, and Valentie De Landro. *Bitch Planet, Vol. 1: Extraordinary Machine.* Berkeley, CA: Image Comics, 2015.

Dee, John. *John Dee: Essential Readings.* Edited by Gerald Suster. Berkeley, CA: North Atlantic, 2003.

Dell, Watt. "Olga Mesmer." *Spicy Mystery Stories* 5.4 (August 1937): 64–65.

Dell, Watt. "Vera Ray." *Spicy Mystery Stories* 9.2 (June 1940): 86–89.

Delle Colonne, Guido. *Historia Destructionis Troiae.* Bloomington, IN: Indiana University Press, 1974.

Dent, Guy. *The Emperor of the If.* London: William Heinemann, 1926.

Dent, Lester. "The Fortress of Solitude." *Doc Savage* 12.2 (October 1938): 11–88.

Dent, Lester. "The Man of Bronze." *Doc Savage* 1.1 (March 1933): 3–93.

Dickens, Charles. *Bleak House.* George H. Ford, and Sylvère Monod, Norton Critical Edition. New York: Norton, 1977.

Dickens, Charles. "On Duty with Inspector Field." *Household Words* 3.64 (June 14, 1851): 265–269.

Dio, Cassius. *Dio's Roman History IX.* Translated by Earnest Carey. London: William Heinemann, 1905.

Ditko, Steve, and Denny O'Neill. "Where Lurks the Menace?" *Beware the Creeper* 1 (May–June 1968): 1–22.

Ditko, Steve, and Steve Skeates. "Prologue." *Showcase* 75 (June 1968): 1–2.

Dixon, Thomas. *The Clansmen.* New York: American New Company, 1905.

Dixon, Thomas. *The Leopard's Spots: A Romance of the White Man's Burden, 1865–1900.* Ridgewood, NJ: Gregg Press, 1967.

Dodsley, Robert, William Carew Hazlitt, and Richard Morris. *A Select Collection of Old English Plays.* 1744. Reprint, New York: B. Blom, 1964.

Doughty, Francis. "Old King Brady the Sleuth-Hound." *New York Detective Library* 241 (November 14, 1885): 1–8.

Doyle, C. W. "The Illumination of Lee Moy." *Lippincott's Magazine* 64.2 (August 1899): 263–270.

Dr. Mabuse, the Gambler. Directed by Fritz Lang. 1922. London: Eureka!, 2004. DVD.

Dracula: Complete Legacy Collection. Universal City, CA: Universal Studios Home Entertainment, 2014. DVD.

Drake, Arnold, and Carmine Infantino. "Who Has Been Lying in My Grave?" *Strange Adventures* 205 (October 1967): 1–16.

Du Terrail, Ponson. *La résurrection de Rocambole.* Paris: E. Dentu, 1866.

Du Terrail, Ponson. *Les Chevaliers du Clair du Lune.* Paris: Manginot-Hellitasse, 1862.

Du Terrail, Ponson. *Les Exploits de Rocambole.* Paris: Proust, 1859.

Dumas, Alexandre. *The Count of Monte Cristo.* Translated by Peter Washington. New York: Knopf, 2009.

Edwards, Ellis. "The Discovery of Gold in California Changed the Foothills of the Sierra Nevada Mountains..." *The Comics Magazine* 1.3 (July 1936): 24–25.

Eisner, Will. "The Old Hex House." *Wonder Comics* 2 (June 1939): 2–10.

Eisner, Will. "The Origin of the Spirit." *Police Comics* 11 (September 1942): 33–39.

Eisner, Will. "The Origin of Wonder Man." *Wonder Comics* 1 (May 1939): 2–15.

Eisner, Will, and Lou Fine. "Captain Flagg's River Pirates." *Wonderworld Comics* 3 (July 1939): 1–7.

Eisner, Will, and Mort Meskin. "Sheena, Queen of the Jungle." *Jumbo Comics* 1 (September 1938): 31–35.

Eisner, Will, and Charles Nicholas. "The Coming of the Blue Beetle." *Mystery Men Comics* 1 (August 1939): 45–48.

Eisner, Will, Bob Powell, and Chuck Cuidera. "The Origin of Blackhawk." *Military Comics* 1 (August 1941): 1–11.

Ellerbrock, G., and William Kent. "Far Off in Space on the Planet Antaclea." *Popular Comics* 46 (December 1939): 6–13.

Ellis, Edward S. *The Steam Man of the Prairies.* New York: Dover Publications, 2016.

Ellis, Sophie Wenzel. "Creatures of the Light." *Astounding Stories of Super-Science* 1.2 (February 1930): 196–220.

Ellis, Warren, and John Cassaday. *Planetary: All over the World, and Other Stories.* La Jolla, CA: WildStorm / DC Comics, 2000.

Ellis, Warren, and Stuart Immonen. *Nextwave, Agents of H.A.T.E.: The Complete Collection.* New York: Marvel, 2015.

Ellis, Warren, and Tom Raney. *Stormwatch Vol. 1.* New York: DC Comics, 2012.

Ellis, Warren, and Darrick Robertson. *Absolute Transmetropolitan Vol. 1.* New York: DC / Vertigo, 2015.

Elven, Sven. "The Rhangwa Pearls." *Detective Comics* 1 (March 1937): 7–12.

Ely, Bill. "Pearl of the Bleeding Heart." *New Adventure Comics* 2.5 (July 1937): 4–7.

England, George Allan. "The Fatal Gift." *All-Story Weekly* 49.1 (September 4, 1915): 1–28.

Englehart, Steve. ". . . Before the Dawn!" *Captain America* 175 (July 1974): 1–18.

Englehart, Steve, and Jim Starlin. *Master of Kung Fu* 17 (April 1974): 1–19.

Ennis, Garth, and Steve Dillon. *Absolute Preacher Vol. 1.* New York: Vertigo, 2016.

Ennis, Garth, and John McCrea. *Hitman Vol. 1: A Rage in Arkham.* New York: DC Comics, 2009.

Ernst, Paul. "Justice, Inc." *The Avenger* 1.1 (September 1939): 9–52.

Evans, Constance M. *The Girl with the X-Ray Eyes.* London, 1935.

Evans, Frank Howel. *The Murder Club.* New York: Burt Company, 1925.

Everett, Bill. "The Human Torch and the Sub-Mariner Meet." *Marvel Mystery Comics* 8 (June 1940): 1–10.

Everett, Bill. "Origin of Amazing-Man." *Amazing-Man Comics* 1.5 (September 1939): 1–10.

Everett, Bill. "Origin of the Sub-Mariner." *Marvel Comics* 1 (October 1939): 26–37.

Everett, Bill. "The Sub-Mariner Returns." *Young Men* 24 (December 1953): 18–26.

Everett, Bill. "The Treasure of Captain Derelict." *Young Men* 27 (April 1954): 18–25.

Falk, Lee, and Phil Davis. *Mandrake the Magician: Mandrake in Hollywood.* New York: Nostalgia Press, 1970.

Farmer, Philip José. *A Feast Unknown.* London: Titan Books, 2012.

Fearn, John Russell. "The Golden Amazon." *Fantastic Adventures* 1.2 (July 1939): 32–43.

Féval, Paul. *The White Wolf of Brittany.* London: C. H. Clarke, 1859.

Filchock, George. "The Ermine Appears." *Star Ranger Funnies* 15 (October 1938): 11–14.

Filchock, Martin. "Origin of Mighty Man." *Amazing Man Comics* 1.5 (September 1939): 59–65.

Finger, Bill, and Syd Shores. "The Crime of the Ages!" *All-Winners Comics* 19 (Fall, 1946): 1–5.

Fitch, Ken, and Bernard Baily. "Introduction 'Miss X.'" *Action Comics* 26 (July 1940): 30–39.

Fitzball, Edward. *The Black Robber: A Romance.* London: A. K. Newman, 1819.

The Flash: The Complete Series. Burbank, CA: Warner Home Video, 2011.

Fleischman, Hy. "Revenge of the Crimson Avenger." *Masked Ranger* 1 (April 1954): 8–13.

Fleming, Homer. "The A-G Gang." *Action Comics* 1 (June 1938): 15–20.

Fleming, Homer. "The Bar S Rustlers." *Detective Comics* 1 (March 1937): 45–50.

Fleming, Homer. "Rajah Maharajah." *New Comics* 5 (June 1936): 16–17.

Fletcher, R. A. *The Quest for El Cid.* New York: Knopf, 1990.

Forrest, Aston. *The Extraordinary Islanders: Being an Authentic Account of the Cruise of the "Asphodel."* London: R. A. Everett, 1903.

Forrester, Andrew, Jr. *The Female Detective.* London, 1864.

Fortune, Dion. *The Secrets of Dr. Taverner.* London: N. Douglas, 1926.

Fox, Gardner, and Everett E. Hibbard. "The First Meeting of the Justice Society of America." *All-Star Comics* 3 (Winter 1940–1941): 1–4.

Fox, Gardner, and Gil Kane. "Birth of the Atom!" *Showcase* 34 (September–October 1961): 1–10.

Fox, Gardner, and Joe Kubert. "Creature of a Thousand Shapes!" *The Brave and the Bold* 34 (February–March 1961): 1–25.

Fox, Gardner, and Dennis Neville. "Origin of Hawkman." *Flash Comics* 1 (January 1940): 22–33.

Fox, Gardner, and Mike Sekowsky. "Starro the Conqueror!" *The Brave and the Bold* 28 (February–March 1960): 1–5.

Fox, Gardner, and Howard Sherman. "The Menace of Wotan." *More Fun Comics* 55 (May 1940): 26–31.

Fox, Gill, and Lou Fine. "The Bombing of Pearl Harbor." *National Comics* 18 (December 1941): 1–9.

Fraction, Matt, and David Aja. *Hawkeye by Matt Fraction and David Aja Omnibus.* New York: Marvel, 2015.

Fraction, Matt, and Gabriel Ba. *Casanova The Complete Edition Volume 1: Luxuria.* Berkeley, CA: Image Comics, 2014.

Fraction, Matt, and Chip Zdarsky. *Sex Criminals, Vol. 1.* Berkeley, CA: Image Comics, 2014.

Frehm, Walter. "A Modern Robin Hood." *Mystery Men Comics* 1 (August 1939): 1–9.

Fulk, R. D., ed. *The Beowulf Manuscript: Complete Texts; and The Fight at Finnsburg.* Cambridge, MA: Harvard University Press, 2010.

Gaiman, Neil, Sam Keith, and Mike Dringenberg. *The Sandman Vol. 1: Preludes & Nocturnes.* New York: DC / Vertigo, 2010.

Galford, Ellen. *Moll Cutpurse, Her True History.* Ithaca, NY: Firebrand Books, 1985.

Gardenhire, S. M. "The Park Slope Mystery." *Saturday Evening Post* 178.4 (July 22, 1905): 6–8.

George, A. R., trans. *The Epic of Gilgamesh: The Babylonian Epic Poem and Other Texts in Akkadian and Sumerian.* London: Penguin, 2003.

Gerber, Steve, and Frank Brunner. "Howard the Barbarian." *Howard the Duck* 1 (January 1976): 1–19.

Gernsback, Hugo. "A New Sort of Magazine." *Amazing Stories* 1.1 (April 1926): 3.

Gernsback, Hugo. "Thought Transmission on Mars." *Electrical Experimenter* 3.9 (January 1916): 474.

Gershwin, Emil. "Origin of the Eagle." *Science Comics* 1 (February 1940): 1–8.

Gibson, Walter. "The Golden Master." *The Shadow* 31.2 (September 15, 1939): 9–52.

Gibson, Walter B. "The Living Shadow." *The Shadow, a Detective Magazine* 1.1 (April 1931): 2–116.

Gibson, Walter B. "The Whispering Eyes." *The Shadow* 55.1 (1949): 6–83.

Giesy, J. U., and Junius Smith. "The Occult Detector." *The Cavalier* 12.3 (February 17, 1912): 441–457.

Gill, Joe, and Steve Ditko. "In This Issue Introducting Captain Atom." *Space Adventures* 33 (March 1960): 8–16.

Gillen, Kieron, and Jamie McKelvie. *Phonogram Volume 1: Rue Britannia*. Berkeley, CA: Image Comics, 2007.

Gillen, Kieron, and Jamie McKelvie. *The Wicked + Divine, Vol. 1: The Faust Act*. Berkeley, CA: Image Comics, 2014.

Gillen, Kieron, and Jamie McKelvie. *Young Avengers Omnibus*. New York: Marvel, 2014.

Godwin, William. *St. Leon: A Tale of the Sixteenth Century*. London: G. G. and J. Robinson, 1800.

Goethe, Johann Wolfgang von. *Faust, Part One*. Translated by David Luke. Oxford: Oxford University Press, 2008.

Golden, Robert Louis. "Origin of the Eternal Brain." *Red Raven Comics* 1 (August 1940): 58–65.

Gordon, R. K. *The Story of Troilus*. New York: Dutton, 1964.

Grant, Alan, and Norm Breyfogle. "Letters to the Editor." *Detective Comics* 608 (November 1989): 1–22.

Grant, Steven, and Mike Zeck. *Punisher: Circle of Blood*. New York: Marvel, 2011.

Greatest American Hero: Season 1. 1981. Golden Valley, MT: Mill Creek Entertainment, 2010. DVD.

Green, Anna Katherine. *The Leavenworth Case*. 1878. Reprint, New York: Penguin Books, 2010.

The Green Hornet. Directed by Ford Beebe and Ray Taylor. 1940. Tulsa, OK: VCI Entertainment, 2011. DVD.

Green, William Child. *The Abbot of Montserrat*. 1826. Reprint, New York: Arno Press, 1977.

Greene, Robert. *The Honourable Historie of Friar Bacon and Friar Bungay*. Gloucester, U.K.: Dodo Press, 2008.

Greener, William. *Rufin's Legacy: A Theosophical Romance*. London: Hutchinson, 1892.

Griffith, George Chetwynd. *The Angel of the Revolution: A Tale of the coming Terror*. London: Tower Publishing Company, 1893.

Griffith, George Chetwynd. *A Honeymoon in Space*. London: C. A. Pearson, 1901.

Grosse, Karl. *Horrid Mysteries: A Story*. 1796. Reprint, London: Folio Press, 1968.

Guardineer, Fred. "The Mystery of the Freight Train Robberies." *Action Comics* 1 (June 1938): 21–32.

Gueullette, Thomas-Simon. *Chinese Tales: Or, The Wonderful Adventures of the Mandarin Fum-Hoam*. London: J. Parsons, 1800.

Gustavson, Paul. "The Sign of the Cricket." *Crack Comics* 1 (May 1940): 19–22.

Gustavson, Paul. "You'd Better Talk, Dillon." *Funny Pages* 2.10 (September 1938): 1–5.

Haggard, H. Rider. *She: A History of Adventure*. New York: Penguin, 2007.

Halsey, Harlan. "Old Sleuth, the Detective: Or, The Bay Ridge Mystery." *Fireside Companion* (June 10, 1872): 1.

Hancock. Directed by Peter Berg. 2008. Culver City, CA: Sony Pictures Home Entertainment, 2008. DVD.

Hand, Learned. *Detective Comics, Inc. v. Bruns Publications, Inc.* 111 F.2d 432 (2nd Cir., Apr. 29, 1940).

Hanks, Fletcher. "No White Man Knows Where the Elephant Goes . . ." *Jungle Comics* 2 (February 1940): 59–65.

Hanshew, Thomas L. *Cleek: The Man of Forty Faces*. New York: Cassell, 1913.

Harr, Will, and Edd Ashe. "The Mosconians Master Plan." *Top-Notch Comics* 5 (May 1940): 1–11.

Harr, Will, and Jack Binder. "Introducing Flexo the Rubber Man." *Mystic Comics* 1 (March 1940): 2–9.

Harrison, Robert L. *The Song of Roland*. New York: Signet Classic, 2012.

Harvey, Alfred, and Barbara Hall. "Origin of the Black Cat." *Pocket Comics* 1 (August 1941): 38–49.

"The Hawk of the Plains." *Surprise* 3.60 (April 1, 1933): 7–10.

Hawks, Chester. "Python Men of Lost City." *Captain Hazzard Magazine* 1.1 (May 1938): 10–60.

Hawthorne, Nathaniel. "The Gray Champion." *Twice-Told Tales*, 13–24. Boston: Fields, Osgood, 1871.

Hayward, William S. *Revelations of a Lady Detective*. London: George Vickers, 1864.

Heilman, Robert Bechtold. *An Anthology of English Drama Before Shakespeare*. New York: Rinehart, 1952.

Hernandez, Gilbert, and Jaime Hernandez. *Love & Rockets Vol. 1: Music for Mechanics*. Seattle, WA: Fantagraphics, 1985.

Heroes: The Complete Series. 2006–2010. Universal City, CA: Universal Home Entertainment, 2015. DVD.

Heron, E., and H. Heron. "The Story of the Spaniards, Hammersmith." *Pearson's Magazine* 5.25 (January 1898): 60–69.

Heron-Allen, Edward, and Selina Dolaro. *The Princess Daphne*. Leyburn: Tartarus, 2001.

Herrtage, Sidney J. H. *Sir Ferumbras*. 1879. Reprint, Oxford: Oxford University Press, 1966.

Heywood, Thomas. *The Fair Maid of the West, or a Girl Worth Gold*. Edited by Kevin Theis. Woodstock, IL: Dramatic Publications, 1995.

Hibbert, Samuel. *Sketches of the Philosophy of Apparitions: Or, an Attempt to Trace Such Illusions to Their Physical Causes*. Edinburgh, 1824.

Hickman, Jonathan, and Esad Ribic. *Secret Wars*. New York: Marvel, 2016.

Hoffmann, E. T. A. *Mademoiselle de Scudéri: A Tale of the Times of Louis XIV.* Translated by Andrew Brown. London: Hesperus, 2002.

Hoffmann, E. T. A. *Tales of Hoffmann.* Translated by Stella Humphries, Vernon Humphries, and R. J. Hollingdale. New York: Penguin, 1982.

Hogg, James, and Douglas Gifford. *The Three Perils of Man: War, Women and Witchcraft.* London: Chatto and Windus, 1972.

Hornung, E. W. *The Complete Short Stories of Raffles—The Amateur Cracksman.* London: Souvenir Press, 1984.

Howe, Irving, and Eliezer Greenberg. *A Treasury of Yiddish Stories.* New York: Viking Press, 1954.

Hughes, Richard, and David Gabrielsen. "Nemesis of Evil." *Exciting Comics* 3.3 (May 1941): 1–15.

Hugo, Victor. *Hans of Iceland.* London, 1825.

Hulme-Beaman, Emeric. *Ozmar the Mystic. A Novel.* London: Bliss, Sands, 1896.

Hulme-Beaman, Emeric. *The Prince's Diamond.* London: Hutchinson, 1898.

Incredible Hulk: Season 1. 1978. Universal City, CA: Universal Studios Home Entertainment, 2006. DVD.

The Incredibles. Directed by Brad Bird. 2004. Burbank, CA: Walt Disney Home Entertainment, 2005. DVD.

The Invisible Ray. Directed by Lambert Hillyer. 1936. Universal City, CA: Universal Studios, 2012.

Iron Man. Directed by Jon Favreau. 2008. Burbank, CA: Buena Vista Home Entertainment, 2013. DVD.

Iron Man 2. Directed by Jon Favreau. 2010. Burbank, CA: Buena Vista Home Entertainment, 2013. DVD.

Isaacs, Mrs. *Ariel, or the Invisible Monitor.* London: Minerva Press, 1801.

Isabella, Tony, and Trevor von Eeden. *Black Lightning* 1 (April 1977): 1–17.

Jackson, Edward Payson. *A Demigod.* New York: Harper & Brothers, 1886.

Jaeger, Muriel. *The Man with Six Senses.* London: The Hogarth Press, 1927.

Jane, Frederick Thomas. *The Violet Flame. A Story of Armageddon and After.* London: Ward, Lock, 1899.

Jesse, F. Tennyson. "Mademoiselle Lamotte of the Mantles." *Metropolitan Magazine* 48.3 (August 1918): 16–22.

Johns, Geoff, and Andy Kubert. *Flashpoint.* New York: DC Comics, 2012.

Johns, Geoff, Grant Morrison, Greg Rucka, and Mark Waid. "Golden Lads and Lasses Must . . ." *52* 1 (July 2006): 1–24.

Johnson, D. Curtis, and J. H. Willliams III. "Baptized in Fire." *Chase* 1 (February 1998): 1–22.

Jones, Neil R. "The Jameson Satellite." *Amazing Stories* 6.4 (July 1931): 334–343.

Judex. Directed by Louis Feuillade. 1917. Los Angeles, CA: Flicker Alley, 2004. DVD.

Jurgens, Dan, and Jerry Ordway. *The Death of Superman.* New York: DC Comics, 2013.

Jussen, Steve. "How Old is Zardi—This Man Who Does Not Die?" *Amazing-Man Comics* 11 (April 1940): 29–34.

Kane, Bob, and Bill Finger. "The Case of the Chemical Syndicate." *Detective Comics* 27 (May 1939): 2–7.

Kane, Bob, and Bill Finger. "The Pirate Ship." *New Adventure Comics* 26 (May 1938): 13–17.

Kane, Bob, and Bill Finger. "Robin the Boy Wonder." *Detective Comics* 38 (April 1940): 1–12.

Kanigher, Robert, and Nick Cardy. "A Penny for a Black Star." *Teen Titans* 26 (March–April 1970): 1–23.

Kanigher, Robert, and Carmine Infantino. "Mystery of the Human Thunderbolt!" *Showcase* 4 (September–October 1956): 1–12.

Kanigher, Robert, and Carmine Infantino. "Nine Worlds to Conquer." *Mystery in Space* 1 (April–May 1951): 1–10.

Kanigher, Robert, and Carmine Infantino. "Terror Rides the Rails!" *Flash Comics* 98 (August 1948): 28–32.

Karig, Walter. *Zotz!* New York: Rinehart, 1947.

Kashuba, Maurice. "In His Famous Mountain-Top Laboratory..." *Popular Comics* 60 (February 1941): 2–9.

Kelland, Clarence Budington. "Still Face." *The Saturday Evening Post* 197.18 (November 1, 1924): 5–7.

Kerruish, Jessie Douglas. *The Undying Monster.* London: Heath Cranston, 1922.

Keyhoe, Donald. "A Squadron Will Perish." *Flying Aces* 9.3 (August 1931): 8–31.

Keyhoe, Donald. "Vultrues of Lost Valley." *Flying Aces* 24.4 (November 1936): 4–8.

Kildale, Malcolm. "Early in the Twenty-First Century, a Cruise Ship." *Planet Comics* 1 (January 1940): 17–22.

Kildale, Malcolm. "Far to the North, Vast Wastes of Land..." *Amazing Mystery Funnies* 2.8 (August 1939): 2–10.

Kildale, Malcolm. "Speed Centaur." *Amazing Mystery Funnies* 2.8 (August 1939): 2–11.

Killigrew, Thomas. *Comedies and Tragedies.* New York: B. Blom, 1967.

Kindt, Matt. *Mind MGMT Volume 1: The Manager.* Milwaukie, OR: Dark Horse Originals, 2013.

Kinney, Arthur F., ed. *Renaissance Drama: An Anthology of Plays and Entertainments.* Malden, MA: Blackwell Publishers, 2005.

Kinsey, Alfred C., Wardell Baxter Pomeroy, and Clyde E. Martin. *Sexual Behavior in the Human Male.* Philadelphia: W. B. Saunders, 1948.

Kirby, Jack. "Orion Fights for Earth!" *New Gods* 1 (February–March 1971): 1–23.

Kirby, Jack, and Joe Simon. "Break the Spy Ring." *Fighting American* 1.1 (April–May 1954): 1–10.

Kirkman, Robert, and Tony Moore. *The Walking Dead, Vol. 1: Days Gone Bye.* Berkeley, CA: Image Comics, 2013.

Kiss, Edmund. *Das Glaeserne Meer.* Leipzig: Koehler & Amelang, G.m.b.H,, 1930.

Klaus Störtebecker, Der Gefürchtete Herrscher der Meere 1 (July 13, 1908): 1–32.

Klein, George. "Holdup! Robbery! Murder!" *All-Winners Comics* 8 (1942–1943): 52–63.

Kolb, John F. "So My Dear Brother Won't Let Me Have More Money." *Amazing Man Comics* 1.5 (September 1939): 37–43.

Lach-Szyrma, Wladyslaw. *A Voice From Another World.* Oxford, 1874.

Lacy, Norris J. *Lancelot-Grail: The Old French Arthurian Vulgate and Post-Vulgate in Translation.* Vol. 1, *Introduction; History of the holy grail; Story of Merlin.* New York: Garland, 1993.

Lanford, Russ. "The Train Wreck." *Mystic Comics* 4 (July 1940): 48–55.

Lawrence, D. H. *Sea and Sardinia.* Cambridge: Cambridge University Press, 2002.

Lawrence, Mort, and Robert Peterson. "Transmutation! The Dream of Centuries Is an Actuality!" *The Atomic Thunderbolt* 1 (February 1946): 1–10.

Lawson, Alfred. *Born Again.* New York: Wox, Conrad Company, 1904.

Le Fanu, J. Sheridan. "Green Tea." In *Green Tea and Other Ghost Stories*, 1–32. New York: Dover, 1993.

Le Queux, William. *The Rainbow Mystery: Chronicles of a Colour-Criminologist, etc.* London: Hodder & Stoughton, 1917.

Leblanc, Maurice, and Michael Sims. *Arsène Lupin, Gentleman-Thief.* New York: Penguin Books, 2007.

Lee, Jim, and Chris Claremont. *X-Men* 1 (October 1991): 1–37.

Lee, Stan, and Gene Colan. "Brother, Take My Hand!" *Daredevil* 47 (December 1968): 1–20.

Lee, Stan, and Gene Colan. "The Coming of . . . the Falcon!" *Captain America* 117 (September 1969): 1–20.

Lee, Stan, and Steve Ditko. "Spider-Man!" *Amazing Fantasy* 15 (September 1962): 2–12.

Lee, Stan, and Bill Everett. "The Origin of Daredevil." *Daredevil* 1 (April 1964): 1–23.

Lee, Stan, and Don Heck. "The Sign of the Serpent." *Avengers* 32 (September 1966): 1–20.

Lee, Stan, and Jack Kirby. "Among Us Hide . . . the Inhumans!" *Fantastic Four* 45 (December 1965): 1–20.

Lee, Stan, and Jack Kirby. "Captain America Joins...The Avengers!" *Avengers* 4 (March 1964): 1–23.

Lee, Stan, and Jack Kirby. "The Black Panther!" *Fantastic Four* 52 (July 1966): 1–20.

Lee, Stan, and Jack Kirby. "The Coming of the Avengers." *The Avengers* 1 (September 1963): 1–22.

Lee, Stan, and Jack Kirby. "The Coming of the Hulk." *The Incredible Hulk* 1 (May 1962): 1–6.

Lee, Stan, and Jack Kirby. "The Fangs of the Desert Fox." *Sgt. Fury* 6 (March 1964): 1–23.

Lee, Stan, and Jack Kirby. "The Fantastic Four!" *Fantastic Four* 1 (November 1961): 2–14.

Lee, Stan, and Jack Kirby. "The Silver Burper." *Not Brand Echh* 1 (August 1967): 2–9.

Lee, Stan, and Jack Kirby. "To Wake the Mangog!" *Thor* 154 (July 1968): 1–20.

Lee, Stan, and Jack Kirby. "X-Men." *The X-Men* 1 (September 1963): 1–23.

Lee, Stan, Larry Lieber, and Jack Kirby. "The Thunder God and the Thug!" *Journey into Mystery* 89 (February 1963): 1–13.

Leland, Charles Godfrey. *The Unpublished Legends of Virgil*. New York: Macmillan, 1900.

Lewis, Bernard, and Stanley Burstein. "The Dream of Nectanebo." In *Land of Enchanters: Egyptian short stories from the earliest times to the present day*, edited by Bernard Lewis and Stanley Burstein, 95–97. Princeton: Markus Wiener Publishers, 2001.

Lieber, Larry, Stan Lee, and Jack Kirby. "I Am the Fantastic Dr. Droom!" *Amazing Adventures* 1 (June 1961): 21–25.

"The Life and Death of Mrs. Mary Frith, Commonly Called Mal Cutpurse." *Rogue's Gallery*. http://www.crimeculture.com/earlyunderworlds/Contents/Cutpurse.html. Accessed on September 28, 2016.

Lippard, George. *The Quaker City: Or the Monks of Monk Hall; A Romance of Philadelphia Life, Mystery, and Crime*. Amherst, MA: University of Massachusetts Press, 1995.

Lipscomb, George. *The Grey Friar and the Black Spirit of the Wye: A Romance*. London: Minerva Press, 1810.

Littell, Jane. "Party Girl." *Underworld Romances* 1.1 (1931): 48–67.

Littleton, Betty J. *Clyomon and Clamydes*. The Hague: Mouton, 1968.

Lois & Clark: The New Adventures of Superman: Season 1. 1993. Burbank, CA: Warner Home Video, 2006. DVD.

Løseth, Eilbert. *Robert le Diable. Roman d'adventures*. 1903. Reprint, New York: Johson, 1968.

Loudon, Mrs., and Alan Rauch. *The Mummy!: A Tale of the Twenty-Second Century*. Ann Arbor, MI: University of Michigan Press, 1994.

Lytton, Edward Bulwer. *The Coming Race*. London: G. Routledge & Sons, 1875.

Lytton, Edward Bulwer. *Night and Morning*. London: G. Routledge & Sons, 1841.

Lytton, Edward Bulwer. *A Strange Story*. London: Sampson Low, Son, 1862.

Lytton, Edward Bulwer. *Zanoni*. London: W. Nicholson & Sons, 1890.

Machen, Arthur. *The Chronicle of Clemendy*. London: Martin Secker, 1925.

Malory, Thomas. *Le Morte d'Arthur*. New York: E. P. Dutton, 1906.

"The Man in the Black Cloak: Or, In Search of the John Street Jewels." *The Boys of New York; A Paper for Young Americans* 11.569 (1886): 1–8.

Man of Steel. Directed by Zack Snyder. 2013. Burbank, CA: Warner Home Video, 2013. DVD.

The Man Who Shot Liberty Valence / Shane Double Feature. Directed by John Ford and George Stevens. 1962 and 1953. Hollywood, CA: Paramount, 2008. DVD.

Manetho, and W. G. Waddell. *Manetho.* Cambridge, MA: Harvard University Press, 1940.

Manning, William Henry. *Lady Jaguar, the Robber Queen: A Romance of the Black Chaparral.* New York: Beadle & Adams, 1882.

Mantlo, Bill, and Sal Buscema. "Arrival!" *Rom* 1 (December 1979): 1–18.

Mantlo, Bill, Michael Golden, and Joe Rubinstein. "Homeworld!" *Micronauts* 1 (January 1979): 1–17.

Marinetti, F. T., Steve Cox, and Carol Diethe. *Mafarka the Futurist: An African Novel.* London: Middlesex University Press, 1998.

The Mark of Zorro. Directed by Fred Niblo. 1920. Mountain View, CA: Rialto Media, 2007. DVD.

Marryat, Frederick. *The Novels of Captain Marryat.* London, 1875.

Marsh, Richard. *The Beetle: A Mystery.* London: Skeffington & Son, 1897.

Marshall, Luther. *Thomas Boobig: A Complete Enough Account of His Life and Singular Disappearance: Narration of His Scribe.* Boston: Lee and Shepard, 1895.

Marston, William Moulton, and Harry G. Peter. "Introducing Wonder Woman." *All-Star Comics* 8 (December 1941–January 1942): 61–68.

Marston, William Moulton, and Harry G. Peter. "The Menace of Dr. Poison." *Sensation Comics* 2 (February 1942): 1–13.

Martin, George R. R., and Edward Bryant. *Wild Cards: A Mosaic Novel.* New York: Bantam Books, 1987.

The Mask. Directed by Chuck Russell. 1994. Los Angeles, CA: New Line Cinema, 2006. DVD.

The Masked Rider. Directed by Aubrey M. Kennedy. 1919. Newtown, PA: Serial Squadron, 2015. DVD.

Masters of the Universe. Directed by Gary Goddard. 1987. Burbank, CA: Warner Home Video, 2009. DVD.

Maturin, Charles. *The Albigenses, A Romance.* London: Hurst, Robinson and Co., 1824.

Maturin, Charles. *Melmoth the Wanderer: A Tale.* 1820. Reprint, Lincoln, NE: University of Nebraska Press, 1961.

Mayer, Robert. *Superfolks: A Novel.* New York: Dial Press, 1977.

Maynard, Guy L. "Senor Red Mask." *Street & Smith's Wild West Weekly* 66.3 (April 2, 1932): 1–12.

Mazzucchelli, David. *Asterios Polyp.* New York: Pantheon Books, 2009.

McCulley, Johnston. "The Big Six." *Detective Story Magazine* 34.4 (September 7, 1920): 2–32.

McCulley, Johnston. *Curse of Capistrano: The Original Adventures of Zorro.* Akron, OH: Summit Classic Press, 2013.

McCulley, Johnston. "Trimble, Trouble Maker." *Detective Story Magazine* 6.5 (March 5, 1917): 1–31.

McKenzie, Roger, and Ernie Colon. "Battlestar Galactica." *Battlestar Galactica* 1 (March 1979): 1–18.

McKenzie, Roger, and Frank Miller. "A Grave Mistake!" *Daredevil* 158 (May 1979): 1–17.

McNeil, Carla Speed. *Finder: Sin-Eater, Vol. 1.* Philadelphia, PA: Kogan Page, 1999.

Meade, L. T., and Robert Eustace. "The Adventures of John Bell—Ghost-Exposer." *Cassell's Family Magazine* 24.1 (June 1897): 78–91.

Meade, L. T., and Robert Eustace. "The Dead Hand." *Pearson's Magazine* 7.2 (1902): 177–186.

Mercer, Marilyn, and Jerry Grandenetti. "The Strange Case of the Absent Floor." *Rangers Comics* 47 (June 1949): 14–21.

Middleton, Thomas, and Thomas Dekker. *The Roaring Girle: Or, Moll Cut-Purse.* Amersham, U.K.: John S. Farmer, 1914.

Miller, Frank. *The Dark Knight Returns 30th Anniversary Edition.* New York: DC Comics, 2016.

Miller, Frank, and Klaus Janson. "Last Hand." *Daredevil* 181 (April 1982): 1–38.

Mills, Tarpe. "In the Sumptuous Office of Steve Harrington . . ." *Amazing Man Comics* 1.5 (September 1939): 12–16.

Mills, Tarpe. "Miss Fury." *Miss Fury* 1 (Winter 1942–1943): 1–57.

Mish, Charles C., ed. *Short Fiction of the Seventeenth Century.* New York: W. W. Norton, 1968.

Modell, Norman, and Lionel March. "The Gold of Garlok." *Colossus Comics* 1 (1940): 39–50.

Moench, Doug, and Bill Sienkiewicz. "The Macabre Moon Knight!" *Moon Knight* 1 (November 1980): 1–24.

Moore, Alan, and Steve Bissette. "Growth Patterns." *Swamp Thing* 37 (June 1985): 1–23.

Moore, Alan, and Dave Gibbons. *Watchmen.* New York: DC Comics, 2014.

Moore, Alan, and Garry Leach. "A Dream of Flying." *Warrior* 1 (March 1982): 3–10.

Moore, Alan, and David Lloyd. *V for Vendetta.* New York: Vertigo/DC Comics, 2005.

Moore, Alan, and Kevin O'Neill. *League of Extraordinary Gentlemen Omnibus.* New York: DC Comics, 2011.

Moore, Edward. *The Mysteries of Hungary: A Romantic History of the Fifteenth Century, etc.* London, 1817.

Moore, Terry. *Strangers in Paradise Omnibus Edition.* Houston, TX: Abstract Studios, 2013.

Morley, Henry, ed. *Early English Prose Romances.* London: G. Routledge and Sons, 1906.

Morrison, Grant. *The Invisibles.* New York: DC / Vertigo, 2012.

Morrison, Grant, and John Nyberg. *The Doom Patrol Omnibus.* New York: DC / Vertigo, 2014.

Morrison, Grant, and Frank Quitely. *All-Star Superman.* New York: DC Comics, 2011.

Morrison, Grant, and Frank Quitely. *WE3*. New York: DC/Vertigo, 2014.

Morrison, Grant, and Chas Truog. *The Animal Man Omnibus*. New York: DC / Vertigo, 2013.

Morrison, Grant, and J. H. Williams III. *Seven Soldiers of Victory, Vol. 1*. New York: DC Comics, 2006.

Munday, Anthony, and M. St. Clare Byrne. *John a Kent & John a Cumber*. Oxford: Oxford University Press, 1923.

Munro, John. *A Trip to Venus*. London: Jarrold & Sons, 1897.

Myler, Lok.. "Ein Mann fällt vom Himmel." *Sun Koh Der Erbe von Atlantis* 1 (May 1933): 1–32.

The Mysterious Doctor Satan. Directed by John English and William Witney. 1940. Golden Valley, MT: Mill Creek Entertainment, 2007. DVD.

Mystery Men. Directed by Kinka Usher. 1999. Universal City, CA: Universal Studios Home Entertainment, 2000. DVD.

Naubert, Christiane B. E. *Herman of Unna: a series of adventures of the fifteenth century, in which the proceedings of the secret tribunal under the emperors Winceslaus and Sigismond, are delineated*. London: G. G. and J. Robinson, 1795–1795.

Nesbit, E. "The Third Drug." *Strand Magazine* 35.206 (February 1908): 179–188.

Newth, Michael A. *The Song of Aliscans*. New York: Garland, 1992.

Nicholson, J. S. *Thoth: A Romance*. Edinburgh: Blackwood and Sons, 1888.

Nietzsche, Friedrich. *Thus Spoke Zarathustra*. Translated by Adrian del Caro and edited by Robert Pippin. Cambridge: Cambridge University Press, 2006.

Nordling, Klaus. "Origin of the Thin Man." *Mystic Comics* 1.4 (July 1940): 19–26.

North, Ryan, and Erica Henderson. *The Unbeatable Squirrel Girl Vol. 1: Squirrel Power*. New York: Marvel, 2015.

Odle, E. V. *The Clockwork Man*. London: William Heinemann, 1923.

"Old Cap. Collier, Chief of Detectives: Or, 'Piping' the New Haven Mystery." *Old Cap. Collier Library* 1 (1883): 1–8.

O'Neill, Denny, and Neal Adams. "No Evil Shall Escape My Sight!" *Green Lantern* 76 (April 1970): 1–23.

O'Neill, Denny, and Mike Sekowsky. "Wonder Woman's Last Battle." *Wonder Woman* 179 (November–December 1968): 1–23.

Orczy, Baroness. *The Scarlet Pimpernel*. Hollywood, FL: Simon & Brown, 2010.

Page, Norvell W. "The Emperor from Hell." *The Spider* 15.2 (July 1938): 4–77.

Parker, Bill, and C. C. Beck. "Introducing Captain Marvel." *Whiz Comics* 2 (February 1940): 1–13.

Parker, Bill, and Pete Costanza. "Origin of Golden Arrow." *Whiz Comics* 2 (February 1940): 22–31.

Pechey, Archibald Thomas. *The Adjusters*. London: Anglo-Eastern Publishing, 1922.

Peddy, Arthur. "The Coming of the Phantom Lady." *Police Comics* 1 (August 1941): 32–37.

Peretz, I. L. *The I. L. Peretz Reader*. New Haven, CT: New Yiddish Library, 2013.

Perez, George, Marv Wolfman, and Pablo Marcos. "The Murder Machine." *The New Teen Titans Annual* 2 (1983): 1–42.

Perez, George, Marv Wolfman, and Romeo Tanghal. "New Teen Titans." *The New Teen Titans* 1 (November 1980): 1–25.

Peters, Daniel. "The Origin of Dynamic Man." *Mystic Comics* 1.1 (March 1940): 54–64.

Peterson, A. L. "Lin Wade Top Waddy of the 'Lazy Y' Ranch . . ." *Star Comics* 1.16 (December 1938): 1–6.

Pinajian, Art. "Fantastic Brain Destroyers." *Zip Jet* 1 (February 1953): 1–7.

Pinajian, Art. "Origin of Madam Fatale." *Crack Comics* 1 (May 1940): 52–56.

Pinajian, Art. "Red Man of the Rockies." *Star Ranger Funnies* 2.5 (October 1939): 1–5.

Pindar. *Pindar: The Nemean and Isthmian Odes.* Translated by Charles Augustus Maude Fennell. Cambridge: Cambridge University Press, 1883.

Plato. *Plato in Twelve Volumes.* Translated by W. R. M. Lamb. Reprint of the 1925 edition. Perseus Digital Library. http://www.perseus.tufts.edu/hopper /text?doc=urn:cts:greekLit:tlg0059.tlg033. Accessed on October 3, 2016.

Plutarch. *Plutarch: Lives of the Noble Grecians and Roman.* Translated by Arthur Hugh Clough. Oxford: Benediction Classics, 2015.

Poe, Edgar Allan. *Complete Stories and Poems of Edgar Allan Poe.* Garden City, NY: Doubleday, 1966.

Polidori, John William. *The Vampyre and Ernestus Berchtold or The Modern Eedipus.* Edited Kathleen Scherf and D. L. Macdonald. Orchard Park, NY: Broadview Press, 2007.

Potter, Robert. *The Germ Growers: The Strange Adventures of Robert Easterley and John Wilbraham.* London: Hutchinson, 1892.

Powell, Bob. "The Flying Circus." *Strongman* 1 (March–April 1955): 1–8.

Powerpuff Girls: The Complete Series—10th Anniversary Collection. 1998–2004. Atlanta, GA: Turner Home Entertainment, 2009. DVD.

Praed, Rosa Caroline. *The Brother of the Shadow: A Mystery of To-day.* London: G. Routledge & Sons, 1886.

Prest, Thomas Peckett, and James Malcolm Rymer. *Varney the Vampyre: Or, The Feast of Blood.* 1847. Reprint, New York: Arno Press, 1970.

Prince, Arnold D. "Life on Our Distant Neighbor Is 'Grand, Intense, Formidable,' Says M. Perrier." *New York Tribune*, February 1920.

Pronzini, Bill. *Werewolf!* New York: Arbor House, 1979.

Pseudo-Callisthenes. *The Greek Alexander Romance.* Translated by Richard Stoneman. London, England: Penguin, 1991.

Pseudo-Callisthenes. *The Romance of Alexander the Great by Pseudo-Callisthenes.* Translated by Albert Mugrdich Wolohojian. New York: Columbia University Press, 1969.

Pulci, Luigi. *Morgante: The Epic Adventures of Orlando and His Giant Friend Morgante.* Translated by Joseph Tusiani. Bloomington: Indiana University Press, 1998.

Pyle, Howard. *The Merry Adventures of Robin Hood of Great Renown in Nottingham-shire.* New York: Charles Scribner's Sons, 1883.

Radcliffe, Ann. *The Italian: Or, The Confessional of the Black Penitents: a Romance.* London: T. Cadell and W. Davies, 1811.

Radcliffe, Ann. *The Mysteries of Udolpho.* New York: Dutton, 1931.

Raymond, P. T. *The Man in the Black Cloak: Or, In Search of the John Street Jewels.* Baldwin, NY: Almond Press, 2009.

Reynolds, Alexander M. "The Mystery of Djara Singh." *The Overland Monthly* 30.179 (1897): 401–406.

Reynolds, G. W. M. *Wagner the Wehr-Wolf.* 1857. Reprint, New York: Dover Publications, 1975.

Rhodius, Apollonius. *Argonautica (Loeb Classical Library).* Translated by William H. Race. Cambridge, MA: Harvard University Press, 2008.

Richmond: Scenes in the Life of a Bow Street Runner, Drawn Up from His Private Memoranda. 1827. Reprint, New York: Dover Publications, 1976.

Rico, Don, and Jack Binder. "The Daredevil, Master of Courage." *Silver Streak Comics* 6 (September 1940): 30–37.

Rittenberg, Max. "The Man Who Lived Again." *The London Magazine* 25.150 (February 1911): 708–719.

Robinson, James, and Tony Harris. *The Starman Omnibus Vol. 1.* New York: DC Comics, 2012.

RoboCop. Directed by Paul Verhoeven. 1987. Los Angeles, CA: MGM, 2001. DVD.

The Rock of Modrec; Or, The Legend of Sir Eltram: An Ethical Romance. Dublin: Thomas Burnside, 1792.

The Rocketeer. Directed by Joe Johnston. 1991. Burbank, CA: Walt Disney Home Video, 1999. DVD.

Rohmer, Sax. "Fu Manchu." In *Meet the Detective,* edited by H. C. McNeile, A. E. W. Mason, and Cecil Madden, 64–67. London: G. Allen & Unwin, 1935.

Romberg, Sigmund, Otto Harbach, Oscar Hammerstein, II, and Frank Mandel. *The Desert Song: A Musical Play in Two Acts.* New York: S. French, 1959.

Romita, John. "Back from the Dead!" *Young Men* 24 (December 1953): 12–17.

Rowcroft, Charles. *The Triumph of Woman: A Christmas Story.* London, 1848.

Saint-Yves, Joseph Alexandre. *Mission de l'Inde en Europe, mission de l'Europe en Asie. La question du Mahatma et sa solution. Ouvrage orné de deux portraits hors texte.* Paris: Dorbon, 1910.

Samachson, Joe, and Joe Certa. "The Strange Experiment of Dr. Erdel." *Detective Comics* 225 (November 1955): 23–28.

Sansone, Leonard. "The Origin of Mystico." *Startling Comics* 1.1 (June 1940): 26–32.

Sargent, Ellen C. "Wee Wi Ping." *The Californian* 5.25 (January 1882): 60–70.

Satrapi, Marjane. *Persepolis: The Story of a Childhood.* New York: Pantheon Books, 2004.

Scanlon, C. K. M. *The Bat Strikes Again and Again!* Boston: Altus Press, 2009.

Schachner, Nat. "Redmask of the Outlands." *Astounding Stories* 12.5 (January 1934): 2–30.

Schachner, Nat. "The Son of Redmask." *Astounding Stories* 15.6 (August 1935): 100–122.

Schiff, Jack, Mort Weisinger, Bernie Breslauer, and George Papp. "Columbus of Space." *Real Fact Comics* 6 (January–February 1947): 7–10.

Schiller, Friedrich. *The Ghost-Seer.* Columbia, SC: Camden House, 1992.

Schiller, Friedrich. *The Robbers and Wallenstein.* Translated by F. J. Lamport. New York: Penguin Books, 1979.

Schurmacher, Emile, and Ed Kressy. "The Scar Bozzi Case." *Miracle Comics* 1.1 (February 1940): 46–53.

Scott, R. T. M. "The Spider Strikes." *The Spider* 1.1 (October 1933): 8–107.

Scott, Walter. *The Black Dwarf.* London: William Blackwood, 1816.

Scott, Walter, and Peter Garside, *Guy Mannering.* Edinburgh: Edinburgh University Press, 1999.

The Searchers. Directed by John Ford. 1956. Burbank, CA: Warner Home Video, 2007. DVD.

Segar, E. C., Kim Thompson, Jules Feiffer, and Bill Blackbeard. *I Yam What I Yam.* Seattle, WA: Fantagraphics, 2006.

Sekowsky, Mike. "The Beginning." *Captain Flash* 1 (November 1954): 1–7.

Serviss, Garrett Putman. *Edison's Conquest of Mars.* Los Angeles: Carcosa House, 1947.

Seuling, Carole, Steve Gerber, and George Tuska. "Shanna the She-Devil!" *Shanna, the She-Devil* 1 (December 1972): 1–21.

The Shadow. Directed by James W. Horne. 1940. Golden Valley, MT: Mill Creek Entertainment, 2012. DVD.

The Shadow. Directed by Russell Mulcahy, 1994. Universal City, CA: Universal Studios, 1997. DVD.

The Shadow Strikes. Directed by Lynn Shores. 1937. Eden Prairie, MN: Alpha Video & Audio, 2003. DVD.

Shakespeare, William. *The Riverside Shakespeare.* Edited by G. Blakemore Evans. Boston: Houghton Mifflin, 1974.

Shaw, Bernard. *Back to Methuselah: A Metabiological Pentateuch.* New York: Brentano's, 1921.

Shelley, Mary. *Frankenstein: The Original 1818 Text.* Edited by D. L. Macdonald, and Kathleen Scherf. Calgary: Broadview Press, 1999.

Shelley, Percy. *St. Irvyne, or the Rosicrucian: A Romance.* London: J. J. Stockdale, 1811.

Shepard, Leslie, ed. *The Dracula Book of Great Vampire Stories.* Secaucus, NJ: Citadel Press, 1977.

Sherman, Harold. *Tahara, Boy Mystic of India.* Chicago: The Goldsmith Publishing Company, 1933.

Shiel, M. P. "The Empress of the Earth." *Short Stories* 475 (February 5, 1898): 161–169.

Shiel, M. P. *The Isle of Lies.* London: T. Werner Laurie, 1909.

Shooter, Jim, and Mike Zeck. *Secret Wars.* New York: Marvel, 2011.

Shorten, Harry, and Irv Novick. "G-Man Extraordinary." *Pep Comics* 1 (January 1940): 1–10.

Shorten, Harry, and George Storm. "The Origin of the Hangman." *Pep Comics* 17 (July 1941): 14–24.

Siddons, Henry. *Reginal di Torby: Or, The Twelve Robbers.* London: Minerva Press, 1803.

Siegel, Jerry. "The Secret Formula." *Approved Comics* 2 (March 1954): 1–8.

Siegel, Jerry, and Bernard Baily. "The Spectre." *More Fun Comics* 52 (February 1940): 1–10.

Siegel, Jerry, and Joe Shuster. "As a Distant Planet Was Destroyed by Old Age . . ." *Action Comics* 1 (June 1938): 2.

Siegel, Jerry, and Joe Shuster. "Introducing Dr. Occult." *New Fun* 6 (October 1935): 13.

Siegel, Jerry, and Joe Shuster. "Toth and the Secret Seven Part 2." *More Fun* 2.2 (October 1936): 36–37.

Simon, Joe, and Louis Cazeneuve. "The Origin of the Red Raven." *Red Raven Comics* 1.1 (August 1940): 2–18.

Simon, Joe, and Jack Kirby. "Case No. 1. Meet Captain America." *Captain America Comics* 1 (March 1941): 2–9.

Simon, Joe, and Jack Kirby. "The Double Life of Private Strong." *The Double Life of Private Strong* 1 (June 1959): 2–5.

Simon, Joe, and Jack Kirby. "The Strange New World of the Fly." *The Fly* 1 (August 1959): 1–8.

Sims, Michael, ed. *Dracula's Guest: A Connoisseur's Collection of Victorian Vampire Stories.* New York: Walker, 2010.

Six Million Dollar Man: The Complete Series. 1974–1978. Universal City, CA: Universal Studios Home Entertainment, 2015. DVD.

The Skeleton Horseman: Or, The Shadow of Death. London, 1866.

Smith, Alexander, and Arthur Lawrence Hayward. *A complete history of the lives and robberies of the most notorious highwaymen, footpads, shoplifts, & cheats of both sexes, wherein their most secret and barbarous murders, unparalleled robberies, notorious thefts, and unheard-of cheats are set in a true light and exposed to public view, for the common benefit of mankind.* 1719. Reprint, London: G. Routledge & Sons, 1926.

Smith, Ralph. "Frank Merriwell vs. Fred Fearnot." *Frank Reade Library* 1.1 (September 1928): 1–6.

"The Space Platform!" *Space Comics* 4 (March–April 1954): 9–15.

Spenser, Edmund. *The Faerie Queene.* Edited by Thomas P. Roche Jr. London: Penguin, 1987.

Spider-Man. Directed by Sam Raimi. 2002. Culver City, CA: Sony Pictures Home Entertainment, 2002. DVD.

Stevenson, Noelle, Shannon Watters, and Brooke A. Allen. *Lumberjanes Vol. 1: Beware the Holy Kitten.* Los Angeles, CA: Boom! Studios, 2015.

Stevenson, Robert Louis. *The Black Arrow: A Tale of the Two Roses.* New York: Scribner, 1987.

Stevenson, Robert Louis. *The Strange Case of Dr. Jekyll and Mr. Hyde.* New York: Pocket Books, 2005.

Stewart, Ritson, and Stanley Stewart. *The Professor's Last Experiment.* London: Swan Sonnenschein, 1888.

Stoker, Bram, and Leslie Klinger. *The New Annotated Dracula.* New York: W. W. Norton, 2008.

Stone, John Mack. "Rogue for a Day." *Detective Story Magazine* 3.6 (June 20, 2016): 2–17.

Storm, George. "The Origin of the Hangman." *Pep Comics* 17 (July 1941): 14–24.

Sue, Eugène, Carolyn Betensky, Jonathan Loesberg, and Peter Brooks. *The Mysteries of Paris.* New York: Penguin Books, 2015.

Superboy: The Complete First Season, special ed. DVD. Burbank, CA: Warner Home Video, 2006.

Superman. Directed by Richard Donner. 1978. Burbank, CA: Warner Home Video, 2006. DVD.

Superman: The 1948 and 1950 Theatrical Serials Collection. 1948. Directed by Spencer Gordon Bennet and Thomas Carr. Burbank, CA: Warner Home Video, 2006. DVD.

Superman II. Directed by Richard Lester and Richard Donner. 1980. Burbank, CA: Warner Home Video, 2006. DVD.

Superman III. Directed by Richard Lester. 1983. Burbank, CA: Warner Home Video, 2006. DVD.

Superman Returns. Directed by Bryan Singer. 2006. Burbank, CA: Warner Home Video, 2008. DVD.

Swamp Thing. Directed by Wes Craven. 1982. DVD. Beverly Hills, CA: MGM, 2005. DVD.

Swamp Thing: The Series. 1990–1993. Eden Prairie, MN: Shout! Factory, 2008. DVD.

Swan, Charles, and Wynnard Hooper. *Gesta Romanorum: Or, Entertaining moral stories.* 1876. Reprint, New York: Dover Publications, 1959.

Swift, Jonathan. *Gulliver's Travels.* Franklin Center, PA: Franklin Library, 1979.

Tasso, Torquato. *Jerusalem Delivered; Gerusalemme Liberata.* Baltimore, MD: Johns Hopkins University Press, 2000.

Thackeray, William Makepeace. *Vanity Fair.* New York: Knopf, 1991.

Thomas, Frank. "The Eye Sees." *Keen Detective Funnies* 2.12 (December 1939): 52–57.

Thomas, Frank. "The Land Beneath the Sea." *Amazing-Man Comics* 5 (September 1939): 44–50.

Thomas, Jean, and Win Mortimer. *Night Nurse* 1 (November 1972): 1–20.

Thomas, Roy. "Stan Lee's Amazing Marvel Interview!" *Alter Ego* 104 (2011): 3–45.

Thomas, Roy, and John Buscema. "Come On In, The Revolution's Fine." *The Avengers* 83 (December 1970): 1–19.

Thomas, Roy, and John Buscema. "The Coming of Red Wolf." *Avengers* 80 (September 1970): 1–19.

Thomas, Roy, and John Buscema. "The Frightful Four—Plus One." *Fantastic Four* 129 (December 1972): 1–20.

Thomas, Roy, and John Buscema. "The Monarch and the Man-Ape!" *Jungle Action* 5 (July 1973): 1–20.

Thomas, Roy, and Howard Chaykin. "Star Wars." *Star Wars* 1 (July 1977): 1–17.

Thomas, Roy, Linda Fite, and Marie Severin. *The Cat* 1 (November 1972): 1–22.

Thomas, Roy, John Romita, Archie Goodwin, and George Tuska. "Out of Hell—A Hero!" *Hero for Hire* 1 (June 1972): 1–23.

Thomas, Roy, and Barry Windsor-Smith. "The Coming of Conan!" *Conan the Barbarian* 1 (October 1970): 2–20.

Thomson, Richard. *Tales of an Antiquary: Chiefly Illustrative of the Manners, Traditions, and Remarkable Localities of Ancient London*. London: H. Colburn, 1828.

Thor. Directed by Kenneth Branagh. 2011. Burbank, CA: Buena Vista Home Entertainment, 2013. DVD.

Tick: The Complete Series. 1994–1996. Eden Prairie, MN: Mill Creek Entertainment, 2014. DVD.

Triem, Paul Ellsworth. "Ting-a-ling's Mousetrap." *Western Story Magazine* 89.5 (September 14, 1929): 103–106.

Tyler, Charles. "Raggedy Ann." *Detective Story Magazine* 13.4 (March 26, 1918): 2–23.

Tyler, Margaret. *The Mirror of Princely Deeds and Knighthood*. Edited by Joyce Leslie Boro. London: Modern Humanities Research Association, 2014.

Udall, Ted. "Enter the Sniper." *Military Comics* 5 (December 1941): 12–17.

Unbreakable. Directed by M. Night Shyamalan. 2000. Burbank, CA: Touchstone Home Entertainment, 2001. DVD.

Underdog: The Complete Series. Directed by W. Watts Biggers. 1964–1967. Santa Monica, CA: Shout! Factory, 2012. DVD.

Van Rensselaer Dey, Frederic. "3,000 Miles by Freight: Or, The Mystery of a Piano Box." *The Nick Carter Library* 13 (1891): 1–8.

Van Rensselaer Dey, Frederic. "Alias the Night Wind." *The Cavalier* 28.3 (May 10, 1913): 385–422.

Van Rensselaer Dey, Frederic. "The Index of Seven Stars: Or, Nick Carter Finds the Hidden City." *New Nick Carter Weekly* 529 (February 16, 1907): 1–24.

Van Rensselaer Dey, Frederic. "The Making of a King: Or, Nick Carter Faces His Greatest Mystery." *New Nick Carter Weekly* 534 (March 23, 1907): 1–24.

Van Vogt, A. E. "Slan." *Astounding Science-Fiction* 26.1 (September 1940): 9–40.

Vaughan, Brian K., and Pia Guerra. *Y: The Last Man, Vol. 1: Unmanned*. New York: DC/Vertigo, 2003.

Vaughan, Brian K., and Fiona Staples. *Saga, Vol. 1*. Berkeley, CA: Image Comics, 2012.

Victor, Metta Victoria, and Catherine Ross Nickerson. *The Dead Letter and the Figure Eight*. Durham, NC: Duke University Press, 2003.

Vidocq, Eugène François. *Vidocq: The Personal Memoirs of the First Great Detective*. Translated by Edwin Gile Rich. Boston: Houghton Mifflin Company, 1935.

Vincent, Joyce. *The Celestial Hand: A Sensational Story.* Sydney: J. C. MacCartie, 1903.

Virgil. *The Aeneid.* Translated by Robert Fagles. New York: Penguin, 2008.

Voight, Charles. "The Coming of the Atomic Man." *Headline Comics* 2.4 (November–December 1945): 33–38.

Voight, Charles. "Many are the Tales of Terror Told of that Legendary Figure Dr. Styx." *Treasure Comics* 2 (August–September 1945): 26–33.

Von Eschenbach, Wolfram. *The Middle High German poem of Willehalm.* Translated by Charles E. Passage. New York: F. Ungar Publishing Company, 1977.

Von Grafenberg, Wirnt. *Wigalois, The Knight of Fortune's Wheel.* Translated by J. W. Thomas. Lincoln, NE: University of Nebraska Press, 1977.

Von Voss, Julius. *Ini: ein Roman aus dem ein und zwanzigsten Jahrhundert; eine Utopie der Goethe-Zeit.* Oberhaid, Germany: Utopica, 2008.

Vulpius, Christian. *The Life, Surprising Adventures, and Most Remarkable Escapes of Rinaldo Rinaldini, Captain of a Banditti of Robbers.* London: Ann Lemoine, 1801.

Waid, Mark, Paolo Manuel Rivera, and Marcos Martin. *Daredevil Vol 1.* New York: Marvel, 2012.

Waid, Mark, and Alex Ross. *Kingdom Come.* New York: DC Comics, 2008.

Walker, Hugh. *The Merry Devil of Edmonton: A Comedy.* London: J. M. Dent, 1897.

Walpole, Horace. *The Castle of Otranto.* 1764. Reprint, New York: Dover Publications, 1966.

Wandrei, Donald. "The Man with the Molten Face." *Detective Action Stories* 7.3 (August–September 1937): 6–37.

Ward, Adolphus William, ed. *Old English Drama: Select Plays.* Oxford: Clarendon Press, 1887.

Waters, Thomas. *The Recollections of a Policeman.* New York, 1853.

Wein, Len, and Bernie Wrightson. "Dark Genesis." *Swamp Thing* 1 (October–November 1972): 1–24.

Wellman, Manly Wade, and Carmine Infantino. "The Haunters from Beyond." *The Phantom Stranger* 1 (August–September 1952): 2–9.

Wells, Carolyn. "The Adventure of the Mona Lisa." *The Century Magazine* 83.3 (January 1912): 478–483.

Wells, H. G. *The Complete Short Stories of H. G. Wells.* New York: St. Martin's Press, 1970.

Wells, H. G. *The First Men in the Moon.* London: G. Newnes, 1901.

Wells, H. G. *The Food of the Gods and How It Came to Earth.* London: Macmillan, 1904.

Wells, H. G. *The Invisible Man.* New York: Signet Classics, 2010.

Wells, H. G. *The Island of Doctor Moreau.* London: W. Heinemann, 1896.

Wells, H. G. "The New Accelerator." In *Twelve Stories and a Dream,* 122–140. Auckland, NZ: Floating Press, 2011.

Wells, H. G. *The Sleeper Awakes, and, Men Like Gods.* London: Odhams Press, 1921.

Wells, H. G. *The Time Machine. An Invention.* London: William Heinemann, 1911.

Wells, H. G. *The War of the Worlds.* London: W. Heinemann, 1898.

Wells, H. G. *When the Sleeper Wakes.* London: Harper & Bros., 1899.

Wheeler, Edward L. *Deadwood Dick, the Prince of the Road.* 1884. Reprint, New York: Garland Publications, 1979.

Williamson, Jack. "Darker Than You Think." *Unknown* 4.4 (December 1940): 9–91.

Wilson, G. Willow, and Adrian Alphona. *Ms. Marvel Volume 1: No Normal.* New York: Marvel, 2014.

Winter, C. A. "Queen of the Lost Empire." *Jungle Comics* 1 (January 1940): 27–34.

Wister, Owen. *The Virginian: A Horseman of the Plains.* London: Macmillan, 1902.

Wolfman, Marv, and George Perez. *Crisis on Infinite Earths.* New York: DC Comics, 2001.

Wolverton, Basil. "The Creeping Death from Neptune." *Target Comics* 1.5 (June 1940): 54–64.

Wolverton, Basil. "The Tunnel That Led to Death." *U.S.A. Comics* 1 (August 1941): 39–47.

Wonder Woman: The Complete Collection. 1975–1979. Burbank, CA: Warner Home Video, 2007. DVD.

Wright, Sewell Peaslee. "From the Ocean's Depths." *Astounding Stories of Super-Science* 1.3 (March 1930): 376–389.

Wright, Sewell Peaslee. "Into the Ocean's Depths." *Astounding Stories of Super-Science* 2.2 (May 1930): 151–165.

Wylie, Philip. *Gladiator.* 1930. Reprint, Westport CT: Hyperion Press, 1974.

Wylie, Philip. *The Savage Gentleman.* Lincoln NE: University of Nebraska Press, 2010.

X-Men. Directed by Bryan Singer. 2000. Century City, CA: 20th Century Fox, 2013. DVD.

X-Men 2. Directed by Bryan Singer. 2003. Century City, CA: 20th Century Fox, 2003. DVD.

X-Men: Animated Series: Volume One. 1992. Culver City, CA: Sony Pictures Home Entertainment, 2012. DVD.

Zschokke, Heinrich. *Die schwarzen Brüder: Eine abenteuerliche Geschichte in drei Bänden.* Berlin: Hofenberg, 2016.

Zschokke, Heinrich. *The Bravo of Venice: A Romance.* Translated by M. G. Lewis. 1805. Reprint, New York: Arno Press, 1972.

Secondary Sources

Adcock, John. "Spring-Heeled Jack in Popular Culture, 1838–2005." *Yesterday's Papers.* http://john-adcock.blogspot.com/2015/10/spring-heeled-jack-in-popular-culture.html. Accessed on October 3, 2016.

Aertsen, Henk. "Beowulf." In *A Dictionary of Medieval Heroes: Characters in Medieval Narrative Traditions and Their Afterlife in Literature, Theatre, and the Visual Arts,* edited by W. P. Gerritsen, A. G Van Melle, and Tanis M. Guest, 54–59. Woodbridge, Suffolk, U.K.: Boydell, 1998.

Allen, Nicholas J. "The Indo-European Background to Greek Mythology." In *A Companion to Greek Mythology*, edited by Ken Dowden and Niall Livingston, 341–356. Chichester, West Sussex: Wiley-Blackwell, 2011.

Almond, Philip C. *The Devil: A New Biography*. Ithaca, NY: Cornell University Press, 2014.

Andrae, Thomas. "From Menace to Messiah: The Prehistory of the Superman in Science Fiction Literature." *Discourse* 2 (1980): 84–112.

Artz, Frederick Binkerd. *The Mind of the Middle Ages, A.D. 200–1500: An Historical Survey*. Chicago: University of Chicago, 1980.

Ashley, Michael. *The Mammoth Book of King Arthur*. New York: Carroll & Graf, 2005.

Bakhtin, Mikhail. *Rabelais and His World*. Translated by Helene Iswolsky. Bloomington, IN: Indiana University Press, 1984.

Bartelmus, Rüdiger. *Heroentum in Israel und seiner Umwelt: eine traditionsgeschichtliche Untersuchung zu Gen. 6, 1–4 und verwandten Texten im Alten Testament und der altorientalischen Literatur*. Zurich: Theologischer Verlag, 1979.

Benton, Mike. *The Comic Book in America: An Illustrated History*. Dallas, TX: Taylor, 1989.

Benton, Mike. *Superhero Comics of the Golden Age: The Illustrated History*. Dallas, TX: Taylor, 1992.

Bjork, Robert E., and Anita Obermeier. "Date, Provenance, Author, Audiences." In *A Beowulf Handbook*, edited by Robert E. Bjork and John D. Niles, 13–34. Lincoln: University of Nebraska, 1997.

Black, Edwin. *War against the Weak: Eugenics and America's Campaign to Create a Master Race*. Washington, DC: Dialog Press, 2012.

Blanning, T. C. W. *The Pursuit of Glory: Europe, 1648–1815*. New York: Viking, 2007.

Bleiler, E. F., and Richard Bleiler. *Science-Fiction, the Early Years: A Full Description of More Than 3,000 Science-fiction Stories from Earliest Times to the Appearance of the Genre Magazines in 1930: With Author, Title, and Motif Indexes*. Kent, OH: Kent State University Press, 1990.

Bleiler, E. F., and Richard Bleiler. *Science-Fiction: The Gernsback Years: A Complete Coverage of the Genre Magazines . . . from 1926 through 1936*. Kent, OH: Kent State University Press, 1998.

Box Office Mojo. *Box Office Mojo*. http://www.boxofficemojo.com/. Accessed on October 3, 2016.

Boyer, Régis. "Virile Women." In *Companion to Literary Myths: Heroes and Archetypes*, edited by Pierre Brunel, 1159–1162. London: Routledge, 1992.

Boyle, John Andrew. "The Alexander Romance in the East and West." *Bulletin of the John Rylands Library* 60 (1977): 13–27.

Braun, Martin. *History and Romance in Graeco-Oriental Literature*. Oxford: B. Blackwell, 1938.

Bridgwater, Patrick. *German Gothic Novel in Anglo-German Perspective*. New York: Rodopi, 2013.

Bruce, Christopher. *Christopher Bruce's Arthurian Name Dictionary.* http://gorddcymru .org/twilight/camelot/bruce_dictionary/index.htm. Accessed on October 3, 2016.

Bruce, J. Douglas. "Human Automata in Classical Tradition and Mediaeval Romance." *Modern Philology* 10.4 (1913): 511–526.

Bryant, Stephanie. "America's Amazons: Women Soldiers of the American Civil War." *History in the Making.* https://historyitm.files.wordpress.com/2013 /08/bryant.pdf. Accessed on October 3, 2016.

Bryant, Tim. "Ages of Comics." In *Encyclopedia of Comic Books and Graphic Novels*, edited by M. Keith Booker, 12–14. Santa Barbara, CA: Greenwood, 2010.

Campbell, Joseph. *The Hero with a Thousand Faces.* 1949. Reprint, Princeton, NJ: Princeton University Press, 1972.

Carpenter, Kevin. "Robin Hood in Boys' Weeklies to 1914." In *Popular Children's Literature in Britain*, edited by Julia Briggs, Dennis Butts, and Matthew Orville Grenby, 47–68. Aldershot, England: Ashgate, 2008.

Castle, Terry. *The Literature of Lesbianism: A Historical Anthology from Ariosto to Stonewall.* New York: Columbia University Press, 2003.

Chaplin, Sue. "De Quincey's Gothic Innovations: 'The Avenger,' 1838." *Romanticism* 17.3 (2011): 319–326.

Clute, John. "Marshall, Luther." *Science Fiction Encyclopedia.* http://www.sf -encyclopedia.com/entry/marshall_luther. Accessed on October 3, 2016.

Clute, John. "Taproot Texts." In *The Encyclopedia of Fantasy*, edited by John Clute and John Grant, 921–922. New York: St. Martin's Press, 1997.

Clute, John. "Technothriller." *Science Fiction Encyclopedia.* http://www.sf-encyclopedia .com/entry/technothriller. Accessed on October 3, 2016.

Clute, John. "Thinning." In *The Encyclopedia of Fantasy*, edited by John Clute and John Grant, 942–943. New York: St. Martin's Press, 1997.

Cohen, Margaret. *Profane Illumination: Walter Benjamin and the Paris of Surrealist Revolution* Berkeley: University of California Press, 1995.

Comfort, William Wistar. "The Saracens in Epic Italian Poetry." *PMLA* 59.4 (1944): 882–910.

Comtois, Pierre. *Marvel Comics in the 1960s: An Issue-by-Issue Field Guide to a Pop Culture Phenomenon.* Raleigh, NC: TwoMorrows, 2009.

Comtois, Pierre. *Marvel Comics in the 1970s: An Issue-by-Issue Field Guide to a Pop Culture Phenomenon.* Raleigh, NC: TwoMorrows, 2011.

Coogan, Peter M. *Superhero: The Secret Origin of a Genre.* Austin, TX: Monkey-Brain, 2006.

Cooper-Oakley, Isabel. *The Comte de St. Germain.* Blauvelt, NY: R. Steiner Publications, 1970.

Costello, Matthew J. *Secret Identity Crisis: Comic Books and the Unmasking of Cold War America.* New York: Continuum, 2009.

Couliano, Ioan P. "Dr. Faust, Great Sodomite and Necromancer." *Revue de l'histoire des religions* 207.3 (1990): 261–288.

Cox, J. Randolph. *The Dime Novel Companion: A Source Book.* Westport, CT: Greenwood, 2000.

Dash, Mike. "Spring-heeled Jack: To Victorian Bugaboo from Suburban Ghost." *Mike Dash.* http://mikedash.com/extras/forteana/shj-about/. Accessed on October 3, 2016.

Davis, Edward B. "Science and Religious Fundamentalism in the 1920s." *American Scientist* 93.3 (2005): 253–260.

De Pisan, Christine. *The Book of the City of Ladies.* New York: Persea Books, 1982.

Derrida, Jacques, and Avitall Ronell. "The Law of Genre." *Critical Inquiry* 7.1 (1980): 55–81.

Dixon-Kennedy, Mike. *Encyclopedia of Greco-Roman Mythology.* Santa Barbara, CA: ABC-CLIO, 1998.

Dowden, Ken. "Telling the Mythology: From Hesiod to the Fifth Century." In *A Companion to Greek Mythology,* edited by Ken Dowden and Niall Livingston, 47–72. Chichester, West Sussex: Wiley-Blackwell, 2011.

Dugaw, Dianne. *Warrior Women and Popular Balladry, 1650–1850.* Chicago: University of Chicago Press, 1996.

Duncan, Randy, and Matthew J. Smith. *The Power of Comics: History, Form, and Culture.* New York: Continuum, 2009.

Dunning, John. *On the Air: The Encyclopedia of Old-Time Radio.* Oxford: Oxford University Press, 1998.

Eco, Umberto. *The Role of the Reader: Explorations in the Semiotics of Texts.* Bloomington, IN: Indiana University Press, 1994.

Engels, L. J. "Aeneas." In *A Dictionary of Medieval Heroes: Characters in Medieval Narrative Traditions and Their Afterlife in Literature, Theatre, and the Visual Arts,* edited by W. P. Gerritsen, A. G. Van Melle, and Tanis M. Guest, 9–12. Woodbridge, Suffolk, U.K.: Boydell, 1998.

Engels, L. J. "Alexander the Great." In *A Dictionary of Medieval Heroes: Characters in Medieval Narrative Traditions and Their Afterlife in Literature, Theatre, and the Visual Arts,* edited by W. P. Gerritsen, A. G. Van Melle, and Tanis M. Guest, 15–24. Woodbridge, Suffolk, U.K.: Boydell, 1998.

Engels, L. J.. "Hector." In *A Dictionary of Medieval Heroes: Characters in Medieval Narrative Traditions and Their Afterlife in Literature, Theatre, and the Visual Arts,* edited by W. P. Gerritsen, A. G. Van Melle, and Tanis M. Guest, 139–145. Woodbridge, Suffolk, U.K.: Boydell, 1998.

Faludi, Susan. *Backlash: The Undeclared War against American Women.* New York: Crown, 1991.

Federal Bureau of Investigation. *Uniform Crime Reports for the United States.* Washington, DC: U.S. Department of Justice, 1947.

Federal Bureau of Investigation. *Uniform Crime Reports for the United States.* Washington, DC: U.S. Department of Justice, 1948.

Federal Bureau of Investigation. *Uniform Crime Reports for the United States.* Washington, DC: U.S. Department of Justice, 1949.

Federal Bureau of Investigation. *Uniform Crime Reports for the United States.* Washington, DC: U.S. Department of Justice, 1950.

Finley, M. I. *The World of Odysseus.* New York: New York Review, 2002.

Flanders, Judith. "Penny Dreadfuls." *Discovering Literature: Romantics and Victorians.* https://www.bl.uk/romantics-and-victorians/articles/penny-dreadfuls. Accessed on October 3, 2016.

Fort, Charles. *Lo!* New York: Cosimo Classics, 2006.

Foster, John L. *Ancient Egyptian Literature: An Anthology.* Austin, TX: University of Texas, 2001.

Frank, Frederick S. *The First Gothics: A Critical Guide to the English Gothic Novel.* New York: Garland Publishing, 1987.

Frazer, James. *The Golden Bough; A Study in Magic and Religion.* New York: The Macmillan Company, 1922.

Friedman, John. *The Monstrous Races in Medieval Art and Thought.* Syracuse, NY: Syracuse University Press, 2000.

Frye, Northrop. *Anatomy of Criticism: Four Essays.* Princeton: Princeton University Press, 1971.

Gabilliet, Jean-Paul, Bart Beaty, and Nick Nguyen. *Of Comics and Men: A Cultural History of American Comic Books.* Jackson, MS: University of Mississippi, 2010.

Galle, Heinz. *Sun Koh, der Erbe von Atlantis und Andere Deutsche Supermänner.* Zurich: SSI, 2013.

Gartenberg, Patricia. "An Elizabethan Wonder Woman: The Life and Fortunes of Long Meg of Westminster." *The Journal of Popular Culture* 17.3 (1983): 49–58.

Gavaler, Chris. *On the Origin of Superheroes: From the Big Bang to Action Comics, Issue 1.* Iowa City, IA: University of Iowa, 2015.

Gelbin, Cathy S. *The Golem Returns: From German Romantic Literature to Global Jewish Culture, 1808–2008.* Ann Arbor: University of Michigan, 2011.

Gerritsen, W. P., A. G. Van Melle, and Tanis M. Guest. *A Dictionary of Medieval Heroes: Characters in Medieval Narrative Traditions and Their Afterlife in Literature, Theatre, and the Visual Arts.* Woodbridge, Suffolk, U.K.: Boydell, 1998.

Gitlin, Todd. *Inside Prime Time.* Berkeley: University of California Press, 2000.

Goethe, Johann Wolfgang von. *Faust, Part One.* Translated by David Luke. Oxford: Oxford University Press, 2008.

Goulart, Ron. *Comic Book Culture: An Illustrated History.* Portland, OR: Collectors, 2000.

"Grand Comics Database Team." *Grand Comics Database.* http://www.comics.org/. Accessed on October 3, 2016.

Green, Peter. *Alexander of Macedon, 356–323 B.C.: A Historical Biography.* Berkeley: University of California Press, 1991.

Grünewald, Thomas. *Bandits in the Roman Empire: Myth and Reality.* London: Routledge, 2004.

Hackett, Helen. "Suffering Saints or Ladies Errant?? Women Who Travel for Love in Renaissance Prose Fiction." *The Yearbook of English Studies* 41.1 (2011): 126–140.

Hajdu, David. *The Ten-Cent Plague: The Great Comic-Book Scare and How It Changed America.* New York: Farrar, Straus and Giroux, 2008.

Halpern, Richard. "Puritanism and Maenadism in *A Mask.*" In *Rewriting the Renaissance: The Discourses of Sexual Difference in Early Modern Europe,* edited by Margaret W. Ferguson, Maureen Quilligan, and Nancy J. Vickers, 88–105. Chicago: University of Chicago Press, 1986.

Hatfield, Charles, Jeet Heer, and Kent Worcester. *The Superhero Reader.* Jackson: University of Mississippi, 2013.

Heckethorn, Charles William. *The Secret Societies of All Ages and Countries.* London: Richard Bentley and Son, 1875.

Heilbron, J. L. "Geometry." In *The Oxford Guide to the History of Physics and Astronomy,* edited by John L. Heilbron, 131–135. Oxford: Oxford University Press, 2005.

Hilton, R. H. "The Origins of Robin Hood." In *Robin Hood: An Anthology of Scholarship and Criticism,* edited by Stephen Knight, 197–210. Woodbridge, Suffolk: D. S. Brewer, 1999.

Hitchcock, Susan Tyler. *Frankenstein: A Cultural History.* New York: W. W. Norton, 2007.

Hoberek, Andrew. *Considering Watchmen: Poetics, Property, Politics.* New Brunswick, NJ: Rutgers University Press, 2014.

Hobsbawm, E. J. *Bandits.* 1969. Reprint, New York: New Press, 2000.

Hodder, Mark. *Blakiana.* http://www.mark-hodder.com/Blakiana/, accessed on October 3, 2016.

Hogetoorn, C. "Fierabras." In *A Dictionary of Medieval Heroes: Characters in Medieval Narrative Traditions and Their Afterlife in Literature, Theatre, and the Visual Arts,* edited by W. P. Gerritsen, A. G. Van Melle, and Tanis M. Guest, 103–105. Woodbridge, Suffolk, U.K.: Boydell, 1998.

Howard, Jacqueline. *Reading Gothic Fiction: A Bakhtinian Approach.* Oxford: Clarendon Press, 1994.

Howe, Sean. *Marvel Comics: The Untold Story.* New York: Harper, 2012.

Husband, Timothy, and Gloria Gilmore-House. *The Wild Man: Medieval Myth and Symbolism.* New York: Metropolitan Museum of Art, 1980.

Hutchisson, James M. *Poe.* Jackson: University of Mississippi, 2005.

Internet Movie Database. http://www.imdb.com/. Accessed on October 3, 2016.

Irving Jr., Edward B. "Christian and Pagan Elements." In *Beowulf,* edited by Harold Bloom, 121–138. New York: Chelsea House, 2007.

Irwin, Robert. *The Arabian Nights: A Companion.* London: I. B. Tauris, 2004.

Jackson-Laufer, Guida M. *Encyclopedia of Literary Epics.* Santa Barbara, CA: ABC-CLIO, 1996.

Jasnow, Richard. "The Greek Alexander Romance and Demotic Egyptian Literature." *Journal of Near Eastern Studies* 56.2 (1997): 95–103.

Jedamski, Doris. *Chewing Over the West: Occidental Narratives in Non-Western Readings.* Amsterdam: Rodopi, 2009.

Johnson-Woods, Toni. "Roman-Feuilleton." In *Encyclopedia of the Novel*, edited by Paul E. Schellinger, Christopher Hudson, and Marijke Rijsberman, 1108–1110. Chicago: Fitzroy Dearborn, 1998.

Jones, Gerard. *Men of Tomorrow: Geeks, Gangsters, and the Birth of the Comic Book*. New York: Basic, 2004.

Jones, Steve. *Antonio Gramsci*. London: Routledge, 2006.

Kang, Minsoo. *Sublime Dreams of Living Machines: The Automaton in the European Imagination*. Cambridge, MA: Harvard University Press, 2011.

Kay, Richard. "The Spare Ribs of Dante's Michael Scot." *Dante Studies, with the Annual Report of the Dante Society* 103 (1985): 1–14.

Kayman, Martin A. "The Short Story from Poe to Chesterton." In *The Cambridge Companion to Crime Fiction*, edited by Martin Priestman, 41–58. Cambridge: Cambridge University Press, 2003.

Keen, Maurice. *The Outlaws of Medieval Legend*. London: Routledge, 2001.

Kennedy, Edward Donald. *King Arthur: A Casebook*. New York: Routledge, 2002.

Kenny, Kevin. *Making Sense of the Molly Maguires*. New York: Oxford University Press, 1998.

Kieckhefer, Richard. *Magic in the Middle Ages*. Cambridge: Cambridge University Press, 2000.

Knight, Stephen. *Merlin: Knowledge and Power through the Ages*. Ithaca: Cornell University Press, 2009.

Knight, Stephen. *The Mysteries of the Cities: Urban Crime Fiction in the Nineteenth Century*. Jefferson, NC: McFarland, 2011.

Knight, Stephen. *Robin Hood: A Complete Study of the English Outlaw*. Oxford: Blackwell, 1994.

Kruk, Remke. "Warrior Women in Arabic Popular Romance: Qannâ a bint Muzâ im and Other Valiant Ladies. Part One." *Journal of Arabic Literature* 24.3 (November 1993): 213–230.

Labalme, Patricia H. *Beyond Their Sex: Learned Women of the European Past*. New York: New York University Press, 1980.

Langford, David. "Lost Races." *Science Fiction Encyclopedia*. http://www.sf-encyclopedia.com/entry/lost_races. Accessed on October 3, 2016.

Levi, Eliphas, and Arthur Edward Waite. *The History of Magic: Including a Clear and Precise Exposition of Its Procedure, Its Rites and Its Mysteries*. Cambridge: Cambridge University Press, 2013.

Lewis, Paul. "Attaining Masculinity: Charles Brockden Brown and the Women Warriors of the 1790s." *Early American Literature* 40.1 (2005): 37–55.

Lincoln, Bruce. "The Indo-European Cattle-Raiding Myth." *History of Religions* 16.1 (1976): 42–65.

LoCicero, Donald. *Superheroes and Gods: A Comparative Study from Babylonia to Batman*. Jefferson, NC: McFarland, 2008.

Lopes, Paul Douglas. *Demanding Respect: The Evolution of the American Comic Book*. Philadelphia: Temple University Press, 2009.

Louden, Bruce. "Aeneas in the Iliad: The One Just Man." Paper Presented at the 102nd Annual Meeting of the Classical Association of the Middle West and South, Gainesville, FL. April 2006.

Lupack, Alan. *The Oxford Guide to Arthurian Literature and Legend*. Oxford: Oxford University Press, 2007.

Mathière, Catherine. "The Golem." In *Companion to Literary Myths: Heroes and Archetypes*, edited by Pierre Brunel, 468–487. London: Routledge, 1992.

Matthews, Victor Harold., and Don C. Benjamin. *Old Testament Parallels: Laws and Stories from the Ancient Near East*. New York: Paulist, 1991.

Mayor, Adrienne. *The Amazons: Lives and Legends of Warrior Women across the Ancient World*. Princeton, NJ: Princeton University Press, 2014.

McCulloch, Lynsey. "Antique Myth, Early Modern Mechanism: The Secret History of Spenser's Iron Man." In *The Automaton in English Renaissance Literature*, edited by Wendy Beth Hyman, 61–76. Farnham, Surrey: Ashgate, 2011.

McKracken, Zak. "Marvel and DC Sales Figures." *Zak-Site.Com*. http://zak-site .com/Great-American-Novel/comic_sales.html. Accessed on October 3, 2016.

McLaughlin, Megan. "The Woman Warrior: Gender, Warfare and Society in Medieval Europe." *Women's Studies* 17 (1990): 193–209.

McPhee, Peter. *A Social History of France, 1789–1914*. New York: Palgrave Macmillan, 2004.

Mellor, Anne K. "*Frankenstein*, Racial Science, and the Yellow Peril." *Nineteenth Century Concepts* 23 (2001): 1–28.

Miller, John Jackson. "Comic Book Sales by Year." *Comichron: The Comics Chronicles*. http://www.comichron.com/yearlycomicssales.html. Accessed on October 3, 2016.

Mobley, Gregory. *Samson and the Liminal Hero in the Ancient Near East*. New York: T & T Clark, 2006.

Mobley, Gregory. "The Wild Man in the Bible and the Ancient Near East." *Journal of Biblical Literature* 116.2 (1997): 217–233.

Moore, Megan. *Exchanges in Exoticism: Cross-Cultural Marriage and the Making of the Mediterranean in Old French Romance*. Toronto: University of Toronto Press, 2014.

Muchembled, Robert, and Jean Birrell. *A History of Violence: From the End of the Middle Ages to the Present*. Cambridge, U.K.: Polity, 2012.

Mulvey, Laura. "Visual Pleasure and Narrative Cinema." *Screen* 16.3 (1975): 6–18.

Murray, Christopher. *Champions of the Oppressed? Superhero Comics, Popular Culture, and Propaganda in America during World War II*. Cresskill, NJ: Hampton, 2011.

Murray, Christopher. "Cold War." In *Encyclopedia of Comic Books and Graphic Novels*, edited by M. Keith Booker, 104–109. Santa Barbara, CA: Greenwood, 2010.

Murray, Will. Introduction to *The Bat Strikes Again and Again!*, by Johnston McCulley, 1–12. Will Murray, 2009.

Neidorf, Leonard. "Beowulf Before *Beowulf*: Anglo-Saxon Anthroponymy and Heroic Legend." *The Review of English Studies* 64.266 (2013): 553–573.

Nevins, Jess. "Captain Future." *Incognito: Bad Influences* 3 (February 2011): 25–28.

Nevins, Jess. *The Encyclopedia of Fantastic Victoriana*. Austin, TX: Monkeybrain, 2004.

Nevins, Jess. *The Encyclopedia of Golden Age Superheroes*. http://jessnevins.com/encyclopedia/characterlist.html. Accessed on October 3, 2016.

Nevins, Jess. *The Encyclopedia of Pulp Heroes*. Hornsea, U.K.: P.S. Publishing, 2016. Manuscript.

Nevins, Jess. "May Day, 1871: The Day 'Science Fiction' Was Invented." *Io9*. http://io9.gizmodo.com/5796919/may-day-1871-the-day-science-fiction-was-invented. Accessed on October 3, 2016.

Nevins, Jess. "Pulp Science Fiction." In *The Oxford Handbook of Science Fiction*, edited by Rob Latham, 93–103. Oxford: Oxford University Press, 2014.

Nevins, Jess. *The Pulps*. Tomball TX: Jess Nevins, 2012.

Ogle, M. B. "The Perilous Bridge and Human Automata." *Modern Language Notes* 35.3 (1920): 129–136.

Ohlgren, Thomas H. *Medieval Outlaws: Ten Tales in Modern English*. Thrupp, Stroud, Gloucestershire: Sutton Pub., 1998.

Overstreet, Robert M. *Official Overstreet Comic Book Price Guide*. Timonium, MD: Gemstone Publishing, 1999.

Peck, Harry Thurston. *Harper's Dictionary of Classical Literature and Antiquities*. London: Osgood, 1897.

People of Color in European Art History. http://medievalpoc.tumblr.com/. Accessed on October 3, 2016.

Perry, B. E. "The Egyptian Legend of Nectanebus." *Transactions and Proceedings of the American Philological Association* 97 (1966): 327–333.

The Personal Library Collection of Edgar Rice Burroughs. http://www.erbzine.com/dan/, accessed on October 3, 2016.

Peterson, Todd Samuel. *Muscular Judaism: The Jewish Body and the Politics of Regeneration*. London: Routledge, 2007.

Priest, Cherie. E-mail message to author, January 17, 2012.

Quarles, Chester L. *The Ku Klux Klan and Related American Racialist and Antisemitic Organizations: A History and Analysis*. Jefferson, NC: McFarland, 1999.

Raber, Karen L. "Warrior Women in the Plays of Cavendish and Killigrew." *Studies in English Literature, 1500–1900* 40.3 (2000): 413–433.

Raglan, Baron. *The Hero: A Study in Tradition, Myth, and Drama*. 1956. Reprint, Westport, CT: Greenwood Press, 1975.

Rainone, Joseph L. Introduction to *The Man in the Black Cloak: Or, In Search of the John Street Jewels*, edited by Joseph L. Rainone, 1–12. Baldwin, NY: Almond Press, 2009.

Rank, Otto. *The Myth of the Birth of the Hero: A Psychological Interpretation of Mythology*. Translated by Drs. F. Robbins and Smith Ely Jelliffe. New York: The Journal of Nervous and Mental Disease Publishing Company,

1914. Originally published as *Der Mythus von der Geburt des Helden: Versuch einer psychologischen Mythendeutung*, 1909.

Reed, James. *Sir Walter Scott: Landscape and Locality.* London: A&C Black, 2014.

Resoort, R. J. "Robert the Devil." In *A Dictionary of Medieval Heroes: Characters in Medieval Narrative Traditions and Their Afterlife in Literature, Theatre, and the Visual Arts*, edited by W. P. Gerritsen, A. G. Van Melle, and Tanis M. Guest, 220–223. Woodbridge, Suffolk, U.K.: Boydell, 1998.

Reynolds, Bryan, and Janna Segal. "The Reckoning of Moll Cutpurse: A Transversal Enterprise." In *Rogues and Early Modern English Culture*, edited by Craig Dionne and Steve Mentz, 62–91. Ann Arbor: University of Michigan, 2004.

Rhoades, Shirrel. *A Complete History of American Comic Books.* New York: Peter Lang, 2008.

Robinson, Lillian. *Monstrous Regiment: The Lady Knight in Sixteenth-Century Epic.* New York: Garland Publications, 1985.

Rollin, Roger B. "Beowulf to Batman: The Epic Hero and Pop Culture." *College English* 31.5 (February 1970): 431–449.

Rosenberg, Robin, and Jennifer Canzoneri. *The Psychology of Superheroes: An Unauthorized Exploration.* Dallas, TX: BenBella, 2008.

Rosenberg, Robin, and Peter Coogan. *What Is a Superhero?* Oxford: Oxford University Press, 2013.

Ruickbie, Leo. *Faustus: The Life and Times of a Renaissance Magician.* Stroud, Gloucestershire, U.K.: The History Press, 2011.

Rutherford, Ian. "The Genealogy of the Boukoloi: How Greek Literature Appropriated an Egyptian Narrative-Motif." *The Journal of Hellenistic Studies* 120 (2000): 106–121.

Rutherford, Ian. "Mythology of the Black Land: Greek Myths and Egyptian Origins." In *A Companion to Greek Mythology*, edited by Ken Dowden and Niall Livingston, 459–470. Chichester, West Sussex: Wiley-Blackwell, 2011.

Sampson, Robert. *Yesterday's Faces: Strange Days.* Bowling Green, OH: Bowling Green University Popular Press, 1984.

Savage, William W. *Commies, Cowboys, and Jungle Queens: Comic Books and America, 1945–1954.* Middletown, CT: Wesleyan University Press, 1990.

Sawday, Jonathan. *Engines of the Imagination: Renaissance Culture and the Rise of the Machine.* London: Routledge, 2007.

Schwarz, Kathryn. "Amazon Reflections in the Jacobean Queen's Masque." *Studies in English Literature, 1500–1900* 35.2 (1995): 293–319.

Seal, Graham. *The Outlaw Legend: A Cultural Tradition in Britain, America, and Australia.* Cambridge, U.K.: Cambridge University Press, 1996.

Shaw, Brent. "Bandits in the Roman Empire." *Past and Present* 105 (1984): 3–52.

Shepherd, Simon. *Amazons and Warrior Women: Varieties of Feminism in Seventeenth-Century Drama.* New York: St. Martin's, 1981.

Sherman, William H. *John Dee: The Politics of Reading and Writing in the English Renaissance.* Amherst, MA: University of Massachusetts Press, 1995.

Simone, Gail. *Women in Refrigerators.* http://lby3.com/wir/. Accessed on October 3, 2016.

Sinha, Madhudya. "Masculinity under Siege: Gender, Empire, and Knowledge in Late Victorian Literature." PhD diss., University of Cincinnati, 2009. ProQuest A AT 304850443.

Solterer, Helen. "Figures of Female Militancy in Medieval France." *Signs: Journal of Women In Culture and Society* 16.3 (1991): 522–549.

Spargo, John Webster. *Virgil the Necromancer: Studies in Virgilian Legends.* Cambridge, MA: Harvard University Press, 1934.

Spock, Benjamin, and Michael B. Rothenberg. *Baby and Child Care.* New York: E. P. Dutton, 1985.

Stableford, Brian. "Science Fiction before Genre." In *The Cambridge Companion to Science Fiction,* edited by Edward James and Farah Mendlesohn, 15–31. Cambridge, U.K.: Cambridge University Press, 2003.

Stock, Lorraine Kochanske. "'Arms and the (Wo)man' in Medieval Romance: The Gendered Arming of Female Warriors in the 'Roman d'Eneas' and Heldris's 'Roman de Silence.'" *Arthuriana* 5.4 (1995): 56–83.

Stok, Fabio. "Virgil between the Middle Ages and the Renaissance." *International Journal of the Classical Tradition* 1.2 (1994): 15–22.

Stoneman, Richard. *Alexander the Great: A Life in Legend.* New Haven: Yale University Press, 2008.

Stoppino, Eleonora. *Genealogies of Fiction: Women Warriors and the Dynastic Imagination in the Orlando Furioso.* New York: Fordham University Press, 2012.

Sutherland, John. *The Longman Companion to Victorian Fiction.* Harlow, England: Pearson Longman, 2009.

Sykes, Heather Jane. *Queer Bodies: Sexualities, Genders, & Fatness in Physical Education.* New York: Peter Lang, 2011.

Thompson, Stith. *Motif-Index of Folk-Literature: A Classification of Narrative Elements in Folktales, Ballads, Myths, Fables, Mediaeval Romances, Exempla, Fabliaux, Jest-Books, and Local Legends.* Bloomington, IN: Indiana University Press, 1955–1958.

Tilley, Carol L. "Seducing the Innocent: Fredric Werthamm and the Falsifications That Helped Condemn Comics." *Information & Culture: A Journal of History* 47.4 (2012), 383–413.

Tomalin, Margaret. "Bradamante and Marfisa: An Analysis of the 'Guerriere' of the 'Orlando Furioso.'" *The Modern Language Review* 71.3 (1976): 540–552.

Tomalin, Margaret. *The Fortunes of the Warrior Heroine in Italian Literature: An Index of Emancipation.* Ravenna: Longo Editore, 1982.

Tondro, Jason. *Superheroes of the Round Table: Comics Connections to Medieval and Renaissance Literature.* Jefferson, NC: McFarland, 2011.

Traister, Barbara Howard. *Heavenly Necromancers: The Magician in English Renaissance Drama.* Columbia: University of Missouri, 1984.

Tresch, John. "The Machine Awakens: The Science and Politics of the Fantastic Automaton." *French Historical Studies* 34.1 (2011): 87–123.

Truitt, E. R. *Medieval Robots: Mechanism, Magic, Nature, and Art*. Philadelphia: University of Pennsylvania Press, 2015.

Tyrrell, William Blake., and Frieda S. Brown. *Athenian Myths and Institutions: Words in Action*. New York: Oxford University Press, 1991.

Ungerer, Gustav. "Mary Frith, Alias Moll Cutpurse, In Life and Literature." *Shakespeare Studies* 28 (2000): 42–84.

Van Lente, Fred, and Ryan Dunlavey. *The Comic Book History of Comics*. San Diego, CA: IDW, 2012.

Vermeulen, Timotheus, and Robin Van Den Akker. "Notes on Metamodernism." *Journal of Aesthetics and Culture* 2 (2010): 1–14. Accessed June 13, 2016. http://www.aestheticsandculture.net/index.php/jac/article/view/5677.

Vinson, Steve. "The Accent's on Evil: Ancient Egyptian 'Melodrama' and the Problem of Genre." *Journal of the American Research Center in Egypt* 41 (2004): 33–54.

Vitullo, Juliann. "Contained Conflict: Wild Men and Warrior Women in the Early Italian Epics." *Annali d'italianistica* 12 (1994): 39–59.

Wahrman, Dror. "Percy's Prologue: From Gender Play to Gender Panic in Eighteenth-Century England." *Past & Present* 159 (May 1998): 113–160.

Wandtke, Terence R. *The Meaning of Superhero Comic Books*. Jefferson, NC: McFarland, 2012.

Wertham, Fredric. *Seduction of the Innocent*. New York: Rinehart, 1954.

West, M. L. *The East Face of Helicon: West Asiatic Elements in Greek Poetry and Myth*. Oxford: Clarendon, 1997.

Westfahl, Gary. "Edmund Spenser." In *The Encyclopedia of Fantasy*, edited by John Clute and John Grant, 889–890. New York: St. Martin's Press, 1997.

Wheelwright, Julie. *Amazons and Military Maids: Women Who Dressed as Men in the Pursuit of Life, Liberty, and Happiness*. Boston: Pandora, 1989.

Winkler, Jack. "Lollianos and the Desperadoes." *The Journal of Hellenic Studies* 100 (1980): 155–181.

Wood, Juliette. "Virgil and Taliesin: The Concept of the Magician in Medieval Folklore." *Folklore* 94.1 (1983): 91–104.

Wright, Bradford W. *Comic Book Nation: The Transformation of Youth Culture in America*. Baltimore, MD: Johns Hopkins University Press, 2003.

Wright, Celeste Turner. "The Amazons in Elizabethan Literature." *Studies in Philology* 37.3 (1940): 433–456.

Žižek, Slavoj. *Violence*. London: Picador, 2008.

Index

About the Author

Jess Nevins is a reference librarian at Lone Star College in Tomball, TX, and author of *The Encyclopedia of Pulp Heroes* (P.S. Publishing, 2016), *The Victorian Bookshelf* (McFarland, 2016), *The Encyclopedia of Golden Age Superheroes* (self-published, 2013), *The Encyclopedia of Fantastic Victoriana* (MonkeyBrain Books, 2004), and numerous other books and articles.